NONVIOLENCE IN AMERICA

NONVIOLENCE IN AMERICA

A Documentary History

Revised edition

Edited by
Staughton Lynd and Alice Lynd

ORBIS BOOKS

Maryknoll, New York 10545

Fifth printing, October 2002

The Catholic Foreign Mission Society of America (Maryknoll) recruits and trains people for overseas missionary service. Through Orbis Books, Maryknoll aims to foster the international dialogue that is essential to mission. The books published, however, reflect the opinions of their authors and are not meant to represent the official position of the society.

Published by Orbis Books, Maryknoll, NY 10545-0308

This is a revised and expanded edition of *Nonviolence in America: A Documentary History* originally published in 1966 by The Bobbs-Merrill Company, Inc.

Manufactured in the United States of America

Library of Congress Cataloging-in-Publication Data

Nonviolence in America : a documentary history / edited by
   Staughton Lynd and Alice Lynd. — Rev. ed.
       p.   cm.
   Includes bibliographical references and index.
   ISBN 1-57075-013-0 — ISBN 1-57075-010-6 (pbk.).
   1. Passive resistance—United States.   I. Lynd, Staughton.
II. Lynd, Alice.
HM278.L9   1995
303.6'1—dc20   94-41973
                                   CIP

CONTENTS

PART IX

DIRECT ACTION FOR CIVIL RIGHTS, POST-WORLD WAR II

PART X

THE VIETNAM WAR

PART XIV

THE GULF WAR

PART XV

HEALING GLOBAL WOUNDS

INTRODUCTION

I

This book attempts to present the history of the idea of nonviolence in the United States.[1] While there are several good anthologies of writings on nonviolence currently in print, few provide a consecutive account of the tradition of nonviolence in this country. Moreover, we know of no volume where one can find the full text of key essays in the tradition—Thoreau's "Civil Disobedience," William James' "The Moral Equivalent of War," and Martin Luther King, Jr.'s "Letter from Birmingham City Jail"—brought together between two covers.

It is often supposed that nonviolence is a philosophy conceived by Gandhi and Tolstoy, and recently imported into the United States by Martin Luther King, Jr. The fact is that a distinctive tradition of nonviolence runs back to the British colonies in the seventeenth century. Thoreau's influence on Gandhi is well-known. Tolstoy, too, was indebted to North American predecessors. In "A Message to the American People," written in 1901, Tolstoy stated that "Garrison, Parker, Emerson, Ballou, and Thoreau . . . specially influenced me."[2]

Three years later Tolstoy wrote that "Garrison was the first to proclaim this principle [of nonresistance to evil] as a rule for the organization of man's life."[3] There is good ground for arguing that the Christian pacifism of the

---

1. We regret that in the first edition of this work, the terms "America" and "American" were used to refer to the "United States of America" and its residents. The United States is only one of many nations in the Americas.

2. Quoted from the *North American Review* (April 1901) in Lev N. Tolstoy, *Miscellaneous Letters and Essays, The Complete Works of Count Tolstoy,* ed. Leo Wiener, XXIII (Boston: Dana Estes & Co., 1905), p. 462. See Ernest J. Simmons, *Leo Tolstoy* (Boston: Little, Brown and Co., 1946), p. 436, for Tolstoy's appreciation of Ballou.

3. "Introduction to a Short Biography of William Lloyd Garrison," *The Kingdom of God and Peace Essays,* trans. Aylmer Maude, in *The Works of Leo Tolstoy,* Tolstoy Centenary Edition, XX (London: Oxford University Press for the Tolstoy Society, 1935), p. 581. Tolstoy made the following comment elsewhere in the same brief essay (p. 578): "Formerly the question was how to free the negroes from the violence of slaveholders; now it is how to free the negroes from the violence of the whites and the whites from the violence of the blacks.

"The solution of this problem in its new form can certainly not be accomplished by lynching negroes, nor by any skilful and liberal measures of American politicians, but only by the application to life of the principle Garrison proclaimed half a century ago."

radical Reformation was kept alive from about 1650 to 1850 primarily by North Americans; and that, in view of the cumulative impact of Penn and Woolman, Garrison and Thoreau, William James and Jane Addams, and now Martin Luther King, Jr., the United States has more often been teacher than student in the history of the nonviolent idea.

That idea has itself changed in the course of its application in North America. Before the Revolution, nonviolence was the conviction of some of the members of a few small Christian sects. They understood nonviolence as literal obedience to the teaching of Jesus concerning nonresistance to evil. In its name they sought reconciliation with the Indians, appealed for the abolition of slavery, and on occasion broke the law rather than disobey conscience. The major development since the Revolution has been a tendency to secularization as people have employed nonviolent tactics for social, political, or economic reasons. An advantage of the historical approach employed in this volume is that it enables the reader to watch the unfolding of nonviolent philosophy as it was brought to bear in a series of specific contexts. William James, for example, introduced a new concern with the psychological roots of nonviolence, emphasizing the need for a positive, constructive expression of the idea. On the other hand, Martin Luther King, Jr., while retaining an emphasis on personal action, has sought to restore the older vision that the springs of nonviolence are ultimately religious. The following documents have been selected on the assumption that the understanding of a tradition that has involved both direct action and sophisticated personal philosophy means including samples of both. This is particularly true when attempting to convey some sense of nonviolent actions on behalf of peace, civil rights, the environment, and other causes, since World War II. Much of this recent experience has not yet been articulated, except in the fugitive form of broadsides and pamphlets. It is history, nonetheless, and must be apprehended in whatever form it can be found.

This experimental emphasis cautions against rigid definition. Nevertheless, it may help the reader to view the term "nonviolence" as including the following overlapping but distinct elements: (1) refusal to retaliate ("pacifism," "nonresistance"); (2) acting-out of conviction by demonstrative action ("direct action"); (3) deliberate lawbreaking for conscience's sake ("civil disobedience"). In this volume "nonviolence" means all these things and something more: the vision of love as an agent for fundamental social change.

QUAKERS

The practice of nonviolent civil disobedience in this country's history began with the struggle for freedom of conscience. It is no accident that most of the pre-twentieth-century authors in this volume were Pennsylvanians or New Englanders. These were the two principal theaters for the early nonviolent movement: Pennsylvania, uniquely tolerant to dissenters but after 1750 no longer pacifist in its Indian policy; Massachusetts, intolerant mother of a long line of rebels, including Garrison and Thoreau.

Before the Revolution of 1776, nonviolence was peculiarly identified with members of the Society of Friends, also known as "Quakers." There were other pacifist sects, of course: John Woolman recorded in his *Journal* the case of a Mennonite who slept in the woods rather than receive hospitality from a slaveholder. But the Quakers were more numerous, and as English persons they were more in touch with the English majority in the colonies than Continental pietists could hope to be. The Quakers, moreover, insisted stubbornly on defying what Roger Williams called "that body-killing, soule-killing, and State-killing doctrine of not permitting, but persecuting all other consciences and wayes of worship. . . ."[4]

There was nothing respectable or middle-class about Quakerism then. In 1660 an act of Virginia referred to the Friends as an

. . . unreasonable and turbulent sort of people . . . teaching and publishing, lies, miracles, false visions, prophecies and doctrines, which have influence upon the communities of men both ecclesiasticall and civil endeavouring and attemp[t]ing thereby to destroy religion, lawes, communities and all bonds of civil societie, leaveing it arbitrarie to everie vaine and vitious person whether men shall be safe, lawes established, offenders punished, and Governours rule, hereby disturbing the publique peace and just interest. . . .[5]

While this was being said in Virginia, Quakers were mounting a nonviolent invasion of Massachusetts Bay.[6] In July 1656, Mary Fisher and Ann Austin arrived in Boston. They were deported, but two days after their ship sailed out eight more Friends sailed in. As described by George Lakey:

These formidable zealots carried the battle to the Puritans, avoiding devious means of spreading their message. They attempted to speak after the sermon in church, made speeches during trials and from jail windows during imprisonments, issued pamphlets and tracts, held illegal

---

4. Roger Williams, "Mr. Cottons Letter Examined and Answered," *Publications of the Narragansett Club,* First Series, I (Providence: Providence Press Co., 1866), p. 328.

5. William W. Hening, ed., *The Statutes at Large,* I (New York: R. & W. & G. Bartow, 1823), pp. 532–533.

6. This description of the Quaker encounter with Massachusetts Bay is drawn from George Lakey, *Nonviolent Action: How It Works,* Pendle Hill Pamphlet No. 129 (Wallingford, Pa.: Pendle Hill, 1963), pp. 11–12. Permission to reprint was granted by Pendle Hill, Wallingford, Pa. Lakey cites Harvey Joseph Daniel Seifert, "The Use by American Quakers of Nonviolent Resistance as a Method of Social Change" (unpublished Ph.D. dissertation, Boston University, 1940).

public meetings, refused to pay fines, and refused to work in prison even though it meant going without food.

Again and again Quakers returned to the Bay Colony, despite whippings and executions. "While William Leddra was being considered for the death penalty, Wenlock Christison, who had already been banished on pain of death, calmly walked into the courtroom. And while Christison was being tried, Edward Wharton, who also had been ordered to leave the colony or lose his life, wrote to the authorities from his home that he was still there.

This early experiment in nonviolence, to use Gandhi's phrase, was successful.

The jailer's fees were often paid by sympathetic citizens and food was brought to the prisoners through the jail window at night. A number of colonists were converted to Quakerism by witnessing the suffering. For example, Edward Wanton, an officer of the guard at the execution of Robinson and Stephenson, was so impressed that he came home saying, "Alas, mother! we have been murdering the Lord's people."

When Hored Gardner prayed for her persecutors after her whipping, a woman spectator was so affected that she said, "Surely if she had not the support of the Lord she could not do this thing."

Governor Endicott was not so easily moved. When Catherine Scott indicated her willingness to die for her faith, the Governor replied, "And we shall be as ready to take away your lives, as ye shall be to lay them down." But the protest against the treatment of the Quakers continued to grow.

After William Brend had been so cruelly beaten that he seemed about to die, even Governor Endicott became so alarmed at the attitude of the people that he announced that the jailer would be prosecuted. The later execution of a woman, Mary Dyer, added to the discontent, and even the General Court began to weaken. Virtual abolition of the death penalty followed; there were problems in getting the constables to enforce laws which became ever milder.

"By 1675," Lakey's account concludes, "Quakers were regularly meeting undisturbed in Boston."

Shortly thereafter, in the early 1680s, William Penn experimented with another form of nonviolence in his treaty with the Delaware Indians. No reliable account of the treaty exists. It may be that there were several treaties which were remembered as one event. According to Indian tradition, which carefully preserved the memory of the treaty as a bright chain to be kept free of rust, the principal points of the agreement included: (1) that all paths should be open and free to both Christians and Indians; (2) that the doors of the Christians' houses should be open to the Indians and the houses of the Indians open to the Christians, and they should make each other welcome as friends; (3) that the Christians should not believe any false rumors or reports of the Indians, nor the Indians believe any such rumors or reports of the Christians, but should first come as brethren to inquire of each other.

There were prudential as well as idealistic motives in Penn's approach to the Delaware Indians. He wrote to the commissioners who went out to Pennsylvania ahead of him: "Be tender of offending the Indians, and hearken by honest spies, if you can hear that any body inveigles them not to sell, or to stand off, and raise the value upon you."[7] Yet the policy appears to have worked. Not only did it keep the peace in Pennsylvania for two generations; it seems to be true also that when, in the mid-eighteenth century, warfare between the colony and the Indians began, Quaker families were spared. The influential English Quaker of the early nineteenth century, Jonathan Dymond, passed on to abolitionist readers the tradition that Friends who refused to arm themselves or to retire to garrisons were left unharmed by the Indians.[8]

Pennsylvania's decision to arm against the Indians prompted another form of nonviolent action: the refusal to pay taxes for military purposes. The issue pitted John Woolman and Anthony Benezet, the best remembered Quakers in the British colonies, against Benjamin Franklin, who led the non-Quakers of Pennsylvania in insisting on military preparations.

John Woolman found the decision to refuse payment of taxes a difficult one. His problem sprang from the very concept of religious tolerance. He was fully convinced that the Catholic Thomas à Kempis and the Protestant John Huss were both acceptable Christians in the sight of God. And if it was "true Charity ... to sincerely Labour for their good, whose belief in all points, doth not agree with ours," how could one be so self-righteous as "to refuse the active payment of a Tax which our Society [of Friends] generally paid"? Woolman was the more perplexed because, while his conscience was clearly uneasy about paying the tax, "Scrupling to pay a tax on account of the application hath seldom been heard of heretofore."[9]

His solution was interesting. Tax refusal was appropriate for Friends in the colonies, Woolman argued, precisely because their religion was so tolerated and secure. In England, where Quakers had no share in civil government, the danger of uniting with their rulers "in things inconsistent with the purity of Truth" had been slight. North American Quakers, "tryed with favour and

---

7. William Penn to William Crispin, John Bezar, and Nathaniel Allen, September 30, 1681, quoted in Samuel M. Janney, *The Life of William Penn; With Selections from his Correspondence and Autobiography* (Philadelphia: Hogan, Perkins & Co., 1852), p. 168.

8. Jonathan Dymond, *Essays on the Principles of Morality, and on the Private and Political Rights and Obligations of Mankind* (New York: Collins, Brother & Co., 1845), pp. 558–559. In 1849 Charles Sumner cited Dymond as the exemplar of absolute pacifism in the "War System of the Commonwealth of Nations," *Charles Sumner; his complete works,* II (Boston: Lee and Shepard, 1900), p. 335.

9. These quotations are from *The Journal and Essays of John Woolman,* ed. Amelia Mott Gummere (New York: The Macmillan Co., 1922), pp. 205–207; see Document 2.

prosperity," were in a different position. Woolman urged his coreligionists to consider tax refusal as a protection against "a Carnal mind," and also against the danger that Quakers in public office might "quench the tender movings of the Holy Spirit in their minds" if they saw Quakers out of office united in paying war taxes.

Woolman died on the eve of the Revolution, but Franklin and Benezet, antagonists over the French and Indian War, differed once more about the War for Independence. Franklin spoke for the majority when he made his well-known proposal for a seal of the United States: Moses lifting up his wand and dividing the Red Sea, Pharaoh in his chariot overwhelmed with the waters, and the motto, "Rebellion to tyrants is obedience to God." Benezet, drawing on the New Testament rather than the Old, expressed the feelings of the pacifist minority in a letter of 1779 to the President of the Continental Congress, John Jay. Benezet asked Jay "to distinguish between such who are active in opposition (to the war), and those who have been restrained from an apprehension of duty, and a persuasion that our common beneficent Father who has the hearts of all men in his power, and has in former times so eminently displayed his goodness in favour of these countries, if properly sought unto, would in his love and mercy have averted the evil effects of any attempt which might have been made to impede our real welfare."[10]

Symbolized by the confrontation of these leaders was the conflict between Quaker nonviolence and the dominant philosophy of Locke. Locke was contemptuous of those whose scruples over violence permitted tyranny to reign unchecked. Thus in his *Second Treatise of Government* Locke declared:

> If the innocent honest Man must quietly quit all he has for Peace sake, to him who will lay violent hands upon it, I desire it may be consider'd, what a kind of Peace there will be in the World, which consists only in Violence and Rapine; and which is to be maintain'd only for the benefit of Robbers and Oppressors. Who would not think it an admirable Peace betwixt the Mighty and the Mean, when the Lamb, without resistance, yielded his Throat to be torn by the imperious Wolf?[11]

Probably at no other time in United States history was nonviolence so alien to the mainstream of this country's social thought as in the Revolutionary

---

10. Anthony Benezet to John Jay, February 7, 1779, quoted in George S. Brookes, *Friend Anthony Benezet* (Philadelphia: University of Pennsylvania Press, 1937), pp. 330–331.

11. John Locke, *Two Treatises of Government,* ed. Peter Laslett (Cambridge, England: Cambridge University Press, 1960), p. 435. The attitude of radical Whigs toward nonviolence in the era of the American Revolution is suggested by the following examples: John Adams called it "the most mischievous of all doctrines";

generation. Even in the nineteenth century only a few pacifists, such as the South Carolina abolitionist Thomas Grimké, were prepared to say flatly that the violence of the Revolution had been wrong.

ABOLITIONISTS

The Lockean Franklin and his Quaker antagonists were united, however, in their concern to abolish slavery. Woolman made long journeys through the South admonishing Quaker slaveholders, and refused to use the products of slave labor. Benezet founded a school for the instruction of free Blacks. In 1790 the aged Franklin set his name at the head of a petition against slavery to the new United States Congress. Southern Congressmen responded by extended reference to the pacifism of Quakers during the Revolution, insisting that the "self-constituted" Society of Friends not be permitted to disturb sectional harmony. "The Northern States adopted us with our slaves," declared Representative William Smith of South Carolina, "and we adopted them with their Quakers."[12] The clash between the Founding Fathers' pragmatic acceptance of slavery and the "fanatical" objections of the Quakers was to reappear writ large in the decades after 1830.

Abolitionism, as it developed in the context of religious revivalism, was at first committed to nonviolence. Nathaniel Macon, Congressman from North Carolina, wrote to a friend in 1818: "We have abolition, colonization, bible and peace societies. . . . The character and spirit of one may without injustice be considered that of all. . . ."[13] In 1815-1860, as in the years since World War II, peace movements and civil rights organizations attracted the same people. Samuel May and William Ellery Channing were advocates of peace before they became abolitionists. Antislavery stalwarts Henry C. Wright, Edmund Quincy, Maria W. Chapman, Lucretia Mott, and Lydia Maria Child

---

John Cartwright spoke of "the dark regions of passive-obedience and non-resistance"; while Richard Price referred to "the odious doctrines of passive obedience, non-resistance, and the divine right of kings" ("A Dissertation On The Canon And Feudal Law," *The Political Writings of John Adams: Representative Selections,* ed. George A. Peek, Jr. [New York: The Bobbs-Merrill Company Inc., The Liberal Arts Press, 1954], p. 10; John Cartwright, *The Legislative Right Of The Commonalty Vindicated; Or, Take Your Choice!* [London, 1777], p. xxvi; Richard Price, *A Discourse On The Love Of Our Country* [London, 1790], p. 35). For nonviolence as a favorite theme of American Tories, see Leonard Labaree, *Conservatism In Early American History* (New York City: New York University Press, 1948), pp. 74–75, 126–130.

12. "On Slavery," Speech of March 17, 1790, *The Debates and Proceedings in the Congress of the United States,* ed. Joseph Gales, Senior, II (Washington: Gales and Seaton, 1834), p. 1508.

13. Nathaniel Macon to Bartlett Yancey, March 8, 1818, quoted in William E. Dodd, *The Life of Nathaniel Macon* (Raleigh, N.C.: Edwards & Broughton, 1903), p. 313.

joined William Lloyd Garrison in launching the New England Non-Resistance Society. Frederick Douglass denounced "the whole naval system" and capital punishment. Charles Sumner made his political debut by condemning war before a Fourth of July audience on the Boston Common, and in 1849, in a speech called "War System of the Commonwealth of Nations," produced the most comprehensive indictment of war by any United States resident in the nineteenth century. William Jay, Lewis Tappan, and Theodore Parker were others prominent in both the peace and antislavery movements.[14]

The manifesto of the American Antislavery Society in 1833 espoused nonviolence in almost the same language as the declaration of the New England Non-Resistance Society in 1838: a natural outcome, since Garrison wrote both. Nor was this nineteenth century nonviolent movement confined to words. Direct action against railroad segregation began almost coincidentally with railroads themselves, in New England, New York, and Pennsylvania.[15] Assisting fugitive slaves was "constructive work" in the best Gandhian sense.

But Garrisonian nonviolence in 1840, like Quaker pacifism in 1776, was open to the charge that it salved the conscience of the individual yet failed to change the structure of power. Garrison disavowed the French Revolution: "We advocate no jacobinical doctrines. The spirit of jacobinism is the spirit of retaliation, violence and murder." The American Antislavery Society asked not only its members but also the slaves of the South to forego the use of violence. Its declaration said that "[we reject and] entreat the oppressed to reject, the use of all carnal weapons for deliverance from bondage; relying solely upon those which are spiritual, and mighty through God to the pulling down of strongholds."[16] As the years passed and the strongholds remained, as the war with Mexico of 1846-1848 was followed by the Fugitive Slave Law of 1850, many abolitionists began to wonder if nonviolence was enough.

One of these was Garrison's lieutenant, Wendell Phillips. In his first public speech, on the murder of abolitionist editor Elijah Lovejoy in 1837, Phillips had dissociated himself from "what are called Peace principles" and justified Lovejoy's use of arms to protect his press. After the Fugitive Slave Law he

---

14. *The Life and Writings of Frederick Douglass,* ed. Philip S. Foner (New York: International Publishers, 1950), II, pp. 13–14; *Sumner . . . works,* I (1889), pp. 5–132 and II, pp. 323–429; *William Lloyd Garrison, 1805–1879: The Story of His Life Told by His Children* (New York: The Century Co., 1885–1889), II, pp. 221–242, 326–328; Merle E. Curti, *The American Peace Crusade, 1815–1860* (Durham: Duke University Press, 1929), pp. 64, 80–82 *et passim.*

15. Leon Litwack, "Non-Violence in Negro Rights Movements of the Ante-Bellum North" and Louis Filler, "Non-Violence and Abolition," papers presented to a conference on nonviolence at Hobart and William Smith College, May 1962.

16. The first quotation is from the "Declaration of Sentiments adopted by the [American] Peace Convention . . . 1838," *Selections from the Writings and Speeches of William Lloyd Garrison* (Boston: R. F. Wallcutt, 1852), p. 75 (see Document 3); for the second, see *William Lloyd Garrison, 1805–1879,* I, p. 409.

went further: "It seems to me that the man who is not conscientiously a non-resistant, is not only entitled, he is bound, to use every means that he has or can get to resist arrest in the last resort." Yet while justifying violence in defense of individuals, Phillips continued to believe in nonviolent abolition of slavery as an institution until the Civil War began. "I think," Phillips then told a cheering audience, "the South is all wrong, and the administration [of Abraham Lincoln] is all right."[17]

A more dramatic conversion to violence was the case of Frederick Douglass. As late as September 1849 Douglass could say: "I am willing at all times to be known as a Garrisonian abolitionist." But earlier that same year Douglass had thrown Faneuil Hall into an uproar by declaring that he would welcome the news of a slave insurrection in the South. In 1854, his attitude hardened by the Fugitive Slave Law, Douglass posed the question, "Is It Right and Wise to Kill a Kidnapper?," and answered, Yes. In 1856 Douglass said of the slave system, "its peaceful annihilation is almost hopeless." In June 1860 the former slave came full circle, stating:

I have little hope of the freedom of the slave by peaceful means. A long course of peaceful slaveholding has placed the slaveholders beyond the reach of moral and humane considerations. . . . The only penetrable point of a tyrant is the *fear of death*.[18]

Henry Thoreau's emphasis, even in "Civil Disobedience," was on lawbreaking not on pacifism. Conscious of writing near Concord Bridge, Thoreau asked, in effect: If violence was justified against a tax on tea, how much more would it be justified to emancipate the slaves? The essay is, in fact, a subtle and ambiguous synthesis of the previously disparate Quaker and Lockean traditions. Thoreau, like Roger Williams or William Penn, affirms the peril of coercion in spiritual matters: he refused to pay a tax for the support of the established church several years before his more celebrated refusal of the Massachusetts poll tax. At the same time Thoreau breaks with Garrison's disavowal of jacobinism, and flatly declares that "all men recognize the right of revolution" and that "it is not too soon for honest men to rebel and revolutionize." Thoreau's condemnation of all government can be misleading here. Thomas Paine's *Common Sense* also began with the conception that "Society in every state is a blessing, but government, even in its best state, is but a necessary evil. . . ." This belief did not prevent Paine from advocating a political revolution; and Thoreau himself tells us that, speaking practically,

17. "The Murder of Lovejoy," in Wendell Phillips, *Speeches, Lectures, and Letters* (Boston: James Redpath, 1863), p. 7; "Sims Anniversary," *ibid.*, p. 89; "Under the Flag," *ibid.*, p. 400.

18. *Life and Writings of Frederick Douglass*, II, pp. 49–51, 284–289.

what he wants is not *no* government, but a better government at once.[19]

In "Civil Disobedience" Thoreau presented individual noncooperation with the state as "the definition of a peaceable revolution, if any such is possible." By 1854, under the hammer of the Fugitive Slave Law, Thoreau was prepared to say: "Show me a free state, and a court truly of justice, and I will fight for them, if need be." In 1859, speaking on the death of John Brown, Thoreau said: "I do not wish to kill nor to be killed, but I can foresee circumstances in which both these things would be by me unavoidable." He squarely supported Brown's violent raid:

> It was his [Brown's] peculiar doctrine that a man has a perfect right to interfere by force with the slaveholder, in order to rescue the slave. I agree with him. . . . I shall not be forward to think him mistaken in his method who quickest succeeds to liberate the slave. I speak for the slave when I say, I prefer the philanthropy of Captain Brown to that philanthropy which neither shoots me nor liberates me.[20]

The collapse of Garrisonian nonviolence is the most striking failure of nonviolence in United States history to date. One can argue endlessly whether it might have been otherwise. Should Garrison have gone into the South, like Woolman, and tried to reason with slaveholders face-to-face rather than condemn them at a distance? The great and unavoidable fact is that the abolitionist movement, virtually unanimous in adhering to nonviolence in the 1830s, was almost equally united in supporting Lincoln when the war came.

Garrison's unctuous explanations for his own change of position hardly help. "Oh, Mr. President," Garrison declared at a July Fourth picnic in the first year of the Civil War,

> . . . how it delights my heart when I think that the worst thing we propose to do for the South is the very best thing that God or men can do! . . . Yes, we will make it possible for them to be a happy and prosperous people, as they have never been, and never can be, with slavery. We will make it possible for them to have free schools, and free presses, and free institutions, as we do at the North. . . . Let us return them good for evil, by seizing this opportunity to deliver them from their deadliest curse—that is Christian.

To Quakers distressed that their sons had joined the Union Army, Garrison said: "They had imagined they were on the plane of the Sermon on the

---

19. Henry Thoreau, "Civil Disobedience," in *A Yankee in Canada, with Anti-Slavery and Reform Papers* (Boston: Ticknor and Fields, 1866), pp. 127, 124 (see Document 5); *The Complete Writings of Thomas Paine,* ed. Philip S. Foner, I (New York: The Citadel Press, 1945), p. 4.

20. "Civil Disobedience," in *A Yankee in Canada,* p. 137; "Slavery in Massachusetts," *ibid.,* p. 112; "A Plea for Captain John Brown," *ibid.,* pp. 175, 174–175.

Mount, and they found they were only up to the level of Lexington and Bunker Hill. . . ."[21]

Perhaps the most significant contribution to the nonviolent tradition between the Revolution and the Civil War was the thinking of Elihu Burritt, one of the few abolitionists to oppose the Civil War on pacifist grounds. Burritt was imaginative in devising techniques of peace agitation. In 1846, when England and the United States came to the brink of war over Oregon, Burritt urged workingmen and merchants to send "friendly addresses" to their English counterparts. In the same year Burritt founded in England the League of Universal Brotherhood, members of which took the following pledge:

> Believing all war to be inconsistent with the spirit of Christianity, and destructive to the best interests of mankind, I do hereby pledge myself never to enlist or enter into any army or navy, or to yield any voluntary support or sanction to the preparation for or prosecution of any war, by whomsoever, for whatsoever proposed, declared or waged. And I do hereby associate myself with all persons, of whatever country, condition, or colour, who have signed, or shall hereafter sign this pledge, in a "League of Universal Brotherhood"; whose object shall be, to employ all legitimate and moral means for the abolition of all war, and all spirit, and all manifestation of war, throughout the world; for the abolition of all restrictions upon international correspondence and friendly intercourse, and of whatever else tends to make enemies of nations, or prevents their fusion into one peaceful brotherhood; for the abolition of all institutions and customs which do not recognize the image of God and a human brother in every man of whatever clime, colour, or condition of humanity.[22]

Finally, Burritt's proposal for a general strike of workingmen against war foreshadowed the mass (as opposed to individual) nonviolence of trade unionists and Blacks in the twentieth century.

ANARCHISTS AND PROGRESSIVES

Nonviolence was quiescent for a generation after 1861, just as it had been after 1776. A few of the prewar reformers, such as Adin Ballou and Henry C. Wright, joined with Alfred Henry Love to form the Universal Peace Union shortly after the war. Its membership was never more than about 10,000.

Anarchism formed an important connecting link between nineteenth- and twentieth-century nonviolence in the United States. Its alien character has

---

21. *William Lloyd Garrison, 1805–1879,* IV, pp. 31–32, 37.
22. Quoted in Curti, *The American Peace Crusade,* p. 145.

been exaggerated. The bitter tone of anarchist writing during the industrial wars of the 1870s and 1880s echoed such prewar antistatists as John Humphrey Noyes, founder of Perfectionism and the Oneida Community, who wrote to his close friend William Lloyd Garrison in 1837:

> When I wish to form a conception of the government of the United States (using a personified representation), I picture to myself a bloated, swaggering libertine, trampling on the Bible—its own Constitution—its treaties with the Indians—the petitions of its citizens; with one hand whipping a negro tied to a liberty-pole, and with the other dashing an emaciated Indian to the ground. ... The question urges itself upon me—"What have I, as a Christian, to do with such a villain?"

"My hope of the millenium," Noyes asserted, "begins where Dr. Beecher's expires—viz., AT THE OVERTHROW OF THIS NATION."[23]

The ultimate goal of all anarchists was a society that would function nonviolently without need of the aggressive state. *The Alarm*, founded by Haymarket anarchist Albert Parsons, printed in 1888 a piece by Gertrude Kelly called: "Passive Resistance. Robbery of the People Based on Force Cannot be Remedied by Force." It contrasted the effect upon the public mind of passive resistance, which causes "the capitalist to stand forth unmasked before the world as the enemy of mankind," and violence, which casts "ourselves [instead of the capitalists] before the world in the light of criminals." A rent strike in tenements owned by the Trinity Church would therefore be better advised than blowing up the Church. Besides, "we must never fail to remember that it is upon an improvement in the moral tone of the people that true progress depends, that, therefore, our means as our ends must be pure." The gentle anarchist concluded by recommending to her readers Parker Pillsbury's *Acts of the Antislavery Apostles*.[24]

Anarchism wavered between an individualist and a communal vision of the good society. Josiah Warren, editor of *The Peaceable Revolutionist*, lived for a time at Robert Owen's New Harmony colony before developing the atomistic doctrine that he passed on to his disciple, Benjamin Tucker. The anarchists presented in this volume shared a more collectivist ideal. The Haymarket anarchists were trade-unionists. Emma Goldman was influenced by the idealization of the peasant village common among the Narodnik revolutionaries with whom she worked in Russia before emigrating to the United States. Bill Haywood espoused a "syndicalist" or "anarcho-syndicalist" future in which workers themselves would collectively manage the economy. Haywood was a well-known spokesperson for the Industrial Workers of the

---

23. John Humphrey Noyes to W. L. Garrison, March 22, 1837, in *William Lloyd Garrison, 1805–1879*, II, pp. 145–148.

24. *The Alarm* (Chicago), July 14, 1888. We owe this reference to the kindness of Professor Herbert Gutman of the University of Buffalo.

World, or "Wobblies." No organization in United States history has been so wholeheartedly dedicated to direct action. The Wobblies believed that labor laws would remain dead letters unless direct action created pressure for enforcement; that the way to fight violations of free speech was to fill the jails; and that the means for destroying capitalism was not electoral politics, but the general strike.

Nonviolence in the United States was also influenced by Tolstoy, who, finding his own Christian pacifism expressed by Garrison and other North Americans, transmitted the Garrisonian doctrine of nonviolence to a new generation of reformers in the United States. Clarence Darrow, William Jennings Bryan, and Jane Addams made the pilgrimage to Tolstoy's home at Yasnaya Polyana to sit at the great man's feet. Hamlin Garland has recorded the influence of Tolstoy upon reformers at the close of the century. From 1888 to 1890, Garland wrote, they received "utterances of such apostolic austerity that they read like encyclicals from the head of a great church—the church of humanity. . . . We quoted Ibsen to reform the drama and Tolstoy to reform society. We made use of every available argument his letters offered."[25] Later, Darrow would help to revolutionize the treatment of criminals with *Resist Not Evil* (1903), and Bryan would resign as Secretary of State in protest against the United States' drift toward war in 1915.

Another powerful influence on prewar nonviolence, but of a quite different character, was the thinking of William James. James, a physiologist and psychologist as well as a philosopher, broke away from the traditional Christian conception that killing and loving service are completely contradictory kinds of action. In his famous essay, "The Moral Equivalent of War," he asserted that war and constructive labor are varying expressions of an impulse to heroic self-sacrifice. Thus war is not all bad. It is "the great preserver of our ideals of hardihood," "the supreme theatre of human strenuousness," the approved social mechanism for calling forth "strenuous honor and disinterestedness." These qualities of military service help to explain why "war-taxes are the only ones men never hesitate to pay."

Jane Addams' *Newer Ideals of Peace* (1907) blended the teachings of Tolstoy and James. Toward the end of the book Ms. Addams told again one of the Russian master's famous anecdotes:

> The Doukhobors are a religious sect in Russia whose creed emphasizes the teaching of non-resistance. A story is told of one of their young men who, because of his refusal to enter the Russian army, was brought for trial before a judge, who reasoned with him concerning the folly of his course and in return received a homily upon the teachings of Jesus. "Quite right you are," answered the judge, "from the point of abstract virtue, but the time has not yet come to put into practice the

---

25. Hamlin Garland, "The Reformer Tolstoy," Introduction to *Recollections and Essays,* by Leo Tolstoy, in *The Works of Leo Tolstoy,* pp. vii–viii.

literal sayings of Christ." "The time may not have come for you, your Honor," was the reply, "but the time has come for us."[26]

In the United States, such conscientious objection to military service is for the most part a twentieth-century phenomenon because conscription itself is a modern practice. During the Civil War both North and South provided for compulsory military service, but it was possible to hire a substitute under the Union law, and to secure exemption by a $500 payment under its Confederate counterpart. During the Spanish-American War there was no conscription law. Hence it was World War I which for the first time brought the objector and the state into unavoidable frontal conflict.

While most prewar pacifists followed John Dewey in supporting President Wilson, others held fast to Wilson's own "peace without victory" doctrine of January 1917. One such was Randolph Bourne, who indignantly struck off the phrase, "War is essentially the health of the State."[27] Another was Jane Addams herself. Compelled to watch immigrants whom she had helped to become citizens resentfully submit to conscription, Jane Addams decided it was necessary that "at least a small number of us should be forced into an unequivocal position."[28] In this belief she supported Henry Ford's Peace Ship, took part in the Women's Congress at the Hague in 1915, and became the first president of the Women's International League for Peace and Freedom (WILPF).

The WILPF was one among many peace organizations founded during World War I. The Fellowship of Reconciliation (FOR) grew out of a pledge between the Kaiser's chaplain, Friedrich Siegmund-Schultze, and an English Quaker, Henry Hodgkin, on the day before the war began, to "keep the bonds of Christian love unbroken across the frontier." Organized in England late in 1914, the FOR set up a branch in the United States in November 1915. The American Civil Liberties Union (ACLU) originated in 1916 as the American Union Against Militarism. The American Friends Service Committee (AFSC) came into being three weeks after United States entry into the war under the leadership of Rufus Jones. The AFSC, prototype of the later Civilian Conservation Corps and Peace Corps, was a practical expression of the philosophy of William James' "The Moral Equivalent of War."

The conscription law of May 1917 provided that members of "well recognized" religious groups "whose existing creed or principles" forbade their members "to participate in war in any form" might be assigned to noncombatant service within the armed forces. According to War Department figures,

---

26. Jane Addams, *Newer Ideals of Peace* (New York: The Macmillan Co., 1907), p. 230.

27. Randolph S. Bourne, *War and the Intellectuals: Collected Essays, 1915–1919*, ed. Carl Resek (New York: Harper & Row, 1964), p. 69.

28. Jane Addams, "Personal Reactions During War," *Peace and Bread in Time of War* (Boston: G. K. Hall, 1960), p. 133; see Document 13.

64,693 claims for noncombatant status under the law were made. Of these, 56,830 claims were accepted by local draft boards; however, only 20,873 of these applicants were actually inducted, and just 3,989 of that number persisted in their position after reaching camp because of the extraordinary harshness with which objectors were treated.[29]

If the war stimulated nonviolence in the form of conscientious objection, it was also a time of spectacular direct action by the women's suffrage movement. Only slightly less radical than their sisters in England, one of whom threw herself under the hooves of the King's horse in the Grand National, Alice Paul and her associates in the United States refused to work and eat in jail when they were denied the status of political prisoners (see Document 12). The suffragettes represented Progressivism's nearest approach to the tradition of civil disobedience and direct action.

BETWEEN THE WARS: THE INFLUENCE OF THE LABOR MOVEMENT

Between the two world wars, antiwar sentiment took its tone not from the essentially religious outlook of Jane Addams, but from the political pacifism of Eugene Debs. As Garrison had placed on the masthead of *The Liberator* the motto of Thomas Paine, "Our country is the world, our countrymen are all mankind," so at the outbreak of World War I Debs said: "I have no country to fight for; my country is the earth, and I am a citizen of the world." Debs was sentenced to ten years in the Atlanta Penitentiary at the age of sixty-five. He responded with "My Prison Creed":

> While there is a lower class I am in it;
> While there is a criminal element I am of it;
> While there's a soul in prison I am not free.[30]

While Debs was in Atlanta Penitentiary, the Unitarian minister John Haynes Holmes began to popularize in the United States the teaching of Gandhi. One expression of the resulting dialogue between pacifism and socialism was Reinhold Niebuhr's brilliant and still unsurpassed inquiry into the meaning of

---

29. Mulford Q. Sibley and Philip E. Jacob, *Conscription of Conscience: The American State and the Conscientious Objector, 1940–1947* (Ithaca: Cornell University Press, 1952), pp. 11–12, citing for their statistics J. S. Easby-Smith, *Statement concerning the Treatment of Conscientious Objectors in the Army,* published by the War Department, June 18, 1919. The same source is credited in Stephen M. Kohn, *Jailed for Peace: The History of American Draft Law Violators, 1658–1985* (Westport, Conn.: Greenwood Press, 1986), pp. 25–26.

30. These words will be found at the beginning of Debs' account of his prison experiences, *Walls and Bars* (Chicago: Socialist Party, 1927), p. 11.

terms such as "violence," "nonviolence," "coercion," and "force" in *Moral Man and Immoral Society*, published in 1932. In this book, the most influential United States theologian of the twentieth century was in transition between his early, socialist and pacifist phase (Niebuhr was at one time national chairman of the Fellowship of Reconciliation), and the later, "neo-orthodox" phase for which he is better known. Demanding that the Christian confront the realities of class struggle, Niebuhr condemned any teaching of nonviolence that permitted the comfortable to make peace with oppression. When used to change society, Niebuhr argued, nonviolence inevitably involves coercion. "Once the principle of coercion and resistance has been accepted as necessary to the social struggle, and pure pacifism has thus been abandoned," Niebuhr continued, "the differences between violence and nonviolence lose some of their significance though they remain important."[31]

Moral Man and Immoral Society also contained a startling prophecy. Writing a generation before the Montgomery bus boycott in the bitter era of the Scottsboro case, Niebuhr declared:

> It is hopeless for the Negro to expect complete emancipation from the menial social and economic position into which the white man has forced him, merely by trusting in the moral sense of the white race. It is equally hopeless to attempt emancipation through violent rebellion.[32]

The alternative was nonviolent mass action. "It will, if persisted in with the same patience and discipline attained by Mr. Gandhi and his followers, achieve a degree of justice which neither pure moral suasion nor violence could gain." The Negro, Niebuhr concluded, "would need only to fuse the aggressiveness of the new and young Negro with the patience and forebearance of the old Negro, to rob the former of its vindictiveness and the latter of its lethargy."[33]

The thought and action of Abraham Johannes ("A.J.") Muste form an instructive counterpoint to the development of Reinhold Niebuhr. Muste, an ordained minister, resigned his pastorate during World War I because of pacifist convictions. He then turned to the organization of labor, as he tells in his account of the 1919 textile strike in Lawrence, Massachusetts. The strike convinced him that "the often expressed idea that Americans cannot understand nonviolence, as Indians (for example) do, is erroneous" (see Document 16).

For a time during the Depression, Muste abandoned both Christianity and nonviolence and became a leader of the Trotskyist movement in the United

---

31. Reinhold Niebuhr, "Is Peace or Justice the Goal?," *The World Tomorrow*, XV, September 21, 1932, p. 277.

32. Reinhold Niebuhr, *Moral Man and Immoral Society* (New York: Charles Scribner's Sons, 1932), p. 252.

33. *Ibid.*, p. 254.

States. While in Paris in 1936 he reconverted to Christian pacifism. He described the experience in a moving letter to Cara Cook:

> War is the central problem for us all today. . . . International war and coercion at home will continue to exist for just so long as people regard these things as suitable, as even conceivable, instruments of policy. . . . The Christian position does not mean to justify or condone the capitalist system. Quite the contrary. It provides the one measure by which the capitalist system stands thoroughly and effectively condemned. It stands condemned because it makes the Christian relation in its full sense, the relation of brotherhood between human beings, impossible. . . . So long, however, as the matter remains on the plane of economics and self-interest, no one is in a position to condemn another. When we feel indignation, as we do even in spite of ourselves, we then enter the realm of standards and values, the realm in which moral judgment is pronounced, the realm in which ethical and spiritual appeals are made . . . the realm of morality and religion.[34]

The labor movement of the 1930s influenced in many ways the nonviolent movement after World War II. A number of leaders, such as Muste, E. D. Nixon of the Montgomery, Alabama bus boycott movement, and James Peck, were active in the labor movement before they became famous as agitators for peace and civil rights.[35] The theme song of Black sit-inners, "We Shall

---

34. Quoted in Nat Hentoff, *Peace Agitator: The Story of A. J. Muste* (New York: The Macmillan Co., 1963), pp. 99–100.

35. When the Montgomery bus boycott began in 1955, E. D. Nixon had served as president of the Alabama branch of the Sleeping Car Porters union for more than twenty-five years. He also served for five years as president of the NAACP chapter in Montgomery, recruiting Rosa Parks, secretary of the chapter at the time of the bus boycott. When Ms. Parks was arrested on December 1, 1955, for refusing to give up her seat to a white passenger, Nixon bailed her out, urged her to fight the matter in the courts, and telephoned Martin Luther King, Jr., to ask him to endorse a bus boycott and to make his church available for meetings. (Taylor Branch, *Parting the Waters: America in the King Years 1954–63* [New York: Simon and Schuster, 1988], pp. 120–133). James Peck, who died as this edition was in preparation, worked as a seaman for several years in the 1930s and was active in the formation of the National Maritime Union. In 1940 he declared himself a conscientious objector. During World War II, he was imprisoned for more than two years at the penitentiary in Danbury, Connecticut, where he helped to organize a strike to protest racial segregation (see Document 21). In 1947, he set fire to his draft card outside the White House and took part in a Journey of Reconciliation, an integrated bus trip through parts of the South. He also participated in the 1961 Freedom Ride. A crowd in Birmingham, Alabama, assaulted him as he tried to enter the lunch room at a bus terminal with a Black man. His injuries required 50 stitches. (Obituary, "James Peck, 78, Union Organizer Who Promoted Civil Rights Causes," *New York Times,* July 13, 1993, p. A13.)

Overcome," had previously been sung by striking Appalachian textile work-ers. And the sit-in itself was unquestionably suggested in part by the sit-down strikes of the 1930's. Rosa Parks acted spontaneously when she refused to move to the back of a bus in Montgomery in December 1955; yet it is also true that she had shortly before returned from a leadership seminar at the Highlander Folk School in Tennessee, the South's principal training center for union organizers.[36]

THE NONVIOLENT MOVEMENT DURING AND AFTER WORLD WAR II

The years before World War II produced a resurgence of religious pacifism. Quaker Larry Gara describes a sequence of experiences that may have been typical of the several thousand war resisters in federal prisons during World War II.

[W]hile in high school, I found a small Fellowship of Reconciliation group which introduced me to antiwar activity. I participated in some anti-draft rallies and on one occasion engaged in a one-person picket line against war. I had read about World War I and the disillusionment which followed it. As a student in a nearby college I, along with three others, failed to stand up when the college administrators, without warning, instituted the pledge of allegiance in convocation. For that I was almost expelled . . . .

My convictions were deepened by . . . joining the Society of Friends, two summers in volunteer AFSC work camps, reading about and later meeting some of the World War I resisters, and especially by partici-pating in a walk from Lancaster, Pennsylvania to New York City during Christmas break of 1940. The Food for Europe Pilgrimage was to dramatize the need for sending food to the people of the Low Countries who were starving under Nazi rule because of the Allied blockade. That walk, along with another the following spring, transformed me from primarily an armchair pacifist to an activist. Among other things it introduced me to A. J. Muste and to several young men who had refused to register for the draft [see Document 19].

By the time I had reached the age of twenty, I knew that I could not in good conscience register for conscription . . . .[37]

When war came, it was accompanied by a draft law more liberal than that of World War I. At least 25,000 persons performed noncombatant service in

---

36. See Branch, *Parting the Waters,* p. 130.

37. Larry Gara, "Testimony of a Peace Activist," an unpublished paper read to Dayton, Ohio area activists as part of a Hiroshima Day Commemoration.

the armed forces and 11,868 reported for alternative service work in Civilian Public Service camps. CPS camps witnessed some small-scale triumphs for nonviolence, as in the encounter with Forest Service foreman Eric Kloppenburg ("a big, rough, tough hater of Germans, Japanese and CO's") narrated by CO poet William Stafford.[38]

But many of those who went to CPS camps came to feel that they had mistakenly allowed themselves to become part of the war system. There were 5,516 prosecutions of war objectors for failure to register, failure to report for induction, walking out of CPS camps, and similar offenses, with more than 5,000 resulting jail sentences.[39]

Pacifism persisted and grew stronger after World War II because of the way the war ended. Early in the morning of August 6, 1945, a United States Air Force pilot named Claude Eatherly flew his B-29 bomber, the *Straight Flush*, over Hiroshima, Japan. "The weather seemed ideal" for dropping the first atomic bomb, the reconnaissance plane reported. A few hours later four-fifths of Hiroshima's population of 245,000 were dead or seriously wounded. Eatherly spoke for many others when he wrote, subsequently, that the bombing of Hiroshima convinced him "that cruelty, hatred, violence and injustice never can and never will be able to create a mental, moral and material millennium. The only road to it is the all giving creative love, trust and brotherhood, not only preached but consistently practiced."[40]

There emerged after World War II a group of persons who had been war resisters (often the organizers of prison strikes and sit-ins) and who threw themselves into nonviolent direct action for peace and racial equality when the war ended. Among these postwar leaders of nonviolence were Bayard Rustin and David Dellinger, who joined with Muste to found the pacifist magazine *Liberation*. The Congress Of Racial Equality (1943), Peacemakers (1948), and the Committee for Nonviolent Action (1957), provided organizational channels for this new nonviolent movement.

James Peck later recalled that the first nonviolent direct action against atmospheric nuclear weapons testing occurred in the summer of 1946. He and forty others led around New York City's Times Square a stuffed goat mounted on roller-skate wheels with a placard around its neck saying, "Today me—Tomorrow you." (The Bikini hydrogen bomb tests, then being con-

---

38. See William Stafford, "The Battle of Anapamu Creek" (Document 20).

39. Sibley and Jacob, *Conscription of Conscience,* pp. 83, 333, 348, 523, citing Selective Service System, *Conscientious Objection,* Special Monograph No. 11, I (Washington, 1950), p. 315, for the total numbers of Selective Service registrants claiming various kinds of conscientious objector status, and Department of Justice figures reported in *The Reporter,* Nov. 1, 1945, p. 3, for prosecutions and convictions.

40. "Claude Eatherly to the Reverend N," August 8, 1960, *Burning Conscience. The case of the Hiroshima pilot, Claude Eatherly, told in his letters to Gunther Anders with a postscript for American readers by Anders* (New York: Monthly Review Press, 1962), p. 82.

ducted, involved the use of goats and other animals for experimental purposes.)

The odds against such a handful of demonstrators changing the course of history must have seemed overwhelming.[41] The protesters persisted, and the movement grew. In the late 1950s, Lawrence Scott resigned from his job as AFSC representative in Chicago and toured the country recruiting pacifists and liberals for a demonstration at the nuclear weapons testing site in Mercury, Nevada. (Scott later created the 1960 vigil against biological and chemical weapons at Fort Detrick, Maryland.) In the summer of 1958, Ted Olsen led a group who protested against the first Atlas missile bases being built near Cheyenne, Wyoming. One of the group was Ken Calkins, a founder of the Student Peace Union. Calkins sat down in protest in front of a truck being used to construct a missile site, was run over, and had his thigh broken.

The next major nonviolent action project against missile systems was Omaha Action in the summer of 1959 (see Document 24). About six persons committed civil disobedience by trespassing on a missile base near Meade, Nebraska, and received six-month federal prison sentences. A picture of the elderly A. J. Muste climbing over a fence just prior to his arrest has become a classic.

Bradford Lyttle, co-coordinator of Omaha Action and another arrestee, tells what happened next.

While in prison in the Medical Center for Federal Prisoners in Springfield, Missouri, as a result of Omaha Action, I thought about what should be the next project against missile systems. At that time, the Navy was ballyhooing its new Polaris missile-launching weapons systems and it seemed to me that that was a natural target. Not only were Polaris submarines the most destructive weapons ever built, capable of incinerating 16 cities in half an hour, but their main construction contractor was Electric Boat Shipyard at Groton, Connecticut, and their main base was the U.S. Submarine Base, just up the Thames River estuary. The location was perfect for a project that could mobilize the resources of the East Coast peace movement. Consequently, I decided that, after being released from prison, I would try to organize a project against Polaris submarines and missiles. . . .

We established an office in the Skid Row area of New London, and began to organize the project. From the beginning, the office was under

---

41. Pete Seeger reports an anecdote from those years. "Back in the 1950's there was a tiny peace demonstration in Times Square. A young Quaker was carrying a sign. A passerby scoffed: 'Do you think you're going to change the world by standing here at midnight with that sign?' 'I suppose not,' said the young man, 'But I'm going to make sure the world doesn't change me'." Pete Seeger, *Where Have All The Flowers Gone: A Singer's Stories, Songs, Seeds, Robberies* (Bethlehem, PA: Sing Out Corporation, 1993), p. 261.

attack from drunken sailors and right-wingers. Within a month, every window had been broken, and intruders had destroyed considerable literature and equipment. Also, they had attacked several participants. Nevertheless, we persisted in organizing a wide variety of projects in Groton and New London, and along the whole East Coast, ranging from Portsmouth, Maine to Norfolk, Virginia. Civil disobedience demonstrations involved trespassing on Electric Boat and the submarine base, and swimming out to newly-launched subs. The project received wide publicity in the media. . . .

. . . Peacemakers decided to hold its annual conference at Waterford, Connecticut, just west of New London, and rented a house, and part of a closed hotel. One Saturday, during a Peacemakers' meeting, two women joined our group. No one knew them. They introduced themselves as Barbara Deming and Mary Weigs, from Wellfleet, Massachusetts [see Documents 25, 45].

In the autumn of 1960, a number of participants in Polaris Action had lunch in a restaurant in New London, and hatched the next project: the San Francisco to Moscow Peace Walk.[42]

An informal moratorium on testing and, after this proved inadequate, a Soviet-American treaty banning atmospheric and underwater tests, were finally achieved.

With the Montgomery bus boycott of 1955-1956 and still more with the student sit-ins of 1960, nonviolence became a more significant social force than at any earlier period in the history of the United States. Bus service in Montgomery was a daily humiliation for the city's 50,000 Blacks. Often they were required to get off the bus and reboard at the rear after paying their fare in front. If there were not enough seats in the section reserved for whites to accomodate the white passengers, then the Blacks had to move further back to other seats, or stand. On December 1, 1955 the city's Black community began to boycott the buses in protest against these conditions. The boycott continued until November 13, 1956, when the United States Supreme Court declared bus segregation in Montgomery illegal. The combination of nonviolent direct action with legal pressure, successful in Montgomery, provided a model in subsequent agitation for equal access to public accomodations and the right to vote.

The genesis of the 1960 sit-ins has been described by Martin Oppenheimer. "On Aug. 9, 1958, the NAACP Youth Council in Oklahoma City began the first formal sit-in by predominantly Negro students." During the next year

---

42. Bradford Lyttle to Staughton and Alice Lynd, Jan. 24, 1994. This letter is also the source for the material in the text about Lawrence Scott, Ted Olsen, and Ken Calkins.

and a half there were several sporadic and unpublicized sit-ins in other border states. Then:

> Among the students at North Carolina Agricultural and Technical College in Greensboro, in the Fall of 1959, were four who were in the habit of getting together in the campus rooms of two of them for "bull-sessions." They assigned each other books to read—Frederick Douglass, Langston Hughes, Gandhi, among others. They watched a T-V documentary on Gandhi that semester. In January, 1960, one of the boys read Robert E. Davis' *The American Negro's Dilemma*, which complains of the Negro's apathy and failure to "do something on his own to alleviate his burdens, . . ." All of the boys were, or at some time had been, members of an NAACP Youth Council, but were not in contact with the NAACP at this point. Some months earlier they had asked for advice on how to run a direct action project, but had not heard from the National Office by the time action was decided on. At 4:30 p.m. on Feb. 1, 1960, the four went into the F. W. Woolworth store in downtown Greensboro, sat down, and waited for service.[43]

By December 31, 1960 sit-in demonstrations had occurred in over one hundred communities. Meantime, in April 1960 more than two hundred delegates, representing fifty-two colleges and high schools in thirty-seven communities in thirteen different states, met in Raleigh, North Carolina, and formed the Student Nonviolent Coordinating Committee (SNCC). It was SNCC that during the next five years led the effort to register unfranchised Blacks in the Deep South. This nonviolent movement between World War II and the mid-1960s resembled in many ways the Garrisonian movement of the 1830s. In one as in the other, peace and civil rights were closely intertwined. Channing and Burritt had their twentieth-century counterparts in a Bayard Rustin, who organized both a direct-action protest against French atomic testing in Africa, and the 1963 March on Washington, or a James Peck, one of four men to sail a small boat into the Pacific testing area in 1958 and also a participant in the 1961 Freedom Ride. When a 1962 Nashville-to-Washington peace walk left Nashville it walked right past a sit-in demonstration. By the time the group reached Washington, moved and heartened by its reception at Black churches along the way, the group had decided there was one issue, not two (see Document 25). Similarly, members of the Quebec-to-Guantanamo peace walk in 1963-1964 spent two months hunger-striking

---

43. Martin Oppenheimer, "The Southern Student Movement: Year I," *The Journal of Negro Education* (Fall 1964), pp. 396–398, summarizing his "The Genesis of the Southern Negro Student Movement (Sit-In Movement): A Study in Contemporary Negro Protest" (unpublished Ph.D. dissertation, University of Pennsylvania, 1963). See also the account of Izell Blair, one of the Greensboro four, in Robert Penn Warren, *Who Speaks for the Negro?* (New York: Random House, 1965), pp. 358–361.

in Albany, Georgia, for the right to walk through the downtown business district where civil rights demonstrations had been forbidden (see Document 26).

The older and newer movements were similar, too, in their underlying philosophies. John Woolman could have affirmed the "discipline" of the Quebec-to-Guantanamo peace walk or the rules of action of the Congress Of Racial Equality (see Documents 26A, 28A). Garrison could have written the declaration of the Student Nonviolent Coordinating Committee at its founding conference in 1960 (see Document 28B).

These very similarities between the old and the new nonviolent movements raised the question: Would nonviolence in the twentieth century, as in the nineteenth century, prove only a passing phase of a movement ending in force and bloodshed? There were many indications in the 1960s that this was so. As Wendell Phillips had justified violence first for individual self-defense, then for the transformation of society, so in the middle of the 1960s civil rights workers in the ghettoes of the North and in the hard-core areas of the South began to arm for self-protection.

The civil rights turmoil of the middle 1960s could, however, be diagnosed in a different way: as a turning toward more fundamental social change, involving masses of people, not just solitary intellectuals. Thoreau had defined individual civil disobedience as the method of peaceable revolution, if such a revolution were possible. The Civil War came, seeming to disprove this possibility; but a generation later Gandhi discovered in South Africa how masses of people—without which no genuine revolution can occur—could use nonviolent action. In the 1930s, the labor movement in the United States coupled the strike, itself an essentially nonviolent technique, with the deliberate civil disobedience of the sit-down. Like the labor movement, the Black protest movement involved thousands of poor, uneducated persons. They asked from nonviolence tangible results: they wanted jobs as well as freedom. The violence encountered in 1963-1964 signified that the direction of nonviolent action was shifting from public accommodations to the twin levers of power in our society, the vote and the job. Because the objectives were more basic, resistance was more bitter and tenacious. Violence increased as the target of the protest became "the system" and "the power structure." Nonviolent action tended to become nonviolent revolution.

In this modern civil rights struggle, nonviolence was referred to both as a "tactic" and as a "way of life." Both are long-standing and essential components of the tradition of nonviolence in the United States. In a nonviolent mass movement, such as the strikes of the 1930s or the civil rights actions of the 1950s and 1960s, most participants have been nonviolent because they were outnumbered and outgunned, and because their refusal to retaliate when attacked won them necessary sympathizers. Yet throughout our history there have always been a few who chose nonviolence because it answered a personal need to live in harmony with universal forces of life and love. For them, nature and nature's God required what Barbara Deming described as "two hands upon the oppressor—one hand taking from him what is not his due, the other slowly calming him, as we do this."[44]

What distinguishes this absolutist strain in the nonviolent tradition is a reluctance to accept a stereotyped image of "the enemy," a refusal to relinquish the conception that the antagonist is human. Yet the most sensitive of this group have also felt compelled to confront the full reality of violence and murder as practiced, for example, in the southern United States, or still more brutally, in parts of Central and South America. If there is a way out of the dilemma, it cannot be found in history books. It will be found only in the action of persons who refuse to choose between justice and love, and seek a way forward that includes both.

The first edition of this book went to press at a time of mingled success and tragedy for nonviolence in the United States. On the one hand, there were victories: the Soviet-American treaty banning nuclear tests in the atmosphere (summer 1963), the civil rights bill (summer 1964), the voting bill (summer 1965). But in Alabama and Mississippi, these years brought death to William Moore, walking from Baltimore to Jackson, Mississippi on behalf of civil rights; to Medgar Evers, shot in the back in Jackson; to four children bombed in a Birmingham, Alabama church; to Michael Schwerner, James Chaney, and Andrew Goodman, murdered on the first day of the 1964 Mississippi Summer Project; to Jimmy Jackson, James Reeb, and Viola Liuzzo in Selma, Alabama.

Speaking at a memorial service for Schwerner, Chaney, and Goodman in August 1964, Robert Moses, director of the Mississippi Summer Project, "emphasized that their bodies were discovered almost simultaneously with the United States bombing of North Vietnam after the Tonkin Bay incident."[45] There was a connection between these events, Moses said. Dark-skinned people were being killed both in Mississippi and in Vietnam. Moses spelled out the connection more fully at the Berkeley Teach-In against the Vietnam War in May 1965.

A couple of months ago, a month and a half, people marched out of the North down to Selma. The incident which triggered them off was the killing of Reverend Reeb. Before Reverend Reeb was killed, a Negro was killed, Jimmy Jackson. His death and his killing didn't trigger anything off, except confusion as to how he was exactly killed. Now we've watched the phenomenon time and again in the South. Before the summer project last summer we watched five Negroes mur-

---

44. Barbara Deming, "Pacifism," *Win*, May 1, 1971, p. 8, reprinted under its original title but slightly edited as "New Men, New Women: Some Notes on Nonviolence," in Barbara Deming, *We Cannot Live Without Our Lives* (New York: Grossman Publishers, 1974).

45. Staughton Lynd, preface to Bob Moses, "Mississippi: 1961–1962," *Liberation* (January 1970), p. 7.

dered in two counties of Mississippi with no reaction from the country. We couldn't get the news out. Then we saw that when the three civil rights workers were killed [Chaney, Schwerner, and Goodman], and two of them were white, the whole country reacted, went into motion. There's a deep problem behind that, and I think that if you can begin to understand what that problem is—why you don't move when a Negro is killed the same way you move when a white person is killed—then maybe you can begin to understand this country in relation to Vietnam and the third world, the Congo and Santo Domingo.

I saw a picture in the AP release. It said, "Marine captured Communist rebel." Now I looked at that picture and what I saw was a little colored boy standing against a wire fence with a big huge white Marine with a gun in his back. But what I knew was that the people in this country saw a Communist rebel. And that we travel in different realities. And that the problem about Vietnam is how to change the reality of this country, which is isolated, how to switch that. That's going to be a very, very deep problem.[46]

Martin Luther King, Jr., also stressed the connection between violence at home, and violence abroad, in a book on the Birmingham demonstrations of 1963:

In measuring the full implications of the civil-rights revolution, the greatest contribution may be in the area of world peace. The concept of nonviolence has spread on a mass scale in the United States as an instrument of change in the field of race relations. To date only a few practitioners of nonviolent direct action have been committed to its philosophy. The great mass have used it pragmatically as a tactical weapon, without being ready to live it.

More and more people, however, have begun to conceive of this powerful ethic as a necessary way of life in a world where the wildly accelerated development of nuclear power has brought into being weapons that can annihilate all humanity. . . .

King summed up: "Nonviolence, the answer to the Negroes' need, may become the answer to the most desperate need of all humanity."[47]

II

After the murder of Dr. King in 1968, the spirit of nonviolence seemed for a time to move outside the United States. During the period 1968-1986,

46. Folkways Records Album No. FD5765, *Berkeley Teach-In: Vietnam,* ed. Louis Menashe (1966), transcript, pp. 5–6.

47. Martin Luther King, Jr., *Why We Can't Wait* (New York: Harper & Row, 1964), pp. 168–169.

nonviolent movements associated with Lech Walesa in Poland, Desmond
Tutu in South Africa, Oscar Romero in El Salvador, and Corazon Aquino in
the Phillipines, made headlines worldwide. In the late 1980s, masses of
unarmed demonstrators carrying candles brought down Communist regimes
throughout Eastern Europe. As we write in early 1994, the nonviolent impulse
in the Third World continues in what Phillipine base communities call "active
nonviolence" and Father Aristide in Haiti has termed the "revolution without arms."[48]

In the United States, meanwhile, after a period (late 1960s, early 1970s)
in which many activists scorned nonviolence as "bourgeois" and sought to
imitate Third World armed guerrillas,[49] there followed years of apparent
apathy and ideological retreat. Under the surface, however, a powerful new
nonviolent movement was germinating. There was no single charismatic
spokesperson like Dr. King. Nor was nonviolent activism focused on civil
rights and peace, as it had been before 1968: new movements associated
with saving the environment, feminism, opposition to nuclear power, farm
workers' rights, divestment from South Africa, sanctuary for Central American refugees, and more, all presented themselves nonviolently. These new
nonviolent movements drew their activists from a generation of young persons
in and out of the armed forces who rejected the Vietnam War. Objection to
the Vietnam War (and, later, to the war in the Persian Gulf) went far beyond
the Hutterites, Mennonites, Brethren, and Quakers who made up the sub-
culture of traditional Protestant pacifism. Many objectors, such as the protesters at the Presidio and Brian Willson (Document 36), were working-class
young men who came to object to these wars because of what they experienced
in the military. Some objectors who were not religious in any conventional
sense found in the Nuremburg and Japanese War Crimes trials the doctrine

---

48. Niall O'Brien, *Island of Tears, Island of Hope: Living the Gospel in a Revolutionary Situation* (Maryknoll, N.Y.: Orbis Books, 1993); Mark Danner, "The Prophet,"
The New York Review of Books, Nov. 18, 1993, p. 31.

49. David Dellinger recounts a paradigmatic incident. During the 1968 demonstration against the Vietnam War at the Democratic Party national convention in Chicago,
Dellinger was attempting to chair a rally punctuated by sporadic violence from the
encircling Chicago police. Rennie Davis, the head of the nonviolent marshals, was
clubbed unconscious from behind, and taken to a hospital.

A half hour or more later, after everything had settled into a series of speeches
uninterrupted by police attacks, Tom Hayden strode up and onto the platform with
a group of four or five others. "We're taking over the microphone," he said angrily.
"The police attacked us and you called for nonviolence. They beat Rennie bloody
and you said to sit down and ignore it. Nonviolence is dead and you're telling the
crowd to be nonviolent. We're taking over the microphone for the rest of the rally.
From now on there will be no calls for nonviolence."

David Dellinger, *From Yale to Jail: The Life Story of a Moral Dissenter* (New
York: Pantheon Books, 1993), p. 330.

of individual responsibility for one's actions.[50] Like historian Howard Zinn (Document 52), a number of those who resisted these wars did not consider themselves pacifists, but concluded that any war waged by the United States under current and foreseeable conditions would be an unjust war.

Daniel Ellsberg is an important example of the way in which the traditional pacifist movement influenced new forms of protest. From 1959 to 1964 Ellsberg was a strategic analyst for the Rand Corporation and a consultant to the Department of Defense, which he joined in 1964. In 1965 he went to Vietnam for the State Department as a member of the team led by counterinsurgency expert Edward G. Lansdale. Returning to the Rand Corporation in 1967, he worked on Defense Secretary McNamara's study of U.S. decision making in Vietnam, now known as the Pentagon Papers, which he released to the press in 1971. In taking this step Ellsberg ended his own professional career and risked years of imprisonment. As he and his wife struggled with the question of what to do, Ellsberg was influenced by the Pentagon demonstration of October 1967 (Document 34), which he witnessed while in the office of Defense Secretary Robert McNamara, where the two of them were drafting plans for a U.S. invasion of North Vietnam[51]; by a conference cosponsored by the American Friends Service Committee in 1968; by reading the autobiographies of Gandhi and King, and Joan Bondurant's *Conquest of Violence*; by a War Resisters League conference to which he was invited by longtime antiwar organizer David McReynolds; and above all, by the example of Randy Kehler, who gave a talk to the conference "filled with hope about the growing understanding of nonviolence, especially among young people," and "mentioned almost casually that as a result of his own expression of nonviolence, he would be going to jail very shortly."[52]

Fed by so many streams of protest, the movement against the war in Vietnam grew during the course of the war to an extent without parallel in United States history. James Tollefson offers a statistical overview:

---

50. See David Mitchell, "What Is Criminal?," in *We Won't Go: Personal Accounts of War Objectors,* ed. Alice Lynd (Boston: Beacon Press, 1968), pp. 92–108.

51. David Dellinger, *From Yale to Jail,* pp. 311–312, basing himself on Ellsberg's testimony in 1987 at a trial of Dellinger and twenty others for having committed civil disobedience in the Capitol Rotunda against United States sponsorship of the Nicaraguan contras.

52. "Does the President Have an Unlimited Right to Lie? An Interview with Daniel Ellsberg," *Win,* Nov. 1, 1972, pp. 7–8. See also Ellsberg's "The Responsibility of Officials in a Criminal War," an expanded version of a lecture delivered at the Community Church in Boston on May 23, 1971, and printed in Daniel Ellsberg, *Papers on the War* (New York: Simon and Schuster, 1972), pp. 275–309. In this talk, delivered just before release of the Papers, Ellsberg analogized his own situation to that of Albert Speer, a policymaker for Nazi Germany. He quoted Speer's words, "I was like a man following a trail of bloodstained footprints through the snow without realizing someone had been injured." *Ibid.,* p. 308.

The total number of individuals receiving deferments from the draft as conscientious objectors during the Vietnam War was approximately 170,000. As many as 300,000 other applicants were denied CO deferments. Nearly 600,000 illegally evaded the draft; about 200,000 were formally accused of draft offenses. . . . Between 30,000 and 50,000 fled to Canada. Another 20,000 fled to other countries or lived underground in America. . . .

As the war dragged on and the legal definition of conscientious objection broadened, the number of COs increased dramatically, from 18,000 in 1964 to 61,000 in 1971. But as the number of men claiming conscientious objection rose, so did the prosecution of those whose claims were rejected. Between 1965 and 1972, the number of federal prosecutions for draft evasion rose from 340 to nearly 5,000 annually. During the height of the prosecutions, draft cases accounted for a tenth of all cases in the federal courts. . . .

Not all CO applications were from men seeking to avoid military service. About 17,000 were from individuals already in the military.[53]

When the United States withdrew its last military forces from Vietnam in 1975, protest refocused as opposition to the nuclear arms race, and continued. Thus Daniel Ellsberg denounced the "nuclear failsafe system"[54] and was arrested at the Rocky Flats testing grounds in Colorado.

Likewise Molly Rush, a Catholic "ultra-resister" (see Document 35), walked into the General Electric weapons assembly plant in King of Prussia, Pennsylvania as part of a group of eight persons in September 1980. The group carried with them hammers, with which they dented the nose cones of two missiles, and bottles of their own blood, which they poured on classified plans that were lying on a desk. We serve weapons as idols, she said, falsely worshipping "not golden calves, but golden nose cones." Symbolically, the group was putting down false idols and beating swords into plowshares, she explained.

Molly Rush believed that if children anywhere in the world were vulnerable, so were her own children, and that women have to break the cycle of violence. In a speech at Indiana University, Molly Rush said of the Plowshares Eight, they wanted

---

53. James W. Tollefson, *The Strength Not to Fight: An Oral History of Conscientious Objectors of the Vietnam War* (Boston: Little, Brown and Company, 1993), pp. 6–7, drawing on Lawrence Baskir and William A. Strauss, *Chance and Circumstance* (New York: Alfred A. Knopf, 1978); John Whiteclay Chambers, *To Raise an Army* (New York: Free Press, 1987); D. Michael Shafer, ed., *The Legacy* (Boston: Beacon, 1990); and David S. Surrey, *Choice of Conscience* (New York: Praeger, 1982).

54. See "Stranger than Strangelove: Dan Ellsberg on the Nuclear Failsafe System," *Win*, Nov. 17, 1977.

to shine a flashlight on the fact that many people go to work every day to build nuclear weapons that are going to kill their children and my kids [and here her voice broke] and I'm not going to let this happen without doing everything I can. . . . Every mother ought to think about the threat that's hanging over her kids and ask what she's going to do about it.[55]

Similarly Elizabeth McAlister, wife of nonviolent activist Philip Berrigan and like Molly Rush a mother with young children,

entered Griffiss Air Force Base in Rome, New York, on Thanksgiving 1983. We went inside the building that housed, among other things, a B-52 bomber that was being outfitted to carry a full complement of cruise missiles. Some of us hammered on the bomb bay doors of the B-52, poured our own blood on the fuselage, spraypainted the phrases "320 Hiroshimas" and "Thou Shalt Not Kill" and "If I Had A Hammer" on it, and taped to it photos of our children, and a "people's indictment" of Griffiss Air Force Base that we had drawn up.[56]

The new nonviolent movements drew on the movements of the 1950s and 1960s in a variety of ways. Consider sanctuary, that is, the practice of offering a place of refuge (usually a church) for those fleeing persecution. On April 20, 1968, the historic Arlington Street Church in Boston offered sanctuary to a draft refuser who had just lost his appeal to the Supreme Court and to an AWOL Vietnam veteran. From there sanctuary spread across the country.[57] Then in the late 1970s and 1980s small groups of concerned persons in Tucson, Arizona and Berkeley, California began meeting about the problem of refugees from El Salvador and Guatemala who were seized by the government, detained under exorbitant bail, and summarily deported, often to face possible death in their countries of origin. In Berkeley, "[o]ne minister reminded the group that during the Vietnam War, his church had declared itself a sanctuary for conscientious objectors who deserted the armed forces." The pastor of All Saints Church in Tucson remembers: "We had gotten a letter from a Lutheran pastor in L.A. who'd had a Salvadoran run into his church, and then be dragged out in handcuffs. We saw that maybe sanctuary was the appropriate tradition for what we were already doing."[58]

---

55. Liane Ellison Norman, "Molly Goes to Jail," *The Mill Hunk Herald* (Oct.–Nov.–Dec. 1980), pp. 7–8.

56. Elizabeth McAlister, "For Love of the Children," in *Swords into Plowshares: Nonviolent Direct Action for Disarmament*, ed. Arthur J. Laflin and Anne Montgomery (San Francisco: Harper & Row, 1987), pp. 157–158.

57. Michael Ferber and Staughton Lynd, *The Resistance* (Boston: Beacon Press, 1971), pp. 188–199, 225–227.

58. Susan Bibler Coutin, *The Culture of Protest: Religious Activism and the U.S. Sanctuary Movement* (Boulder: Westview Press, 1993), pp. 23–31.

The new nonviolence overflowed into many forms of community organizing. It was enriched by a new Catholicism that sprang up all over the world in the aftermath of the Second Vatican Council, 1962-1965, and the conference of Latin American bishops at Medellin in 1968 (Documents 37-41). It took surprising form in the consciously nonviolent leadership of farm worker organizer Cesar Chavez, and vice president Cecil Roberts of the United Mine Workers (Documents 42-43). These men led nonviolent labor struggles among people more accustomed to using dynamite, baseball bats, and squirrel rifles. Chavez was influenced by Gandhi. Both Chavez and Roberts modeled themselves on Dr. King, whose last address was to striking sanitation workers in Memphis.[59]

The new nonviolent movements also confronted United States imperialism, recognizing that approximately 5 percent of the world's population live in the United States, consume about half the world's resources, and use any means to keep things that way, as in the 1991 Gulf War (Documents 44-52).

Learning at last from the first inhabitants of this continent, the new nonviolent movements sought to preserve the fragile ecology of the earth, as well as to rediscover the harmony with all being set forth in many Native American traditions (Documents 53-56). Simon J. Ortiz has written: "The United States will not be able to survive unless it comes to truly know and accept its indigenous reality."[60]

We set forth as best we can the special characteristics of these various strands of the new nonviolence in the documents and headnotes that follow. (Some documents we would have liked to include do not appear because of problems getting permission to reprint.) A few general comments may be in order.

A SPIRITUAL BASIS?

Practitioners of nonviolence have continued to be uncertain whether their action requires a spiritual basis, and if so, what that basis should be. We

---

59. Martin Luther King, Jr., "I See the Promised Land," in *The Eyes on the Prize Civil Rights Reader: Documents, Speeches, and Firsthand Accounts from the Black Freedom Struggle, 1954–1990*, ed. Clayborne Carson and others (New York: Blackside, Inc., 1991), pp. 409–419. Dr. King said in part:

Now, what does all of this mean in this great period of history? It means that we've got to stay together. We've got to stay together and maintain unity. You know, whenever Pharoah wanted to prolong the period of slavery in Egypt, he had a favorite, favorite formula for doing it. What was that? He kept the slaves fighting among themselves. . . .

Secondly, let us keep the issues where they are. The issue is injustice. The issue is the refusal of Memphis to be fair and honest in its dealings with its public servants, who happen to be sanitation workers. . . . [The press] very seldom got around to mentioning the fact that one thousand, three hundred sanitation workers were on strike, and that Memphis is not being fair to them. . . . *(Ibid.,* pp. 411–412.)

60. Simon J. Ortiz, *Woven Stone* (Tucson: University of Arizona Press, 1992), p. 32.

suggest that in a society as diverse as the United States, participants in a nonviolent movement must be able to define the term "spiritual" in many, not necessarily religious, ways.

Gregory Calvert, national secretary of Students for a Democratic Society (SDS) in the mid-1960s, discusses the rise and fall of the civil rights movement of the early 1960s in his book *Democracy from the Heart*. He affirms that the "spiritual vision of nonviolence" gave Black people and their white allies the courage to struggle.

> It was the spiritual conviction that love is stronger than hate that made it possible for civil rights activists to imagine that a redemptive community of faith could overturn, through active nonviolence, a social order based on racism . . . . The notion of "black and white together" was the result of spiritual belief, not of materialist analysis.[61]

The founding statement of the Student Nonviolent Coordinating Committee (SNCC) (see Document 28B) sought to articulate this spiritual vision of nonviolence, Calvert continues. But while the statement was a moving description of nonviolence ("Through nonviolence, courage displaces fear; love transforms hate") it also cast that experience in the language of Judaeo-Christian belief in a personal God. Calvert asks: Why did draftsperson James Lawson, who was familiar with Gandhi's ecumenical spirit, narrowly refer to "Nonviolence as it grows from Judaic-Christian traditions"? Why not have been satisfied with the assertion that "Love is the central motif of nonviolence," instead of adding that "Love is the force by which God binds man to Himself"?

The problem with the religious narrowness of these formulations, according to Calvert, is that from the beginning SNCC promulgated a language with which most of its members did not fully agree. This meant that the SNCC founding statement could "not serve as a serious point of reference or a basis for discussion when SNCC organizers faced crises of faith and direction." Moreover, the character of the SNCC founding statement made it (as Calvert describes) easy for SNCC activists at the time and for subsequent historians of SNCC like Clayborne Carson to dismiss the language of nonviolence as mere "rationale" or "rhetoric."[62]

Calvert raises the profound question as to why the movement of the 1960s (including SNCC) tore itself to pieces, and whether this disintegration may not have had something to do with a loss of genuine, inner faith in nonviolence. May it not have been the case

---

61. Gregory Nevala Calvert, *Democracy From The Heart: Spiritual Values, Decentralism, and Democratic Idealism in the Movement of the 1960s* (Eugene, Oregon: Communitas Press, 1991), p. 58.

62. *Ibid.*, pp. 76–78, quoting and discussing Clayborne Carson, *In Struggle: SNCC and the Black Awakening of the 1960s* (Cambridge: Harvard University Press, 1981).

that the beliefs and values of morally and spiritually inspired nonviolence had been the most authentic expression of the Movement and its constituencies and the only coherent set of values that could hold a racially diverse political movement together? And that once those spiritual values had been downgraded to "rhetoric," the possibility of sustaining the measure of unity necessary to a functioning democratic community had also been destroyed?[63]

The question of whether nonviolence requires explicit spiritual underpinning is presented with equal force by liberation theology.

On the one hand, liberation theology—especially as developed in Latin America—offers a powerful new synthesis of Christianity and the need for social revolution. Liberation theology calls on pastoral agents to practice a "preferential option for the poor." It denounces the "institutional violence" of existing social and economic structures. It urges the poor and those assisting them to form "base communities": small, face-to-face groups in particular villages and barrios, including both men and women, that read the Gospel together, apply it to their own lives, and on that basis plan appropriate common action. It stands for the propositions that grinding poverty and exploitation are not God's will, and that it is our personal responsibility to help bring into being the kinds of relationships and conditions which express the will of God.

On the other hand, liberation theology is a form of Catholicism, ultimately requiring belief in Jesus Christ as the Son of God, the virgin birth, the resurrection of the flesh, and papal authority. It therefore presents the problem Calvert describes in his discussion of the SNCC founding statement: it makes affirmations in which many persons cannot wholeheartedly join.

Certain practitioners of nonviolence represented in this volume have sought to resolve that dilemma. Brian Willson is a Vietnam veteran, raised as a fundamentalist Christian, who lost both legs when he sought to block a train carrying munitions to a dock for shipment to Central America (see Document 48). When Willson recovered consciousness in a hospital, and understood that he was still alive, he addressed himself to a "Great Spirit" and to "Mother Earth" in the manner of many Native Americans, rather than to a personal God.

Oh Great Spirit, what dost thou have in store for me? Thank you for the gift of a second life. Can I become a closer cooperator with the infinite wisdom of the Great Spirit and Mother Earth? Do I have the strength and capacity to stand up to the demonic values and policies of my government and culture? Will I be creative and courageous enough to live out an alternative, even if experimental, vision, while

---

63. *Ibid.*, p. 78.

noncooperating with dangerous entrenched status quo values and policies?[64]

ACCOMPANIMENT

Liberation theology has also been unclear how persons personally committed to nonviolence should relate to violent movements of the poor for justified social transformation. Here David Dellinger and Barbara Deming each have something to say. David Dellinger, in an essay with which we ended the first edition of this book (see Document 44), states that those

> who are convinced that nonviolence can be used in *all* conflict situations have a responsibility to devise concrete methods by which it can be made effective. For example, can we urge the Negroes of Harlem or the *obreros* and *campesinos* (workers and peasants) of Latin America to refrain from violence if we offer them no positive method of breaking out of the slums, poverty, and cultural privation that blight their lives and condemn their children to a similar fate? It is contrary to the best tradition of nonviolence to do so. Gandhi often made the point that it is better to resist injustice by violent methods than not to resist at all.

The major advances in nonviolence, Dellinger continues, have come not from persons who approached nonviolence "as an end in itself" but from persons "who were passionately striving to free themselves from social injustice." Before the term was publicized by liberation theology, Dellinger denounced "the built-in institutional violence" imposed on the poor. Nonviolence cannot be used successfully to "protect special privileges," he argues. Nonviolence requires renunciation of all claims to special privilege and power at the expense of other people. Nonviolence "simply cannot defend property rights over human rights."

Dellinger also writes that the key attitudes in practicing nonviolence "stem from a feeling of solidarity for all human beings." Nonviolence may begin, as it did for Gandhi in South Africa, as a technique for wresting gains from an unloved and unlovely oppressor. "But somewhere along the line," the strategy of a nonviolent movement "must flow from a sense of the underlying unity of all human beings."

Barbara Deming says something very similar in her essay on "Pacifism."

> A remark of Che Guevara is often quoted: "Let me say, at the risk of seeming ridiculous, that the true revolutionary is guided by great feelings of love." Even those revolutionaries who speak of the necessity of

---

64. S. Brian Willson, *On Third World Legs* (Chicago: Charles H. Kerr Publishing Co., 1992), p. 85.

violence acknowledge again and again that the release of feelings of love for one another (which includes, of course, love, true respect, for ourselves) gives the movement for change its deepest energy. ... In the speech he made at his court martial in Bolivia, Regis Debray spoke at length about "the respect for human beings" Che Guevara always showed even in the midst of battle. He reported, for example, how Che gave instructions that "whatever the cost, the enemy wounded must be treated, even when they were in a hopeless condition. ... If necessary, the [medical] supplies on hand should all be used up."

The soldiers on the other side deserve this treatment for two reasons. First, because they too are poor workers and peasants, who do not hold, and abuse, real power. And second, because they are human beings.[65]

Perhaps we can synthesize these observations about revolutionary violence and the role of the nonviolent advocate with the help of Archbishop Oscar Romero.[66]

In his last Pastoral Letter, Romero asserted that the advocate of nonviolence must take sides in the struggle between rich and poor. Such an advocate should *prefer* the poor, and live amongst them. So situated, however, the advocate of nonviolence should not pretend to be anything he or she is not. The advocate should listen to the voice of conscience, despite pressure from popular organizations to give uncritical support to revolutionary projects. The essential task of the nonviolent advocate is to be present: to "accompany"

---

65. Barbara Deming, "Pacifism," *Win*, May 1, 1971, p. 7.

66. Romero was not a pacifist, yet eloquently expressed a strong belief in nonviolence. To begin with, he distinguished between different kinds of violence. There is the institutionalized violence "of a socio-economic and political system that takes it for granted that progress is impossible unless the majority of the people are used as a productive force under the control of a privileged minority." There is the repressive violence of the state. There is the "seditious or terrorist violence" of guerrilla warfare, which is "wrongly thought of as the final and only effective way to change a social situation," and is a violence "that produces and provokes useless and unjustifiable bloodshed, abandons society to explosive tensions beyond the control of reason, and disparages in principle any form of dialogue as a possible means of solving social conflicts." There is spontaneous violence, and there is violence in legitimate self-defense, which "seeks to neutralize, or at least to bring under effective control—not necessarily to destroy—an imminent, serious, and unjust threat." Quoting the Medellin statement, Romero also expressly legitimized insurrectional violence "in the very exceptional circumstances of an evident, prolonged tyranny that seriously works against human rights and seriously damages the common good of the country," while at the same time cautioning that like all other forms of violence, insurrectional violence can lead to "new injustices . . . new imbalances . . . new disasters." Applying this analysis to the task of social transformation, Romero called for "profound, urgent, but nonviolent changes." Archbishop Oscar Romero, *Voice of the Voiceless: The Four Pastoral Letters and Other Statements* (Maryknoll, N.Y.: Orbis Books, 1985), Third Pastoral Letter, pp. 106–109.

the poor, and with them seek appropriate means for our common liberation. Only if we ourselves are involved in the situation can we understand the dynamics of what is going on and participate in generating new ideas that can, perhaps, break through to humane resolutions.[67]

Many such accompaniers are represented in the new material in this volume. Some, like Sister Helen Prejean (Document 41), are Catholics. More, like Reverend Jim Sessions (Document 43), or the predominantly Protestant and Jewish activists who built the sanctuary movement (Document 47), are not. All share a belief in the healing and transformation of our world by means of struggle together with the poor and oppressed. Accompaniment offers a practice and experience through which all of us—Christian, Jew, Muslim, Buddhist, atheist, and agnostic—can join hands in discovering the meaning of nonviolence.

CLINGING TO THE TRUTH

Nonviolence, then, is not defined by the words we use, but by our common experience. It is not merely a technique and ought not to be limited by expressions such as "CD" (for "civil disobedience"). Nonviolence is breaking through to the deepest level of human communication by creative means. It is a way of being, as well as of doing.

Indeed, the greatest practitioners of nonviolence have viewed it not so much as a way to encounter adversaries, or even to change the world, but rather as a journey in search of truth. Gandhi entitled his autobiography an "experiment with truth." He described the reality in the universe on which he placed his faith as "satyagraha," or "clinging to the truth." Quakers, similarly, have referred to what they do as "speaking truth to power."

Viewed in this way, accompaniment is a way of testifying by conduct to the truth of oppression and injustice. And it witnesses, not just to a negative, but also to the infinite potentiality of all human beings to live lives that are dignified, loving, useful, and self-governing.

Nonviolence is the very opposite of one person imposing his (or her) truth on another. In nonviolent action, one seeks a truth larger than the truth that can be glimpsed by a single human being at a particular time. That truth which is perceived at a given moment is *offered* to others by means of acting it out. This may mean making it through one more day in prison; or a clear

---

67. Oscar Romero, *Voice of the Voiceless,* Fourth Pastoral Letter, pp. 127, 139, 147, 155–156. In the radio address of March 23, 1980, that appears to have been the immediate cause of his death, Archbishop Romero called on government soldiers not to obey orders to kill their brothers and sisters among the people. "In the name of God, then, and in the name of this suffering people whose cries rise daily more loudly to heaven, I plead with you, I beg you, I order you in the name of God: put an end to this repression!" *Ibid.,* Introduction by Ignacio Martin-Baro, p. 18.

word in a confused meeting; or silence; or putting one's body in the way. Regardless, it is truth exemplified in such a fashion that both the actor and the person acted upon can learn and change through the experience.

III

This book is dedicated to Helen Michalowski. Helen co-edited with Robert Cooney *The Power of the People: Active Nonviolence in the United States* (Culver City, Cal.: Peace Press, Inc., 1977), a magnificent survey of its subject with over 400 photographs.[68] Dying of cancer as this book was being edited, Helen Michalowski wrote to her friends: "During my adult life, I increasingly developed the conviction that changing the world for the better necessitated changing actual material conditions, not simply changing consciousness."

We would also like to thank the many people who suggested pieces for inclusion in this new edition or gave us permission to use pieces that they wrote, among whom we particularly wish to mention: Gregory Nevala Calvert, David Dellinger, Ralph DiGia, Robert Ellsberg, Larry Gara, Vincent Harding, Martha Lynd, Bradford Lyttle, David McReynolds, Roxanne Dunbar Ortiz, George Taylor, James Tollefson, Michael True, Brian Willson, Arthur Wiser, and Howard Zinn.

Staughton Lynd
Alice Lynd

---

68. *The Power of the People* can be obtained from New Society Publishers, 4527 Springfield Avenue, Philadelphia, PA 19143.

PART I

QUAKERS

DOCUMENT 1

William Penn,
First Letter to the Delaware Indians

William Penn (1644–1718), son of an English admiral, came in contact with Quakers while he was a student at Oxford University. After joining the Friends, he was arrested and jailed several times under Restoration laws that restricted nonconformity. (One of these cases, in 1670, settled the legal precedent that a jury's verdict of "not guilty" shall prevail despite a contrary instruction from the judge.) His radicalism notwithstanding, in 1681 Penn was given Pennsylvania as a proprietary province.

Document 1 is a letter of October 18, 1681, which Penn gave the commissioners who preceded him to Pennsylvania to read to the Indians on their arrival. The result was the famous treaty or treaties of peace between Penn and the Delaware Indians.

"William Penn's First Letter to the Indians," *Annals of Pennsylvania, from the Discovery of the Delaware, 1609–1682*, ed. Samuel Hazard (Philadelphia: Hazard and Mitchell, 1850), pp. 532–533.

1

London, 18th of 8th Month, 1681

MY FRIENDS—There is one great God and power that hath made the world and all things therein, to whom you and I, and all people owe their being and well-being, and to whom you and I must one day give an account for all that we do in the world; this great God hath written his law in our hearts, by which we are taught and commanded to love and help, and do good to one another, and not to do harm and mischief one to another. Now this great God hath been pleased to make me concerned in your parts of the world, and the king of the country where I live hath given unto me a great province, but I desire to enjoy it with your love and consent, that we may always live together as neighbours and friends, else what would the great God say to us, who hath made us not to devour and destroy one another, but live soberly and kindly together in the world? Now I would have you well observe, that I am very sensible of the unkindness and injustice that hath been too much exercised towards you by the people of these parts of the world, who sought themselves, and to make great advantages by you, rather than be examples of justice and goodness unto you, which I hear hath been matter of trouble to you, and caused great grudgings and animosities, sometimes to the shedding of blood, which hath made the great God angry; but I am not such a man, as is well known in my own country; I have great love and regard towards you, and I desire to win and gain your love and friendship, by a kind, just, and peaceable life, and the people I send are of the same mind, and shall in all things behave themselves accordingly; and if in any thing any shall offend you or your people, you shall have a full and speedy satisfaction for the same, by an equal number of just men on both sides, that by no means you may have just occasion of being offended against them. I shall shortly come to you myself, at what time we may more largely and freely confer and discourse of these matters. In the mean time, I have sent my commissioners, to treat with you about land, and a firm league of peace. Let me desire you to be kind to them and the people, and receive these presents and tokens which I have sent to you, as a testimony of my good will to you, and my resolution to live justly, peaceably, and friendly with you.

I am your loving friend,

WILLIAM PENN.

John Woolman

The most significant figure in the early history of nonviolence in the North American colonies is John Woolman (1720–1772). A member of the Society of Friends, or Quakers, his thought belonged to the tradition of the radical Reformation, with its insistence on pacifism, civil disobedience, and community of goods, and its mystical intuition of the oneness of creation.

Woolman's best-known work, his Journal *(first published in 1774), tells the story of his life. Unlike the aristocratic William Penn, but like William Blake, William Lloyd Garrison, and Elihu Burritt, Woolman belonged to the class of self-educated craftsmen and small shopkeepers then known as "mechanics and tradesmen." A keen sense of social concern drove him to leave his New Jersey home for long trips to admonish Quaker slaveholders in the South, to visit the Indians, and finally to England, where he died shortly before the American Revolution.*

These excerpts from the Journal *illustrate the development of Woolman's thought in response to encounters in daily life. Thus, his objection to slavery sprang from occasions on which neighbors asked him to write legal documents relating to their human chattels. The French and Indian War led Woolman as well as Anthony Benezet and other Quakers to refuse to pay taxes in support of war. Woolman's account of his tax refusal reveals how new a practice it was, even among Friends. Believing that "conduct is more convincing than language," Woolman also refused free hospitality from slaveholders and gave up the use of commodities, such as cotton cloth and sugar, which were made with slave labor.*

"A Plea for the Poor," first published in 1793, expresses the full scope of Woolman's social philosophy: that if human beings would regard their daily bread as a gift from God, and be content with necessities, then wars caused by the strife for luxuries would end, and exploitation would give way to universal love.

A. Journal

[*SLAVERY*]

About the twenty third year of my age I had many fresh and heavenly openings, in respect to the care and providence of the Almighty over his creatures in general, and over man as the most noble amongst those which are visible, and Being clearly convinced in my Judgmt that to place my whole trust in God was best for me, I felt renewed engagements that in all things I might act on an inward principle of Virtue, and pursue worldly business no further than as Truth open'd my way therein. . . .

. . . My Employer having a Negro woman sold her, and directed me to write a bill of Sale, The man being waiting who had bought her. The thing was Sudden, and though the thoughts of writing an Instrument of Slavery for one of my fellow creatures felt uneasie, yet I remembered I was hired by the year; that it was my master who [directed] me to do it, and that it was an Elderly man, a member of our society who bought her, so through weakness I gave way, and wrote it, but at the Executing it I was so Afflicted in my mind, that I said before my Master and the friend, that I believed Slavekeeping to be a practice inconsistent with the Christian Religion: this in some degree abated my uneasiness, yet as often as I reflected seriously upon it I thought I should have been clearer, if I had desired to be Excused from it, as a thing against my conscience, for such it was. [And] some time after this a young man of our Society, spake to me to write [an instrument of Slavery], he having lately taken a Negro into his house. I told him I was not easie to write it, for though many [people] kept slaves in our society as in others, I still believed the practice was not right, and desired to be excused from doing the writing. I spoke to him in good will, and he told me, that keeping slaves was not altogether agreable to his mind, but that the slave being a gift made to his wife, he had accepted of her. . . .

. . . Feeling an exercise in relation to a visit to the Southern parts to increase upon me, I acquainted our monthly meeting therewith, and Obtained their Certificate. . . .

As the people in this and the southern provinces, live much on the labour of Slaves, many of whom are used hardly, my concern was, that I might

---

"The Journal of John Woolman," *The Journal and Essays of John Woolman,* edited from the original manuscripts with a biographical introduction by Amelia Mott Gummere (New York: The Macmillan Company, 1922), pp. 160–162, 187–190, 204–207, 248–249, 254–256. The slavery excerpts were written in 1743 and 1757; tax refusal in 1757; treatment of Indians in 1763. Bracketed material in the text, but not the subheadings, was supplied by Mrs. Gummere. Reprinted with the permission of Richard M. Gummere for the Estate of F. B. Gummere.

attend with singleness of heart to the Voice of the True Shepherd, and be so supported as to remain unmoved at the faces of men.

As it is common for Friends on a visit to have Entertainment free cost, a difficulty arose in my mind with respect to saveing my own money by kindness received, which to me appeared to be the gain of Opression.

Receiving a gift, considered as a gift, brings the receiver under Obligations to the Benefactor, and has a natural tendency to draw the Obliged into a party with the giver. To prevent difficulties of this kind, and to preserve the minds of Judges from any byas, was that Divine Prohibition "Thou shalt not receive any gift, for a gift blindeth the wise, and perverteth the words of the Righteous." Exod. xxiii. 8. As the Disciples were sent forth without any Provision for their Journey, and our Lord said, the workman is worthy of his meat, Their labour in the Gospel was considered as a reward for their Entertainment, and therefore not received as a gift: yet in regard to my present Journey I could not see my way clear in that respect—the odds appeared thus: The entertainment the disciples met with, was from such whose hearts God had opened to receive them, from a Love to them, and the Truth which they published: But we, considered as members of the same society, look upon it as a piece of Civility to receive each other in such visits, and Such reception, at times, is partly in regard to reputation, and not from an inward Unity of heart and Spirit.

Conduct is more convincing than language; and where people by their actions manifest that the Slave trade is not so disagreeable to their principles but that it may be encouraged, there is not a Sound uniting with some Friends who Visit them.

The prospect of so weighty a work & being so distinguished from many whom I Esteemed before myself, brought me verry low, & Such were the conflicts of my Soul, that I had a near sympathy with the profet in the time of his weakness, when he said "If thou deal thus with me, kill me, I pray thee out of hand if I have found favour in thy Sight," but I soon saw that this proceeded from the want of a full resignation to Him. Many were the afflictions which attended me and in great Abasement, with many tears, my Cries were to the Almighty for his Gracious and Fatherly assistance, and then, after a Time of Deep Tryals I was favoured to understand the state mentioned by the psalmist more clearly than ever I had before, to wit: "My Soul is even as a weaned child."

Being thus helped to sink down into Resignation I felt a deliverance from that Tempest in which I had been sorely Exercised, and in Calmness of mind went forward Trusting that the Lord Jesus Christ, as I faithfully attended to Him, would be a Councellor to me in all Difficulties, and that by his Strength I should be enabled even to leave money with the members of Society where I had Entertainment, when I found that omiting of it would Obstruct that work to which I believed he had called me. And as I copy this after my return [from that Journey] I may here add, that oftentimes I did so, Under a sense of duty. The Manner in which I did it was thus: when I expected soon to leave a Friend's house where I had Entertainment, if I believed that I should not keep clear from the gain of Oppression without leaving some money, I spoke to One of the heads of the Family privately, and desired them to accept of them pieces of Silver, and give them to such of their Negroes as they believ'd would make the best use of them; And at other times, I gave them to the Negroes myself, [according] as the way looked clearest to me. As I expected this before I came out, I had provided a large number of small pieces [of silver] and thus offering them to Some who appeared to be wealthy people was a tryal both to me and them: But the [Exercise of my mind was Such and the] fear of the Lord so covered me at times, that way was made easier than I expected, and few, if any, manifested any resentment at the offer, and most of them, after some [little] talk, accepted of them. . . .

[TAX REFUSAL]

A few years past, money being made current in our province for carrying on wars, and to be sunk by Taxes laid on the Inhabitants, my mind was often affected with the thoughts of paying such Taxes, and I believe it right for me to preserve a memorandum concerning it.

I was told that Friends in England frequently paid Taxes when the money was applied to such purposes. I had [conference] with several Noted Friends on the subject, who all favoured the payment of such taxes, Some of whom I preferred before myself, and this made me easier for a time: yet there was in the deeps of my mind, a scruple which I never could get over; and, at certain times, I was greatly distressed on that account.

I all along believed that there were some upright-hearted men who paid such taxes, but could not see that their Example was a Sufficient Reason for me to do so, while I believed that the Spirit of Truth required of me as an individual to suffer patiently the distress of goods, rather than pay actively.

I have been informed that Thomas à Kempis lived & died in the profession of the Roman Catholick Religion, and in reading his writings, I have believed him to be a man of a true Christian spirit, as fully so as many who died Martyrs because they could not join with some superstitions in that Church.

All true Christians are of [one and] the same spirit, but their gifts are diverse; [Jesus] Christ appointing to each one their peculiar Office, agreeable to his Infinite Wisdom.

John Huss Contended against the Errors crept into the Church, in oposition to the Council of Constance, which the historian reports to have consisted of many thousand persons. He modestly vindicated the cause which he believed was right, and though his language and Conduct toward his Judges appear to have been respectfull, yet he never could be moved from the principles settled in his mind. To use his own words: "This I most humbly require and desire of you all, even for His sake who is the God of us all, that I be not compelled to the thing which my Conscience doth repugn or strive against." And again in his answer to the emperor "I refuse nothing, most noble Emperor whatsoever the council shall decree or determine upon me, this only one thing I except, that I do not offend God and my Conscience." At length rather than act contrary to that which he believed the Lord required of Him, he chose to Suffer death by fire. Thomas à Kempis, without disputing against the Articles then generally agreed to, appears to have laboured, by a Pious Example as well as by Preaching & writing to promote Virtue and the Inward Spiritual Religion, and I believe they were both sincere-hearted followers of Christ. [To me it looks likely that they were both in their proper places.]

True Charity is an excellent Virtue, and to sincerely Labour for their good, whose belief in all points, doth not agree with ours, is a happy case. To refuse the active payment of a Tax which our Society generally paid, was exceeding disagreeable; but to do a thing contrary to my Conscience appeared yet more dreadfull. When this exercise came upon me I knew of none under the like difficulty, and in my distress I besought the Lord to enable me to give up all, that so I might follow him wheresoever he was pleased to lead me, and under this Exercise I went to our Yearly Meeting at Philada, in 1755, at which a Committee was appointed, some from each Quarter to Correspond with the meeting for Sufferings in London, and another to Visit our Monthly and Quarterly meetings, and after their appointment before the last Adjournment of the meeting, it was agreed on in the meeting that these two Committees should meet together in Friends School House in the Citty, at a time [when the Meeting stood adjourned] to consider some [cases] in which the cause of Truth was concerned: and these Committees meeting together had a weighty conferrence in the fear of the Lord, at which time I perceived there were many Friends under a Scruple like that before mentioned.

As Scrupling to pay a tax on account of the application[1] hath seldom been heard of heretofore, even amongst men of Integrity, who have Steadily born their testimony against outward wars in their time, I may here note some things which have opened on my mind, as I have been inwardly Exercised on that account.

From the Steady oposition which Faithfull Friends in early times made to wrong things then approved of, they were hated and persecuted by men living in the Spirit of this world, & Suffering with firmness, they were made a Blessing to the Church, & the work prospered. It equaly concerns men in every age to take heed to their own Spirit: & in comparing their Situation with ours, it looks to me there was less danger of their being infected with the Spirit of this world in paying their taxes, than there is of us now. They had little or no Share in Civil Government, neither Legislative nor Executive & many of them declared they were through the power of God separated from the Spirit in which wars were, and being Afflicted by the Rulers on account

---

1. Christians refused to pay taxes to support Heathen Temples. See Cave's Primitive Christianity, part iii, page 327. [Note by Woolman. Ed.]

of their Testimony, there was less likelyhood of uniting in Spirit with them in things inconsistent with the purity of Truth. We, from the first settlement of this Land have known little or no troubles of that sort. The profession, which for a time was accounted reproachfull, at length the uprightness of our predecessors being understood by the Rulers, & their Innocent Sufferings moving them, our way of Worship was tolerated, and many of our members in these colonies became active in Civil Government. Being thus tryed with favour and prosperity, this world hath appeared inviteing; our minds have been turned to the Improvement of our Country, to Merchandize and Sciences, amongst which are many things usefull, being followed in pure wisdom, but in our present condition that a Carnal mind is gaining upon us I believe will not be denied.

Some of our members who are Officers in Civil Government are in one case or other called upon in their respective Stations to Assist in things relative to the wars, Such being in doubt whether to act or crave to be excused from their Office, Seeing their Brethren united in the payment of a Tax to carry on the said wars, might think their case [nearly like theirs, &] so quench the tender movings of the Holy Spirit in their minds, and thus by small degrees there might be an approach toward that of Fighting, till we came so near it, as that the distinction would be little else but the name of a peaceible people.

It requires great self-denial and Resignation of ourselves to God to attain that state wherein we can freely cease from fighting when wrongfully Invaded, if by our Fighting there were a probability of overcoming the invaders. Whoever rightly attains to it, does in some degree feel that Spirit in which our Redeemer gave his life for us, and, through Divine goodness many of our predecessors, and many now living, have learned this blessed lesson, but many others having their Religion chiefly by Education, & not being enough acquainted with that Cross which Crucifies to the world, do manifest a Temper distinguishable from that of an Entire trust in God.

In calmly considering these things it hath not appeared strange to me, that an exercise hath now fallen upon some, which as to the outward means of it is different from what was known to many of those who went before us. . . .

[*TREATMENT OF INDIANS*]

Having many years felt Love in my heart towards the Natives of this Land, who dwell far back in the Wilderness, whose Ancestors were the owners and possessors of the [Country] where we dwell, and who for a very small consideration Assigned their Inheritance to us ... I felt inward drawings toward a Visit to that place. . . .

... And as I rode over the barren Hills my meditations were on the Alterations of the Circumstances of the Natives of this land since the coming in of the English. The Lands near the Sea are Conveniently scituated for fishing. The lands near the Rivers where the tides flow, and some above, are in many places fertile, and not mountainous; while the Runing of the Tides makes passing up and down easie with any kind of Traffick. Those natives have in some places for [small] considerations sold their Inheritance so favourably Scituated and in other places been driven back by superior force. So that in many places as their way of Clothing themselves is now altered from what it was, and they far remote from us have to pass over Mountains, Swamps, and Barran deserts, where Traveling is very troublesome, in bringing their furs & skins to trade with us.

By the Extending of English Settlements and partly by English Hunters, those wild Beasts they chiefly depend on for a subsistence are not so plenty as they were. And people too often for the Sake of gain open a Door for them to waste their Skins & furs, in purchasing a Liquor which tends to the ruin of y^m [them] & their Families.

My own will and desire being now very much broken, and my heart with much earnestness turned to the Lord, to whom alone I looked for help in the dangers before me, I had a prospect of the English along the Coast for upwards of nine hundred miles where I have traveled. And the favourable Situation of the English, and the difficulties attending the natives [and the Slaves amongst us,] were open before me, and a weighty and Heavenly care came over my mind, and love filled my heart toward all mankind, in which I felt a Strong Engagement that we might be [faithful] to the Lord while His mercies [are yet extended] to us, and so attend to pure Universal Righteousness as to give no just cause of offence to the gentiles who do not profess christianity, Whither the Blacks from Africa, or the Native Inhabitants of this Continent: And here I was led into a close, laborious Enquiry, whether I as an individual kept clear from all things which tended to Stir up, or were connnected with wars, Either in this Land or Africa, and my heart was deeply concerned that in future I might in all things keep steadily to the pure Truth, & live and walk in the plainness and Simplicity of a Sincere follower of Christ. And in this lonely Journey, I did this day greatly bewail the spreading of a wrong Spirit, believing that the prosperous Conveniant Scituation of the English, requires a Constant Attention to Divine love & wisdom, to guide and Support us in a way answerable to the will of that Good, Gracious, & Almighty Being who hath an Equal regard to all mankind. And here Luxury and Covetousness, with the numerous Opressions and other evils attending them, appeared very Afflicting to me, and I felt in that which is Immutable that the Seeds of great Calamity and desolation are Sown & growing fast on this Continent. Nor have I words sufficient to set forth that longing I then felt, that we who are placed along the Coast, & have tasted the Love and Goodness of God, might arise in his Strength, and like faithful Messengers Labour to check the growth of those Seeds that they may not ripen to the Ruin of our posterity.

B. "A Plea for the Poor"

CHAPTER X

"Are not two Sparrows sold for a Farthing, and one of them shall not fall to the Ground without your Father."

The way of Carrying on Wars, common in the world, is so far distinguishable from the purity of Christ's Religion, that many scruple to joyn in them. Those who are so redeemed from the Love of the World, as to possess nothing in a Selfish Spirit, their "Life is hid with Christ in God," and these he preserves in resignedness, even in times of Commotion.

As they possess nothing but what pertains to His family, anxious thoughts about wealth or dominion hath little or nothing in them to work upon, and they learn contentment in being disposed of according to His Will, who being Omnipotent, and always mindful of his Children, causeth all things to work for their good. But where that spirit works which loves Riches; works, & in its working gathers wealth, and cleaves to customs which have their Root in self pleasing. This Spirit thus separating from Universal Love, seeks help from that power which stands in the Separation, and whatever name it hath, it still desireth to defend the Treasures thus gotten. This is like a Chain, where the end of one link encloses the end of another. The rising up of a desire to obtain wealth is the beginning. This desire being cherished moves to action, and riches thus gotten pleace self and while self hath a life in them it desires to have them defended.

Wealth is attended with Power, by which Bargains and proceedings contrary to Universal Righteousness are Supported, and here Oppression, carried on with worldly policy & order, cloathes itself with the name of Justice, and becomes like a seed of Discord in the soyl: and as this spirit which wanders from the pure Habitation prevails, so the seed of War Swells & Sprouts and grows & becomes Strong, till much fruit are ripened. Thus cometh the Harvest spoken of by the prophet, which "is a Heap, in the Day of Grief & of desperate Sorrow."

Oh! that we who declare against wars, and Acknowledge our trust to be in God only, may walk in the Light, and therein examine our Foundation & motives in holding great Estates: May we look upon our Treasures, and the furniture of our Houses, and the Garments in which we array ourselves, and

---

"A Plea for the Poor," *The Journal and Essays of John Woolman,* ed. Amelia Mott Gummere (New York: The Macmillan Company, 1922), Chapters X, XI. This essay of sixteen chapters is presumed by Mrs. Gummere to have been written in 1763. Bracketed material in the text was supplied by Mrs. Gummere. Reprinted with the permission of Richard M. Gummere for the Estate of F. B. Gummere.

try whether the seeds of war have any nourishment in these our possessions, or not. Holding Treasures in the Self pleasing Spirit is a Strong plant, the fruit whereof ripens fast.

A day of outward Distress is coming, and Divine Love calls to prepare for it. Hearken then, O ye Children who have known the Light, and come forth! Leave every thing which our Lord Jesus Christ does not own. Think not his pattern too plain or too coarse for you. Think not a Small portion in this life too little: but let us live in His Spirit, & walk as he walked, and he will preserve us in the greatest Troubles.

CHAPTER XI

"The Heaven, even the Heavens are the Lord's; but the Earth hath he given to the children of men." Psal. 115:16.

As Servants of God, what Land or Estates we hold, we hold under him as his gifts; and in applying the profits, it is our duty to act consistently with the Design of Our Benefactor. Imperfect men may give on motives of Misguided Affection, but Perfect Wisdom & Goodness gives agreeable to his own Nature; nor is this gift absolute, but conditional, for us to occupy as dutiful Children, and not otherwise; for he alone is the true proprietor. "The World," saith He, "is mine, and the fulness thereof." Psal. xxiv. 1.

The Inspired Law giver directed that such of the Israelites as sold their Inheritance, should sell it for a term only; and that they or their Children should again enjoy it in the year of Jubilee, settled on every Fiftieth year. "The land shall not be sold for ever; for the Land is mine, saith the Lord, for ye are Strangers, and Sojourners with me." Levit. xxv. 23. The design of which was to prevent the Rich from Oppressing the poor, by too much engrossing the Land. And Our Blessed Redeemer said, "Till heaven and earth pass, one jot or one Tittle shall in no wise pass from the Law till all be fulfilled."

Where Divine love takes place in the Hearts of any people, and they steadily act on a principle of Universal Righteousness, there the true intent of the Law is fulfilled, though their outward modes of proceeding may be distinguishable from one another: But where men are possessed by that Spirit hinted at by the Prophet, and looking over their wealth, say in their hearts, "Have we not taken to us Horns by our own Strength?" Here they deviate from the Divine Law, and do not account their possessions so strictly God's, nor the weak & poor entitled to so much of the increase thereof, but that they may indulge their desires in conforming to worldly pomp. And thus where House is joined to House, and Field laid to Field, till there is no place, and the poor are thereby straitened; though this be done by Bargain & Purchase, yet so far as it Stands distinguished from Universal Love, so far that WO, prefixed by the Prophet will accompany their proceedings.

As He who first formed the Earth out of nothing was then the true Proprietor of it, so He still remains; and though he hath given it to the Children of men, so that multitudes of people have had sustenance from it, while they continued here, yet he hath never Aliened it, but his Right to give is as good as the first, nor can any apply the increase of their possessions contrary to Universal Love: nor dispose of Lands in a way which they know tends to Exalt some, by Oppressing others, without being justly chargeable with Usurpation.

PART II

ABOLITIONISTS

DOCUMENT 3

William Lloyd Garrison,
"Declaration of Sentiments, 1838"

Quiescent for a generation after the American Revolution, nonviolence revived during the widely unpopular War of 1812. After the war the abolitionist movement, under the influence of William Lloyd Garrison, adopted nonviolence as part of its creed.

Garrison (1805–1879) espoused the abolition of capital punishment, abstention from politics, and opposition to all war, as well as emancipation of the slaves. Prompted by these beliefs, Garrison and a few abolitionist friends split the American Peace Society in 1838 to found the New England Non-Resistance Society. The Society's statement of principles, which he drafted, illustrates the fact that Garrison might eschew physical violence but was never hesitant to "assail iniquity" with words.

"Declaration of Sentiments adopted by the [American] Peace Convention, held in Boston, September 18, 19 and 20, 1838," *Selections from the Writings and Speeches of William Lloyd Garrison* (Boston: R. F. Wallcutt, 1852), pp. 72–77.

13

Assembled in Convention, from various sections of the American Union, for the promotion of peace on earth and good will among men, we, the undersigned, regard it as due to ourselves, to the cause which we love, to the country in which we live, and to the world, to publish a Declaration, expressive of the principles we cherish, the purposes we aim to accomplish, and the measures we shall adopt to carry forward the work of peaceful and universal reformation.

We cannot acknowledge allegiance to any human government; neither can we oppose any such government, by a resort of physical force. We recognize but one King and Lawgiver, one Judge and Ruler of mankind. We are bound by the laws of a kingdom which is not of this world; the subjects of which are forbidden to fight; in which Mercy and Truth are met together, and Righteousness and Peace have kissed each other; which has no state lines, no national partitions, no geographical boundaries; in which there is no distinction of rank, or division of caste, or inequality of sex; the officers of which are Peace, its exactors Righteousness, its walls Salvation, and its gates Praise; and which is destined to break in pieces and consume all other kingdoms.

Our country is the world, our countrymen are all mankind. We love the land of our nativity, only as we love all other lands. The interests, rights, and liberties of American citizens are no more dear to us, than are those of the whole human race. Hence, we can allow no appeal to patriotism, to revenge any national insult or injury. The Prince of Peace, under whose stainless banner we rally, came not to destroy, but to save, even the worst of enemies. He has left us an example, that we should follow his steps. 'God commendeth his love towards us, in that while we were yet sinners, Christ died for us.'

We conceive, that if a nation has no right to defend itself against foreign enemies, or to punish its invaders, no individual possesses that right in his own case. The unit cannot be of greater importance than the aggregate. If one man may take life, to obtain or defend his rights, the same license must necessarily be granted to communities, states, and nations. If he may use a dagger or a pistol, they may employ cannon, bomb-shells, land and naval forces. The means of self-preservation must be in proportion to the magnitude of interests at stake, and the number of lives exposed to destruction. But if a rapacious and blood-thirsty soldiery, thronging these shores from abroad, with intent to commit rapine and destroy life, may not be resisted by the people or magistracy, then ought no resistance to be offered to domestic troublers of the public peace, or of private security. No obligation can rest upon Americans to regard foreigners as more sacred in their persons than themselves, or to give them a monopoly of wrong-doing with impunity.

The dogma, that all the governments of the world are approvingly ordained of God, and that the powers that be in the United States, in Russia, in Turkey, are in accordance with His will, is not less absurd than impious. It makes the impartial Author of human freedom and equality, unequal and tyrannical.

It cannot be affirmed, that the powers that be, in any nation, are actuated by the spirit, or guided by the example of Christ, in the treatment of enemies: therefore, they cannot be agreeable to the will of God: and, therefore, their overthrow, by a spiritual regeneration of their subjects, is inevitable.

We register our testimony, not only against all wars, whether offensive or defensive, but all preparations for war; against every naval ship, every arsenal, every fortification; against the militia system and a standing army; against all military chieftains and soldiers; against all monuments commemorative of victory over a foreign foe, all trophies won in battle, all celebrations in honor of military or naval exploits; against all appropriations for the defence of a nation by force and arms on the part of any legislative body; against every edict of government, requiring of its subjects military service. Hence, we deem it unlawful to bear arms, or to hold a military office.

As every human government is upheld by physical strength, and its laws are enforced virtually at the point of the bayonet, we cannot hold any office which imposes upon its incumbent the obligation to do right, on pain of imprisonment or death. We therefore voluntarily exclude ourselves from every legislative and judicial body, and repudiate all human politics, worldly honors, and stations of authority. If *we* cannot occupy a seat in the legislature, or on the bench, neither can we elect *others* to act as our substitutes in any such capacity.

It follows, that we cannot sue any man at law, to compel him by force to restore any thing which he may have wrongfully taken from us or others; but, if he has seized our coat, we shall surrender up our cloak, rather than subject him to punishment.

We believe that the penal code of the old covenant, An eye for an eye, and a tooth for a tooth, has been abrogated by Jesus Christ; and that, under the new covenant, the forgiveness, instead of the punishment of enemies, has been enjoined upon all his disciples, in all cases whatsoever. To extort money from enemies, or set them upon a pillory, or cast them into prison, or hang them upon a gallows, is obviously not to forgive, but to take retribution. 'Vengeance is mine—I will repay, saith the Lord.'

The history of mankind is crowded with evidences, proving that physical coercion is not adapted to moral regeneration; that the sinful disposition of man can be subdued only by love; that evil can be exterminated from the earth only by goodness; that it is not safe to rely upon an arm of flesh, upon man, whose breath is in his nostrils, to preserve us from harm; that there is great security in being gentle, harmless, long-suffering, and abundant in mercy; that it is only the meek who shall inherit the earth, for the violent, who resort to the sword, shall perish with the sword. Hence, as a measure of sound policy, of safety to property, life, and liberty, of public quietude and private enjoyment, as well as on the ground of allegiance to Him who is King of kings, and Lord of lords, we cordially adopt the non-resistance principle; being confident that it provides for all possible consequences, will ensure all things needful to us, is armed with omnipotent power, and must ultimately triumph over every assailing force.

We advocate no jacobinical doctrines. The spirit of jacobinism is the spirit of retaliation, violence and murder. It neither fears God, nor regards man. We would be filled with the spirit of Christ. If we abide by our principles, it is impossible for us to be disorderly, or plot treason, or participate in any evil work: we shall submit to every ordinance of man, for the Lord's sake; obey all the requirements of government, except such as we deem contrary to the commands of the gospel; and in no wise resist the operation of law, except by meekly submitting to the penalty of disobedience.

But, while we shall adhere to the doctrines of non-resistance and passive submission to enemies, we purpose, in a moral and spiritual sense, to speak and act boldly in the cause of God; to assail iniquity in high places and in low places; to apply our principles to all existing civil, political, legal, and ecclesiastical institutions; and to hasten the time, when the kingdoms of this world shall become the kingdoms of our Lord and of his Christ, and he shall reign for ever.

It appears to us a self-evident truth, that, whatever the gospel is designed to destroy at any period of the world, being contrary to it, ought now to be abandoned. If, then, the time is predicted, when swords shall be beaten into plough-shares, and spears into pruning-hooks, and men shall not learn the art of war any more, it follows that all who manufacture, sell, or wield those deadly weapons, do thus array themselves against the peaceful dominion of the Son of God on earth.

Having thus briefly, but frankly, stated our principles and purposes, we proceed to specify the measures we propose to adopt, in carrying our object into effect.

We expect to prevail through the foolishness of preaching—striving to commend ourselves unto every man's conscience, in the sight of God. From the press, we shall promulgate our sentiments as widely as practicable. We shall endeavor to secure the co-operation of all persons, of whatever name or sect. The triumphant progress of the cause of Temperance and of Abolition in our land, through the instrumentality of benevolent and voluntary associations, encourages us to combine our own means and efforts for the promotion of a still greater cause. Hence we shall employ lecturers, circulate tracts and publications, form societies, and petition our state and national governments in relation to the subject of Universal Peace. It will be our leading object to devise ways and means for effecting a radical change in the views, feelings and practices of society respecting the sinfulness of war, and the treatment of enemies.

In entering upon the great work before us, we are not unmindful that, in its prosecution, we may be called to test our sincerity, even as in a fiery ordeal. It may subject us to insult, outrage, suffering, yea, even death itself. We anticipate no small amount of misconception, misrepresentation, calumny. Tumults may arise against us. The ungodly and violent, the proud and pharisaical, the ambitious and tyrannical, principalities and powers, and spiritual wickedness in high places, may combine to crush us. So they treated the Messiah, whose example we are humbly striving to imitate. If we suffer with him, we know that we shall reign with him. We shall not be afraid of their terror, neither be troubled. Our confidence is in the Lord Almighty, not in man. Having withdrawn from human protection, what can sustain us but that faith which overcomes the world? We shall not think it strange concerning the fiery trial which is to try us, as though some strange thing had happened unto us; but rejoice, inasmuch as we are partakers of Christ's sufferings. Wherefore, we commit the keeping of our souls to God, in well-doing, as unto a faithful Creator. 'For every one that forsakes houses, or brethren, or sisters, or father, or mother, or wife, or children, or lands, for Christ's sake, shall receive an hundred fold, and shall inherit everlasting life.'

Firmly relying upon the certain and universal triumph of the sentiments contained in this Declaration, however formidable may be the opposition arrayed against them, in solemn testimony of our faith in their divine origin, we hereby affix our signatures to it; commending it to the reason and conscience of mankind, giving ourselves no anxiety as to what may befall us, and resolving, in the strength of the Lord God, calmly and meekly to abide the issue.

DOCUMENT 4

Adin Ballou,
Christian Non-Resistance

Adin Ballou (1803–1890) was another of those early nineteenth-century reformers who made the eradication of sin—whether in the form of war, slavery, or intemperance—the business of their lives. Ballou founded one of the first American utopian communities at Hopedale, Massachusetts. It lasted from 1841 to 1856. In 1839, at a meeting of the New England Non-Resistance Society, he delivered a lecture on "Non-Resistance in Relation to Human

From Adin Ballou, *Christian Non-Resistance, in All Its Important Bearings, Illustrated and Defended* (Philadelphia: J. Miller M'Kim, 1846).

Governments"; later he expanded these thoughts into a book, Christian Non-Resistance, *here excerpted. Ballou's work contains many of the ideas made famous by Thoreau's more celebrated essay.*

The almost universal opinion and practice of mankind has been on the side of resistance of injury *with* injury. It has been held justifiable and *necessary,* for individuals and nations to inflict any amount of *injury* which would effectually resist a supposed greater injury. The consequence has been universal suspicion, defiance, armament, violence, torture and bloodshed. The earth has been rendered a vast slaughter-field—a theatre of reciprocal cruelty and vengeance—strewn with human skulls, reeking with human blood, resounding with human groans, and steeped with human tears. Men have become drunk with mutual revenge; and they who could inflict the greatest amount of injury, in pretended defence of life, honor, rights, property, institutions and laws, have been idolized as the heroes and rightful sovereigns of the world. Non-resistance explodes this horrible delusion; announces the impossibility of overcoming evil with evil; and, making its appeal directly to all the *injured* of the human race, enjoins on them, in the name of God, never more to *resist injury with injury;* assuring them that by adhering to the law of love under all provocations, and scrupulously suffering wrong, rather than inflicting it, they shall gloriously "overcome evil with good," and exterminate all their enemies by turning them into faithful friends. . . .

WHAT A CHRISTIAN NON-RESISTANT CANNOT CONSISTENTLY DO

It will appear from the foregoing exposition, that a true Christian non-resistant *cannot,* with deliberate intent, knowledge or conscious voluntariness, compromit his principles by either [any] of the following acts.

1. He cannot kill, maim or otherwise *absolutely injure* any human being, in personal self-defence, or for the sake of his family, or any thing he holds dear.

2. He cannot participate in any lawless conspiracy, mob, riotous assembly, or disorderly combination of individuals, to cause or countenance the commission of any such absolute personal injury.

3. He cannot be a member of any voluntary association, however orderly, respectable or allowable by law and general consent, *which declaratively* holds as *fundamental truth,* or claims as an essential right, or distinctly inculcates as sound doctrine, or approves as commendable in practice, *war, capital* punishment, or any other absolute personal injury.

4. He cannot be an *officer* or *private,* chaplain or retainer, in the army, navy or militia of any nation, state, or chieftain.

5. He cannot be an officer, elector, agent, legal prosecutor, passive constituent, or approver of any government, as a sworn or otherwise pledged supporter thereof, whose civil constitution and fundamental laws, require, authorize or tolerate war, slavery, capital punishment, or the infliction of any absolute personal injury.

6. He cannot be a member of any chartered corporation, or body politic, whose articles of compact oblige or authorize its official functionaries to resort for compulsory aid, in the conducting of its affairs, to a government of constitutional violence.

7. Finally, he cannot do any act, either in person or by proxy; nor abet or encourage any act in others; nor demand, petition for, request, advise or approve the doing of any act, by an individual, association or government, *which* act would inflict, *threaten* to inflict, or *necessarily* cause to *be* inflicted *any absolute personal injury,* as herein before defined. . . .

ROBERT BARCLAY AND LEONARD FELL

Robert Barclay, the celebrated apologist of the Quakers, and Leonard Fell, a member of the same Society, were severally attacked by highwaymen in England, at different times. Both faithfully adhered to their non-resistance principles, and both signally triumphed. The pistol was levelled at Barclay, and a determined demand made for his purse. Calm and self-possessed, he looked the robber in the face, with a firm but meek benignity, assured him he was *his* and every man's friend, that he was willing and ready to relieve his wants, that he was free from the fear of death through a divine hope in immortality, and therefore was not to be intimidated by a deadly weapon; and then appealed to him, whether he could have heart to shed the blood of one who had no other feeling or purpose but to do him good. The robber was confounded; his eye melted; his brawny arm trembled; his pistol fell to his side; and he fled from the presence of the non-resistant hero whom he could no longer confront.

Fell was assaulted in a much more violent manner. The robber rushed upon him, dragged him from his horse, rifled his pockets, and threatened to blow out his brains on the spot, if he made the least resistance. This was the work of a moment. But Fell experienced no panic. His principles raised him above the fear of man and of death. Though forbidden to speak, he calmly but resolutely reproved the robber for his wickedness, warned him of the consequences of such a course of life, counselled him to reform, and assured him that while he forgave this wanton outrage on himself, he hoped for *his own* sake he would henceforth betake himself to an upright calling. His expostulation was so fearless, faithful and affectionate, that the robber was struck with compunction, delivered back his money and horse, and bade him go in peace. Then, with tears filling his eyes, he exclaimed,—"May God have mercy on a sinful wretch," and hastened out of sight. . . .

... Perhaps the severest test to which the peace principles were ever put, was in Ireland, during the memorable rebellion of 1798. During that terrible conflict, the Irish Quakers were continually between two fires. The protestant party viewed them with suspicion and dislike because they refused to fight or to pay military taxes; and the fierce multitude of insurgents deemed it sufficient cause of death, that they would neither profess belief in the Catholic religion nor help them fight for Irish freedom. Victory alternated between the two contending parties, and, as usual in civil war, the victors made almost indiscriminate havoc of those who did not march under their banners. It was a perilous time for all men; but the Quakers alone were liable to a raking fire from both sides. Foreseeing calamity, they had, nearly two years before the war broke out, publicly destroyed all their guns, and other weapons used for game. But this pledge of pacific intentions was not sufficient to satisfy the government, which required warlike assistance at their hands. Threats and insults were heaped upon them from all quarters; but they steadfastly adhered to their resolution of doing good to both parties, and harm to neither. Their houses were filled with widows and orphans, with the sick, the wounded and the dying, belonging both to the loyalists and the rebels. Sometimes, when the Catholic insurgents were victorious, they would be greatly enraged to find Quaker houses filled with Protestant families. They would point their pistols and threaten death, if their enemies were not immediately turned into the street to be massacred. But the pistol dropped, when the Christian mildly replied, "Friend, do what thou wilt, I will not harm thee, or any other human being." Not even amid the savage fierceness of civil war, could men fire at one who spoke such words as these. They saw that this was not cowardice, but bravery very much higher than their own.

On one occasion, an insurgent threatened to burn down a Quaker house unless the owner expelled the Protestant women and children who had taken refuge there. "I cannot help it," replied the Friend; "so long as I have a house, I will keep it open to succor the helpless and distressed, whether they belong to thy ranks, or to those of thy enemies. If my house is burned, I must be turned out with them, and share their affliction." The fighter turned away and did the Christian no harm.

The Protestant party seized the Quaker school-master of Ballitore, saying they could see no reason why he should stay at home in quiet, while they were obliged to defend his property. "Friends, I have asked no man to fight for me," replied the school-master. But they dragged him along, swearing that he should at least stop a bullet. His house and schoolhouse were filled with women and children, who had taken refuge there; for it was an instructive fact, throughout this bloody contest, that *the houses of the men of peace were the only places of safety.* Some of the women followed the soldiers, begging them not to take away their friend and protector, a man who expended more for the sick and starving, than others did for arms and ammunition. The school-master said, "Do not be distressed, my friends. I forgive these neighbors; for what they do, they do in ignorance of my principles and feelings. They may take my life, but they cannot force me to do injury to one of my fellow creatures." As the Catholics had done, so did the Protestants; they went away, and left the man of peace safe in his divine armor.

The flames of bigotry were, of course, fanned by civil war. On one occasion, the insurgents seized a wealthy old Quaker, in very feeble health, and threatened to shoot him, if he did not go with them to a Catholic priest to be christened. They had not led him far, before he sank down from extreme weakness. "What do you say to our proposition?" asked one of the soldiers, handling his gun significantly. The old man quietly replied, "If thou art permitted to take my life I hope our Heavenly Father will forgive thee." The insurgents talked apart for a few moments, and then went away, restrained by a power they did not understand.

Deeds of kindness added strength to the influence of gentle words. The officers and soldiers of both parties had had some dying brother tended by the Quakers, or some starving mother who had been fed, or some desolate little ones who had been cherished. Whichever party marched into a village victorious, the cry was, "Spare the Quakers! They have done good to all, and harm to none." While flames were raging, and blood flowing in every direction, the houses of the peace makers stood uninjured. . . .

DOCUMENT 5

Henry David Thoreau, "Civil Disobedience"

Henry Thoreau (1817–1862) wrote his essay on civil disobedience after he served a night in jail, in 1846, for refusing to pay the Massachusetts poll tax. He believed that the war with Mexico, then going on, was intended to spread slavery; and that those who wished to do more than wish godspeed to the right as it went by them (as he put it) would have to put their bodies in the way.

Thoreau's essay owed much to the Christian anarchism of Garrison and Ballou. But while Garrison and Ballou disavowed "jacobinism" (violent

Henry D. Thoreau, "Civil Disobedience," *A Yankee in Canada, with Anti-Slavery and Reform Papers* (Boston: Ticknor and Fields, 1866), pp. 123–151.

revolution), Thoreau deliberately proclaimed the need for revolution, albeit a revolution of one. And in contrast to the religious perfectionism of his predecessors, Thoreau put forward his doctrine as a creed for citizens: ". . . to speak practically and as a citizen, unlike those who call themselves no-government men, I ask for, not at once no government, but at once a better government." In effect Thoreau synthesized two previously divergent traditions: the Christian concept of civil disobedience, and John Locke's justification of revolution. The essay on civil disobedience was first published in 1849 under the title "Resistance to Civil Government."

I heartily accept the motto,—"That government is best which governs least"; and I should like to see it acted up to more rapidly and systematically. Carried out, it finally amounts to this, which also I believe,—"That government is best which governs not at all"; and when men are prepared for it, that will be the kind of government which they will have. Government is at best but an expedient; but most governments are usually, and all governments are sometimes, inexpedient. The objections which have been brought against a standing army, and they are many and weighty, and deserve to prevail, may also at last be brought against a standing government. The standing army is only an arm of the standing government. The government itself, which is only the mode which the people have chosen to execute their will, is equally liable to be abused and perverted before the people can act through it. Witness the present Mexican war, the work of comparatively a few individuals using the standing government as their tool; for, in the outset, the people would not have consented to this measure.

This American government,—what is it but a tradition, though a recent one, endeavoring to transmit itself unimpaired to posterity, but each instant losing some of its integrity? It has not the vitality and force of a single living man; for a single man can bend it to his will. It is a sort of wooden gun to the people themselves. But it is not the less necessary for this; for the people must have some complicated machinery or other, and hear its din, to satisfy that idea of government which they have. Governments show thus how successfully men can be imposed on, even impose on themselves, for their own advantage. It is excellent, we must all allow. Yet this government never of itself furthered any enterprise, but by the alacrity with which it got out of its way. *It* does not keep the country free. *It* does not settle the West. *It* does not educate. The character inherent in the American people has done all that has been accomplished; and it would have done somewhat more, if the government had not sometimes got in its way. For government is an expedient by which men would fain succeed in letting one another alone; and, as has been said, when it is most expedient, the governed are most let alone by it. Trade and commerce, if they were not made of India-rubber, would never manage to bounce over the obstacles which legislators are continually putting in their way; and, if one were to judge these men wholly by the effects of their actions and not partly by their intentions, they would deserve to be classed and punished with those mischievous persons who put obstructions on the railroads.

But, to speak practically and as a citizen, unlike those who call themselves no-government men, I ask for, not at once no government, but *at once* a better government. Let every man make known what kind of government would command his respect, and that will be one step toward obtaining it.

After all, the practical reason why, when the power is once in the hands of the people, a majority are permitted, and for a long period continue, to rule, is not because they are most likely to be in the right, nor because this seems fairest to the minority, but because they are physically the strongest. But a government in which the majority rule in all cases cannot be based on justice, even as far as men understand it. Can there not be a government in which majorities do not virtually decide right and wrong, but conscience?—in which majorities decide only those questions to which the rule of expediency is applicable? Must the citizen ever for a moment, or in the least degree, resign his conscience to the legislator? Why has every man a conscience, then? I think that we should be men first, and subjects afterward. It is not desirable to cultivate a respect for the law, so much as for the right. The only obligation which I have a right to assume, is to do at any time what I think right. It is truly enough said, that a corporation has no conscience; but a corporation of conscientious men is a corporation *with* a conscience. Law never made men a whit more just; and, by means of their respect for it, even the well-disposed are daily made the agents of injustice. A common and natural result of an undue respect for law is, that you may see a file of soldiers, colonel, captain, corporal, privates, powder-monkeys, and all, marching in admirable order over hill and dale to the wars, against their wills, ay, against their common sense and consciences, which makes it very steep marching indeed, and produces a palpitation of the heart. They have no doubt that it is a damnable business in which they are concerned; they are all peaceably inclined. Now, what are they? Men at all? or small movable forts and magazines, at the service of some unscrupulous man in power? Visit the Navy-Yard, and behold a marine, such a man as an American government can make, or such as it can make a man with its black arts,—a mere shadow and reminiscence of humanity, a man laid out alive and standing, and already, as one may say, buried under arms with funeral accompaniments, though it may be,—

"Not a drum was heard, not a funeral note,
As his corse to the rampart we hurried;
Not a soldier discharged his farewell shot
O'er the grave where our hero we buried."

The mass of men serve the state thus, not as men mainly, but as machines, with their bodies. They are the standing army, and the militia, jailers, constables, posse comitatus, &c. In most cases there is no free exercise whatever of the judgment or of the moral sense; but they put themselves on a level with wood and earth and stones; and wooden men can perhaps be manufactured that will serve the purpose as well. Such command no more respect than men of straw or a lump of dirt. They have the same sort of worth only as horses and dogs. Yet such as these even are commonly esteemed good citizens. Others,—as most legislators, politicians, lawyers, ministers, and officeholders,—serve the state chiefly with their heads; and, as they rarely make any moral distinctions, they are as likely to serve the Devil, without *intending* it, as God. A very few, as heroes, patriots, martyrs, reformers in the great sense, and *men,* serve the state with their consciences also, and so necessarily resist it for the most part; and they are commonly treated as enemies by it. A wise man will only be useful as a man, and will not submit to be "clay," and "stop a hole to keep the wind away," but leave that office to his dust at least:—

> "I am too high-born to be propertied,
> To be a secondary at control,
> Or useful serving-man and instrument
> To any sovereign state throughout the world."

He who gives himself entirely to his fellow-men appears to them useless and selfish; but he who gives himself partially to them is pronounced a benefactor and philanthropist.

How does it become a man to behave toward this American government to-day? I answer, that he cannot without disgrace be associated with it. I cannot for an instant recognize that political organization as *my* government which is the *slave's* government also.

All men recognize the right of revolution; that is, the right to refuse allegiance to, and to resist, the government, when its tyranny or its inefficiency are great and unendurable. But almost all say that such is not the case now. But such was the case, they think, in the Revolution of '75. If one were to tell me that this was a bad government because it taxed certain foreign commodities brought to its ports, it is most probable that I should not make an ado about it, for I can do without them. All machines have their friction; and possibly this does enough good to counterbalance the evil. At any rate, it is a great evil to make a stir about it. But when the friction comes to have its machine, and oppression and robbery are organized, I say, let us not have such a machine any longer. In other words, when a sixth of the population of a nation which has undertaken to be the refuge of liberty are slaves, and a whole country is unjustly overrun and conquered by a foreign army, and subjected to military law, I think that it is not too soon for honest men to rebel and revolutionize. What makes this duty the more urgent is the fact, that the country so overrun is not our own, but ours is the invading army.

Paley, a common authority with many on moral questions, in his chapter on the "Duty of Submission to Civil Government," resolves all civil obligation into expediency; and he proceeds to say, "that so long as the interest of the whole society requires it, that is, so long as the established government cannot be resisted or changed without public inconveniency, it is the will of God that the established government be obeyed, and no longer. . . . This principle being admitted, the justice of every particular case of resistance is reduced to a computation of the quantity of the danger and grievance on the one side, and of the probability and expense of redressing it on the other." Of this, he says, every man shall judge for himself. But Paley appears never to have contemplated those cases to which the rule of expediency does not apply, in which a people, as well as an individual, must do justice, cost what it may. If I have unjustly wrested a plank from a drowning man, I must restore it to him though I drown myself. This, according to Paley, would be inconvenient. But he that would save his life, in such a case, shall lose it. This people must cease to hold slaves, and to make war on Mexico, though it cost them their existence as a people.

In their practice, nations agree with Paley; but does any one think that Massachusetts does exactly what is right at the present crisis?

> "A drab of state, a cloth-o'-silver slut,
> To have her train borne up, and her soul trail in the dirt."

Practically speaking, the opponents to a reform in Massachusetts are not a hundred thousand politicians at the South, but a hundred thousand merchants and farmers here, who are more interested in commerce and agriculture than they are in humanity, and are not prepared to do justice to the slave and to Mexico, *cost what it may.* I quarrel not with far-off foes, but with those who, near at home, co-operate with, and do the bidding of, those far away, and without whom the latter would be harmless. We are accustomed to say, that the mass of men are unprepared; but improvement is slow, because the few are not materially wiser or better than the many. It is not so important that many should be as good as you, as that there be some absolute goodness somewhere; for that will leaven the whole lump. There are thousands who are *in opinion* opposed to slavery and to the war, who yet in effect do nothing to put an end to them; who, esteeming themselves children of Washington and Franklin, sit down with their hands in their pockets, and say that they know not what to do, and do nothing; who even postpone the question of freedom to the question of free-trade, and quietly read the prices-current along with the latest advices from Mexico, after dinner, and, it may be, fall asleep over them both. What is the price-current of an honest man and patriot to-day? They hesitate, and they regret, and sometimes they petition; but they do nothing in earnest and with effect. They will wait, well disposed, for others to remedy the evil, that they may no longer have it to regret. At most, they give only a cheap vote, and a feeble countenance and Godspeed, to the right, as it goes by them. There are nine hundred and ninety-nine patrons of virtue to one virtuous man. But it is easier to deal with the real possessor of a thing than with the temporary guardian of it.

All voting is a sort of gaming, like checkers or backgammon, with a slight moral tinge to it, a playing with right and wrong, with moral questions; and betting naturally accompanies it. The character of the voters is not staked. I cast my vote, perchance, as I think right; but I am not vitally concerned that that right should prevail. I am willing to leave it to the majority. Its obligation, therefore, never exceeds that of expediency. Even voting *for the right* is *doing* nothing for it. It is only expressing to men feebly your desire that it should prevail. A wise man will not leave the right to the mercy of chance, nor wish it to prevail through the power of the majority. There is but little virtue in the action of masses of men. When the majority shall at length vote for the abolition of slavery, it will be because they are indifferent to slavery, or because there is but little slavery left to be abolished by their vote. *They* will then be the only slaves. Only *his* vote can hasten the abolition of slavery who asserts his own freedom by his vote.

I hear of a convention to be held at Baltimore, or elsewhere, for the selection of a candidate for the Presidency, made up chiefly of editors, and men who are politicians by profession; but I think, what is it to any independent, intelligent, and respectable man what decision they may come to? Shall we not have the advantage of his wisdom and honesty, nevertheless? Can we not count upon some independent votes? Are there not many individuals in the country who do not attend conventions? But no: I find that the respectable man, so called, has immediately drifted from his position, and despairs of his country, when his country has more reason to despair of him. He forthwith adopts one of the candidates thus selected as the only *available* one, thus proving that he is himself *available* for any purposes of the demagogue. His vote is of no more worth than that of any unprincipled foreigner or hireling native, who may have been bought. O for a man who is a *man*, and, as my neighbor says, has a bone in his back which you cannot pass your hand through! Our statistics are at fault: the population has been returned too large. How many *men* are there to a square thousand miles in this country? Hardly one. Does not America offer any inducement for men to settle here? The American has dwindled into an Odd Fellow,—one who may be known by the development of his organ of gregariousness, and a manifest lack of intellect and cheerful self-reliance; whose first and chief concern, on coming into the world, is to see that the Almshouses are in good repair; and, before yet he has lawfully donned the virile garb, to collect a fund for the support of the widows and orphans that may be; who, in short, ventures to live only by the aid of the Mutual Insurance company, which has promised to bury him decently.

It is not a man's duty, as a matter of course, to devote himself to the eradication of any, even the most enormous wrong; he may still properly have other concerns to engage him; but it is his duty, at least, to wash his hands of it, and, if he gives it no thought longer, not to give it practically his support. If I devote myself to other pursuits and contemplations, I must first see, at least, that I do not pursue them sitting upon another man's shoulders. I must get off him first, that he may pursue his contemplations too. See what gross inconsistency is tolerated. I have heard some of my townsmen say, "I should like to have them order me out to help put down an insurrection of the slaves, or to march to Mexico;—see if I would go"; and yet these very men have each, directly by their allegiance, and so indirectly, at least, by their money, furnished a substitute. The soldier is applauded who refuses to serve in an unjust war by those who do not refuse to sustain the unjust government which makes the war; is applauded by those whose own act and authority he disregards and sets at naught; as if the State were penitent to that degree that it hired one to scourge it while it sinned, but not to that degree that it left off sinning for a moment. Thus, under the name of Order and Civil Government, we are all made at last to pay homage to and support our own meanness. After the first blush of sin comes its indifference; and from immoral it becomes, as it were, *un*moral, and not quite unnecessary to that life which we have made.

The broadest and most prevalent error requires the most disinterested virtue to sustain it. The slight reproach to which the virtue of patriotism is commonly liable, the noble are most likely to incur. Those who, while they disapprove of the character and measures of a government, yield to it their allegiance and support, are undoubtedly its most conscientious supporters, and so frequently the most serious obstacles to reform. Some are petitioning the State to dissolve the Union, to disregard the requisitions of the President. Why do they not dissolve it themselves,—the union between themselves and the State,—and refuse to pay their quota into its treasury? Do not they stand in the same relation to the State, that the State does to the Union? And have not the same reasons prevented the State from resisting the Union, which have prevented them from resisting the State?

How can a man be satisfied to entertain an opinion merely, and enjoy *it?* Is there any enjoyment in it, if his opinion is that he is aggrieved? If you are cheated out of a single dollar by your neighbor, you do not rest satisfied with knowing that you are cheated, or with saying that you are cheated, or even with petitioning him to pay you your due; but you take effectual steps at once to obtain the full amount, and see that you are never cheated again. Action from principle, the perception and the performance of right, changes things and relations; it is essentially revolutionary, and does not consist wholly with anything which was. It not only divides states and churches, it divides families; ay, it divides the *individual,* separating the diabolical in him from the divine.

Unjust laws exist: shall we be content to obey them, or shall we endeavor to amend them, and obey them until we have succeeded, or shall we transgress them at once? Men generally, under such a government as this, think that they ought to wait until they have persuaded the majority to alter them. They think that, if they should resist, the remedy would be worse than the evil. But it is the fault of the government itself that the remedy *is* worse than the evil. *It* makes it worse. Why is it not more apt to anticipate and provide for reform? Why does it not cherish its wise minority? Why does it cry and resist before it is hurt? Why does it not encourage its citizens to be on the alert to point out its faults, and *do* better than it would have them? Why does it always crucify Christ, and excommunicate Copernicus and Luther, and pronounce Washington and Franklin rebels?

One would think, that a deliberate and practical denial of its authority was the only offence never contemplated by government; else, why has it not assigned its definite, its suitable and proportionate penalty? If a man who has no property refuses but once to earn nine shillings for the State, he is put in prison for a period unlimited by any law that I know, and determined only by the discretion of those who placed him there; but if he should steal ninety times nine shillings from the State, he is soon permitted to go at large again.

If the injustice is part of the necessary friction of the machine of government, let it go, let it go: perchance it will wear smooth,—certainly the machine will wear out. If the injustice has a spring, or a pulley, or a rope, or a crank, exclusively for itself, then perhaps you may consider whether the remedy will not be worse than the evil; but if it is of such a nature that it requires you to be the agent of injustice to another, then, I say, break the law. Let your life be a counter friction to stop the machine. What I have to do is to see, at any rate, that I do not lend myself to the wrong which I condemn.

As for adopting the ways which the State has provided for remedying the evil, I know not of such ways. They take too much time, and a man's life will be gone. I have other affairs to attend to. I came into this world, not chiefly to make this a good place to live in, but to live in it, be it good or bad. A man has not everything to do, but something; and because he cannot do *everything*, it is not necessary that he should do *something* wrong. It is not my business to be petitioning the Governor or the Legislature any more than it is theirs to petition me; and, if they should not hear my petition, what should I do then? But in this case the State has provided no way: its very Constitution is the evil. This may seem to be harsh and stubborn and unconciliatory; but it is to treat with the utmost kindness and consideration the only spirit that can appreciate or deserves it. So is all change for the better, like birth and death, which convulse the body.

I do not hesitate to say, that those who call themselves Abolitionists should at once effectually withdraw their support, both in person and property, from the government of Massachusetts, and not wait till they constitute a majority of one, before they suffer the right to prevail through them. I think that it is enough if they have God on their side, without waiting for that other one. Moreover, any man more right than his neighbors constitutes a majority of one already.

I meet this American government, or its representative, the State government, directly, and face to face, once a year—no more—in the person of its tax-gatherer; this is the only mode in which a man situated as I am necessarily meets it; and it then says distinctly, Recognize me; and the simplest, the most effectual, and, in the present posture of affairs, the indispensablest mode of treating with it on this head, of expressing your little satisfaction with and love for it, is to deny it then. My civil neighbor, the tax-gatherer, is the very man I have to deal with,—for it is, after all, with men and not with parchment that I quarrel,—and he has voluntarily chosen to be an agent of the government. How shall he ever know well what he is and does as an officer of the government, or as a man, until he is obliged to consider whether he shall treat me, his neighbor, for whom he has respect, as a neighbor and well-disposed man, or as a maniac and disturber of the peace, and see if he can get over this obstruction to his neighborliness without a ruder and more impetuous thought or speech corresponding with his action. I know this well, that if one thousand, if one hundred, if ten men whom I could name,—if ten *honest* men only,—ay, if *one* HONEST man, in this State of Massachusetts, *ceasing to hold slaves,* were actually to withdraw from this copartnership, and be locked up in the county jail therefor, it would be the abolition of slavery in America. For it matters not how small the beginning may seem to be: what is once well done is done forever. But we love better to talk about it: that we say is our mission. Reform keeps many scores of newspapers in its service, but not one man. If my esteemed neighbor, the State's ambassador, who will devote his days to the settlement of the question of human rights in the Council Chamber, instead of being threatened with the prisons of Carolina, were to sit down the prisoner of Massachusetts, that State which is so anxious to foist the sin of slavery upon her sister,—though at present she can discover only an act of inhospitality to be the ground of a quarrel with her,—the Legislature would not wholly waive the subject the following winter.

Under a government which imprisons any unjustly, the true place for a just man is also a prison. The proper place to-day, the only place which Massachusetts has provided for her freer and less desponding spirits, is in her prisons, to be put out and locked out of the State by her own act, as they have already put themselves out by their principles. It is there that the fugitive slave, and the Mexican prisoner on parole, and the Indian come to plead the wrongs of his race, should find them; on that separate, but more free and honorable ground, where the State places those who are not *with* her, but *against* her,—the only house in a slave State in which a free man can abide with honor. If any think that their influence would be lost there, and their voices no longer afflict the ear of the State, that they would not be as an enemy within its walls, they do not know by how much truth is stronger than error, nor how much more eloquently and effectively he can combat injustice who has experienced a little in his own person. Cast your whole vote, not a strip of paper merely, but your whole influence. A minority is powerless while it conforms to the majority; it is not even a minority then; but it is irresistible when it clogs by its whole weight. If the alternative is to keep all just men in prison, or give up war and slavery, the State will not hesitate which to choose. If a thousand men were not to pay their tax-bills this year, that would not be a violent and bloody measure, as it would be to pay them, and enable the State to commit violence and shed innocent blood. This is, in fact, the definition of a peaceable revolution, if any such is possible. If the tax-gatherer, or any other public officer, asks me, as one has done, "But what shall I do?" my answer is, "If you really wish to do anything, resign your office." When the subject has refused allegiance, and the officer has resigned his office, then the revolution is accomplished. But even suppose blood should flow. Is there not a sort of blood shed when the conscience is wounded? Through this wound a man's real manhood and immortality flow out, and he bleeds to an everlasting death. I see this blood flowing now.

I have contemplated the imprisonment of the offender, rather than the seizure of his goods,—though both will serve the same purpose,—because they who assert the purest right, and consequently are most dangerous to a corrupt State, commonly have not spent much time in accumulating property. To such the State renders comparatively small service, and a slight tax is wont to appear exorbitant, particularly if they are obliged to earn it by special labor with their hands. If there were one who lived wholly without the use of money, the State itself would hesitate to demand it of him. But the rich man,—not to make any invidious comparison,—is always sold to the institution which makes him rich. Absolutely speaking, the more money, the less virtue; for money comes between a man and his objects, and obtains them for him; and it was certainly no great virtue to obtain it. It puts to rest many questions which he would otherwise be taxed to answer; while the only new question which it puts is the hard but superfluous one, how to spend it. Thus his moral ground is taken from under his feet. The opportunities of living are diminished in proportion as what are called the "means" are increased. The best thing a man can do for his culture when he is rich is to endeavor to carry out those schemes which he entertained when he was poor. Christ answered the Herodians according to their condition. "Show me the tribute-money," said he;—and one took a penny out of his pocket;—if you use money which has the image of Caesar on it, and which he has made current and valuable, that is, *if you are men of the State,* and gladly enjoy the advantages of Caesar's government, then pay him back some of his own when he demands it; "Render therefore to Caesar that which is Caesar's, and to God those things which are God's,"—leaving them no wiser than before as to which was which; for they did not wish to know.

When I converse with the freest of my neighbors, I perceive that, whatever they may say about the magnitude and seriousness of the question, and their regard for the public tranquillity, the long and the short of the matter is, that they cannot spare the protection of the existing government, and they dread the consequences to their property and families of disobedience to it. For my own part, I should not like to think that I ever rely on the protection of the State. But, if I deny the authority of the State when it presents its tax-bill, it will soon take and waste all my property, and so harass me and my children without end. This is hard. This makes it impossible for a man to live honestly, and at the same time comfortably, in outward respects. It will not be worth the while to accumulate property; that would be sure to go again. You must hire or squat somewhere, and raise but a small crop, and eat that soon. You must live within yourself, and depend upon yourself always tucked up and ready for a start, and not have many affairs. A man may grow rich in Turkey even, if he will be in all respects a good subject of the Turkish government. Confucius said: "If a state is governed by the principles of reason, poverty and misery are subjects of shame; if a state is not governed by the principles of reason, riches and honors are the subjects of shame." No: until I want the protection of Massachusetts to be extended to me in some distant Southern port, where my liberty is endangered, or until I am bent solely on building up an estate at home by peaceful enterprise, I can afford to refuse allegiance to Massachusetts, and her right to my property and life. It costs me less in every sense to incur the penalty of disobedience to the State, than it would to obey. I should feel as if I were worth less in that case.

Some years ago, the State met me in behalf of the Church, and commanded me to pay a certain sum toward the support of a clergyman whose preaching my father attended, but never I myself. "Pay," it said, "or be locked up in the jail." I declined to pay. But, unfortunately, another man saw fit to pay it. I did not see why the schoolmaster should be taxed to support the priest, and not the priest the schoolmaster; for I was not the State's schoolmaster, but I supported myself by voluntary subscription. I did not see why the lyceum should not present its tax-bill, and have the State to back its demand, as well as the Church. However, at the request of the selectmen, I conde-scended to make some such statement as this in writing:—"Know all men by these presents, that I, Henry Thoreau, do not wish to be regarded as a member of any incorporated society which I have not joined." This I gave to the town clerk; and he has it. The State, having thus learned that I did not wish to be regarded as a member of that church, has never made a like demand on me since; though it said that it must adhere to its original presumption that time. If I had known how to name them, I should then have signed off in detail from all the societies which I never signed on to; but I did not know where to find a complete list.

I have paid no poll-tax for six years. I was put into a jail once on this account, for one night; and, as I stood considering the walls of solid stone, two or three feet thick, the door of wood and iron, a foot thick, and the iron grating which strained the light, I could not help being struck with the foolishness of that institution which treated me as if I were mere flesh and blood and bones, to be locked up. I wondered that it should have concluded at length that this was the best use it could put me to, and had never thought to avail itself of my services in some way. I saw that, if there was a wall of stone between me and my townsmen, there was a still more difficult one to climb or break through, before they could get to be as free as I was. I did not for a moment feel confined, and the walls seemed a great waste of stone and mortar. I felt as if I alone of all my townsmen had paid my tax. They plainly did not know how to treat me, but behaved like persons who are underbred. In every threat and in every compliment there was a blunder; for they thought that my chief desire was to stand the other side of that stone wall. I could not but smile to see how industriously they locked the door on my meditations, which followed them out again without let or hindrance, and *they* were really all that was dangerous. As they could not reach me, they had resolved to punish my body; just as boys, if they cannot come at some person against whom they have a spite, will abuse his dog. I saw that the State was half-witted, that it was timid as a lone woman with her silver spoons, and that it did not know its friends from its foes, and I lost all my remaining respect for it, and pitied it.

Thus the State never intentionally confronts a man's sense, intellectual or moral, but only his body, his senses. It is not armed with superior wit or honesty, but with superior physical strength. I was not born to be forced. I will breathe after my own fashion. Let us see who is the strongest. What force has a multitude? They can only force me who obey a higher law than I. They force me to become like themselves. I do not hear of *men* being *forced* to live this way or that by masses of men. What sort of life were that to live? When I meet a government which says to me, "Your money or your life," why should I be in haste to give it my money? It may be in a great strait, and not know what to do: I cannot help that. It must help itself; do as I do. It is not worth the while to snivel about it. I am not responsible for the successful working of the machinery of society. I am not the son of the engineer. I perceive that, when an acorn and a chestnut fall side by side, the one does not remain inert to make way for the other, but both obey their own laws, and spring and grow and flourish as best they can, till one, perchance, overshadows and destroys the other. If a plant cannot live according to its nature, it dies; and so a man.

The night in prison was novel and interesting enough. The prisoners in their shirt-sleeves were enjoying a chat and the evening air in the doorway, when I entered. But the jailer said, "Come, boys, it is time to lock up"; and so they dispersed, and I heard the sound of their steps returning into the hollow apartments. My room-mate was introduced to me by the jailer, as "a first-rate fellow and a clever man." When the door was locked, he showed me where to hang my hat, and how he managed matters there. The rooms were whitewashed once a month; and this one, at least, was the whitest, most simply furnished, and probably the neatest apartment in the town. He naturally wanted to know where I came from, and what brought me there; and, when

I had told him, I asked him in my turn how he came there, presuming him to be an honest man, of course; and, as the world goes, I believe he was. "Why," said he, "they accuse me of burning a barn; but I never did it." As near as I could discover, he had probably gone to bed in a barn when drunk, and smoked his pipe there; and so a barn was burnt. He had the reputation of being a clever man, had been there some three months waiting for his trial to come on, and would have to wait as much longer; but he was quite domesticated and contented, since he got his board for nothing, and thought that he was well treated.

He occupied one window, and I the other; and I saw, that, if one stayed there long, his principal business would be to look out the window. I had soon read all the tracts that were left there, and examined where former prisoners had broken out, and where a grate had been sawed off, and heard the history of the various occupants of that room; for I found that even here there was a history and a gossip which never circulated beyond the walls of the jail. Probably this is the only house in the town where verses are composed, which are afterward printed in a circular form, but not published. I was shown quite a long list of verses which were composed by some young men who had been detected in an attempt to escape, who avenged themselves by singing them.

I pumped my fellow-prisoner as dry as I could, for fear I should never see him again; but at length he showed me which was my bed, and left me to blow out the lamp.

It was like travelling into a far country, such as I had never expected to behold, to lie there for one night. It seemed to me that I never had heard the town-clock strike before, nor the evening sounds of the village; for we slept with the windows open, which were inside the grating. It was to see my native village in the light of the Middle Ages, and our Concord was turned into a Rhine stream, and visions of knights and castles passed before me. They were the voices of old burghers that I heard in the streets. I was an involuntary spectator and auditor of whatever was done and said in the kitchen of the adjacent village-inn,—a wholly new and rare experience to me. It was a closer view of my native town. I was fairly inside of it. I never had seen its institutions before. This is one of its peculiar institutions; for it is a shire town. I began to comprehend what its inhabitants were about.

In the morning, our breakfasts were put through the hole in the door, in small oblong-square tin pans, made to fit, and holding a pint of chocolate, with brown bread, and an iron spoon. When they called for the vessels again, I was green enough to return what bread I had left; but my comrade seized it, and said that I should lay that up for lunch or dinner. Soon after he was let out to work at haying in a neighboring field, whither he went every day, and would not be back till noon; so he bade me good-day, saying that he doubted if he should see me again.

When I came out of prison,—for some one interfered, and paid that tax,—I did not perceive that great changes had taken place on the common, such as he observed who went in a youth, and emerged a tottering and gray-headed man; and yet a change had to my eyes come over the scene,—the town, and State, and country,—greater than any that mere time could effect. I saw yet more distinctly the State in which I lived. I saw to what extent the people among whom I lived could be trusted as good neighbors and friends; that their friendship was for summer weather only; that they did not greatly propose to do right; that they were a distinct race from me by their prejudices and superstitions, as the Chinamen and Malays are; that, in their sacrifices to humanity, they ran no risks, not even to their property; that, after all, they were not so noble but they treated the thief as he had treated them, and hoped, by a certain outward observance and a few prayers, and by walking in a particular straight though useless path from time to time, to save their souls. This may be to judge my neighbors harshly; for I believe that many of them are not aware that they have such an institution as the jail in their village.

It was formerly the custom in our village, when a poor debtor came out of jail, for his acquaintances to salute him, looking through their fingers, which were crossed to represent the grating of a jail window, "How do ye do?" My neighbors did not thus salute me, but first looked at me, and then at one another, as if I had returned from a long journey. I was put into jail as I was going to the shoemaker's to get a shoe which was mended. When I was let out the next morning, I proceeded to finish my errand, and having put on my mended shoe, joined a huckleberry party, who were impatient to put themselves under my conduct; and in half an hour,—for the horse was soon tackled,—was in the midst of a huckleberry field, on one of our highest hills, two miles off, and then the State was nowhere to be seen.

This is the whole history of "My Prisons."

I have never declined paying the highway tax, because I am as desirous of being a good neighbor as I am of being a bad subject; and, as for supporting schools, I am doing my part to educate my fellow-countrymen now. It is for no particular item in the tax-bill that I refuse to pay it. I simply wish to refuse allegiance to the State, to withdraw and stand aloof from it effectually. I do not care to trace the course of my dollar, if I could, till it buys a man or a musket to shoot one with,—the dollar is innocent,—but I am concerned to trace the effects of my allegiance. In fact, I quietly declare war with the State, after my fashion, though I will still make what use and get what advantage of her I can, as is usual in such cases.

If others pay the tax which is demanded of me, from a sympathy with the State, they do but what they have already done in their own case, or rather they abet injustice to a greater extent than the State requires. If they pay the tax from a mistaken interest in the individual taxed, to save his property, or prevent his going to jail, it is because they have not considered wisely how far they let their private feelings interfere with the public good.

This, then, is my position at present. But one cannot be too much on his guard in such a case, lest his action be biased by obstinacy, or an undue regard for the opinions of men. Let him see that he does only what belongs to himself and to the hour.

I think sometimes, Why, this people mean well; they are only ignorant; they would do better if they knew how: why give your neighbors this pain to treat you as they are not inclined to? But I think again, this is no reason why I should do as they do, or permit others to suffer much greater pain of a different kind. Again, I sometimes say to myself, When many millions of men, without heat, without ill will, without personal feeling of any kind, demand of you a few shillings only, without the possibility, such is their constitution, of retracting or altering their present demand, and without the possibility, on your side, of appeal to any other millions, why expose yourself to this overwhelming brute force? You do not resist cold and hunger, the winds and the waves, thus obstinately; you quietly submit to a thousand similar necessities. You do not put your head into the fire. But just in proportion as I regard this as not wholly a brute force, but partly a human force, and consider that I have relations to those millions as to so many millions of men, and not of mere brute or inanimate things, I see that appeal is possible, first and instantaneously, from them to the Maker of them, and secondly, from them to themselves. But, if I put my head deliberately into the fire, there is no appeal to fire or to the Maker of fire, and I have only myself to blame. If I could convince myself that I have any right to be satisfied with men as they are, and to treat them accordingly, and not according, in some respects, to my requisitions and expectations of what they and I ought to be, then, like a good Mussulman and fatalist, I should endeavor to be satisfied with things as they are, and say it is the will of God. And, above all, there is this difference between resisting this and a purely brute or natural force, that I can resist this with some effect; but I cannot expect, like Orpheus, to change the nature of the rocks and trees and beasts.

I do not wish to quarrel with any man or nation. I do not wish to split hairs, to make fine distinctions, or set myself up as better than my neighbors. I seek rather, I may say, even an excuse for conforming to the laws of the land. I am but too ready to conform to them. Indeed, I have reason to suspect myself on this head; and each year, as the tax-gatherer comes round, I find myself disposed to review the acts and position of the general and State governments, and the spirit of the people, to discover a pretext for conformity.

> "We must affect our country as our parents;
> And if at any time we alienate
> Our love or industry from doing it honor,
> We must respect effects and teach the soul
> Matter of conscience and religion,
> And not desire of rule or benefit."

I believe that the State will soon be able to take all my work of this sort out of my hands, and then I shall be no better a patriot than my fellow-countrymen.

Seen from a lower point of view, the Constitution, with all its faults, is very good; the law and the courts are very respectable; even this State and this American government are, in many respects, very admirable and rare things, to be thankful for, such as a great many have described them; but seen from a point of view a little higher, they are what I have described them; seen from a higher still, and the highest, who shall say what they are, or that they are worth looking at or thinking of at all?

However, the government does not concern me much, and I shall bestow the fewest possible thoughts on it. It is not many moments that I live under a government, even in this world. If a man is thought-free, fancy-free, imagination-free, that which *is not* never for a long time appearing *to be* to him, unwise rulers or reformers cannot fatally interrupt him.

I know that most men think differently from myself; but those whose lives are by profession devoted to the study of these or kindred subjects, content me as little as any. Statesmen and legislators, standing so completely within the institution, never distinctly and nakedly behold it. They speak of moving society, but have no resting-place without it. They may be men of a certain experience and discrimination, and have no doubt invented ingenious and even useful systems, for which we sincerely thank them; but all their wit and usefulness lie within certain not very wide limits. They are wont to forget that the world is not governed by policy and expediency. Webster never goes behind government, and so cannot speak with authority about it. His words are wisdom to those legislators who contemplate no essential reform in the existing government; but for thinkers, and those who legislate for all time, he never once glances at the subject. I know of those whose serene and wise speculations on this theme would soon reveal the limits of his mind's range and hospitality. Yet, compared with the cheap professions of most reformers, and the still cheaper wisdom and eloquence of politicians in general, his are almost the only sensible and valuable words, and we thank Heaven for him. Comparatively, he is always strong, original, and, above all, practical. Still his quality is not wisdom, but prudence. The lawyer's truth is not Truth, but consistency, or a consistent expediency. Truth is always in harmony with herself, and is not concerned chiefly to reveal the justice that may consist with wrong-doing. He well deserves to be called, as he has been called, the Defender of the Constitution. There are really no blows to be given by him but defensive ones. He is not a leader, but a follower. His leaders are the men of '87. "I have never made an effort," he says, "and never propose to make an effort; I have never countenanced an effort, and never mean to countenance an effort, to disturb the arrangement as originally made, by which the various States came into the Union." Still thinking of the sanction which the Constitution gives to slavery, he says, "Because it was a part of the original compact,—let it stand." Notwithstanding his special acuteness and ability, he is unable to take a fact out of its merely political relations, and behold it as it lies absolutely to be disposed of by the intellect,—what, for instance, it behooves a man to do here in America today with regard to slavery, but ventures, or is driven, to make some such desperate answer as the following, while professing to speak absolutely, and as a private man,— from which what new and singular code of social duties might be inferred? "The manner," says he, "in which the governments of those States where slavery exists are to regulate it, is for their own consideration, under their responsibility to their constituents, to the general laws of propriety, humanity, and justice, and to God. Associations formed elsewhere, springing from a feeling of humanity, or any other cause, have nothing whatever to do with it. They have never received any encouragement from me, and they never will."

They who know of no purer sources of truth, who have traced up its stream no higher, stand, and wisely stand, by the Bible and the Constitution, and drink at it there with reverence and humility; but they who behold where it comes trickling into this lake or that pool, gird up their loins once more, and continue their pilgrimage towards its fountain-head.

No man with a genius for legislation has appeared in America. They are rare in the history of the world. There are orators, politicians, and eloquent men, by the thousand; but the speaker has not yet opened his mouth to speak, who is capable of settling the much-vexed questions of the day. We love eloquence for its own sake, and not for any truth which it may utter, or any heroism it may inspire. Our legislators have not yet learned the comparative value of free-trade and of freedom, of union, and of rectitude, to a nation. They have no genius or talent for comparatively humble questions of taxation and finance, commerce and manufacturers and agriculture. If we were left solely to the wordy wit of legislators in Congress for our guidance, uncorrected by the seasonable experience and the effectual complaints of the people, America would not long retain her rank among the nations. For eighteen hundred years, though perchance I have no right to say it, the New Testament has been written, yet where is the legislator who has wisdom and practical talent enough to avail himself of the light which it sheds on the science of legislation?

The authority of government, even such as I am willing to submit to,—for I will cheerfully obey those who know and can do better than I, and in many things even those who neither know nor can do so well,—is still an impure one: to be strictly just, it must have the sanction and consent of the governed. It can have no pure right over my person and property but what I concede to it. The progress from an absolute to a limited monarchy, from a limited monarchy to a democracy, is a progress toward a true respect for the individual. Even the Chinese philosopher was wise enough to regard the individual as the basis of the empire. Is a democracy, such as we know it, the last improvement possible in government? Is it not possible to take a step further towards recognizing and organizing the rights of man? There will never be a really free and enlightened State, until the State comes to recognize the individual as a higher and independent power, from which all its own power and authority are derived, and treats him accordingly. I please myself with imagining a State at last which can afford to be just to all men, and to treat the individual with respect as a neighbor; which even would not think it inconsistent with its own repose, if a few were to live aloof from it, not meddling with it, nor embraced by it, who fulfilled all the duties of neighbors and fellow-men. A State which bore this kind of fruit, and suffered it to drop off as fast as it ripened, would prepare the way for a still more perfect and glorious State, which also I have imagined, but not yet anywhere seen.

DOCUMENT 6

Elihu Burritt,
"Passive Resistance"

Elihu Burritt (1810–1879) snatched time from his work as a blacksmith to learn Latin, Greek, French, Spanish, Italian, German, Hebrew, Chaldaic, Samaritan, Ethiopic, and a number of other languages. During one three-month period he studied near (but not at) Yale University; later he took a foundry job in Worcester, Massachusetts, so as to be able to borrow grammars and lexicons from the American Antiquarian Society.

As Burritt's learning became publicly recognized, he devoted himself increasingly to writing and lecturing on behalf of temperance, abolitionism, and world peace. Never forgetting his own origins, Burritt also called on workingmen for a worldwide general strike against war. "We hope," he declared in 1867, "the day will come when the working-men of Christendom will form one vast Trades Union, and make a universal and simultaneous strike against the whole war system." The concern for mass use of nonviolence, as opposed to the individual action of a Woolman or Thoreau, is evident through-out Burritt's essays on "Passive Resistance."

From Elihu Burritt, *Thoughts and Things at Home and Abroad* (Boston: Phillips, Sampson, and Co., 1854).

THE POWER OF PASSIVE RESISTANCE

The full power revealed and prescribed in that simple and sublime precept of the Gospel, *"overcome evil with good,"* has never been tested by any people, population, or community, in subduing the evils and enemies that beset and oppressed them, either from within or without. To put it into full operation, requires a capacity of good-will, of forgiveness of injuries, of abnegation of natural instincts, which the population of no town, or province, or state, has ever acquired. But, at long intervals, and a little more frequently of late, a case has occurred here and there, in which a considerable community has acquired the ability of sustaining for awhile the lowest, feeblest, manifestation of this power, or a condition of *passive resistance* to oppression, armed with a force which could instantly crush any violent opposition they might attempt to array against it. Within the last two or three years, several of these cases have transpired in different parts of the world. In one of these, a little English colony at the Cape of Good Hope, *passively,* but successfully, *resisted* the great Government of the British empire, backed with all its navies and armies, in its attempt to make the home of their small population a receptacle of criminals, crime, and convicts from England. Then, almost simultaneously with this successful experiment with the force of passive resistance, there comes the report of another, from the distant islands of the Pacific Ocean, tried under circumstances of more imminent peril and oppression, and crowned with more illustrious triumph. The weak little Government of the Sandwich Islands, in order to diminish the use and effect of intoxicating liquors among their people, imposed a heavy tax upon French brandy and wine. This irritated the French, and they sent thither a great ship of war to compel the government to remove the tax; and the captain gave them but a few hours to comply with the demand. But they absolutely refused to obey. Then they must take the consequences, and these would be terrible. The lady of the French consul—good, kind, compassionate woman—went with her husband from house to house, and entreated the foreign residents to take refuge on board the French ship, for the island was to be blown up, or sunk, to punish the wicked government for taxing French brandy, and making drunkenness a dearer luxury to the people! But not a single person accepted of the refuge. The government held fast to its resolution without wavering for a moment. The French commander landed with his marines in battle array. Men with lighted matches stood at the great cannons of the ship. The hour of vengeance had come. Poor little people! what will become of you now? What will you do to defend yourselves against this resistless force? Do? do nothing but *endure.* "The King," says the report, "gave peremptory orders to his people to *oppose no resistance* to the Frenchmen. The gallant commander, therefore, landed his marines and took possession of the fort, custom-house, and some other Government buildings, *no resistance being offered.* All was still and peaceful in the streets, business going on as usual.

Here they remained for some days; when, finding that the government would not accede at all to their demands, though they offered to leave the whole question to an umpire, the chivalrous Frenchmen went to work to dismantle the fort, and destroyed everything within its walls. After having finished this Vandal-like work, they marched off with flying colors." How full of illustration is this case of passive resistance! The simple, quiet force of *endurance* which the government opposed to the French, wet their powder and turned their bayonets to straw. Against this unexpected force the marines were powerless. They had no arms to contend with such an enemy. All their weapons, and discipline, and bravery, were fitted only to overcome brute force; and of this they found none, except its shadow in the fort and its equipments; and with great valor they fell upon this shadow, and mutilated it terribly, and then marched back with flying colors! So far was this invasion of bayonet-power from inducing a settlement to the advantage of the French, that the government even refused their offer to submit the question to arbitration, or to put the law at any hazard of modification, in face of all the brute force that France could marshal against it.

These are examples of the irresistible power of *passive resistance,* when opposed by a people to foreign enemies and oppression. But almost simultaneously with these, we have examples of this kind of resistance when arrayed against domestic oppression, or the despotic acts of dynasties that have at their command vast military organizations, ready to do their will. The most striking of these is the case of Hesse Cassel. Here, the force of resistance has been tested for a longer period, and by a larger population than ever have illustrated its virtue before. The result has not yet transpired, nor can we conclude what it will be. We can hardly believe that it will be crowned with complete success; for we cannot believe that the Hessians will be able to *endure* unto the end which they seek. We fear they will lose their impregnable strength, by being seduced into a manifestation of brute force. But the teaching of their experiment, even up to this stage, will be invaluable to the people and the cause of popular freedom everywhere on the Continent of Europe. It has established the fact that despotism, backed by the mightiest armies, cannot serf or subdue a people or a population, or rob them of their rights, or barricade their way to rational freedom, if they can only acquire the capacity of a *passive resistance,* which the most aggravated oppression can never weary out. Up to this hour, the Hessians have manifested this capacity, and practised this virtue; and the bristling bayonets which virtually surrounded them have become as stubble. While they possess their souls in patience, and refrain from the slightest act of violence, the whole soldiery of the continent will be powerless against them. How full of glorious illustration and consequence is this spectacle! The eyes of despotism, like those of beasts of prey, are glaring upon them from every side, watching to spring upon them at a single bound, the first moment that they venture from their stronghold of *passive resistance!* What a sublime sight in the moral world! It is said that the poor peasants, and the poorest day-laborers in Cassel have signed a pledge to abstain from intoxicating drinks, and that they are watching over each other with the keenest vigilance, lest, in an evil hour, some sudden act of oppression should make them mad, and they should fall from the grace of patience, and peril their country's all by a deed of violence! Contrast that discipline with the spirit and deeds of a brute-force revolution! How the people rise, rise, rise to the highest stature of moral being, under such a process of self-education! "Better is he that ruleth his spirit than he that taketh a city." Yes; the Elector may take the city of Cassel, with 60,000 Austrian and Bavarian troops; but they will be to him as mere shadows, so long as the Hessians shall be able to rule their spirits after this fashion. The cause of popular freedom, progress, and prosperity has an immense interest at stake in the issue of this grand experiment with a force which the God of the poor and the oppressed has given to them in his great Gospel of love:—"I SAY UNTO YOU, RESIST NOT EVIL, BUT OVERCOME EVIL WITH GOOD."

PART III

ANARCHISTS

DOCUMENT 7

Michael Schwab and August Spies, Speeches in Court, 1886

On May 3, 1886, Chicago police fired into a crowd of strikers at the McCormick Harvester works. A protest meeting was held the next day in front of the Haymarket. Somebody threw a bomb which killed seven policemen. Michael Schwab, August Spies, and six other anarchist leaders were arrested, tried, and convicted, despite a total lack of evidence as to the murderer's identity. Spies was hanged; Schwab's sentence was commuted to life imprisonment, and in 1893 he was pardoned by Illinois Governor John Peter Altgeld.

The Haymarket Anarchists were hardly advocates of nonviolence. Yet, while urging that workers arm themselves in response to the habitual violence of businessmen, they also envisioned a society in which the coercion of governments and armies would wither away.

The obvious injustice in this incident shocked reform-minded Americans. Among authors represented in this volume, Emma Goldman and William

The Chicago Martyrs. The Famous Speeches Of The Eight Anarchists In Judge Gary's Court, October 7, 8, 9, 1886 ... (San Francisco: Free Society, Publishers, 1899), pp. 14, 19–20.

Haywood both considered Haymarket the decisive event in shaping their radical convictions.

[SCHWAB]

"Anarchy" is Greek, and means, verbatim, without rulership; not being ruled. According to our vocabulary, anarchy is a state of society in which the only government is reason; a state of society in which all human beings do right for the simple reason that it is right, and hate wrong because it is wrong. In such a society, no laws, no compulsion will be necessary. The attorney of the State was wrong when he said: "Anarchy is dead." Anarchy, up to the present day, has existed only as a doctrine, and Mr. Grinnell has not the power to kill any doctrine whatever. You may call anarchy, as defined by us, an idle dream, but that dream was dreamed by Gotthold Ephraim Lessing, one of the three great German poets and the most celebrated German critic of the last century. If anarchy were the thing the State's attorney makes it out to be, how could it be that such eminent scholars as Prince Kropotkine and the greatest living geographer, Elisee Reclus, were avowed anarchists, even editors of anarchistic newspapers? Anarchy is a dream, but only in the present. It will be realized. Reason will grow in spite of all obstacles. Who is the man that has the cheek to tell us that human development has already reached its culminating point? I know that our ideal will not be accomplished this or next year, but I know that it will be accomplished as near as possible, some day, in the future. It is entirely wrong to use the word anarchy as synonymous with violence. Violence is one thing and anarchy another. In the present state of society violence is used on all sides, and, therefore, we advocated the use of violence against violence, but against violence only, as a necessary means of defence.

[SPIES]

Society will reclaim its own, even though you erect a gibbet on every street corner. And anarchism, this terrible "ism," deduces that under a co-operative organization of society, under economic equality and individual independence, the "state"—the political state—will pass into barbaric antiquity. And we will be where all are free, where there are no longer masters and servants, where intellect stands for brute force; there will no longer be any use for the policemen and militia to preserve the so-called "peace and order"—the order that the Russian general speaks of when he telegraphed to the Czar after he had massacred half of Warsaw, "Peace reigns in Warsaw." Anarchism does not mean bloodshed; does not mean, robbery, arson, etc. These monstrosities are, on the contrary, the characteristic features of capitalism. Anarchism means peace and tranquility to all. Anarchism means the reorganization of society upon scientific principles and the abolition of causes which produce vice and crime.

DOCUMENT 8

Emma Goldman, "Anarchism: What It Really Stands For"

Emma Goldman (1869–1940) was born in Russia, and moved to St. Petersburg at the age of thirteen, one year after the assassination of Czar Alexander II. In 1886 she emigrated to the United States where she obtained work in a clothing factory at a wage of $2.50 a week. In 1892 her companion Alexander Berkman attempted to assassinate Henry Clay Frick of Carnegie Steel during the Homestead strike. Arrested for sedition in June 1917, Goldman was deported to revolutionary Russia two years later. Emma Goldman's disappointment with the Russian Revolution is recorded in My Disillusionment in Russia *(1923) and other books.*

Toward the end of her life this fiery but compassionate rebel reconsidered her attitude to violence, writing to Berkman in 1928 that she wished that she could adopt the nonviolence of Gandhi and Tolstoy: "I feel violence in whatever form never has and probably never will bring constructive results." Anarchism's most important contribution to the nonviolent tradition was its doctrine of "direct action," which Ms. Goldman here expounds.

. . . As to methods. Anarchism is not, as some may suppose, a theory of the future to be realized through divine inspiration. It is a living force in the affairs of our life, constantly creating new conditions. The methods of Anarchism therefore do not comprise an iron-clad program to be carried out under all circumstances. Methods must grow out of the economic needs of each place

From Emma Goldman, "Anarchism: What It Really Stands For," *Anarchism And Other Essays* (New York: Mother Earth Publishing Association, 1910).

and clime, and of the intellectual and temperamental requirements of the
individual. The serene, calm character of a Tolstoy will wish different methods
for social reconstruction than the intense, overflowing personality of a Michael
Bakunin or a Peter Kropotkin. Equally so it must be apparent that the economic
and political needs of Russia will dictate more drastic measures than would
England or America. Anarchism does not stand for military drill and unifor-
mity; it does, however, stand for the spirit of revolt, in whatever form, against
everything that hinders human growth. All Anarchists agree in that, as they
also agree in their opposition to the political machinery as a means of bringing
about the great social change.

"All voting," says Thoreau, "is a sort of gaming like checkers, or backgammon, a playing with right and wrong; its obligation never exceeds that of
expediency. Even voting for the right thing is doing nothing for it. A wise
man will not leave the right to the mercy of chance, nor wish it to prevail
through the power of the majority." A close examination of the machinery
of politics and its achievements will bear out the logic of Thoreau.

What does the history of parliamentarism show? Nothing but failure and
defeat, not even a single reform to ameliorate the economic and social stress
of the people. Laws have been passed and enactments made for the improvement and protection of labor. Thus it was proven only last year that Illinois,
with the most rigid laws for mine protection, had the greatest mine disasters.
In States where child labor laws prevail, child exploitation is at its highest,
and though with us the workers enjoy full political opportunities, capitalism
has reached the most brazen zenith.

Even were the workers able to have their own representatives, for which
our good Socialist politicians are clamoring, what chances are there for their
honesty and good faith? One has but to bear in mind the process of politics
to realize that its path of good intentions is full of pitfalls: wire-pulling,
intriguing, flattering, lying, cheating; in fact, chicanery of every description,
whereby the political aspirant can achieve success. Added to that is a complete
demoralization of character and conviction, until nothing is left that would
make one hope for anything from such a human derelict. Time and time
again the people were foolish enough to trust, believe, and support with their
last farthing aspiring politicians, only to find themselves betrayed and cheated.

It may be claimed that men of integrity would not become corrupt in the
political grinding mill. Perhaps not; but such men would be absolutely helpless
to exert the slightest influence in behalf of labor, as indeed has been shown
in numerous instances. The State is the economic master of its servants.
Good men, if such there be, would either remain true to their political faith
and lose their economic support, or they would cling to their economic master
and be utterly unable to do the slightest good. The political arena leaves one
no alternative, one must either be a dunce or a rogue.

The political superstition is still holding sway over the hearts and minds
of the masses, but the true lovers of liberty will have no more to do with it.
Instead, they believe with Stirner that man has as much liberty as he is willing

to take. Anarchism therefore stands for direct action, the open defiance of, and resistance to, all laws and restrictions, economic, social, and moral. But defiance and resistance are illegal. Therein lies the salvation of man. Everything illegal necessitates integrity, self-reliance, and courage. In short, it calls for free, independent spirits, for "men who are men, and who have a bone in their backs which you cannot pass your hand through."

Universal suffrage itself owes its existence to direct action. If not for the spirit of rebellion, of the defiance on the part of the American revolutionary fathers, their posterity would still wear the King's coat. If not for the direct action of a John Brown and his comrades, America would still trade in the flesh of the black man. True, the trade in white flesh is still going on; but that, too, will have to be abolished by direct action. Trade unionism, the economic arena of the modern gladiator, owes its existence to direct action. It is but recently that law and government have attempted to crush the trade union movement, and condemned the exponents of man's right to organize to prison as conspirators. Had they sought to assert their cause through begging, pleading, and compromise, trade unionism would today be a negligible quantity. In France, in Spain, in Italy, in Russia, nay even in England (witness the growing rebellion of English labor unions) direct, revolutionary, economic action has become so strong a force in the battle for industrial liberty as to make the world realize the tremendous importance of labor's power. The General Strike, the supreme expression of the economic consciousness of the workers, was ridiculed in America but a short time ago. Today every great strike, in order to win, must realize the importance of the solidaric general protest.

Direct action, having proved effective along economic lines, is equally potent in the environment of the individual. There a hundred forces encroach upon his being, and only persistent resistance to them will finally set him free. Direct action against the authority in the shop, direct action against the authority of the law, direct action against the invasive, meddlesome authority of our moral code, is the logical, consistent method of Anarchism.

Will it not lead to a revolution? Indeed, it will. No real social change has ever come about without a revolution. People are either not familiar with their history, or they have not yet learned that revolution is but thought carried into action.

Anarchism, the great leaven of thought, is today permeating every phase of human endeavor. Science, art, literature, the drama, the effort for economic betterment, in fact every individual and social opposition to the existing disorder of things, is illumined by the spiritual light of Anarchism. It is the philosophy of the sovereignty of the individual. It is the theory of social harmony. It is the great, surging, living truth that is reconstructing the world, and that will usher in the Dawn.

DOCUMENT 9

William Haywood,
Testimony Before The Industrial Relations Commission, 1915

In this remarkable testimony before a government commission studying labor strife in 1915, William ("Big Bill") Haywood (1869–1928) also sketched the story of his early life. Born in Salt Lake City, he lost an eye at the age of nine as a child laborer in the mines. Emerging as a leader of the Western Federation of Miners during a series of violent strikes, he also helped to organize the Industrial Workers of the World, or "Wobblies," in 1905. In 1906 Haywood ran as Socialist candidate for governor of Colorado while imprisoned on a false charge of assassinating the ex-governor of Idaho. Prominent both in the IWW and in the radical wing of the Socialist Party, Haywood opposed America's entry into World War I and was arrested for "sedition" in September 1917. He jumped bail by going to the Soviet Union in 1921. There, like Emma Goldman, he was disillusioned with the first fruits of the revolutionary movement he had sacrificed so much to create.

The IWW, and Haywood as its principal spokesman, are important to the history of nonviolence because of their thoroughgoing syndicalism: the vision of a future society in which workers would control their own industrial destinies, created by the direct action of a general strike. In his testimony Haywood also stresses the need for direct action to ensure that laws are enforced, a conviction shared by civil rights workers half a century later. "Filling the jails" was a tactic introduced to America not by SNCC but by Wobblies like Haywood.

Testimony of William D. Haywood Before The Industrial Relations Commission (Chicago: I. W. W. Publishing Bureau, [ca. 1915]), pp. 3–5, 8–17, 23–24, 26–29, 35–37, 43–47, 54–56, 70–71.

Chairman Walsh: Will you please state your full name?

Mr. Haywood: William D. Haywood.

Chairman Walsh: Where do you reside, Mr. Haywood?

Mr. Haywood: Denver is my home.

Chairman Walsh: Denver, Colo.?

Mr. Haywood: Yes, sir.

Chairman Walsh: Where were you born?

Mr. Haywood: Salt Lake City, Utah.

Chairman Walsh: And what is your Age?

Mr. Haywood: Born in 1869—February.

Chairman Walsh: At what age did you begin work?

Mr. Haywood: Nine years old.

Chairman Walsh: And in what industry, or what occupation?

Mr. Haywood: In the mining industry.

Chairman Walsh: Whereabouts?

Mr. Haywood: Utah—Ophir Canyon.

Chairman Walsh: Would you be kind enough, Mr. Haywood, just to sketch your history as a worker and a miner, up to the time you became a member of the association of the Western Federation of Miners?

Mr. Haywood: Well, after the first short period, we moved from there back to Salt Lake City, where I worked at different kinds of work until I went to the State of Nevada, when I was 15 years old.

Chairman Walsh: Well, now, in a general way, what sort of work did you work at, between the ages of 9 and 15?

Mr. Haywood: Why, I worked at driving delivery wagons, as a messenger boy, in a hotel as elevator boy and bell boy. It was when I was in the latter part of it, the fifteenth year, that I went to Nevada, and went to work in the mines permanently.

Chairman Walsh: At the age of 15?

Mr. Haywood: Yes, sir.

Chairman Walsh: Will you kindly pitch your voice a little louder; the reporters seem to have difficulty in hearing you, and there are a number of spectators who would like to hear you. So you will speak a little louder.

Mr. Haywood: I went to work for the Ohio Mining Company in Willow Creek, Nevada, and worked there until I was 19; and then drifted around into the different mining camps of Utah, Colorado, Idaho, and back to Nevada again.

Chairman Walsh: Are you familiar with the formation of the Western Federation of Miners?

Mr. Haywood: Yes; being a miner, of course I kept acquainted with what the miners were doing and remember when that federation of miners was organized, and have since become acquainted with all of the circumstances that brought about the federation of miners.

Chairman Walsh: Will you please describe the conditions that led to the formation of the Western Federation of Miners?

Mr. Haywood: It was organized as the result of a strike that occurred in the Coeur d'Alene.

Chairman Walsh: What form of organization did they have prior to that time, if any?

Mr. Haywood: Local unions, and mostly branches or assemblies of the Knights of Labor.

The miners of the Coeur d'Alene had gone on strike against a reduction of wages, and the mine owners called in armed thugs, armed men from outside territory. There was a pitched battle between these guards and the miners, and in the course of the fight there was a mill blown up. This was charged to the miners, and the mine owners called on the governor for the militia. The militia was sent in there and martial law was declared, and nearly 1,000 men were arrested and placed in what they called the "bull pen." That was a hurriedly erected two-story structure built out of rough lumber, and these men were crowded in there with scarcely room to lie down—so many— with cracks in the floor above permitting the excrement from the men to drop on those below. The result of that incarceration, there were many of them who sickened and died from the diseases that they caught there. At one period of this strike an injunction was issued and 14 of the leaders were arrested and sent to Ada County; 2 of them, I think, were sent to Detroit to serve terms.

It was while these men were in Boise that they conceived the idea of federating all of the miners of the West into one general organization. After they were released, being in jail for six or seven months, they called a convention, that was held in Butte, in May, 1893, and it was there the Western Federation of Miners was started. . . .

. . . In 1902 and 1903 came the strike that is so well known as the Cripple Creek strike, and that strike was in the nature of a sympathetic strike. The men who were working in the mills in Colorado City, although entitled to the benefits of the 8-hour law which had been passed in Colorado at that time, were working 12 hours a day 11 hours on the day shift and 13 hours on the night shift.

This condition prevails in the smelting plants of Colorado at the present time, and in some of the milling plants. They went out on strike in September, I think, 1902.

Chairman Walsh: Was the attention of the authorities called to the condition—that is, that the law was being violated with reference to the hours of labor?

Mr. Haywood: Oh, yes, indeed.

Chairman Walsh: Was the law inoperative, or why didn't they prosecute the officials?

Mr. Haywood: The smelter officials, or mine owners, do you mean?

Chairman Walsh: Yes.

Mr. Haywood: Did you ever hear of a mine owner or of a manufacturer being prosecuted for violation of a law? Well, they were not, anyway. The courts don't work that way.

In the following March the miners of Cripple Creek who were producing the ore that was reduced at Colorado City, went on strike. . . .

. . . They were striking as they struck ten years before, for the enforcement of a state law. The laws at that time were inoperative at Cripple Creek. The militia ran the district. They threw the officers out of office. Sheriff Robinson, I remember, had a rope thrown at his feet and was told to resign or they would hang him; and others officers were treated in the same way, and some 400 men were deported from their homes. Seventy-six of them were placed aboard trains and escorted by soldiers over into the State of Kansas, where they were dumped out on the prairie and told that they must never come back. Habeas corpus was denied. I recall Judge Seed's court, where he had three men brought in that were being held by the militia. While his court was in session it was surrounded by soldiers who had their gatling guns and rifles trained on the door. He ordered those three prisoners released, and the soldiers went after them and they were taken back to jail. That strike was not won. . . .

. . . It was during the period of those strikes that the Western Federation of Miners realized the necessity of labor getting together in one big union. We were on strike in Cripple Creek, the miners; the mill men were on strike in Colorado Springs. There were scabs in the mines and scabs in the mills, and there were union railroaders that were the connecting link between those two propositions. There seemed to be no hope for such a thing as that among any of the existing labor organizations, and in 1905 the officials of the Western Federation of Miners took part in a conference we called—the convention of the Industrial Workers of the World. That convention was held in Chicago in June, 1905, and the Western Federation of Miners, among other labor organizations, became a part of that movement. . . . The Industrial Workers, when organized, became first involved in a strike of serious proportions at McKees Rocks, Pa. There was the first time that we went up against what were called the Cossacks, the black plague of that State. The Industrial Workers met them on a different basis to what other labor organizations had done, and told them, "For every man you kill of us, we will kill one of you," and with the death of one or two of the Cossacks their brutality became less.

I am trying to think of these incidents in sequence, as near as I can.

I think the next instance where the Industrial Workers had to contend with the law was perhaps the free speech fight in Spokane, where the members of the organization insisted on speaking on the streets in front of the employment agency offices. They were telling what the employment sharks—what they were doing; how they would employ men; that these men would go up to take jobs that they had picked for them; that they would be discharged and other gangs sent out. The authorities of the city took up the side of the employment sharks, and between 500 and 600 men and women, members of the organization, were thrown into prison. Several of them were killed. They were put in the hot box and then removed and put into a cold cell. Several died from pneumonia. They got no relief from the court, but, as the members of the organization persisted in carrying on the fight, finally the

City of Spokane compromised by saying that they would let them all out of jail provided that the organization would not prosecute certain cases that had been made against the officers. I think that it was the following year that the free speech fight occurred in Fresno, California. There the authorities started to arrest men merely for speaking on the street corner, not causing a congestion of traffic. If I have it correctly, there was between 150 and 200 men thrown into prison there. They were crowded to more than the capacity of the prison. The hose of the fire department was turned on them. I am told that one night they were compelled to stand up to their knees in water, but they won that fight. . . .

. . . I think this will bring us down to the time of the Lawrence strike, in which the Industrial Workers took charge. There, of course, as everywhere, I might say, that I have seen courts in action; they took the side of the capitalists. There were between 800 and 900 people arrested—men and women, girls and boys—there were some convictions, but a small proportion for the large number that were arrested. In Massachusetts they have a system of State Police, something similar to that of Pennsylvania, though they are not mounted. When the strike was called the State police came, and the park police, the municipal police from other cities, and then they brought in the militia. Several of the strikers were killed, none of the employers were, but they arrested two of the leaders of the strike for the death of Anna————; she was one of the girls that was on strike. They had those men in jail for nine months and would probably have convicted them if it had not been for the general strike on the part of the workers. After the strike had been settled and the demands had been gained, they added to their former demands that Ettor, Caruso, and Giovannitti be released from prison; they were finally acquitted. During the Lawrence strike there were strikes at Clinton and many other places in the textile industry.

At Clinton the police were again used by the mill owners, and they shot into a crowd of striking girls, wounding many of them seriously. In Little Falls the same treatment was accorded the strikers by the police, which is also true of the great strike at Paterson. Nearly everyone is acquainted with the details of that strike and its outcome.

Since the Paterson strike there has been trouble in Wheatland, California, where members of the Industrial Workers of the World organized 2,500 hop pickers, asking for better conditions in the hop fields of the Durst Brothers ranches. As the outcome of that demand two young married men, Ford and Suhr, were arrested and charged with the killing of the district attorney. They were convicted, and have been sentenced to prison for life terms.

This, I think, briefly outlines the main strikes of the organization that I have been affliated with and, I think, clearly portrays a condition that this commission should understand, and that is that there is a class struggle in society, with workers on one side of that struggle and the capitalists on the other; that the workers have nothing but their labor power and the capitalists have the control of and the influence of all branches of government—

legislative, executive, and judicial; that they have on their side of the question all of the forces of law; they can hire detectives, they can have the police force for the asking or the militia, or the Regular Army.

There are workers who have come to the conclusion that there is only one way to win this battle. We don't agree at all with the statement that you heard reiterated here day after day—that there is an identity of interests between capital and labor. We say to you frankly that there can be no identity of interests between labor, who produces all by their own labor power and their brains, and such men as John D. Rockefeller, Morgan, and their stock-holders, who neither by brain or muscle or by any other effort contribute to the productivity of the industries that they own. We say that this struggle will go on in spite of anything that this commission can do or anything that you may recommend to Congress; that the struggle between the working class and the capitalist class is an inevitable battle; that it is a fight for what the capitalistic class has control of—the means of life, the tools and machinery of production. These, we contend should be in the hands of and controlled by the working class alone, independent of anything that capitalists and their shareholders and stockholders may say to the contrary.

Personally, I don't think that this can be done by political action. First, for the very good reason that the wage earner or producing class are in the minority; second, that they are not educated in the game of politics; that their life is altogether industrial. That while they are the only valuable unit of society, still their efforts must be confined to the jobs where they work. A dream that I have in the morning and at night and during the day is that there will be a new society sometime in which there will be no battle between capitalist and wage earner, but that every man will have free access to land and its resources. In that day there will be no political government, there will be no States, and Congress will not be composed of lawyers and preachers as it is now, but it will be composed of experts of the different branches of industry, who will come together for the purpose of discussing the welfare of all the people and discussing the means by which the machinery can be made the slave of the people instead of a part of the people being made the slave of machinery or the owners of machinery.

I believe that there will come a time when the workers will realize what the few of us are striving for—and that is industrial freedom.

Chairman Walsh: In how many of these places that you have spoken of—

Commissioner O'Connell: Just let me carry out this point if you please, Mr. Chairman. You say you don't believe it can be done by political action?

Mr. Haywood: No, sir.

Commissioner O'Connell: Have you in mind some other method by which it can?

Mr. Haywood: Yes sir; I think it can be done by direct action. I mean by organization of the forces of labor. Take, for instance, the organization that you know, the United Mine Workers of America. They have about one-half of the miners of this country organized. At least a sufficient number to control them all. I think the United Mine Workers can say to the mine owners, "You must put these mines in order, in proper shape, or we won't work in them." They can compel the introduction of safety appliances, of ventilation systems, and save in that way thousands of lives every year. I don't think anybody will deny that they have that power to bring about that improvement. If they have the power to bring that about by direct action, they have the power to reduce their hours; they have the power to increase or at least to better the laboring conditions around the mines and have better houses. It seems to me there is no reason in the world why the miner should not enjoy, even in a mining camp, some of the advantages that the worker has in the city. And I think that free organization of miners, organized in one big union, having no contract with the boss, have no right to enter into a contract with the employer or any other combination of labor, to my mind. There can be each division of industry, each subdivision, be brought into a whole, and that will bring about the condition that I have described to you.

Commissioner O'Connell: You mean by that, that these economic organizations would create, or control questions of hours and things of that kind you spoke of, but as to the ownership, the right of ownership, what is the method that you have in mind of your organization in connection with the method of taking over?

Mr. Haywood: Taking over through the organization. If you are strong enough to exact the things I speak of, you are strong enough to say, "Here, Mr. Stockholder, we won't work for you any longer. You have drawn dividends out of our hides long enough; we propose that you shall go to work now, and under the same opportunities that we have had."

Commissioner O'Connell: Well, you propose by your strength and numbers to declare ownership?

Mr. Haywood: Yes; exactly; through the organized efforts of the working class. . . .

Commissioner Weinstock: Well, then, summing up we find that I. W. W.'ism teaches the following:

(a) That the workers are to use any and all tactics that will get the results sought with the least possible expenditure of time and energy.

(b) The question of right or wrong is not to be considered.

(c) The avenging sword is to be unsheathed, with all hearts resolved on victory or death.

(d) The workman is to help himself when the proper time comes.

(e) No agreement with an employer is to be considered by the worker as sacred or inviolable.

(f) The worker is to produce inferior goods and kill time in getting tools repaired and in attending to repair work; all by a silent understanding.

(g) The worker is to look forward to the day when he will confiscate the factories and drive out the owners.

(h) The worker is to get ready to cause national industrial paralysis with a view of confiscating all industries, meanwhile taking forcible possession of all things that he may need.

(i) Strikers are to disobey and to treat with contempt all judicial injunction.

If that is the creed of the I. W. W., do you think the American people will ever stand for it? . . .

Mr. Haywood: Read me that over again.

Commissioner Weinstock (reading): "(a) That the workers are to use any and all tactics that will get the results sought with the least possible expenditure of time and energy."

Mr. Haywood: Yes; I believe in the worker using any kind of tactics that will get the results. I do not care what those tactics are when the working class had arrived at that stage of efficiency and organization, I do not care whether it means revolution. That is exactly the very—

Commissioner Weinstock (interrupting): "(b) The question of right or wrong is not to be considered."

Mr. Haywood: What is right and wrong? What I think is right in my mind or what you think is right in your mind?

Commissioner Weinstock: "(c) The avenging sword is to be unsheathed, with all hearts resolved on victory or death."

Mr. Haywood: What that means is a general strike.

Commissioner Weinstock: "(d) The workman is to help himself when the proper time comes."

Mr. Haywood: When the proper time comes, when he needs it let him go and get it.

Commissioner Weinstock: "(e) No agreement with an employer of labor is to be considered by the worker as sacred or inviolable."

Mr. Haywood: No agreement?

Commissioner Weinstock: Yes.

Mr. Haywood: He never wants to enter into an agreement. Let me explain something about an agreement. I heard you talk to Kobylak yesterday. What would a union man say if some member of that union entered into an agreement with the boss? He would say he was a bad man, wouldn't he? And that he ought to stand by the rest of the members of his union. Now, we say that union has only a little nucleus of industry; we say that a union has no right to enter into an agreement because the rest of the men employed in that industry ought to be considered. We say that no union has a right to enter into an agreement with the employers because they are members of the working class; and finally we say that the working class has no right to enter into an agreement because it is the inherent mission of the working class to overthrow capitalism and establish itself in its place.

You can let that about contract and agreement stand.

Commissioner Weinstock: "(f) The worker is to produce inferior goods and kill time"—we will cut that out, that which relates to the production of inferior goods and killing time; that is out of the subject.

Mr. Haywood: Yes.

Commissioner Weinstock: "(g) The worker is to look forward to the day when he will confiscate the factories and drive out the owners."

Mr. Haywood: I would drive them in instead of out.

Commissioner Weinstock: I think that was your own quotation.

Mr. Haywood: I would make an arrangement to take every owner on the inside and give him a job alongside of me.

Commissioner Weinstock: Have you changed your views any since you delivered this speech on March 16, 1911, in which, among other things, you said this:

"I hope to see the day when the man who goes out of the factory will be the one who will be called a scab, when the good union man will stay in the factory, whether the capitalists like it or not; when we lock the bosses out and run the factories to suit ourselves. That is our program. We will do it." Are your views the same today as when you said that?

Mr. Haywood: I hope we can do that tomorrow.

Commissioner Weinstock: The next is, "(h) The worker is to get ready to cause national industrial paralysis, with a view of confiscating all industries, meanwhile taking forcible possession of all things that he may need."

Mr. Haywood: I do not understand the necessity of causing industrial paralysis; that is, when the workers are sufficiently organized they have got control of the machinery; you never saw a capitalist with his hand on the throttle; you never saw him on the stormy end of a No. 2 shovel; you read of him on his way to Europe and going down with the Lusitania or the Titanic; they are not interested in work. It is the workers who have control now of all of the machinery if they would only make up their minds to hold that control and maintain it for themselves.

Commissioner Weinstock: I take it, then, that you take no issue as a member of the I. W. W. with that statement here?

Mr. Haywood: No; I will let that go.

Commissioner Weinstock: And the last is, "(i) Strikers are to disobey and treat with contempt all judicial injunction."

Mr. Haywood: Well, I have been plastered up with injunctions until I do not need a suit of clothes, and I have treated them with contempt.

Commissioner Weinstock: And you advocate that?

Mr. Haywood: I do not believe in that kind of law at all. I think that is a usurpation on the part of the courts of a function that was never vested in the courts by the Constitution.

Commissioner Weinstock: Therefore you would have no hesitancy in advising your fellow I. W. W.'ists to do as you have done.

Mr. Haywood: I do not like to advise too much, but I would do it myself. . . .

Commissioner Weinstock: Let me see if I understand the distinction correctly between socialism and I. W. W.'ism.

As I understand it, I. W. W.'ism is socialism, with this difference—

Mr. Haywood (interrupting): With its working clothes on.

Commissioner Weinstock: As an I. W. W., are you a believer in free speech?

Mr. Haywood: Yes, sir.

Commissioner Weinstock: Are you a believer in free press?

Mr. Haywood: Yes, sir.

Commissioner Weinstock: Now, if your idea prevails and you went to bed tonight under the capitalistic system and woke up tomorrow morning under your system, the machinery of production and distribution would belong to all the people?

Mr. Haywood: Under our system it would be under the management of the working class.

Commissioner Weinstock: There would be collective ownership?

Mr. Haywood: Yes, sir.

Commissioner Weinstock: Of course, you are not anarchistic, you believe in organization, you believe in government?

Mr. Haywood: Yes, sir.

Commissioner Weinstock: Well, the anarchists believe in individualism, and carries it to the limit, without government?

Mr. Haywood: Yes, sir.

Commissioner Weinstock: And if you believe in government, then you would have to have a ruler—

Mr. Haywood: Would you?

Commissioner Weinstock: You would have to have superiors; otherwise, how could you have government?

Mr. Haywood: It has been run at times without bosses.

Commissioner Weinstock: Without any officials of any kind?

Mr. Haywood: Without any officials; it was the glass workers of Italy.

Commissioner Weinstock: Taking society as we find it, as you know it and I know it, if you have organization you have to have officers?

Chairman Walsh: Let us have the glass workers' illustration; I never heard of it.

Mr. Haywood: The glass workers of Italy went on strike, and while on strike they determined to run competitive factories, and they built factories of their own, owned by the members of the glass blowers' union. They went to work in those factories; each man knew his work—what there was to do. If you have any surplus and different interests to divide up, then there is some occasion for a boss; but if—suppose, now, that these men who are working in glass factories cooperate, as in this instance, and had some occasion for a boss, they would elect him wouldn't they?

Commissioner Weinstock: Yes, sir; they would elect him, that is guaranteed, and would put certain responsibilities on him to carry out certain rules and regulations or laws that they might adopt.

Mr. Haywood: I cannot conceive of much rules and regulations that would need to be applied with a man of common sense. There would be sanitary regulations around the mine. They would not shoot during shift; they would keep the places well ventilated and clean and well timbered. What other regulations do you want?

Commissioner Weinstock: If this group in this room organized, it can not reasonably be expected to carry out its object unless it elected representatives and officers to carry out its wishes.

Mr. Haywood: But you take a motly group like this; no one can carry out its wishes, because they change every time they turn around.

But you take the workers that work in one industry; their interests can be well carried out.

Commissioner Weinstock: Now, would you confine this great army of workers, organized in one body, would you confine their functions and their efforts to industrial matters pure and simple, or would you at the same time have them also deal with the political conditions, with the government of our municipalities, of our Commonwealths, or our Republic?

Mr. Haywood: There would be neither county or State or National lines.

Commissioner Weinstock: There would be no political sub-division?

Mr. Haywood: Only what existed in the community.

Commissioner Weinstock: That is incomprehensible to me, Mr. Haywood; you will have to explain it a little more definitely.

Mr. Haywood: What is the government of the country? The government of many cities have been changed to the commission form.

Commissioner Weinstock: Yes, sir.

Mr. Haywood: The commissioner has the fire department, the public safety, and public improvement. Those are the different divisions. Why not have that same thing under industrial—

Commissioner Weinstock: Have it nationally?

Mr. Haywood: You have no community that is national in scope.

Commissioner Weinstock: How, then, would you have it?

Mr. Haywood: Have this group or this community wherever the industry was located. Do you suppose under normal conditions that there would be communities like New York or Chicago with great skyscrapers sticking up in the air?

Commissioner Weinstock: What would you say would be the size of the community?

Mr. Haywood: Some 50,000 or 60,000, where the people in that industry would dwell. There would be no lawyers or preachers or stockholders like built New York. . . .

Commissioner Weinstock: Let me make sure, Mr. Haywood, that I certainly understand the objective of I. W. W.'ism. I have assumed,—I will admit that I have assumed in my presentation to you—that I. W. W.'ism was socialism with a plus; that is, that I. W. W.'ism in—

Mr. Haywood (interrupting): I would very much prefer that you would eliminate the reference to socialism in referring to I. W. W.'ism, because from the examples we have, for instance, in Germany, socialism has, or at least the Social Democratic Party, has been very much discredited in the minds of workers of other countries. They have gone in for war, and those of us who believe we are Socialists are opposed to war. So if you don't mind we will discuss industrialism on its own basis.

Commissioner Weinstock: Well, in order that I at least may better understand the purpose, aims, and objects of industrialism, I must, in order to bring out the differences and compare it with the socialistic doctrine—you may not believe in the socialistic doctrine any more, and I do not; but my purpose is, so that we do not have a misunderstanding of the meaning of words. Now, let me briefly state to you what I understand socialism stands for, and what I understand I. W. W.'ism stands for. The Socialist, as I understand it, is striving for the cooperative commonwealth, striving to bring about a situation whereby all the machinery of production and distribution shall be owned by all the people, where there shall be but one employer, and that employer shall be all the people, and everything shall be conducted substantially as the Army and Navy are conducted under our form of government. I understand that I. W. W.'ism believes in exactly the same objectives but differs in the methods—

Mr. Haywood, (interrupting): In the first place, I. W. W.'ism has no such thing as an army or navy, and certainly not as the Army and Navy are conducted at the present time.

Commissioner Weinstock: Well, I did not say that the Socialists believe in a continuation of the Army and Navy—

Mr. Haywood, (interrupting): Some of them do.

Commissioner Weinstock: I said that they believed that everything would be managed as we now manage the Army and Navy. All the people manage the Army and Navy—

Mr. Haywood (interrupting): But you make a statement that is not true.

Commissioner Weinstock: The soldier and sailor has but one employer, and that employer is all the people. Now the only distinction that I have been able to discover between the aims and objects of those representing the I. W. W. doctrine, and those representing the so-called socialistic doctrines, is the methods of getting to the ends. The Socialists believe in getting it through education and political action, and you believe in doing it through direct action—

Mr. Haywood, (interrupting): And education.

Commissioner Weinstock, (continuing): And the general strike.

Mr. Haywood: Yes.

Commissioner Weinstock: Therefore, the ends are the same, but to be reached through different pathways?

Mr. Haywood: No; the ends are not the same. Now, Socialists, while they present an industrial democracy, they hope to follow the forms of existing governments, having industries controlled by the government, eventually, however, sloughing the State. They will tell you the State is of no further use; and when industries are controlled by the workers the State will no longer function.

Commissioner Weinstock: Well, then, am I to understand this, Mr. Haywood? I want that made very clear to me, because if the objective is as I understand you have tried to indicate, then I have been laboring under a misapprehension. Am I to understand that it is not the objective of the I. W. W. to have the State-owned industries?

Mr. Haywood: It certainly is not.

Commissioner Weinstock: I see. Then there is a radical difference between the I. W. W.'s and the Socialists, Mr. Haywood?

Mr. Haywood: Yes.

Commissioner Weinstock: The Socialist wants the State to own all the industries.

Mr. Haywood: Yes, sir.

Commissioner Weinstock: And the I. W. W., then, as you now explain it, proposes to have those industries not owned by the State but by the workers—

Mr. Haywood, (interrupting): By the workers.

Commissioner Weinstock, (continuing): Independent of the State.

Mr. Haywood: Independent of the State. There will be no such thing as the State or States. The industries will take the place of what are now existing States. Can you see any necessity for the States of Rhode Island and Connecticut, and two capitols in the smallest State in the Union?

Commissioner Weinstock: Except that of home rule.

Mr. Haywood: Well, you have home rule anyhow, when you place it in the people who are interested, and that is in the industries.

Commissioner Weinstock: Well, then, will you briefly outline to us, Mr. Haywood, how would you govern and direct the affairs under your proposed system of 100,000,000 of people, as we are in this country today?

Mr. Haywood: Well, how are the affairs of the hundred million people conducted at the present time? The workers have no interest, have no voice in anything except the shops. Many of the workers are children. They certainly have no interest and no voice in the franchise. They are employed in the shops, and of course my idea is that children who work should have a voice in the way they work—in the hours they work, in the wages that they should receive—that is, under the present conditions children should have that voice, children who labor. The same is true of women. The political state, the Government, says that women are not entitled to vote—that is, except in the 10 free States of the West; but they are industrial units; they are productive units; from millions of women. My idea is that they should have a voice in the control or disposition of their labor power, and the only place where they can express themselves is in their labor union halls, and there they express themselves to the fullest as citizens of industry, if you will, as to the purpose of their work and the conditions under which they will labor. Now, you recognize that in conjunction with women and children.

The black men of the South are on the same footing. They are all citizens of this country, but they have no voice in its government. Millions of black men are disfranchised, who if organized would have a voice in saying how they should work and how the conditions of labor should be regulated. But unorganized they are as helpless and in the same condition of slavery as they were before the war. This is not only true of women and children and black men, but it extends to the foreigner who comes to this country and is certainly a useful member of society. Most of them at once go into industries, but for five years they are not citizens. They plod along at their work and have no voice in the control or use of their labor power. And as you have learned through this commission there are corporations who direct the manner in which these foreigners shall vote. Certainly you have heard something of that in connection with the Rockefeller interests in the Southern part of Colorado. You know that the elections there were never carried on straight, and these foreigners were directed as to how their ballot should be placed.

They are not the only ones who are disfranchised, but there is also the workingman who is born in this country, who is shifted about from place to place by industrial depressions; their homes are broken up and they are compelled to go from one city to another, and each State requires a certain period of residence before a man has the right to vote. Some States say he must be a resident 1 year, others say 2 years; he must live for a certain length of time in the county; he must live for 30 days or such a matter in the precinct before he has any voice in the conduct of government. Now, if a man was not a subject of a State or Nation, but a citizen of industry, moving from place to place, belonging to his union, wherever he went he would step in the union hall, show his card, register, and he at once has a voice in the conduct of the affairs pertaining to his welfare. That is the form of society I want to see, where the men who do the work, and who are the only people who are worth while—understand me, Mr. Weinstock, I think that the workingman, even doing the meanest kind of work, is a more important member of society than any judge on the Supreme Bench and other useless members of society. I am speaking for the working class, and I am a partisan to the workers. . . .

Commissioner Harriman: Mr. Haywood. I understand from what you have said today, and from what you have said before, that you do not believe in war. Now, if you don't believe in war, why do you believe in violence in labor disputes? One is war between nations, and the other is war between—

Mr. Haywood, (interrupting): You say I believe in violence?

Commissioner Harriman: Yes, sir; one of your contemporaries, I think St. John, I asked him the direct question last spring, if the I. W. W. believed in violence, and he said yes.

Mr. Haywood: But you said I believe in violence?

Commissioner Harriman: I thought you did.

Mr. Haywood: Probably I do; but I don't want it to be taken for granted without giving me an opportunity to explain what violence means. I think you will agree that there is nothing more violent that you can do to the capitalist than to drain his pocketbook. In that sort of violence I believe, and we are trying to make it impossible for the growth of more capitalists, and to make useful citizens out of the existing capitalists. I give you an illustration of what I think violence is:

In Sioux City, Iowa, last month the authorities of that town came to the hall of the union and told a man, a member of the Industrial Workers of the World, that the chief wanted to see him. He said, knowing his rights as an

American citizen, he said, "If the chief wants to see me, tell him where I am." He said, "No; you will have to go to the office." He said, "Have you a warrant?" "No." "Well, I will not go." The detective went downstairs and got a crowd of uniformed policemen and they came to the hall and took this man and all the other members that were in the hall and went to headquarters with them. The men were put in jail temporarily without a hearing. They were all thrown into jail, and the next morning refused a jury trial, refused a change of venue, and were sentenced to $100 fine or 30 days in jail. One of them remarked to the judge, "Why don't you make it a hundred?" And he said, "In your case, I will just double the sentence." Those men were put in jail, and word went out to the other locals throughout the country, and footloose members started for Sioux City. They came in groups of twos and threes, and tens and fifteens, and fifties and hundreds, until the Sioux City jails, both the city and the county were crowded to capacity. The authorities thinking to make use of the labor power of these men purchased from Sioux Falls, South Dakota, three carloads of granite, which they expected the members of the I. W. W. to break, making little ones out of big ones. This they refused to do. They went on hunger strike. Some 75 of those men were 86 hours without eating. The authorities found that they could not do anything with them, so they appointed a committee, or a commission, to go to see the men in jail, and asked them up on what terms things could be settled. The men said, "Unequivocal release from prison, the re-establishment of the right of free speech," and one of the boys said, "New clothes for the ones the 'bulls' have destroyed," and upon those terms they were released. Those men were released from the prison in the face of the fact that they had been sentenced to jail by judges. That I regard as action more violent than the discharge of bombs in St. Patrick's Cathedral in New York, because they enforced the rights that this country gave to them; they compelled the authorities who are supposed to uphold those rights in seeing that they were granted. I believe in that kind of violence . . .

Chairman Walsh: That is all, Mr. Haywood, and you will be excused permanently, We thank you.

Mr. Haywood: I have here the Preamble of the Industrial Workers of the World that I wanted to make a part of the record, I would like to read it in.

Chairman Walsh: We will be very glad to have it put in the record.

Mr. Haywood, (reading): "Mr. Chairman, in view of the attempt on the part of Commissioner Weinstock yesterday to create an erroneous impression relative to the methods and aims of the I. W. W., and in view of the further fact that Commissioner Weinstock read into the record in the form of questions propounded to me portions of a biased report on the I. W. W. prepared some years ago by himself in California, I desire at this time to read for the enlightenment of the commission the very brief Preamble of the Industrial Workers of the World.

I. W. W. PREAMBLE

"The working class and the employing class have nothing in common.

"There can be no peace so long as hunger and want are found among millions of the working people, and the few who make up the employing class have all the good things of life.

"Between these two classes a struggle must go on until the workers of the world organize as a class, take possession of the earth, and the machinery of production, and abolish the wage system.

"We find that the centering of the management of industries into fewer and fewer hands makes the trade-unions unable to cope with the ever-growing power of the employing class.

"The trade-unions foster a state of affairs which allows one set of workers to be pitted against another set of workers in the same industry, thereby helping to defeat one another in wage wars.

"Moreover the trade-unions aid the employing class to mislead the workers into the belief that the working class have interests in common with their employers.

"These conditions can be changed and the interests of the working class upheld only by an organization formed in such a way that all its members in any one industry, or in all industries, if necessary, cease work whenever a strike or lockout is on in any department thereof, thus making an injury to one an injury to all.

"Instead of the conservative motto, 'A fair day's wage for a fair day's work,' we must inscribe on our banner the revolutionary watchword, 'Abolition of the wage system.'

"It is the historic mission of the working class to do away with capitalism.

"The army of production must be organized, not only for the everyday struggle with the capitalists, but also to carry on production when capitalism shall have been overthrown.

"By organizing industrially we are forming the structure of a new society within the shell of the old."

PART IV

PROGRESSIVES

DOCUMENT 10

William James,
"The Moral Equivalent of War"

Next to Thoreau's essay on civil disobedience, "The Moral Equivalent of War"
by William James (1842–1910) is probably the most influential statement in
the history of American nonviolence. The American Friends Service Commit-
tee, the Civilian Conservation Corps, and the Peace Corps all derive from
the central thought of James' argument.

According to James, the pacifist will never succeed merely by preaching
against war. His task must be to find another mode whereby the energies of
men can be elicited, involving risk, voluntary poverty, and service to the
state. James suggested that young people be conscripted for a period of years
in a war against nature rather than against man. Such labor would redirect
warlike impulses toward more constructive ends: "Great indeed is Fear; but
it is not . . . the only stimulus known for awakening the higher ranges of
men's spiritual energy."

William James, *The Moral Equivalent of War* (New York: American Association for International Conciliation, 1910), Leaflet No. 27.

First written as a pamphlet for the American Association for International Conciliation, "The Moral Equivalent of War" was also published in 1910 by McClure's Magazine *and* The Popular Science Monthly.

———————————

The war against war is going to be no holiday excursion or camping party. The military feelings are too deeply grounded to abdicate their place among our ideals until better substitutes are offered than the glory and shame that come to nations as well as to individuals from the ups and downs of politics and the vicissitudes of trade. There is something highly paradoxical in the modern man's relation to war. Ask all our millions, north and south, whether they would vote now (were such a thing possible) to have our war for the Union expunged from history, and the record of a peaceful transition to the present time substituted for that of its marches and battles, and probably hardly a handful of eccentrics would say yes. Those ancestors, those efforts, those memories and legends, are the most ideal part of what we now own together, a sacred spiritual possession worth more than all the blood poured out. Yet ask those same people whether they would be willing in cold blood to start another civil war now to gain another similar possession, and not one man or woman would vote for the proposition. In modern eyes, precious though wars may be, they must not be waged solely for the sake of the ideal harvest. Only when forced upon one, only when an enemy's injustice leaves us no alternative, is a war now thought permissible.

It was not thus in ancient times. The earlier men were hunting men, and to hunt a neighboring tribe, kill the males, loot the village and possess the females, was the most profitable, as well as the most exciting, way of living. Thus were the more martial tribes selected, and in chiefs and peoples a pure pugnacity and love of glory came to mingle with the more fundamental appetite for plunder.

Modern war is so expensive that we feel trade to be a better avenue to plunder; but modern man inherits all the innate pugnacity and all the love of glory of his ancestors. Showing war's irrationality and horror is of no effect upon him. The horrors make the fascination. War is the *strong* life; it is life *in extremis;* war-taxes are the only ones men never hesitate to pay, as the budgets of all nations show us.

History is a bath of blood. The Iliad is one long recital of how Diomedes and Ajax, Sarpedon and Hector *killed.* No detail of the wounds they made is spared us, and the Greek mind fed upon the story. Greek history is a panorama of jingoism and imperialism—war for war's sake, all the citizens being warriors. It is horrible reading, because of the irrationality of it all—save for the purpose of making "history"—and the history is that of the utter ruin of a civilization in intellectual respects perhaps the highest the earth has ever seen.

Those wars were purely piratical. Pride, gold, women, slaves, excitement, were their only motives. In the Peloponnesian war, for example, the Athenians ask the inhabitants of Melos (the island where the "Venus of Milo" was found), hitherto neutral, to own their lordship. The envoys meet, and hold a debate which Thucydides gives in full, and which, for sweet reasonableness of form, would have satisfied Matthew Arnold. "The powerful exact what they can," said the Athenians, "and the weak grant what they must." When the Meleans say that sooner than be slaves they will appeal to the gods, the Athenians reply: "Of the gods we believe and of men we know that, by a law of their nature, wherever they can rule they will. This law was not made by us, and we are not the first to have acted upon it; we did but inherit it, and we know that you and all mankind, if you were as strong as we are, would do as we do. So much for the gods; we have told you why we expect to stand as high in their good opinion as you." Well, the Meleans still refused, and their town was taken. "The Athenians," Thucydides quietly says, "thereupon put to death all who were of military age and made slaves of the women and children. They then colonized the island, sending thither five hundred settlers of their own."

Alexander's career was piracy pure and simple, nothing but an orgy of power and plunder, made romantic by the character of the hero. There was no rational principle in it, and the moment he died his generals and governors attacked one another. The cruelty of those times is incredible. When Rome finally conquered Greece, Paulus Aemilius was told by the Roman Senate to reward his soldiers for their toil by "giving" them the old kingdom of Epirus. They sacked seventy cities and carried off a hundred and fifty thousand inhabitants as slaves. How many they killed I know not; but in Etolia they killed all the senators, five hundred and fifty in number. Brutus was "the noblest Roman of them all," but to reanimate his soldiers on the eve of Philippi he similarly promises to give them the cities of Sparta and Thessalonica to ravage, if they win the fight.

Such was the gory nurse that trained societies to cohesiveness. We inherit the warlike type; and for most of the capacities of heroism that the human race is full of we have to thank this cruel history. Dead men tell no tales, and if there were any tribes of other type than this they have left no survivors. Our ancestors have bred pugnacity into our bone and marrow, and thousands of years of peace won't breed it out of us. The popular imagination fairly fattens on the thought of wars. Let public opinion once reach a certain fighting pitch, and no ruler can understand it. In the Boer war both governments began with bluff, but couldn't stay there, the military tension was too much for them. In 1898 our people had read the word WAR in letters three inches high for three months in every newspaper. The pliant politician McKinley was swept away by their eagerness, and our squalid war with Spain became a necessity.

At the present day, civilized opinion is a curious mental mixture. The military instincts and ideals are as strong as ever, but are confronted by reflective criticisms which sorely curb their ancient freedom. Innumerable writers are showing up the bestial side of military service. Pure loot and mastery seem no longer morally avowable motives, and pretexts must be found for attributing them solely to the enemy. England and we, our army and navy authorities repeat without ceasing, arm solely for "peace," Germany and Japan it is who are bent on loot and glory. "Peace" in military mouths to-day is a synonym for "war expected." The word has become a pure provocative, and no government wishing peace sincerely should allow it ever to be printed in a newspaper. Every up-to-date Dictionary should say that "peace" and "war" mean the same thing, now *in posse,* now *in actu.* It may even reasonably be said that the intensely sharp competitive *preparation* for war by the nations *is the real war,* permanent, unceasing; and that the battles are only a sort of public verification of the mastery gained during the "peace"-interval.

It is plain that on this subject civilized man has developed a sort of double personality. If we take European nations, no legitimate interest of any one of them would seem to justify the tremendous destructions which a war to compass it would necessarily entail. It would seem as though common sense and reason ought to find a way to reach agreement in every conflict of honest interests. I myself think it our bounden duty to believe in such international rationality as possible. But, as things stand, I see how desperately hard it is to bring the peace-party and the war-party together, and I believe that the difficulty is due to certain deficiencies in the program of pacifism which set the militarist imagination strongly, and to a certain extent justifiably, against it. In the whole discussion both sides are on imaginative and sentimental ground. It is but one utopia against another, and everything one says must be abstract and hypothetical. Subject to this criticism and caution, I will try to characterize in abstract strokes the opposite imaginative forces, and point out what to my own very fallible mind seems the best utopian hypothesis, the most promising line of conciliation.

In my remarks, pacificist tho' I am, I will refuse to speak of the bestial side of the war-régime (already done justice to by many writers) and consider only the higher aspects of militaristic sentiment. Patriotism no one thinks discreditable; nor does any one deny that war is the romance of history. But inordinate ambitions are the soul of every patriotism, and the possibility of violent death the soul of all romance. The militarily patriotic and romantic-minded everywhere, and especially the professional military class, refuse to admit for a moment that war may be a transitory phenomenon in social evolution. The notion of a sheep's paradise like that revolts, they say, our higher imagination. Where then would be the steeps of life? If war had ever stopped, we should have to reinvent it, on this view, to redeem life from flat degeneration.

Reflective apologists for war at the present day all take it religiously. It is a sort of sacrament. Its profits are to the vanquished as well as to the victor; and quite apart from any question of profit, it is an absolute good, we are told, for it is human nature at its highest dynamic. Its "horrors" are a cheap price to pay for rescue from the only alternative supposed, of a world of clerks and teachers, of co-education and zoophily, of "consumer's leagues" and "associated charities," of industrialism unlimited, and feminism unabashed. No scorn, no hardness, no valor any more! Fie upon such a cattleyard of a planet!

So far as the central essence of this feeling goes, no healthy minded person, it seems to me, can help to some degree partaking of it. Militarism is the great preserver of our ideals of hardihood, and human life with no use for hardihood would be contemptible. Without risks or prizes for the darer, history would be insipid indeed; and there is a type of military character which every one feels that the race should never cease to breed, for every one is sensitive to its superiority. The duty is incumbent on mankind, of keeping military characters in stock—of keeping them, if not for use, then as ends in themselves and as pure pieces of perfection,—so that Roosevelt's weaklings and molly-coddles may not end by making everything else disappear from the face of nature.

This natural sort of feeling forms, I think, the innermost soul of army-writings. Without any exception known to me, militarist authors take a highly mystical view of their subject, and regard war as a biological or sociological necessity, uncontrolled by ordinary psychological checks and motives. When the time of development is ripe the war must come, reason or no reason, for the justifications pleaded are invariably fictitious. War is, in short, a permanent human *obligation*. General Homer Lea, in his recent book "the Valor of Ignorance," plants himself squarely on this ground. Readiness for war is for him the essence of nationality, and ability in it the supreme measure of the health of nations.

Nations, General Lea says, are never stationary—they must necessarily expand or shrink, according to their vitality or decrepitude. Japan now is culminating; and by the fatal law in question it is impossible that her statesmen should not long since have entered, with extraordinary foresight, upon a vast policy of conquest—the game in which the first moves were her wars with China and Russia and her treaty with England, and of which the final objective is the capture of the Philippines, the Hawaiian Islands, Alaska, and the whole of our Coast west of the Sierra Passes. This will give Japan what her ineluctable vocation as a state absolutely forces her to claim, the possession of the entire Pacific Ocean; and to oppose these deep designs we Americans have, according to our author, nothing but our conceit, our ignorance, our commercialism, our corruption, and our feminism. General Lea makes a minute technical comparison of the military strength which we at present could oppose to the strength of Japan, and concludes that the islands, Alaska, Oregon, and Southern California, would fall almost without resistance, that San Francisco must surrender in a fortnight to a Japanese investment, that in three or four months the war would be over, and our republic, unable to regain what it had heedlessly neglected to protect sufficiently, would then "disintegrate," until perhaps some Caesar should arise to weld us again into a nation.

A dismal forecast indeed! Yet not unplausible, if the mentality of Japan's statesmen be of the Caesarian type of which history shows so many examples, and which is all that General Lea seems able to imagine. But there is no reason to think that women can no longer be the mothers of Napoleonic or Alexandrian characters; and if these come in Japan and find their opportunity, just such surprises as "the Valor of Ignorance" paints may lurk in ambush for us. Ignorant as we still are of the innermost recesses of Japanese mentality, we may be foolhardy to disregard such possibilities.

Other militarists are more complex and more moral in their considerations. The "Philosophie des Krieges," by S. R. Steinmetz is a good example. War, according to this author, is an ordeal instituted by God, who weighs the nations in its balance. It is the essential form of the State, and the only function in which peoples can employ all their powers at once and convergently. No victory is possible save as the resultant of a totality of virtues, no defeat for which some vice or weakness is not responsible. Fidelity, cohesiveness, tenacity, heroism, conscience, education, inventiveness, economy, wealth, physical health and vigor—there isn't a moral or intellectual point of superiority that doesn't tell, when God holds his assizes and hurls the peoples upon one another. *Die Weltgeschichte ist das Weltgericht;* and Dr. Steinmetz does not believe that in the long run chance and luck play any part in apportioning the issues.

The virtues that prevail, it must be noted, are virtues anyhow, superiorities that count in peaceful as well as in military competition; but the strain on them, being infinitely intenser in the latter case, makes war infinitely more searching as a trial. No ordeal is comparable to its winnowings. Its dread hammer is the welder of men into cohesive states, and nowhere but in such states can human nature adequately develop its capacity. The only alternative is "degeneration."

Dr. Steinmetz is a conscientious thinker, and his book, short as it is, takes much into account. Its upshot can, it seems to me, be summed up in Simon Patten's word, that mankind was nursed in pain and fear, and that the transition to a "pleasure-economy" may be fatal to a being wielding no powers of defense against its disintegrative influences. If we speak of the *fear of emancipation from the fear-regime,* we put the whole situation into a single phrase; fear regarding ourselves now taking the place of the ancient fear of the enemy.

Turn the fear over as I will in my mind, it all seems to lead back to two unwillingnesses of the imagination, one aesthetic, and the other moral: unwillingness, first to envisage a future in which army-life, with its many elements of charm, shall be forever impossible, and in which the destinies of peoples shall nevermore be decided quickly, thrillingly, and tragically, by force, but only gradually and insipidly by "evolution"; and, secondly, unwillingness to see the supreme theatre of human strenuousness closed, and the splendid military aptitudes of men doomed to keep always in a state of latency and never show themselves in action. These insistent unwillingnesses, no less than other esthetic and ethical insistencies have, it seems to me, to be listened to and respected. One cannot meet them effectively by mere counter-insistency on war's expensiveness and horror. The horror makes the thrill; and when the question is of getting the extremest and supremest out of human nature, talk of expense sounds ignominious. The weakness of so much merely negative criticism is evident—pacificism makes no converts from the military party. The military party denies neither the bestiality nor the horror, nor the expense; it only says that these things tell but half the story. It only says that war is *worth* them; that, taking human nature as a whole, its wars are its best protection against its weaker and more cowardly self, and that mankind cannot *afford* to adopt a peace-economy.

Pacificists ought to enter more deeply into the esthetical and ethical point of view of their opponents. Do that first in any controversy, says J. J. Chapman, *then move the point,* and your opponent will follow. So long as anti-militarists propose no substitute for war's disciplinary function, no *moral equivalent* of war, analogous, as one might say, to the mechanical equivalent of heat, so long they fail to realize the full inwardness of the situation. And as a rule they do fail. The duties, penalties, and sanctions pictured in the utopias they paint are all too weak and tame to touch the military-minded. Tolstoy's pacificism is the only exception to this rule, for it is profoundly pessimistic as regards all this world's values, and makes the fear of the Lord furnish the moral spur provided elsewhere by the fear of the enemy. But our socialistic peace-advocates all believe absolutely in this world's values; and instead of the fear of the Lord and the fear of the enemy, the only fear they reckon with is the fear of poverty if one be lazy. This weakness pervades all the socialistic literature with which I am acquainted. Even in Lowes Dickinson's exquisite dialogue, high wages and short hours are the only forces invoked for overcoming man's distaste for repulsive kinds of labor. Meanwhile men at large still live as they always have lived, under a pain-and-fear economy— for those of us who live in an ease-economy are but an island in the stormy ocean—and the whole atmosphere of present-day utopian literature tastes mawkish and dishwatery to people who still keep a sense for life's more bitter flavors. It suggests, in truth, ubiquitous inferiority.

Inferiority is always with us, and merciless scorn of it is the keynote of the military temper. "Dogs, would you live forever?" shouted Frederick the Great. "Yes," say our utopians, "let us live forever, and raise our level gradually." The best thing about our "inferiors" to-day is that they are as tough as nails, and physically and morally almost as insensitive. Utopianism would see them soft and squeamish, while militarism would keep their callousness, but transfigure it into a meritorious characteristic, needed by "the service," and redeemed by that from the suspicion of inferiority. All the qualities of a man acquire dignity when he knows that the service of the collectivity that owns him needs them. If proud of the collectivity, his own pride rises in proportion. No collectivity is like an army for nourishing such

PROGRESSIVES

pride; but it has to be confessed that the only sentiment which the image of pacific cosmopolitan industrialism is capable of arousing in countless worthy breasts is shame at the idea of belonging to *such* a collectivity. It is obvious that the United States of America as they exist to-day impress a mind like General Lea's as so much human blubber. Where is the sharpness and precipitousness, the contempt for life, whether one's own, or another's? Where is the savage "yes" and "no," the unconditional duty? Where is the conscription? Where is the blood-tax? Where is anything that one feels honored by belonging to?

Having said thus much in preparation, I will now confess my own utopia. I devoutly believe in the reign of peace and in the gradual advent of some sort of a socialistic equilibrium. The fatalistic view of the war-function is to me nonsense, for I know that war-making is due to definite motives and subject to prudential checks and reasonable criticisms, just like any other form of enterprise. And when whole nations are the armies, and the science of destruction vies in intellectual refinement with the sciences of production, I see that war becomes absurd and impossible from its own monstrosity. Extravagant ambitions will have to be replaced by reasonable claims, and nations must make common cause against them. I see no reason why all this should not apply to yellow as well as to white countries, and I look forward to a future when acts of war shall be formally outlawed as between civilized peoples.

All these beliefs of mine put me squarely into the anti-militarist party. But I do not believe that peace either ought to be or will be permanent on this globe, unless the states pacifically organized preserve some of the old elements of army-discipline. A permanently successful peace-economy cannot be a simple pleasure-economy. In the more or less socialistic future towards which mankind seems drifting we must still subject ourselves collectively to those severities which answer to our real position upon this only partly hospitable globe. We must make new energies and hardihoods continue the manliness to which the military mind so faithfully clings. Martial virtues must be the enduring cement; intrepidity, contempt of softness, surrender of private interest, obedience to command, must still remain the rock upon which states are built—unless, indeed, we wish for dangerous reactions against commonwealths fit only for contempt, and liable to invite attack whenever a centre of crystallization for military-minded enterprise gets formed anywhere in their neighborhood.

The war-party is assuredly right in affirming and reaffirming that the martial virtues, although originally gained by the race through war, are absolute and permanent human goods. Patriotic pride and ambition in their military form are, after all, only specifications of a more general competitive passion. They are its first form, but that is no reason for supposing them to be its last form. Men now are proud of belonging to a conquering nation, and without a murmur they lay down their persons and their wealth, if by so doing they may fend off subjection. But who can be sure that *other aspects of one's country* may not, with time and education and suggestion enough, come to be regarded with similarly effective feelings of pride and shame? Why should men not some day feel that it is worth a blood-tax to belong to a collectivity superior in *any* ideal respect? Why should they not blush with indignant shame if the community that owns them is vile in any way whatsoever? Individuals, daily more numerous, now feel this civic passion. It is only a question of blowing on the spark till the whole population gets incandescent, and on the ruins of the old morals of military honour, a stable system of morals of civic honour builds itself up. What the whole community comes to believe in grasps the individual as in a vise. The war-function has graspt us so far; but constructive interests may some day seem no less imperative, and impose on the individual a hardly lighter burden.

Let me illustrate my idea more concretely. There is nothing to make one indignant in the mere fact that life is hard, that men should toil and suffer pain. The planetary conditions once for all are such, and we can stand it. But that so many men, by mere accidents of birth and opportunity, should have a life of *nothing else* but toil and pain and hardness and inferiority imposed upon them, should have *no* vacation, while others natively no more deserving never get any taste of this campaigning life at all,—*this* is capable of arousing indignation in reflective minds. It may end by seeming shameful to all of us that some of us have nothing but campaigning, and others nothing but unmanly ease. If now—and this is my idea—there were, instead of military conscription a conscription of the whole youthful population to form for a certain number of years a part of the army enlisted against *Nature,* the injustice would tend to be evened out, and numerous other goods to the commonwealth would follow. The military ideals of hardihood and discipline would be wrought into the growing fibre of the people; no one would remain blind as the luxurious classes now are blind, to man's real relations to the globe he lives on, and to the permanently sour and hard foundations of his higher life. To coal and iron mines, to freight trains, to fishing fleets in December, to dish-washing, clothes-washing, and window-washing, to road-building and tunnel-making, to foundries and stoke-holes, and to the frames of skyscrapers, would our gilded youths be drafted off, according to their choice, to get the childishness knocked out of them, and to come back into society with healthier sympathies and soberer ideas. They would have paid their blood-tax, done their own part in the immemorial human warfare against nature, they would tread the earth more proudly, the women would value them more highly, they would be better fathers and teachers of the following generation.

Such a conscription, with the state of public opinion that would have required it, and the many moral fruits it would bear, would preserve in the midst of a pacific civilization the manly virtues which the military party is so afraid of seeing disappear in peace. We should get toughness without callousness, authority with as little criminal cruelty as possible, and painful work done cheerily because the duty is temporary, and threatens not, as now, to degrade the whole remainder of one's life. I spoke of the "moral equivalent" of war. So far, war has been the only force that can discipline a whole community, and until an equivalent discipline is organized, I believe that war must have its way. But I have no serious doubt that the ordinary prides and shames of social man, once developed to a certain intensity, are capable of organizing such a moral equivalent as I have sketched, or some other just as effective for preserving manliness of type. It is but a question of time, of skillful propagandism, and of opinion-making men seizing historic opportunities.

The martial type of character can be bred without war. Strenuous honour and disinterestedness abound elsewhere. Priests and medical men are in a fashion educated to it, and we should all feel some degree of it imperative if we were conscious of our work as an obligatory service to the state. We should be *owned,* as soldiers are by the army, and our pride would rise accordingly. We could be poor, then, without humiliation, as army officers now are. The only thing needed henceforward is to inflame the civic temper as past history has inflamed the military temper. H. G. Wells, as usual, sees the centre of the situation. "In many ways," he says, "military organization is the most peaceful of activities. When the contemporary man steps from the street, of clamorous insincere advertisement, push, adulteration, underselling and intermittent employment, into the barrack-yard, he steps on to a higher social plane, into an atmosphere of service and co-operation and of infinitely more honourable emulations. Here at least men are not flung out of employment to degenerate because there is no immediate work for them to do. They are fed and drilled and trained for better services. Here at least a man is supposed to win promotion by self-forgetfulness and not by self-seeking. And beside the feeble and irregular endowment of research by commercialism, its little short-sighted snatches at profit by innovation and scientific economy, see how remarkable is the steady and rapid development of method and appliances in naval and military affairs! Nothing is more striking than to compare the progress of civil conveniences which has been left almost entirely to the trader, to the progress in military apparatus during the last few decades. The house-appliances of to-day for example, are little better than they were fifty years ago. A house of today is still almost as ill-ventilated, badly heated by wasteful fires, clumsily arranged and furnished as the house of 1858. Houses a couple of hundred years old are still satisfactory places of residence, so little have our standards risen. But the rifle or battleship of fifty years ago was beyond all comparison inferior to those we possess; in power, in speed, in convenience alike. No one has a use now for such superannuated things."

Wells adds that he thinks that the conceptions of order and discipline, the tradition of service and devotion, of physical fitness, unstinted exertion, and universal responsibility, which universal military duty is now teaching European nations, will remain a permanent acquisition, when the last ammunition has been used in the fireworks that celebrate the final peace. I believe as he does. It would be simply preposterous if the only force that could work ideals of honour and standards of efficiency into English or American natures should be the fear of being killed by the Germans or the Japanese. Great indeed is Fear; but it is not, as our military enthusiasts believe and try to make us believe, the only stimulus known for awakening the higher ranges of men's spiritual energy. The amount of alteration in public opinion which my utopia postulates is vastly less than the difference between the mentality of those black warriors who pursued Stanley's party on the Congo with their cannibal war-cry of "Meat! Meat!" and that of the "general-staff" of any civilized nation. History has seen the latter interval bridged over: the former one can be bridged over much more easily.

DOCUMENT 11

Clarence Darrow, Crime and Punishment

Clarence Darrow (1857–1938) came to Chicago in the late 1880s and took part in the campaign for amnesty to the surviving Haymarket Anarchists. He was named corporation counsel for the city of Chicago, then general attorney for the Chicago and Northwestern Railroad. But when his employer became involved in the great railway strike of 1894, Darrow resigned to represent Eugene Debs and the striking workers.

Thus began his celebrated career as "attorney for the damned." Among the criminals he defended were Nathan Leopold and Richard Loeb, wealthy Chicago youths, and "Big Bill" Haywood, poor and persecuted leader of Western miners. Darrow's interest in nonviolence grew from his observation of crime and punishment in American courts and jails. In the excerpts that follow, from a debate between Darrow and the Socialist Arthur Lewis concerning the relative merits of the Marxist and Tolstoyan social philosophies, he presents nonviolence as "the opposite to the theory of punishment, or the theory of vengeance," and goes on to argue that while the state "was born

From *Marx vs Tolstoi. A Debate Between Clarence S. Darrow and Arthur M. Lewis,* People's Pocket Series No. 157 (Girard, Kansas: Appeal to Reason [*ca.* 1910]), pp. 5–16, 38–40.

in force and violence" yet "the only force that can win is determination, non-resistance, peaceable force." These views earned Darrow a reputation as America's foremost exponent of nonviolence in the years just prior to World War I. He expounded them more at length in books such as Resist Not Evil *(1903) and* An Eye for an Eye *(1905).*

———————————

As this is Sunday morning, and a semi-religious question, I take for my text the 38th and 39th verses in the 5th chapter of Matthew. I cannot quote it literally. It is quite a time since I have read it. But I know the import of it.

"Ye have heard it hath been said," I am quoting from Matthew, "An eye for an eye, and a tooth for a tooth. But I say unto you: Resist not evil. But whosoever shall smite you on the right cheek, turn to him the other also."

I do not quote this because Matthew wrote it. I really do not know whether he did or not; and I care a great deal less. I could not find out whether Matthew wrote it, unless I should read Professor Foster's works on religion, and that would take too long. But I quote it because throughout all the Western world this has been the accepted statement of the doctrine of non-resistance. It is, perhaps, as good a statement of that theory as one can find in a few short sentences. Matthew had no patent on it, of course. There are very few thoughts in this world that are patented, and those are not worth it. It was undoubtedly very old before Matthew lived—if he lived. And it has been repeated a great many times since he died—if he died.

The theory of non-resistance is taken, generally, as the opposite to the theory of punishment, or the theory of vengeance, which, up to the time of the Christian religion, was the theory of the world—and since that time has been doubly the theory of the world. Its announcement, as generally admitted by those who have written and spoken upon the subject, has reference, first, to the treatment of those whom society calls criminals; next, perhaps, to governments in their relations to each other and to their subjects; and then to women and children, insane, prisoners, and the like. It relates to the way those who have the power have generally exercised that power in relation to the rest of the world.

Now, I might say in the beginning that I am not quite sure of this theory, or of any other theory. I used to be a good deal more positive than I am today. And especially, I am not at all sure that there is any theory in philosophy, or morals (or laws), that works out in sociology. The science of society, if there is such a science, is not an exact science. You cannot demonstrate any theory of society the way you can demonstrate the multiplication table, unless it is Socialism—and you cannot demonstrate that in the same way unless you are speaking to an audience of Socialists. You might demonstrate Single Tax to a Single Taxer, but you could not do it to anybody else. Exact science has little to do—something to do, but little to do, with the ways in which man organizes himself on the planet. He does not move in straight lines, or in regular curves, or even in crooked lines, that can be depended upon. When he learns what the crooked line is he goes straight. And no theory of life, no theory of society can be worked out as to communal life, in the same way that you can work out the science of mathematics, or of astronomy, or geology, or any science dealing with anything that keeps still.

But the question is, whether the theory of punishment, as opposed to the theory of non-resistance, is most in harmony with life, and tends to the progress of the world; whether human life in its slow evolution is going toward the theory of non-resistance, or is going toward the theory of violence, and force, and punishment.

If one looks back to the origin of the State we do not find that it had the immaculate birth that most people believe. It was born in force and violence. The strong took a club and made a state for himself. It was a simple state, kept there by the force of the strong man's club and his will. From that it has gone on until it takes a good many strong clubs, together with a good many armies, navies, policemen, lawyers, judges, etc., to keep the state in order. But through it all has run the theory of force, and through it all the power has come not from the people who ask it, but from the people who took it because they were the stronger. In the beginning the chief preserved order and the law, by saying what should be the law and enforcing order himself with his club.

In modern society the controlling forces arrange things as they want them, and provide that certain things are criminal. Sometimes those things have a semblance of natural crime, and sometimes not. The largest number of crimes are crimes against property. Sometimes you may trace them more or less directly to the violation of some law that is in the natural world. But the fact is that the class which rules society come together and say what men must do, and what they must not do. And the man who violates it commits crime.

There are in society, and always have been, a large number of people, due mainly to conditions of society, who are what we call defectives; who are anti-social in their nature; whose life and conduct tend toward the disintegration of society, instead of the life of society. Very largely the treatment of crime is a question of treatment of these anti-social individuals. It is a question of treatment of those who persevere, in one way or another, in violating the rules of the game which society has made.

Way back under the Mosaic Law—and Moses did not have a patent on it either, but under the law of the world, the doctrine of an "Eye for an eye, a tooth for a tooth," prevailed. If a man killed another his life should be taken. If he stole something he should be punished. If he burglarized, then it meant something else, generally death. If he did something, the world would do something to him. And they would do that something that the world at that time thought was the right thing to do to him. In this way, even down to a hundred years ago, there were in England about two hundred crimes punishable by death. Almost everything that could be conceived was punished by death. And the lawyers, and judges, and preachers of that day had no thought that society could hang together if men were not hanged regularly for stealing sheep and anything that happened. The old doctrine of an eye for an eye, and a tooth for a tooth, was the common doctrine of the world, and that doctrine prevails today.

All penal codes are really built upon that doctrine. When you trace penal codes back to the beginning, they mean one thing, and only one, i. e., vengeance. . . . In the early stages, if some one slew another, the members of his tribe had the right to go and take the life of any member of the other tribe in return. It did not matter whether he had been guilty or not. It was the law of vengeance, the law of punishment—and punishment and vengeance have always meant the same thing in the world, no matter where it has been.

Punishments of crimes have always been arbitrary. One man would say that for stealing a horse the somebody stealing it should go to jail for thirty days. Another would say that he should go to the penitentiary for a year; another would say five years; and somebody else would say he should be hanged by the neck until dead. Punishments have never depended upon the act done, but upon the man who saw the act done and the mind possessed by the ruling power. Or half a dozen judges given authority to administer punishment for a certain act no two judges would administer the same kind of punishment. One would say thirty days, another thirty years; just according to the mind he has. Some judge might give you less after breakfast than he would before. And another judge might give you more if he had attended a banquet through the small hours in the morning preceding, and did not feel well when he administered the sentence. All those things enter into it, and when you come to sum it all up, the real theory of it is a question of vengeance: The individual has done something. How much shall we do to him in return? How much will we make him suffer, because he has made some one else suffer?

Now, the non-resistant says, there is no such thing as crime, i. e., some of them say that. And they say that all punishment is bad, not heavy punishment alone—but all punishment; that man has no right to punish his fellow man, that only evil results from it; that the theory of vengeance and the theory of punishment is wrong; that it cures nobody, it does not tend to benefit society, it does not tend to change the defective, it does not tend to build up society. It is wrong and untrue in its whole theory; and the theory of non-resistance is the true theory as to crime. Whatever you may think of the theory, the world has been steadily going that way. It has been abolishing the death penalty, until today in most civilized countries there are only one or two crimes punishable by death; and it is very rarely that death is meted out for those.

Punishment has been growing less severe, and the methods of inflicting punishment are less severe. Of course, in the old day when men were less squeamish and more honest they had their hangings in broad daylight. Today we do not do it, not because we are better, but because we are squeamish.

We have hangings in the jail, so that the effects of the punishment will be entirely lost to the community.

Our terms of imprisonment are not so long. Our methods of treating the imprisoned are more humane. We sentence a man to prison. Of course, in the old time he used to be put into a vile place, where he would be half clad and half fed, and where he would be covered with rags full of vermin, and where he would suffer all sorts of physical pain. Today we send him to jail, and we have the jail steam heated and electric lighted. We have a doctor to take care of him if so, perchance, the penalty is death he won't die before his time comes; and if he is to be hanged he gets better food than he ever did before. So far as men are entrusted with the power of carrying out these provisions they do it as humanely as they can do it.

In the old times the insane were treated like criminals. They were locked up in cells; they were loaded with chains; they WERE criminals, because the rest of the world did not understand them. We have gotten over that. We have learned to treat them as human beings, and to treat them as those suffering from ailment, whereas once in the history of the world they were visited with the old law of vengeance, the law of force. The world some time will learn to treat all of its defectives, and all those who violate the code, the same as they treat the insane and the ill today. And we are learning it, more and more, every day.

The theory of non-resistance does not, necessarily, say that a man cannot be restrained, although very likely that would not be necessary under any decent law of society. It is possible there are some who are so born, and have been so treated by society, that they would need to be restrained just as those afflicted with small-pox may be restrained in a hospital. But to restrain them and treat them until cured is one thing; to say that men because of some inherent wickedness deserve punishment is another thing. It would be absurd to restrain men suffering from small-pox and turn them out from a hospital in six weeks, whether cured or not. If hospitals were run in the same way as jails, we would send them up for thirty days; and if they got well in a week we would keep them there.

The whole theory of punishment, so far as there is any theory in it—and there is not much in it, except the idea of vengeance—but the whole theory, so far as there is one, comes from the religious conception; that some people are made inherently bad, that their minds are evil, or their souls for that matter, or whatever is the intangible thing about them that makes them evil. And they deserve punishment, because they have a "wicked, abandoned and malignant heart." We always have to put that "wicked, abandoned and malignant heart" in the indictment; otherwise it is no good. If he has that in his heart he can be punished. When twelve jurors and a judge get together, how can they tell whether his heart is bad or not? You could tell better if you dissect him. It goes upon the theory that man is apart from all the other beings that inhabit the universe; that he is a free moral agent; that he is a sort of a wild train running at large through the universe; that he is not governed by rules and conditions like the rest of the universe about us. But that the Lord created him, put a mind in him, a good heart in some of them; a wicked, abandoned and malignant heart in others; and sent them out to run wild independent of all the universe about them. And whenever the good people catch up with these wicked, abandoned and malignant people then we punish the wicked because, intrinsically, they are bad, because they chose the evil instead of the good. They could do better if they wanted to be better but they did not choose. Society sends them to jail, just as brutal parents whip their children because they are bad instead of good. As a matter of fact, science and evolution teach us that man is an animal, a little higher than the other orders of animals; that he is governed by the same natural laws that govern the rest of the universe; that he is governed by the same laws that govern animal life, aye, and plant life; that free moral agency is a myth, a delusion, and a snare. It teaches us that he is surrounded by environment the product of all the past, the product of all the present; that he is here just like any other subject of natural law; and that it is not goodness, it is not badness, that makes him what he is. It is the condition of life in which he lives. And if he lives unwisely, if he is a defective, if he is anti-social, it is not that he chose it; but it is due to a thousand conditions over which he has not the slightest control. And the wise society seeks to change his environment, to place him in harmony with life. They know that they can only change the man by changing the conditions under which he lives; that good and evil, so far as he is concerned, do not exist; that right and wrong are religious myths; that it is a question of the adaptability of the individual to society life, and a gradual change of the environment under which he lives.

With the state is the same thing. The theory of force and violence applied to the state has drenched the world in blood. It has built great navies, and great armies. One nation builds a great navy and a great army, and destroys the resources of its people to build armies and navies. And another nation must build a greater navy and a greater army, because of the first. It makes of the nations of the earth armed camps, and the stronger the one arms itself, the stronger must the rest. England builds her wonderful navy out of the toil of the poor, out of what should buy food for the men who produce it. And when she builds it, then Germany must build one as large, and so must France and so must Russia build one, too. And of course patriotic America must build one. We need a navy for fear that a band of Senegambians might send a fleet to devastate Chicago some night. The theory of force and violence as applied to political states has built up the navies and armies of the world, and has caused most of the bloodshed of the human race. Is there any doubt but what nations would be stronger if they burned their battleships instead of building new ones? Can you increase the power of one nation by building ships when you simply make others build larger? You never change the relative proportion, which alone makes the strength. If instead of adding to the navies the world over, we gradually got rid of them, the relative strength would be what it was before.

In industrial life it is the same thing. The reign of force, and the reign of violence, means competition, means industrial strife; is responsible for the greed and selfishness and avarice for the fortunes of the great and the poverty of the poor. It is only in these later days, when the world is looking to something better, when they are learning that force and violence is wrong, that it is wrong that merchants compete and cut each other's throats and workmen compete against each other to show how much less they can work for; and that it is better to organize society on a co-operative basis where each man is to help his fellowman instead of fighting his fellowman.

The dreams of the world may be far off, and we must fit every dream to every reality. For the world is imperfect. But if, as society progresses, there shall one day be a civilization better than the world has known, it will be a society where force and violence and bloodshed and cruelty have disappeared. It will be a world of brotherhood. A world not of destruction, of competition, of violence, of hatred, of enmity; but a world of co-operation, of mutual help, of love, of brotherliness; and that alone makes for the progress of the world.

... Those who think that non-resistance is a milk-and-water theory have got another guess. It is not. I was talking the other day with a man who had been a colonel in the war. I said: "I do not know how you could get up courage to go up in the face of cannons and bayonets and take your life in your hands." He says: "I did it because I was too big a coward to run away." And that is why most all men go to war. They are too big cowards to stay at home. That is why men fight. They are too big cowards not to fight. Do you think it is a brave man who fights; or is it the brave man who does not fight? I will show you ten thousand men who are willing to go up in the face of hostile cannon, where you cannot find one man who will take one stick of criticism in a daily newspaper. There is not anything on earth so cheap as physical courage. Why even a bulldog can fight, but it has not got much brain. Fighting has nothing to do with the labor question, or with the question of capital and labor. How is it applied to the question as it exists today?

In order to change social conditions you say you must get rid of the ruling class, by force or some other way—one way or the other. Now, the weak are the poorest ones in the world to fight. They have no guns; the other fellow has them all. They have no organization. They have no chance in a fight. But they can fight. Workingmen of today can fight. If all of them would refuse to work or the great majority would refuse to work and enter into passive resistance—non-resistance—quit feeding the race; that is all you need to do. You cannot, of course. Wait until you can. You can get a small minority to arm themselves with brickbats and guns. What happens? You are sending a small force, poorly armed and equipped, against all the power of the state, and you cannot succeed, and you never have succeeded.

The only force that can win is determination, non-resistance, peaceable force. There is such a thing as peaceable force that is more forcible than forcible force.

Let me give you a few illustrations. What makes life? The cold, hard, stern winter; or the sunshine and the warm rain of the summer and the spring? The one means death, and the other means life. Repression and death go together. Love and sunshine and life are born together. Do you want to change the conduct of men, whether grown individuals or children; take a child and whip a child, can you change his conduct? You may change his conduct, but can you change his heart? Conduct is only the outward manifestation of the inward individual. To change the individual you must change the heart, and then the conduct must be free. Can you cure hatred with hatred? Everybody knows it in their own life. You may force men against their will to do certain things, but their hearts are a seething mass waiting for a time when they may accomplish other things by violence. Do you think you can do something for a man by sending him to the penitentiary? Gentleness is the law that makes life. Cruelty and hatred and coldness is the law that makes death. The question of non-resistance or resistance means a choice between those two laws.

DOCUMENT 12

Suffragettes, Letters from Prison, 1917

The struggle for women's rights began as a phase of the abolitionist movement. Garrison insisted that women be permitted to participate in antislavery meetings, and women leaders such as Susan B. Anthony and Lucretia Mott urged freedom for both the slave and the unfranchised female. After the Civil War most male abolitionists concluded that the vote for women should be deferred so that the vote for the Negro could be won. Victory in the women's suffrage struggle came fifty years later, during World War I.

Doris Stevens, *Jailed For Freedom* (New York: Boni and Liverwright, 1920), pp. 175, 177–178, 184–191.

Led now by a new and more militant group of spokeswomen, such as Alice Paul, the suffragettes did not hesitate to press their domestic concern in a world at war. They picketed persistently in Washington, D. C. When arrested, they continued their protest in jail. The following passages, from a book by a participant in the movement, describe prison protest, first by petition, then by a refusal to work and eat. The suffering of the suffragettes moved the nation, prompted the resignation of the Collector of Customs for the Port of New York, contributed to the passage of the Nineteenth Amendment, and established significant precedents for later nonviolent demonstrators.

POLITICAL PRISONERS

Finding that a Suffrage Committee in the House and a report in the Senate had not silenced our banners, the Administration cast about for another plan by which to stop the picketing. This time they turned desperately to longer terms of imprisonment. They were indeed hard pressed when they could choose such a cruel and stupid course.

Our answer to this policy was more women on the picket line, on the outside, and a protest on the inside of prison.

We decided, in the face of extended imprisonment, to demand to be treated as political prisoners. We felt that, as a matter of principle, this was the dignified and self-respecting thing to do, since we had offended politically, not criminally. We believed further that a determined, organized effort to make clear to a wider public the political nature of the offense would intensify the Administration's embarrassment and so accelerate their final surrender.

It fell to Lucy Burns, vice chairman of the organization, to be the leader of the new protest. . . . She had no sooner begun to organize her comrades for protest than the officials sensed a "plot," and removed her at once to solitary confinement. But they were too late. Taking the leader only hastened the rebellion. A forlorn piece of paper was discovered, on which was written their initial demand. It was then passed from prisoner to prisoner through holes in the wall surrounding leaden pipes, until a finished document had been perfected and signed by all the prisoners.

This historic document—historic because it represents the first organized group action ever made in America to establish the status of political prisoners—said:

To the Commissioners of the District of Columbia:

As political prisoners, we, the undersigned, refuse to work while in prison. We have taken this stand as a matter of principle after careful consideration, and from it we shall not recede.

This action is a necessary protest against an unjust sentence. In reminding President Wilson of his pre-election promises toward woman suffrage we were exercising the right of peaceful petition, guaranteed by the Constitution of the United States, which declares peaceful picketing is legal in the District of Columbia. That we are unjustly sentenced has been well recognized—when President Wilson pardoned the first group of suffragists who had been given sixty days in the workhouse, and again when Judge Mullowny suspended sentence for the last group of picketers. We wish to point out the inconsistency and injustice of our sentences—some of us have been given sixty days, a later group thirty days, and another group given a suspended sentence for exactly the same action.

Conscious, therefore, of having acted in accordance with the highest standards of citizenship, we ask the Commissioners of the District to grant us the rights due political prisoners. We ask that we no longer be segregated and confined under locks and bars in small groups, but permitted to see each other, and that Miss Lucy Burns, who is in full sympathy with this letter, be released from solitary confinement in another building and given back to us.

We ask exemption from prison work, that our legal right to consult counsel be recognized, to have food sent to us from outside, to supply ourselves with writing material for as much correspondence as we may need, to receive books, letters, newspapers, our relatives and friends.

Our united demand for political treatment has been delayed, because on entering the workhouse we found conditions so very bad that before we could ask that the suffragists be treated as political prisoners, it was necessary to make a stand for the ordinary rights of human beings for all the inmates. Although this has not been accomplished we now wish to bring the important question of the status of political prisoners to the attention of the commissioners, who, we are informed, have full authority to make what regulations they please for the District prison and workhouse.

The Commissioners are requested to send us a written reply so that we may be sure this protest has reached them.

Signed by,

MARY WINSOR, LUCY BRANHAM, ERNESTINE HARA, HILDA BLUMBERG, MAUD MALONE, PAULINE F. ADAMS, ELEANOR A. CALNAN, EDITH AINGE, ANNIE ARNEIL, DOROTHY J. BARTLETT, MARGARET FOTHERINGHAM.

The Commissioners' only answer to this was a hasty transfer of the signers and the leader, Miss Burns, to the District Jail, where they were put in solitary confinement. The women were not only refused the privileges asked but were denied some of the usual privileges allowed to ordinary criminals. . . .

THE HUNGER STRIKE—A WEAPON

When the Administration refused to grant the demand of the prisoners and of that portion of the public which supported them, for the rights of political prisoners, it was decided to resort to the ultimate protest-weapon inside prison. A hunger strike was undertaken, not only to reinforce the verbal demand for the rights of political prisoners, but also as a final protest against unjust imprisonment and increasingly long sentences. This brought the Administration face to face with a more acute embarrassment. They had to choose between more stubborn resistance and capitulation. They continued for a while longer on the former path.

Little is known in this country about the weapon of the hunger strike. And so at first it aroused tremendous indignation. "Let them starve to death," said the thoughtless one, who did not perceive that that was the very thing a political administration could least afford to do. "Mad fanatics," said a kindlier critic. The general opinion was that the hunger strike was "foolish."

Few people realize that this resort to the refusal of food is almost as old as civilization. It has always represented a passionate desire to achieve an end. There is not time to go into the religious use of it, which would also be pertinent, but I will cite a few instances which have tragic and amusing likenesses to the suffrage hunger strike.

According to the Brehon Law,[1] which was the code of ancient Ireland by which justice was administered under ancient Irish monarchs (from the earliest record to the 17th century), it became the duty of an injured person, when all else failed, to inflict punishment directly, for wrong done. "The plaintiff 'fasted on' the defendant." He went to the house of the defendant and sat upon his doorstep, remaining there without food to force the payment of a debt, for example. The debtor was compelled by the weight of custom and public opinion not to let the plaintiff die at his door, and yielded. Or if he did not yield, he was practically outlawed by the community, to the point of being driven away. A man who refused to abide by the custom not only incurred personal danger but lost all character.

If resistance to this form of protest was resorted to it had to take the form of a counter-fast. If the victim of such a protest thought himself being unjustly coerced, he might fast in opposition, "to mitigate or avert the evil."

"Fasting on a man" was also a mode of compelling action of another sort. St. Patrick fasted against King Trian to compel him to have compassion on his [Trian's] slaves.[2] He also fasted against a heretical city to compel it to become orthodox.[3] He fasted against the pagan King Loeguire to "constrain him to his will."[4]

This form of hunger strike was further used under the Brehon Law as compulsion to obtain a request. For example, the Leinstermen on one occasion fasted on St. Columkille till they obtained from him the promise that an extern King should never prevail against them.

---

1. Joyce, *A Social History of Ancient Ireland,* Vol. I, Chapter VIII.
2. *Tripartite Life of St. Patrick,* CLXXVII, p. 218.
3. *Ibid.,* CLXXVII, p. 418.
4. *Ibid.,* CLXXVII, p. 556.

It is interesting to note that this form of direct action was adopted because there was no legislative machinery to enforce justice. These laws were merely a collection of customs attaining the force of law by long usage, by hereditary habit, and by public opinion. Our resort to this weapon grew out of the same situation. The legislative machinery, while empowered to give us redress, failed to function, and so we adopted the fast.

The institution of fasting on a debtor still exists in the East. It is called by the Hindoos "sitting dharna."

The hunger strike was continuously used in Russia by prisoners to obtain more humane practices toward them. Kropotkin[5] cites an instance in which women prisoners hunger struck to get their babies back. If a child was born to a woman during her imprisonment the babe was immediately taken from her and not returned. Mothers struck and got their babies returned to them.

He cites another successful example in Kharkoff prison in 1878 when six prisoners resolved to hunger strike to death if necessary to win two things—to be allowed exercise and to have the sick prisoners taken out of chains.

There are innumerable instances of hunger strikes, even to death, in Russian prison history. But more often the demands of the strikers were won. Breshkovsky[6] tells of a strike by 17 women against outrage, which elicited the desired promises from the warden.

As early as 1877 members of the Land and Liberty Society[7] imprisoned for peaceful and educational propaganda, in the Schlusselburg Fortress for political prisoners, hunger struck against inhuman prison conditions and frightful brutalities and won their points.

During the suffrage campaign in England this weapon was used for the double purpose of forcing the release of imprisoned militant suffragettes, and of compelling the British government to act.

Among the demonstrations was a revival of the ancient Irish custom by Sylvia Pankhurst, who in addition to her hunger strikes within prison, "fasted on" the doorstep of Premier Asquith to compel him to see a deputation of women on the granting of suffrage to English women. She won.

Irish prisoners have revived the hunger strike to compel either release or trial of untried prisoners and have won. As I write, almost a hundred Irish prisoners detained by England for alleged nationalist activities, but not brought to trial, hunger struck to freedom. As a direct result of this specific hunger strike England has promised a renovation of her practices in dealing with Irish rebels.

And so it was that when we came to the adoption of this accelerating tactic, we had behind us more precedents for winning our point than for losing. We were strong in the knowledge that we could "fast on" President Wilson and his powerful Administration, and compel him to act or "fast back."

---

5. See *In Russian and French Prisons,* P. Kropotkin.
6. *For Russia's Freedom,* by Ernest Poole,—An Interview with Breshkovsky.
7. See *The Russian Bastille,* Simon O. Pollock.

Among the prisoners who with Alice Paul led the hunger strike was a very picturesque figure, Rose Winslow (Ruza Wenclawska) of New York, whose parents had brought her in infancy from Poland to become a citizen of "free" America. At eleven she was put at a loom in a Pennsylvania mill, where she wove hosiery for fourteen hours a day until tuberculosis claimed her at nineteen. A poet by nature she developed her mind to the full in spite of these disadvantages, and when she was forced to abandon her loom she became an organizer for the Consumers' League, and later a vivid and eloquent power in the suffrage movement.

Her group preceded Miss Paul's by about a week in prison.

These vivid sketches of Rose Winslow's impressions while in the prison hospital were written on tiny scraps of paper and smuggled out to us, and to her husband during her imprisonment. I reprint them in their original form with cuts but no editing.

"If this thing is necessary we will naturally go through with it. Force is so stupid a weapon. I feel so happy doing my bit for decency—for *our* war, which is after all, real and fundamental."

"The women are all so magnificent, so beautiful. Alice Paul is as thin as ever, pale and large-eyed. We have been in solitary for five weeks. There is nothing to tell but that the days go by somehow. I have felt quite feeble the last few days—faint, so that I could hardly get my hair brushed, my arms ached so. But to-day I am well again. Alice Paul and I talk back and forth though we are at opposite ends of the building and a hall door also shuts us apart. But occasionally—thrills—we escape from behind our iron-barred doors and visit. Great laughter and rejoicing!"

[To her husband]

"My fainting probably means nothing except that I am not strong after these weeks. I know you won't be alarmed.

"I told about a syphilitic colored woman with one leg. The other one was cut off, having rotted so that it was alive with maggots when she came in. The remaining one is now getting as bad. They are so short of nurses that a little colored girl of twelve, who is here waiting to have her tonsils removed, waits on her. This child and two others share a ward with a syphilitic child of three or four years, whose mother refused to have it at home. It makes you absolutely ill to see it. I am going to break all three windows as a protest against their confining Alice Paul with these!

"Dr. Gannon is chief of a hospital. Yet Alice Paul and I found we had been taking baths in one of the tubs here, in which this syphilitic child, an incurable, who has his eyes bandaged all the time, is also bathed. He has been here a year. Into the room where he lives came yesterday two children to be operated on for tonsillitis. They also bathed in the same tub. The syphilitic woman has been in that room seven months. Cheerful mixing, isn't it? The place is alive with roaches, crawling all over the walls, everywhere. I found one in my bed the other day. . . ."

"There is great excitement about my two syphilitics. Each nurse is being asked whether she told me. So, as in all institutions where an unsanitary fact is made public, no effort is made to make the wrong itself right. All hands fall to, to find the culprit, who made it known, and he is punished."

"Alice Paul is in the psychopathic ward. She dreaded forcible feeding frightfully, and I hate to think how she must be feeling. I had a nervous time of it, gasping a long time afterward, and my stomach rejecting during the process. I spent a bad, restless night, but otherwise I am all right. The poor soul who fed me got liberally besprinkled during the process. I heard myself making the most hideous sounds. . . . One feels so forsaken when one lies prone and people shove a pipe down one's stomach."

"This morning but for an astounding tiredness, I am all right. I am waiting to see what happens when the President realizes that brutal bullying isn't quite a statesmanlike method for settling a demand for justice at home. At least, if men are supine enough to endure, women—to their eternal glory—are not.

"They took down the boarding from Alice Paul's window yesterday, I heard. It is so delicious about Alice and me. Over in the jail a rumor began that I was considered insane and would be examined. Then came Doctor White, and said he had come to see 'the thyroid case.' When they left we argued about the matter, neither of us knowing which was considered 'suspicious.' She insisted it was she, and, as it happened, she was right. Imagine any one thinking Alice Paul needed to be 'under observation!' The thick-headed idiots!"

"Yesterday was a bad day for me in feeding. I was vomiting continually during the process. The tube has developed an irritation somewhere that is painful.

"Never was there a sentence[8] like ours for such an offense as ours, even in England. No woman ever got it over there even for tearing down buildings. And during all that agitation *we* were busy saying that never would such things happen in the United States. The men told us they would not endure such frightfulness."

"Mary Beard and Helen Todd were allowed to stay only a minute, and I cried like a fool. I am getting over that habit, I think.

"I fainted again last night. I just fell flop over in the bathroom where I was washing my hands and was led to bed when I recovered, by a nurse.

---

8. Sentence of seven months for "obstructing traffic."

I lost consciousness just as I got there again. I felt horribly faint until 12 o'clock, then fell asleep for awhile."

"I was getting frantic because you seemed to think Alice was with me in the hospital. She was in the psychopathic ward. The same doctor feeds us both, and told me. Don't let them tell you we take this well. Miss Paul vomits much. I do, too, except when I'm not nervous, as I have been every time against my will. I try to be less feeble-minded. It's the nervous reaction, and I can't control it much. I don't imagine bathing one's food in tears very good for one.

"We think of the coming feeding all day. It is horrible. The doctor thinks I take it well. I hate the thought of Alice Paul and the others if I take it well."

"We still get no mail; we are 'insubordinate.' It's strange, isn't it; if you ask for food fit to eat, as we did, you are 'insubordinate'; and if you refuse food you are 'insubordinate.' Amusing. I am really all right. If this continues very long I perhaps won't be. I am interested to see how long our so-called 'splendid American men' will stand for this form of discipline.

"All news cheers one marvelously because it is hard to feel anything but a bit desolate and forgotten here in this place.

"All the officers here know we are making this hunger strike that women fighting for liberty may be considered political prisoners; we have told them. God knows we don't want other women ever to have to do this over again."

There have been sporadic and isolated cases of hunger strikes in this country but to my knowledge ours was the first to be organized and sustained over a long period of time. . . .

PART V

CONSCIENTIOUS OBJECTORS, WORLD WAR I

DOCUMENT 13

Jane Addams,
"Personal Reactions During War"

An important opponent of the First World War was Jane Addams (1860–1935).
Best known as the founder of one of America's first settlement houses, Hull
House, Jane Addams also helped to organize the Women's International
League for Peace and Freedom and in 1931 received the Nobel Prize. Her
"Personal Reactions During War" is a moving statement of a liberal driven
to radicalism by persevering in her convictions in time of crisis.

Jane Addams, "Personal Reactions During War," *Peace and Bread in Time of War,*
Chapter VII (Boston: G. K. Hall, 1960), pp. 132–151. Permission has been given to
quote copyrighted material from *Peace and Bread in Time of War,* copyright 1922
by the Macmillan Company, 1945 by the Women's International League for Peace
and Freedom of which Jane Addams was the first international president.

After the United States had entered the war there began to appear great divergence among the many types of pacifists, from the extreme left, composed of non-resistants, through the middle-of-the-road groups, to the extreme right, who could barely be distinguished from mild militarists. There were those people, also, who although they felt keenly both the horror and the futility of war, yet hoped for certain beneficent results from the opportunities afforded by the administration of war; they were much pleased when the government took over the management of the railroads, insisting that governmental ownership had thus been pushed forward by decades; they were also sure that the War Labor Policies Board, the Coal Commission and similar war institutions would make an enormous difference in the development of the country, in short, that militarism might be used as an instrument for advanced social ends. Such justifications had their lure and one found old pacifist friends on all the war boards and even in the war department itself. Certainly we were all eager to accept whatever progressive social changes came from the quick reorganization demanded by war, and doubtless prohibition was one of these, as the granting of woman suffrage in the majority of the belligerent nations, was another. But some of us had suspected that social advance depends as much upon the process through which it is secured as upon the result itself; if railroads are nationalized solely in order to secure rapid transit of ammunition and men to points of departure for Europe, when that governmental need no longer exists what more natural than that the railroads should no longer be managed by the government?

My temperament and habit had always kept me rather in the middle of the road; in politics as well as in social reform I had been for "the best possible." But now I was pushed far toward the left on the subject of the war and I became gradually convinced that in order to make the position of the pacifist clear it was perhaps necessary that at least a small number of us should be forced into an unequivocal position. If I sometimes regretted having gone to the Woman's Congress at The Hague in 1915, or having written a book on Newer Ideals of Peace in 1911 which had made my position so conspicuously clear, certainly far oftener I was devoutly grateful that I had used such unmistakable means of expression before the time came when any spoken or written word in the interests of Peace was forbidden.

It was on my return from The Hague Congress in July, 1915, that I had my first experience of the determination on the part of the press to make pacifist activity or propaganda so absurd that it would be absolutely without influence and its authors so discredited that nothing they might say or do would be regarded as worthy of attention. I had been accustomed to newspaper men for many years and had come to regard them as a good natured fraternity, sometimes ignorant of the subject on which they asked an interview, but usually quite ready to report faithfully albeit somewhat sensationally. Hull-House had several times been the subject of sustained and inspired newspaper attacks, one, the indirect result of an exposure of the inefficient sanitary service in the Chicago Health Department had lasted for many months; I had of course known what it was to serve unpopular causes and throughout a period of campaigning for the Progressive Party I had naturally encountered the "opposition press" in various parts of the country, but this concerted and deliberate attempt at misrepresentation on the part of newspapers on all shades of opinion was quite new in my experience. After the United States entered the war, the press throughout the country systematically undertook to misrepresent and malign pacifists as a recognized part of propaganda and as a patriotic duty. We came to regard this misrepresentation as part of the war technique and in fact an inevitable consequence of war itself, but we were slow in the very beginning to recognize the situation, and I found my first experience which came long before the United States entered the war rather overwhelming.

Upon our return from the Woman's International Congress at The Hague in 1915, our local organization in New York City with others, notably a group of enthusiastic college men, had arranged a large public meeting in Carnegie Hall. Dr. Anna Howard Shaw presided and the United States delegates made a public report of our impressions in "war stricken Europe" and of the moral resources in the various countries we visited that might possibly be brought to bear against a continuation of the war. We had been much impressed with the fact that it was an old man's war, that the various forms of doubt and opposition to war had no method of public expression and that many of the soldiers themselves were far from enthusiastic in regard to actual fighting as a method of settling international difficulties. War was to many of them much more anachronistic than to the elderly statesmen who were primarily responsible for the soldiers' presence in the trenches.

It was the latter statement which was my undoing, for in illustration of it I said that in practically every country we had visited, we had heard a certain type of young soldier say that it had been difficult for him to make the bayonet charge (enter into actual hand to hand fighting) unless he had been stimulated; that the English soldiers had been given rum before such a charge, the Germans ether and that the French were said to use absinthe. To those who heard the address it was quite clear that it was not because the young men flinched at the risk of death but because they had to be inflamed to do the brutal work of the bayonet, such as disembowelling, and were obliged to overcome all the inhibitions of civilization.

Dr. Hamilton and I had notes for each of these statements with the dates and names of the men who had made them, and it did not occur to me that the information was new or startling. I was, however, reported to have said that no soldier could go into a bayonet charge until he was made half drunk, and this in turn was immediately commented upon, notably in a scathing letter written to the New York Times by Richard Harding Davis, as a most choice specimen of a woman's sentimental nonsense. Mr. Davis himself had recently returned from Europe and at once became the defender of the heroic soldiers who were being traduced and belittled. He lent the weight of his name and his very able pen to the cause, but it really needed neither, for the misstatement was repeated, usually with scathing comment, from one end of the country to the other.

I was conscious, of course, that the story had struck athwart the popular and long-cherished conception of the nobility and heroism of the soldier as such, and it seemed to me at the time that there was no possibility of making any explanation, at least until the sensation should have somewhat subsided. I might have repeated my more sober statements with the explanation that whomsoever the pacifist held responsible for war, it was certainly not the young soldiers themselves who were, in a sense, its most touching victims, "the heroic youth of the world whom a common ideal tragically pitted against each other." Youth's response to the appeal made to their self-sacrifice, to their patriotism, to their sense of duty, to their high-hearted hopes for the future, could only stir one's admiration, and we should have been dull indeed had we failed to be moved by this most moving spectacle in the world. That they had so responded to the higher appeals only confirms Ruskin's statement that "we admire the soldier not because he goes forth to slay but to be slain." The fact that many of them were obliged to make a great effort to bear themselves gallantly in the final tests of "war's brutalities" had nothing whatever to do with their courage and sense of devotion. All this, of course, we had realized during our months in Europe.

After the meeting in Carnegie Hall and after an interview with President Wilson in Washington, I returned to Chicago to a public meeting arranged in the Auditorium; I was met at the train by a committee of aldermen appointed as a result of a resolution in the City Council. There was an indefinite feeling that the meeting at The Hague might turn out to be of significance, and that in such an event its chairman should have been honored by her fellow citizens. But the bayonet story had preceded me and every one was filled with great uneasiness. To be sure, a few war correspondents had come to my rescue— writing of the overpowering smell of ether preceding certain German attacks; the fact that English soldiers knew when a bayonet charge was about to be ordered because rations of rum were distributed along the trenches. Some people began to suspect that the story, exaggerated and grotesque as it had become, indicated not cowardice but merely an added sensitiveness which the modern soldier was obliged to overcome. Among the many letters on the subject which filled my mail for weeks, the bitter and abusive were from civilians or from the old men to whom war experiences had become a reminiscence, the larger number and the most understanding ones came from soldiers in active service.

Only once did I try a public explanation. After an address in Chautauqua, New York, in which I had not mentioned bayonets, I tried to remake my original statement to a young man of the associated press only to find it once more so garbled that I gave up in despair, quite unmoved by the young man's letter of apology which followed hard upon the published report of his interview.

I will confess that the mass psychology of the situation interested me even then and continued to do so until I fell ill with a serious attack of pleuro-pneumonia, which was the beginning of three years of semi-invalidism. During weeks of feverish discomfort I experienced a bald sense of social opprobrium and wide-spread misunderstanding which brought me very near to self pity, perhaps the lowest pit into which human nature can sink. Indeed the pacifist in war time, with his precious cause in the keeping of those who control the sources of publicity and consider it a patriotic duty to make all types of peace propaganda obnoxious, constantly faces two dangers. Strangely enough he finds it possible to travel from the mire of self pity straight to the barren hills of self-righteousness and to hate himself equally in both places.

From the very beginning of the great war, as the members of our group gradually became defined from the rest of the community, each one felt increasingly the sense of isolation which rapidly developed after the United States entered the war into that destroying effect of "aloneness," if I may so describe the opposite of mass consciousness. We never ceased to miss the unquestioning comradeship experienced by our fellow citizens during the war, nor to feel curiously outside the enchantment given to any human emotion when it is shared by millions of others. The force of the majority was so overwhelming that it seemed not only impossible to hold one's own against it, but at moments absolutely unnatural, and one secretly yearned to participate in "the folly of all mankind." Our modern democratic teaching has brought us to regard popular impulses as possessing in their general tendency a valuable capacity for evolutionary development. In the hours of doubt and self-distrust the question again and again arises, has the individual or a very small group, the right to stand out against millions of his fellow countrymen? Is there not a great value in mass judgment and in instinctive mass enthusiasm, and even if one were right a thousand times over in convic-tion, was he not absolutely wrong in abstaining from this communion with his fellows? The misunderstanding on the part of old friends and associates and the charge of lack of patriotism was far easier to bear than those dark periods of faint-heartedness. We gradually ceased to state our position as we became convinced that it served no practical purpose and, worse than that, often found that the immediate result was provocative.

We could not, however, lose the conviction that as all other forms of growth begin with a variation from the mass, so the moral changes in human affairs may also begin with a differing group or individual, sometimes with the one who at best is designated as a crank and a freak and in sterner moments is imprisoned as an atheist or a traitor. Just when the differing individual becomes the centro-egotist, the insane man, who must be thrown out by society for its own protection, it is impossible to state. The pacifist was constantly brought sharply up against a genuine human trait with its biological basis, a trait founded upon the instinct to dislike, to distrust and finally to destroy the individual who differs from the mass in time of danger. Regarding this trait as the basis of self-preservation it becomes perfectly natural for the mass to call such an individual a traitor and to insist that if he is not for the nation he is against it. To this an estimated nine million people can bear witness who have been burned as witches and heretics, not by mobs, for of the people who have been "lynched" no record has been kept, but by order of ecclesiastical and civil courts.

There were moments when the pacifist yielded to the suggestion that keeping himself out of war, refusing to take part in its enthusiasms, was but pure quietism, an acute failure to adjust himself to the moral world. Certainly nothing was clearer than that the individual will was helpless and irrelevant. We were constantly told by our friends that to stand aside from the war mood of the country was to surrender all possibility of future influence, that we were committing intellectual suicide, and would never again be trusted as responsible people or judicious advisers. Who were we to differ with able statesmen, with men of sensitive conscience who also absolutely abhorred war, but were convinced that this war for the preservation of democracy would make all future wars impossible, that the priceless values of civilization which were at stake could at this moment be saved only by war? But these very dogmatic statements spurred one to alarm. Was not war in the interest of democracy for the salvation of civilization a contradiction of terms, whoever said it or however often it was repeated?

Then, too, we were always afraid of fanaticism, of preferring a consistency of theory to the conscientious recognition of the social situation, of a failure to meet life in the temper of a practical person. Every student of our time had become more or less a disciple of pragmatism, and its great teachers in the United States had come out for the war and defended their positions with skill and philosophic acumen. There were moments when one longed desperately for reconciliation with one's friends and fellow citizens; in the words of Amiel, "Not to remain at variance with existence but to reach that understanding of life which enables us at least to obtain forgiveness." Solitude has always had its demons, harder to withstand than the snares of the world, and the unnatural desert into which the pacifist was summarily cast out seemed to be peopled with them. We sorely missed the contagion of mental activity, for we are all much more dependent upon our social environment and daily newspaper than perhaps any of us realize. We also doubtless encountered, although subconsciously, the temptations described by John Stuart Mill: "In respect to the persons and affairs of their own day, men insensibly adopt the modes of feeling and judgment in which they can hope for sympathy from the company they keep."

The consciousness of spiritual alienation was lost only in moments of comradeship with the like minded, which may explain the tendency of the pacifist in war time to seek his intellectual kin, his spiritual friends, wherever they might be found in his own country or abroad.

It was inevitable that in many respects the peace cause should suffer in public opinion from the efforts of groups of people who, early in the war, were convinced that the country as a whole was for peace and who tried again and again to discover a method for arousing and formulating the sentiment against war. I was ill and out of Chicago when the People's Council held a national convention there, which was protected by the city police but threatened with dispersion by the state troops, who, however, arrived from the capital several hours after the meeting had adjourned. The incident was most sensational and no one was more surprised than many of the members of the People's Council who thus early in the war had supposed that they were conducting a perfectly legitimate convention. The incident gave tremendous "copy" in a city needing rationalizing rather than sensationalizing at that moment. There is no doubt that the shock and terror of the "anarchist riots" occurring in Chicago years ago have left their traces upon the nervous system of the city somewhat as a nervous shock experienced in youth will long afterwards determine the action of a mature man under widely different circumstances.

On the whole, the New York groups were much more active and throughout the war were allowed much more freedom both of assembly and press, although later a severe reaction followed expressed through the Lusk Committee and other agencies. Certainly neither city approximated the freedom of London and nothing surprised me more in 1915 and again in 1919 than the freedom of speech permitted there.

We also read with a curious eagerness the steadily increasing number of books published from time to time during the war, which brought a renewal of one's faith or at least a touch of comfort. These books broke through that twisting and suppressing of awkward truths, which was encouraged and at times even ordered by the censorship. Such manipulation of news and motives was doubtless necessary in the interest of war propaganda if the people were to be kept in a fighting mood. Perhaps the most vivid books came from France, early from Romain Rolland, later from Barbusse, although it was interesting to see how many people took the latter's burning indictment of war merely as a further incitement against the enemy. On the scientific side were the frequent writings of David Starr Jordan and the remarkable book of Nicolai on "The Biology of War." The latter enabled one, at least in one's own mind, to refute the pseudo-scientific statement that war was valuable in securing the survival of the fittest. Nicolai insisted that primitive man must necessarily have been a peaceful and social animal and that he developed his intelligence through the use of the tool, not through the use of the weapon; it was the primeval community which made the evolution of man possible, and coöperation among men is older and more primitive than mass combat which is an outgrowth of the much later property instinct. No other species save ants, who also possess property, fights in masses against other masses of its own kind. War is in fact not a natural process and not a struggle for existence in the evolutionary sense. He illustrated the evolutionary survival of the fittest by two tigers inhabiting the same jungle or feeding ground, the one who has the greater skill and strength as a hunter survives and the other starves, but the strong one does not go out to kill the weak one, as the war propagandist implied; or by two varieties of mice living in the same field or barn; in the biological struggle, the variety which grows a thicker coat survives the winter while the other variety freezes to extinction, but if one variety of mice should go forth to kill the other, it would be absolutely abnormal and quite outside the evolutionary survival which is based on the adjustment of the organism to its environment. George Nasmyth's book on Darwinism and the Social Order was another clear statement of the mental confusion responsible for the insistence that even a biological progress is secured through war. Mr. Brailsford wrote constantly on the economic results of the war and we got much comfort from John Hobson's "Toward International Government," which gave an authoritative account of the enormous amount of human activity actually carried on through international organizations of all sorts, many of them under governmental control. Lowes Dickenson's books, especially the spirited challenge in "The Choice Before Us," left his readers with the distinct impression that "war is not inevitable but proceeds from definite and removable causes." From every such book the pacifist was forced to the conclusion that none save those interested in the realization of an idea are in a position to bring it about and that if one found himself the unhappy possessor of an unpopular conviction, there was nothing for it but to think as clearly as he was able and be in a position to serve his country as soon as it was possible for him to do so.

But with or without the help of good books a hideous sensitiveness remained, for the pacifist, like the rest of the world, has developed a high degree of suggestibility, sharing that consciousness of the feelings, the opinions and the customs of his own social group which is said to be an inheritance from an almost pre-human past. An instinct which once enabled the man-pack to survive when it was a question of keeping together or of perishing off the face of the earth, is perhaps not underdeveloped in any of us. There is a distinct physical as well as moral strain when this instinct is steadily suppressed or at least ignored.

The large number of deaths among the older pacifists in all the warring nations can probably be traced in some measure to the peculiar strain which such maladjustment implies. More than the normal amount of nervous energy must be consumed in holding one's own in a hostile world. These older men, Kier Hardie and Lord Courtney in England, Jenkin Lloyd Jones, Rauchen-busch, Washington Gladden in the United States, Lammasch and Fried in Austria, had been honored by their fellow citizens because of marked ability to interpret and understand them. Suddenly to find every public utterance wilfully misconstrued, every attempt at normal relationship repudiated, must react in a baffled suppression which is health-destroying even if we do not accept the mechanistic explanation of the human system. Certainly by the end of the war we were able to understand, although our group certainly did not endorse the statement of Cobden, one of the most convinced of all internationalists: "I made up my mind during the Crimean War that if ever I lived in the time of another great war of a similar kind between England

and another power, I would not as a public man open my mouth on the subject, so convinced am I that appeals to reason, conscience or interest have no force whatever on parties engaged in war, and that exhaustion on one or both sides can alone bring a contest of physical force to an end."

On the other hand there were many times when we stubbornly asked ourselves, what after all, has maintained the human race on this old globe despite all the calamities of nature and all the tragic failings of mankind, if not faith in new possibilities, and courage to advocate them. Doubtless many times these new possibilities were declared by a man who, quite unconscious of courage, bore the "sense of being an exile, a condemned criminal, a fugitive from mankind." Did every one so feel who, in order to travel on his own proper path had been obliged to leave the traditional highway? The pacifist, during the period of the war could answer none of these questions but he was sick at heart from causes which to him were hidden and impossible to analyze. He was at times devoured by a veritable dissatisfaction with life. Was he thus bearing his share of blood-guiltiness, the morbid sense of contradiction and inexplicable suicide which modern war implies? We certainly had none of the internal contentment of the doctrinnaire, the ineffable solace of the self-righteous which was imputed to us. No one knew better than we how feeble and futile we were against the impregnable weight of public opinion, the appalling imperviousness, the coagulation of motives, the universal confusion of a world at war. There was scant solace to be found in this type of statement: "The worth of every conviction consists precisely in the steadfastness with which it is held," perhaps because we suffered from the fact that we were no longer living in a period of dogma and were therefore in no position to announce our sense of security! We were well aware that the modern liberal having come to conceive truth of a kind which must vindicate itself in practice, finds it hard to hold even a sincere and mature opinion which from the very nature of things can have no justification in works. The pacifist in war time is literally starved of any gratification of that natural desire to have his own decisions justified by his fellows.

That, perhaps, was the crux of the situation. We slowly became aware that our affirmation was regarded as pure dogma. We were thrust into the position of the doctrinnaire, and although, had we been permitted, we might have cited both historic and scientific tests of our so-called doctrine of Peace, for the moment any sanction even by way of illustration was impossible.

It therefore came about that ability to hold out against mass suggestion, to honestly differ from the convictions and enthusiasms of one's best friends did in moments of crisis come to depend upon the categorical belief that a man's primary allegiance is to his vision of the truth and that he is under obligation to affirm it.

DOCUMENT 14

Roger Baldwin and Others, Statements of Conscientious Objection, 1917–1918

Of the approximately 4,000 persons who persisted in their conscientious objection to World War I, some 1,300 eventually entered noncombatant military service, a similar number were given furloughs to do farm work, about 100 were assigned to Quaker war relief work in France, and 500 were court-martialed and sentenced to prison (Mulford Q. Sibley and Philip E. Jacob, Conscription of Conscience: The American State and the Conscientious Objector, 1940–1947 *[Ithaca: Cornell University Press, 1952], p. 14, and Walter Guest Kellogg,* The Conscientious Objector *[New York: Boni and Liveright, 1919], p. 127, citing figures reported by the Adjutant General's Office, Dec. 24, 1918). Seventeen persons were sentenced to death. None of the death sentences were actually carried out, and in 1933 President Roosevelt pardoned all those still in prison. But at least seventeen objectors died in jail as a direct consequence of torture or barbaric prison conditions (Stephen M. Kohn,* Jailed for Peace: The History of American Draft Law Violations, 1658–1985 *[Westport, CT: Greenwood Press, 1986], pp. 29, 42 [listing the names of those who died]). The statements of conscientious objectors that follow illustrate the variety of their motives. The political objector, Carl Haessler, and the religious objector, Maurice Hess, were or became college professors; Roger Baldwin was then director of the Civil Liberties Bureau and later became president of the American Civil Liberties Union.*

From Norman Thomas, *The Conscientious Objector in America* (New York: B. W. Huebsch, 1923), pp. 23–28. Reprinted with the permission of Norman Thomas.

I [Carl Haessler]

I, Carl Haessler, Recruit, Machine Gun Company, 46th Infantry, respectfully submit the following statement in extenuation in connection with my proposed plea of guilty to the charge of violation of the 64th Article of War, the offense having been committed June 22, 1918, in Camp Sheridan, Ala.

The offense was not committed from private, secret, personal, impulsive, religious, pacifist or pro-German grounds. An admixture of quasi-personal motives is admitted, but they were in no sense the guiding or controlling factors. I have evidence for each of these assertions, should it be required.

The willful disobedience of my Captain's and of my Lieutenant-Colonel's orders to report in military uniform arose from a conviction which I hesitate to express before my country's military officers but which I nevertheless am at present unable to shake off, namely, that America's participation in the World War was unnecessary, of doubtful benefit (if any) to the country and to humanity, and accomplished largely, though not exclusively, through the pressure of the Allied and American commercial imperialists.

Holding this conviction, I conceived my part as a citizen to be opposition to the war before it was declared, active efforts for a peace without victory after the declaration, and a determination so far as possible to do nothing in aid of the war while its character seemed to remain what I thought it was. I hoped in this way to help bring the war to an earlier close and to help make similar future wars less probable in this country.

I further believe that I shall be rendering the country a service by helping to set an example for other citizens to follow in the matter of fearlessly acting on unpopular convictions instead of forgetting them in time of stress. The crumbling of American radicalism under pressure in 1917 has only been equalled by that of the majority of German socialist leaders in August, 1914.

Looking at my case from the point of view of the administration and of this court, I readily admit the necessity of exemplary punishment. I regret that I have been forced to make myself a nuisance and I grant that this war could not be carried on if objections like mine were recognized by those conducting the war. My respect for the administration has been greatly increased by the courteous and forbearing treatment accorded me since having been drafted, but my view of international politics and diplomacy, acquired during my three years of graduate study in England, has not altered since June, 1917, when I formally declared that I could not accept service if drafted. Although officers have on three occasions offered me noncombatant service if I would put on the uniform, I have regretfully refused each time on the ground that "bomb-proof" service on my part would give the lie to my sincerity (which was freely granted by Judge Julian Mack when he and his colleagues examined me at Camp Gordon). If I am to render any war services, I shall not ask for special privileges.

I wish to conclude this long statement by reiterating that I am not a pacifist or pro-German, not a religious or private objector, but regard myself as a patriotic political objector, acting largely from public and social grounds.

I regret that, while my present view of this war continues, I cannot freely render any service in aid of the war. I shall not complain about the punishment that this court may see fit to mete out to me.

II [Maurice Hess]

I do not believe that I am seeking martyrdom. As a young man, life and its hopes and freedom and opportunities for service are sweet to me. I want to go out into the world and make use of what little talent I may have acquired by long and laborious study.

But I know that I dare not purchase these things at the price of eternal condemnation. I know the teaching of Christ, my Savior. He taught us to resist not evil, to love our enemies, to bless them that curse us, and do good to them that hate us. Not only did he teach this, but he also practiced it in Gethsemane, before Pilate, and on Calvary. We would indeed be hypocrites and base traitors to our profession if we would be unwilling to bear the taunts and jeers of a sinful world, and its imprisonment, and torture or death, rather than to participate in war and military service. We know that obedience to Christ will gain for us the glorious prize of eternal life. We cannot yield, we cannot compromise, we must suffer.

Two centuries ago our people were driven out of Germany by religious persecution, and they accepted the invitation of William Penn to come to his colony where they might enjoy the blessing of religious liberty which he promised them. This religious liberty was later confirmed by the Constitution of Pennsylvania, and the Constitution of the United States.

If the authorities now see fit to change those fundamental documents and take away our privilege of living in accordance with the teaching of the scriptures of God, then we have no course but to endure persecution as true soldiers of Christ.

If I have committed anything worthy of bonds or death, I do not refuse to suffer or to die.

I pray God for strength to remain faithful.

III [Roger N. Baldwin]

The compelling motive for refusing to comply with the draft act is my uncompromising opposition to the principle of conscription of life by the state for any purpose whatever, in time of war or peace. I not only refuse to obey the present conscription law, but I would in future refuse to obey any similar statute which attempts to direct my choice of service and ideals. I regard the principle of conscription of life as a flat contradiction of all our cherished ideals of individual freedom, democratic liberty, and Christian teaching.

I am the more opposed to the present act, because it is for the purpose of conducting war. I am opposed to this and all other wars. I do not believe in the use of physical force as a method of achieving any end, however good. . . .

I am not complaining for myself or others. I am merely advising the court that I understand full well the penalty of my heresy, and am prepared to pay it. The conflict with conscription is irreconcilable. Even the liberalism of the President and Secretary of War in dealing with objectors leads those of us who are "absolutists" to a punishment longer and severer than that of desperate criminals.

But I believe most of us are prepared even to die for our faith, just as our brothers in France are dying for theirs. To them we are comrades in spirit—we understand one another's motives, though our methods are wide apart. We both share deeply the common experience of living up to the truth as we see it, whatever the price.

Though at the moment I am of a tiny minority, I feel myself just one protest in a great revolt surging up from among the people—the struggle of the masses against the rule of the world by the few—profoundly intensified by the war. It is a struggle against the political state itself, against exploitation, militarism, imperialism, authority in all forms. . . .

Having arrived at the state of mind in which those views mean the dearest things in life to me, I cannot consistently, with self-respect, do other than I have, namely, to deliberately violate an act which seems to me to be a denial of everything which ideally and in practice I hold sacred.

DOCUMENT 15

Prisoners for Peace

Ammon Hennacy opposed World War I as a socialist but was converted to Christian pacifism while in prison. Later he became a leader of the Catholic Worker movement, founded in 1933 by Peter Maurin and Dorothy Day (see Document 37).

Among those mistreated because of their refusal to serve in the armed forces were four members of the Hutterite church, David, Michael, and Joseph Hofer, and Joseph Wipf. They were drafted into the army against their will, and, upon their refusal to cooperate, were court-martialed and imprisoned. Joseph and Michael Hofer died.

Resisters during World War I started a tradition of prison protest campaigns and strikes by conscientious objectors. According to Stephen M. Kohn, Jailed for Peace: The History of American Draft Law Violations, 1658–1985 *(Westport, CT: Greenwood Press, 1986), p. 33: "Small nonviolent prison strikes and protest actions occurred at a scattering of prison camps during the war. But serious trouble unfolded when the vast majority of COs were collected from around the country and herded into the Fort Leavenworth 'concentration camp' in November 1918." Kohn's account of the Fort Leavenworth general strike is based primarily on an article in* Survey, *February 15, 1919, by a reporter who witnessed the event.*

A.   Ammon Hennacy, "Atlanta Prison—1917"

I was arrested when I spoke against the coming war at Broad and High in Columbus, Ohio before about 10,000 people on the evening of April 5, 1917. The next day war was declared and I was released for trial May 30. Meanwhile I distributed leaflets over Ohio for the Socialist Party, advising young men to refuse to register for the draft. When I was picked up again I asked to see a lawyer but was told I could not see one. Detective Wilson said that unless I registered for the draft by June 5th, which was registration day, I was to be shot on orders from Washington. I was shown a copy of the local paper with headlines "Extreme Penalty for Traitors." I only saw it through the bars and was not allowed to read it. The detective said that the young Socialists arrested with me for refusing to register had all given in and registered. (Later I found out that he had also told them that I had registered.) I felt that if they gave in someone had to stick, and I was that one. Spike Moore, an I.W.W., the radical union of that day: the Industrial Workers of the World, founded by Debs, Haywood and others, from Pittsburgh who was in Columbus, sneaked me a note and a clipping from the paper in which a reporter asked my mother if she was not frightened because I was to be shot soon. Her reply was that the

---

From *Two Agitators: Peter Maurin—Ammon Hennacy,* ed. Ammon Hennacy (New York: *The Catholic Worker,* 1959), pp. 6–19. Reprinted with the permission of *The Catholic Worker.*

only thing she was afraid of was that they might scare me to give in. This gave me added courage. June 5th passed and no move was made to shoot me. Detective Wilson said that the Government had postponed my execution thinking I would give the names of those who had helped me distribute the leaflets. I pled guilty for my refusal to register. My partner and I each got 2 years in Atlanta. After this term was served I was to do 9 months in Delaware, Ohio County Jail nearby for refusal to register. The two guards who accompanied us to Atlanta chained us to our Pullman berths and gave us sandwiches prepared by their women folks, kidding us that they were marking up good meals on their expense accounts.

Friday, July 3, 1917 was the date of my arrival in Atlanta. My number was 7438. I was sent to the top floor of the old cell house, to a certain cell. This was occupied by someone else it seemed, for pictures of chorus girls were on the wall, and magazines and cigarette stubs on the floor. This cell was 8 feet long, 8 feet high, and $4^1/_2$ feet wide and was made of steel. In half an hour a large, burly, but good natured man of about 40 came in.

"Hello kid, my name's Brockman, Peter Brockman from Buffalo, doin' a six bit for writing my name on little pieces of paper. Got one to go yet. How do you like our little home? What's your name?"

The next morning after breakfast, Blackie, the runner in the block, brought me a note, saying that he knew the prisoner who had written the note, and had done time with him in Alleghaney prison years ago. I read:

"Blackie, who gave you this note is o.k. See me in the yard this afternoon if it does not rain; otherwise come to the Catholic Mass tomorrow and I will talk to you there. Your cell mate has paid $5 worth of tobacco to the screw in your cell block to get the first young prisoner coming in to be his cell mate. You are the 'lucky' one. Watch him, for he is one of the worst perverts in the prison. There is no use making a fuss for you may 'accidentally' fall down four tiers. Get $5 worth of tobacco from the store and give it to Blackie and he will give it to the guard and pull strings to have you transferred out of the cell. This will take weeks; meantime get along the best you can.

Yours for the revolution, A. B."

A note from Alexander Berkman, the great Anarchist! I read it over and over again and then destroyed it, per the first rule in prison: don't keep any unnecessary contraband. For the first time in my life when I had read a book I had sat down at once and written to the author. This was in Warren, Ohio, in 1916, when I had read Berkman's *Memoirs*. I did not get an answer, but now I was to meet him personally. Hundreds of workers had been killed by the Pinkertons, a notorious detective agency, at Homestead, Pa. Frick was manager of Carnegie Steel at Homestead. Berkman, then a young anarchist, had stabbed and shot Frick, and had done 14 years and ten months actual time in Alleghaney prison, $3^1/_2$ years of this in solitary in a dark hole. He had been in prison before I was born and here he was again with a fighting spirit that jails could not kill. I had read his paper *The Blast*. I had but a faint idea of the word pervert, and I wondered how and why I could talk to Berkman in a Catholic chapel.

The sun shone brightly that afternoon on the packed ground of the prison yard. In the shadow along one prison wall Blackie had pointed out Berkman to me. I hastened to greet him. His kindly smile made me feel that I had a friend. He told me of a means of getting out letters, *sub rosa,* and explained how to talk in your throat without moving your lips. He said that on rainy Saturdays, when we could not meet, we could see each other at the Catholic chapel, as the chaplain was an ex-prizefighter who was sympathetic to workers and did not mind those who came to visit each other. He gave me four things to remember. "(1) Don't tell a lie. (2) Don't tell on another prisoner; it's the job of the screws to find out what is going on, not yours. (3) Draw your line as to what you will do and will not do and don't budge, for if you begin to weaken they will beat you. (4) Don't curse the guards. They will try to get you to strike them and they will have the excuse to beat you up; and if one can't, two can; and if two can't, ten can. They are no good or they wouldn't take such a job. Just smile. Obey them in unimportant details but never budge an inch on principle. Don't be seen talking to me very often, for the guards are watching and will make trouble. Write to me by way of Blackie and I will do the same."

John, in my cell, was boss of the paint gang and was from Columbus, Ohio. He had me transferred to his gang, and when he left in about six months I was made boss of the gang. I had a pass to go anywhere I wanted inside the prison. The editor of the prison paper, *Good Words,* asked me to give him something to print. I told him that was what I got in for, printing things in papers, and that my ideas were too radical for him. He insisted so I gave this quote which, believe it or not, appeared in a box underneath the editorial caption of the Department of Justice on April 1, 1918: "*A prison is the only house in a slave state where a free man can abide with honor.*" Thoreau. This had the o.k. of the warden and was not sneaked in. The ignorant official thought it praised prisons. *The Conservator,* edited by the radical Horace Traubel, literary executor of Walt Whitman, was allowed in because they thought it was conservative. The *Irish World* which was much against the war came to the Catholic chaplain and he got copies to us radicals through John Dunn, a conscientious objector and Catholic, from Providence, R.I., who was boss of the plumbing gang.

The conscientious objectors were scattered in different gangs and cell houses over the prison. The warden told me that the orders from Washington were to put us all in one place, but he knew better and scattered us out, for if we were in one place we would plot. This reminded me of the farmer who caught the ground-mole and said, "Hanging's too good; burning's too good; I'll bury you alive." So we conscientious objectors were scattered around where we could do propaganda instead of being segregated where we would argue among ourselves. John Dunn and I were good friends. His number was 7979 and he got 20 years. After his release he studied for the priesthood and is now a priest in Portsmouth, Ohio, and a reader of the *Catholic Worker*. Paul was a young, Russian born Socialist who had quit a good job to come to prison. Morris was a quiet, very short Russian Jewish anarchist, whom I met often at the vegetarian diet table. Louis was just the opposite; an erratic boisterous Nietzschean who felt that everything that you had was his and what he had was his own. Morris was deported at the same time as Emma Goldman and Alexander Berkman, after the war. Louis after many years came to an appreciation of God, but finally committed suicide. Tony was a Russian who did not speak English, but whose quiet manner marked him as some kind of a religious sectarian. Walter was a college man who came from an old anarchist family, and who had despised his father's ideas until the crisis of war brought him to prison. His partner was John, a seaman who belonged to the I.W.W. maritime branch. He had been banished from Australia as a radical, and had refused to register for the draft. Theodore and Adolph were young Socialists from Rhode Island who were enthusiastic and helpful in any prison rebellion. Gilbert was an Italian I.W.W. who spoke little English. He worked in the stone gang. I never met him personally; we just smiled from a distance. Al and Fred were two older comrades who had unwittingly been sent to prison. They were not left wingers, but were in official position in the Socialist Party, where the extreme conservatism of their communities made them martyrs. They were not active in any plans that we younger rebels formed. Francisco was the only local comrade from Atlanta in prison against the war; he was a Puerto Rican and had the advantage of his family coming to see him often. The young Hollander from Vermont was not a radical in the accepted sense of the term; he simply refused to fight against relatives who were in the German army. Fritz was a young Russian Socialist who was also quiet, but who went along with us in any of our plans.

The Russelites came along later when I was in solitary and I never saw any of them. Their leader Judge Rutherford was with them and they came to be called Jehovah's Witnesses. Nicholas, the Mexican, was dying of tuberculosis. I only saw him from a distance for he lived by himself in a tent the year around. He was a Mexican revolutionist. Two Negro objectors from some Holiness sect in the Carolinas would not mix with us. I sent candy to them but they did not respond. We were not religious and I suppose we shocked them. My especial friend was William McCoy of the McCoy-Hatfield feudists in Kentucky. He claimed to have killed six Hatfields. He could not write and I wrote his letters home for him. He had started out with Phillips, a friend, to shoot up the government when he heard that a war was on. The warden told me he was afraid of him.

Before the transfer had come through for my work on the paint gang I had worked with hundreds of others on the construction gang, wheeling "Georgia buggies," a slang for wheel-barrows, full of concrete mixture and pouring it into the foundation walls for a mill to make duck for mail sacks. There were about 80 of us in a line. The platforms had been built in such a way that we had to make a mighty run to get to the top. Complaining did no good. So John, the "wob" from Australia and I took turns slowing up the line; stopping to tie a shoe lace, to look intently at the wheel as if something was wrong with it, etc. About the time one of us would have the whole line waiting he would behave and the other one would take up the sabotage action. One afternoon of this and the boss took the hint and made the runways like they should have been in the first place. . . .

. . . A white man and a Negro had been killed by guards and I was incensed about it. My cell mates laughed and said I should worry about the living, for the dead were dead and no one could do anything about it. That if I wanted anything to do I should raise a fuss about the poor fish served on Fridays by the new mess guard, who was accused of making his rake-off by charging for good food and giving us junk. Accordingly I got cardboard from John Dunn and painted signs which I put up in all of the toilets around the place telling the prisoners to work on Fridays, but to stay in their cells and refuse to go to dinner or to eat the rotten fish. The guards and stoolpigeons tore the signs down, but I made others and put them up. The first Friday 20 of us stayed in our cells. The guards came around and asked us if we were sick. We said we were sick of that damn fish. The next Friday 200 stayed in their cells; and the next Friday 600. That was too many people thinking alike, so on the next Thursday the warden came to the second mess and said that those who did not come to dinner the next day would be put in the hole. Some kid squeaked out in a shrill voice: "You can't do it warden; there's only 40 solitary cells and there's a thousand of us." The next day 900 out of the 1,100 who ate at this shift stayed in their cells.

The next Monday I was called to the office and was told that I had been seen plotting to blow up the prison with dynamite, and was promptly sent to the dark hole. This was on June 21, 1918. I was left in my underwear, and lying in the small, three cornered, dark hole. I got a slice of cornbread and a cup of water each day. I kept a count of the days as I heard the men marching to work, and at the end of ten days I was put in the light hole. White bread, which I got then, tasted like cake. This cell was on the ground floor, back of the deputy's office. It was about 18 feet long, 15 feet high, and 6 feet wide. A small dirty window near the top to the east faced a tall building, which kept sunlight from coming in, except on very bright days. A bunk was attached to the wall to the right; a plain chair and a small table, with a spoon, plate, and cup on it. There was a toilet; and a wash basin attached to the wall. A small 20 watt light was screwed in the high ceiling and was turned off and on from the outside. There was a door of bars and an extra wooden door with a funnel shaped peephole through which guards could watch me at any time. I walked around examining my new home. The cell was exactly $8\frac{1}{2}$ steps from corner to corner. The walls were dirty, and initials and home made calendars with days crossed off had been left by former inmates.

After the dark hole this cell was a relief. A Negro lifer brought in meals, three times a day, and ladled grits, beans, raisins, etc. out of a large bucket onto my plate, while Johnson, the fat guard, stood at the door. The Negro found out that I did not eat meat and he always grabbed my portion. Perhaps this helped him in his favorable attitude toward me, for he gave me notes and candy from Berkman and Dunn, and took my notes in return. The first morning I said "hello" to the guard, but he did not answer me; after a few days of silence on his part I ceased to bother him with a greeting.

When I had first come to prison I had met the Protestant chaplain. My red-headed cousin Georgia, who was his daughter-in-law, had told him about me. He wanted to know what church I belonged to, and when I told him I was an atheist he would have nothing to do with me, even when I was in solitary. Catholics were taken care of by the priest and the Protestant had all the rest, so I sent a note to him for a Bible to read in solitary, for I was not allowed anything else, or to send or receive mail. After a few weeks a Bible with good print and maps and references in the back was sent to me. After a few days this was taken away and one with very small print and no maps was given to me in its place. I asked Johnson, the guard, why I was given a Bible with small print, as this was more difficult to read with the small light 15 feet above me, and he simply grunted. The colored trusty later spoke, down in his throat without moving his lips, in the manner we all learned, and told me that anything was done which would make it more difficult for those in solitary. I do not think that the chaplain had anything to do with this; probably the deputy or the guard took this means of teasing one of their caged animals. You hear the groans of fellow prisoners and when you do not know how many months you may remain in solitary you have a weight over you that precludes any joyfulness of spirit.

Here is the way my day went in solitary:

I hear the six o'clock gong ring for the early mess. I know at 7:20 I will get my mush. I am not sleepy, but I stretch out and relax. In a minute I wash and pull on my few articles of clothing. I pick up my chair and swing it thirty times—up-right-left-down; up-right-left-down. Then I walk 100 steps back and forth in my cell—arms-up-arms-out-arms-clenched-arms-down, as I walk back and forth. This I repeat several times. It is now 7 o'clock. I make my bed and then wash my face and hands again. Then I hear the clanging of the door and I know that breakfast is on the way. I hear the doors open and shut and the jangling of the keys and the rattling of utensils. I sit and watch the door like a cat watching a mouse. The shadows of the guard and the Negro trusty lengthen under my door; the key turns in the lock; the wooden door opens and Johnson, the fat guard, stands back after he has opened the iron barred door. The Negro steps in and ladles out my oatmeal, hands me a couple slices of bread, and pours out a large cup of coffee. Today he has no note for me; tomorrow he may have one. He smiles to me as he turns his back to Johnson and I smile in return. I look up at Johnson but he scowls; no fraternizing it seems. The trusty leaves and the doors are locked. I am not very hungry, and I prolong the breakfast as much as possible to take up my time. At last the food is gone. I leisurely wash the dishes and dry them. Perhaps I spin my plate a dozen times, and see how long I can count before it falls to the floor off the table. I lean back in my chair and think of Selma, my girl in Milwaukee, and of my folks at home. Then I realize that I am within these four walls: a jail in a jail. I walk back and forth for 5 or 10 minutes and then throw myself on my bunk; take off my shoes and hunch up on my bunk. In a few minutes I am restless and turn on my side. I hear the men marching to work and stand near the outer wall hoping to hear a word or two but I only hear mumbled voices and the shouts of the guards. I hear the whistle of the train in the distance. I kneel by the door and strain my eyes seeking to discern someone in the tailor shop on the second floor next door, but everything is a blur. I walk around the walls reading the poetry I have written on the wall and all the inscriptions others have engraved.

I try to figure out what the possible history of this or that initial may mean, but soon give it up as waste time. I hear the voice of the deputy in the hall greeting the guard in charge. It is now 9 a.m. and according to my schedule, time to read the Bible. I lie on my bunk for half an hour reading the chapter for that morning. Then I sit on the toilet and take my pencil which I found the first day hidden in a small crack in the plaster, back of the toilet. A pencil is precious, you either have one or you don't. The toilet is near the door and the only place in the cell where a full view of the occupant cannot be gained through the peephole. I do not want to be caught with my precious pencil. I place the toilet paper on which I have written my notes in the Bible and sit on my chair and study what I have written. Then I return to the toilet seat and write some conclusions. Then I lie on my bunk and with my eyes closed think over what I have read.

I try to sleep for half an hour but become restless and walk back and forth in my cell for a mile and a half and take my exercises. I spin my plate again. I look up to the dirty window many times but can see nothing. For fifteen minutes I look steadily, after I have noticed a bird flying near the window, hoping that it may return. But why should a bird stop by my dusty window? It is now 11:15 and the guards are outside watching the men enter for the first mess. I feel that this is the opportune time to write a few words, which I have not finished, on the wall. I sharpen my spoon on the floor and stealthily carve two letters when I hear a step in the hall and cease my carving. I walk aimlessly around my cell for fifteen minutes and then sit and wait for the door to open for my dinner. Beans, oleo, bread and coffee. I eat the beans carefully, for often I break my teeth from biting against the stones which are included in the beans. I again wash my dishes leisurely, rest on my bunk for half an hour, then become restless again and walk to and fro for a mile or two. I read for an hour as the afternoon passes slowly. Then make notes and think about the subject matter for a time. I hear the train at 2 p.m. I am tired of thinking and tired of exercising. I again walk aimlessly about my cell, examining the walls. Perhaps I take some toilet paper, wet it, and wash a section of the wall to see if there is a message written underneath the grime; perhaps I figure out a calendar six months ahead to discover on what day of the week Selma's birthday occurs.

I think again of those on the outside and of the radical movement. An hour passes by in this manner and I try to sleep for half an hour but turn from one side to the other. I hear Popoff rattle his chains and groan in the next cell. He is a Bulgarian, a counterfeiter. He invented some kind of a gun and offered the plans to the War Department but they never answered him. He does not speak English and did not explain his sickness to the doctor so it could be understood at once, and was put into solitary for faking. He had sent a poem to the prison paper and this was sent back. He sassed the guards and was beaten up. What with all this he thought if he knocked the deputy warden down someone would then come from Washington and then he could tell them about his invention. He struck harder than he thought and the deputy died. He got life imprisonment, but it was not supposed to be hanging by his wrists from the bars. He was not a pacifist or a radical, and when he called the guards names they strung him up.

I take strenuous exercises punching an imaginary punching bag; I try walking on my hands; I sing a song or recite some poetry for another hour. Finally a break in my day comes with the first mess marching by at 4:30. Supper comes and is soon over. I walk aimlessly around my cell. The guards change for the night shift. Now the other fellows in jail, outside of solitary, are getting their evening papers and mail; visiting with each other; playing games on the sly and having a good time. It is dark and the night guard, Dean, turns on the light. Again I read the Bible for an hour and take notes on what I have read. I rest on my bunk; sing some songs; perhaps curse a little if I feel like it; walk back and forth. Finally it is 8:30 p.m. and my light is turned out. I undress and go to bed. The lonesome whistle of the train howls in the distance. I lie on my back; then on one side; then on the other. Sometimes I cry; sometimes I curse; sometimes I pray to whatever kind of God listens to those in solitary. I think it must be night when the door opens and Dean flashes the light on to see if I am in my cell and shouts to the other guard, "o.k. all in at 10 p.m." I toss about, am nearly asleep when the bedbugs commence. I finally pass a night of fitful sleeping and dreaming. Again it is 6 a.m. and I cross off another day on my calendar.

I had read the Bible once when I belonged to the Baptist church, and now that was all I had to read. I commenced with Genesis and read at least twenty chapters a day. I also walked what I figured was four and a half miles a day. Berkman sent me a copy of Edwin Markham's "The Man with the Hoe," and I learned it by heart and recited it aloud several times a day. For the first few weeks the time did not go so slowly, as I was busy planning a routine. I found that on one day, perhaps a Thursday or Friday, I would suddenly be called by the guard to go across the hall and get a bath. Meanwhile my cell would be searched for contraband. For three minutes at some other odd time in the week I would be taken across the hall to be shaved. It was summer time and I asked to have my hair shaved off to make my head cooler. I could not see myself and whatever the trusty or Johnson thought of my appearance did not make any difference to me. Once when I was going to get a shave

I saw Popoff entering his cell with his head bandaged. This must have been the result of the blows which I had heard faintly the day before. He was mistreated for a year or more until he went insane. Selma and I visited him in 1921 at St. Elizabeth's Hospital in Washington, D.C. He did not recognize me until I said "Johnson, the guard." I sent notes to my sister Lola for the newspapers about the treatment of Popoff. I heard the chains fall which bound him to the bars and then the thump of his body to the floor. I was told that papers in Atlanta printed something about it but no official investigation was ever made. My mood was to curse the damned capitalist system, the guards and everyone connected with the government and prisons. Once in a while I would crouch by the door of my cell, on bright sunny mornings, and see the top of Berkman's bald head as he worked at his regular table by the west window of the tailor shop on the second floor of the building next to my solitary. I thought that if he did $3\frac{1}{2}$ years in solitary, in Alleghaney prison, in a cell with slimy walls, I could do the balance of my time in this comparatively clean dry cell.

It was now nearly three months that I had been in solitary. Fred Zerbst, the warden, came in and asked me to sign a paper. It was registration for the second war draft. I told him that I had not changed my mind about the war. He said I wouldn't get anything around here acting that way. I told him that I wasn't asking for anything around here: I was just doing time. He said that I would get another year back in the hole for this second refusal to register. I told him that was o.k. It was September 21, 1918. The warden came in again and said this was all the longer they kept prisoners in solitary and that he would let me out in the regular prison the next day; if I would not plot to blow up any more prisons.

"You know I didn't do that," I said.

"I know you didn't," he replied, "but what do you suppose I am warden for? If I had told the prisoners that you were put in solitary for leading in that food sit-down, all of them would be your friends. When you are accused of plotting to blow up the prison they are all afraid to know you. Why didn't you come and tell me about the food?"

"Why didn't you come in the kitchen and find out? No one but stoolies go to your office," I answered. He left hurriedly.

In about five minutes he returned, saying, "I forgot to ask you something, Hennacy. I'll leave you out tomorrow just the same."

"What's on your mind?" I asked.

"Have you been sneaking any letters out of this prison?" he asked in an angry tone.

"Sure," I replied, smiling.

"Who is doing it for you?" he demanded.

"A friend of mine," I answered.

"What is his name?" was the query.

"That is for you and your guards and stool pigeons to find out."

He stormed around my cell, somewhat taken back by the fact that I had not lied or given in.

"You'll stay in here all your good time and get another year, you stubborn fool," he said as he left.

I picked up the Bible and threw it in a corner, pacing back and forth, thinking and mumbling to myself: the liars, the double-crossers, tempting me with freedom and then telling me the only way to obtain it was by being a rat. This was bad enough, but to talk the Golden Rule and religion, as they did whenever outsiders came around. Love your enemies, turn the other cheek; fine stuff, after they frame you, and admit it. The world needs a Samson to pull down their whole structure of lies. Debs is arrested near my home town in Ohio for defending my comrades Ruthenberg, Wagenknecht and Baker who were doing time in Canton jail and he will come to Atlanta soon. He did time when he was a young man. He's not so bitter; but then, he's older, and won't allow the capitalist class to tramp on him either.

That night I was nervous and tore the buttons from my clothing in order to have something to do to sew them on again. I paced my eight and a half steps back and forth for hours and finally flung myself on the bunk. It must have been the middle of the night when I awoke. I had not had a note from anyone for a month. Were my friends forgetting me? I felt weak, lonesome and alone in the world. Here I had been singing defiance at the whole capitalist world but a few hours before, and had boasted to the warden how I would bravely do my time; now I wondered if anyone really cared. Perhaps by this time Selma might be married to someone else with a real future ahead of him instead of being lost in a jail. The last letter I had received from her was rather formal. Would she understand why I did not write; and could I be sure that some of the letters I had sent her had been received, with the officials opening the mail I had sent to my sister Lola? How could one end it all? The sharp spoon with which I had carved poems and my calendar on the wall could cut my wrist and I would bleed to death before a guard arrived. But then that would be such a messy death. Then the warden would be sorry for the lies he had told me and the tricks he had tried to play. The last thing I could remember before falling asleep was the long wailing whistle of the freight train as it echoed in the woods nearby.

The next day the deputy came to my cell and said that I was looking very pale, that number 7440, a man just two numbers from me who had come in the same day with me, had died of the flu, and that thirty others were buried that week. If I did not get out and breathe the fresh air it was likely that I would die sooner than the others, he said. Why should I not tell what I knew and get out? In reply I asked the deputy to talk about the weather, as I was not interested in achieving the reputation of a rat. He asked me if it was a prisoner or a guard who had sent out my letters. I walked up to him closely and in a confidential tone said, "It was a prisoner or a guard." I did not know the nature of the flu but thought that this might be a good way to die if I could only get it. Fate seemed to seal me up in a place where I couldn't get any germs. Late that afternoon I was called across the hall to take a bath. The guard accidently left my wooden door open when he was called to answer a telephone. I could not see anywhere except across the hall to the solid door of another cell, but I could hear Popoff in the next cell groaning and calling for water. He was still hanging from his hands for the eight hours a day as he had been for months. As the guard came down the hall he opened Popoff's door, dipping his tin cup in the toilet and threw the dirty water in Popoff's face. Then he came and slammed my door shut and locked it. How soon would I be strung to the bars? How long could a fellow stand such treatment? As soon as it was dark I sharpened my spoon again and tried it gently on my wrist. The skin seemed to be quite tough, but then I could press harder. If I cut my wrist at midnight I could be dead by morning. I thought I ought to write a note to Selma and my mother and I couldn't see to do it until morning. Well, I had waited that long, I could wait a day longer. That night my dreams were a mixture of Victor Hugo's stories of men hiding in the sewers of Paris; I.W.W. songs; blood flowing from the pigs that had been butchered on the farm when I was a boy; and the groans of Popoff.

The sun shone brightly in my cell the next morning for the first time in weeks. I crouched again by the door and saw Berkman's bald head. Tears came into my eyes and I felt ashamed of myself for my cowardly idea of suicide just because I had a few reverses. Here was Berkman who had passed through much more than I would ever have to endure if I stayed two more years in solitary. How was the world to know more about the continued torture of Popoff and others if I gave up? The last two verses of the I.W.W. prison song now had a real meaning to me as I sang them again. I was through with despair. I wanted to live to make the world better. Just because most prisoners, and for all that, most people on the outside, did not understand and know what solitary meant was all the more reason why I should be strong. I sang cheerfully:

> "By all the graves of Labor's dead,
> By Labor's deathless flag of red,
> We make a solemn vow to you,
> We'll keep the faith, we will be true.
> For freedom laughs at prison bars,
> Her voice reechoes from the stars;
> Proclaiming with the tempest's breath
> A Cause beyond the reach of death."

Two months later I heard the whistles blow and shouts resound throughout the prison. The war was over. The Armistice had been signed. It was not until then that I was informed in a note from Berkman that November 11 was also an anarchist anniversary: the date of the hanging of the Chicago anarchists of the Haymarket in 1887. I had ceased by this time my nervous running back and forth like a squirrel in my cell and was now taking steady walks in my cell each day, and also hours of physical exercise. I was going to build myself up and not get sick and die. I would show my persecutors that I would be a credit to my ideals. I had painted the ceiling of the Catholic chapel in flat work before I got in solitary, and had left no brush marks. The priest appreciated my good work. He knew I was an Irishman who was not a Catholic, but he never tried to convert me. Now, as I studied the Bible, I was not thinking of any church but just wanted to see what might be worthwhile in it. I had now read it through four times and had read the New Testament many times and the Sermon on the Mount scores of times. I had made up games with pages and chapters and names of characters in the Bible to pass away the time. I had memorized certain chapters and that I liked. As I read of Isaiah, Ezekiel, Micah and other of the prophets and of Jesus, I could see that they had opposed tyranny. I had also spent many days reviewing all of the historical knowledge that I could remember and trying to think through a philosophy of life. I had passed through the idea of killing myself. This was an escape, not any solution to life. The remainder of my two years in solitary must result in a clear-cut plan whereby I could go forth and be a force in the world. I could not take any halfway measures. If assassination, violence and revolution was the better way, then military tactics must be studied and a group of fearless rebels organized. I remembered again what Slim, the sort of Robin Hood Wobblie who was in on some larceny charge, had told me once to the effect that one could not be a good rebel unless he became angry and vengeful. Then I heard Popoff curse the guards and I heard them beat him. I remembered the Negro who had sworn at the guard in the tailor shop and was killed. I had read of riots in prison over food and I remembered the peaceful victory which we had in our strike against the spoiled fish. I also remembered what Berkman had said about being firm, but quiet. He had tried violence but did not believe in it as a wholesale method. I read of the wars and hatred in the Old Testament. I also read of the courage of Daniel and the Hebrew children who would not worship the golden image: of Peter who chose to obey God rather than the properly constituted authorities who placed him in jail; and of the victory of these men by courage and peaceful methods. I read of Jesus, who was confronted with a whole world empire of tryanny and chose not to overturn the tyrant and make Himself King, but to change the hatred in the hearts of men to love and understanding—to overcome evil with goodwill.

I had called loudly for the sword and mentally listed those whom I desired to kill when I was free. Was this really the universal method which should be used? I would read the Sermon on the Mount again. When a child I had been frightened by hell fire into proclaiming a change of life. Now I spent months making a decision; there was no sudden change. I had all the time in the world and no one could talk to me or influence me, I was deciding this idea for myself. Gradually I came to gain a glimpse of what Jesus meant when He said, "The Kingdom of God is within you." In my heart now after six months I could love everybody in the world but the warden, but if I did not love him then the Sermon on the Mount meant nothing at all. I really saw this and felt it in my heart but I was too stubborn to admit it in my mind. One day I was walking back and forth in my cell when, in turning, my head hit the wall. Then the thought came to me: "Here I am locked up in a cell. The warden was never locked up in any cell and he never had a chance to know what Jesus meant. Neither did I until yesterday. So I must not blame him. I must love him." Now the whole thing was clear. This Kingdom of God must be in everyone: in the deputy, the warden, in the rat and the pervert—and now I came to know it—in myself. I read and reread, the Sermon on the Mount: the fifth, sixth and seventh chapters of Matthew thus became a living thing to me. I tried to take every sentence and apply it to my present problems. The warden had said that he did not understand political prisoners. He and the deputy, in plain words, did not know any better; they had put on the false face of sternness and tyranny because this was the only method which they knew. It was my job to teach them another method: that of goodwill overcoming their evil intentions, or rather habits. The opposite of the Sermon on the Mount was what the whole world had been practicing, in prison and out of prison; and hate piled on hate had brought hate and revenge. It was plain that this system did not work. I would never have a better opportunity than this to try out the Sermon on the Mount right now in my cell. Here was deceit, hatred, lust, murder, and every kind of evil in this prison. I reread slowly and pondered each verse: "ye have heard that it hath been said an eye for an eye, and a tooth for a tooth . . . whoever shall smite thee on thy right cheek turn to him the other also . . . take therefore no thought for the morrow . . . therefore all things whatsoever ye would that men should do to you, do ye even so to them."

I fancied what my radical friends in and out of prison would say when I spoke of the above teachings of Jesus. I knew that I would have to bear their displeasure, just as I had born the hysteria of the patriots and the silence of my friends when I was sent to prison. This did not mean that I was going to "squeal" and give in to the officials, but in my heart I would try to see the good in them and not hate them. Jesus did not give in to His persecutors. He used strong words against the evil doers of His time, but He had mercy for the sinner. I now was not alone fighting the world for I had Him as my helper. I saw that if I held this philosophy for myself I could not engage in violence for a revolution—a good war, as some might call it—but would have to renounce violence even in my thought. Would I be ready to go the whole way? At that time I had not heard of Tolstoy and his application of Christ's teachings to society. Berkman had just mentioned his name along with other anarchists and he might have told me more if I had had a lengthy conversation with him; but I never saw him again. I could see the warden's honesty in admitting that he had "framed" me. I could even see that the deputy had only been used to violence in his years of supervising the chain gang. I did not know much about the outside world and it was up to me now day by day to solve this problem of repressed hatred, and when I was finally released to see in what manner I could apply my new ideals to conditions as I found them. The most difficult animosity for me to overcome was a dislike of the hypocrites and church people who had so long withheld the real teachings of Jesus. I could see no connection between Jesus and the church.

I continued my study of the Bible. Popoff was still being manhandled. My teeth ached much of the time in solitary and I asked the deputy to allow the prison dentist to fix my teeth. The prison doctor gave one pint of dreadful tasting salts for whatever ailed a prisoner. Very few men would fake a sick call with this dose in view. However, the dentist could not give me a pint of physic for my toothache, and neither could he bring his dental chair to solitary. The deputy replied that I knew how I could get my teeth fixed; that was to tell what I knew; otherwise I could ache for all he cared. So loving my enemies was not altogether a theoretical matter.

It was now in February of 1919 and I had been in solitary for $7^{1}/_{2}$ months. Mr. Duehay, Superintendent of Federal Prisons from Washington, and his secretary, and Warden Zerbst came to my cell. Duehay wanted to know why I was being held so long here. I told him I was telling the world of evil conditions in the prison and would not divulge the source of my outlet for contraband mail. He felt that I was an intelligent and educated man who was foolish to endanger my health in solitary by trying to better the conditions for a lot of bums in prison who would sell me for a dime. I told him I was learning to take it. I had read a poem in *The Appeal to Reason* years before and had remembered it and written it on the wall. He and the warden read it and laughed.

SURPLUS VALUE

The Merchant calls it Profit and winks the other eye;
The Banker calls it Interest and heaves a cheerful sigh;
The Landlord calls it Rent as he tucks it in his bag;
But the honest old Burglar he simply calls it Swag.

Duehay changed his tactics and began to swing his arms and berate me as a fool and a coward. The warden had called me names often but he disliked to hear an outsider do so.

"If he's a fool or a coward he must be a different kind, for no one ever stood more than three months in the hole without giving in. He must be a God's fool or a God's coward."

Years later I was to write an account of my prison life and call it "God's coward." Portions of it were printed in the November and December *Catholic Worker* in 1941. It must have seemed especial advice for those about to oppose World War II.

I did not lose my temper or fight back at the warden and Mr. Duehay; just smiled and held my ground. Suddenly Duehay turned to the warden saying,

"Let's make out parole papers for this stubborn fellow. Half of the time I can't trust my own men. This Hennacy is honest and can't be bribed. I will give him a job in the secret service."

The warden nodded and smiled, I shook my head saying I wanted no job hunting down radicals and criminals for I was on their side and not that of the oppressor. The secretary of Duehay was taking all this down in shorthand. Finally they left. The next morning a runner came down from the office to measure me for an outgoing suit, saying: "The warden told us, 'that damn Hennacy wouldn't tell anything in $7\frac{1}{2}$ months; he won't tell anything in $7\frac{1}{2}$ years. Get him the hell out of here; give him back his good time and let him go to his other jail. He is too much of a nuisance.' "

The next month went very quickly. It was now March 19, 1919, and I was to be released the next day. That night the deputy came in and said:

"Going out tomorrow, Hennacy?"

"That's what they say; sure a fine feeling," I replied.

"We give; we take. You tell who is getting out your contraband mail or you'll stay here another $5\frac{1}{2}$ months and lose your good time and then another year for refusing to register. You don't think we will allow anyone to get by in bucking us, do you?"

Tears came to my eyes as I chokingly replied, "I can do it. Go away and don't bother me any more." After he left I wept, but I was at the stage where I felt strong enough to take it.

The next morning after breakfast I wrote on the wall that I was beginning to do the "good time" that I had lost, when the door opened suddenly and old Johnson smiled for once, saying, "Going out of this jail, Hennacy." I did not believe him; and even while the barber was shaving me I thought it was some trick to bedevil me. I was given my outgoing suit and an overcoat. It is customary for the warden to shake hands with those who leave and to admonish them to live a good life out in the world. A guard gave me my $10 outgoing money and a bundle of letters that had come to me while I was in solitary, but the warden never appeared.

When I walked out of prison a plain clothes man met me saying that I was being arrested for refusing to register for the draft in August 1918 and would be taken to the county tower to await trial. We took a street car there, at the end of South Pryor street and walked a few blocks before we got to the tower. A second hand clothing merchant noticed my prison clothes and asked if I wanted to sell my overcoat. I was not handcuffed but I guess my white face from my months of solitary was sign enough to anyone as to my being an ex-convict.

I was ushered into a cell where Joe Webb, a mountain boy, also slept. He had been found guilty of murder, and was to be executed. Through influential friends I was able to get him a new trial, and he got life on the chain gang instead. I asked for radical books to read and among other books Tolstoy's *Kingdom of God Is Within You* was brought.

Debs had entered Moundsville, West Virginia prison to start his twenty years. He could not be allowed to receive letters from another convict so I wrote to his brother Theodore in Terre Haute expressing my admiration for one who in his old age was still a rebel. Sam Castleton, who was to be Debs lawyer in Atlanta, was also my lawyer. My case came up for trial after seven weeks. Castleton told me that if I was not too radical he might get me off with six months. I was asked if I had really refused to register for the first and second drafts and if I had not changed my mind and would I be ready to register for the third draft if and when it came along. I replied that I had entered prison an atheist and not a pacifist. I would fight in a revolution but not in a capitalist war. I had got locked up with the Bible in solitary and read it and became a Christian and a pacifist. If I had been locked up with the phone book, the cook book, or the Book of Mormon I might have come out an expert on these, but my study of the Bible had made me see that Christ was the greatest Revolutionist. And a few weeks ago I had read Tolstoy and had become an anarchist.

"What's an anarchist?" asked the judge. My lawyer shook his head and put his finger to his lips as a warning for me not to be too radical.

"An anarchist is one who doesn't have to have a cop to make him behave. It is the individual, the family, or the small cooperative group as a unit rather than the State." And, I continued for about ten minutes to quote Tolstoy to the effect that one had to obey God rather than man. The District Attorney, Hooper Alexander, an old fashioned looking southerner, came up to the judge and whispered, and the judge said, "case dismissed." I looked around to see whose case it was and it was mine. My lawyer seemed bewildered and so was I. I had approached the court this time with love for my enemy and had never thought I would get my freedom, for he allowed me to go 10 days on my own before I reported to the court in Columbus, Ohio, to do my 9 months in Delaware County jail for my first refusal to register.

B. J. George Ewert,
"Christ or Country?"

When the four Hutterites traveled from their home in South Dakota to the military camp, their troubles began right away because of their beards. . . . The other young men on the train tried to cut the Hutterites' hair and beards, treating them roughly and with contempt. The brothers wept over these indignities because they seemed to be a token of what was to come.

J. George Ewert, "Christ or Country?," *The Plough*, No. 4, May 1984. Reprinted with permission of The Plough Publishing House, Farmington, PA.

Upon their arrival at the military camp in Lewis, Washington, they were asked to sign a card promising obedience to all military commands. As absolute objectors to all military service on the basis of their religious convictions, they refused any service within the military. They were commanded to line up with the others and march to the exercise grounds. This they also refused, and they did not accept the uniform either. Therefore the four men were straightaway put in the guard house. Particularly painful for them was the terrible swearing and cursing they heard all the time.

After two months in the guard house they were condemned by the court-martial to thirty-seven years, which was reduced by the commanding general to twenty years. The place where they were to serve their term was the military prison on the island of Alcatraz in San Francisco Bay.

Chained together two by two, hands and feet, they were sent there under the guard of four armed men. By day the fetters on their ankles were unlocked, but never the handcuffs. At night they had to lie two by two, flat on their backs, doubly chained together. There was not much sleep during the two nights of the journey, just sighing and weeping.

Upon their arrival at Alcatraz their own clothes were taken from them by force. They were ordered to put on the military uniform, which they again refused to do. Then they were taken to the dungeon into dark, dirty, stinking cells for solitary confinement. The uniforms were thrown down next to them with the warning, "If you don't give in, you'll stay here till you die, like the four we dragged out of here yesterday." So they were locked up wearing nothing but their light underwear.

The first four and a half days they got nothing at all to eat, only half a glass of water every twenty-four hours. At night they had to sleep on the wet and cold concrete floor without blankets. (Their cell at Alcatraz was below sea level, and the water oozed through the walls.) The last one and a half days they had to stand with their hands tied together crosswise above their heads and fastened to iron rods so high that they could barely touch the floor with their feet. This strained the tendons in their arms so badly that David Hofer said after his release that he could still feel the effects in his sides. He described how he tried to ease the terrible pain by pushing the toilet bucket toward himself with one foot and then standing on it. This relieved the strain in his arms a little. During this time the brothers could not speak to each other because they were too far apart, but once David heard Jacob Wipf cry out: "O Almighty God!"

At the end of five days the four were brought out of the dungeon into the yard, where a group of other prisoners stood. Some of them were moved with compassion at the sight of the Hutterites. One said with tears in his eyes: "Isn't it a shame to treat people like that?" The men were covered with a rash, badly bitten by insects, and their arms so swollen that they could not get their jackets on. They also had been beaten with clubs. Michael Hofer was once beaten so severely that he passed out.

That fifth day, after they were let out of the dungeon, they still got nothing to eat until evening when they finally got their supper. After that they were locked up again in their cells day and night. Only on Sundays they were allowed to walk for an hour in the fenced-in courtyard, but under heavy guard. This way they spent four months in the prison of Alcatraz.

In late November, guarded by six armed sergeants and again chained together two by two, they were transferred from Alcatraz to Fort Leavenworth in Kansas. This trip went through Texas and took four days and five nights. They arrived at eleven o'clock at night in Leavenworth and were loudly driven up the street with bayonets, like pigs. Chained together at the wrists, they carried their bags in their free hand and their Bibles and an extra pair of shoes under the arm. They were hurriedly driven up the hill to the military prison. By the time they reached the gate they were sweating so much that even the hair on their heads was wet. In this condition, in the raw winter air, they had to take off their clothes in order to put on the prison garb that was to be brought to them. By the time the clothes came, about two hours later, they were chilled to the bone. Early in the morning, at five o'clock, they again had to stand outside a door in the cold wind and wait. Joseph and Michael Hofer could bear it no longer; they had such severe pain that they had to be taken to hospital.

Jacob Wipf and David Hofer were put in solitary confinement because they again refused to take up prison work under military control. Their hands were stretched out through the iron bars and chained together. That way they had to stand nine hours a day, getting only bread and water. This lasted two weeks; then they received regular meals for two weeks, and so on alternately.

When the two Hofer brothers became critically ill, Jacob Wipf sent a telegram home to their wives who left their children and traveled the same night, accompanied by a relative. Owing to confusion at the railroad station they were delayed one day, and when they finally reached Fort Leavenworth at eleven o'clock at night, they found their husbands close to death and hardly able to speak.

The next morning, when they were allowed to come in again, Joseph Hofer was already dead and his body in a coffin. They were told he could not be seen anymore. But his wife Maria made her way to the commanding officer in spite of guards and doors and pleaded for permission to see her husband once more. They showed her where the body was. She went there and looked through tears into the coffin, but to her horror she saw that her beloved husband had been put into the military uniform he had so valiantly refused to wear while living, in order to remain faithful to his convictions.

His brother Michael, who died a few days later, was dressed in his own clothes, according to the strongly expressed wish of his father, who had arrived in the meantime. When Michael died, his father, his wife, and his brother David were present. Shortly before his end he stretched out his arms and said, "Come, Lord Jesus! Into Thy hands I commend my spirit."

After the relatives had left with the body, David Hofer was brought back to his solitary cell and chained. Later he reported, "The whole next day I stood there and wept. But I could not even wipe away my tears, because my hands were chained to the prison bars." No one seemed to have any compassion for him. But the next morning one of the guards was willing to take a message from David to the commanding officer. David asked for permission to have a cell closer to his friend Jacob Wipf, so that they could at least see each other, even if they would not be allowed to speak together. The guard took the message to the commanding officer. An hour later he returned and told David to pack up his things—he had been released!

This message was so unexpected that David could not believe it. The guard then took him to the officer, who told him the same thing and gave him his release papers. . . . David Hofer told the guard that he would have liked to say good-bye to his friend Jacob Wipf. The guard told him to write a few lines on a piece of paper, and he would deliver it to Jacob the very same day, which he did.

On December 6, 1918, the Secretary of War issued an order prohibiting the handcuffing and chaining of military prisoners as well as other brutal punishments. But about five days later, when two Hutterite brothers went to Fort Leavenworth to visit Jacob Wipf, they found him still in solitary confinement, his hands chained to the iron bars, standing there nine hours a day. At seven in the morning he received bread and water for breakfast. At noon they took the chains off for thirty minutes so he could eat his dinner of bread and water. At six in the afternoon he received the same, and at this time the chains were taken off for the night. He was given four blankets for the night but had to sleep on the concrete floor.

Jacob Wipf sent the following message home with the visitors: "Sometimes I envy the three who have already been released from this torment. Then I think, why is the hand of the Lord so heavy upon me? I have always tried to be faithful and hardworking and have hardly ever made any trouble for the Brotherhood. Why must I go on suffering all alone? But then there is joy too, so that I could weep for joy when I think that the Lord considers me worthy to suffer for His sake. And I must confess that my life here, compared with our previous experiences [at Alcatraz] is like living in a palace."

On December 12, 1918, the chaining of military prisoners was finally discontinued in accordance with the order of the Secretary of War. The solitary prisoners also got some planks on the floor to sleep on, making it considerably warmer than the bare concrete floor. There were more improvements after Christmas, when the Department of War received many petitions on behalf of the prisoners.

Jacob Wipf became sick and was in hospital a few days. He was finally released on April 13, 1919.

C. Stephen M. Kohn,
The Fort Leavenworth General Strike

In November 1918, the Leavenworth COs staged their first work strike. Twenty-four objectors refused to work in order to protest the gross mistreatment of Molokan religious COs. The Molokans, members of a small Russian pacifist religious sect, could neither speak nor write English. Consequently, they were almost totally isolated from outside support. Remaining true to the principles of their church, the Molokans refused all work assignments at Fort Leavenworth. As a result, they were placed in solitary confinement, manacled to their cell walls for nine hours every day, placed on a diet of bread and water, and badly beaten by guards.

The CO population at Leavenworth became concerned over the plight of the Molokans. Evan Thomas, a religious objector and the brother of the famous socialist leader Norman Thomas, complained to Leavenworth Warden Colonel Sedgwick Rice and insisted on the release of the Molokans from solitary confinement. Colonel Rice rejected Thomas' plea. In a display of solidarity with the Molokans, Thomas refused to work. He was joined by twenty-three other objectors. All were sent into the "hole."

The striking COs secretly slipped information blasting the inhuman conditions in solitary to their nonstriking comrades within the prison population. Clark Getts, who along with Carl Haessler was reputed to be the mastermind of prison mail smuggling, leaked reports of the conditions to the National Civil Liberties Bureau. In one such report, dated November 14, 1918, Getts wrote:

> The Hole in our jail [is a] black cold place in the subbasement. The men there are chained by their wrists to their cell doors for nine hours a day. They sleep on a cold cement floor between folded blankets and are given bread and water if they will eat at all. There is brutality enough, too. I saw one man dragged by his collar across the right corridor floor, screaming and choking. . . . Several [Molokans] have been hunger striking in the Hole. Two of them were beaten so beastly that even the authorities were shocked . . . other beatings and tortures are matters of general knowledge.

From Stephen M. Kohn, *Jailed for Peace: The History of American Draft Law Violations, 1658–1985,* copyright 1986 by Stephen M. Kohn, pp. 34–40, an imprint of Greenwood Publishing Group, Inc., Westport, CT. Reprinted with permission.

Getts pleaded with outside supporters to pressure the government in Washington to stop the mistreatment. The objectors' supporters issued vehement protests before the government and Department of War. These efforts resulted in a Department of War memorandum dated December 6, 1918, which abolished forever the military policy of manacling defiant prisoners in solitary confinement to the walls of their cells. Shortly thereafter, all of the Molokans and protesting objectors were released from solitary confinement. The War Department commuted Thomas' sentence and ordered his release from Leavenworth. After two months, the first prison strike at Leavenworth had been a complete success. Emboldened by this example, the entire inmate population gained a new respect for the war resisters. The stage was set for the Leavenworth general strike.

Interspersed among the general prison population of over 3,000 were approximately 300 COs. Abhorrent prison conditions confronted both COs and regular prisoners alike. The prison was overcrowded; working, eating, recreation facilities, and living conditions were archaic. Discipline was extreme. Adding to this tension was the feeling among prisoners that they had been sentenced in excess of what their "crimes" deserved. Abysmal conditions and ridiculously long sentences (twenty years for refusing to peel potatoes) affected COs and non-COs alike.

The strike was precipitated by the death of two members of the Huttrian Brotherhood, a branch of the Mennonite Church. The Huttrians were transferred to Leavenworth after a long and debilitating stay in solitary confinement at Alcatraz. Although sick and physically broken from their Alcatraz punishments, the Huttrians continued to refuse all work. They were sent into the Leavenworth "hole." Within a period of days, two of the Huttrians died. This incident outraged the prison population.

On Wednesday, January 29, 1919, one hundred and fifty members of the "first work gang" spontaneously walked off their jobs. Leaderless, they returned to their cells. The prison officials made no attempt to force these inmates back to work. That evening the entire prison population was humming with talk of rebellion and general strike. Everyone felt the frustration of confinement and yet did not know how to direct these energies:

> No one had formulated that afternoon any statement of what was wanted. One prisoner wanted more tobacco; another wanted better food . . . a fifth wanted the privilege of writing more letters . . . absorption in small desires, and utter disagreement of one man to another, characterized the early stages of the strike.

Colonel Rice, the warden, met informally with the inmates the next morning. He informed them that mass refusal to work was mutiny—a crime punishable by death. Rice threatened to call out 4,000 troops, warning that a strike would be futile and counterproductive. By the time Rice finished threatening the inmates, the obstacles confronting them appeared insurmountable.

That afternoon, 2,300 inmates were lined up for work. When an officer called for the first work gang, a yell came back from the prisoners: "There ain't no first gang!" All the inmates stood silently, many with their arms folded defiantly. Colonel Rice called for an inmate to state the strikers' demands. No one moved. All feared being identified as the leader and being shot as an organizer of the "mutiny." The tension was broken when a young objector, W. Oral James, stepped forward and addressed the warden:

I am in no sense a leader of these men. I can speak for myself, however, and I think I speak for many others in these silent ranks when I say that our object in thus seeming to oppose authority is that this is the only way in which we can make articulate our demand to know what is to become of us?

I am a conscientious objector. I realize that in thus separating myself from this mass I make myself a marked man among your officers. I am willing to do this, sir, if I can enlighten this protest.

James went on to state that the prisoners' sentences were too long. He ended the speech with a plea to Colonel Rice to make their protest heard in Washington.

Rice issued a final order for the inmates to report to work. An estimated one hundred inmates broke rank and reported. The remaining 2,200 were marched back into their cells. That evening both the military authorities and the prisoners organized. Colonel Rice received permission to use the troops of the 49th Infantry Regiment to "maintain discipline." One thousand armed soliders were readied for combat and sent to the prison gate.

A reporter from *Survey* magazine coincidentally was present in Leavenworth writing a story about prison conditions when the strike broke out. According to his accounts, the inmates perfected their organization in the seventh wing of Leavenworth and duplicated a similar internal organization throughout the prison's remaining wings. Each wing elected its own committee and one inmate to serve on a general inmate committee. Demands were formulated and sent via messengers to the various wings for negotiation, discussion, and consolidation. The *Survey* reporter, Winthrop Lane, described some of the action unfolding in the seventh wing:

Simmons [a CO] mounted a box. . . . He told [the strikers] that the strike had been organized in other wings. . . . He told them that theirs was the just cause of self-government now being fought for throughout the civilized world. . . . He declared that no authority could withstand the power of a united body of men. . . . "Violence accomplishes nothing," [Simmons said]. "Solidarity accomplishes all things. The watchword of the working men throughout the world today is solidarity. Say nothing, do nothing, but stand like this." The speaker folded his arms. "A man who commits no overt act, but stands like this, is immovable."

The Survey reporter recollected:

As he spoke, I thought of the thick walls that shut these men in, and of the barred doors between them and their fellows. I wondered what was the mysterious power by which the speaker and his listeners thought they could control their own destinies.

The following morning Colonel Rice met with the elected general strike committee. Rice was presented with three demands: (1) amnesty for the strike leaders and release of all inmates from solitary; (2) recognition of the permanent grievance committee; and (3) a recommendation by the colonel to the War Department in Washington, D.C., that all the military prisoners be released immediately.

Rice shocked the inmates. First, he read from a telegram he had already sent to Washington urging the reduction of excessive military sentences. He informed the committee that he would personally go to Washington to deliver the strikers' message. He agreed to the amnesty demand and to the recognition of an elected inmate grievance committee. Within four hours the prisoners voted unanimously to return to work.

Following Rice's return from Washington, 60.6 percent of the COs had their sentences reduced; another 33 percent were released immediately; and only 6.4 percent of the COs did not receive a sentence reduction. As a result of these commutations, the last of the COs was released from miltary prison in November 1920. None of the long sentences was carried out.

A General Prison Conference Committee was elected. It accomplished the following reforms:

- The internal prison judicial system was revamped. Sentences for infractions were reduced, and prisoners were granted the right to present evidence and to be represented by another inmate.
- A campaign to eliminate bed-bugs was initiated.
- Food was improved. The grains and cattle raised on the prison farm were allocated to the inmates as well as to the military officers who previously were their sole consumers.
- Letter writing privileges were expanded, and censorship was limited.

A nonviolent prison rebellion had succeeded. This "mutiny" was the pinnacle of the movement of World War I war resisters for nonviolent direct action. The strike reinforced the faith of many resisters in nonviolent action and was one of the few bright spots in their tortuous experiences during that war.

But the progressive results of the strike were short-lived. Once the COs were transferred out of Leavenworth, the prison administration reneged on the reforms. By July 1919 all strike leaders had either been released or transferred. The vast majority of COs also had been removed from the institution. In addition, over 1,000 new military prisoners were added to the general population. Many of these new inmates, fresh from the front lines in France, were reportedly in an "ugly" mood. The military had promised these soldiers early release, but instead they found themselves crowded into Fort Leavenworth. The situation was tense.

On July 20, 1919, a minor incident (the transfer of a popular inmate from Leavenworth to Alcatraz) triggered a work strike. The administration's response was swift and repressive. Every prisoner, even those who did not support the strike, was locked up and placed on a bread and water diet. The elected inmate committee was disbanded, and the prison was transformed into a battle ground. According to an account:

> In the riot-galleries, high over the door of each wing, sat sentries with shotguns across their knees. Through the windows they [the inmates] saw scores of sentries posted on the walls with machine guns pointed into the yard.

The prisoners were kept in lock-up on restricted diets. No one was allowed to bathe. Once a guard opened fire into the cell block, killing one inmate and wounding several others. After ten days the cells were individually searched; all nonprison-authorized materials were confiscated—including books, soap, and clothing. The inmates were informed that they had lost all their "good-time" and would be denied parole. Their spirits were completely broken. When the prisoners were finally taken from their cells, their heads were shaven. When ordered by the guards to work, none refused. The experiment in prison democracy had ended.

PART VI

TRADE UNIONISM
BETWEEN THE WARS

DOCUMENT 16

A. J. Muste,
"The Lawrence Strike of 1919"

*Abraham Johannes, or as he always called himself, A. J. Muste (1885–1967),
was born in the Netherlands. In 1891 the family emigrated to Grand Rapids,
Michigan. There Muste's father got a job as a teamster at a local furniture
factory. He worked sixty hours a week for $6.00.*

*Muste was educated to be a minister. During World War I he resigned as
pastor of a Congregational Church in Newton, Massachusetts, rather than
keep silent about his pacifist convictions. A little later he became involved
in the dramatic strike narrated here (not to be confused with the earlier
Lawrence strike of 1912, which gave rise to the song "Bread and Roses").*

*After the Lawrence strike of 1919, Muste served from 1921 to 1933 as
director of Brookwood Labor College. Thereafter he took part in the rank-
and-file labor organizing of the early 1930s.*

A. J. Muste, "The Lawrence Strike of 1919," *Liberation*, Feb., Mar., and Apr.
1958. Reprinted with permission.

From the late 1930s until his death in 1967, Muste was a guiding spirit of the Fellowship of Reconciliation (FOR), the War Resisters League, the Committee for Nonviolent Action, Peacemakers, the magazine Liberation *which he helped to found in 1956, and a series of national coalitions against the Vietnam war. He refused to pay war taxes, and was one of the principal participants in a campaign in the late 1950s to refuse to take shelter during "civil defense" drills in New York City. In May 1966, Muste traveled to South Vietnam in company with Barbara Deming and Bradford Lyttle, and was deported for demonstrating against the war in the streets of Saigon.*

It was quite an experience to be, in effect, driven out of a pulpit which for my predecessors had proved a stepping stone to highly distinguished careers in the ministry, and to find myself marked as a pacifist and possibly dangerous character. It was, however, as nothing compared to the transition from preaching in the somewhat old fashioned, though sturdy and courageous, Quaker Meeting in Providence to the leadership, early in 1919, of a turbulent strike of 30,000 textile workers in Lawrence, Massachusetts. . . .

Harold L. Rotzel, with his wife and their three-year-old daughter, occupied the apartment on the top floor of 99 Appleton. The Mustes and our three-year-old daughter lived on the floor below. Harold, a Methodist minister who had been forced to leave his church near Worcester, Massachusetts, and I were members of a loosely organized group of men and women who called themselves "The Comradeship." The emphasis was on the noun, not on the article. Another member was Cedric Long, a young Congregationalist minister, who had been unable to get a church on account of his pacifism. . . .

SEARCH FOR COMMUNITY

Those of us identified with The Comradeship in late 1918 and early 1919 were wrestling with the question of how to organize our lives so that they would truly express the teachings and spirit of Jesus, or, in other terms, faith in the way of truth, nonviolence and love. We were thinking of a place in the country where some members of the community might live and also of places in the city where other members would live, organize cooperatives, and generally enter into the neighborhood life. We talked of a possible economic tie between the community on the land and the community in the city. We were all agreed that we did not want to shut ourselves off from the struggle against war, and for economic justice and racial equality, in the competitive society. I suppose it might be said that this latter was our undoing or our salvation, depending on how you look at it. . . .

During that winter, after the November 11 Armistice, Harold Rotzel and I got up about five o'clock every morning for several weeks. When the chill of the apartment made it necessary, we bundled ourselves in our overcoats while we read the New Testament, especially the Sermon on the Mount, together, analyzed the passages, meditated on each phrase, even each word, prayed, and asked ourselves what obedience to these precepts meant for us, then and there. Insofar as we were thinking of an organized future, it was in terms of an "intentional community" along the lines I have mentioned. Indeed, at that time, we, together with members of the F.O.R. and a number of Quakers, *did* constitute a "fellowship of sharing and concern," in a very substantial measure. During most of the period when we were holding the early morning sessions, strikes were not in our thoughts at all; there was certainly no idea that we should become involved. However, in a psychological and spiritual sense, those hours of meditation and self-searching constituted ideal preparation for what we were to face in the nearby city of Lawrence shortly after the start of 1919.

LAWRENCE IN 1912

There had been an I.W.W.-led strike in Lawrence in 1912. It had been a general strike of textile workers, textile being virtually the only industry the city had. The names of Elizabeth Gurley Flynn, Carlo Tresca, Joseph Ettar and the Italian poet Arturo Giovanitti—and to a lesser extent, Bill Haywood—are associated with that strike. It had been conducted with the flair the I.W.W. had for dramatizing social issues and the human aspects of the labor struggle. When the strike had dragged on and starvation threatened the strikers, scores of Lawrence children had been taken out of Lawrence and into the homes of sympathizers in other cities. The strike had received world-wide publicity. When rumors began to fly, in January, 1919, that another general strike was likely to break out, a number of Comradeship people met at "99 Appleton" to talk over the situation. Our discussions about community had sprung out of a feeling that somehow we had to try to translate the ideal of brotherhood into reality. We had also a feeling that nonviolence had to prove itself in actual struggle; otherwise it was a mere abstraction or illusion. I recall that some of us felt the sting of the charge that during the war, while others risked their lives, we had stood on the side-lines and "had it easy." Here a struggle was developing at our own back door. Did our nonviolence have any relevance to the impending conflict? It would probably be risky to get embroiled in this business, and certainly none of us had any experience whatsoever in the field. So, was one to stay on the sidelines once more?

One bleak winter day three of us, Harold Rotzel (who was then teaching chemistry at Simmons College), Gorham Harris (a member of my old church in Newtonville) and I went from Boston to Lawrence to see for ourselves.

On this visit, and on later visits, we found terrific tension and excitement. This was partly because of the memory of the clashes between strikers and police, the bitterness, of the 1912 strike. There was much more reason for excitement, however, in the immediate situation. A little over a year before, the Bolshevik Revolution had taken place in Russia. Many believed that in the aftermath of the war that revolution would spread, certainly in Europe, perhaps to America. In Winnipeg, Canada, and in Seattle, Washington, there had been general strikes which had received national and international publicity.

We found that among members of the very conservative Quaker Meeting in Lawrence, for example, and indeed in all middle class and native elements of that predominantly proletarian and immigrant section, there was a firm conviction that if a general strike were to break out, it would signal the beginning of the Bolshevik Revolution in America, or at least in Massachusetts; certainly in Lawrence. The workers would seize the city hall, the police station, the mills. . . .

WAR PROFITEERING

We went to see those officials of the great textile companies who would see us. We did actually see William Wood Jr., son of the head of the American Woolen Company, which employed 16,000 people in its four huge mills. At the outset the officials had been rather pleased that we were coming to town, because they assumed that as pacifists we would urge the workers not to strike. When it became clear that we did not condone starvation wages and union smashing, and that, while we opposed violence, we conceived of nonviolence as a form of resistance and not of submission they changed their attitude toward us.

What we found out about the reasons for the impending strike in Lawrence had to do with very specific and painful actualities on the spot, and only remotely, if at all, with global revolution. The average wage of textile workers in the city was $11.00 for a 54-hour week. Eleven dollars a week was quite a lot more money then than it would be now. But even then it was miserable pay. With the end of the war, unemployment had set in. The mill owners had proposed to cut hours to 48 per week but not to adjust hour or piece rates; in other words, to institute a more than ten percent reduction in take-home pay. The slogan of the strike had become "54–48," that is "54 hours' pay for 48 hours' work." Housing conditions were appalling. Moreover, we and our friends dug up the facts about unconscionable war profiteering on the part of the industrialists, facts which in later years became common property. We put these facts into a leaflet and passed it out from house to house. This also did not endear us to the mill owners. There was a story, which was true as to substance, that the American Woolen Company had sold raincoats at a good price to the United States Army. The coats had not kept out the rain, so the division to which they had been sold had returned them. American Woolen had promptly sold the lot again out of the front door at a somewhat stiffer price, to another division of the Army.

The only union organizations in the mills were a couple of craft locals, of skilled loomfixers and spinners, belonging to the United Textile Workers of America, an affiliate of the American Federation of Labor. The men in the craft locals, of English and Scotch and, in a few cases, Irish descent, had no contacts with, or interest in, the great mass of foreign-born workers. The A.F. of L. was opposed to the strike.

The meetings which led to the formation of a provisional strike committee were organized by some middle aged Belgian, Polish and Italian weavers who had been involved in the 1912 strike, a radical-minded carpenter of English descent named Sam Bramhall, whose command of English made him the chairman, and a number of young men who had been from twelve to sixteen years old at the time of the 1912 strike and were hero-worshippers of the leaders of that strike. One was a Jewish lad named Irve Kaplan, and he served as committee secretary. . . .

STRIKE LEADERSHIP

Most of these workers were the kind of people who constitute the heart and backbone of every large-scale radical movement: men of devotion, courage, integrity; men of good judgment in matters within the field of their experience, and living close to their fellow workers. Some of them were remarkably well informed, considering the limited character of their education and their lack of leisure for reading. They had the confidence of their fellow workers, and without their mediation top leadership would have been unable to function.

However, none of these men were able, singly or as part of a group, to provide general leadership for a strike of 30,000 previously unorganized people. Most of them spoke English brokenly or not at all. This in itself was a severe handicap in dealing with liberal groups whose moral and financial support was needed, or with public officials and mill managements. They had almost no contacts outside the mills and their respective language groups. They had no experience or training in organization techniques or in publicity.

No other leadership was in sight. The A.F. of L., as I have already mentioned, was opposed to the strike. No Socialists from Masssachusetts or elsewhere seemed able or willing to undertake the responsibility of leadership in an "outlaw strike"; though a leading Boston socialist, George E. Roewer, rendered brilliant and sacrificial service as an attorney, after the strike had got underway. The Wilson administration . . . had practically wiped out the I.W.W. leadership.

When Harold Rotzel, Cedric Long and I spoke to meetings in Lawrence in the days before the strike was actually called, it was to tell the workers that we believed in their cause and that we would do all we could to raise relief money in case of a strike. This we did on our own behalf and also in the name of other members of The Comradeship who had "encouraged" us to become active in the situation. The strike was called for the first Monday in February of 1919. We were invited to sit in on strike committee meetings, and we accepted. We were mostly silent observers for a few days, except when manifestos or statements to the press had to be put into English. Each night we went back to Boston to interpret the strike and to raise relief money. When people have been working for an $11.00 weekly wage, some need relief by the end of the first week.

I have said something about the tense atmosphere which prevailed in Lawrence. On the Sunday evening before the strike began the Commissioner of Public Safety (sic) and the Chief of Police briefed the police in Lawrence and squads from the surrounding cities which had been called in to quell the revolution. The commissioner instructed them to this effect: "If you do not get these people on the picket-line tomorrow morning first, they will get you."

POLICE TERROR

So there was a blood bath on Monday morning. As the vast picket lines formed before the silent mills in the gray dawn, police, on foot and mounted, waded into the lines, clubbing right and left. In at least a couple of cases police broke into homes near the mills, pulled the covers off women in bed and beat them, alleging that the women had been near the line, had thrown stones at the police, and had then fled home. A score or so of those who had got the worst beating were brought to the little hall belonging to some Polish benefit society which the strike committee had hired as its headquarters. It was after these men and women had been given first aid and reports had been received about other beatings that the strike committee convened to deliberate on the next move.

The reports also showed that the strike was almost 100 percent effective. The decision was to picket the mills again en masse that afternoon and the next morning. The next morning and the next, police brutalities were re-enacted.

Before the end of that week, I was asked to become Executive Secretary of the strike committee, which meant taking on the general leadership. Both Rotzel and Long were invited to become voting members of the committee. Some of the reasons for this move on the part of the worker members of the committee I have already suggested. Under pressure of the police brutality and the adverse press in Lawrence and Boston, these local people came to feel a desperate need for a "front," a cover of people who could not so easily be disregarded, discounted and beaten up; of people whose education and contacts might qualify them in spite of their inexperience to interpret the struggle to the public and to help in developing basic strategy. Of course, our record of dissent during the war plus the fact that we had not stopped coming to Lawrence when the police got ugly, had inspired confidence.

The last thing in the world that any of us had expected, when we first went to Lawrence, had been that such a call as this would be made upon us.

But when the proposition was made, we clearly had either to undertake the ominous responsibility or else to leave Lawrence altogether. There was no middle course. So we accepted the invitation. It would be more accurate to say that, though we had never learned to swim, we three young preachers and devotees of peace and nonviolence were tossed into a raging ocean—and we swam. I was "leader" of 30,000 strikers of twenty or more nationalities. Harold took over the relief organization. Cedric looked after youth activities, entertainment, and some aspects of public relations.

Cedric was still a youth, considerably younger than Harold and me, who were thirty-four. He was tall, athletic, handsome, and possessed of a winning smile. He was a pure spirit, a noble being. In later years he was for some time secretary of the Cooperative League of America. One of the best "entertainments" he put on during the strike was a personal one for the benefit of the relief fund. Before he became a pacifist he had been in the state militia. He was a crack shot and had got a heap of medals for his marksmanship. He auctioned off the medals himself one day. Seeing a pacifist sharpshooter auction off his medals made a lot of people feel good, and I guess it taught some of them some kind of lesson about courage and nonviolence.

JAILED FOR THE FIRST TIME

Union leaders nowadays seldom appear on picket lines—for various reasons. Back in the jungle era in 1919 and for some years thereafter, strike leaders did not ordinarily go out on picket lines, for the same reason that staff generals don't go into the front lines: they would be picked off. However, a few days after we had become full members of the strike committee, the strikers were beginning to wilt under the beating to which scores of them were being subjected every morning and afternoon. It was decided that something drastic had to be done to boost morale, namely, that a number of local leaders, along with Cedric and myself, should head the picket line on a certain afternoon.

It might moderate the police brutality somewhat. If we should be beaten up, the fact that we had gotten it too would nerve others to stay on the line, whatever might come. Utmost precautions were taken to instruct those who were going on the line that day to refuse absolutely to be provoked into counter-violence. This was done publicly so that the labor spies, who infested the strike . . . , would carry the word to the police.

Shortly after four o'clock that afternoon the procession left the hall which served as headquarters, with Cedric and myself at the head. In a few minutes we were on the street opposite the Arlington Mill. As soon as we got there, police on foot, on horseback, and in sidecars, swarmed into the neighborhood as if to quell a raging mob that had gotten out of hand. We took one turn back and forth before the Arlington. There were no incidents and there was no shouting. Shortly after we started the second lap, Cedric and I reached a point where a street branched off to the left and then almost immediately took another bend to the left. Thus people on the main street could not witness what happened in the side street.

At that moment several mounted cops suddenly cut Cedric and me off from the picketers behind us, all of whom were forced by other police to keep walking straight ahead. As soon as we had been shunted into the side street, they began beating us. One of them made the mistake of hitting Cedric at once on the back of the neck and knocking him unconscious, so that he had to be lifted and carried into the patrol wagon, which was conveniently waiting nearby. They beat me around the body and legs with their clubs, taking care not to knock me unconscious, and forced me to keep walking slowly in order to avoid being trampled by the horses.

We were passing a barn that seemed to be shut tight, but suddenly a door opened, an arm shot out, grabbed mine, pulled me into the shed, and slammed the door shut again. In the half light I saw that it was a woman. She could not speak English. She hurried me to a side door of the barn, while the police clamored and cursed outside. She tried to hurry me from the barn into her house, which adjoined it. The police were too quick for her. Some of them had leaped into the yard. They grabbed me as she tried, in vain, to hang on. She let go and cursed them in their turn.

The cops got me back on the sidewalk and resumed the systematic beating, with the result that before long I was too exhausted to keep on my feet and was deposited in the wagon by the side of Cedric, who was slowly coming back to consciousness.

In the police headquarters downtown we were placed in separate cells. The one I occupied was at the end of the row. The wall, along which was a wooden bench, the only place to sit or recline, was made of metal. Policemen in relays beat a steady tattoo on that wall. There was a brief interruption when a police captain from Newton, who had been loaned to Lawrence for strike duty and whose son had been a member of my Bible class in Central Church, took his stand before the cell door and looked at me through the bars. He spoke scathingly of the disgrace of a minister of the gospel's behaving in such a way that he "had to be thrown into jail." When he left, hammering on the cell wall was resumed. But shortly before nine o'clock, about three hours after we landed in jail, we were told that bail had been posted and we could go out. It was an immense relief, for at nine o'clock prisoners were transferred for the night to the prison on the outskirts of the town and it was more or less routine that *en route* prisoners "tried to escape and had to be beaten into submission"—with no witness on hand except the police who did the beating. That is why our fellow committee members had worked so desperately to get the cash before the deadline. . . .

The incident . . . served to heighten and steady the morale of the strikers. When the case against us for "disturbing the peace" came before the city court about a week later, the judge dismissed it. In spite of the fact that we were acquitted because of testimony which clearly indicated that it was the police who had disturbed the peace, the judge lectured Cedric and me, telling us that Lawrence was no place for young ministers to visit at that time and that we should not be caught again, as we had been the week before, on a picket line. . . .

For several weeks . . . the strike settled down. Management made no special effort to get workers back. In the strike committee we concentrated on raising funds for relief, bringing influential people from Boston and elsewhere to observe the situation for themselves, and holding daily meetings in several languages.

When, however, the strike had lasted over a month and there were no signs of a break, conditions again became more tense. One night the police mounted machine guns at the head of the principal streets. This was done in spite of the fact that on the workers' side the strike had been remarkably free from violence. Over a hundred strikers were arrested during the sixteen weeks the struggle lasted. Because these cases were heard during, or after, the close of the strike, no one was sentenced to as much as a day in jail or paid even a one-dollar fine. Bringing in the machine guns was clearly an act of provocation. It was hoped that the strikers would resort to violence and that thereupon the strike could be discredited and broken.

This statement is not based on mere speculation. The morning the machine guns appeared, the strike committee met to discuss the strategy for dealing with this development. One of the members got up and made a heated speech, the import of which was: "The police are only a couple of hundred. We are thirty thousand. Let's seize the machine guns this afternoon and turn them on the police." Very likely, this could have been done. Among the strikers and their families were a good many young men who had been taught guerilla tactics during the war, and how to operate machine guns. They were bitter enough over the cut in wages with which they had been confronted as soon as the war was over, without the added provocation of having the quarters of the town where they lived besieged with machine guns, as if they were a conquered people.

The three young pacifist ministers who sat there listening to that speech were inwardly shaken and apprehensive as to what might happen. However, one after another the local members of the committee, ordinary workers in the mills, made remarks to this effect: "The guns were put there to provoke us; why play into the hands of the mill management and the police? It would only discredit the strike. They can't weave wool with machine guns. All we have to do is to continue to stand together." This view prevailed. The man who made the provocative speech was suspected of being a labor spy. Within two weeks I encountered him in the police headquarters of Lawrence under circumstances which proved that he was either in the employ of the police or in their confidence as an operative of some detective agency. . . .

In the afternoon, about two o'clock, those of the strikers who could crowd into the one hall which would hold fifteen or sixteen hundred people, all standing and packed as closely as possible, met there, as they did every afternoon when the weather did not permit an outdoor meeting. The air was electric, as it is whenever large numbers of men meet in a crisis in the midst of a struggle. Speakers addressed them in several languages. Then it was my turn to try to explain the policy of refraining from violence, refusing to be provoked, which had been decided upon by the strike committee in the morning. They had, of course, to be persuaded that it was a sound policy and to follow it enthusiastically: otherwise their morale would be hopelessly undermined. Men and women who, many of them, had already been clubbed on the picket line, whose savings had long since been used up, whose children no longer had shoes to wear to go to school, had to accept bitter defeat or a split in their ranks which could only lead to early defeat—or else had to embrace nonviolent resistance.

When I began my talk by saying that the machine guns were an insult and a provocation and that we could not take this attack lying down, the cheers shook the frame building. Then I told them, in line with the strike committee's decision, that to permit ourselves to be provoked into violence would mean defeating ourselves; that our real power was in our solidarity and in our capacity to endure suffering rather than give up the fight for the right to organize; that no one could "weave wool with machine guns"; that cheerfulness was better for morale than bitterness and that therefore we would smile as we passed the machine guns and the police on the way from the hall to the picket lines around the mills. I told the spies, who were sure to be in the audience, to go and tell the police and the mill management that this was our policy. At this point the cheers broke out again, louder and louder, and the crowds left, laughing and singing:

> Though cowards flinch and traitors sneer,
> We'll keep the Red Flag flying here.

I have had other such experiences which have convinced me that the often expressed idea that Americans cannot understand nonviolence as Indians (for example) do is erroneous. Under certain circumstances, American workers will practice nonviolent resistance, as the Negroes of Montgomery did a year or two ago in their bus protest.

. . . [D]esperate efforts to break the strike did not cease because it was peacefully conducted. The attempt to provoke mass violence having failed, terrorization of the leaders was again resorted to. More or less friendly newspaper reporters from out of town hinted that my life was in danger and that, since the strike had dragged out so long that it could not end victoriously, no harm would be done if I left town. Not long after these warnings, a group of men, some of whom were reliably identified as members of the Lawrence police force, in the middle of the night entered the hotel where I occasionally stayed and broke the door of the room which I had rented for the week. It happened that I had left town unexpectedly and unannounced that afternoon to go to New York for a conference with officers of the Amalgamated Clothing Workers Union. Surprisingly, no spies or plainclothesmen had seen me leave town, or if any did, they had decided to keep it quiet. So the thugs missed their prey.

That night they did succeed in routing out a young Italian organizer, Anthony Capraro, . . . and took him in a car into the country. They gave him a frightful beating and left him senseless in a ditch near Andover, a town adjoining Lawrence. Fortunately, it was a comparatively mild spring night. Tony recovered consciousness as day began to dawn, and crawled out of the ditch and onto the road. As he was crawling along the road, a milkwagon driver noticed him in time to avoid side-swiping him. The driver carried him to a nearby house, where the people took him in and called a doctor. . . .

GLOOM—AND VICTORY

As the days passed . . . it became increasingly difficult to keep the strike going. The American Woolen Company opened a couple of its mills in other cities. In Lawrence it offered any workers who would come back an increase in piece or hourly rates to compensate for the cut in hours from fifty-four to forty-eight per week. The temptation to return as individuals, without gaining recognition of the right to appoint shop grievance committees, became very strong. On the week end, at the close of the fifteenth week of the struggle, we held a series of conferences and mass meetings in a final effort to keep the workers out on Monday. It was well known that the first day of the new working week was crucial; if they did not stampede back into the mills Monday, they would remain out the rest of the week. We succeeded. The workers, with only a handful of exceptions, had the magnificent courage to remain on strike.

However, on Monday afternoon the completely trustworthy members of the strike committee held a long conference and decided that we had no right to call on the workers for further sacrifices. The following week end, therefore, we would make no special effort to bring pressure on them. There being no settlement in sight, we anticipated that on the following Monday the workers—those who were not on the company blacklists—would go to work; all would be over, and the strike lost.

Some weeks before, a convention of textile workers from Lawrence, New York, Paterson, Passaic and a couple of other centers, had set up an independent union, the Amalgamated Textile Workers of America. I had been elected national secretary. The Lawrence committee decided that it was my job to go to the other locals and prepare them for the shock which the collapse of the Lawrence strike was sure to cause them. On a lovely Tuesday afternoon in the middle of May, therefore, I was disconsolately making my way to the railroad station to take the train to Boston, and thence to New York. I was walking down the street on which was located the little hall where for four months we had held our daily strike committee meetings. As I approached the hall, I noticed a large automobile standing in front of the building. It was unoccupied. I slackened my step, wondering what that car, standing on the otherwise deserted street, might mean. I had just come abreast of the car when the door of our hall opened and a man whom I recognized as a friendly milk dealer, who had probably saved many babies' lives, because he had sold quantities of milk on credit to the strikers, stepped onto the sidewalk. He recognized me at the same instant and motioned to me to come over.

"Lamont wants to see you," he said. Lamont, who was not related to the J. Pierpont Morgan partner, was the head of the American Woolen Company Mills in Lawrence. "What does he want to see me for?" I asked. The milk dealer answered that the only possible reason could be to talk about settling the strike.

He had arranged with Lamont to bring me to the latter's home in Andover shortly after five o'clock. It was then about two. We agreed that I should keep out of circulation during the interval, since it would be catastrophic to have it leak out that there might be a settlement and then have the hope dashed.

We met again at five, and he drove me into the spacious yard of Lamont's home. All about were trees in blossom. Lamont drove into the yard directly behind us, having approached from another direction. There on the lawn beside the cars the three of us met. The moment he laid eyes on me, Lamont began to excoriate me as "the outside agitator who has brought all this needless trouble and suffering to Lawrence." When he paused for a moment, I said, "Is this what you brought me here for?" He said, "No; how can we settle this damn strike?" It appeared that at the very moment when we felt we had to give up, the mill management had decided that, with orders coming in again, they could not hold out, either.

I replied that, of course, we two couldn't "settle" it. The conditions were well known: a twelve-per-cent increase in hour and piece rates and recognition in all departments, to shop committees, through which the union would have a voice in settling grievances. Lamont said that the American Woolen Company agreed. I asked him if he could speak for the other mill corporations also. He answered that he did. Then I told him that it would be necessary for the management of each mill to meet a committee of strikers from its mill on Wednesday morning and formally assure the committee that our terms were accepted. He agreed. We parted without shaking hands on it.

When I showed up later that evening in the relief station, where the strike committeemen usually got together informally, they thought they were seeing a ghost. By that time I was supposed to be well on the way to New York. When I told them of the encounter with the milk dealer and Lamont, they were sure, at first, that the strain of the long weeks of strike and the anticipation of failure had been too much for me and that I was out of my head. I stuck to my story and seemed on the whole sober and in my right mind. When someone who had slipped out to telephone the milk dealer came back and confirmed my story, it was finally accepted.

Even so, the joy was restrained. These workers, who had gone through so much this year and in 1912 and earlier, were not sure that the managements were not up to some trick. They were not going to let their joy really break out until the committees had met the managements and confirmed the settlement. Early Wednesday morning, word was passed around that workers were to meet by mills. The report of the meeting with Lamont was given. Committees were selected and went off to their respective mills. They returned promptly and reported that in each case agreement had been quickly reached.

That evening there was a great outdoor mass meeting, where the strikers as a body formally ratified the settlement and authorized those who were needed to put the machinery back in operation after a sixteen weeks lay-off to return to work the next morning. They sang:

> Arise, ye prisoners of starvation. . . .
> We have been nought; we shall be all.

And that was that.

DOCUMENT 17

Joel Seidman,
Sit-Down

The campaigns of the Congress of Industrial Organizations (CIO) to organize workers in mass production industries had as a dramatic by-product the "sit-down strike." In a sit-down, workers stopped working but refused to leave the factory. Sustained by food from friends and relations outside the plant, sit-downers attempted to live and sleep at their work place until the demand for union recognition was granted.

Sit-down strikes reached their peak between September 1936 and May 1937, when 485,000 workers were involved. Like the activists of the 1960s, these strikers of the 1930s were accused of trespassing on private property. Like the later "sit-inners," sit-downers maintained that human rights come first. This report by the League for Industrial Democracy graphically describes the methods and spirit of the sit-down strike.

From Joel Seidman, *Sit-Down* (New York: The League for Industrial Democracy, 1937). Reprinted with the permission of the League for Industrial Democracy, Inc.

When they tie the can to a union man,
   Sit down! Sit down!
When they give him the sack, they'll take him back,
   Sit down! Sit down!
       Chorus
Sit down, just take a seat,
Sit down, and rest your feet,
Sit down, you've got 'em beat.
   Sit down! Sit down!

EARLY USES OF THE SIT-DOWN IN AMERICA

It is impossible to determine accurately when and where the sit-down strike was first used. It seems such a logical tactic for workers to employ that there are probably many unrecorded instances, each one short in duration, going back almost as far as our modern industrial civilization. The wonder is that its use did not become widespread much earlier.

In at least two American industries it has long been common for workers to stop work without leaving their place of employment. In the anthracite coal fields the breaker boys, whose task it was to remove impurities from the coal, early formed the practice of stopping work without leaving their places when they were dissatisfied. Similarly miners have stopped loading coal when they were not adequately supplied with timber for safety protection.

In the women's garment industry, as far back as 1910, workers have ceased operations without leaving the shop. Partly this has been done when a contract forbade strikes, the workers arguing that a mere stoppage was not a violation. These stoppages, as they were called, attracted little attention because they were usually settled within a few hours, and lacked the drama and publicity value of a picket line. Seldom, if ever, did the workers remain at their places over night, though stoppages often continue for several days. In the Schenectady, N. Y., plant of the General Electric Company, similarly, a sit-down strike occurred as early as 1906. In 1933, 2,500 employees of the Hormel Packing Company in Austin, Minnesota, sat down for three days and won their strike against speed-up, for shorter hours and better wages. Many other instances doubtless occurred in other industries. During the depression the unemployed in New Jersey and elsewhere, took possession of legislative chambers, in an effort to dramatize their plight and force more adequate relief policies.

Seamen used the sit-down strike on the Pacific coast early in 1936. Seamen on the Panama Pacific liner *California* had signed on at the Atlantic coast rates. In an effort to obtain the higher Pacific coast rates, they struck for three days while the ship was at the San Pedro, California docks. The men remained on board, but refused to work. Had they struck while the ship was at sea, they would have been subject to a charge of mutiny. As it was, they narrowly escaped arrest on that charge. The line refused to reemploy the strikers when the ship reached New York, and a long strike against the International Mercantile Marine Company was the result.

RUBBER WORKERS SIT DOWN

It remained for the Akron rubber workers to popularize the sit-down in the United States. According to Louis Adamic it was first used by ball teams of union rubber workers, who sat down on the grass or on benches and refused to play until they were provided with an umpire who was a union man. Later a dozen of them remembered this technique when they were dissatisfied with working conditions. The paralysis spread through the plant, and within an hour the dispute was settled.

The sit-down played a part in the circumstances that led up to the big Goodyear Tire and Rubber Company strike of February-March, 1936. Fundamentally it was insecurity, speed-up, the threat of lower wages and longer hours, and the refusal of the company to engage in genuine collective bargaining that caused the strike. The immediate cause was the laying off of 70 men in the tire division, which convinced the workers that the company planned to change from the six-hour to the eight-hour day. In protest against the lay-off 137 men engaged in a sit-down strike, whereupon they were dismissed. Mass meetings were called, and the company under pressure agreed to rehire the 137 and reconsider the suspension of the 70. Nevertheless a strike acquired momentum and mass picketing closed down the entire plant, with 14,000 workers idle. The strike was started spontaneously and was then officially sanctioned by the union.

The rubber workers are new and enthusiastic unionists. The sit-down technique works, and so they use it as soon as an issue arises. Their officers are urging them not to stop production without first bringing their grievance to the attention of the union and the company through the regular channels. During 1936 there was scarcely a week that did not witness at least one sit-down in the rubber plants. In a single plant in less than a year no less than 58 were counted, ranging in length from an hour or less to two or three days. Following one sit-down 31 Goodyear strikers were charged with inciting to riot, but the charges were later dismissed. As the rubber workers become more experienced and more disciplined unionists, the sit-downs over petty issues will doubtless disappear.

U. A. W. A.; 1937 MODEL

... Automobile workers took the new weapon, adapted and developed it, and with its aid brought the powerful and anti-union General Motors Corporation to terms.

A short sit-down strike had occurred in the automobile industry as early as spring, 1934, in the White plant in Cleveland. This strike was settled within several hours. The first strike in which automobile workers stayed in the plant over night occurred in the Bendix plant in South Bend, Indiana. On November 17, 1936, workers in several Bendix departments, influenced by the successful sit-downs in the Akron rubber industry, stopped work but remained at their machines. The company ordered all workers to assemble outside the plant, to decide whether they wished to work. To forestall this attempted lockout, the Bendix workers determined to remain in the plant until the management came to terms. In a week victory was won.

The same day the Bendix strike ended, 900 workers in the Midland Steel plant in Detroit sat down. This strike had been planned as a stay-in, to utilize the technique used so effectively in South Bend. This strike marked the first use of the stay-in technique by automobile workers in Michigan. Again the strike ended in a smashing victory for the union. In mid-December the sit-down movement spread to the workers of the Kelsey-Hayes Wheel Company of Detroit. Two short sit-downs ended with the company's promise to negotiate; on its failure to live up to its promise the workers sat down again, this time with the determination not to resume work until they had won their demands. There was also a brief sit-down strike in the Windsor, Ontario, plant of the Kelsey Wheel Company, Ltd., a subsidiary of the Kelsey-Hayes Wheel Company. In the meantime other sit-downs were occurring in Detroit, in the plants of the Aluminum Company of America, Bohn Aluminum, and Gordon Bakery. Thus the stage was set for the big sit-down strike in Flint.

In November and December, 1936, the campaign of the United Automobile Workers of America to organize the General Motors Corporation workers was nearing a climax. The auto workers enjoyed the backing of the progressive unions of the Committee for Industrial Organization. In the warfare between non-union mass production industry and the C.I.O., the General Motors strike was the first major battle. Realizing that much might depend upon the outcome, both sides unstintingly threw their resources into the struggle.

In December the union requested a conference with the heads of the General Motors Corporation, to engage in collective bargaining on behalf of all the corporation's employees. This request was denied, and the union was told to take up grievances with individual plant managers. At this point, in the Fisher Body plant of the corporation in Flint, Michigan, a sit-down that began inauspiciously enough was destined to have far-reaching consequences.

On December 29 the union presented a proposed contract to the plant manager, in Flint, requesting an answer within a week. The next morning a sit-down began in the No. 2 plant, when inspectors were transferred to other jobs because they would not leave the union. Late the same day the men in No. 1 were alarmed to see dies placed on box cars bound for Pontiac and Grand Rapids, where the union is weaker. To protect their jobs they kept the line from starting up again, and remained in possession of the plant. Slowly the tie-up spread through the vast General Motors system, as more and more plants were affected by strikes or the shortage of necessary parts. By early February almost all of the 200,000 General Motors employees were idle, and the weekly production of cars had declined to 1,500 from the mid-December peak of 53,000.

Behind the General Motors strike there was a long record of efforts by the United Automobile Workers of America to bargain collectively, with delays and evasions on the part of the corporation. Especially did the workers rebel against the speeding up of production and the spy system employed by the company. Repeated efforts of the union to win recognition and obtain a union contract came to naught, and in the meantime discrimination against union members continued. Complaints were made to the National Labor Relations Board that General Motors had violated the law by discharging employees for union activity, using industrial spies, and dominating a company union in its St. Louis plant. Scarcely had the hearing gotten under way when the corporation sought an injunction to restrain the board from proceeding further. The injunction was denied in the federal district court, but a subsequent appeal and stay prevented the board from proceeding. Six months later, when the strike began, the hands of the board were still bound.

From the first the corporation officials insisted that they would not negotiate so long as the strikers held the plants. The men suspected a ruse, knowing that if they left the plants they would lose their power to prevent production. They agreed to leave, however, if the company pledged itself not to try to operate the plant or to move machinery while negotiations were in progress. The company refused.

INJUNCTIONS AND TEAR GAS IN FLINT

On January 2 the struggle entered a new phase. Upon the company's petition, Judge Edward S. Black issued a sweeping injunction restraining the union from continuing to remain in the plant, from picketing, and from interfering in any manner with those who wished to enter the plant to work. To obey the injunction would be to concede the loss of the strike. The injunction exposed the hollowness of the company's complaint against possession of its plant, for a stay-out strike would have been crushed as surely as the sit-down, had the writ been obeyed. Later, in Cleveland, the corporation was to seek an injunction against strikers who had left the plant to form a picket line. Small wonder that when the sheriff read the injunction to the Flint strikers and asked them to leave voluntarily he was laughed out of the plant. Three days later it was discovered that the injunction judge owned stock in

General Motors. The union charged that he owned 3,665 shares, worth $219,900 at the current market quotation, and the judge admitted ownership of 1,000 shares. The union thereupon petitioned the state legislature to impeach Judge Black, for his violation of the statute forbidding a judge from sitting in a case in which he has an interest. The company, sensing its weak position, did not apply for the writs of body attachment which would have required the sheriff to attempt to arrest the sit-down strikers for contempt of court.

Suddenly, on January 11, the company changed its tactics. Heat in the plant was shut off, and city police mobilized in the area. Company police attempted to starve out the sit-downers, attacking carriers of food and removing the ladders by means of which food had been brought in. The sit-downers, in return, captured the gates from the company police. The city police, who had cleared nearby streets in advance, then attacked in an effort to recapture the gates. Tear gas bombs were hurled against the sit-downers and their sympathizers outside. Strikers used the fire hoses within the plant to direct streams of water on the police and on the gas bombs. During the battle the sit-downers, who had until then occupied only the second floor of the plant, took possession of the entire building. For four hours the strikers fought the police, who used clubs, tear gas, and riot guns. Fourteen workers were wounded by the police gunfire, one of them seriously, and dozens were tear-gassed. Within the sound truck union organizers took turns at the microphone, shouting encouragement to the strikers, and giving direction to the battle. When the battle ended the strikers remained in victorious possession of the plants.

The county prosecuting attorney, who owned 61 shares of General Motors stock, jailed the wounded as they were released from the hospital, and obtained 1,200 John Doe warrants under which any strike sympathizer could be arrested. Seven of the Flint strike leaders were arrested, charged with unlawful assembly and malicious destruction of property. The union demand for the arrest of the police, company guards, and others who had been responsible for the attack was disregarded. In the meantime National Guardsmen were mobilized and sent to Flint.

At this point, the public was relieved to learn that a truce had been arranged. General Motors agreed to enter into negotiations with the union in an effort to settle the strike, and the union in return agreed to evacuate all plants held by it, whether in Flint or elsewhere. One of the most important matters to be considered in the negotiations was whether the United Automobile Workers should be recognized as the sole bargaining agency for the workers. Thirty minutes before the sit-downers were to march out of the Flint plants, and after other plants had already been evacuated, the union discovered that W. S. Knudsen, executive vice-president of the corporation, had agreed to bargain collectively with the Flint Alliance, a semi-company union, semi-vigilante strikebreaking organization inspired by the company. Regarding this as a violation of the truce, the union refused to evacuate the plants, and General

Motors thereupon cancelled the scheduled conference. Several days later the corporation announced that 110,000 workers had signed petitions asking to be returned to work, but this number was exaggerated and the union showed that large numbers of the signatures had been obtained by intimidation.

On February 1 came the turning point in the strike. General Motors had taken the offensive, and the union had suffered defeats in Anderson, Indiana, and Saginaw, Michigan. Hearings on another application for an injunction were in progress, this time before Judge Gadola. The Flint Alliance was becoming dangerous, and there was some fear that the back-to-work movement inspired by the company might spread. Something had to be done to bolster morale. The union had again to take the offensive.

The Chevrolet plant in Flint, the scene of discrimination against union members provided the opportunity. Of most strategic importance was plant No. 4, in which all Chevrolet motors are assembled. A hundred feet from this plant, however, was the personnel building, headquarters of company police and hired gunmen. The strategy decided upon was to make a sham attack upon plant No. 9, in the far corner of the tract. At 3:30 p.m. a sit-down started there, and the excitement brought the company police on the run. At 3:35 the union men in plant No. 6, starting to No. 9 to help, were instead directed by union leaders in the sound truck into No. 4, where a sit-down simultaneously began. The Company police arrived too late, and the union was in control of the key plant, without which no production was possible. The Women's Emergency Brigade, made up of wives, mothers and sisters of the strikers, played a heroic and important part in the battle, both at No. 9 and No. 4. They smashed windows of the plant to keep the men from being suffocated by tear gas, and with locked arms barred the police attack upon the main gate of No. 4.

On the following day Judge Gadola issued the injunction requested by the company. Though not a stockholder, as Judge Black had been, he proved himself just as willing a servant. His injunction, similar in many ways to that issued by Judge Black a month before, was much more drastic. It ordered the union officers and the sit-downers, under penalty of $15,000,000 to evacuate the plants by 3 p.m. the following day, and to refrain from picketing and from interfering with the operation of the plants or the entry of strikebreakers. The sheriff was ordered to evacuate the plants within 24 hours. Again the strikers refused to budge, and the judge ordered them all arrested. Sheriff Wolcott, explaining that he lacked a sufficient number of deputies, refused to carry out the order unless Governor Murphy provided the aid of the National Guard.

Meanwhile sit-downers within Fisher Body plant No. 2 and Chevrolet No. 4 were in a virtual state of siege. National Guardsmen surrounded the plants, and refused to allow friends and relatives to speak to the men at the factory gates. A hunger siege at first imposed by the Guardsmen was lifted in less than a day. Reporters who tried to speak to the strikers at the gates were escorted out of the military zone at the point of bayonets. At Fisher No. 1, on the contrary, the strikers were able to receive visitors and come and go as they pleased, under no restrictions except those imposed by their own shop council.

The stumbling block to peaceful settlement of the strike remained the issue of recognition. The union, which first asked recognition as sole bargaining agent for all General Motors employees, later surrendered that claim and asked merely to be sole bargaining agent in 20 plants closed by the strike. The union proposed that, if this was agreed upon, all plants immediately resume operations, and all other points at issue be settled in conference. This the company likewise refused. Company spokesmen favored a plebiscite to determine the wishes of the men, but refused to recognize the union as sole bargaining agent in those plants where it might win a majority.

Finally, on February 11, an agreement was reached and the strike ended. Much of the credit for its settlement without further bloodshed belonged to Governor Murphy, who proved a skillful and patient mediator. Under the agreement the United Automobile Workers was recognized as bargaining agent for its members, and the company agreed not to bargain on matters of general corporate policy with any other group from 20 struck plants without the governor's sanction. There was to be no discrimination against union men, and all court proceedings were to be dropped. Collective bargaining negotiations were to begin on February 16. The union, on its part, was to evacuate the occupied plants, refrain from recruiting on company property, and exhaust every possibility of negotiating before calling any other strike. At the same time the company announced an increase in the average wage rate of five cents an hour, swelling its normal annual wage bill by $25,000,000.

The strikers hailed the settlement as a signal victory for them. For the first time the giant General Motors Corporation had been fought to a stand-still by its workers, and forced to engage in collective bargaining with them. After 44 days the sit-downers marched out of the plant, heads and spirits high, singing "Solidarity Forever." Out they came, two by two, with a large American flag at the head of the procession, to the cheers of 2,000 sympathizers assembled at the plants.

KEEPING COMFORTABLE

Sit-downers have had a host of new problems to solve, not the least of which have been living in factory buildings. Food, sleeping quarters, and sanitation are matters that must be properly attended to if morale is to be kept up and health maintained for long. The necessary work must be done, and facilities for recreation provided. In all of these respects our experience with sit-downs, brief though it has been, is illuminating.

With hundreds or perhaps several thousands of sit-downers in a plant, the problem of food becomes urgent. The union must assume responsibility for seeing that the workers receive three meals a day. This is a severe strain on the union treasury, but thus far adequate meals have been furnished. Indeed, in some strikes most of the sit-downers have gained weight. One of the most important committees in many sit-down strikes is the chiseling committee, which seeks donations from food merchants. It calls for resourcefulness when the committee is unable to obtain the food for the menu as planned, and the cook must prepare whatever is brought back. The Midland Steel Products Company sit-downers in Detroit were aided by a daily donation of 30 gallons of milk by the milk drivers' union. Often the meals furnished by the union are supplemented by food brought to individual strikers by their families or friends.

Usually the food is cooked in a nearby hall or restaurant, and brought in milk cans, kettles, or other large containers to the plant. In the case of the Wahl-Eversharp Pen Company of Chicago, police refused to allow friends of the strikers to bring food into the plant. The sit-downers then lowered a rope from an upper window to the roof of an adjoining bakery, and obtained food in this fashion. The menu of sit-downers is usually simple, but adequate. Barrels, kegs, and whatever else is suitable are used for chairs, and tables are likewise improvised. Newspapers sometimes serve as tablecloths. Liquor is strictly forbidden.

Usually the cooking is done by a committee of the strikers' wives. In large strikes, however, a professional cook may be obtained. The cook in the Flint strike, for example, was sent there to help by the Cooks' Union of Detroit. He had previously cooked for four other sit-down strikes. For the Flint strike the union installed new kitchen equipment worth more than $1,000.

"The food goes into the factories in twenty kettles of various sizes," the cook reported. "The amount of food the strikers use is immense. Five hundred pounds of meat, one thousand pounds of potatoes, three hundred loaves of bread, one hundred pounds of coffee, two hundred pounds of sugar, thirty gallons of fresh milk, four cases of evaporated milk!"

In Detroit a cooperative kitchen was established to feed 800 sit-down strikers in the Bohn Aluminum, Cadillac, and Fleetwood plants:

> The kitchen runs on efficient lines, not speed-up, in two shifts. About 50 men and women comprise the working crew; the first shift working from 7:00 until 2:00 in the afternoon, the second from 11:00 in the morning until 6:00 in the afternoon. Everyone attends the meetings held at 2:00 o'clock daily at I.A.S. Hall where the various committees make their reports. There is the kitchen committee, which takes care of preparing the food, with a chef from the Cooks' Union, Local No. 234, to supervise the preparation of it. Then there is a finance committee, with two treasurers, working in shifts, one from the Cadillac plant and one from the Bohn Aluminum plant.

Other important committees were the drivers' committee, which delivered the food, and the chiseling committee, which covered the city for donations of food or money. About two-thirds of the supplies were obtained in this fashion.

One of the important problems is to obtain comfortable sleeping quarters. Sit-down strikers in an automobile body or final assembly plant are fortunate in this regard, for they may sleep on the floor of the cars, removing the seats if necessary or arranging the seats between the conveyor lines. In the Midland steel plant some of the men tied burlap to machines, and so rigged up cots. Elsewhere tables have been made to serve. Sometimes cots have been brought to the plants by friends, and usually all have obtained blankets after the first night. Standard Cotton Products Company sit-downers in Flint built houses of cardboard packing boxes, and made beds of cotton padding designed for automobile seats. Their houses were in two rows, one labeled "Union Street" and the other "Cotton Street."

Most visitors to sit-down strikes have been impressed by the neatness of the men and the tidy appearance of the plants. One of the important jobs is to see that the factories are kept clean. The machinery is kept in good order, for the sit-downers wish to return to work as soon as possible after the strike ends. Often a former barber is found among the strikers, and he is made to resume his old trade. In the Kelsey-Hayes plant a wheelbarrow on a platform served as a barber chair. In one sit-down strike where there were women employees, a beauty parlor was opened for them by a former worker in such an establishment. Washing is often a problem, however, for in most plants only ordinary washbowls are available. One sit-down, in the Detroit plant of the Aluminum Company of America, had to be transformed into a walk-out because a number of the men became ill and lack of sufficient sanitary facilities made further stay in the plant hazardous to health.

OBEYING THE RULES

A certain amount of work is required, for meals must be served, the place kept clean, a watch kept, and discipline maintained. For recreation the men play cards, listen to the radio, or provide their own entertainment program. There are dancers, singers, and musicians in every large group, and often an orchestra can be formed. Frequently the sit-downers write songs about their own strikes. A bowling alley was set up in one plant, and horse shoes pitched in others. Basket-ball courts have been improvised, hockey games played, and boxing and wrestling matches promoted. Where the company has provided a recreation room, with ping-pong tables and other games, these facilities are used to the utmost.

Those who are studiously inclined may prefer to read. The educational director of the United Automobile Workers has organized regular classes for the sit-downers, with parliamentary procedure, public speaking, and trade unionism among the popular subjects. Even where no formal classes are organized the sit-down has considerable educational value, for the workers must set up their own community government, and solve the many problems that arise. In some cases church services have been held regularly. Loud speaker systems are rigged up, so that announcements made at the gate or in the nearby union office may be heard by all. Pep speeches are made in the same manner, and entertainment is similarly broadcast. Often the sit-downers amuse themselves, at the very start of the strike, by hanging up the "No Help Wanted" sign.

Where both men and women are employed, the sit-downers must be extremely careful to avoid the charge of immorality. Usually the women have been sent home, partly for this reason and partly because the hardships were more difficult for them. Often the married women had to leave in any event, because of their family responsibilities. Where women have stayed in the plant, strict chaperonage rules have been established. In the Kelsey-Hayes strike the girls were not permitted to leave their dormitory after 11 p.m. The sit-downers asked that two of the regular plant matrons be placed in charge of the women's dormitory, and this request was complied with. The girls in this strike were not permitted to go through a dark tunnel that connected two buildings. Sit-down strikers of the Brownhill-Kramer Hosiery Company of Philadelphia included both men and women. The latter entered the factory each morning at 8 and stayed until 6 p.m., and only the men remained in the plant all night. Most sit-downers have not permitted women to enter the buildings at all. In several cases, however, the overwhelming majority of the sit-down strikers have been women. This was true, for example, in the cigar plant of Webster-Eisenlohr, Inc., of Detroit. "This is a woman's sit-down," said one of the strikers. "The men are just around—that's all."

Discipline and morale are of vital importance. Those who do not conform to the rules may be sentenced to extra clean-up duty for minor offenses, and ejected for serious violations. In the General Motors strike in Flint, court was held each morning, with bringing in liquor and circulating rumors the most frequent offenses. Elsewhere it may be overstaying leaves that is most frequently punished. In the Standard Cotton Products Company strike in Flint the judge himself was twice convicted of breaking the rules, and had to do extra dish washing as the penalty. Sometimes foremen and other company officials are allowed to converse only with union officers, for fear that they may adversely affect the strikers' morale. In some instances subterfuges have been employed by strikers or their wives in order to get out of the plant. Serious illness has been reported at home, or a birth in the family. Where too many such cases seemed to be reported a check was made, and the member immediately dropped. In some cases foremen have visited wives of sit-downers, making false reports of illness or hardships within the plant, in order to break down morale.

Except when trouble is feared, sit-downers are usually permitted to leave the plant for short intervals, under rules that they decide upon. In most cases they are required to return by a specified hour, and a check is made as they go and come. If an outside picket line is maintained as well, the strikers take turns staying within the plant. In one case a sit-downer who belonged to the National Guard was released for strike duty with the Guard.

Visitors are admitted only after a careful check of their credentials. Usually a pass signed by a responsible union officer is required. In many plants everyone who enters must submit to a search for weapons, and a similar search is made of all who leave. A communications system calls to the gate those who have visitors. A post office is sometimes set up to handle the mail, which may be censored. Gates and doors are often barricaded against a surprise attack, with guards on duty at all times. In Flint, sentries, in six-hour watches were on duty twenty-four hours a day, with an alarm system to warn quickly of impending danger. Sometimes metal strips are welded across doorways and windows, to make police entry more difficult, and to provide protection from gas bombs and bullets. In some plants pickets assigned to make the rounds have had to punch the time clock as they went on or off duty.

Heat, light, and water are important to the health and comfort of the strikers. Usually the companies have permitted these services to be maintained. The cutting off of these facilities has precipitated some of the most bitter battles yet fought by sit-downers. In some instances the employer has alternately turned the heat off and on.

Race relations may be another problem faced by sit-downers. In the Midland plant in Detroit both whites and negroes were employed. Workers of both races occupied the plant, and worked together in harmony throughout the strike.

In Flint an amusing episode occurred while the sit-downers were in possession of the plants. Chevrolet plant No. 4 had just been seized and considerable disorder had occurred. Following the seizure everything was peaceful, and the many camera men on the scene had little to do. They therefore engaged in a baseball game, with the still camera men playing the movie camera operators. The umpires were several hundred sit-downers on the roof of plant No. 4, and the spectators were the National Guardsmen on duty. One team, displeased with a decision, sat down on the ball field, and promptly won a reversal, amid cheers, from the union umpires. Several innings later the other team was similarly dissatisfied. Its tactics were to sing "Solidarity Forever;" and the umpires, after joining in the song, again reversed the decision.

Marching out of a plant when the strike has been won or a truce arranged offers opportunity for a colorful demonstration, as in Flint. The Bendix strikers marched out in military order, headed by their own drum and bugle corps, and paraded to the union hall. After the settlement proposals had been adopted, the strikers paraded through the business section of South Bend, headed by the effigy of the Bendix company union hanging on a long pole.

A TYPICAL SET OF RULES

Sit-downers must govern their community, and solve each problem as it arises. Fundamentally these problems are similar, though new situations will arise in each plant. The rules adopted by the sit-down strikers in the Standard

Cotton Products Company in Flint, Michigan, may be taken as fairly typical. With fewer than a hundred strikers, they were able to transact business in a full meeting held at 10 o'clock each morning, without the more complex and elaborate organization that a large plant would require. A strike committee of five members was placed in charge. Other officers included a chairman, a secretary, a judge, a press agent, and three clerks. There was a patrol committee of two, a food committee of two, a clean-up committee of three, and an entertainment committee of one.

Posted on the wall of the mess hall were the following rules, which were added to from time to time by majority vote:

RULES AND REGULATIONS

Rule No. 1. Any man who disturbs anyone while sleeping without good reason will have to wash the dishes and mop floor for one day.

Rule No. 2. Any man found drinking or looking for arguments will wash dishes and mop floor for one day—1st offense.

Rule No. 3. Every man who leaves must get a pass from the committee and check with the clerk. Passes must be shown to the doorman when going in and out, and on returning must check with the clerk. The doorman must obey these rules very strictly.

Rule No. 4. Doormen answer the phone and if the call is important he calls a committee man. No long-distance calls shall be made. All local calls are allowed. No profane language used over phone.

Rule No. 5. When photographers or outsiders come in no one speaks to them but a committee man.

Rule No. 6. Everyone must line up single file before meals are served. Dishwashers will be appointed before each meal by the clean-up committee. Every man must serve his turn.

Rule No. 7. Anyone eating between meals must wash his own dishes.

Rule No. 8. Every man must attend meetings.

Rule No. 9. No standing on tables.

Rule No. 10. No passes will be issued after 12:00 P. M.—except emergency calls.

Rule No. 11. Judge's decision on all broken rules will be regarded as final.

Rule No. 12. No conversation about the strike to the management. Any information concerning the strike will be furnished by the committee.

Rule No. 13. No more than a two-hour grace period allowed on passes. No grace period on a 20-minute leave.

Rule No. 14. No women allowed in the plant at any time.

Rule No. 15. No passes issued during meals and not until the dishes are done unless it is business.

Rule No. 16. All committees must attend meetings and report their activities.

Rule No. 17. No card playing or walking around or any disturbance during meetings.

WHAT OF THE LAW?

... Wyndham Mortimer, vice-president of the United Automobile Workers, has thus stated the case for the sit-down strike:

> Is it wrong for a worker to stay at his job? The laws of the state and nation recognize, in a hundred ways, that the worker has a definite claim upon his job; more fundamentally, it is recognized that every workman has a moral right to continue on his job unless some definite misconduct justifies his discharge. These sit-down strikers are staying at their work-places; no one has a better right to be there than have these men themselves. No one else, certainly, has any right to those positions. But the sit-down strikers have performed valuable services in those factories; General Motors and the public alike have profited by those services. To call them trespassers now, and to deny their right as human beings to remain with their jobs, is logically unsound and is manifestly unjust.

The union asserts that the workers have a property right in their jobs which is superior to the company's right to the use of the property. This theory will be rejected by most judges today, but in time it may be accepted as good law. The legal concept of property rights has changed and developed with usage. In Flint the union also argued that General Motors was not entitled to an injunction on the ground that it had itself violated the laws relating to collective bargaining, and therefore did not come into court with clean hands. Judge Gadola rejected this theory, though other judges have applied this general principle of equity to labor injunction cases. Gadola did not justify General Motors' actions, but merely asked whether one wrong could be righted by another wrong. This attitude is contrary to the principles of equity.

The sit-down strike has served notice on society that mere ownership does not carry with it all possible rights with reference to a factory. Those who work in it, who make it produce with their labor and who depend upon it for their livelihood, should likewise have a voice in its control. Those who invest their lives in an industry have at least as much at stake as those who merely invest their money. The sit-down strike brings these facts forcibly to public attention. It is interesting to note that, in the sit-down strike, workers are re-establishing the control over the tools of production that they lost with the Industrial Revolution.

The ethical case for the sit-down strike has well been presented by Rabbi Edward L. Israel, former chairman of the Social Justice Commission of the Central Conference of American Rabbis. The problem involved, Rabbi Israel asserts, is one of the comparative emphasis of human rights over against property rights. The entire struggle of the human race from bondage toward freedom, he points out, has been a constant battling against vested interests.

The ethical issue in the sit-down strike concerns itself with the right of an employee to his job. According to the average standard of wages in industry today, practically every working family is only a few days removed from starvation. We must therefore ask ourselves whether the right of hiring and firing, at a time when jobs are at a premium, can possibly be construed to be surrounded by such absolutistic and unassailable property prerogatives that it can literally place within the hands of an employer the power of life and death over the men who work for him.

No social conscience will grant any man such a right. By the same token, the worker has certain rights in his job. If he feels that collective bargaining through a national labor union is necessary for the preservation of those rights, he is definitely entitled to pursue such orderly methods as may force the employer to meet with his representatives in collective bargaining.

The argument that a worker has a property right in his job has thus been stated by Homer Martin, president of the automobile workers union:

What more sacred property right is there in the world than the right of a man in his job? This property right involves the right to support his family, feed his children and keep starvation away from the door. This property right is the very foundation stone of American homes. It is the most sacred, most fundamental property right in America. It means more to the stabilization of American life, morally, socially and economically, than any other property right.

Sit-down strikes, like other types of strikes, occur when long-standing grievances of workers have brought them to the breaking point. These employers who recognize unions and deal with them fairly need have little fear of sit-downs. If all employers recognized the right of workers to organize and bargain collectively, and obtain a fair share of the fruits of industry, few strikes would occur. If, when a strike occurred, the employer made no effort to operate with strike-breakers, there would be no need for a seizure of the plant. Employers will make more progress by removing the just grievances of workers than by attacking them on the basis of property laws framed in an earlier social situation, and designed for other purposes.

The sit-down strike is here to stay. Of that workers are resolved. The law may change slowly, but change it must.

DOCUMENT 18

John Sargent,
A Union without a Contract

John Sargent was the first president of Local 1010, United Steelworkers of America, at Inland Steel in East Chicago, Indiana, during the 1930s. The local had 18,000 members and was one of the largest in the nation. Sargent was re-elected in 1943, 1944, 1946, and, despite vicious Red-baiting, 1964.

Sargent describes how in the late 1930s at Inland Steel the union was not yet recognized by the company, and there was no collective bargaining agreement. He insists that "[w]ithout a contract we secured for ourselves agreements on working conditions and wages that we do not have today." This occurred, he argues, because "you had a series of strikes, wildcats, shut-downs, slow-downs, anything working people could think of to secure for themselves what they decided they had to have."

Labor historians have established that not only did Sargent accurately describe what happened at Inland Steel, but a similar situation existed at other large CIO unions (for example, in the electrical and rubber industries) during their early years.

Sargent presented these remarks to a community forum on "Labor History From The Viewpoint Of The Rank And File," at St. Joseph's College in East Chicago, Indiana, in March 1970.

————————————

I was hired at the Inland Steel Company in 1936. And I remember I was hired at 47 cents an hour, which was the going rate, and at a time when there were no such things as vacations, holidays, overtime, insurance, or any of the so-called fringe benefits everybody talks about today. But the worst thing—the thing that made you most disgusted—was the fact that if you came to work and the boss didn't like the way you looked, you went home;

John Sargent, "Your Dog Don't Bark No More," in Alice and Staughton Lynd, eds., *Rank and File: Personal Histories by Working-Class Organizers* (New York: Monthly Review Press, 1988), pp. 98–102.

and if he did like the way you looked, you got a promotion. Anything and everything that happened to you was at the whim and will of the fellow who was your boss and your supervisor. . . . As a matter of fact, in order to get a promotion—and sometimes even in order to work—you had to bring the boss a bottle of whiskey, or you had to mow the boss's lawn, or you had to do something to make yourself stand out from the other people he saw. This was the type of condition that existed as late as 1936 in the steel mills in this region.

When the CIO came in, the people were ready to accept a change. And because they were ready to accept a change, it was not a difficult task to organize the people in the steel mills. Thousands upon thousands of them, in a spontaneous movement, joined the steelworkers' organization at that time. And they did it because conditions in the mill were terrible, and because they had become disgusted with the political set-up in this country and the old tales told by the Republican Party about the free enterprise system in this country in which any man was his own boss, and there was no sense in having an organization, and organizations and unions were anti-American, and so on. All this feel off the backs of the people at that time. They realized that there was going to be a change—both a political and an economic change—in this country, and there was.

John L. Lewis had an agreement with the U. S. Steel Corporation, and they signed a contract. Little Steel—which was Youngstown Sheet and Tube, Republic Steel, Inland Steel, and other independent companies—had no contract with the Steelworkers Union. As a result in 1937 there was a strike called on Little Steel. And one of the things that happened during the strike was the massacre in South Chicago, the Chicago cops beating and shooting the people. The strike was not won. We did not win a contract. Neither Youngstown Sheet and Tube, nor Republic Steel, nor Inland Steel won a contract with the company. What we did get was an agreement through the governor's office that the company would recognize the Steelworkers Union and the company union and any other organization that wanted to represent the people in the steel industry. And we went back to work with this governor's agreement signed by various companies and union representatives in Indiana. At Inland Steel we had a company union; we had our own Steelworkers Union. When we got back to work we had company union representatives and Steelworkers Union representatives, and we had no contract with the company. But the enthusiasm of the people who were working in the mills made this settlement of the strike into a victory of great proportions.

Without a contract, without any agreement with the company, without any regulations concerning hours of work, conditions of work, or wages, a tremendous surge took place. We talk of a rank-and-file movement; the beginning of union organization was the best kind of rank-and-file movement you could think of. John L. Lewis sent in a few organizers, but there were no organizers at Inland Steel, and I'm sure there were no organizers at Youngstown Sheet and Tube. The union organizers were essentially workers in the mill who were so disgusted with their conditions and so ready for a change that they took the union into their own hands.

For example, what happened at Inland Steel I believe is perhaps representative of what happened throughout the steel industry. Without a contract we secured for ourselves agreements on working conditions and wages that we do not have today, and that were better by far than what we do have today in the mill. For example as a result of the enthusiasm of the people in the mill you had a series of strikes, wildcats, shut-downs, slow-downs, anything working people could think of to secure for themselves what they decided they had to have. If their wages were low there was no contract to prohibit them from striking, and they struck for better wages. If their conditions were bad, if they didn't like what was going on, if they were being abused, the people in the mills themselves—without a contract or any agreement with the company involved—would shut down a department or even a group of departments to secure for themselves the things they found necessary.

We made an agreement with Inland Steel way back in '38 or '39 that the company would not pay less than any of its competitors throughout the country. We never had it so good, I assure you of that. All you had to do as a union representative was come into the company and say, "Look, we have a group of people working in the pickle line, and at Youngstown, Ohio or Youngstown Sheet and Tube in East Chicago people are getting more money than we're getting for the same job." And if that was a fact, we were given an increase in wages at Inland. In those departments where you had a strong group of union members, where they were most active, we had the highest rates in the country. We were never able to secure conditions of this kind after we secured contracts.

What I'm trying to get at is the spontaneous action of people who are swept up in a movement they know is right and correct and want to do something about. Our union now has a grievance committee of twenty-five people. In those days there were more than twenty assistant grievers and hundreds of stewards. The grievance committee set-up could handle the affairs of the people on every shift and every turn with every group. Where you did have contracts with the companies (at U. S. Steel, for example) you had a limited grievance procedure. The U. S. Steel plant in Gary, the largest steel plant of the largest steel company, had a grievance committee of only eleven. Where union officials did not take over the union through a contract with the company (as they did with U. S. Steel), you had a broader, bigger, more effective, and more militant organization that set an example for unions throughout the country. Where the union and the company got together through union contracts (as at U. S. Steel), you had a smaller, more restrictive, less militant union that provided less representation for the people in the mill. U. S. Steel has never had a strike (so far as I know) since the unions organized, whereas unions like the Inland Steel union had a whole series of strikes in order to protect their conditions and prevent the company from taking over or taking back the things they had earned.

What happens to a union? And what happened to the United Steelworkers of America? What makes me mad, and what makes thousands of other people in the mill mad, is that the companies became smart and understood that in order to accommodate themselves to a labor organization they could not oppose that labor organization. What they had to do was recognize that labor organization. And when they recognized a labor union they had to be sure they recognized the national and international leadership of that labor union and took the affairs of that labor union out of the hands of the ordinary elected officials on a local scale.

Now Little Steel was not smart. Little Steel had people like the president of Republic Steel, who said he would go out and pick apples before he would recognize the union. And our own dear Inland Steel Company said they would do nothing, they would rather shut their place down forever than recognize the Steelworkers Union. Now what happened to these companies that did not recognize the union, that forced the union to act against the company, was that the workers developed the most militant and the most inspiring type of rank-and-file organization that you can have. Now when the companies realized that this was what was happening, they quickly saw that they had gone off in the wrong direction, and they recognized the leadership of the union.

We used to bargain locally with the Inland Steel Company, and we had our own contract with the company. We let a representative of the international union sit in, but we bargained right in Indiana Harbor and settled our differences right there. But soon Inland began to realize that this was not the way, because they were up against a pretty rough bunch of people who had no ambitions to become political leaders and labor representatives on a national scale. They realized that the best way to handle the situation was to work with the international leadership of this union. And today, the company and the international union get along pretty well.

The union has become a watchdog for the company. The local union has become the police force for the contracts made by the international union. If a local union tries to reject a contract in the Steelworkers Union, the contract is put into effect and the local union acts as the police to see that the men live up to the contract, even if it is rejected by the entire committee [of the local union] which negotiates the contract.

This is, I think, the normal growth which occurs when labor unions and most other organizations become legitimate and old and part of the general situation of the country. . . .

PART VII

CONSCIENTIOUS OBJECTORS, WORLD WAR II

DOCUMENT 19

Donald Benedict and Others, *Why We Refused to Register*

Unlike the legislation of World War I, the Burke-Wadsworth Bill of 1940 provided an alternative to military service for conscientious objectors in the form of Civilian Public Service camps.

Some objectors, however, felt that planting trees or fighting fires under government auspices was an inadequate testimony. In October 1940 eight students at Union Theological Seminary in New York City, who had been living in voluntary poverty in Harlem while pursuing their studies, refused even to register for the draft. The statement by some of this group to the court is the selection which follows.

Excerpts from the joint statement of Donald Benedict, Joseph J. Bevilacqua, Meredith Dallas, David Dellinger, George M. Houser, William H. Lovell, Howard E. Spragg, and Richard J. Wichlei, *Why We Refused to Register,* published jointly by the Fellowship of Reconciliation, Keep America Out of War Congress, National Council for Prevention of War, Youth Committee Against War, Young Peoples Socialist League, and War Resisters League (New York, 1941[?]).

It is impossible for us to think of the conscription law without at the same time thinking of the whole war system, because it is clear to us that conscription is definitely a part of the institution of war. . . .

To us, the war system is an evil part of our social order, and we declare that we cannot cooperate with it in any way. War is an evil because it is in violation of the Way of Love as seen in God through Christ. It is a concentration and accentuation of all the evils of our society. War consists of mass murder, deliberate starvation, vandalism, and similar evils. Physical destruction and moral disintegration are the inevitable result. The war method perpetuates and compounds the evils it purports to overcome. It is impossible, as history reveals, to overcome evil with evil. The last World War is a notorious case of the failure of the war system, and there is no evidence to believe that this war will be any different. It is our positive proclamation as followers of Jesus Christ that we must overcome evil with good. We seek in our daily living to reconcile that separation of man from man and man from God which produces war.

We have also been led to our conclusion on the conscription law in the light of its totalitarian nature. It is a totalitarian move when our government insists that the manpower of the nation take a year of military training. It is a totalitarian move for the President of the nation to be able to conscript industry to produce certain materials which are deemed necessary for national defense without considering the actual physical needs of the people. We believe, therefore, that by opposing the Selective Service law, we will be striking at the heart of totalitarianism as well as war. . . .

We feel a deep bond of unity with those who decide to register as conscientious objectors, but our own decision must be different for the following reasons:

If we register under the act, even as conscientious objectors, we are becoming part of the act. The fact that we as conscientious objectors may gain personal exemption from the most crassly un-Christian requirements of the act does not compensate for the fact that we are complying with it and accepting its protection. If a policeman (or a group of vigilantes) stops us on the street, our possession of the government's card shows that we are "all right"—we have complied with the act for the militarization of America. If that does not hurt our Christian consciences, what will? If we try to rationalize on the theory that we must go along with the act in order to fight the fascism and militarism of which it is a part, it seems to us that we are doing that very thing which all pacifist Christians abhor: we are consciously employing bad means on the theory that to do so will contribute to a good end. . . .

In similar vein, it is urged that great concessions have been won for religious pacifists and that we endanger these by our refusal to accept them. Fascism, as it gradually supplanted democracy in Germany, was aided by the decision of Christians and leftists to accept a partial fascism rather than to endanger those democratic concessions which still remained. It is not alone for our own exemption from fighting that we work—it is for freedom of the American people from fascism and militarism.

Partial exemption of conscientious objectors has come about partly through the work of influential pacifists and partly through the open-mindedness of certain non-pacifists. But it has also been granted because of the fear of the government that, without such a provision, public opposition to war would be too great to handle. In particular, it seems to us that one of the reasons the government has granted exemption to ministers and theological students is to gain a religious sanction for its diabolical war. Where actual support could not be gained, it hoped to soothe their consciences so that they could provide no real opposition.

We do not contend that the American people maliciously choose the vicious instrument of war. In a very perplexing situation, they lack the imagination, the religious faith, and the precedents to respond in a different manner. This makes it all the more urgent to build in this country and throughout the world a group trained in the techniques of non-violent opposition to the encroachments of militarism and fascism. Until we build such a movement, it will be impossible to stall the war machine at home. When we do build such a movement, we will have forged the only weapon which can ever give effective answer to foreign invasion. Thus in learning to fight American Hitlerism we will show an increasing group of war-disillusioned Americans how to resist foreign Hitlers as well.

For these reasons we hereby register our refusal to comply in any way with the Selective Training and Service Act. We do not expect to stem the war forces today; but we are helping to build the movement that will conquer in the future.

DOCUMENT 20

William Stafford,
"The Battle of Anapamu Creek"

Prize-winning poet William Stafford was also a conscientious objector during World War II. His memoir of his experience in Civilian Public Service (CPS) camps was first published in 1947. In a Foreword to the second edition of the book, entitled "A Side Glance at History," Stafford wrote in part:

No one knew, in that spell while war came on in the 1930's—no one knew how civilization would find ways to destroy itself. The Nazis and the Communists would join and then explode apart. In the hardening of war, death camps would come into being. Both sides would go trance-like into spasms of effort to kill; bombing of cities would begin and increase till the end when a vast new bomb would devastate areas inconceivable when the war began.

Losers would be tried and executed. Years would pass. The spell of that war would endure. And even today on hair-trigger alert nations are ready to begin that sequence again.

No one knew. And today when the steps that led into that spell are studied, refinements are created—how if an army had been early prepared, or tactics anticipated, or the selfish concerns of one nation had been more carefully thought out so as to accomplish its own purposes. . . .

Back then—and now—one group stays apart from the usual ways of facing war. They exist now—and they did then—in all countries. Those who refuse the steps along that way are a small group. . . .

William Stafford, "The Battle of Anapamu Creek," *Down in My Heart* (Swarthmore: The Bench Press, 1985), pp. 28–35.

The Forest Service was going to send a spike camp of about a dozen men back into the chaparral, into the back country; and the foreman was to be Eric Kloppenburg, a big, rough, tough hater of Germans, Japanese and CO's.

All had been going well at the new camp, a cluster of long green board buildings near the river where it cut down to the foot of a big cliff in the live-oak foothills thirty miles back of Santa Barbara. At first some of the Forest Service men had talked largely, among themselves when some of our men had happened to overhear, about their enmity for CO's; and I myself had overheard one man, later our friend, say in the ranger station, "I wish I was superintendent of that camp; I'd line 'em up and uh-uh-uh-uh"—he made the sound of a machine gun. I went ahead with my clerical work, and regaled the boys with the story that night.

The situation was, nevertheless, not funny. One superintendent had patrolled the camp after dark with a shotgun; one had reached for his pistol and shouted, during those first days at the camp, at a lagging CO, "Don't run, or I'll shoot!" In our late sessions in the barracks, over a pot of coffee or some cookies from home, we had laughed at the incidents. One Forest Service man had told me with the greatest seriousness that he had gone out with a gang and killed a "German" within twenty miles of our camp one night just after the beginning of the war.

"But," I protested, "that's unconstitutional; the man was living here; that's downright fascistic."

"Son," he said, impressively lowering his voice, "when it's a matter of defending my country I'll do anything—law or not."

And as I listened to our camp-meeting discussion of the new Anapamu Creek spike camp I thought of the conversation at the ranger station when a local cowman was applying for a permit to enter the back country, where our defenseless pacifists would be going:

"Will you be armed?"

"No—I'll have my .38."

All in all, it looked wise to send our champion pacifists, in an attempt to win, nonviolently of course, against the antagonism of Eric. Ken would go; he was our greatest mystic, a small, intense, serious man who dwelt in the eternal. Bob, our vegetarian-Thoreau-noncompromiser, would go. Jack would go, to sing and to build up his musician muscles. Alfred, our champion worker and non-complainer, would go, of course. Lennie, our most forthright and blunt man, would go. (When a ranger asked him why he wasn't in the army, he said: "Do you have two hours to give to that question? Well, then, forget it—I'm tired trying to set right in two minutes what the radio and the papers and the movies have been setting wrong for years.") George would go, because he saw the importance of the reconciliation project and wanted to participate in it.

It was our first team; and it was our first, and crucial, battle. Could we learn to work and live in such a way—even far back in tents in the chaparral—that differences with an avowed opponent could be settled and personalities reconciled? We had to win our kind of battle, and Anapamu Creek was the test.

The expedition was ready to start two mornings after our meeting. There was Eric on horseback at the head of the line; there were the pack mules, with the tents and food supplies and tools for the trail-building project; and there at the end of the line on foot and carrying personal possessions came the CO's, a various trail crew in varied costumes, all jolly and adventurous. Ken, barefooted, had his boots slung over his shoulder and wore shorts made of overalls cut off above the knees; he was relatively unencumbered, for he had smuggled his belongings, including a typewriter, into the luggage carried by the mules. The line moved off, waded the river at the rocky ford, and wound away up Oso Canyon and into the back country—a little potential drama ready to go off.

We waited at camp and wondered. Once a week Henry took supplies in to the group by pack train. We learned the story bit by bit, from him, from a man sent back with a case of poison oak, and finally from the group when they had finished their work and come back—weeks later.

The issue came—in every tense situation there always came some such crisis—between Ken, acting as cook, and Eric, with his frank antagonism for CO's. In the morning Eric would get up early and yell out some doggerel mixed with profanity (shocking to the conservative Alfred), ending, "Get up—it's daylight in the swamp!" Then Eric would go into the dining tent and beat on his tin plate with his spoon, calling out to Ken, who, by getting up at dawn, would have breakfast almost ready: "Hey, Chink! Hurry up, Chink! Chow! . . ."

Ken, back in his crowded cook tent, as likely as not with his typewriter loaded with some letter or bit of philosophy or story he had worked on the night before, his breakfast partly cooked, would hurry. He would bring in the food. The other men would straggle in from their two sleeping tents just below the dining tent. Eric would eat and talk and criticize the food, interspersing his performance with further beating of his spoon and calls for "Chink!"

One day Ken, a pacifist for society but not by any means one to expect negative measures to bring in the kingdom, sat down while the others were out on their trail work, and typed out a sheet of minimum conditions under which he would continue to cook. He mentioned some bigger pans for stewing; no more beating on plates; no more griping about the food, although he was willing to take suggestions; and no more calling the cook "Chink." Ken presented the document to Eric at the end of the working day, and Eric took it to his tent to read. George had been doing his laundry in the stream before supper; and, as the topic did not come up then, he was surprised when Eric called him aside after the meal and appointed him cook in Ken's place. George accepted and went into the dining tent, where the men congregated for reading, writing, and talking under the gasoline lanterns. There George learned about the reason for the change; and the group counseled, out there in the chaparral, far from home and custom, while Eric sat by himself in his own tent, separate from the only society for miles around.

George stepped out of the warm lighted dining tent full of his friends and walked through the dark to Eric's tent. He called to Eric, went inside the tent, and there said that he was sorry but he wouldn't be able to take the cooking job under the conditions as he now saw them. Eric threatened him with dismissal and return to main camp with charges of insubordination. George was sorry; he wished that he could help, but he saw nothing he could do, conscientiously, under the circumstances. Eric walked with George to the dining tent, and they went inside. And Eric, the boss of the camp, sat down in the circle of men, the only society for miles, not one of whom would utter a harsh word at Eric, but not one of whom would volunteer, or even consent, to take Ken's job. And nonviolence began its work.

Everyone knew that Eric could order the camp struck and the whole crew back, and everyone would have obeyed, of course. Eric knew that he could issue orders and even insults, up to a certain point; and nothing would happen in retaliation; the CO's had a primary interest in living comfortably with Eric; they were not interested in retaliation. They wanted to make the camp a success. And—in the background for Eric all the time—it was Eric's job, after all, to succeed in accomplishing his task for the Forest Service.

Everyone sat. No one read; no one talked. They all just thought. They were trying to figure a way out of the problem, and they let Eric know that they were.

Eric was not the kind who could stand silence. He had to talk; he had to issue orders, and he had to justify himself. Everyone listened courteously—and was non-committal. Eric's words grew more and more infrequent.

Finally he said, finishing up a long speech against Ken's stubbornness, "All right, if none of you will cook, I'll cook myself. It's easy. Hell. I don't mind; I'll show you how it can be done."

No one said anything. They sat there in the tent, miles from civilization, and thought. Eric looked from one to the other.

"Well, go on," he said, "go on and read or something—it's all settled."

No one moved. After a few seconds George said, "I guess we are just afraid you don't feel right about it. It just doesn't seem all settled to us. It isn't settled for us until everyone feels all right. I wish we could figure out a better way."

There was another silence, during which Eric began to get restive again. George broke the silence.

"Is it something in Ken's statement you don't like? Is there a part that offends you?"

Well, yes there was, Eric said. He just didn't like the statement.

"Maybe if you'd read us the part, we could do something about it," Bob said. Everyone nodded, as Eric looked around the circle. Lennie pumped up one of the lanterns, which was growing dim, and set it beside Eric, on the table. Ken got out a copy of his statement and put it by the lamp. Eric looked at the paper and around the circle again.

"Here," George said, "I'll read it aloud. 'To continue as cook I'll have to have two more stew pans and a cleaver.' Is that a part that's bad?" George turned to Eric. Everyone looked at Eric.

"Sure it is, damn it," Eric muttered, growing more and more forceful as he went along. "How can I get the stuff? What can I do about it?" Ken pursed his lips. "I can order the stuff," Eric hurried on, "but it can't get here before a week from Saturday, at least."

George turned to Ken. "That's right, isn't it, Ken? You'd have to get along for more than a week longer." Ken shrugged and said he guessed he would.

George read on: " 'I can't continue to cook and be called "Chink," a word that is used disrespectfully of a race and a word that implies an attitude that I find extremely distasteful.' " This time everyone looked at Eric. No one said anything.

"Hell, what's the difference!" Eric bellowed. He looked around the circle—society at Anapamu Creek.

"I guess it makes more difference to some than to others," Bob said; "I don't know. . . . It's just. . . ."

"All right, what the hell!" Eric said.

George looked around the circle. Bob nodded; Ken pursed his lips; Lennie pumped up the lamp and said, "Let's go on."

The rest of the points were settled about the same way—a reading, a pondering, a group decision. At the end of the page George said, "With this new understanding would you stay on as cook, Ken, if Eric says so?" Ken nodded. "What do you say, Eric?" asked George.

Everyone looked at Eric. "You can make another try, Ken," he said.

"Try some of that pie again," Bob said quickly. "Here, put the lamp by the checkerboard. Your move, Len."

Two days later the district ranger rode out to Anapamu Creek to stay overnight. At supper he sat down beside Eric and said, "Well, how's it been going?" Ken went on dishing out the potatoes; George carefully lined up his knife and fork and asked Jack for the salt.

"Everything's just fine," said Eric, "just fine." He looked around at the society he lived in at Anapamu Creek. "I was off my feed for a while, but going good again. . . . How's everything with you?"

DOCUMENT 21

Mulford Sibley and Asa Wardlaw,
Conscientious Objectors in Prison

This selection describes the dramatic techniques of civil disobedience employed to protest racial segregation and other objectionable aspects of prison life by some of those imprisoned as conscientious objectors. The demonstrations formed a bridge between the labor sit-ins of the depression years and the use of nonviolence in the civil rights movement after the war ended.

Clearly the men who went to prison faced further problems of conscience inside the gates. Here, as outside, some felt impelled to resist the demands of authority. An absolutist objector might continue his non-cooperation with the system of war and conscription in protest, not primarily against "abuses" of the prison system, but against the very idea of imprisoning objectors. Individual non-cooperation was climaxed in the course adopted by Corbett Bishop, who refused not only to eat but also to walk or carry out any order of the penal authorities. His action, or inaction, according to observers, was maintained without personal hostility or resentment. Other men, as a symbol of protest, refused on particular occasions to cooperate. One Socialist objector announced that he would refuse to work on May Day, 1944, "Because I wish to demonstrate loyalty to my fellow-workers and because I wish to protest the imprisonment of men of principle."

Non-cooperators sometimes expressed regret for the personal inconvenience they caused to prison officials, while justifying their course on principle. Although non-cooperators did not succeed invariably in keeping their attitudes on this high plane, the intention to do so is revealed in a number of personal records.

Mulford Sibley and Asa Wardlaw, *Conscientious Objectors in Prison 1940–1945* (Philadelphia: Pacifist Research Bureau, 1945), pp. 42–48. Reprinted by permission.

While complete non-cooperation was rare, protests and refusals at certain points in the prison routine were more common. Assignment to work obviously connected with the war brought individual refusals. Individual hunger strikes were undertaken, for varying reasons. James W. Ball, who was serving his second sentence, conducted a 30-day fast in July, 1943. The call to abstain from food came to him, according to his own statement, only after he had received his sentence, and he desired "to protest against the injustice which our government is doing in removing men from occupations to which they have been called by God." Several objectors refused to sign the power of attorney which would permit the prison censor to read their mail. As a result their correspondence privileges were denied.

To the Bureau of Prisons, those conscientious objectors who were active in the major prison strikes were primarily reformers "with a zeal for changing the social, political, economic, and cultural order." Some, according to the same source, were "bewildered and frustrated in their efforts to find a constructive answer to the complex problems of a world in conflict, and finding none, satisfy some inner need through protest and escape from reality." The Bureau held that the conscientious objector reformer's "motivation frequently stem from an overprotective home or a mother fixation, or from a revolt against authority as typified in the home and transferred to society at large. He is a problem child—whether at home, at school, or in prison." On the other hand, many pacifists looked upon prison strike leaders as among the most able, conscientious, and "normal" of all those men who had been attracted to the pacifist movement. Their fellow-prisoners, in so far as they were articulate, thought highly of the majority of strike leaders; and in a number of cases wardens and prison officials testified to their personal respect for the inmates who helped create so many perplexing problems.

The first strike at the Danbury Correctional Institution presumably arose because the warden had withdrawn his permission to a group of conscientious objectors to abstain from lunch on April 23, 1941, in order to hold a demonstration against war. When the sixteen, all of whom had been sentenced for refusal to register in the original draft, heard of the warden's action they refused to report for work the morning of April 23. They also refused to eat or observe any of the routine prescribed for inmates. Their punishment was solitary confinement for two days and confinement to cells for another thirty. There was one report that the strikers had previously made demands for abolition of racial segregation in the prison, and some maintained that they had planned to refuse work all along.

The second strike at Danbury involved the 82-day fast of Stanley Murphy and Louis Taylor . . .

A third strike began on August 11, 1943, when nineteen men initiated a "work strike" in protest against the policy of racial segregation at meals. They were immediately confined to their cells and, with forty minutes a day for exercise and the official "monotonous" diet for food, remained there for

133 days, or until December 23, 1943. The visiting hour usually permitted each month was cut in half, and visits were held under the close scrutiny of guards. After the warden had promised to institute a cafeteria system for the dining room—a scheme which was to be introduced only gradually—the strikers returned to work in the hope that the policy of segregation in the dining room would be permanently eliminated.

Meanwhile, on May 13, 1943, a protest—variously called "work strike" and "hunger strike," but in reality neither—began at the Lewisburg Penitentiary as a demonstration against forced segregation of inmates on the basis of color. There had been some protest against segregation both at the main institution and at the prison farm. When a new group of Negroes came to the farm, making too many for the segregated table in the dining room, one was sent to the kitchen to eat, and even there required to sit at a separate table from the kitchen workers. Immediately, eight conscientious objectors in that section protested by declining to eat in the dining room. They either went without food or subsisted on what they could buy from the prison commissary.

After four days on such a limited diet—only certain types of food could be obtained at the commissary—the men felt too weak to work. Statement of this fact to the prison authorities was construed as refusal to work, for which they were sent to the "hole." There they accepted the usual "monotonous" diet. A little later they were placed together in one room, segregated from the remaining prison population, and their writing privileges limited to one letter a week.

In the meantime, five conscientious objectors from the main prison had gone on strike in sympathy with their fellows of the farm dormitory. They also were sent to the "hole" where they accepted the diet, and were then transferred to the segregation room with the other eight. For a few days the thirteen went on hunger strike after writing to Director Bennett and Attorney General Biddle, demanding abolition of racial segregation in prison.

By August 11, 1943, the so-called "work strike" of conscientious objectors had, for some of the participants, broadened out from protest of racial segregation into a strike against the prison system in general. The number of strikers had decreased to seven. On September 28, five of them (later six) focused upon a protest against prison censorship practices—through a real hunger strike. Paton Price, Jack Dixon, William Kuenning, Thomas Woodman, David Dellinger, and William Lovett thus strove to secure reform of what they termed the "cruel, unnecessary and discriminatory" system whereby prison officials denied inmates certain types of literature and arbitrarily censored their letters.

In a letter to James Bennett, Director of the Bureau of Prisons, the six fasters asked recognition of two "basic rights" for all prison inmates—not merely conscientious objectors. "The first," they said, "is the right of every prisoner to free correspondence with the outside world, at all times, regardless of his prison status. The second is the right of every prisoner to access to uncensored materials for reading and writing at all times, regardless of his prison status." The strikers agreed that it was legitimate for prison censors to open letters in order to detect plots and discover drug smuggling, as well as to exclude pornographic materials. They held that it was not legitimate for censors to exclude expressions of social or religious opinion or descriptions of conditions in prison.

Late in October, 1943, the hunger strikers had become so weakened as a result of their self-imposed discipline that officials began to feed them forcibly. Reports of the conflict attracted public interest. Pacifist and non-pacifist groups alike attempted to gain some settlement from the Bureau of Prisons. Some pacifists, it may be noted, were highly critical of the methods of the strikers, and others expressed doubts, while still others commended their course.

In November Director Bennett, through the Warden of Lewisburg, suggested certain modifications in prison rules regarding censorship. After certain clarifications of these proposed changes, the strikers, on December 1, concluded their fast. The result of the strike, in retrospect, appears to have been a compromise. The Bureau of Prisons refused to promise that library, correspondence, and reading and writing privileges would be allowed to those in punishment status ("the hole" or other forms of restriction). Here wide administrative discretion was to be given to the warden. On the other hand, there was a definite promise that "inspection" of mail should not be interpreted to include the right of censorship of religious or political opinion. The strikers did *not* gain all they asked; but it seems equally clear that the prison authorities *did* modify inspection and literature regulations considerably.

In June, 1944, three conscientious objectors in Petersburg went on work strike, against racial segregation and the war-connected prison industry. They were placed in the "hole" on June 11, 1944. In the meantime, a large group in Danbury had begun a strike against the parole system—and one additional striker a week was, by agreement, to be added to the list. The prison authorities replied by transferring a number of the strikers from Danbury to Lewisburg, where seven of those transferred then began a hunger strike against being deprived of "good time" for failure to work. This continued to October 14, 1944, when one of the group was released, with the restoration of a part of the "good time" formerly denied, and another was reported paroled. Those remaining were joined by five others in a "rotation" strike, whereby five men would refuse to eat for a definite period, their places to be taken by another five for a similar (unannounced) term. Again the purpose was to secure definite promises from the Bureau of Prisons that men would not lose "good time" for refusal to work. A hunger strike of sympathy was begun in Danbury on October 4, 1944, and ended October 8, 1944.

In Ashland, a group began, in the fall of 1944, to protest racial segregation by a program of non-cooperation. This had been preceded by more than a year of effort to secure improvements gradually. The strike action brought little progress and the efforts of the men were somewhat relaxed until May 22, 1945, when a new group of objectors entered Ashland. On June 11, fifteen men refused to eat in the dining room and were placed in administrative segregation. Six were transferred to other prisons. In August, new difficulties at Lewisburg were precipitated by the reduction of "good time" of two non-objector inmates. Ten C.O.'s protested to the Warden and later refused to work, whereupon they also were deprived of thirty days "good time," and placed in segregation.

Meanwhile, both at Danbury and at Lewisburg a group of objectors, changing in numbers as some were released and others entered, followed a permanent policy of non-cooperation. At Milan also several men were carrying on simultaneously a program of non-cooperation, with varying individual reasons. Two were Negroes who refused to eat at racially segregated tables.

PART VIII

DIRECT ACTION FOR PEACE, POST-WORLD WAR II

DOCUMENT 22

Maurice McCrackin, "Pilgrimage of a Conscience"

In 1948 individuals inclined to radical direct action against nuclear war drew together in a group called Peacemakers. This organization revived Woolman's and Thoreau's practice of nonpayment of war taxes. Peacemakers also encouraged refusal to register for the draft. One of those Peacemakers who refused to pay income taxes was the Reverend Maurice McCrackin.

As a student, McCrackin was impressed by the stand of the Union Theological Seminary students who refused to register for the draft in 1940 (see Document 19). After the war McCrackin, pastor of a Presbyterian church in Cincinnati, began systematic nonpayment of income taxes. In 1958 he was

Maurice McCrackin, "Pilgrimage of a Conscience" (Cincinnati: 1961), mimeographed, pp. 9–11.

arrested and served a six months' prison sentence. In May 1961 the Cincinnati Presbytery suspended McCrackin indefinitely from his position as pastor.

I decided that I would never again register for the draft nor would I consent to being conscripted by the government in any capacity. Nevertheless each year around March 15 without protest I sent my tax payments to the government. By giving my money I was helping the government do what I so vigorously declared was wrong. I would never give my money to support a house of prostitution or the liquor industry, a gambling house or for the purchase and distribution of pornographic literature. Yet year after year I had unquestionably been giving my money to an evil infinitely greater than all of these put together since it is from war's aftermath that nearly all social ills stem.

Income tax paid by the individual is essential to the continuance of the war machine. Over 50% of the military budget is paid for by individuals through their income tax payments and 75% to 80% of every dollar he pays via income tax goes for war purposes.

Again I examined what the principle of personal commitment to Jesus meant to me. Through the years I have tried to achieve a personal relationship with Jesus. This is the burden of the Christian gospel, that Jesus can be known personally and that he can bring a saving power into a man's life. For us as Christians to know Jesus personally has reality only as we try earnestly to grow more like him "unto the measure of the stature of His fullness." If we follow Jesus afar off, if we praise his life and teachings but conclude that neither apply to our daily living, what are we doing but denying and rejecting him? Jesus speaks with authority and with love to every individual, "Follow me. Take up your cross. Love one another as I have loved you." What would Jesus *want* me to do in relation to war? What *must* I do if I am his disciple? This was the conclusion I reached: If I can honestly say that Jesus would support conscription, throw a hand grenade, or with a flame thrower drive men out of caves, to become living torches—if I believe he would release the bomb over Hiroshima or Nagasaki, then I not only have the right to do these things as a Christian, I am even obligated to do them. But if, as a committed follower, I believe that Jesus would do none of these things, I have no choice but to refuse at whatever personal cost, to support war. This means that I will not serve in the armed forces nor will I voluntarily give my money to help make war possible.

Having had this awakening, I could no longer in good conscience continue full payment of my federal taxes. At the same time I did not want to withdraw my support from the civilian services which the government offers. For that reason I continued to pay the small percentage now allocated for civilian use. The amount which I had formerly given for war I now hoped to give to such causes as the American Friends Service Committee's program and to other works of mercy and reconciliation which help to remove the roots of war.

As time went on I realized, however, that this was not accomplishing its purpose because year after year the government ordered my bank to release money from my account to pay the tax I had held back. I then closed my checking account and by some method better known to the Internal Revenue Service than to me, it was discovered that I had money in a savings and loan company. Orders were given to this firm, under threat of prosecution, to surrender from my account the amount the government said I owed. I then realized suddenly how far government is now invading individual rights and privileges: money is given in trust to a firm to be kept in safety and the government coerces this firm's trustees into a violation of that trust. But even more evil than this invasion of rights is the violence done to the individual conscience in forcing him to give financial support to a thing he feels so deeply is wrong. I agree wholeheartedly with the affirmation of Presbytery made in February of 1958, that, "A Christian citizen is obligated to God to obey the law but when in conscience he finds the requirements of law to be in direct conflict with his obedience to God, he must obey God rather than man."

Disobedience to a civil law is an act against government, but obedience to a civil law that is evil is an act against God.

At this point it came to me with complete clarity that by so much as filing tax returns I was giving to the Revenue Department assistance in the violation of my own conscience, because the very information I had been giving on my tax forms was being used in finally making the collection. So from this point on, or until there is a radical change for the better in government spending, I shall file no returns.

DOCUMENT 23

Albert Bigelow,
"Why I Am Sailing into the Pacific Bomb-Test Area"

The Committee for Nonviolent Action (CNVA) was formed in 1957 with a dozen members. In 1958, CNVA promoted the voyage of a 30-foot sailing boat, The Golden Rule, *into the forbidden nuclear testing area of the Western Pacific. In this document the boat's captain, former naval commander Albert Bigelow, describes the motives prompting the venture, which ended with the arrest and imprisonment of the crew in Honolulu.*

My friend Bill Huntington and I are planning to sail a small vessel westward into the Pacific H-bomb test area. By April we expect to reach nuclear testing grounds at Eniwetok. We will remain there as long as the tests of H-bombs continue. With us will be two other volunteers.

Why? Because it is the way I can say to my government, to the British government, and to the Kremlin: "Stop! Stop this madness before it is too late. For God's sake, turn back!"

How have I come to this conviction? Why do I feel under compulsion, under moral orders, as it were, to do this?

The answer to such questions, at least in part, has to do with my experience as a Naval officer during World War II. The day after Pearl Harbor was attacked, I was at the Navy recruiting offices. I had had a lot of experience in navigating vessels. Life in the Navy would be a glamorous change from the dull mechanism of daily civilian living. My experience assured me of success. All this adventure ahead and the prospect of becoming a hero into the bargain.

Albert S. Bigelow, "Why I am Sailing into the Pacific Bomb-Test Area," *Liberation* (February 1958), pp. 4–6.

I suppose, too, that I had an enormous latent desire to conform, to go along with the rest of my fellows. I was swayed by the age-old psychology of meeting force with force. It did not really occur to me to resist the drag of the institution of war, the pattern of organized violence, which had existed for so many centuries. This psychology prevailed even though I had already reflected on the fantastic wastefulness of war—the German *Bismarck* hunting the British *Hood* and sending it to the bottom of the sea, and the British Navy hunting the *Bismarck* and scuttling it.

I volunteered, but instead of being sent to sea, I was assigned to 90 Church Street in New York and worked in project "plot" establishing the whereabouts of all combat ships in the Atlantic. In a couple of months I escaped from this assignment and was transferred to the Naval Training Station at Northwestern University.

I had not been at Northwestern very long when I sensed that because of my past experience I would be made an instructor there and still not get to sea. So I deliberately flunked an examination in navigation and before long was assigned to a submarine chaser in the Atlantic.

THE TURKEY SHOOT

From March to October of 1943 I was in command of a submarine chaser in the Solomon Islands, during the fighting. It was during this period that more than 100 Japanese planes were shot down in one day. This was called "the Turkey Shoot." The insensitivity which decent men must develop in such situations is appalling. I remember that the corpse of a Japanese airman who had been shot down was floating bolt upright in one of the coves, a position resulting from the structure of the Japanese life belts, which were different from our Mae Wests. Each day as we passed the cove we saw this figure, his face growing blacker under the terrific sun. We laughingly called him Smiling Jack. As a matter of fact, I think I gave him that name myself and felt rather proud of my wit.

Later in World War II, I was Captain of the destroyer escort *Dale W. Peterson*—DE 337—and I was on her bridge as we came into Pearl Harbor from San Francisco when the first news arrived of the explosion of an atomic bomb over Hiroshima. Although I had no way of understanding what an atom bomb was I was absolutely awestruck, as I suppose all men were for a moment. Intuitively it was then that I realized for the first time that morally war is impossible.

I don't suppose I had the same absolute realization with my whole being, so to speak, of the immorality and "impossibility" of nuclear war until the morning of August 7, 1957. On that day, I sat with a score of friends, before dawn, in the Nevada desert just outside the entrance to the Camp Mercury testing grounds. The day before, eleven of us, in protest against the summer-long tests, had tried to enter the restricted area. We had been arrested as we stepped one after another over the boundary line, and had been carried off to a ghost town which stands at the entrance to Death Valley. There we had been given a speedy trial under the charge of trespassing under the Nevada laws. Sentencing had been suspended for a year, and later in the afternoon we had returned to Camp Mercury to continue the Prayer and Conscience Vigil along with others who had remained there during our civil disobedience action.

In the early morning of August 7 an experimental bomb was exploded. We sat with our backs to the explosion site. But when the flash came I felt again the utterly impossible horror of this whole business, the same complete realization that nuclear war must go, that I had felt twelve years before on the bridge of U. S. S. *Dale W. Peterson,* off Pearl Harbor.

I think also that deep down somewhere in me, and in all men at all times, there is a realization that the pattern of violence meeting violence makes no sense, and that war violates something central in the human heart—"that of God," as we Quakers sometimes say. For example, when each of us at the trial the afternoon before had told why we were committing civil disobedience against nuclear tests, our attorney, Francis Heisler, said: "There isn't one of us in this court room who doesn't wish that he had walked into the testing grounds with these people this morning." Everybody, including the police and court officers, nodded assent.

SOCIETY OF FRIENDS

However, I am ahead of my story. At the close of the War, in spite of what I had felt on the bridge of that destroyer, I did not break away from my old life. For a time I was Housing Commissioner of Massachusetts. Like many other people who had been through the War, I was seeking some sort of unified life-philosophy or religion. I did a good deal of religious "window-shopping." I became impressed by the fact that in one way or another the saints, the wise men, those who seemed to me truly experienced, all pointed in one direction—toward nonviolence, truth, love, toward a way and a goal that could not be reconciled with war. For quite a while, to use a phrase of Alan Watts', I "sucked the finger instead of going where it pointed." But finally I realized that I did have to move in that direction, and in 1952 I resigned my commission in the Naval Reserve. It was promptly and courteously accepted. I felt a bit proud of doing it a month before I would have come into a pension. Such little things we pride ourselves on!

I came into contact with the Quakers, the Society of Friends. My wife, Sylvia, had already joined the Society in 1948. As late as 1955 I was still fighting off joining the Society, which seemed to me to involve a great, awesome commitment. I suppose I was like the man in one of Shaw's plays who wanted to be a Christian—but not yet.

THE HIROSHIMA MAIDENS

Then came the experience of having in our home for some months two of the Hiroshima maidens who had been injured and disfigured in the bombing of August 6, 1945. Norman Cousins and other wonderful people brought them to this country for plastic surgery. There were two things about these girls that hit me very hard and forced me to see that I had no choice but to make the commitment to live, as best I could, a life of nonviolence and reconciliation. One was the fact that when they were bombed in 1945 the two girls in our home were nine and thirteen years old. What earthly thing could they have done to give some semblance of what we call justice to the ordeal inflicted upon them and hundreds like them? What possible good could come out of human action—war—which bore such fruits? Is it not utter blasphemy to think that there is anything moral or Christian about such behavior?

The other thing that struck me was that these young women found it difficult to believe that *we,* who were not members of their families, could love *them.* But *they* loved *us;* they harbored no resentment against us or other Americans. How are you going to respond to that kind of attitude? The newly-elected president of the National Council of Churches, Edwin T. Dahlberg, said in his inaugural talk that instead of "massive retaliation" the business of Christians is to practice "massive reconciliation." Well, these Hiroshima girls practiced "massive reconciliation" on us, on me, who had laughed derisively at "Smiling Jack." What response can one make to this other than to give oneself utterly to destroying the evil, war, that dealt so shamefully with them and try to live in the spirit of sensitivity and reconciliation which they displayed?

As I have said, I think there is that in all men that abhors and rejects war and knows that force and violence can bring no good thing to pass. Yet men are bound by old patterns of feeling, thought and action. The organs of public opinions are almost completely shut against us. It seems practically impossible, moreover, for the ordinary person by ordinary means to speak to, and affect the action of, his government. I have had a recent experience of this which has strengthened my conviction that it is only by such acts as sailing a boat to Eniwetok and thus "speaking" to the government right in the testing area that we can expect to be heard.

TELL IT TO THE POLICEMAN

I was asked by the New England office of the American Friends Service Committee to take to the White House 17,411 signatures to a petition to cancel the Pacific tests. Ten thousand signatures had previously been sent in. I realize that even a President in good health cannot see personally everyone who has a message for him. Yet the right of petition exists—in theory—and is held to be a key factor in democratic process. And the President presumably has assistants to see to it that all serious petitions are somehow brought to his attention. For matters of this kind, there is Maxwell Rabb, secretary to the cabinet.

Twenty-seven thousand is quite a few people to have signed a somewhat unusual petition. The A. F. S. C. is widely known and recognized as a highly useful agency. I am known to Maxwell Rabb with whom I worked in Republican politics in Massachusetts. I was a precinct captain for Eisenhower in the 1952 primaries. Yet a couple of days work on the part of the staff of the Friends Committee on National Legislation failed to secure even an assurance that some time on Tuesday, December 31, the day I would be in Washington, Max Rabb would see me to receive the petitions. On that day I made five calls and talked with his secretary. Each time I was assured that she would call me back within ten minutes. Each time the return call failed to come and I tried again. The last time, early in the afternoon, I held on to the telephone for ten minutes, only to be told finally that the office was about to close for the day.

Each time I telephoned, including the last, I was told I could, of course, leave the petitions with the policeman at the gate. This I refused to do. It seems terrible to me that Americans can no longer speak to or be seen by their government. Has it become their master, not their servant? Can it not listen to their humble and reasonable pleas? This experience may in one sense be a small matter but I am sure it is symptomatic—among other things—of a sort of fear on the part of officials to listen to what in their hearts they feel is right but on which they cannot act without breaking with old patterns of thought. At any rate, the experience has strengthened in me the conviction that we must, at whatever cost, find ways to make our witness and protest heard.

I AM GOING BECAUSE ...

I am going because, as Shakespeare said, "Action is eloquence." Without some such direct action, ordinary citizens lack the power any longer to be seen or heard by their government.

I am going because it is time to *do something* about peace, not just *talk* about peace.

I am going because, like all men, in my heart I know that *all* nuclear explosions are monstrous, evil, unworthy of human beings.

I am going because war is no longer a feudal jousting match; it is an unthinkable catastrophe for all men.

I am going because it is now the little children, and, most of all, the as yet unborn who are the front line troops. It is my duty to stand between them and this horrible danger.

I am going because it is cowardly and degrading for me to stand by any longer, to consent, and thus to collaborate in atrocities.

I am going because I cannot say that the end justifies the means. A Quaker, William Penn, said, "A good end cannot sanctify evil means; nor must we ever do evil that good may come of it." A Communist, Milovan Djilas, says, "As soon as means which would ensure an end are shown to be evil, the end will show itself as unrealizable."

I am going because, as Gandhi said, "God sits in the man opposite me; therefore to injure him is to injure God himself."

I am going to witness to the deep inward truth we all know, "Force can subdue, but love gains."

I am going because however mistaken, unrighteous, and unrepentant governments may seem, I still believe all men are really good at heart, and that my act will speak to them.

I am going in the hope of helping change the hearts and minds of men in government. If necessary I am willing to give my life to help change a policy of fear, force and destruction to one of trust, kindness, and help.

I am going in order to say, "Quit this waste, this arms race. Turn instead to a disarmament race. Stop competing for evil, compete for good."

I am going because I have to—if I am to call myself a human being.

When you see something horrible happening, your instinct is to do something about it. You can freeze in fearful apathy or you can even talk yourself into saying that it isn't horrible. I can't do that. I have to act. This is too horrible. We know it. Let's all act.

DOCUMENT 24

Wilmer Young,
Visible Witness

In 1959 the Committee for Nonviolent Action organized a demonstration against land-launched missiles near Omaha, Nebraska. Among those arrested

Wilmer J. Young, *Visible Witness: A Testimony for Radical Peace Action*, Pendle Hill Pamphlet No. 118 (Wallingford, PA: Pendle Hill, 1961), pp. 3–17. Reprinted with the permission of Pendle Hill, Wallingford, PA.

was Wilmer Young, an elderly Quaker, who tells of his experience in this document.

On July 6, 1959, I found myself in jail in Omaha, Nebraska. Having lived for over seventy years without ever being in jail before, I have been asked to explain. Many men who, for one reason or another, have to beg for their daily bread have this experience often. But I, who had never been really hungry in my life and had lived by the accepted rules of society . . . !

Yet this did not just happen. It came after years of travail of spirit, and if I was foolish or unwise, it may be partly because, as a friend once said to me, "Thee is the most naïve person I have ever known." But it just might be for some better reason, and I'd like to see if I can explain it in a way that may make sense to some who are more sophisticated.

Just before going to Omaha, I had written to my three children that I was going out to help a group of people who were planning to protest the construction of a missile site. I said that I did not yet know what I myself would do there, but felt that I could probably be useful in some way, perhaps drive a car or help with the accounts.

I arrived at Omaha late Saturday night, June 19. The opening public meeting of the project called *Omaha Action* was scheduled to be held that night at the YMCA. I went directly there and found that the clerk at the desk knew nothing of the meeting. But, when I pressed him more, he did admit that he knew of one that was being held at a hotel not far away. His manner, together with the change of place, gave me my first evidence that things were not going to be entirely smooth.

At the hotel, where the meeting was already nearly over, there was an atmosphere of tension. In spite of considerable advertising, only about thirty people had come, and half of them were from our own group. The reporters who were there took pictures of the empty chairs and called special attention to the fact that very few Omaha people attended. It was clear that we were not being welcomed to Omaha. (Well, why should we be?)

A few days earlier, the one local paper had published a long editorial which attacked one of our members who had once been a Trotskyite, and failed to mention that this connection had been repudiated many years ago. Thus the stage was set for fear; no church in the city was found willing to hear any of us.

Sunday morning, some of our group of about fifteen went to hand out our *Omaha Action* leaflets on the streets; others attended church services. I went to the small Friends Meeting held in the YMCA, and found there some cousins who were sympathetic and did what they could to help us throughout our stay. In the afternoon, we met in an office that had been rented when the forerunners of the *Action* first arrived, and there made plans for the next few days. We divided into two groups, one group to go to Lincoln and walk the forty miles from there to the Mead Ordnance Base, the other to remain in Omaha overnight and, on Monday morning, start walking the thirty miles to the same spot.

Three days were allotted for this march. I was errand boy for the Omaha contingent, taking them food and their sleeping equipment at proper hours, and finding them places to sleep. This latter job proved to be another eye-opener for me. We were in open country, with many beautiful farms and farm homes, the kind of country where I grew up three hundred miles farther east, in Iowa. But to find a place where these walkers could get permission to sleep on somebody's ground required some looking around. Word had got around that we were coming, and nobody had any latchstrings out. For the first night, I found a wood where we were allowed to sleep. But the next night, I could not find any place where the owners would allow it, so the night was spent on a railway right-of-way. By this time, we had become somewhat apprehensive, but after getting the group settled, I returned the twenty-five miles to Omaha. Around midnight, two of us started back to call on both groups, to see if all was well. Everything was quiet and peaceful under the stars, and nothing more had happened than that a few epithets and firecrackers had been hurled their way.

On the third day, the groups converged and completed their march to the entrance of the Base nearest the missile site. They set up camp on a little bluff in some tall grass on the edge of a clover field. A round-the-clock vigil was then started which lasted over a week, and was continued in daytime until July 21, when the little camp was torn up at night by hostile youngsters.

The Mead Ordnance Base is twenty-six square miles in area, much of it leased for farming to people who formerly had their homes here but had been forced (in some cases) to sell to the Defense Department. This is near the headquarters of the Strategic Air Command. Our vigil site was just outside the entrance, where there was a very ordinary farm gate, and just inside, a little shelter for two guards was set up after we came. In normal times, the gate usually stood open and there were no guards.

I shall not soon forget a meeting held the next week, at which each person of our group gave his decision as to what part he would take in the actions of the following days. Fifteen persons (this perhaps counts a few who came later) said they planned to do some form of civil disobedience, as their part of the protest. When it came my turn, I found myself saying, somewhat to my surprise, that I too planned to offer civil disobedience. Having said it, I found I was quite calm about it and, what is even more surprising to me, I have never since regretted the decision, although it committed me to a form of action that was completely new to me. I shall try to explain this phenomenon later, in so far as I can.

As the vigil continued, we learned more about the situation. The construction of the missile site was still in a very early stage. Probably not over a hundred men were actually at work there, and they lived in the surrounding area of farms and small towns, some as far away as Omaha. Perhaps fifty cars and trucks went in and out of the Base each day. The men would hardly have dared stop and talk with us in the presence of the guards, or take our leaflets, even if they had wanted to. They could hardly fail to read our signs, but that was all. The signs were brief and easily read:

END MISSILE RACE
LET MANKIND LIVE

and

NON-VIOLENT PROTEST
AGAINST NUCLEAR MISSILE POLICY

It is significant that of all the newspaper pictures taken of us, so far as I saw them, only two showed the signs so that they could be read. Nor were they printed in the newspaper stories.

We were acutely conscious that, in this situation, we were only protesting. We could not find a way even to suggest that we did have a positive program in mind, calling for the strengthening of the United Nations, making use of the World Court, studying nonviolent resistance to evil and training for its use. We asked permission to address the workers at the Base during their lunch-hour or give them our literature. This was refused. We asked for their names, so that we might call on them in their homes. This too was refused. There seemed to be only one way in which we could present our positive program to anybody, and that was to hand out leaflets in Omaha and in the towns, and talk with individuals whenever we could. But you cannot present a whole theory on a four-page leaflet; and the channels we are used to using, such as the local newspaper, the churches, the radio, and TV, were all closed to us, as far as presenting any constructive program was concerned.

What could we do?

Let us remind ourselves for a moment that this condition would be pretty much true in every town and city in America. We are not always aware of it, because we do not often make the attempt to challenge the thought patterns of our neighbors, and to get radical peace messages on the radio or into the papers. The only way we could see to get our message to the people was to dramatize our protest by getting arrested for illegal entry of the Base.

A few days after the meeting where the decisions for civil disobedience had been made, on July 1 at 10 a.m., we held a meeting for worship "after the manner of Friends" at the vigil site. This was a very solemn half hour for us, as it was the preliminary to three of us "going in" to the Base and thus breaking a law. None of us knew what the penalty incurred or even what the charge would be; nor did we know under what court the trial would come.

An 80-year-old man, extremely lively for that age, had come over the road in dramatic fashion, evidently expected by some of the onlookers. He carried a small American flag around our circle a couple of times, causing an occasional guffaw among our visitors, but he did not otherwise disturb our silent meeting. After the meeting, A. J. Muste came to the side of the road and preached a pacifist sermon to the people there. I have attended many meetings, and heard many sermons, but none I think more impressive. Facing him on the left, inside the fence, were perhaps thirty Air Force officers and the Federal Marshal. Opposite him across the road, stood some fifteen members of the American Legion who had come with placards of their own to picket us. There were possibly forty other people from nearby and from Omaha, including reporters and TV operators.

A. J. and the two others who were committed to offer civil disobedience that day then walked over to the gate, where Air Force officers and the Marshal were waiting for them. As is done in all such cases, we had given advance information to all officials likely to be involved.

It is difficult to describe the excitement for us in a simple first action of this kind. Later, these protests by disobedience of the law took on a quite routine character for us; but this time there were so many unknown factors of possibility. For instance, we had been holding the vigil on land next to that belonging to the Base. After considerable inquiry, we had found that this land belonged to another Federal Bureau, which had no office in Omaha and presumably no representative, so we had been using it without getting permission. Might not the Air Force, in cooperation with this Bureau, have us all arrested together for trespassing, or on some other charge, as soon as the first group of our people entered the Base? In case this were done, we thought it might be well for a couple of us to be away from the group and out on the highway, so as to go and notify our friends of what had happened. It had been decided, then, that as soon as A. J.'s sermon was finished, I was to leave immediately for a car parked some distance away, and another person was to keep away from the group but wait to find out what was done, and then come and join me. This now seems naïve—even to me!—but it seemed sensible at the time. We felt we were a long way from most of our friends.

A. J. Muste and the two others climbed over the gate, and were at once informed by the Air Force officers that the maximum penalty for entering was six months in prison and $500 fine. The officers then took them gently but firmly by the arm and led them out and shut the gate. Then the three again climbed over the gate and were immediately arrested by the Federal Marshal and taken to Omaha. This was termed "re-entry after warning" and the charge was "trespassing." They were put into the local jail in Omaha.

I had already volunteered, along with David Wyman, a young man from New York City, to do a similar action on July 6. We both wrote out statements, as did all the others later, of our reasons for offering civil disobedience, and presented them to the radio and press. For the most part, they were ignored. After our usual meeting for worship at the vigil site, and before going into the Base, I read mine to the group instead of preaching a sermon as A. J. had done. About sixty persons were in the audience, including relatives of mine who had come from a Monthly Meeting of Friends in Iowa and, as before, a delegation of about eleven men from the nearby American Legion Post.

As we went up to the gate, the old man who had carried the little flag around our meeting on the first day came up and tried to stamp on my toes. He was very excited and failed to land on them, but his action disconcerted me a little and, as I crawled through the barbed wire fence, I put out one hand to shield myself. After getting through, I was surprised to see him lying flat on the ground. I realized at once that this incident would be used by the press; and, of course, not having any idea what had happened, I said the wrong thing, which was: "I'm sorry!" This of course seemed to imply that I had pushed him. The incident was thoroughly publicized by the Omaha paper, which said, under the headline PACIFIST WINS MEAD TUSSLE, that ". . . two elders with a combined age of 151 years brought violence to the non-violence demonstration of the Omaha Action pacifists;" and after describing the incident: " 'Sorry I pushed you,' said the septuagenarian to the octogenarian." This incident provoked the only notice the *New York Times* ever took of us, except when a congressman's son was sent to prison. It said: "What was supposed to be a nonviolent demonstration produced a tussle between two elderly men." It was sometime afterward that we learned that the old gentleman had candidly told the paper published at Wahoo, Nebraska, that he had not been pushed—he had just lost his balance. It was a relief to have the error cleared up in the press—of Wahoo, Nebraska.

After David Wyman and I had gone through our formal entry and re-entry of the Base, we were taken promptly and put into a "tank" in the Omaha jail. It was designed for twelve men but we found there only our three predecessors, A. J. Muste, Ross Anderson, and Karl Meyer. We five spent two very stimulating days in conversation together there before being called before Federal Judge Robinson. By that time, two more of our comrades had joined us. A. J. presented our defense to the court. As had been previously decided, we pled "technically but not morally guilty" and of course were told that it had to be either "guilty" or "not guilty." We had also decided not to have a lawyer and not to give bail. I pled "guilty" to trespass.

The Judge's sentence was six months and $500 fine, with sentence suspended and one year on probation. I had not expected this and took some time to decide what to do. But Karl Meyer, a Catholic and the son of a congressman, knew at once what he would do. He told the probation officer that he could not accept probation, and probably would be out at the Base next day when two others of our group were planning to make their protest. True to his prediction, he went out the next day. The authorities were nervous about this, and they handcuffed him and obviously wanted to rough him up, but they did not. Apparently the Judge realized now for the first time that we were not the type of people that the press had tried to make out; he was quite angry with Karl and sent him to federal prison at once, warning the other members of *Omaha Action* at the same time that they need expect no leniency from that Court.

In the meantime, I had decided that I could not accept probation. Among several other stipulations, it meant monthly reports to a probation officer and staying away from all military installations for one year. So I addressed the Judge in a letter. After pointing out the direction that I believed our military policy is taking us, I said: "In view of these and other factors which I shall not go into here, what shall I do? I am an old man. I have had a happy life and found it interesting. That I should have my life ended now in a war is of small moment. But I have many young friends. I have three married children and eight lovely grandchildren. I'd like them all to have the opportunity for life as I have had. My one desire in this time is to make a maximum protest against the unnecessary descent of mankind into oblivion. I believe that, at the present time and under the circumstances of today, this protest requires me to spend this time in prison.—If I were an orator or a great writer or a diplomat, perhaps I would not need to do this. But for me, the processes of education, of speaking, of conferences, of writing, alone, seem likely to be 'too little and too late.' There come times in history when action is essential to break through the hard crust of inertia and custom. I believe this is one of those times.—It is in the tradition of my people, Quakers, to go to prison rather than take part in war. I believe the time has come for me, as a Quaker and a human being, to go to prison as a protest against preparation for war.

"You told me the other day that you were turning the prison key over to me. By my own act, in joining a vigil at the Mead Ordnance Plant, I propose to turn that key."

On July 21, therefore, I was arrested again at the Mead Base, this time for violation of the terms of probation. Before our meeting for worship began, the Chief Probation Officer simply asked me to come with him in his car. We had a very friendly talk on the 30-mile drive to Omaha. He said that if I didn't mind, he'd like to make some suggestions. Instead of stirring things up this way, why did we not do educational work in the usual way, write books and articles for magazines, give lectures, use the radio? This would not make people angry and excited, and they could think more clearly. I assured him that we had been trying to do these things for 25 years, and here he didn't even know it!—but I reminded him that one could not get the radio or any of the mass media to accept and use what we were offering. I told him that the very fact that he knew nothing about the writing and lecturing on peace that had been going on for years was a clear indication that other methods are needed.

He informed me that the Judge was away for a vacation and a conference, so that I would have to wait several days in jail. Later we learned that the Judge's conference was in order to get counsel about what his attitude toward *Omaha Action* ought to be.

My next six days with 34 other men in a "tank" designed for 32 was not as pleasant as the previous internment had been. A young man, Arthur Harvey, was with me this time. As we entered, carrying our mattresses, all eyes were upon us, and almost immediately a voice cried out, "Are you those pacifists?"

Arthur replied "Yes!" with what seemed to me rather more gusto than the situation was likely to warrant. And sure enough, there was no gathering around to discuss our experiences. We were left to our own thoughts. The men would not look us in the eye if they could avoid it, nor greet us unless we spoke first.

The "tank" was about fifty feet long and sixteen wide, with two stories of nine cells each on one side, leaving a freeway of 8 × 50 feet on the main floor, for walking back and forth. There were benches to sit on along one side, and a narrow walkway and guard rail in front of the upper tier of cells. To get exercise one had to walk up and down past the cell doors in front of men who were sitting there reading or talking or smoking, or just sitting.

After a day or two, a man would now and then ask a question, and eventually some became rather friendly. The loneliness that one can feel in such a situation is very real. It was heightened one evening when three men asked about my sentence—this was a routine question—and after some discussion, one of the men said: "If I'd been the judge, I'd of given you twenty years." While the others talked, he kept shaking his head and muttering: "You mustn't let your country down." After six days and nights, a few showed signs of seeing some light on pacifism, and many had become friendly, but I saw more clearly than ever how deep is the hold of the military mind in our country.

Getting letters was a tremendous help, but it made one feel all the more sympathy for many of the men who never got any letters at all; some of them had no contact with anyone outside. The many letters I got obviously caused considerable speculation among the men and really puzzled them. This particular "tank" was filled with men who were in for the more premeditated offences, such as forgery, robbery, sexual crimes and murder; there were few alcoholics. The men were relatively young, intelligent, and good-looking. This, as is almost inevitable in our prison system, was a fine school for teaching criminals to be more clever.

It was a county jail, reasonably well run as such jails go. I did not feel the urge, as some sincerely do, to protest the jail treatment, particularly to make things difficult for the jailers. There is a place for protest against the cruelties of prisons, but I wanted to make it as clear as possible that what I was protesting was the building of a missile base, and that I was trying to bear witness to a way of life that renounces war. The real cruelty of the prison system is that it is an arm of a larger system which protects the rich and powerful at the expense of the poor. A cardinal point in nonviolent resistance to evil is willingness to take on oneself the chief part of the suffering, and taking it cheerfully.

When I was called before the Judge again, a little farce was enacted. We both knew that I had been arrested the second time because I had appeared at the Base in violation of the terms of a probation I had stated I would not comply with, and that the Marshal had taken me away before the silent vigil began that morning. "Mr. Young," said the judge, "did you attend the vigil?"

I smiled at him: "No, I was not allowed to do so." He then asked me if I had been in jail the last few days; and then he said, "Mr. Young, in view of the fact that you did not attend the vigil, I am going to continue you on probation." This, although it was clear that I had refused compliance with the terms of probation! A few days later we had another vigil at the entrance of the Base, and a number of Friends from the area joined us. Almost as soon as the meeting started, a man whom I did not know came up to me and said: "Mr. Young, the Attorney said to tell you that you will not be arrested."

It was now clear that if I were to reinforce my witness by serving a prison term at this time, I should have to repeat the entrance into the Ordnance Base, and thus force the hand of the Judge. Marjorie Swann, the mother of four children, and Arthur Harvey were in the same situation. We decided to spend ten days in making our decisions.

Several Friends from the Meeting at Paullina, Iowa, had come to visit us at various times and take part in the vigil. Most of them I had known for a long time, so I went there and we had a conference, in which I stated my dilemma and asked their advice. They were very sympathetic, but no one wanted to advise me to repeat my protest by civil disobedience. They thought that having made my position clear, I might now be satisfied. I also visited some other relatives, including our son Bill in Wyoming. He had spent three years in Civilian Public Service and later on had served a year and a day in a Federal prison for refusing to register for the military draft. After my visit, he wrote his mother: "I did not feel like discouraging Dad from going ahead." But in the end I refrained, largely because of my wife's strong feeling against a repetition of the illegal action in the circumstances. Marj Swann and Art Harvey did "go in" a second time and were sent to prison. The Judge was obviously very reluctant to put Marj or me into prison. The younger men, who were for the most part relatively free of responsibilities, he felt no particular compunction about, and in one or two cases said as much.

Looking back, I am inclined to feel that both Marj's decision and mine were right for ourselves. Her protest made far more impact than mine, and it may be pure rationalization on my part to think that what little impact mine made would not have been greatly augmented by my actually serving six months in prison. But in her case, the serving of the term while her husband took care of the children did make a great deal of difference and many hearts were deeply touched by their joint sacrifice.

DOCUMENT 25

Barbara Deming,
"Southern Peace Walk: Two Issues or One?"

In the early 1960s, CNVA's main activity was peace walks. In October 1961, after ten months of walking, thirty-one members of the San Francisco to Moscow Walk for Peace entered Red Square in Moscow. The walk covered about 3,900 miles in the United States. The core group varied in size from a dozen to more than 50. In major cities, hundreds sometimes participated, and in London a rally drew 7,000. Contrary to the predictions of virtually every prominent personality in the United States peace movement, the walk was admitted to Communist countries. In the Soviet Union, the walkers held a major press conference, met with Mrs. Khrushchev as well as students and professors at Moscow University, took part in auditorium meetings with thousands of people organized by the Soviet Peace Committee, and freely distributed leaflets.

The smaller and less-publicized walk from Nashville, Tennessee to Washington in 1962 confronted a different barrier: racism. The walk was one of three simultaneous walks, beginning in New Hampshire, Chicago, and Nashville, and designed to converge in Washington on the same day for civil disobedience at the Pentagon. One of the participants was Barbara Deming (1917–1984), a descendant of Elihu Burritt, who joined CNVA in 1960 and became perhaps the most brilliant theorist of nonviolence in the United States during the decades that followed.

The man took a leaflet and read a few lines. "This is the Nashville, Tennessee to Washington, D. C. Walk for Peace," it began; " 'Since 650 B. C. there have been 1,656 arms races, only sixteen of which have not ended in war. The remainder have ended in economic collapse.' " He looked up. "Are you walking with that nigger?" he asked.

Barbara Deming, "Southern Peace Walk: Two Issues or One?," *Liberation*, July-Aug. 1962. Reprinted by permission.

This kind of discussion of our message had been anticipated by the Committee for Nonviolent Action, when it decided that the walk should be integrated. "Token integrated," somebody later commented. Of thirteen young men and women committed to walk the whole distance, Robert Gore was the only Negro, though we hoped others might join before Washington. Whether they did or not, it was assumed that in the many talks about war and peace we would attempt to provoke along the way, we were sure to be asked a good many times whether we would be happy to see Robert married to our sisters. Before we headed south, we discussed the question of just how distracting our obvious attitude to race relations might be, and the proper way to cope with the problem. Events then proved our tentative conclusions to have been utterly inadequate.

Most of those advising us felt that battle on the two issues simply could not be combined. Of course we ought never to deny our belief in racial brotherhood; but Robert's presence was enough to confirm it. We should try to avoid talking about it; we were there to talk about *peace*. And it would be folly to seek to associate ourselves too closely with the people down there who were struggling for integration. Many people would then shy away from us. And they, the Negroes, could be harmed by it even more than we. They had enough of a burden to bear, already, without our giving their opponents added ammunition—the charge of their being "unpatriotic."

I supposed that the advice was practical, but it depressed me. I think we all left the meeting feeling unsatisfied—wondering a little why, then the walk *was* to be integrated. We'd talked about the fact that this could lead us into danger. The South was unpredictable, it was stressed: we might not run into any trouble at all; on the other hand, we just might all get killed. In a cause we were not to appear to be battling for?

I had felt for a long time that the two struggles—for disarmament and for Negro rights—were properly parts of the one struggle. The same nonviolent tactic joined us, but more than this: our struggles were fundamentally one—to commit our country in act as well as in word to the extraordinary faith announced in our Declaration of Independence: that all men are endowed with certain rights that must not be denied them. *All* men, including those of darker skin, whom it has been convenient to exploit; including those in other countries, with whose policies we quarrel; among those rights which are not to be questioned, the right to be free to pursue happiness, and among them the right not to be deprived of life. In short, the Christian faith, still revolutionary, that men are brothers and that—no matter what—our actions must respect the fact. The only mode of battle that does, implicitly, respect this fact is that of nonviolence, and I had heard that for more and more of those in the civil rights as well as in the peace movement, the very attempt to practice it had implanted a corresponding faith, however tentative. But of course it is possible to hold a faith and yet not recognize all its implications, to be struggling side by side with others and yet be unaware of them. Perhaps it wasn't realistic to think of joining ranks.

We started out, in Nashville, with only a wistful look in the direction of the integration movement. We marched past a sit-in demonstration at a "Simple Simon's" and "smiled in." We didn't even picket for a few minutes; didn't pause in our marching. "There they are"—we turned our heads. We caught a glimpse of a row of young people at a counter—a glimpse, as in a flash photograph, of young heads held in a certain proud and patient fashion; and then we had marched past. A few steps away, in front of a movie theatre, several adolescent toughs loitered—faces furtive, vacant. Did they plan trouble? In a minute, we were out of sight. It felt unnatural, I think, to all of us.

That afternoon we held a small open meeting at Scarritt College for Christian Workers. Two Negro leaders were among those present—James Lawson and Metz Rollins. Members of the group staging the sit-in—the Student Nonviolent Coordinating Committee—had been invited; but none came. Was this because they *were* shy of association with us? Or was it perhaps because, as one walker suggested, they felt that we should have done more to demonstrate solidarity with them? Rollins inclined his head, smiled. "It may well be."

Lawson spoke that afternoon. In the course of his talk, he remarked, "There is a clearcut relation between the peace walk and what some of us are seeking to do in the emerging nonviolent movement in the South. Some people have tried to classify our effort here as one that is of and for and by the Negro. They have tried to define the struggle for integration as a struggle to gain the Negro more power. I maintain that it is not the case. Go among the common ordinary people . . . for the 'leading Negroes' are not the leaders of this movement. . . . Listen to their prayers and to their speech. They are constantly thinking not in terms of civil rights but in terms of the kingdom of God on earth, the brotherhood of all men. . . . What is behind it is an effort to build a community for all of us . . . 'the beloved community.' I say that this work is related to the work for peace. . . . It might be a prototype to speak to the whole world. . . . And the peace walk is related to the task of building community here. . . . The movements are related to each other, in a sense are one and the same enterprise."

I took down the words he spoke, in my notebook, nodding, "Yes"; and at the same time, disregarding them—perhaps because I was tired from the long drive south, and the process of breaking myself in again to group life, to sleeping on the floor, to packing up and moving each day; or perhaps because the meeting room was very nearly empty: the peace movement and the civil rights movement were certainly not visibly related here.

On Easter afternoon, we walked out of Nashville, heading out along Route 70N toward Knoxville. Two Fisk students, members of S.N.C.C., did appear just before starting time, to walk with us for a little while. Their presence was well noted. The signs we carried were unconventional: "If your conscience demands it, refuse to serve in the armed forces," ". . . refuse to pay taxes for war." "Defend freedom with nonviolence"; but more conspicuous than our signs, quite obviously, were the Negro students—while they remained with us—and after a while the single figure of Robert Gore. Robert carried the

"lollipop" sign that simply labelled the walk: NASHVILLE TO WASHING-
TON; but he was in himself our most provocative, most instantly legible
sign—walking along very quietly; dressed, carefully, not in hiking clothes but
sober sports jacket and slacks; head held high, a quiet tension in his bearing.

We encountered a certain amount of Southern courtesy—"Well, have a
nice walk!"; and now and then expression of active sympathy—"God go
with you!" "You mean you agree with us?" "I sure do!" But less friendly
messages were of course more common—"Boo!", "Get out of here!" As we
held out our leaflets, car windows were rolled up swiftly; some cars actually
backed off from us in a rush; citizens on foot stepped quickly behind shop
doors. Approaching a leaflet victim, one tried, by remaining very calm oneself,
and looking him quietly in the eye, to prevent his flight, and infect him with
corresponding calm; but the exercise was difficult. Soon the "hot rod gang"
began to face us in the field. Parking their cars by the roadside, they would
line up, leaning against them, awaiting our approach, assuming looks that
were meant to kill—expressions glowering and at the same time pathetically
vacant. We would offer leaflets, walk past; they would hop into their cars,
speed past us, line up again by the roadside. And now the first warnings
began to be delivered to us. I handed a leaflet to the manager of a garage,
and to the Negro employee who stood beside him. "I hear they're going to
shoot you a little farther down the line," the white man told me softly. "They
don't like niggers there, you see." He turned and smiled fixedly into the eyes
of the black man by his side—"That's what I hear." The Negro made no
answer, returning the stare but allowing nothing to come to the surface of
his look—his shining eyes fathomless. The white man turned back to me. "I
just hope you'll be all right," he said—not pretending not to pretend. I told
him, as brightly as I could, "Keep hoping."

That first night we slept on the floors of a white church near Old Hickory;
the next night our "advance worker" had arranged for us to stay in a Negro
church in Lebanon. Lebanon was a small town which had lately seen much
violence. Fifteen months before, a young Negro minister, Reverend Cordell
Sloan, had been assigned to the town to try to build a Negro Presbyterian
church. He had felt called, as well, to try to build a sit-in movement. This
was the first small town in the South in which the struggle had been taken
up; and it involved not college but high school students. Retaliation had been
vigorous. Just recently the headquarters of the group had been demolished
with rocks, while the Negroes themselves stood pressed against the walls
inside, and the police looked on. This day, as we filed along the highway, a
car slowed down in passing, a young man leaned his head out: "You walking
into Lebanon?" "That's right." "Good place for you to be walking. We're
going to hang you all there." It was a bright beautiful day. Fruit trees were
coming into bloom; the purple redbud was out. Horses and goats and litters
of many-colored pigs ran in mixed company through the long Tennessee
fields. The fields were vivid with flowering mustard. We marched along,
trying not to straggle out, but to keep fairly close together. Just before mid-

day a car approaching us suddenly whizzed into a side-road and stopped; the doors flew open, and several men leaped out. Well here it is, I thought; may we all behave well. Then I saw that their faces were dark. They were students from Lebanon, two of them come to walk into town with us. More planned to join us later. They held out their hands for signs to carry.

We stopped by the side of the road and shared a picnic lunch. We bought a carton of milk at a nearby store, and in a shy ritual gesture passed it from hand to hand, each drinking from the spout. On the road again, we walked past an all-Negro primary school, set high on a hill. The entire school stood out in the yard, waving to us. I ran up the hill with leaflets. A sweet-faced teacher asked me—so softly that I could hardly catch the words: "How many colored are with you?" I told her that two of the young men she saw were from Lebanon. "I thought I recognized J. T.," she said; and in her voice, in her face, was a contained, tremulous pride and excitement. A few miles further on, more students waited by the road to join us; a little further on, more; and at the town's edge, still more. As we stepped onto the sidewalks of the town, more of us were black than white.

A car sped by, an arm jerked out of the window and slung an empty coke bottle. The youngest of the team, Henry Wershaw, gave a little cry: he had been hit in the ankle. He was able soon to limp on. We kept close ranks, to be ready for worse than that; but everyone was stepping lightly; the mood among us was almost gay. One small boy, Sam, strode with us, eyes sparkling. A pretty young woman named Avis, in a light-colored summer dress, almost skipped along the street. The citizens of the town, as usual, stepped back from us in dread; withdrew behind their doors and peered out, through the glass panes, in amazement and dread, as the unarmed troop of us passed. There were several among us who bore the marks of violence at the hands of townspeople. The skull of one of the young Negroes showed, beneath his close-cropped hair, an intricate tracery of scars: he had been hit with a wrench during one of the sit-ins. There were others walking, too, who had suffered such blows; and none had ever struck back. They walked along the street now, lighthearted, as if secure, faces extraordinarily bright, while those who had, in one way or another, condoned the blows struck, drew back, in the reflex of fear. Before we headed south, the women had been cautioned against walking in public next to a Negro man; it might make things dangerous for him. At any rate, we were told, best to take our cue from the man himself. I had carefully made no move to walk next any of these students. But now one after another, as we moved through the town, stepped alongside me, to introduce himself, to exchange a few words—free of caution. They had made their choice, had entered a fight, and if one was in it, then one was in it—ready to take what might come. At lunch one of them talked about this a little: "When you see those hoodlums arriving, you just divorce yourself from your body—prepare your body for anything: spit, fists, sticks, anything—"

Police cars had begun to drive past us at frequent intervals; but our friends remarked that we mustn't assume that they were there for our protection.

During recent trouble, one woman had asked an officer whether the police intended to protect them from the mob. "We're hired to protect the city, not individuals," had been his reply. We headed for the town square now, preparing ourselves for "anything." We walked through uneventfully. Within our hearing, an officer in a squad car pulled up next to a car full of young toughs and told the driver, "Not today, Hank, not today." We turned the corner and limped the final block to Picketts Chapel Methodist Church.

In the white churches where we had stayed so far, we had had the use of the church kitchen in which to fix our meals, from supplies we carried about with us; once the pastor's wife had kindly fixed us sandwiches and lemonade; and evenings, after supper, as many as five members of the congregation had sometimes dropped in to ask questions. This day, as we sat in the churchyard easing our feet, women began to appear from the four points of the compass, carrying bowls and platters; all who had walked were soon summoned into the room behind the church to a feast: fried chicken, garden peas, turnip greens, two kinds of potato salad, three kinds of pie. After we had sat down together to eat, we were invited into the church itself; word of a meeting had been spread through the community; the door kept opening, and soon the church had filled up.

The shape this meeting took swiftly dissolved any remaining anxieties about the harm we might do to the integrationists and to ourselves if we sought association with them. Reverend Sloan spoke first—a thin handsome man with gentle but stubborn demeanor, and the luminous wide eyes of a man who is almost blind but who sees what it is that he wants to do. "I hope the town never gets over what it saw today," he began. What the town had seen of course, as we walked through its streets together, was the first integrated gathering that had ever occurred in Lebanon. The white community had seen, and the Negro community had seen, too, the brotherhood of which Sloan preached made visible—turned fact. "I hope it gets into its system, I hope it gets to the bone," said Sloan. It was clear that he meant both white community and Negro. We learned, at the end of the meeting, that this was the largest audience he had ever had there. He had made great headway with students, but adults had been largely apathetic. Because of the drama of our arrival, many adults were present tonight, gazing about them in quiet astonishment, and he was addressing them particularly.

He spoke of the struggles in which he and his followers had been involved; he spoke of the opposition they had encountered—sprayed with insecticides, hit with ketchup bottles, threatened with pistols, run down with lawn mowers, "Name it, we've had it." "The proficient, efficient, sufficient police" had been on the scene. He smiled wryly. "We like to get killed." Many had been arrested. He asked those who had been to jail to stand. A large number stood. The leader of the peace walk, Bradford Lyttle, here interrupted to ask those among the peace walkers who had been to jail to stand, too; and an equal number rose. "Let no one be afraid of going to jail," the minister urged: "It has become an honor. . . . It's easy to say, isn't it? But come and try it." They shouldn't be afraid, he repeated; they should be afraid of being slaves any longer. "The only thing I'm afraid of is going back into the old way of living again. We've gone too far." He reminded those in the audience who had not been fighting that when freedom came, they too would enjoy it—unless perhaps they'd feel too guilty to enjoy it. They had better begin to get the feeling of it right now. Then he got very specific about the ways in which they could help, and the ways in which they had been doing the movement harm.

After he had spoken, Bradford Lyttle spoke about the work of the C.N.V.A. He spoke at ease, his words briefer than they often were—so much obviously could be assumed to be understood by this audience. He felt very strongly, he told them, that America was in a desperate situation today. Here were the most prosperous and happily situated people who had ever lived, on the verge of giving up their souls—for we were professing ourselves quite willing to murder hundreds of millions of other human beings to try to preserve our own standards of life. Many Americans were beginning to demonstrate in protest—to name themselves *un*willing. He urged them to join the protest. C.N.V.A. believed in disarming unilaterally, and in training for defense through nonviolent resistance. Heads nodded. No one stood up to hurl the familiar challenge: Are we supposed to lie down and let the Russians walk right over us? Of all the signs we carry, the sign that usually remains the most abstract for those who read it is "Defend freedom through nonviolent resistance"; but when the students of Lebanon walked through their town carrying that banner, the message could not remain abstract. If our walking beside them had made visible for the community the substance of what Reverend Sloan had been preaching, their walking beside us had made visible the substance of what Bradford Lyttle preached. Forty-five people in that audience came forward to put their names on C.N.V.A.'s mailing list.

Reverend Sloan called for a collection to be taken up for both causes. Many who had little enough to spare opened their purses. Some who had never given before gave this night. We stood and clasped hands and sang the hymn that has become the theme song of the movement in the South: "We shall overcome some day! . . . Black and white together. . . . We shall live in peace!" The words seemed to belong to both our causes.

The next day we were scheduled to walk to the small town of Carthage, set on the bluffs of the Cumberland River. A number of the people who had walked into town with us the day before turned up to see us on our way. Reverend Sloan was among them, and a leader among the students, Bobby, and Sloan's right-hand-man, a tall very homely newspaper reporter, Finley, a man of wit and feeling; and quite a few others. We expected to be escorted to the town's edge and I rather think they had expected to walk only this far, themselves; but most of them ended by walking with us all the way to Carthage. Passing motorists again leaned out of their cars to shout threatening or vile remarks. "Let not your hearts be troubled," Reverend Sloan advised, in his soft rather lilting voice. He and Finley left for a while to ride up ahead with Bradford and find a place for us to stay that night. They found it at

Braden Methodist Church, where Sloan knew the assistant minister, Beulah Allen. "How could we turn you out?" she said to Bradford; "You can never tell when the stranger will be the Lord."

After we had entered Carthage with our banners, Sloan and Finley and Bobby took a little stroll about its streets. The walk had now linked them dramatically with *that* town; and who knows when their battle may not be taken up there?

Again, this evening, women of the community appeared, arms laden; a feast was spread for us in the church basement. Again, after dinner together, we moved into the "sanctuary"; and again the church filled up. It was the first integrated meeting that had ever taken place here, too. That night, the women in our group slept in the house of Beulah Allen's sister, Dona. As we tiptoed through her room, Dona's old mother woke, and Dona introduced us. "Honey, they look white," Dona's mother whispered to her. "Mama, they are," said Dona. "Lord bless us!" said the old lady.

Braden's Methodist Church was set up on a little rise just above the large town square, and as we gathered noisily first in the basement and then in the church proper, a good many of the white people of the town and of the country round the town gathered in the square and stood glaring up. A few of them had thrown some rotten fruit and vegetables, as we sat outside before dinner; a few had walked past, holding empty coke bottles—but not quite bringing themselves to throw those. During the meeting, the door would open and shut, open and shut, as more and more of the Negro community kept arriving; and one was never quite sure that some of the crowd below might not be arriving at last. But again there were a lot of cops around, and again they had decided to keep order. The crowd just stood, until past midnight, glaring up at the small frame building which resounded with our talk and laughter and singing and prayer. Dona reported to us afterward that she had gone outside once and found several white boys loitering and had asked them in. "They don't understand," she explained to us; "They've never even been outside the county." If the resistance movement had not yet taken root among the Negroes of Carthage, they hardly needed to be introduced to the idea of nonviolence. They had found it long ago in the New Testament.

This meeting was above all an old-fashioned prayer meeting. Bradford Lyttle talked again briefly—drawing a picture of the world-wide nonviolent movement. And he issued a rather shy invitation to them to walk with us the next day. Reverend Sloan then rose and declared that he would be less shy about it: he would simply tell them that they *should* walk with us. Robert Gore asked Beulah Allen if he could say a few words from the pulpit, and he spoke of how the message of Jesus—to love one's enemies—was a strange message, a revolutionary one. "That's right," came from the audience— "Amen!" But it was Beulah Allen who led the meeting, and who spoke the prayers. I think few of us had ever before this evening felt that we were being prayed for. The days we were now approaching on the walk promised to be the most trying. We were about to enter Cumberland County, where—we had been told by both friends and antagonists—no Negro was supposed to remain after nightfall. The last Negro family that had tried to build had been burned out; the last Negro who had tried to walk through the county had been found dead by the side of the road. Beulah Allen had heard these stories too. She stood solidly before the altar rail, spread out her arms, raised up her voice—half in a piercing shout, half in a song—and addressing God as though He were indeed there just above us, just beyond the roof—"Heavenly FATHER! . . . Heavenly FATHER!"—she asked Him to give us courage, and also a good night's sleep that night, asked Him to teach all of us, including the people out there in the square, and the people along the road we were going to walk, how best to behave. The words themselves vanish now in my memory, having entered too deeply that evening into my flesh. I looked about me, and the other walkers, too, were sitting up, stock still. We had all of us heard, before, theatrical versions of such prayer—intended sometimes to be funny or sometimes to be endearing; and Beulah's prayer retained for us of course something of the extravagance of theatre; but now we were in the play; we were at the heart of it, amazed.

Again we sang together. Dona, accompanying us at the upright piano, hit the keys with a heavily-pouncing, laboring but joyful, heart-felt emphasis of her own. The rhythm was always almost jazz, and as we nodded our heads, tapped our feet, our weariness and the nudging fears we'd kept down all the past days dissolved. Again, at Reverend Sloan's prompting, we sang the integration hymn—reaching out and taking hands: "We shall overcome some day!" "Now this is difficult," Reverend Sloan said, with a flickering smile, and prompted, "Black and white together some day." He prompted, "We are not afraid *today*." At the end of the meeting, Beulah Allen gave us a blessing, and exclaimed, "It's been so sweet!" At that moment, I recalled the words of James Lawson about "the beloved community." It seemed that we had been living in that community this past hour.

The next morning I learned to my astonishment that our evening's meeting had not caused the breach between us and the white community that might have been supposed. I entered one of the shops on the square to buy some things, expecting to be served with glum hostility. The young woman behind the counter—who clearly knew who I was—was full of both curiosity and warmth. She chattered eagerly about the peculiar weather they had been having this past year, and "It's the times, I think," she ventured. I asked whether she felt that atomic tests were disrupting the weather, and she nodded: "There's One who is more powerful; we forget that." As I left, "I hope you come back and see us again," she said.

In the course of the next few days, we walked into mythical Cumberland County and walked out of it, unharmed. Two Quaker couples who bravely put us up received middle-of-the-night telephone calls, threatening "roast nigger for breakfast"; one night the fire department arrived in the yard, summoned by false alarm; one night local high school students swarmed up to the house—but when invited in, sat and talked until late, quietly enough, their curiosity about us obviously deeper than their hostility. (As they left, they were arrested by the police—as eager to protect them from us as to protect us from them.) It was actually at the edge of the county, the first night after we left Carthage, that we had our nearest brush with violence. Reverend Sloan and Finley and Bobby and others had walked with us again this third day, but had taken their final leave of us at a little one-room Negro church by the side of the road, way out "nowhere," between towns. No one was in the church, but we had been told that we could spend the night there. We had crawled into our sleeping bags, scattered out on the floor between the pews, and were listening sleepily to the small country noises in the air, when abruptly the ruder sound of rocks hitting the building brought us full awake. Two of the men stepped outside and called into the dark, inviting the besiegers to come and talk to us about it. The hail of rocks stopped and the people rustled off into the dark. We could hear the crickets again for a while and then the barrage began again; a rock came crashing through one of the windows. Another two stepped outside, this time carrying flashlights aimed at themselves, to show the strangers where they were and that they were unarmed. We could hear their voices and we could hear the stones still flying and suddenly we heard a small gasping cry. Eric Weinberger had been hit on the side of the head and knocked off his feet. He staggered up, and called to them again. "It's all right. You hit me in the head, but it's all right. But now why don't you come and talk with us?"—and seven or eight young men finally emerged out of the dark and consented to talk. They were young workingmen from around there. They talked for a good while, and finally they said that well, they might perhaps agree with some of the things we said about war and peace, but they couldn't understand our walking around with a nigger, and all sleeping in the same building with him. And then one of them asked the time-worn question: "Would you let a nigger marry your sister?" The question was posed to Sam Savage, who is a Southerner himself. When he answered that yes, he would; the decision would, after all, be hers to make—they exclaimed in sudden anger and disgust: well he was no real Southerner then, and there was no use talking about anything further; and they stamped off into the dark. At which point, one might have said that the advice we had been given before starting out on the walk had now been proved to be correct: the two issues of race relations and of war and peace could not be discussed together. However, there is a final chapter to this story. After a short time, the young men returned, wanting to talk further. The talk this time went on until the one who had done the most arguing remarked that they must be up early to work and had better get some sleep. But would we be there the next evening? he wanted to know. (We had of course, unfortunately, to move on.) As they left, he shook hands with Sam, who had said that yes, he'd let his sister marry a black man. It is my own conviction that these men listened to us as they did, on the subject of peace, just *because* Robert Gore was travelling with us. It made it more difficult for them to listen, of course; it made the talk more painful; but it also snatched it from the realm of the merely abstract. For the issue of war and peace remains fundamentally the issue of whether or not one is going to be willing to respect one's fellow man.

DOCUMENT 26

Quebec-Washington-Guantanamo
Walk for Peace, 1963–1964

This peace walk from Canada to Cuba was conceived by Bradford Lyttle, National Secretary of the Committee for Nonviolent Action, who also coordinated the San Francisco to Moscow Walk for Peace in 1960–1961. In this walk, as in the Nashville-to-Washington walk that preceded it (see Document 25), the issues of peace and race converged.

A letter by peace walker Katherine Havice described an incident involving David Dellinger and Barbara Deming:

[W]e were walking along the road at the very end of a long hard day and the Walk passed some little kids aged 5–7 hauling and struggling with huge buckets and gallon jugs of water the half mile to their shack up the road. Dave Dellinger, big man that he is, caught up and overtook the first little boy. He reached down with his free hand that wasn't carrying his sign and took the bucket to carry it. Barbara Deming came up behind the littlest and took the gallon jug from him and walked on. The kids were startled at first but soon were skipping along beside their buckets and jugs at the side of the line of walkers, looking up every few steps and grinning at us.

The walk became involved in a dramatic contest with Laurie Pritchett, police chief of Albany, Georgia. Forbidden to proceed through the downtown business district lest it create a precedent for civil rights demonstrations, the peace marchers defied the city ordinance and were arrested two days before Christmas, 1963. In jail they fasted until their release on January 16, 1964. After negotiations with the city authorities once more proved unsuccessful, the walkers again entered the restricted area, were again arrested, and again fasted for about three weeks, until, finally, a compromise was reached.

This document contains: (A) the statement of discipline which the walkers adopted; (B) an explanation of the walkers' fast, written by Bradford Lyttle who suggested the fast.

A. Discipline of Nonviolence

1. Our attitude toward officials and others who may oppose us will be one of sympathetic understanding of the burdens and responsibilities they carry.

2. No matter what the circumstances or provocation, we will not respond with physical violence to acts directed against us.

3. We will not call names or make hostile remarks.

4. We will adhere as closely as we are able to the letter and spirit of truth in our spoken and written statements.

5. We will always try to speak to the best in all men, rather than seeking to exploit their weaknesses to what we may believe is our advantage.

6. We will always attempt to interpret as clearly as possible to anyone with whom we are in contact—and especially to those who may oppose us—the purpose and meaning of our actions.

B. Bradford Lyttle,
"The Peacewalkers' Struggle in Albany, Georgia"

The issues are twofold. There is a question of civil liberties over which the walkers have been arrested and imprisoned. Of far deeper significance is *the challenge which the walkers constitute for the system of oppression used to maintain institutions of racial segregation* and other forms of social, political and economic inequality and injustice in "hard core" segregationist cities.

The civil liberties issue is simple and, on the surface, almost trifling. The authorities in Albany have designated a route through the city which they insist the walkers take. The route does not permit the Walk to pass through

---

"Discipline of Nonviolence for the Quebec-Washington-Guantanamo Walk for Peace" (New York: Committee for Nonviolent Action), mimeographed, n.d. [1963].

Bradford Lyttle, "The Peacewalkers' Struggle in Albany, Georgia" (New York: Committee for Nonviolent Action), mimeographed [January 22, 1964].

a number of commercial areas and along main thoroughfares where the walkers can distribute their leaflets and display their signs to considerable advantage. But it skirts the main, downtown shopping areas. The walkers have chosen a route that passes through these downtown areas. The authorities have arrested them and resisted a 24 day fast to deny them this route.

Why? No clear reason has ever been given. A parade permit issued by the authorities referred to traffic congestion due to an influx of Christmas shoppers in the downtown area. A reason commonly talked about by white people in Albany is that if the police let the walkers parade downtown they will have to allow other groups like the Nazis, Communists and Ku Klux Klan do so also. And many of these groups can become violent.

Almost certainly, the real and unexpressed reason is that if the walkers—a racially integrated group—are permitted to demonstrate downtown, the same right, heretofore grimly and desperately denied, will have to be granted to Albany's Negroes, to the Albany Movement. Albany Police Chief Laurie Pritchett stated it this way, "We will not have minority groups dictating policies to the city." And within the category of "minority groups" Negroes as well as peacewalkers certainly would be placed.

Intense segregationist feeling permeates Albany's history. Albany is an old slave trading center situated in the middle of the black belt. Over 42% of its population of 63,000 are Negroes, and segregation has been so ruthlessly maintained that Dougherty County, whose seat is Albany, is one of the five Georgia counties with the highest number of lynchings. Negroes are denied all but traditional, menial jobs.

In 1961, Martin Luther King organized a mass integration movement in Albany that drew worldwide attention. More than 1200 Negroes poured into the city's jail, arrested in the course of parading and demonstrations of all kinds. But the segregationists resisted the Albany Movement, made no concessions, even refused to negotiate with or otherwise recognize the Negroes' militant leaders. King eventually withdrew, the Movement's swell broke, then ebbed and Albany became the symbol of hard core segregationist resistance to the mass demonstration technique.

The Albany Movement was prevented from achieving its goal of integration by a system of police control that was able to blunt the overwhelming and disruptive effect of demonstrations. Working in close cooperation with the city's segregationist courts, the police arrested the Negro leadership, dispersed crowds with a minimum of violence. When the Movement tried to fill Albany's jails, hundreds of Negroes were farmed out to nearby county, state and city prisons. Soon the Movement lost its drive and ceased to be a threat. Later, the federal government instigated suits against several of the Movement's leaders. An all white jury in Macon has returned guilty-verdicts, which, if upheld, carry sentences of more than a year.

Creator of these successful tactics was Albany Police Chief Laurie Pritchett, whose fame as the man who had stopped the Negroes and King spread throughout the country.

Despite its severe setbacks and failure to achieve official recognition or any concrete success, the Albany Movement remains, sustaining a partially successful boycott against downtown stores, holding weekly mass meetings and occasional small protest demonstrations.

The significance of our struggle in Albany lies in its relation to the system of police oppression described below—

THE SYSTEM OF POLICE OPPRESSION

This has been carefully shaped to deal with Negro demonstrations. It is protected against every possible attack. At its foundation is the social and economic fabric of the city. Until 1940, Albany was controlled by fewer than half a dozen extremely wealthy families whose fortunes either antidated the Civil War or had been amassed early in the Century. Part of Albany constituted a "company town" for one giant textile industry. After the Second World War other businesses moved in and their owners began to have a voice in the city's affairs. Military influence grew. Turner Airforce Base, a SAC and MATS base, and the Marine Corps Supply Center, which serves the entire southeastern section of the United States, became the largest employers and economic element in the Albany area.

Politically, control of the city has always rested in the hands of rigid segregationists whose pride and financial security make them indifferent to international, national and even state criticisms of their unrelenting refusal of Negro demands for recognition and equal treatment. Albany has a Mayor and five City Commissioners who appoint a City Manager. He, in turn, appoints the Chief of Police. Although the Commissioners live in different districts of Albany, they are elected by the citizens at large. So effectively do they control the election apparatus that not one of the Commissioners is a Negro, although half of the population are.

The City Court with its judge appointed by the Commissioners assists the police force in repressing racial protests. The Peacewalkers have been in Albany's court many times now and have seen and experienced legal processes so arbitrary as to be ludicrous if their effects weren't so painful and unjust. One receives the impression that sentences are determined by the Chief of Police and served before the trials take place. Probation documents are drawn up before evidence is heard, verdicts rendered. In one trial, our judge denied every objection of a Negro attorney, sustained all made by the City Attorney. Frequent whispered conferences took place between the Judge, City Attorney and Chief of Police. Local white attorneys, who might be in a position to object to these violations of due process, are unwilling publicly to comment upon matters which might embarrass the police and courts. "There's less justice in the Albany court than in Mississippi," was the astonished comment of a SNCC worker imprisoned with us.

This pattern of oppression is common enough to many cities in the Deep South. A difference in Albany, and one of its sources of even greater effectiveness, is the unusual policy of "nonviolence" which Chief Pritchett demands of his officers. Police brutality and violence to whites or Negroes, drunks, prostitutes, thiefs, demonstrators, peacewalkers, he condemns and seems to minimize in public and the jail. Negroes report cruel exceptions to the policy and believe Pritchett holds it, when he does, only to present a "good image" to the public and create the impression that he is a responsible, progressive law enforcement official. Chief Pritchett himself claims to believe in nonviolence in principle, "I'm a nonviolent man," he told me once, and as a tactic, "We know all about nonviolence in Albany. We beat Dr. King with it." He justifies the system he serves on the grounds that it maintains law and order. Without it, he claims, mob violence and police brutality would rule. He is a proud and complex person, at once a man who meticulously fashions his police and legal apparatus to hold the segregationist line and at the same time never calls a Negro "nigger." His wife, a Catholic, teaches in an integrated school.

THE NONVIOLENT WEAPON OF THE PEACEWALKERS

One may ask, what possible chance does a small, racially integrated group of 20–30 peacewalkers have against such a system? Their pacifist, integrationist views and method of vigorous public demonstration strike abhorrence and fear in the hearts of Albany's rulers. No Albany judge recognizes their civil liberties, rights of free speech, as guaranteed by the 1st and 14th Amendments and sustained by innumerable Supreme Court decisions. Back in South Carolina, from where "northern agitators" come to Albany, a newspaper reporter smilingly told me, "You're not in Supreme Court country, son." Without blushing, Albany has endured waves of indignant protests from clergymen, liberals and others during Dr. King's integration protests. Gaining a bad reputation seems to mean little to the power structure. The daily newspaper is a kingpin in the segregation mechanism. So are the radio stations. All white Protestant churches are segregated, their ministers refrain from social action. A calm indifference and "stand offishness" pervades the white citizenry when even major racial and civil liberties conflicts develop. Georgia's Governor seems to have little influence over Albany's affairs.

Most of us in the Quebec-Washington-Guantanamo Walk for Peace believe we have only one powerful weapon with which we can battle for our civil liberties, our right to proclaim on the streets of Albany our vision of truth. That is the fast or hunger strike. If we are arrested we refuse to eat and within a period of time the authorities are faced with recognizing our rights and granting us our freedom or having on their hands people slowly dying of starvation, people who generate not only intense interest throughout the nation and even the world but stir the hearts of white citizens in Albany to doubt and misgivings. And it is expensive to hospitalize and force feed 20 people. Within a few days, thousands of dollars must be committed.

To be successful, the fast must be maintained steadily towards death by as many people as possible. They must be willing to endure emaciation, scurvy, extreme weakness, muscle deterioration, the pain of intravenous and tube feeding. They must be willing to risk fatal errors in judgment by police or doctors, or outbursts of violence from men driven to desperation by a protest that they cannot suppress.

The prolonged fast is our chief weapon. We have others. A number of walkers practice kinds of civil disobedience other than fasting. Some refuse to walk into their cells. They oppose the prison system in principle. Others will not walk to court. They cannot recognize an apparatus created in the name of justice for the purpose of denying justice. By these acts they offset, indeed annihilate and make ridiculous, the mantle of power and authority that the Albany court has gathered about itself.

Outside the jail and hospital we maintain an office and administrative center. We send news reports to the mass media, bulletins to hundreds of people, groups and organizations throughout the nation and world who sympathize with us. These friends respond by writing letters and sending telegrams on our behalf. In addition to interpreting the project to people outside of Albany, our staff does similar work within the city itself, visiting the newspaper editors, ministers and others, negotiating with officials, mustering local support wherever it can be found.

In Albany, a great source of strength and support comes from the Negro people who understand that the fight for our civil liberties is for theirs as well. They have provided a house for our office and living quarters. They help in many other ways and encourage us.

In our first engagement with the Albany power structure, 22 people were imprisoned. Nine fasted 24 days, three went to the hospital, two were fed intravenously, all the long term fasters eventually were given vitamin injections. It is our impression that the authorities were seriously worried by the protest and released us in the hope that we would depart. They have not, however, granted us the right to walk through the city's main shopping area. Recent conversations we have had with Chief Pritchett and City Manager S. A. Roos have convinced us that they deeply understand that our project and technique of fasting threaten their entire system—their power. They will go to great lengths to win. The struggle will be desperate.

IS IT WORTH IT?

Why risk your health and life to walk through downtown Albany? For those of us who probably will go to prison, the answer is that we believe we owe it to the struggle against racial injustice to do so. The horrible evil for which Albany has become a symbol is intolerable and must be ended even at great cost. If God, fate, or the science of nonviolence permits truth to win, we shall have shown that Albany's hitherto invincible system of oppression has a flaw: that a few people willing and able to couple prolonged, deliberately accepted suffering with an efficient medium of public communication and interpretation can generate enough sympathy in the hearts of their opponents and enough public support to make this carefully constructed machinery of oppression ineffective. The achievement of this in Albany would help the Negro people here—and the white too, by freeing them partly from the bonds of an inhuman system. But its larger implications may be even more important, for we will have created a technique of nonviolent struggle that can be used by others in other cities, North and South, even throughout the world. By this experiment, the science of nonviolence can be expanded, as it must rapidly be everywhere if our world is not to perish before the onslaught of weapons without which men believe they are naked before the power of cruelty and injustice. We write and talk about extending freedom and demo-cratic institutions against totalitarianism by means of nonviolence. Albany, Georgia, has a totalitarian government. We should not skirt this challenge; we should make an experiment with the power of nonviolent action.

The struggle has a close relationship to our concern for American-Cuban relationships too, the main theme of the Walk. We will demonstrate unmistak-ably to the Cuban people and government where we stand in regard to racism and denials of free speech in the United States. We hope thereby to win their deep respect and increase the likelihood that we will be welcomed in Cuba even if we maintain a critical attitude towards some policies of the Cuban government. There is evidence that already this respect is being won, for on January 7 Radio Havana devoted a substantial part of a news broadcast to describing the Walk, its purpose, and its imprisonment and protest in Albany.

There are reasons why our battle for truth in Albany, Georgia, is important. We enter it in a spirit of the deepest comradeship, fully aware of each others weakness and strength, for behind us lie thousands of miles of walking in Canada and the United States, of cold, heat, dust and rain, fear of the unknown, the barren dirty walls of prisons in nine cities, a cattle prod in the hands of sadistic men, hurled eggs and rocks and countless threats and curses. Through all we have seen the power of nonviolence, of persistence, patience, entreaty, forgiveness, win out time and time again. Not one of us doubts that though our struggle here may carry us down to frightening depths, the eternal forces of truth that we are striving to release will in the end break forth and prevail at least in part. . . .

PART IX

DIRECT ACTION FOR CIVIL RIGHTS, POST-WORLD WAR II

DOCUMENT 27

Martin Luther King, Jr., "Pilgrimage to Nonviolence"

Martin Luther King, Jr. was born in Atlanta in 1929. He graduated from Morehouse College in 1948, received the B.D. from Crozer Theological Seminary in 1951 and the Ph.D. in 1955 from Boston University, in the field of systematic theology. Just before graduation Reverend King was appointed pastor at the Dexter Avenue Baptist Church in Montgomery, Alabama, where he was catapulted into national prominence as leader of the 1955–1956 Montgomery bus boycott.

"Pilgrimage to Nonviolence" deals not so much with the Montgomery boycott as with the intellectual and spiritual evolution which led King, its

Martin Luther King, Jr., "Pilgrimage to Nonviolence," *Stride Toward Freedom* (New York: Harper & Bros., 1958), pp. 90–107. *Stride Toward Freedom: The Montgomery Story* by Martin Luther King, Jr. Copyright © by Martin Luther King. Reprinted by permission of Harper & Row, Publishers, Incorporated.

leader, to a commitment to nonviolence. Particularly significant are (1) the distinction between varieties of love (eros, philia, and agape), and (2) the emphasis upon creating and restoring "community" as the purpose of nonviolent action. Elsewhere in his writings, King speaks of creating the "blessed community," a phrase which has become widely current.

Often the question has arisen concerning my own intellectual pilgrimage to nonviolence. In order to get at this question it is necessary to go back to my early teens in Atlanta. I had grown up abhorring not only segregation but also the oppressive and barbarous acts that grew out of it. I had passed spots where Negroes had been savagely lynched, and had watched the Ku Klux Klan on its rides at night. I had seen police brutality with my own eyes, and watched Negroes receive the most tragic injustice in the courts. All of these things had done something to my growing personality. I had come perilously close to resenting all white people.

I had also learned that the inseparable twin of racial injustice was economic injustice. Although I came from a home of economic security and relative comfort, I could never get out of my mind the economic insecurity of many of my playmates and the tragic poverty of those living around me. During my late teens I worked two summers, against my father's wishes—he never wanted my brother and me to work around white people because of the oppressive conditions—in a plant that hired both Negroes and whites. Here I saw economic injustice first-hand, and realized that the poor white was exploited just as much as the Negro. Through these early experiences I grew up deeply conscious of the varieties of injustice in our society.

So when I went to Atlanta's Morehouse College as a freshman in 1944 my concern for racial and economic justice was already substantial. During my student days at Morehouse I read Thoreau's *Essay on Civil Disobedience* for the first time. Fascinated by the idea of refusing to coöperate with an evil system, I was so deeply moved that I reread the work several times. This was my first intellectual contact with the theory of nonviolent resistance.

Not until I entered Crozer Theological Seminary in 1948, however, did I begin a serious intellectual quest for a method to eliminate social evil. Although my major interest was in the fields of theology and philosophy, I spent a great deal of time reading the works of the great social philosophers. I came early to Walter Rauschenbusch's *Christianity and the Social Crisis,* which left an indelible imprint on my thinking by giving me a theological basis for the social concern which had already grown up in me as a result of my early experiences. Of course there were points at which I differed with Rauschenbusch. I felt that he had fallen victim to the nineteenth-century "cult of inevitable progress" which led him to a superficial optimism concerning man's nature. Moreover, he came perilously close to identifying the Kingdom of God with a particular social and economic system—a tendency which should never befall the Church. But in spite of these shortcomings Rauschenbusch had done a great service for the Christian Church by insisting that the gospel deals with the whole man, not only his soul but his body; not only his spiritual well-being but his material well-being. It has been my conviction ever since reading Rauschenbusch that any religion which professes to be concerned about the souls of men and is not concerned about the social and economic conditions that scar the soul, is a spiritually moribund religion only waiting for the day to be buried. It well has been said: "A religion that ends with the individual, ends."

After reading Rauschenbusch, I turned to a serious study of the social and ethical theories of the great philosophers, from Plato and Aristotle down to Rousseau, Hobbes, Bentham, Mill, and Locke. All of these masters stimulated my thinking—such as it was—and, while finding things to question in each of them, I nevertheless learned a great deal from their study.

During the Christmas holidays of 1949 I decided to spend my spare time reading Karl Marx to try to understand the appeal of communism for many people. For the first time I carefully scrutinized *Das Kapital* and *The Communist Manifesto*. I also read some interpretive works on the thinking of Marx and Lenin. In reading such Communist writings I drew certain conclusions that have remained with me as convictions to this day. First I rejected their materialistic interpretation of history. Communism, avowedly secularistic and materialistic, has no place for God. This I could never accept, for as a Christian I believe that there is a creative personal power in this universe who is the ground and essence of all reality—a power that cannot be explained in materialistic terms. History is ultimately guided by spirit, not matter. Second, I strongly disagreed with communism's ethical relativism. Since for the Communist there is no divine government, no absolute moral order, there are no fixed, immutable principles; consequently almost anything—force, violence, murder, lying—is a justifiable means to the "millennial" end. This type of relativism was abhorrent to me. Constructive ends can never give absolute moral justification to destructive means, because in the final analysis the end is preëxistent in the mean. Third, I opposed communism's political totalitarianism. In communism the individual ends up in subjection to the state. True, the Marxist would argue that the state is an "interim" reality which is to be eliminated when the classless society emerges; but the state is the end while it lasts, and man only a means to that end. And if any man's so-called rights or liberties stand in the way of that end, they are simply swept aside. His liberties of expression, his freedom to vote, his freedom to listen to what news he likes or to choose his books are all restricted. Man becomes hardly more, in communism, than a depersonalized cog in the turning wheel of the state.

This deprecation of individual freedom was objectionable to me. I am convinced now, as I was then, that man is an end because he is a child of God. Man is not made for the state; the state is made for man. To deprive man of freedom is to relegate him to the status of a thing, rather than elevate him to the status of a person. Man must never be treated as a means to the end of the state, but always as an end within himself.

Yet, in spite of the fact that my response to communism was and is negative, and I considered it basically evil, there were points at which I found it challenging. The late Archbishop of Canterbury, William Temple, referred to communism as a Christian heresy. By this he meant that communism had laid hold of certain truths which are essential parts of the Christian view of things, but that it had bound up with them concepts and practices which no Christian could ever accept or profess. Communism challenged the late Archbishop and it should challenge every Christian—as it challenged me—to a growing concern about social justice. With all of its false assumptions and evil methods, communism grew as a protest against the hardships of the underprivileged. Communism in theory emphasized a classless society, and a concern for social justice, though the world knows from sad experience that in practice it created new classes and a new lexicon of injustice. The Christian ought always to be challenged by any protest against unfair treatment of the poor, for Christianity is itself such a protest, nowhere expressed more eloquently than in Jesus' words: "The Spirit of the Lord is upon me, because he hath anointed me to preach the gospel to the poor; he hath sent me to heal the brokenhearted, to preach deliverance to the captives, and recovering of sight to the blind, to set at liberty them that are bruised, to preach the acceptable year of the Lord."

I also sought systematic answers to Marx's critique of modern bourgeois culture. He presented capitalism as essentially a struggle between the owners of the productive resources and the workers, whom Marx regarded as the real producers. Marx interpreted economic forces as the dialectical process by which society moved from feudalism through capitalism to socialism, with the primary mechanism of this historical movement being the struggle between economic classes whose interests were irreconcilable. Obviously this theory left out of account the numerous and significant complexities—political, economic, moral, religious, and psychological—which played a vital role in shaping the constellation of institutions and ideas known today as Western civilization. Moreover, it was dated in the sense that the capitalism Marx wrote about bore only a partial resemblance to the capitalism we know in this country today.

But in spite of the shortcomings of his analysis, Marx had raised some basic questions. I was deeply concerned from my early teen days about the gulf between superfluous wealth and abject poverty, and my reading of Marx made me ever more conscious of this gulf. Although modern American capitalism had greatly reduced the gap through social reforms, there was still need for a better distribution of wealth. Moreover, Marx had revealed the danger of the profit motive as the sole basis of an economic system: capitalism is always in danger of inspiring men to be more concerned about making a living than making a life. We are prone to judge success by the index of our salaries or the size of our automobiles, rather than by the quality of our service and relationship to humanity—thus capitalism can lead to a practical materialism that is as pernicious as the materialism taught by communism.

In short, I read Marx as I read all of the influential historical thinkers—from a dialectical point of view, combining a partial yes and a partial no. In so far as Marx posited a metaphysical materialism, an ethical relativism, and a strangulating totalitarianism, I responded with an unambiguous "no"; but in so far as he pointed to weaknesses of traditional capitalism, contributed to the growth of a definite self-consciousness in the masses, and challenged the social conscience of the Christian churches, I responded with a definite "yes."

My reading of Marx also convinced me that truth is found neither in Marxism nor in traditional capitalism. Each represents a partial truth. Historically capitalism failed to see the truth in collective enterprise and Marxism failed to see the truth in individual enterprise. Nineteenth-century capitalism failed to see that life is social and Marxism failed and still fails to see that life is individual and personal. The Kingdom of God is neither the thesis of individual enterprise nor the antithesis of collective enterprise, but a synthesis which reconciles the truths of both.

During my stay at Crozer, I was also exposed for the first time to the pacifist position in a lecture by Dr. A. J. Muste. I was deeply moved by Dr. Muste's talk, but far from convinced of the practicability of his position. Like most of the students of Crozer, I felt that while war could never be a positive or absolute good, it could serve as a negative good in the sense of preventing the spread and growth of an evil force. War, horrible as it is, might be preferable to surrender to a totalitarian system—Nazi, Fascist, or Communist.

During this period I had about despaired of the power of love in solving social problems. Perhaps my faith in love was temporarily shaken by the philosophy of Nietzsche. I had been reading parts of *The Genealogy of Morals* and the whole of *The Will to Power.* Nietzsche's glorification of power—in his theory all life expressed the will to power—was an outgrowth of his contempt for ordinary morals. He attacked the whole of the Hebraic-Christian morality—with its virtues of piety and humility, its other-worldliness and its attitude toward suffering—as the glorification of weakness, as making virtues out of necessity and impotence. He looked to the development of a superman who would surpass man as man surpassed the ape.

Then one Sunday afternoon I traveled to Philadelphia to hear a sermon by Dr. Mordecai Johnson, president of Howard University. He was there to preach for the Fellowship House of Philadelphia. Dr. Johnson had just returned from a trip to India, and to my great interest, he spoke of the life and teachings of Mahatma Gandhi. His message was so profound and electrifying that I left the meeting and bought a half-dozen books on Gandhi's life and works.

Like most people, I had heard of Gandhi, but I had never studied him seriously. As I read I became deeply fascinated by his campaigns of nonviolent resistance. I was particularly moved by the Salt March to the Sea and his numerous fasts. The whole concept of "Satyagraha" (*Satya* is truth which equals love, and *agraha* is force; "Satyagraha," therefore, means truth-force or love force) was profoundly significant to me. As I delved deeper into the philosophy of Gandhi my skepticism concerning the power of love gradually diminished, and I came to see for the first time its potency in the area of social reform. Prior to reading Gandhi, I had about concluded that the ethics of Jesus were only effective in individual relationship. The "turn the other cheek" philosophy and the "love your enemies" philosophy were only valid, I felt, when individuals were in conflict with other individuals; when racial groups and nations were in conflict a more realistic approach seemed necessary. But after reading Gandhi, I saw how utterly mistaken I was.

Gandhi was probably the first person in history to lift the love ethic of Jesus above mere interaction between individuals to a powerful and effective social force on a large scale. Love for Gandhi was a potent instrument for social and collective transformation. It was in this Gandhian emphasis on love and nonviolence that I discovered the method for social reform that I had been seeking for so many months. The intellectual and moral satisfaction that I failed to gain from the utilitarianism of Bentham and Mill, the revolutionary methods of Marx and Lenin, the social-contracts theory of Hobbes, the "back to nature" optimism of Rousseau, and the superman philosophy of Nietzsche, I found in the nonviolent resistance philosophy of Gandhi. I came to feel that this was the only morally and practically sound method open to oppressed people in their struggle for freedom.

But my intellectual odyssey to nonviolence did not end here. During my last year in theological school, I began to read the works of Reinhold Niebuhr. The prophetic and realistic elements in Niebuhr's passionate style and profound thought were appealing to me, and I became so enamored of his social ethics that I almost fell into the trap of accepting uncritically everything he wrote.

About this time I read Niebuhr's critique of the pacifist position. Niebuhr had himself once been a member of the pacifist ranks. For several years, he had been national chairman of the Fellowship of Reconciliation. His break with pacifism came in the early thirties, and the first full statement of his criticism of pacifism was in *Moral Man and Immoral Society*. Here he argued that there was no intrinsic moral difference between violent and non-violent resistance. The social consequences of the two methods were different, he contended, but the differences were in degree rather than kind. Later Niebuhr began emphasizing the irresponsibility of relying on nonviolent resistance when there was no ground for believing that it would be successful in preventing the spread of totalitarian tyranny. It could only be successful, he argued, if the groups against whom the resistance was taking place had some degree of moral conscience, as was the case in Gandhi's struggle against the British. Niebuhr's ultimate rejection of pacifism was based primarily on the doctrine of man. He argued that pacifism failed to do justice to the reformation doctrine of justification by faith, substituting for it a sectarian perfectionism which believes "that divine grace actually lifts men out of the sinful contradictions of history and establishes him above the sins of the world."

At first, Niebuhr's critique of pacifism left me in a state of confusion. As I continued to read, however, I came to see more and more the shortcomings of his position. For instance, many of his statements revealed that he interpreted pacifism as a sort of passive nonresistance to evil expressing naïve trust in the power of love. But this was a serious distortion. My study of Gandhi convinced me that true pacifism is not nonresistance to evil, but nonviolent resistance to evil. Between the two positions, there is a world of difference. Gandhi resisted evil with as much vigor and power as the violent resister, but he resisted with love instead of hate. True pacifism is not unrealistic submission to evil power, as Niebuhr contends. It is rather a courageous confrontation of evil by the power of love, in the faith that it is better to be the recipient of violence than the inflicter of it, since the latter only multiplies the existence of violence and bitterness in the universe, while the former may develop a sense of shame in the opponent, and thereby bring about a transformation and change of heart.

In spite of the fact that I found many things to be desired in Niebuhr's philosophy, there were several points at which he constructively influenced my thinking. Niebuhr's great contribution to contemporary theology is that he has refuted the false optimism characteristic of a great segment of Protestant liberalism, without falling into the anti-rationalism of the continental theologian Karl Barth, or the semi-fundamentalism of other dialectical theologians. Moreover, Niebuhr has extraordinary insight into human nature, especially the behavior of nations and social groups. He is keenly aware of the complexity of human motives and of the relation between morality and power. His theology is a persistent reminder of the reality of sin on every level of man's existence. These elements in Niebuhr's thinking helped me to recognize the illusions of a superficial optimism concerning human nature and the dangers of a false idealism. While I still believed in man's potential for good, Niebuhr made me realize his potential for evil as well. Moreover, Niebuhr helped me to recognize the complexity of man's social involvement and the glaring reality of collective evil.

Many pacifists, I felt, failed to see this. All too many had an unwarranted optimism concerning man and leaned unconsciously toward self-righteousness. It was my revolt against these attitudes under the influence of Niebuhr that accounts for the fact that in spite of my strong leaning toward pacifism, I never joined a pacifist organization. After reading Niebuhr, I tried to arrive at a realistic pacifism. In other words, I came to see the pacifist position not as sinless but as the lesser evil in the circumstances. I felt then, and I feel now, that the pacifist would have a greater appeal if he did not claim to be free from the moral dilemmas that the Christian nonpacifist confronts.

The next stage of my intellectual pilgrimage to nonviolence came during my doctoral studies at Boston University. Here I had the opportunity to talk to many exponents of nonviolence, both students and visitors to the campus. Boston University School of Theology, under the influence of Dean Walter Muelder and Professor Allen Knight Chalmers, had a deep sympathy for pacifism. Both Dean Muelder and Dr. Chalmers had a passion for social justice that stemmed, not from a superficial optimism, but from a deep faith in the possibilities of human beings when they allowed themselves to become coworkers with God. It was at Boston University that I came to see that Niebuhr had over-emphasized the corruption of human nature. His pessimism concerning human nature was not balanced by an optimism concerning divine nature. He was so involved in diagnosing man's sickness of sin that he overlooked the cure of grace.

I studied philosophy and theology at Boston University under Edgar S. Brightman and L. Harold DeWolf. Both men greatly stimulated my thinking. It was mainly under these teachers that I studied personalistic philosophy—the theory that the clue to the meaning of ultimate reality is found in personality. This personal idealism remains today my basic philosophical position. Personalism's insistence that only personality—finite and infinite—is ultimately real strengthened me in two convictions: it gave me metaphysical and philosophical grounding for the idea of a personal God, and it gave me a metaphysical basis for the dignity and worth of all human personality.

Just before Dr. Brightman's death, I began studying the philosophy of Hegel with him. Although the course was mainly a study of Hegel's monumental work, *Phenomenology of Mind,* I spent my spare time reading his *Philosophy of History* and *Philosophy of Right.* There were points in Hegel's philosophy that I strongly disagreed with. For instance, his absolute idealism was rationally unsound to me because it tended to swallow up the many in the one. But there were other aspects of his thinking that I found stimulating. His contention that "truth is the whole" led me to a philosophical method of rational coherence. His analysis of the dialectical process, in spite of its shortcomings, helped me to see that growth comes through struggle.

In 1954 I ended my formal training with all of these relatively divergent intellectual forces converging into a positive social philosophy. One of the main tenets of this philosophy was the conviction that nonviolent resistance was one of the most potent weapons available to oppressed people in their quest for social justice. At this time, however, I had merely an intellectual understanding and appreciation of the position, with no firm determination to organize it in a socially effective situation.

When I went to Montgomery as a pastor, I had not the slightest idea that I would later become involved in a crisis in which nonviolent resistance would be applicable. I neither started the protest nor suggested it. I simply responded to the call of the people for a spokesman. When the protest began, my mind, consciously or unconsciously, was driven back to the Sermon on the Mount, with its sublime teachings on love, and the Gandhian method of nonviolent resistance. As the days unfolded, I came to see the power of nonviolence more and more. Living through the actual experience of the protest, nonviolence became more than a method to which I gave intellectual assent; it became a commitment to a way of life. Many of the things that I had not cleared up intellectually concerning nonviolence were now solved in the sphere of practical action.

Since the philosophy of nonviolence played such a positive role in the Montgomery Movement, it may be wise to turn to a brief discussion of some basic aspects of this philosophy.

First, it must be emphasized that nonviolent resistance is not a method for cowards; it does resist. If one uses this method because he is afraid or merely because he lacks the instruments of violence, he is not truly nonviolent. This is why Gandhi often said that if cowardice is the only alternative to violence, it is better to fight. He made this statement conscious of the fact that there is always another alternative: no individual or group need submit to any wrong, nor need they use violence to right the wrong; there is the way of nonviolent resistance. This is ultimately the way of the strong man. It is not a method of stagnant passivity. The phrase "passive resistance" often gives the false impression that this is a sort of "do-nothing method" in which the resister quietly and passively accepts evil. But nothing is further from the truth. For while the nonviolent resister is passive in the sense that he is not physically aggressive toward his opponent, his mind and emotions are always active, constantly seeking to persuade his opponent that he is wrong. The method is passive physically, but strongly active spiritually. It is not passive nonresistance to evil, it is active nonviolent resistance to evil.

A second basic fact that characterizes nonviolence is that it does not seek to defeat or humiliate the opponent, but to win his friendship and understanding. The nonviolent resister must often express his protest through noncoöperation or boycotts, but he realizes that these are not ends themselves; they are merely means to awaken a sense of moral shame in the opponent. The end is redemption and reconciliation. The aftermath of nonviolence is the creation of the beloved community, while the aftermath of violence is tragic bitterness.

A third characteristic of this method is that the attack is directed against forces of evil rather than against persons who happen to be doing the evil. It is evil that the nonviolent resister seeks to defeat, not the persons victimized by evil. If he is opposing racial injustice, the nonviolent resister has the vision to see that the basic tension is not between races. As I like to say to the people in Montgomery: "The tension in this city is not between white people and Negro people. The tension is, at bottom, between justice and injustice, between the forces of light and the forces of darkness. And if there is a victory, it will be a victory not merely for fifty thousand Negroes, but a victory for justice and the forces of light. We are out to defeat injustice and not white persons who may be unjust."

A fourth point that characterizes nonviolent resistance is a willingness to accept suffering without retaliation, to accept blows from the opponent without striking back. "Rivers of blood may have to flow before we gain our freedom, but it must be our blood," Gandhi said to his countrymen. The nonviolent resister is willing to accept violence if necessary, but never to inflict it. He does not seek to dodge jail. If going to jail is necessary he enters it "as a bridegroom enters the bride's chamber."

One may well ask: "What is the nonviolent resister's justification for this ordeal to which he invites men, for this mass political application of the ancient doctrine of turning the other cheek?" The answer is found in the realization that unearned suffering is redemptive. Suffering, the nonviolent resister realizes, has tremendous educational and transforming possibilities. "Things of fundamental importance to people are not secured by reason alone, but have to be purchased with their suffering," said Gandhi. He continues: "Suffering is infinitely more powerful than the law of the jungle for converting the opponent and opening his ears which are otherwise shut to the voice of reason."

A fifth point concerning nonviolent resistance is that it avoids not only external physical violence but also internal violence of spirit. The nonviolent resister not only refuses to shoot his opponent but he also refuses to hate him. At the center of nonviolence stands the principle of love. The nonviolent resister would contend that in the struggle for human dignity, the oppressed people of the world must not succumb to the temptation of becoming bitter or indulging in hate campaigns. To retaliate in kind would do nothing but intensify the existence of hate in the universe. Along the way of life, someone must have sense enough and morality enough to cut off the chain of hate. This can only be done by projecting the ethic of love to the center of our lives.

In speaking of love at this point, we are not referring to some sentimental or affectionate emotion. It would be nonsense to urge men to love their oppressors in an affectionate sense. Love in this connection means understanding, redemptive good will. Here the Greek language comes to our aid. There are three words for love in the Greek New Testament. First, there is *eros*. In Platonic philosophy *eros* meant the yearning of the soul for the realm of the divine. It has come now to mean a sort of aesthetic or romantic love. Second, there is *philia* which means intimate affection between personal friends. *Philia* denotes a sort of reciprocal love; the person loves because he is loved. When we speak of loving those who oppose us, we refer to neither *eros* nor *philia;* we speak of a love which is expressed in the Greek word *agape*. *Agape* means understanding, redeeming good will for all men. It is an overflowing love which is purely spontaneous, unmotivated, groundless, and creative. It is not set in motion by any quality or function of its object. It is the love of God operating in the human heart.

Agape is disinterested love. It is a love in which the individual seeks not his own good, but the good of his neighbor (I Cor. 10:24). *Agape* does not begin by discriminating between worthy and unworthy people, or any qualities people possess. It begins by loving others *for their sakes*. It is an entirely "neighbor-regarding concern for others," which discovers the neighbor in every man it meets. Therefore, *agape* makes no distinction between friend and enemy; it is directed toward both. If one loves an individual merely on account of his friendliness, he loves him for the sake of the benefits to be gained from the friendship, rather than for the friend's own sake. Consequently, the best way to assure oneself that Love is disinterested is to have love for the enemy-neighbor from whom you can expect no good in return, but only hostility and persecution.

Another basic point about *agape* is that it springs from the *need* of the other person—his need for belonging to the best in the human family. The Samaritan who helped the Jew on the Jericho Road was "good" because he responded to the human need that he was presented with. God's love is eternal and fails not because man needs his love. St. Paul assures us that the loving act of redemption was done "while we were yet sinners"—that is, at the point of our greatest need for love. Since the white man's personality is greatly distorted by segregation, and his soul is greatly scarred, he needs the love of the Negro. The Negro must love the white man, because the white man needs his love to remove his tensions, insecurities, and fears.

Agape is not a weak, passive love. It is love in action. *Agape* is love seeking to preserve and create community. It is insistence on community even when one seeks to break it. *Agape* is a willingness to sacrifice in the interest of mutuality. *Agape* is a willingness to go to any length to restore community. It doesn't stop at the first mile, but it goes the second mile to restore community. It is a willingness to forgive, not seven times, but seventy times seven to restore community. The cross is the eternal expression of the length to which God will go in order to restore broken community. The resurrection is a symbol of God's triumph over all the forces that seek to block community. The Holy Spirit is the continuing community creating reality that moves through history. He who works against community is working against the whole of creation. Therefore, if I respond to hate with a reciprocal hate I do nothing but intensify the cleavage in broken community. I can only close the gap in broken community by meeting hate with love. If I meet hate with hate, I become depersonalized, because creation is so designed that my personality can only be fulfilled in the context of community. Booker T. Washington was right: "Let no man pull you so low as to make you hate him." When he pulls you that low he brings you to the point of working against community; he drags you to the point of defying creation, and thereby becoming depersonalized.

In the final analysis, *agape* means a recognition of the fact that all life is interrelated. All humanity is involved in a single process, and all men are brothers. To the degree that I harm my brother, no matter what he is doing to me, to that extent I am harming myself. For example, white men often refuse federal aid to education in order to avoid giving the Negro his rights; but because all men are brothers they cannot deny Negro children without harming their own. They end, all efforts to the contrary, by hurting themselves. Why is this? Because men are brothers. If you harm me, you harm yourself.

Love, *agape,* is the only cement that can hold this broken community together. When I am commanded to love, I am commanded to restore community, to resist injustice, and to meet the needs of my brothers.

A sixth basic fact about nonviolent resistance is that it is based on the conviction that the universe is on the side of justice. Consequently, the believer in nonviolence has deep faith in the future. This faith is another reason why the nonviolent resister can accept suffering without retaliation. For he knows that in his struggle for justice he has cosmic companionship. It is true that there are devout believers in nonviolence who find it difficult to believe in a personal God. But even these persons believe in the existence of some creative force that works for universal wholeness. Whether we call it an unconscious process, an impersonal Brahman, or a Personal Being of matchless power and infinite love, there is a creative force in this universe that works to bring the disconnected aspects of reality into a harmonious whole.

DOCUMENT 28

CORE and SNCC, Statements of Principle

The use of mass nonviolence in Montgomery fanned into flame a spark which had been kept alive for more than a decade by members of the Congress Of Racial Equality (CORE). In February 1942 James Farmer, then race relations secretary of the Fellowship of Reconciliation, proposed the formation of a group composed of both pacifists and nonpacifists to take nonviolent action against racial discrimination. That same year the Chicago Committee of Racial Equality began to use against segregated facilities the sit-in techniques devised by labor organizers during the depression. In 1943 the Congress Of Racial Equality (a name reminiscent of the Congress of Industrial Organizations) was formed.

CORE's organizing procedures were strongly influenced by its philosophy of nonviolence (see Document 28A). The same spirit was evident in the statement of purpose of the Student Nonviolent Coordinating Committee

(SNCC), formed in 1960 to coordinate the activities of thousands of students using the sit-in, "kneel-in," "jail-in," and other nonviolent techniques to integrate public accommodations facilities (see Document 28B).

A. "CORE Rules for Action"

GUARANTEES OF THE INDIVIDUAL TO THE GROUP

1. A CORE member will investigate the facts carefully before determining whether or not racial injustice exists in a given situation.

2. A CORE member will seek at all times to understand both the attitude of the person responsible for a policy of racial discrimination, and the social situation which engendered the attitude. The CORE member will be flexible and creative, showing a willingness to participate in experiments which seem constructive, but being careful not to compromise CORE principles.

3. A CORE member will make a sincere effort to avoid malice and hatred toward any group or individual.

4. A CORE member will never use malicious slogans or labels to discredit any opponent.

5. A CORE member will be willing to admit mistakes.

6. He will meet the anger of any individual or group in the spirit of good will and creative reconciliation: he will submit to assault and will not retaliate in kind either by act or word.

7. A member will never engage in any action in the name of the group except when authorized by the group or one of its action units.

8. When in an action project a CORE member will obey the orders issued by the authorized leader or spokesman of the project, whether these orders please him or not. If he does not approve of such orders, he shall later refer the criticism back to the group or to the committee which was the source of the project plan.

9. No member, after once accepting the discipline of the group for a particular action project, shall have the right of withdrawing. However, should a participant feel that under further pressure he will no longer be able to adhere to the *Rules for Action,* he shall then withdraw from the project and leave the scene immediately after notifying the project leader.

Congress Of Racial Equality, "CORE Rules for Action," flier (New York: n.d. [1963]). Reprinted with the permission of the Congress Of Racial Equality.

10. Only a person who is a recognized member of the group or a participant accepted by the group leader in a particular project shall be permitted to take part in that group action.

GUARANTEES FROM THE LOCAL GROUP TO
THE INDIVIDUAL

11. Each member has the right to dissent from any group decision and, if dissenting, need not participate in the specific action planned.

12. Each member shall understand that all decisions on general policy shall be arrived at only through democratic group discussion.

13. A CORE member shall receive the uncompromising support of his CORE group as he faces any difficulties resulting from his authorized CORE activities.

B.   Student Nonviolent Coordinating Committee,
Statement of Purpose

We affirm the philosophical or religious ideal of nonviolence as the foundation of our purpose, the presupposition of our faith, and the manner of our action. Nonviolence as it grows from the Judaeo-Christian tradition seeks a social order of justice permeated by love. Integration of human endeavor represents the crucial first step towards such a society.

Through nonviolence, courage displaces fear; love transforms hate. Acceptance dissipates prejudice; hope ends despair. Peace dominates war; faith reconciles doubt. Mutual regard cancels emnity. Justice for all overcomes injustice. The redemptive community supercedes systems of gross social immorality.

Love is the central motif of nonviolence. Love is the force by which God binds man to himself and man to man. Such love goes to the extreme; it remains loving and forgiving even in the midst of hostility. It matches the capacity of evil to inflict suffering with an even more enduring capacity to absorb evil, all the while persisting in love.

By appealing to conscience and standing on the moral nature of human existence, nonviolence nurtures the atmosphere in which reconciliation and justice become actual possibilities.

The Student Nonviolent Coordinating Committee, *Constitution* (as revised in Conference, April 29, 1962 [originally adopted Raleigh, N.C., April, 1960]). Mimeographed, n.d., on file at SNCC office, Atlanta, Georgia.

DOCUMENT 29

Thomas Gaither,
Jailed-In

The first national CORE project was a Journey of Reconciliation in which twenty-five persons spent two weeks testing bus segregation in the upper South. This was in 1947. CORE workers, such as the Reverend James Lawson of Nashville, were also prominent in the lunch-counter sit-ins of 1960. The sit-ins began as the spontaneous action of four students at North Carolina A. and T. College in Greensboro, North Carolina on February 1, 1960. By September 1960 the sit-ins had involved 70,000 students, 3,600 of whom were arrested. A number of these demonstrators, such as Thomas Gaither, elected not only to commit civil disobedience but to refuse bail when arrested. This technique became known as "jail-in," or "jail no bail."

Eight Friendship Junior College students and I served 30 days on the York County road gang for the "crime" of sitting-in at McCrory's lunch counter in Rock Hill, South Carolina. While hundreds of students have been jailed since the start of the sit-in movement, we were the first to be committed to a road gang, which is the present-day version of the dreaded southern chain gang.

We could have paid $100 fines, or we could have posted $200 bail each and gone out pending appeal. Instead, we chose to be jailed-in. All nine of us felt that this would strengthen the impact of our protest. Furthermore, instead of the city being $900 richer for the injustice it had committed, it would have to pay the expense of boarding and feeding us for 30 days.

Thomas Gaither, *Jailed-In* (New York: League for Industrial Democracy, 1961). Reprinted with the permission of the Congress Of Racial Equality.

WHAT HAPPENED BEFORE

The story behind our case opens on Lincoln's Birthday, 1960. This was the date of the first sit-ins at Rock Hill, which were also the first in the state of South Carolina. Immediately following the original sit-in at Greensboro, North Carolina, on February 1, students at Friendship Junior College in Rock Hill expressed interest in joining the south-wide protest movement. Under the very able leadership of Abe Plummer and Arthur Hamm, they sought advice from Rev. C. A. Ivory and other local civil rights leaders. CORE Field Secretary James T. McCain, who has worked for civil rights in South Carolina for most of his life, was dispatched to Rock Hill to help train the students in sit-ins and other nonviolent techniques. A Student Civic Committee was established for the purpose of planning and coordination. By Lincoln's Birthday, preparations for the first sit-in were complete.

On that date groups of students entered the Woolworth and McCrory stores and sat down at the lunch counters. A gang of whites rapidly gathered, some of them armed with homemade ammonia bombs, which were hurled at the sit-inners. A counterman kept wiping the surfaces with an ammonia-soaked rag. The students remained quietly in their seats.

Violence by whites continued in the days that ensued. Negro adults, who were not involved in sit-ins in any way, were assaulted on the streets. Rev. Ivory received repeated threatening phone calls.

On March 15, Friendship Junior College students joined a mass protest demonstration in Orangeburg in which 350 were arrested and herded into an open-air stockade. Being a student at Claflin College, I was among those jailed on that day. It was on this occasion that Governor Hollings asserted that no such demonstrations would be tolerated, adding: "*They think they can violate any law, especially if they have a Bible in their hands.*"

In Rock Hill, sit-ins and picketing continued throughout the school year. After the college students left for summer vacation, a number of high school students became involved. Arthur Hamm, one of the college student leaders, remained in town to give them direction. On June 7, Hamm was arrested while sitting-in at McCrory's. Arrested with him was Rev. Ivory, who had the courage to engage in this type of action even though he is crippled and confined to a wheelchair. The gross indignity of arresting a crippled minister in a wheelchair gave this incident nationwide publicity. Wheeling Rev. Ivory out the rear entrance and across the street to the jail, was an awkward task for Police Captain Honeysucker. Shaking-down the minister in his wheelchair for concealed weapons and taking him downstairs for fingerprinting also presented a problem. Finally, after going through all the procedures of being booked, Rev. Ivory was rolled into a cell where he stayed until his attorney got him out on bail. Hamm, too, was released. Next day he was back at his sit-ins and picketing with a group of high school students. Before the end of June, Hamm had to leave Rock Hill for a summer job with the American Friends Service Committee.

During July and August the campaign slowed down. But with September and the reopening of college, sit-ins were resumed. At about this same time, I went to work as a CORE field secretary and one of the first places to which I was dispatched was Rock Hill.

THE TOWN OF ROCK HILL

This textile manufacturing town of 33,000 people was not new to me. Both my father and mother had attended Friendship Junior College. As a child, I used to come into town often. I even recall visiting the McCrory and Woolworth stores, now the focal points of the struggle for lunch counter integration in Rock Hill. I never bought more than a bag of popcorn or some cashews but it occurred to me even then to wonder why we couldn't ever sit down and get something to eat at the counter. Of course, I didn't realize why.

By the time of the memorable Montgomery bus boycott, I was 17 and I well remember the sympathy action taken by Negroes in Rock Hill. Following the lead of Montgomery, they too decided to stop riding the buses until they were free to sit where they chose. Within a few months the bus company went out of business. The job of furnishing transportation for Negroes was undertaken by a special committee, initiated by Rev. Ivory. The committee eventually bought two buses, one of which is still running today.

As I walked up the street upon arrival in Rock Hill last fall, a little Negro boy suddenly rushed out in front of me. He was dirty, ragged and suffering from a severe cold. We got to talking. His mother is a domestic worker who in addition brings home wash. His father has worked for years in the bleachery. He has never been promoted and never will be. His wage scale is low: unions have somehow not been able to make inroads at Rock Hill. The total weekly income of both he and his wife is less than $45. I describe this family because it seems to me so typical of the Negro's lot in a town like Rock Hill.

It is a town of many churches, but the worship of God is on a strictly segregated basis. Rock Hill's first kneel-ins occurred only recently, on the Sunday of the big supporting demonstration on our behalf when we were on the road gang. The Negro kneel-inners were admitted at three of the white churches but barred at two others. Even the Christian so-called liberals in Rock Hill feel that Negroes should be satisfied with second class citizenship. One exception is the Catholic school in town, which desegregated without incident—and without any outcry from the segregationists. In addition to Friendship, the town has another small Negro church-run college, Clinton, and a state-operated white girls' college, Winthrop. The heads of the two Negro colleges were at first fairly neutral in regard to the local sit-ins. They did not come out in public support, but neither did they pressure students against participation, as was the case in Baton Rouge and in some other

Negro college communities. However, as the situation developed, James Goudlock, president of Friendship College took a strong position in support of the sit-ins.

As for the public officials, they have been blatantly prosegregation and opposed to any compromise. Rock Hill's mayor has flatly refused to set up a bi-racial committee of the type which has been established in some southern communities as an outcome of the student protests. Much of the ill-will evidenced by whites when the Rock Hill sit-ins started, was brought on by the segregationist agitation of local and state political leaders.

My familiarity with Rock Hill, coupled with my experience in the student movement in South Carolina, were factors in CORE's dispatching me there soon after I took the field secretary's job. Upon arrival, it didn't take me long to conclude that the most urgent need was for training student leaders. The Friendship students who had become involved in sit-ins and picketing at the start of the 1960–61 school year were mostly freshmen. I suggested that CORE hold an action workshop. This took place on the weekend of Dec. 9–11 at the college from which I had graduated the previous year: Claflin, in Orangeburg. One outcome was a full understanding by the students of the effectiveness of jail-ins, as opposed to accepting bail or paying fines. Immediately after the workshop a really intensified program of sit-ins and picketing got under way in Rock Hill.

As Robert McCullough, one of our jail-inners, later told the press regarding the month of January preceding our arrest: *"City officials pointed out that we had staged 19 demonstrations during January and suddenly we felt sort of ashamed of ourselves that we hadn't staged 31. After all, there are 31 days in January, so what had we been doing the other 12 days?"*

HOUR OF DECISION

The 26th day of January had been selected as the date for the sit-in, which inevitably would lead to the jail-in. Rev. Diggs, the college chaplain had suggested that the students involved should first register for the spring term to make sure of being able to return to classes following release from jail. To facilitate this the sit-in date was changed to the 31st. From Sumter, where I had been working with students at Morris College, I returned to Rock Hill on January 25.

On the 29th we held a meeting in an attempt to enroll more students in the action. Two members of the basketball team, Mack Workman and David "Scoop" Williamson signed up. The way some of the original members of our group felt was summarized by John Gaines when he said: *"I will go to jail and stay there, even if no one else does."*

Making a decision to go to jail for the first time was not easy. In some cases, it meant leaving a girl friend; in others, antagonizing parents who had little understanding of nonviolent action and much fear for their children's safety. There was also the danger that parents might be fired from their jobs as a result of their children's action.

On the night before the scheduled sit-in . . . in fact at about one in the morning . . . Clarence Graham, who had been considering the matter for some days, reached his final decision and got out of bed to write a letter of explanation to his mother and father.

"Try to understand that what I'm doing is right," the letter said. *"It isn't like going to jail for a crime like stealing or killing, but we are going for the betterment of all Negroes."*

Came January 31, the nine of us committed to be jailed-in and one who was to come out on appeal as a legal test, assembled in the college lounge. Willie McCleod was prepared to the extent of carrying his toothbrush in his pocket. Surprised to see Willy Massey, a student with a goatee and dressed like a typical cool cat, I asked why he had come to the meeting. *"Man, I'm going to jail!"* was his reply. An atmosphere of parting sorrow filled the room. Girlfriends were there to say goodbye and, in some cases, to ask their boyfriends to reconsider.

At the end of the meeting we headed uptown for McCrory's and Woolworth's. Woolworth's lunch counter had been discontinued in the course of the month-long intensive campaign and had been replaced with a flower counter, but picketing continued. McCrory's lunch counter was still open. It closed down the day after our demonstration. As we walked uptown, some of us wondered whether any of our group would change his decision on the way and withdraw. None did.

As we approached the stores we were stopped briefly by Police Captain Honeysucker and an official of the South Carolina Law Enforcement Division, who advised us to return to the campus, and avoid *"getting in trouble."* Instead, we established picket lines at the two stores. Fifteen minutes later, our group entered McCrory's and took seats at the lunch counter.

ARREST AND TRIAL

The manager, who was perspiring and obviously jittery, told us *"We can't serve you here."* Hardly were the words out of his mouth when city and state police who were standing by roughly pushed us off our stools and hauled us out the back door onto a parking lot area and across the street to jail. We were first searched and then locked in cells. We started singing freedom songs and spirituals. An hour or so later we were joined by another Negro prisoner named NuNu, who had been picked up for being drunk. At 5:30 we were fed a piece of cold barbecued chicken and cold coffee without sugar. Then we received a visit from Rev. Ivory and Rev. Diggs. We slept on bare steel bunks, which bruised our bones but not our morale. At dawn we were awakened by a prisoner on the white side asking for a cigaret. He kept yelling and banging on the walls.

It was February 1 and, as I noted mentally, the first anniversary of the south-wide sit-in movement. We were taken into the courtroom for trial. The charge was trespassing.

On direct examination, Lieutenant Thomas admitted that he had given us only between 3 and 15 *seconds* to leave the store. However, he changed this to between 3 and 15 *minutes* when cross-examined by our attorney, Ernest A. Finney, Jr. So confused did the lieutenant become with his two stories, that he requested and obtained permission to rest a little before proceeding. Finally, even Judge Billy Hayes stated that according to the evidence, we had not been given sufficient time to leave the store, even if we had wanted to take the opportunity of doing so. Police Captain Honeysucker, who was seated to the judge's right, looked dejected. An atmosphere of indecision prevailed. Were we finally going to win a legal case in a lower court in the deep south? We were called upon to enter our pleas. We pleaded not guilty. Hardly were the words out of our mouths, when the judge pronounced us guilty and sentenced us to 30 days hard labor on the road gang or $100 fines. Surprise and shock filled the courtroom when it became known that we had chosen to be jailed-in. The only thing they had to beat us over the head with was a threat of sending us to jail. So we disarmed them by using the only weapon we had left . . . jail without bail. It was the only practical thing we could do. It upset them considerably.

"YOU'RE ON THE CHAIN GANG NOW"

From the courtroom we were taken to the York County road gang stockade. We got there about four in the afternoon. It consisted of two large dormitories, one for whites the other for Negroes. It was like a barracks except for the bars and mesh-wire which made it unmistakably like a jail.

First, we were taken to the clothing room to get our prison clothes. In charge was Captain Dagler, who, as we learned later, was one of the toughest guards in the camp. *"Boy, cut that thing from under your chin and pull off that jitterbug hat,"* he said to Willy Massey. *"You're on the chain gang now!"* Meanwhile, "Scoop" Williamson was trying to scoop a pair of shoes out of the huge pile on the middle of the floor. He finally found a pair that fitted.

Inside the prison, our initial feeling was one of uncertainty. As we entered the Negro dormitory, we were met with curious stares from the other prisoners. Some already knew, via the grapevine, why we were there; others didn't.

"THE STUFF IS ON"

One prisoner commented *"The stuff is on, now!"* Others echoed the slogan. By the *"stuff"* they meant anti-Negro hatred. They explained that the *"stuff"* had been *"on"* only recently in the white dormitory, following the much-publicized marriage of the Negro singer-actor, Sammy Davis, Jr. and the white screen star, May Britt.

"*If anybody bothers you, let us know; we can handle them,*" volunteered one of the prisoners in talking to James Wells. The latter explained that all in our group believe in nonviolence. Our would-be protector seemed surprised.

As it turned out, the Negro prisoners' fears regarding our effect on the white prisoners, proved unfounded. Most of us worked in integrated gangs (until after we were put in solitary) without incident. In fact, when we were in solitary, a white prisoner took the initiative of writing the FBI that he considered this unjust. Another white prisoner volunteered to assert that it was wrong to single-out Negro prisoners only—including us students—to go out on Lincoln's Birthday, a Sunday, and erect a barbed wire fence in anticipation of the crowds expected to visit us on that occasion. By the end of our stretch, some of the white prisoners would actually request us to sing one of the freedom hymns which we had sung at our morning devotional services.

The only "*stuff*" which did occur was a single incident in which a white prisoner serving life, upon coming in from work one day, started cursing at Clarence Graham and Robert McCullough and finally drew a knife on them. The two simply looked at him and walked on. When the Negro prisoners heard about it, some of them were ready to fight. Again, we had to try to explain our adherence to nonviolence.

"A PRISON—NOT A DAMNED SCHOOL"

As to the Negro prisoners, they held us in high esteem. We were called upon repeatedly to serve as final authorities in arguments. Our presence prompted frequent discussions of world problems. We conducted classes in English and Current Events.

But we were barred from keeping up with our studies. On our sixth day in jail, Captain Dagler ordered me to gather up all the college textbooks which the students had brought along and carry them up-front. He said that the books were being taken away from us because the prison did not want to be responsible for them. I assured him that each of us was willing to assume responsibility for his own books. He retorted that he was simply carrying out orders. I then inquired who had given the orders, to which he answered:

"*Quit asking questions. This is a prison—not a damned school. If this was a school, we'd have teachers here.*"

Obviously, it was a prison. We got up at 5:30 in the morning, ate a breakfast of grits, fatback with flour gravy and black coffee. Then, we went out for the day's labor. On our first day, the temperature was 24°.

My first job was loading sand onto a truck. There was one white prisoner on my gang; the rest were Negroes. Among them was NuNu, who had been thrown into our cell at the city jail the day we were arrested. NuNu was always the center of attention. He had apparently been involved in numerous petty difficulties with the law.

The guards' attitudes toward us ranged from indifference to hostility. Captain Jim, the guard bossing my work gang was a fat, jovial type who seemed to me surprisingly broad-minded. I discovered he had been raised among Negroes. He frequently recalled how, when he was a youth, he used to play baseball with Negro kids on Sundays and whenever there was spare time. He usually referred to Negroes as "darkies," not seeming to realize that the term is derogatory.

On February 7 we were joined by a student from Charlotte, North Carolina and one from Petersburg, Virginia. Along with two female students from Nashville and Atlanta, Diane Nash and Ruby Smith, they had sat-in at a Rock Hill lunch counter. Like us, all four had been sentenced to 30 days and had refused to pay fines. There being no road gang for women, the two girls were confined to the women's county jail.

With the addition of the two new students—Charles Jones and Charles Sherrod—the jail-inners on our road gang totaled 11. Our original group included John Gaines, Clarence Graham, Willie McCleod, Robert McCullough, Willy Massey, James Wells, David Williamson, Mack Workman and myself.

SOLITARY

February 7 was memorable for us because we spent the entire morning in solitary confinement. The periodic shouting, cursing and other loud noises which emanated from the prisoners' quarters apparently did not bother the officials. However, for several days they had objected to our singing hymns at the morning devotional services which we had initiated.

One line that particularly irritated them was *"Before I'll be a slave, I'll be buried in my grave."* No sooner would we start to sing, than a guard would order us to *"cut out that damned fuss!"* Of course, we refused and simply kept on singing. When this happened on February 7, Captain Maloney, the prison superintendent, put us in solitary.

He accused us of *"trying to run the prison."* I tried to explain that we were simply exercising our right of religious freedom. He replied: *"If y'all are that religious, why ain't y'all preachers?"* I explained that two of us were actually studying for the ministry.

At this point, Charles Jones, as a goodwill gesture, stepped forward and presented the prison superintendent with a box of chocolates which he had received as a present. Maloney slammed it down on a table outside the solitary cell door and proceeded to lock us in.

We found ourselves in a 12-by-12 foot, dark room furnished with a commode, a small sink and one lone drinking cup. Obscuring the window was a metal sheet and steel bars. Lights went on at mealtimes only and meals consisted of bread and water.

But on this occasion we never got a chance to taste this sumptuous food. Shortly after noon, Captain Maloney unlocked our door and asked if we were ready to go back to work. He fully realized that we had no intention of ceasing our morning hymn-singing, but in order to save face, he did not raise the issue.

We were given a meal of beans, cornbread, milk and a peach, and were driven under heavy guard to the city dump, where the county maintains a topsoil pit. We eleven students were now on a separate work gang. It soon became clear that in putting us back to work, rather than keeping us in solitary, the prison officials' strategy was to "*work-the-hell*" out of us. By quiting time we had shoveled 14 loads of topsoil onto the 7-ton dump trucks. It was backbreaking work.

VISITING

The parents' difficulty at grasping what we were trying to accomplish did not deter them from coming to the camp on visiting days. I mentioned earlier how Clarence Graham had been so worried about his parents' reactions that he drafted an explanatory letter to them at 1 a.m. of the day we were to be arrested. Both his father and mother came to visit. So did John Gaines's 95-year-old great-grandmother, who is in a wheelchair. She brought $200 cash just in case John should want to change his mind and accept bail.

"*I don't think I ever got it explained completely to my great-grandmother,*" Gaines explained. "*She was afraid they'd work me too hard and that I couldn't stand it. She was still puzzled when I told her that it was a privilege for a Negro to go to jail for his rights.*"

Regarding his grandmother, who is a cook at the college, Gaines said: "*She told me I was disobedient when I said I had to go to jail. But once I got locked up, she was quite changed. She came to jail and asked me if I was all right or needed anything.*"

Gaines's grandmother's attitude was typical of many of the parents who came to visit. In addition to relatives, friends and supporters came from many parts of the country. This gave us great encouragement. On our first Sunday, a caravan of 60 cars and a bus brought more than 300 Negro and white visitors to the isolated road camp.

The following Sunday, Lincoln's Birthday, over 1,000 local citizens and students from other states participated in a pilgrimage to Rock Hill on behalf of our cause. It was early that morning that we were ordered to erect a barbed-wire fence around the compound. From the dormitory window, I could see an endless line of highway patrol cars. Some residents in the vicinity had posted their property in such a way that if Negroes should step on it, they could be accused of trespassing. A few white hoodlums speeded their cars up and down the road in an attempt at intimidation. But the pilgrimage was not deterred. Guards, posted between us and our visitors, started to take notes on what was being said. They failed to dampen our enthusiasm over this significant demonstration of support for our efforts. We were additionally encouraged to learn that since our arrest, the jail-ins had spread to Atlanta and Lynchburg bringing the total number of students involved—including us—to almost 100.

SPEED-UP

As the days went by, following our return to work from solitary, it became increasingly clear that we were the victims of a speed-up. Starting the second day, we were expected to load 36 trucks of topsoil, or double the workload of other prisoners. I was cited by the captain as an experienced chain gang man—possibly because I was the oldest in the group—and singled-out to lead the pace. In a kidding vein, Massey kept yelling at me to shovel faster. *"Come on Moses!"* he would say.

We decided to refuse to go along with the speedup. Two of our gang, Jones and Sherrod had gotten sick, the former with an injured shoulder muscle. On February 13 our work output decreased considerably. The following morning, the prison superintendent warned us that unless we worked faster we would be transferred to the state penitentiary. When we reached the topsoil pit, we found an additional truck had been dispatched for us to load. We worked at a moderate pace and after about an hour and a half, a group of prison officials arrived to inspect us. As they departed, John Gaines waved to them in a joking manner. His wave was misinterpreted as a threatening gesture, and Gaines was ordered into the officials' car.

The rest of us stopped work and planted our shovels in the topsoil. We started toward the officials to inquire where they were taking Gaines. They told us to resume work—or join Gaines. We chose the latter, as a move of solidarity. We were then loaded onto one of the dump trucks, and driven back to camp.

BACK INTO SOLITARY

Upon arrival at the stockade, we found ourselves back in solitary confinement for a second time. But before locking us in, a guard came and took Gaines away. Our attempts to inquire where he was being taken proved fruitless. Aware of what might happen to a lone Negro "agitator" in the hands of white southern prison guards, we feared for Gaines's safety. We decided to go on a hunger strike until we learned his whereabouts. This did not constitute too much of a sacrifice, since the only food in solitary was bread—three times a day. But it was at least some demonstration of our concern.

Furthermore it had an impact on the guards. They seemed quite disturbed at the end of the first day to discover there were 24 pieces of corn bread to be removed from our cell. Lying on the floor in this cramped space, with only our jackets on or under us—and with Mack Workman's snoring—we didn't get too much sleep during our first night in solitary. The lack of sleep added to the gnawing of the hunger strike on our stomachs made us feel miserable on the second day. Some of us had stomach aches; others felt as if our bellies had shrunk. Graham described it as "*a turbulent dispute between my backbone and my stomach.*" We kidded ourselves with graphic descriptions of our favorite things to eat.

In the course of the third day, we were finally told what had happened to Gaines. He had been transferred to the county jail and was unharmed. Upon learning this, we decided to end our hunger strike. The superintendent and the guards had become so worried over the hunger strike that when we resumed eating, they were happier than we were. They brought us seconds on everything. We were ordered back to work.

JAIL TERM ENDS—STRUGGLE GOES ON

The labor was not easy, but the speed-up plan prescribed for us earlier was no longer in evidence. During our last few days on the road gang, we worked laying drainage pipes under rural roads. Prison officials were anxious to avoid any publicity or supporting demonstrations on the day of our release. Captain Dagler made this known to us on our final day, March 2. After only half a day's work, he took us back to the stockade. We were given lunch, ordered to change into our regular clothes and loaded aboard a caged truck. The prison superintendent and his assistant escorted us to the Rock Hill city limits.

There we were set free and walked in a group to the Friendship campus. Our 30 days on the road gang were over, but not our struggle to end lunch counter discrimination in Rock Hill.

As Clarence Graham expressed it at our first major press conference after getting out: "*If requesting first class citizenship in the south is to be regarded as a crime, then I will gladly go back to jail again.*"

One of our group, Willy Massey, *was* back in jail again less than two weeks later. He and four other students were arrested March 14 while picketing a drug store with a segregated lunch counter. Like our group, they refused to pay fines. The day before, two other members of our group—John Gaines and Robert McCullough—were assaulted on the picket line by white hoodlums. Gaines was clubbed unconscious and taken to York County hospital.

Two hours later, he and McCullough resumed picketing accompanied with three others of our group—Clarence Graham, James Wells and me.

These students are determined to carry on the nonviolent action campaign until Rock Hill's lunch counters desegregate. Our jail-in has strengthened—not weakened—that determination. Unfortunately, I cannot stay with them. CORE field secretaries have to cover considerable territory and I will be dispatched elsewhere. For me, Rock Hill was my second jail-in. My first was in Miami, Florida, in August when seven of us at CORE's Interracial Action Institute remained 10 days in jail rather than accept bail. The Rock Hill experience has fortified my conviction in the effectiveness of jail-ins in cases of unjust arrests.

DOCUMENT 30

William Mahoney, "In Pursuit of Freedom"

In 1961 CORE initiated the Freedom Rides, modeled on the earlier Journey of Reconciliation. This time the riders ventured into the Deep South, meeting mob violence at Anniston, Birmingham and Montgomery, Alabama. A number of riders were arrested in Jackson, Mississippi and imprisoned in the state penitentiary at Parchman. In this document, William Mahoney, leader of the Washington, D. C. Nonviolent Action Group, recounts his experience.

In early May I heard from fellow Howard University students that the Congress on Racial Equality was looking for volunteers to ride from Washington, D.C. to New Orleans by bus to determine whether bus station facilities were integrated in compliance with Supreme Court rulings. I was sympathetic to the idea, but approaching final examinations and a 34-hour-a-week job made my participation at that time out of the question.

William Mahoney, "In Pursuit of Freedom," *Liberation* (September 1961), pp. 7–11. Reprinted with the permission of *Liberation* magazine.

I forgot about the CORE-sponsored trip, known as the Freedom Ride, until Monday, May 15th, when the morning papers were delivered to the dormitory desk at which I was working and I saw pictures of a fellow Howard student with whom I had participated the past year and a half in the Non-Violent Action Group (N.A.G.) of Washington, leaving a flaming bus on the outskirts of Anniston, Alabama. The caption said that the student, whose name is Henry Thomas, had been struck on the head as he left the bus. I was infuriated.

In protest against the savagery displayed by segregationist mobs at Anniston, Birmingham, and Montgomery, I joined N.A.G. in picketing the White House and also spent a few hours on a CORE picket line at Trailways bus terminal. Pedestrians didn't coldly pass by our signs as they usually do, but stopped and stared, deep in thought.

Late one evening, two members of N.A.G., Paul Detriecht and John Moody, called at my room to say goodbye before leaving for Montgomery. Paul and John joined the Freedom Riders in time to attend the meeting, at the Montgomery First Baptist Church, which became the target of an angry mob. The National Guard was called out and the Freedom Riders went into hiding to avoid possible arrest and segregationist fury. While in hiding, Paul called N.A.G. and pleaded for as many as possible from the District to come down to Montgomery. The project seemed to be at its most trying stage and my brothers in the South needed every person they could possibly muster, so I decided to go. I could quit the 60-cent-an-hour job and either take exams early or have them put off until I returned.

The next few days were a sleepless scramble to have exam dates changed, find some place to leave my clothes and books, resign from my job, constantly debate my reasons for going, and continue my regular studies. I knew that my parents would oppose my decision, so I wrote them a letter of explanation (which I mailed while already on the way to Alabama). I consoled myself with the thought that all revolutions have created such conflicts within families: even Gandhi and Tolstoy had to further the nonviolent movement against the wishes of their families.

At 11 p.m. on Friday, May 26th, Frank Hunt, also a N.A.G. member, and I boarded a Greyhound bus in Washington with tickets for Montgomery. Frank is a recent graduate of the University of Maryland and was on the Freedom Ride during a vacation from his job as an *Afro-American News* reporter.

At our first stop in Virginia Frank and I were confronted with what the Southern white has called "separate but equal." A modern rest station with gleaming counters and picture windows was labelled "White," and a small wooden shack beside it was tagged "Colored." The colored waiting room was filthy, in need of repair, and overcrowded. When we entered the white waiting room Frank was promptly but courteously, in the Southern manner, asked to leave. Because I am a fair-skinned Negro I was waited upon. I walked back to the bus through the cool night trembling and perspiring. This was the pattern at all rest stations from Washington to Jackson, Mississippi.

During our one-day journey Frank and I discussed race problems and eavesdropped on other passengers' conversations. An Air Force man just back from overseas sat in front of us talking to three other white passengers about the Freedom Riders. The consensus was that the integrationists should be hung from the nearest tree. At this point Frank pulled his straw hat over his face and sank down in his seat, and I resumed work on a take-home mathematics exam. At one point a woman spoke loudly about the hardship she was suffering as a Negro, saying that she was the last hired at a job, the worst paid and the first fired. She complained about the high rents one had to pay even to live in a slum. The whites in the front showed no reaction to the woman's loud tale of despair. It was as though the bus riders were from two different worlds, the inhabitants of each being invisible to those of the other.

The Montgomery bus station was surrounded by Army jeeps, trucks, and the National Guard in battle gear. Some of the soldiers, who could be seen as they moved from the shadows into the light of the station, had fierce looking beards, which had been grown for the coming Civil War Centennial celebration. We found the people from the Christian Leadership Council who had been sent to meet us and drove away cautiously, realizing that the least traffic violation would be an excuse for our arrest. We eluded the detectives following us and, winding our way through the city, went to Reverend and Mrs. Abernathy's house, where we met seven other people with whom we were to continue. The house was protected by the National Guard. We didn't meet Reverend Abernathy, for he had been taken to jail with other leaders.

ARRIVAL AND ARREST

At 7:00 Sunday morning, we entered the Montgomery bus station amidst a confusion of photographers, reporters, National Guardsmen and bus passengers. The white lunch counter was closed before we arrived and when we entered the colored waiting room, its lunch counter was quickly shut down.

With two rifle-carrying Guardsmen in the front seat and jeeps leading and following the bus we sped to the border. Waiting rooms at all stops along the way were closed. At the state line the commanding officer of the Guard boarded the bus and in a pleasant voice wished us luck, saying that we could expect a long stay in Mississippi.

Once across the state line we passed a couple of police cars, which began to follow us. At our first stop the station was cordoned off a block in every direction. A police officer jumped on the bus and forbade anyone to move. One woman, who was a regular passenger, frantically tried to convince the police that she was not involved with us. After checking her ticket the police let her get off.

As we rolled toward Jackson, every blocked-off street, every back road taken, every change in speed caused our hearts to leap. Our arrival and speedy arrest in the white bus station in Jackson, when we refused to obey a policeman's order to move on, was a relief. A paddy wagon rushed us down the street to the police station.

While being interrogated I asked the detective if he knew that legally and by the moral standards America professes to the world we had a right to act as we did and that his actions were helping to tear down any respect the world might have had for our country. He said that this might be so but that the South had certain traditions which must be respected.

While waiting in line to be fingerprinted and photographed we were watched by huge policemen who repeatedly inspected their pistols. As a Negro inmate walked past on an errand an officer stamped his foot, which sent the fellow scurrying away like a whipped puppy. The giant men with stars on their chest roared with laughter, having displayed the brand of Southern hospitality we might expect.

At 2 p.m. on May 29th, after spending the night in a barracks-like room of which I can only remember, with trepidation, a one-foot-high sign written on the wall in blood, "I love Sylvia," our group joined nine other Freedom Riders in court. The others were from Tennessee and were among those who had been attacked in Birmingham and Montgomery. In the court's opening exercises Judge Spencer repeated frequently that, "This is a regular Monday afternoon court."

We were charged with a breach of the peace and then the tall, wiry state prosecutor examined Police Chief Wray, the only witness called to the stand. Chief Wray said that we had been orderly but had refused to move on when ordered to do so by his men. Mr. Young, our lawyer, asked if he would have required us to move on if we had entered the colored waiting room. Chief Wray said no. Mr. Young concluded that we must have been arrested for integrating the white waiting room. Chief Wray's face turned from its usual dirty white to a rose red.

The judge picked up a piece of paper and *read* the verdict: "Guilty as charged . . . two-hundred dollar fine or work it off in jail at three dollars a day." We refused to pay Mississippi a continental.

REUNION IN JACKSON

On Tuesday, we were taken across the street to the county jail and locked up with the first group to have been arrested in Jackson. I had finally caught up with Henry Thomas, John Moody, and other friends. Paul Detriech was held in the city jail with other white Freedom Riders. Henry told me that a couple of days earlier they had been taken to the county penal farm. While there several of them, including a young lady, had been beaten with blackjacks for not replying "yes, sir" to the warden's queries. When the F.B.I. learned of the incident, the Riders were returned to the county jail, and the warden brought before a prison board. The warden justified his actions by saying that he had struck all of them, including the frail woman, in self-defense. The board acquitted him.

The thirty or more of us occupied five cells and a dining hall on the top floor. At night we slept on lumpy bags of cotton and were locked in small, dirty, blood-spattered, roach-infested cells. Days were passed in the hot, overcrowded dining room playing cards, reading, praying and, as was almost inevitable, fighting among ourselves over the most petty things. The sermons offered during our self-imposed devotional period by such men as the Reverends Lawson, Vivien and Dunn were refreshing. But I guess any invocation of freedom and equality sounds excellent to a man behind bars. In the evening one of the prisoners in the cell block below ours sang Negro spirituals with the voice of a lonely, wild animal. At every rift one could feel the pain that must have inspired it.

Time crawled painfully, 15 days becoming 45 meals, 360 hours, 100 card games or 3 letters from home. The killing of a roach or the taking of a shower became major events, the subjects of lengthy debate. But morale remained high; insults and brutality became the subject of jokes and skits. The jailers' initial hostility was broken down by responding to it with respect and with good humor. Mr. Young later informed us that the treatment of all prisoners in Jackson jails improved after our matriculation.

On June 12th, a man named Leon Horne was put in with us, and was readily accepted. The next day, after spending the night sleeping in his clothes on an unmade bed in my cell, he was taken away by the turnkey. We never saw him again until we managed to smuggle a newspaper into the jail and found his picture on the front page. In a press conference he had called us everything from Communists to embezzlers of publicly solicited funds. We learned later from our lawyer that Horne had formed the first N.A.A.C.P. chapter in Jackson and run off with its funds. The authorities continued to hold him and one day two of our fellows were placed in a cell close enough to talk with him. He told them that he had been forced into making the statements. This is believable, for the authorities put pressure on two others to make similar statements. In one case, a Negro woman was intimidated by a white woman prisoner who beat her with a shoe, while the authorities pressed her, but she failed to yield.

The police were more successful in their tactics with Reverend Gleason. They took him out, brought him cokes, candy and a meal at a local restaurant and the good Reverend told the Southern newspapers just about anything they wanted to hear. When he got to his home in Chicago he denied all that he had said in Jackson.

The jails began to bulge as even Mississippi Negroes, who according to Southern whites are happy, began to join in the protest. To relieve the crowding, about fifty of us were piled into trucks at 2 a.m. June 15th and sped off into the night. It was rumored that in spite of a law against putting persons convicted of misdemeanors into a penitentiary, we were going to the state penitentiary.

PARCHMAN PENITENTIARY

In the light before sunrise a small caravan of trucks led by a police car sped north on Highway 49 over the flat Mississippi land. Two Negro children walking through a field of young cotton were silhouetted against an orange and blue horizon as they stopped and knowingly pointed to the swiftly moving prison trucks. The procession turned on to the grounds of Parchman Penitentiary, stopped briefly at the main gate, and then moved directly to a restricted area of the sprawling plantation.

One of the larger vehicles, containing twenty-six of the political prisoners, had broken down and was being towed the last few miles to the prison by a pick-up truck which carried luggage. The little pick-up towed its monstrous burden past an observation tower, through a barbed-wire-fence gate, and came to rest in a muddy yard by the front door of a squat, modern red-brick building.

The barked commands of a law officer sent all except two of the Freedom Riders scurrying from the truck into a double line at the front of the building. Surrounded by a group of gun brandishing hecklers, tired unshaven men helplessly listened as sun-reddened faces, sagging from age and dissipation, spat vile remarks at them.

TORTURE

Terry Sullivan and Felix Singer, the two white men who remained in the truck, were refusing to cooperate with their captors. So far their limp bodies had been carefully handled. Hearing a commotion behind them, the men in line turned around in time to see Terry and Felix being thrown from the van onto the wet sand-and-gravel drive. They were then dragged through wet grass, mud puddles, and across a rough cement walk to the rear of the group. There was both pain and conviction in their faces. One of their tormentors laughed:

"Ain't no newspapermen out here, what you actin' like that for?"

Terry replied: "We refuse to cooperate because we have been unjustly imprisoned."

As they were pulled down the walk and into the building, a fat red-faced man wearing cowboy boots ran after them, stamping on the corrugated bottom of Felix's canvas shoes and yelling, "Pull them by the feet, pull them by the feet."

A guard with a serious face under his Stetson hat, examining a long black, rubber-handled tube, walked through the gate, past the smiling guards and police, and the curious, worried prisoners, and into the building.

The black tube was a cattle-shocker, which delivers a powerful charge of electricity when applied to the flesh. After the two passive resisters refused to obey a command to undress, the instrument was applied to their bodies.

When they realized that the men squirming in pain on the cement floor were not going to yield to the torture, the official ripped the clothes from their bodies and threw them into a cell. All of this even though the law forbids corporal or any unusual punishment of recalcitrant prisoners.

The group outside was brought into the hallway, asked to undress, and then herded, two per cell, into the little six-by-ten compartments they were to occupy for the next month or more. The cells were segregated but the cell blocks were not.

A six-foot, three-inch, two-hundred-fifty-pound brute stuffed shorts and tee-shirts through the bars to them. These were the only garments they were to wear while inmates of the maximum-security unit of Parchman Penitentiary.

The guard that handed out the uniforms brought the noon meal and sometimes engaged in heated debates about the philosophy of nonviolence and related issues. He was lovingly named Spike. One of our fellows gave him two stamps. One had a picture of Gandhi on it and the other a picture of Robert E. Lee. He said: "Here are two men. One led his nation to freedom through nonviolence, the other left his nation in ruin through the use of violence." From the thick lips of Spike's grizzled baby face came the profound reply: "If your movement would get rid of trash like you it might have a chance of succeeding." The next day Spike elaborated upon his criticism of the movement. He asked either Abraham Bassford or Price Chatham (it was hard to tell who was talking for we couldn't see each other) why he had come to the South stirring up trouble. The reply was: "Thoreau says in his *Essay on Civil Disobedience,* that under a government which imprisons any unjustly the true place for a just man is also a prison."

Spike rebutted: "If you all wouldn't read so many comic books and look at so much television you wouldn't be in the trouble you are now," and marched down the hall pushing a rattling cart of dishes, another intellectual triumph under his belt.

Processing of the prisoners continued with fingerprinting and photographing. They came for Terry and Felix last.

Their naked bodies were pulled down the row of cells by a Negro inmate in prison stripes to a room at the end of the cell block. There were muffled sounds of furious motion and a frightening scream which reverberated down the steel-and-cement corridor, leaving indelible marks upon the minds of all who heard it. Then came more cries above the snickering of the guards.

"They're breaking my arm, they're breaking my arm."

"They're beating my head against the cement."

On Saturday, June 24th the guards decided that the Freedom Riders' singing was too loud and took their mattresses away as punishment. At first this was taken as a joke and songs were made up about the incident, but after three days of sleeping on a cement floor or steel shelf with an air-conditioning system on full blast the cell block became silent and gloomy. Another time when the Riders sang too loud for the guards, six of them were dragged down the hall with wrist-breakers (clamps tightened upon the wrists) and thrown into dark six-by-six boxes for a couple of days. As the spunky fellows were being taken to solitary they sang, "I'm Going to Tell God How You Treat Me."

When fellow prisoner Jim Farmer, national director of CORE, went before the superintendent to protest the treatment he was told that if we didn't cooperate conditions would deteriorate. A request was made for a written statement of rules to define what was meant by cooperation, but none was ever issued. Consequently the imprisoned men drew up their own code of minimum standards for they felt that although they were obligated to respect the authorities, the authorities had an obligation to treat them as human beings. The code was:

Having, after due consideration, chosen to follow without reservation the principles of nonviolence, we resolve while in any prison:

to practice nonviolence of speech and thought as well as
     action
to treat even those who may be our captors as brothers
to engage in a continual process of cleansing of the mind
     and body in rededication to our wholesome cause
to intensify our search for orderly living even when in the
     midst of seeming chaos.

Most felt that the search for order and meaning in life could best be carried out in group devotion, where sermons could be delivered and group singing take place. Phrases pertaining to the Freedom Rides were put to the tune of Negro spirituals, work songs, and union songs. When Henry Thomas finished with Harry Belafonte's "Day Oh," it became:

Freedom, Freedom
Freedom come and I gonna go home.
I took a trip down Mississippi way (Hey)
Freedom come and I gonna go home.
Met much violence on Mother's Day[1] (Hey)
Freedom come and I gonna go home. . . .

PROTEST AND PURIFICATION

Cleansing of the mind and body included fasting for some. Fasts were also engaged in as protest. The purpose and extent of these acts of dedication

---

1. The attacks at Anniston and Birmingham occurred on Mother's Day.

were misrepresented to the public. For example the press reported that Price Chatham lost three pounds. Actually he lost about thirty-five pounds.

Some prisoners refused to fast and flaunted the fact in front of others who were fasting, perhaps in order to compensate for their guilt. Others gave in to their hunger after a few days and soon became boisterous eaters. A few fasted until there was a thin veil between them and death.

Questions have been raised as to the character of people who willingly withstand such punishment. Are they publicity seekers? Are they Communists?

In cell 14 was a middle-aged art dealer from Minneapolis who had three dollars to his name and had come on the Freedom Ride "because it is one way of fighting a system which not only hurts the Negro but is a threat to world peace and prosperity. Some of the same men in whose interest it is to have segregation, so it is for them to have war industries, to recklessly speculate in other countries and in general to meticulously exploit masses of peoples. I also came because I wanted to see for myself what is happening in the South."

My cellmate, a Negro worker, came because he had been chased home by white toughs once too often, because his sister was determined to come, and because a friend of his, William Barbee, had been almost killed by a mob while on a Freedom Ride. He admits that his behavior is not ordinarily disciplined, but he readily accepted any restrictions required of him by the movement. He had sung professionally and took the lead in many of our group songs.

On my right, in cell 12, was the son of a well-to-do business man who had come because it was his moral duty. His aim was to "change the hearts of my persecutors through the sympathy and understanding to be gained by nonviolent resistance." He spoke proudly of his father who had fought hard and "made it," and was constantly defending North America's economic and political system from the attacks made upon it by myself and the art dealer. We never changed each other's views but the arguments passed time and gave us mental exercise.

These three philosophies—political, emotional, and moralist—represent the three major viewpoints I found while spending forty days in various Mississippi prisons.

The name of Gandhi was constantly on the minds and lips of most of the imprisoned Riders. Anything Gandhi had said or done was interpreted and reinterpreted to be applied to the situation in Mississippi. As with all religious movements, from Christianity to Marxism, factions arose which read their prophet's teaching as best suited them. Those who went on long fasts justified this by Gandhi's remark that at times he had to fast in spite of his followers' refusals to join him; others, who would fast only when there were numbers large enough to be politically effective, said that they took this stand in accord with Gandhi's practice of only making *meaningful* sacrifices.

At 5 p.m. on July 7th those remaining of the first and second groups were released on appeal bonds after 40 days in jail. When we left, the number of Freedom Riders in jail was close to a hundred. We were taken back to the city jail to sign our bonds in a little pick-up led by a police car.

Colored workers were leaving the fields as we sped down the highway. The women were clad in gay-colored prints, making me think of pictures the old people used to paint in my mind of slave days. How my heart hurt every time we passed a car driven by a Negro, for he would, upon hearing our police escort's siren, come to a stop in the grass by the side of the road, whereas a white driver would only move to the edge of the road and reduce his speed.

Before parting for our various destinations we stood in a circle, grasped hands and sang a song called "We Will Meet Again." As I looked round the circle into my companions' serious faces and saw the furrowed brows of the 19- and 20-year-old men and women, I knew that we *would* meet again.

DOCUMENT 31

Voter Registration, Mississippi and Georgia

The Student Nonviolent Coordinating Committee (SNCC), formed in 1960 to coordinate sit-in activities, decided in 1961 to concentrate on voter registration. The areas selected for registration drives were rural regions with Black majorities: southwestern Georgia and the state of Mississippi.

The persistence and self-sacrifice of SNCC workers in these "hardcore" areas of the South called forth an answering courage from local Black communities.

In Pike, Walthall, and Amite counties of southwestern Mississippi, white Mississippians pistol-whipped John Hardy and murdered Reverend Herbert Lee, local leader of the registration drive (see Document 31A). Two students at the Burgland High School in McComb, Mississippi, were expelled for attempting to integrate the Greyhound bus station. Their expulsion led to a boycott of the school by their fellow-students with strong support from parents (see Document 31B). SNCC workers Robert Moses, Charles McDew, and Dion Diamond taught mathematics, science and history to the expelled and boycotting students at "Nonviolent High," the first Mississippi "freedom school," in a room above a McComb grocery store. Late in October 1961 the entire SNCC staff was imprisoned; unable to pay bail, their spirit remained defiant (see Document 31C).

SNCC's southwest Georgia project led to the Albany, Georgia demonstrations of 1961–1962, in which local police made more than 1,000 arrests. After the great wave of marches, the heroic everyday routine of voter registration continued (see Documents 31D and E).

Except for Document 31A, all the following documents were copied from originals on file at the Student Nonviolent Coordinating Committee office in Atlanta, Georgia.

A.   Mississippi Violence vs Human Rights

CHRONOLOGY OF VIOLENCE AND INTIMIDATION IN MISSISSIPPI 1961

... AUGUST 15, AMITE COUNTY: Robert Moses, Student Non-Violent Coordinating Committee (SNCC) registration worker, and three Negroes who had tried unsuccessfully to register in Liberty, were driving toward McComb when a county officer stopped them. He asked if Moses was the man " ... who's been trying to register our niggers." All were taken to court and Moses was arrested for "impeding an officer in the discharge of his duties," fined $50 and spent two days in jail.

AUGUST 22, AMITE COUNTY: Robert Moses went to Liberty with three Negroes, who made an unsuccessful attempt to register. A block from the courthouse, Moses was attacked and beaten by Billy Jack Caston, the sheriff's first cousin. Eight stitches were required to close a wound in Moses' head. Caston was acquitted of assault charges by an all-white jury before a justice of the peace.

AUGUST 26, MC COMB, PIKE COUNTY: Hollis Watkins, 20, and Elmer Hayes, 20, SNCC workers, were arrested while staging a sit-in at the F. W. Woolworth store and charged with breach of the peace. They spent 36 days in jail.

AUGUST 27 and 29, MC COMB, PIKE COUNTY: Five Negro students from a local high school were convicted of breach of the peace following a sit-in at a variety store and bus terminal. They were sentenced to a $400 fine each and eight months in jail. One of these students, a girl of 15, was turned

---

Committee for the Distribution of the Mississippi Story, *Mississippi Violence vs Human Rights* [Atlanta: 1963].

over to juvenile authorities, released, subsequently rearrested, and sentenced to 12 months in a state school for delinquents.

AUGUST 29, MC COMB, PIKE COUNTY: Two Negro leaders were arrested in McComb as an aftermath of the sit-in protest march on city hall, charged with contributing to the delinquency of minors. They were Curtis C. Bryant of McComb, an official of the NAACP, and Cordelle Reagan, of SNCC. Each arrest was made on an affidavit signed by Police Chief George Guy, who said he had information that the two ". . . were behind some of this racial trouble."

AUGUST 30, MC COMB, PIKE COUNTY: SNCC workers Brenda Travis, 16, Robert Talbert, 19, and Isaac Lewis, 20, staged a sit-in in the McComb terminal of the Greyhound bus lines. They were arrested on charges of breach of the peace and failure to obey a policeman's order to move on. They spent 30 days in jail.

SEPTEMBER 5, LIBERTY, AMITE COUNTY: Travis Britt, SNCC registration worker, was attacked and beaten by whites on the courthouse lawn. Britt was accompanied at the time by Robert Moses. Britt said one man hit him more than 20 times. The attackers drove away in a truck.

SEPTEMBER 7, TYLERTOWN, WALTHALL COUNTY: John Hardy, SNCC registration worker, took two Negroes to the county courthouse to register. The registrar told them he ". . . wasn't registering voters" that day. When the three turned to leave, Registrar John Q. Wood took a pistol from his desk and struck Hardy over the head from behind. Hardy was arrested and charged with disturbing the peace.

SEPTEMBER 13, JACKSON, HINDS COUNTY: Fifteen Episcopal ministers (among them three Negroes) were arrested for asking to be served at the lunch counter of the Greyhound bus terminal. They were charged with inviting a breach of the peace. They were found not guilty of the charge on May 21, 1962, by County Judge Russell Moore.

SEPTEMBER 25, LIBERTY, AMITE COUNTY: Herbert Lee, a Negro who had been active in voter registration, was shot and killed by white state representative E. H. Hurst in downtown Liberty. No prosecution was undertaken, the authorities explaining that the representative had shot in self-defense.

OCTOBER 4, MC COMB, PIKE COUNTY: The five students who were arrested as a result of the August 29 sit-in in McComb returned to school, but were refused admittance. At that, 116 students walked out and paraded downtown to the city hall in protest. Police arrested the entire crowd, but later released all but 19, all of whom were 18 years old or older. They were charged with breach of the peace and contributing to the delinquency of minors and allowed to go free on bail totalling $3,700. At the trial on October 31, Judge Brumfield, finding the students guilty, and sentencing each to a $500 fine and six months in jail, said: "Some of you are local residents, some of you are outsiders. Those of you who are local residents are like sheep being led to the slaughter. If you continue to follow the advise of outside agitators, you will be like sheep and be slaughtered."

B.   A Statement from the Burgland High School Students

We the Negro youth of Pike County feel that Brenda Travis and Isaac Lewis should not be barred from an education for protesting against injustice. We feel that as a member of Burgland High School they have fought this battle for us. To prove that we appreciate them for doing this, we will suffer whatever punishment they have to take with them.

In school we are taught democracy, but the rights that democracy has to offer have been denied to us by our oppressor: we have not had the right to vote; we have not had a balanced school system; we have not had an opportunity to participate in any of the branches of our local, state and federal government.

However, we are children of God, who makes the sun shine on the just and unjust. So we petition all our fellowmen to love rather than hate, to build rather than tear down, to bind our nation with love and justice without regard to race, color or creed.

C.   Robert Moses, Message from Jail

We are smuggling this note from the drunk tank of the county jail in Magnolia, Mississippi. Twelve of us are here, sprawled out along the concrete bunker; Curtis Hayes, Hollis Watkins, Ike Lewis and Robert Talbert, four veterans of the bunker, are sitting up talking—mostly about girls; Charles McDew ("Tell the story") is curled into the concrete and the wall; Harold Robinson, Stephen Ashley, James Wells, Lee Chester Vick, Leotus Eubanks, and Ivory Diggs lay cramped on the cold bunker; I'm sitting with smuggled pen and paper, thinking a little, writing a little; Myrtis Bennett and Janie Campbell are across the way wedded to a different icy cubicle.

Later on, Hollis will lead out with a clear tenor into a freedom song, Talbert and Lewis will supply jokes, and McDew will discourse on the history of the black man and the Jew. McDew—a black by birth, a Jew by choice, and a revolutionary by necessity—has taken on the deep hates and deep loves which America and the world reserve for those who dare to stand in a strong sun and cast a sharp shadow. . . .

This is Mississippi, the middle of the iceberg. Hollis is leading off with his tenor, "Michael row the boat ashore, Alleluia; Christian brothers don't be slow, Alleluia; Mississippi's next to go, Alleluia." This is a tremor in the middle of the iceberg—from a stone that the builders rejected.

D. Statement by a High School Student

My name is Roychester Patterson, II. My age is seventeen (17), and I am a high school senior. I live at 601 First Avenue, S.E. I went to Carver High School. I was an honor student for (10) years. My mother's name is Mrs. Carolyn Daniels. My father's name is Mr. Roychester Patterson.

The school I attended was unequipped and incapable of furnishing a qualified education for students who plan to go out to college. It is incapable of giving students the necessary knowledge with which to compete with other students from better schools. Our school needs typewriters, science equipment, library books, text books, home economics equipment, more buses, maps, and math facilities. We also need an auditorium and gymnasium. These are the things that three other students and I went to the principal, E. E. Sykes, and asked for. He told us, there was nothing he could do, so we went to the Supt. Frank Christie, who said that he did something for the colored schools every year. We then mentioned the funds that the State Department of Education sends to every County to supply the school needs. He then told us there was nothing he could do. So the next day we criticized the administration for its inefficiency. The day after that, the Supt. Christie came to the school and called me in a conference and threatened me, "Patterson if you don't change your attitude, you'll have to leave Terrell County. You're sitting on a keg of dynamite whether you know it or not."

A few weeks later P.T.A. meeting was coming up, so we went around and got the parents to come out to P.T.A., we tried to explain to them what the school needed, but the Principal, E. E. Sykes, exploaded and wouldn't let us finish, so we made a house to house campaign.

We later told the State Department about these lack of necessary facilities and they threatened to send in the Fact Finding Committee and the Supt. ordered thousands of dollars worth of facilities for our school.

Then SNCC came into Terrell for Voter Registration and asked for our help, so we gave him our support, we tried to get all of the students who were eligible to register and vote. I made a speech to this affect to an assemblage of students trying to get the students to register, I made the speech to a group of students during lunch hour on the basketball court when the principal came out and tried to break-up the meeting, but the students refused to go to class unless they be given the priviledge to listen to my speech. So he allowed me to finish, meanwhile he called the cops, four of them came. The sheriff, L. T. Matthews, the deputy, Mathis, the chief of Police, Cherry, and the Revenue, Hancock. They came to the school and threatened us with vulgar language. Later that day I went to Albany, while the demonstrations were going strong. Upon seeing several of friends in the line I immediately joined the march, because I felt very close; I had been a student at Monroe High during my junior year.

I spent two days in jail, on Friday I went to school only to find that I had been expelled from school. Because the students thought that they had me in Dawson's jail, they boycotted the lunchroom, wouldn't go to class, and wouldn't participate in school activities.

So I dropped out of school and went to work for SNCC on Voter Registration and no violence had erupted until on Saturday, February 3, 1962. A friend and I took a lady up to register and a white brother decided as long as no one did anything to me, I would be an obstacle in the way of their racket.

All of this happened because almost everybody said, to crack Terrell County was impossible and I've always wanted to do the impossible. I did what I did because I have a conviction that each man should be judged by his personal worth and not for the color of his skin. I admire men like M. L. King, Roy Wilkins and Thurgood Marshall.

I did this because I am deeply attached to my peeple and I want them to know freedom and enjoy rights as human beings.

All of this happened between September 7, 1961 and February 3, 1962.

E.   [Jack] Chatfield, Lee County Report

TO: SNCC
               Atlanta, Ga.
FROM: Chatfield
               Leesburg, Ga.
SUBJECT: Lee County Report

Tuesday, April 16
Chico and I went to Lee County. We were joined by a local Albany lad, James Crawford ... Crawford had just gotten out of jail after a three week stay; he was jailed, ostensibly, for "investigation" (72 hours is the law). He told us he had been expelled from school because he had missed so many days; I told him he could come to Lee County; he came.

Wednesday, April 17
Chico, Crawford and I went to Terrell County; we have arranged that everybody goes to Terrell on Wednesday, which is Terrell tent-meeting day. We went to Bronwood, spoke to people there.

Went to Terrell Meeting that night, in tent in Sasser.

Friday, April 19

We canvassed in Leesburg; asked one lady who owns well-known (only) cafe-service station-grocery store whether or not we could put a poster up on her wall. She said, no, that would not be practical, what with the situation in the South today, and whatall. Later on we talked to her son, who showed more hope.

Saturday, April 20

The four Lee County girls—Brenda Hurd, Gloria Hawkins, Jackie Shinault, Katie Mae James—plus one older girl, Claritha Coven, and the three of us went to downtown Leesburg. . . . The four girls were wearing something they had made in home economics class: "Freedom" headbands or "Freedom sashes"; two of them wore sashes with Freedom written on them; two wore headbands with same. All four had occasion to walk into the registrar's office when he left at 11:15 instead of 12:00.

They went into the office and were told that the deputy registrar was an old man and that he had to leave early all the time.

We were able to get two young boys to go into the courthouse, knowing full well that Mr. Yeoman wasn't there. Soon we will have to protest Mr. Yeoman's absence, and have to have a reason. The boys entered ostensibly to register; but in reality to build a case. They will go next Saturday, they say.

We chalked up more promises than we had had in a long time. There were no incidents. I went for a short time to the home of Willie Frank Bell (who stays with the Burney family) to ask him whether he would sign an affidavit saying he went to the courthouse and was told that the deputy registrar would not be in except for Fridays and Saturdays. He said he would have to ask his parents, who were not home. He said he would attempt to register again shortly.

Monday, April 22

Chico, James Crawford and I carried two Smithville people down to the courthouse. . . .

We heard from Willie Frank Bell that he and one other boy had gone to the courthouse that morning, but that 8 or 10 white men had stepped out into the hall as they entered; the two boys left, apparently they thought the white men might make a bit of trouble.

Thursday, April 25

We picked up one lady in Smithville and headed to Leesburg. James and Eddie went into the courthouse with Mrs. Geraldine Johnson, while I sat in the car.

According to James Crawford, this is what happened:

The three walked into courthouse. James said, "This lady wants to register."

White lady (sheriff's wife) said, "Have a seat outside."

James and Mrs. Johnson went outside (Eddie Moore was in corridor). The lady started to sit down but James told her not to sit down, because there were seats inside the office. Just then Sol Yeoman, deputy registrar came out of office across the hall:

"What do you want?" he asked.

James said: "I brung this lady down to register."

Yeoman told them to come inside. He handed the lady a card, instructed her to fill out the front, sign her name on the back. He told her to go outside into the hall, which the lady did.

Yeoman said to James: "Why did you bring this lady down here?"

James said: "Because she wants to be a first class citizen like y'all."

Yeoman said, "Where are you from?"

James: "Albany."

Yeoman: "Who do you work for?"

James: "SNCC."

Yeoman: "What is that?"

James: "Student Non-Violent Coordinating Committee."

Yeoman: asked if he and the lady were kinfolk; James told him they were not. Then Yeoman asked him why he had brought her down here.

James: "I brung her down to register and vote."

Yeoman: "Who are you to bring people down to register?"

James: "It's my job to bring people down to register."

Yeoman asked him whether or not he had heard about the boy in Mississippi who was shot in the head. James told him he had not.

Yeoman: "Suppose you get two bullets in your head right now?"

James: "I got to die anyhow."

Yeoman: "If I don't do it I can get somebody else to do it."

Yeoman again: "Are you scared?"

James: "No."

Yeoman: "Suppose somebody came in that door and shoot you in the back of the head right now. What would you do?"

James: "I couldn't do nothing. If they shoot me in the back of the head there are people coming from all over the world."

Yeoman: "What people?"

James: "The people I work for."

The lady was trembling and had put "Sumter County" where she should have "Smithville". James told her to write Smithville in the slot. Yeoman got angry, said, "Now you're through" to the lady. He told her to put her name on the back of the card. As they left the courthouse, James turned back and said, "I'll be back, I'll be back Saturday. That's what I'm here for—to die or live."

We then took the lady back to Smithville. From Smithville we went to Koinonia Farm, where I was supposed to pick up Don Harris and take him to Albany. When we got there we heard about Ralph's getting beaten and started into Albany.

Our car broke down on the way to Smithville. The white man who owned the land where the car had stopped said for us to move down the road, off his property. We rolled the car down, locked it, and hitched a ride into Smithville on the back of a truck. We went straight to the Burney's house because they had a phone. We called Albany and told them what the story was.

About fifteen minutes after we arrived, two white men in a two-tone 1955 Chevrolet pulled up in front and asked for Robert Burney, the owner of the house. He was not at home. The men left. I was told that the same men (who are Field Smith and Williard Smith) had come yesterday and had told Robert Burney that we ("that white boy") had better not come back; they had told Mr. Burney that it was no good that their boys play basketball with "that white boy".

Shortly thereafter, a second car with four men in it pulled up. It was black 1953 Ford. James Crawford says he was sure that the men had guns. I got on the telephone to Albany.

The Ford came back down the second time, after having driven around the block. Mr. Robert Burney, in the meantime, had come home after having gone to the store up the street and been told that we had better get out of his house.

A third car, a 1954 two-tone Oldsmobile, pulled up. We had been told that Sherrod was on the way. Willie Frank Bell had loaded his shotgun. Gracie Bell, age 13 or 14, was in the living room watching TV.

"Do you mind being shot at?" I asked her.

"No," she said. "Not if it's for our country."

Finally Sherrod arrived. Just before this Mr. Burney, tears in his eyes, had told us to leave the house. We had started out across a field (it was dark) when we saw Sherrod and the other car pulling up. We ran back across the field and got in.

As we were going through Smithville we saw the 1954 Oldsmobile parked and a group of people near it. They saw us, got into the car, and someone shouted something. Then they moved behind us again, picked up a bit of speed, and rammed us from behind. Marion Gaines was crying in my arms, hysterically (we were sitting facing the car behind us, in the back section of the Rambler, so that we could see the car behind us moving toward us and hit us).

They followed us a few minutes longer and left. A nice evening. Six people had applied for registration.

Birmingham, Alabama

1963 was a climactic year for the nonviolent movement in the United States. President John Kennedy negotiated a ban on atmospheric nuclear tests with the Soviet Union. The eloquent Birmingham Manifesto (Document 32A), released on April 3, 1963, launched turbulent demonstrations that shocked national public opinion.

Birmingham touched the nation's conscience because it was so violent. Day after day Black children faced dogs and fire hoses, and on more than one occasion Reverend Martin Luther King, Jr. and local civil rights leaders lost control of the demonstrators. King's "Letter from Birmingham City Jail" (Document 32B) responded sharply to a communication from eight Alabama religious leaders which said: "When rights are consistently denied, a cause should be pressed in the courts and in negotiations among local leaders, and not in the streets." King's letter expressed disillusion with white moderates, and asserted that, while individuals could always be redeemed, "history is the long and tragic story of the fact that privileged groups seldom give up their privileges voluntarily."

Although this crisis produced little change in Birmingham, it precipitated the peaceful "March on Washington" of August 1963, and the subsequent enactment by Congress of the Civil Rights Act of 1964 and the Voting Rights Act of 1965.

A.   Birmingham Manifesto, 1963

The patience of an oppressed people cannot endure forever. The Negro citizens of Birmingham for the last several years have hoped in vain for some evidence of good faith resolution of our just grievances.

F. L. Shuttlesworth and N. H. Smith, "The Birmingham Manifesto." Reprinted with permission from *Freedomways* magazine, Winter 1964, pp. 20–21.

Birmingham is part of the United States and we are *bona fide* citizens. Yet the history of Birmingham reveals that very little of the democratic process touches the life of the Negro in Birmingham. We have been segregated racially, exploited economically, and dominated politically. Under the leadership of the Alabama Christian Movement for Human Rights, we sought relief by petition for the repeal of city ordinances requiring segregation and the institution of a merit hiring policy in city employment. We were rebuffed. We then turned to the system of the courts. We weathered set-back after set-back, with all of its costliness, finally winning the terminal, bus, parks and airport cases. The bus decision has been implemented begrudgingly and the parks decision prompted the closing of all municipally-owned recreational facilities with the exception of the zoo and Legion Field. The airport case has been a slightly better experience with the exception of hotel accommodations and the subtle discrimination that continues in the limousine service.

We have always been a peaceful people, bearing our oppression with superhuman effort. Yet we have been the victims of repeated violence, not only that inflicted by the hoodlum element but also that inflicted by the blatant misuse of police power. Our memories are seared with painful mob experience of Mother's Day 1961 during the Freedom Rides. For years, while our homes and churches were being bombed, we heard nothing but the rantings and ravings of racist city officials.

The Negro protest for equality and justice has been a voice crying in the wilderness. Most of Birmingham has remained silent, probably out of fear. In the meanwhile, our city has acquired the dubious reputation of being the worst big city in race relations in the United States. Last fall, for a flickering moment, it appeared that sincere community leaders from religion, business and industry discerned the inevitable confrontation in race relations approaching. Their concern for the city's image and commonweal of all its citizens did not run deep enough. Solemn promises were made, pending a postponement of direct action, that we would be joined in a suit seeking the relief of segregation ordinances. Some merchants agreed to desegregate their rest-rooms as a good-faith start, some actually complying, only to retreat shortly thereafter. We hold in our hands now, broken faith and broken promises.

We believe in the American Dream of democracy, in the Jeffersonian doctrine that "all men are created equal and are endowed by their Creator with certain inalienable rights, among these being life, liberty and the pursuit of happiness."

Twice since September we have deferred our direct action thrust in order that a change in city government would not be made in the hysteria of community crisis. We act today in full concert with our Hebraic-Christian tradition, the law of morality and the Constitution of our nation. The absence of justice and progress in Birmingham demands that we make a moral witness to give our community a chance to survive. We demonstrate our faith that we believe that The Beloved Community can come to Birmingham.

We appeal to the citizenry of Birmingham, Negro and white, to join us in this witness for decency, morality, self-respect and human dignity. Your individual and corporate support can hasten the day of "liberty and justice for all." This is Birmingham's moment of truth in which every citizen can play his part in her larger destiny. The Alabama Christian Movement for Human Rights, in behalf of the Negro community of Birmingham.

F. L. SHUTTLESWORTH, President
N. H. SMITH, Secretary

B.   Martin Luther King, Jr.,
Letter from Birmingham City Jail

MARTIN LUTHER KING, JR.
Birmingham City Jail
April 16, 1963

Bishop C. C. J. CARPENTER
Bishop JOSEPH A. DURICK
Rabbi MILTON L. GRAFMAN
Bishop PAUL HARDIN
Bishop NOLAN B. HARMON
The Rev. GEORGE M. MURRAY
The Rev. EDWARD V. RAMAGE
The Rev. EARL STALLINGS

My dear Fellow Clergymen,

While confined here in the Birmingham City Jail, I came across your recent statement calling our present activities "unwise and untimely." Seldom, if ever, do I pause to answer criticism of my work and ideas. If I sought to answer all of the criticisms that cross my desk, my secretaries would be engaged in little else in the course of the day and I would have no time for constructive work. But since I feel that you are men of genuine goodwill and your criticisms are sincerely set forth, I would like to answer your statement in what I hope will be patient and reasonable terms.

I think I should give the reason for my being in Birmingham, since you have been influenced by the argument of "outsiders coming in." I have the

---

Martin Luther King, Jr., *Letter from Birmingham City Jail* (Philadelphia: American Friends Service Committee, 1963), pp. 3–14. Reprinted with the permission of Martin Luther King, Jr.

honor of serving as president of the Southern Christian Leadership Conference, an organization operating in every Southern state with headquarters in
Atlanta, Georgia. We have some eighty-five affiliate organizations all across
the South—one being the Alabama Christian Movement for Human Rights.
Whenever necessary and possible we share staff, educational, and financial
resources with our affiliates. Several months ago our local affiliate here in
Birmingham invited us to be on call to engage in a nonviolent direct action
program if such were deemed necessary. We readily consented and when the
hour came we lived up to our promises. So I am here, along with several
members of my staff, because we were invited here. I am here because I
have basic organizational ties here. Beyond this, I am in Birmingham because
injustice is here. Just as the eighth century prophets left their little villages
and carried their "thus saith the Lord" far beyond the boundaries of their
home town, and just as the Apostle Paul left his little village of Tarsus and
carried the gospel of Jesus Christ to practically every hamlet and city of the
Graeco-Roman world, I too am compelled to carry the gospel of freedom
beyond my particular home town. Like Paul, I must constantly respond to
the Macedonian call for aid.

Moreover, I am cognizant of the interrelatedness of all communities and
states. I cannot sit idly by in Atlanta and not be concerned about what happens
in Birmingham. Injustice anywhere is a threat to justice everywhere. We are
caught in an inescapable network of mutuality tied in a single garment of
destiny. Whatever affects one directly affects all indirectly. Never again can
we afford to live with the narrow, provincial "outside agitator" idea. Anyone
who lives inside the United States can never be considered an outsider
anywhere in this country.

You deplore the demonstrations that are presently taking place in Birmingham. But I am sorry that your statement did not express a similar concern
for the conditions that brought the demonstrations into being. I am sure that
each of you would want to go beyond the superficial social analyst who
looks merely at effects, and does not grapple with underlying causes. I would
not hesitate to say that it is unfortunate that so-called demonstrations are
taking place in Birmingham at this time, but I would say in more emphatic
terms that it is even more unfortunate that the white power structure of this
city left the Negro community with no other alternative.

In any nonviolent campaign there are four basic steps: (1) collection of
the facts to determine whether injustices are alive; (2) negotiation; (3) self-
purification; and (4) direct action. We have gone through all of these steps
in Birmingham. There can be no gainsaying of the fact that racial injustice
engulfs this community. Birmingham is probably the most thoroughly segregated city in the United States. Its ugly record of police brutality is known
in every section of this country. Its unjust treatment of Negroes in the courts
is a notorious reality. There have been more unsolved bombings of Negro
homes and churches in Birmingham than any city in this nation. These are
the hard, brutal, and unbelievable facts. On the basis of these conditions

Negro leaders sought to negotiate with the city fathers. But the political leaders consistently refused to engage in good faith negotiation.

Then came the opportunity last September to talk with some of the leaders of the economic community. In these negotiating sessions certain promises were made by the merchants—such as the promise to remove the humiliating racial signs from the stores. On the basis of these promises Rev. Shuttlesworth and the leaders of the Alabama Christian Movement for Human Rights agreed to call a moratorium on any type of demonstrations. As the weeks and months unfolded we realized that we were the victims of a broken promise. The signs remained. As in so many experiences of the past we were confronted with blasted hopes, and the dark shadow of a deep disappointment settled upon us. So we had no alternative except that of preparing for direct action, whereby we would present our very bodies as a means of laying our case before the conscience of the local and national community. We were not unmindful of the difficulties involved. So we decided to go through a process of self-purification. We started having workshops on nonviolence and repeatedly asked ourselves the questions, "Are you able to accept blows without retaliating? Are you able to endure the ordeals of jail?"

We decided to set our direct action program around the Easter season, realizing that with the exception of Christmas, this was the largest shopping period of the year. Knowing that a strong economic withdrawal program would be the by-product of direct action, we felt that this was the best time to bring pressure on the merchants for the needed changes. Then it occurred to us that the March election was ahead, and so we speedily decided to postpone action until after election day. When we discovered that Mr. Connor was in the run-off, we decided again to postpone action so that the demonstrations could not be used to cloud the issues. At this time we agreed to begin our nonviolent witness the day after the run-off.

This reveals that we did not move irresponsibly into direct action. We too wanted to see Mr. Connor defeated; so we went through postponement after postponement to aid in this community need. After this we felt that direct action could be delayed no longer.

You may well ask, "Why direct action? Why sit-ins, marches, etc.? Isn't negotiation a better path?" You are exactly right in your call for negotiation. Indeed, this is the purpose of direct action. Nonviolent direct action seeks to create such a crisis and establish such creative tension that a community that has constantly refused to negotiate is forced to confront the issue. It seeks so to dramatize the issue that it can no longer be ignored. I just referred to the creation of tension as a part of the work of the nonviolent resister. This may sound rather shocking. But I must confess that I am not afraid of the word tension. I have earnestly worked and preached against violent tension, and there is a type of constructive nonviolent tension that is necessary for growth. Just as Socrates felt that it was necessary to create a tension in the mind so that individuals could rise from the bondage of myths and half-truths to the unfettered realm of creative analysis and objective appraisal, we must see the need of having nonviolent gadflies to create the kind of tension in society that will help men rise from the dark depths of prejudice and racism to the majestic heights of understanding and brotherhood. So the purpose of the direct action is to create a situation so crisis-packed that it will inevitably open the door to negotiation. We, therefore, concur with you in your call for negotiation. Too long has our beloved Southland been bogged down in the tragic attempt to live in monologue rather than dialogue.

One of the basic points in your statement is that our acts are untimely. Some have asked, "Why didn't you give the new administration time to act?" The only answer that I can give to this inquiry is that the new administration must be prodded about as much as the outgoing one before it acts. We will be sadly mistaken if we feel that the election of Mr. Boutwell will bring the millennium to Birmingham. While Mr. Boutwell is much more articulate and gentle than Mr. Connor, they are both segregationists dedicated to the task of maintaining the status quo. The hope I see in Mr. Boutwell is that he will be reasonable enough to see the futility of massive resistance to desegregation. But he will not see this without pressure from the devotees of civil rights. My friends, I must say to you that we have not made a single gain in civil rights without determined legal and nonviolent pressure. History is the long and tragic story of the fact that privileged groups seldom give up their privileges voluntarily. Individuals may see the moral light and voluntarily give up their unjust posture; but as Reinhold Niebuhr has reminded us, groups are more immoral than individuals.

We know through painful experience that freedom is never voluntarily given by the oppressor; it must be demanded by the oppressed. Frankly I have never yet engaged in a direct action movement that was "well timed," according to the timetable of those who have not suffered unduly from the disease of segregation. For years now I have heard the word "Wait!" It rings in the ear of every Negro with a piercing familiarity. This "wait" has almost always meant "never." It has been a tranquilizing thalidomide, relieving the emotional stress for a moment, only to give birth to an ill-formed infant of frustration. We must come to see with the distinguished jurist of yesterday that "justice too long delayed is justice denied." We have waited for more than three hundred and forty years for our constitutional and God-given rights. The nations of Asia and Africa are moving with jet-like speed toward the goal of political independence, and we still creep at horse and buggy pace toward the gaining of a cup of coffee at a lunch counter.

I guess it is easy for those who have never felt the stinging darts of segregation to say wait. But when you have seen vicious mobs lynch your mothers and fathers at will and drown your sisters and brothers at whim; when you have seen hate filled policemen curse, kick, brutalize, and even kill your black brothers and sisters with impunity; when you see the vast majority of your twenty million Negro brothers smothering in an air-tight cage of poverty in the midst of an affluent society; when you suddenly find your tongue twisted and your speech stammering as you seek to explain to your six-year-old daughter why she can't go to the public amusement park that has just been advertised on television, and see tears welling up in her little eyes when she is told that Funtown is closed to colored children, and see the depressing clouds of inferiority begin to form in her little mental sky, and see her begin to distort her little personality by unconsciously developing a bitterness toward white people; when you have to concoct an answer for a five-year-old son asking in agonizing pathos: "Daddy, why do white people treat colored people so mean?"; when you take a cross country drive and find it necessary to sleep night after night in the uncomfortable corners of your automobile because no motel will accept you; when you are humiliated day in and day out by nagging signs reading "white" men and "colored"; when your first name becomes "nigger" and your middle name becomes "boy" (however old you are) and your last name becomes "John," and when your wife and mother are never given the respected title "Mrs."; when you are harried by day and haunted by night by the fact that you are a Negro, living constantly at tip-toe stance never quite knowing what to expect next, and plagued with inner fears and outer resentments; when you are forever fighting a degenerating sense of "nobodiness";—then you will understand why we find it difficult to wait. There comes a time when the cup of endurance runs over, and men are no longer willing to be plunged into an abyss of injustice where they experience the bleakness of corroding despair. I hope, sirs, you can understand our legitimate and unavoidable impatience.

You express a great deal of anxiety over our willingness to break laws. This is certainly a legitimate concern. Since we so diligently urge people to obey the Supreme Court's decision of 1954 outlawing segregation in the public schools, it is rather strange and paradoxical to find us consciously breaking laws. One may well ask, "How can you advocate breaking some laws and obeying others?" The answer is found in the fact that there are two types of laws; there are *just* laws and there are *unjust* laws. I would be the first to advocate obeying just laws. One has not only a legal but moral responsibility to obey just laws. Conversely, one has a moral responsibility to disobey unjust laws. I would agree with Saint Augustine that "An unjust law is no law at all."

Now what is the difference between the two? How does one determine when a law is just or unjust? A just law is a man-made code that squares with the moral law or the law of God. An unjust law is a code that is out of harmony with the moral law. To put it in the terms of Saint Thomas Aquinas, an unjust law is a human law that is not rooted in eternal and natural law. Any law that uplifts human personality is just. Any law that degrades human personality is unjust. All segregation statutes are unjust because segregation distorts the soul and damages the personality. It gives the segregator a false sense of superiority and the segregated a false sense of inferiority. To use the words of Martin Buber, the great Jewish philosopher, segregation substitutes an "I-it" relationship for the "I-thou" relationship, and ends up relegating persons to the status of things. So segregation is not only politically, economically, and sociologically unsound, but it is morally wrong and sinful. Paul Tillich has said that sin is separation. Isn't segregation an existential expression of man's tragic separation, an expression of his awful estrangement, his terrible sinfulness? So I can urge men to obey the 1954 decision of the Supreme Court because it is morally right, and I can urge them to disobey segregation ordinances because they are morally wrong.

Let us turn to a more concrete example of just and unjust laws. An unjust law is a code that a majority inflicts on a minority that is not binding on itself. This is *difference* made legal. On the other hand a just law is a code that a majority compels a minority to follow that it is willing to follow itself. This is *sameness* made legal.

Let me give another explanation. An unjust law is a code inflicted upon a minority which that minority had no part in enacting or creating because they did not have the unhampered right to vote. Who can say the legislature of Alabama which set up the segregation laws was democratically elected? Throughout the state of Alabama all types of conniving methods are used to prevent Negroes from becoming registered voters and there are some counties without a single Negro registered to vote despite the fact that the Negro constitutes a majority of the population. Can any law set up in such a state be considered democratically structured?

These are just a few examples of unjust and just laws. There are some instances when a law is just on its face but unjust in its application. For instance, I was arrested Friday on a charge of parading without a permit. Now there is nothing wrong with an ordinance which requires a permit for a parade, but when the ordinance is used to preserve segregation and to deny citizens the First Amendment privilege of peaceful assembly and peaceful protest, then it becomes unjust.

I hope you can see the distinction I am trying to point out. In no sense do I advocate evading or defying the law as the rabid segregationist would do. This would lead to anarchy. One who breaks an unjust law must do it *openly, lovingly* (not hatefully as the white mothers did in New Orleans when they were seen on television screaming "nigger, nigger, nigger") and with a willingness to accept the penalty. I submit that an individual who breaks a law that conscience tells him is unjust, and willingly accepts the penalty by staying in jail to arouse the conscience of the community over its injustice, is in reality expressing the very highest respect for law.

Of course there is nothing new about this kind of civil disobedience. It was seen sublimely in the refusal of Shadrach, Meshach, and Abednego to obey the laws of Nebuchadnezzar because a higher moral law was involved. It was practiced superbly by the early Christians who were willing to face hungry lions and the excruciating pain of chopping blocks, before submitting to certain unjust laws of the Roman Empire. To a degree academic freedom is a reality today because Socrates practiced civil disobedience.

We can never forget that everything Hitler did in Germany was "legal" and everything the Hungarian freedom fighters did in Hungary was "illegal."

It was "illegal" to aid and comfort a Jew in Hitler's Germany. But I am sure that, if I had lived in Germany during that time, I would have aided and comforted my Jewish brothers even though it was illegal. If I lived in a communist country today where certain principles dear to the Christian faith are suppressed, I believe I would openly advocate disobeying these anti-religious laws.

I must make two honest confessions to you, my Christian and Jewish brothers. First I must confess that over the last few years I have been gravely disappointed with the white moderate. I have almost reached the regrettable conclusion that the Negroes' great stumbling block in the stride toward freedom is not the White Citizens' "Counciler" or the Ku Klux Klanner, but the white moderate who is more devoted to "order" than to justice; who prefers a negative peace which is the absence of tension to a positive peace which is the presence of justice; who constantly says "I agree with you in the goal you seek, but I can't agree with your methods of direct action"; who paternalistically feels that he can set the time-table for another man's freedom; who lives by the myth of time and who constantly advises the Negro to wait until a "more convenient season." Shallow understanding from people of good will is more frustrating than absolute misunderstanding from people of ill will. Lukewarm acceptance is much more bewildering than outright rejection.

I had hoped that the white moderate would understand that law and order exist for the purpose of establishing justice, and that when they fail to do this they become the dangerously structured dams that block the flow of social progress. I had hoped that the white moderate would understand that the present tension in the South is merely a necessary phase of the transition from an obnoxious negative peace, where the Negro passively accepted his unjust plight, to a substance-filled positive peace, where all men will respect the dignity and worth of human personality. Actually, we who engage in nonviolent direct action are not the creators of tension. We merely bring to the surface the hidden tension that is already alive. We bring it out in the open where it can be seen and dealt with. Like a boil that can never be cured as long as it is covered up but must be opened with all its pusflowing ugliness to the natural medicines of air and light, injustice must likewise be exposed, with all of the tension its exposing creates, to the light of human conscience and the air of national opinion before it can be cured.

In your statement you asserted that our actions, even though peaceful, must be condemned because they precipitate violence. But can this assertion be logically made? Isn't this like condemning the robbed man because his possession of money precipitated the evil act of robbery? Isn't this like condemning Socrates because his unswerving commitment to truth and his philosophical delvings precipitated the misguided popular mind to make him drink the hemlock? Isn't this like condemning Jesus because His unique God consciousness and never-ceasing devotion to His will precipitated the evil act of crucifixion? We must come to see, as federal courts have consistently affirmed, that it is immoral to urge an individual to withdraw his efforts to gain his basic constitutional rights because the quest precipitates violence. Society must protect the robbed and punish the robber.

I had also hoped that the white moderate would reject the myth of time. I received a letter this morning from a white brother in Texas which said: "All Christians know that the colored people will receive equal rights eventually, but is it possible that you are in too great of a religious hurry? It has taken Christianity almost 2000 years to accomplish what it has. The teachings of Christ take time to come to earth." All that is said here grows out of a tragic misconception of time. It is the strangely irrational notion that there is something in the very flow of time that will inevitably cure all ills. Actually time is neutral. It can be used either destructively or constructively. I am coming to feel that the people of ill will have used time much more effectively than the people of good will. We will have to repent in this generation not merely for the vitriolic words and actions of the bad people, but for the appalling silence of the good people. We must come to see that human progress never rolls in on wheels of inevitability. It comes through the tireless efforts and persistent work of men willing to be co-workers with God, and without this hard work time itself becomes an ally of the forces of social stagnation.

We must use time creatively, and forever realize that the time is always ripe to do right. Now is the time to make real the promise of democracy, and transform our pending national elegy into a creative psalm of brotherhood. Now is the time to lift our national policy from the quicksand of racial injustice to the solid rock of human dignity.

You spoke of our activity in Birmingham as extreme. At first I was rather disappointed that fellow clergymen would see my nonviolent efforts as those of the extremist. I started thinking about the fact that I stand in the middle of two opposing forces in the Negro community. One is a force of complacency made up of Negroes who, as a result of long years of oppression, have been so completely drained of self-respect and a sense of "somebodiness" that they have adjusted to segregation, and of a few Negroes in the middle class who, because of a degree of academic and economic security, and because at points they profit by segregation, have unconsciously become insensitive to the problems of the masses. The other force is one of bitterness and hatred and comes perilously close to advocating violence. It is expressed in the various black nationalist groups that are springing up over the nation, the largest and best known being Elijah Muhammad's Muslim movement. This movement is nourished by the contemporary frustration over the continued existence of racial discrimination. It is made up of people who have lost faith in America, who have absolutely repudiated Christianity, and who have concluded that the white man is an incurable "devil." I have tried to stand between these two forces saying that we need not follow the "do-nothingism" of the complacent or the hatred and despair of the black nationalist. There is the more excellent way of love and nonviolent protest. I'm grateful to God that, through the Negro church, the dimension of nonviolence entered our struggle. If this philosophy had not emerged I am convinced that by now many streets of the South would be flowing with floods of blood. And I am further convinced that if our white brothers dismiss us as "rabble rousers" and "outside agitators"—those of us who are working through the channels of nonviolent direct action—and refuse to support our nonviolent efforts, millions of Negroes, out of frustration and despair, will seek solace and security in black nationalist ideologies, a development that will lead inevitably to a frightening racial nightmare.

Oppressed people cannot remain oppressed forever. The urge for freedom will eventually come. This is what has happened to the American Negro. Something within has reminded him of his birthright of freedom; something without has reminded him that he can gain it. Consciously and unconsciously, he has been swept in by what the Germans call the *Zeitgeist,* and with his black brothers of Africa, and his brown and yellow brothers of Asia, South America, and the Caribbean, he is moving with a sense of cosmic urgency toward the promised land of racial justice. Recognizing this vital urge that has engulfed the Negro community, one should readily understand public demonstrations. The Negro has many pent-up resentments and latent frustrations. He has to get them out. So let him march sometime; let him have his prayer pilgrimages to the city hall; understand why he must have sit-ins and freedom rides. If his repressed emotions do not come out in these nonviolent ways, they will come out in ominous expressions of violence. This is not a threat; it is a fact of history. So I have not said to my people, "Get rid of your discontent." But I have tried to say that this normal and healthy discontent can be channeled through the creative outlet of nonviolent direct action. Now this approach is being dismissed as extremist. I must admit that I was initially disappointed in being so categorized.

But as I continued to think about the matter I gradually gained a bit of satisfaction from being considered an extremist. Was not Jesus an extremist in love? "Love your enemies, bless them that curse you, pray for them that despitefully use you." Was not Amos an extremist for justice—"Let justice roll down like waters and righteousness like a mighty stream." Was not Paul an extremist for the gospel of Jesus Christ—"I bear in my body the marks of the Lord Jesus." Was not Martin Luther an extremist—"Here I stand; I can do none other so help me God." Was not John Bunyan an extremist—"I will stay in jail to the end of my days before I make a butchery of my conscience." Was not Abraham Lincoln an extremist—"This nation cannot survive half slave and half free." Was not Thomas Jefferson an extremist— "We hold these truths to be self evident that all men are created equal." So the question is not whether we will be extremist but what kind of extremist will we be. Will we be extremists for hate or will we be extremists for love? Will we be extremists for the preservation of injustice—or will we be extremists for the cause of justice? In that dramatic scene on Calvary's hill three men were crucified. We must never forget that all three were crucified for the same crime—the crime of extremism. Two were extremists for immorality, and thus fell below their environment. The other, Jesus Christ, was an extremist for love, truth, and goodness, and thereby rose above His environment. So, after all, maybe the South, the nation, and the world are in dire need of creative extremists.

I had hoped that the white moderate would see this. Maybe I was too optimistic. Maybe I expected too much. I guess I should have realized that few members of a race that has oppressed another race can understand or appreciate the deep groans and passionate yearnings of those that have been oppressed, and still fewer have the vision to see that injustice must be rooted out by strong, persistent, and determined action. I am thankful, however, that some of our white brothers have grasped the meaning of this social revolution and committed themselves to it. They are still all too small in quantity, but they are big in quality. Some like Ralph McGill, Lillian Smith, Harry Golden, and James Dabbs have written about our struggle in eloquent, prophetic, and understanding terms. Others have marched with us down nameless streets of the South. They have languished in filthy, roach-infested jails, suffering the abuse and brutality of angry policemen who see them as "dirty nigger lovers." They, unlike so many of their moderate brothers and sisters, have recognized the urgency of the moment and sensed the need for powerful "action" antidotes to combat the disease of segregation.

Let me rush on to mention my other disappointment. I have been so greatly disappointed with the white Church and its leadership. Of course there are some notable exceptions. I am not unmindful of the fact that each of you has taken some significant stands on this issue. I commend you, Rev. Stallings, for your Christian stand on this past Sunday, in welcoming Negroes to your worship service on a non-segregated basis. I commend the Catholic leaders of this state for integrating Springhill College several years ago.

But despite these notable exceptions I must honestly reiterate that I have been disappointed with the Church. I do not say that as one of those negative critics who can always find something wrong with the Church. I say it as a minister of the gospel, who loves the Church; who was nurtured in its bosom; who has been sustained by its spiritual blessings and who will remain true to it as long as the cord of life shall lengthen.

I had the strange feeling when I was suddenly catapulted into the leadership of the bus protest in Montgomery several years ago that we would have the support of the white Church. I felt that the white ministers, priests, and rabbis of the South would be some of our strongest allies. Instead, some have been outright opponents, refusing to understand the freedom movement and misrepresenting its leaders; all too many others have been more cautious than courageous and have remained silent behind the anesthetizing security of stained glass windows.

In spite of my shattered dreams of the past, I came to Birmingham with the hope that the white religious leadership of this community would see the justice of our cause and, with deep moral concern, serve as the channel through which our just grievances could get to the power structure. I had hoped that each of you would understand. But again I have been disappointed.

I have heard numerous religious leaders of the South call upon their worshippers to comply with a desegregation decision because it is the law, but I have longed to hear white ministers say follow this decree because integration is morally right and the Negro is your brother. In the midst of blatant injustices inflicted upon the Negro, I have watched white churches stand on the sideline and merely mouth pious irrelevancies and sanctimonious trivialities. In the midst of a mighty struggle to rid our nation of racial and economic injustice, I have heard so many ministers say, "Those are social issues with which the Gospel has no real concern," and I have watched so many churches commit themselves to a completely other-worldly religion which made a strange distinction between body and soul, the sacred and the secular.

So here we are moving toward the exit of the twentieth century with a religious community largely adjusted to the status quo, standing as a tail light behind other community agencies rather than a headlight leading men to higher levels of justice.

I have travelled the length and breadth of Alabama, Mississippi, and all the other Southern states. On sweltering summer days and crisp autumn mornings I have looked at her beautiful churches with their spires pointing heavenward. I have beheld the impressive outlay of her massive religious education buildings. Over and over again I have found myself asking: "Who worships here? Who is their God? Where were their voices when the lips of Governor Barnett dripped with words of interposition and nullification? Where were they when Governor Wallace gave the clarion call for defiance and hatred? Where were their voices of support when tired, bruised, and weary Negro men and women decided to rise from the dark dungeons of complacency to the bright hills of creative protest?"

Yes, these questions are still in my mind. In deep disappointment, I have wept over the laxity of the Church. But be assured that my tears have been tears of love. There can be no deep disappointment where there is not deep love. Yes, I love the Church; I love her sacred walls. How could I do otherwise? I am in the rather unique position of being the son, the grandson, and the great grandson of preachers. Yes, I see the Church as the body of Christ. But, oh! How we have blemished and scarred that body through social neglect and fear of being nonconformist.

There was a time when the Church was very powerful. It was during that period when the early Christians rejoiced when they were deemed worthy to suffer for what they believed. In those days the Church was not merely a thermometer that recorded the ideas and principles of popular opinion; it was a thermostat that transformed the mores of society. Wherever the early Christians entered a town the power structure got disturbed and immediately sought to convict them for being "disturbers of the peace" and "outside agitators." But they went on with the conviction that they were a "colony of heaven" and had to obey God rather than man. They were small in number but big in commitment. They were too God-intoxicated to be "astronomically intimidated." They brought an end to such ancient evils as infanticide and gladiatorial contest.

Things are different now. The contemporary Church is so often a weak, ineffectual voice with an uncertain sound. It is so often the arch-supporter of the status quo. Far from being disturbed by the presence of the Church, the power structure of the average community is consoled by the Church's silent and often vocal sanction of things as they are.

But the judgment of God is upon the Church as never before. If the Church of today does not recapture the sacrificial spirit of the early Church, it will lose its authentic ring, forfeit the loyalty of millions, and be dismissed as an irrelevant social club with no meaning for the twentieth century. I am meeting young people every day whose disappointment with the Church has risen to outright disgust.

Maybe again I have been too optimistic. Is organized religion too inextricably bound to the status quo to save our nation and the world? Maybe I must turn my faith to the inner spiritual Church, the church within the Church, as the true *ecclesia* and the hope of the world. But again I am thankful to God that some noble souls from the ranks of organized religion have broken loose from the paralyzing chains of conformity and joined us as active partners in the struggle for freedom. They have left their secure congregations and walked the streets of Albany, Georgia, with us. They have gone through the highways of the South on torturous rides for freedom. Yes, they have gone to jail with us. Some have been kicked out of their churches and lost the support of their bishops and fellow ministers. But they have gone with the faith that right defeated is stronger than evil triumphant. These men have been the leaven in the lump of the race. Their witness has been the spiritual salt that has preserved the true meaning of the Gospel in these troubled times. They have carved a tunnel of hope through the dark mountain of disappointment.

I hope the Church as a whole will meet the challenge of this decisive hour. But even if the Church does not come to the aid of justice, I have no despair about the future. I have no fear about the outcome of our struggle in Birmingham, even if our motives are presently misunderstood. We will reach the goal of freedom in Birmingham and all over the nation, because the goal of America is freedom. Abused and scorned though we may be, our destiny is tied up with the destiny of America. Before the pilgrims landed at Plymouth, we were here. Before the pen of Jefferson etched across the pages of history the majestic words of the Declaration of Independence, we were here. For more than two centuries our foreparents labored in this country without wages; they made cotton "king"; and they built the homes of their masters in the midst of brutal injustice and shameful humiliation—and yet out of a bottomless vitality they continued to thrive and develop. If the inexpressible cruelties of slavery could not stop us, the opposition we now face will surely fail. We will win our freedom because the sacred heritage of our nation and the eternal will of God are embodied in our echoing demands.

I must close now. But before closing I am impelled to mention one other point in your statement that troubled me profoundly. You warmly commended the Birmingham police force for keeping "order" and "preventing violence." I don't believe you would have so warmly commended the police force if you had seen its angry violent dogs literally biting six unarmed, nonviolent Negroes. I don't believe you would so quickly commend the policemen if you would observe their ugly and inhuman treatment of Negroes here in the city jail; if you would watch them push and curse old Negro women and young Negro girls; if you would see them slap and kick old Negro men and young Negro boys; if you will observe them, as they did on two occasions, refuse to give us food because we wanted to sing our grace together. I'm sorry that I can't join you in your praise for the police department.

It is true that they have been rather disciplined in their public handling of the demonstrators. In this sense they have been rather publicly "nonviolent." But for what purpose? To preserve the evil system of segregation. Over the last few years I have consistently preached that nonviolence demands that the means we use must be as pure as the ends we seek. So I have tried to make it clear that it is wrong to use immoral means to attain moral ends. But now I must affirm that it is just as wrong, or even moreso, to use moral means to preserve immoral ends. Maybe Mr. Connor and his policemen have been rather publicly nonviolent, as Chief Pritchett was in Albany, Georgia, but they have used the moral means of nonviolence to maintain the immoral end of flagrant racial injustice. T. S. Eliot has said that there is no greater treason than to do the right deed for the wrong reason.

I wish you had commended the Negro sit-inners and demonstrators of Birmingham for their sublime courage, their willingness to suffer, and their amazing discipline in the midst of the most inhuman provocation. One day the South will recognize its real heroes. They will be the James Merediths, courageously and with a majestic sense of purpose, facing jeering and hostile mobs and the agonizing loneliness that characterizes the life of the pioneer. They will be old, oppressed, battered Negro women, symbolized in a seventy-two year old woman of Montgomery, Alabama, who rose up with a sense of dignity and with her people decided not to ride the segregated buses, and responded to one who inquired about her tiredness with ungrammatical profundity: "My feets is tired, but my soul is rested." They will be young high school and college students, young ministers of the gospel and a host of the elders, courageously and nonviolently sitting in at lunch counters and willingly going to jail for conscience sake. One day the South will know that when these disinherited children of God sat down at lunch counters they were in reality standing up for the best in the American dream and the most sacred values in our Judeo-Christian heritage, and thus carrying our whole nation back to great wells of democracy which were dug deep by the founding fathers in the formulation of the Constitution and the Declaration of Independence.

Never before have I written a letter this long (or should I say a book?). I'm afraid that it is much too long to take your precious time. I can assure you that it would have been much shorter if I had been writing from a comfortable desk, but what else is there to do when you are alone for days in the dull monotony of a narrow jail cell other than write long letters, think strange thoughts, and pray long prayers?

If I have said anything in this letter that is an overstatement of the truth and is indicative of an unreasonable impatience, I beg you to forgive me. If I have said anything in this letter that is an understatement of the truth and is indicative of my having a patience that makes me patient with anything less than brotherhood, I beg God to forgive me.

I hope this letter finds you strong in the faith. I also hope that circumstances will soon make it possible for me to meet each of you, not as an integrationist or a civil rights leader, but as a fellow clergyman and a Christian brother. Let us all hope that the dark clouds of racial prejudice will soon pass away and the deep fog of misunderstanding will be lifted from our fear-drenched communities and in some not too distant tomorrow the radiant stars of love and brotherhood will shine over our great nation with all of their scintillating beauty.

Yours for the cause of
Peace and Brotherhood
MARTIN LUTHER KING, JR.

PART X

THE VIETNAM WAR

DOCUMENT 33

We Won't Go

Nonviolent protest against the Vietnam War took a variety of forms, many of them without precedent in the country's history.

In 1965 about 6,000 persons signed a declaration (Document 33A) pledging "conscientious refusal to cooperate with the United States government in the prosecution of the war in Vietnam." In late Spring 1965, the statement was broadened to include "refusal to cooperate with U.S. military intervention in the Dominican Republic, or the affairs of any other nation."

The signers included such veterans of the nonviolent movement as David Dellinger, Dorothy Day, Ammon Hennacy, Bradford Lyttle, A. J. Muste, and Robert Swann; well-known leaders of the civil rights movement such as James Bevel, John Lewis, Robert Moses, A. Phillip Randolph, and Bayard Rustin; and a number of clergymen, academics, and intellectuals, among them Kenneth Boulding, W. H. Ferry, Erich Fromm, Paul Goodman, Nobel Prize-winning Linus Pauling, and Staughton Lynd.

Whereas many Black Americans had seen the Civil War and World Wars I and II as an opportunity to prove that they deserved to be first-class citizens, the Student Nonviolent Coordinating Committee (SNCC) and later, Dr. Martin Luther King, Jr., came out against the Vietnam War. The first call for draft resistance from within the civil rights movement was a leaflet distributed in

July 1965 in McComb, Mississippi (Document 33B). McComb was the town in which SNCC's voter registration work in Mississippi began in 1961 (see Document 31A). The leaflet was written by a group of Blacks in the community after learning that a classmate of theirs, John D. Shaw, had been killed in action in Vietnam. Shaw had taken part in the 1961 demonstrations in McComb in support of students expelled from the local high school for protesting segregation at the McComb bus station (see Document 31 B,C).

Women as well as men took part in many forms of noncooperation with the Vietnam War. Marjorie Swann, author of "Noncooperation" (Document 33C), was born on a farm in Cedar Rapids, Iowa in 1921. She was arrested for the first time while protesting outside the British Embassy in Washington, D.C. on behalf of Indian independence in the early 1940s. During World War II, she worked as administrative secretary of the National Committee on Conscientious Objection. A founder of the Committee for Nonviolent Action (CNVA), she was arrested in 1959 during Omaha Action (see Document 24) and was sentenced to six months in federal prison.

A. Declaration of Conscience Against the War in Vietnam

Because the use of the military resources of the United States in Vietnam and elsewhere suppresses the aspirations of the people for political independence and economic freedom;

Because inhuman torture and senseless killing are being carried out by forces armed, uniformed, trained and financed by the United States;

Because we believe that all peoples of the earth, including both Americans and non-Americans, have an inalienable right to life, liberty, and the peaceful pursuit of happiness in their own way; and

Because we think that positive steps must be taken to put an end to the threat of nuclear catastrophe and death by chemical or biological warfare, whether these result from accident or escalation—

We hereby declare our conscientious refusal to cooperate with the United States government in the prosecution of the war in Vietnam.

We encourage those who can conscientiously do so to refuse to serve in the armed forces and to ask for discharge if they are already in.

Those of us who are subject to the draft ourselves declare our own intention to refuse to serve.

Declaration Of Conscience Against The War In Vietnam (New York: published jointly by the Catholic Worker, the Committee for Nonviolent Action, the Student Peace Union, and the War Resisters League, 1965).

We urge others to refuse and refuse ourselves to take part in the manufacture or transportation of military equipment, or to work in the fields of military research and weapons development.

We shall encourage the development of other nonviolent acts, including acts which involve civil disobedience, in order to stop the flow of American soldiers and munitions to Vietnam.

NOTE: *Signing or distributing this Declaration of Conscience might be construed as a violation of the Universal Military Training and Service Act, which prohibits advising persons facing the draft to refuse service. Penalties of up to 5 years imprisonment, and/or a fine of $5,000 are provided. While prosecutions under this provision of the law almost never occur, persons signing or distributing this declaration should face the possibility of serious consequences.*

B. Leaflet, McComb, Mississippi

No Mississippi Negroes should be fighting in Viet Nam for the White Man's freedom, until all the Negro People are free in Mississippi.

Negro boys should not honor the draft here in Mississippi. Mothers should encourage their sons not to go.

We will gain respect and dignity as a race only by forcing the United States Government and the Mississippi Government to come with guns, dogs and trucks to take our sons away to fight and be killed protecting Miss., Ala., Ga., and La.

No one has a right to ask us to risk our lives and kill other Colored People in Santo Domingo and Viet Nam, so that the White American can get richer. We will be looked upon as traitors by all the Colored People of the world if the Negro people continue to fight and die without a cause.

Last week a white soldier from New Jersey was discharged from the Army because he refused to fight in Viet Nam he went on a hunger strike. Negro boys can do the same thing. We can write and ask our sons if they know what they are fighting for. If he answers Freedom, tell him thats what we are fighting for here in Mississippi. And if he says Democracy, tell him the truth—we don't know anything about Communism, Socialism, and all that, but we do know that Negroes have caught hell here under this *American Democracy.*

Michael Ferber and Staughton Lynd, *The Resistance* (Boston: Beacon Press, 1971), pp. 31–32.

C. Marjorie Swann, "Noncooperation"

As civil disobedience and other actions, not specifically intended to be civil disobedience but which lead to arrest, increase in the context of protest against the war in Vietnam, the incidence of noncooperation with arrest and even with court and prison procedures will mount.

An example is that of the 20 persons who were arrested on May 12 at the Pentagon. None of these individuals cooperated with the arrest, and many of them continued their noncooperation in the jails and in court.

It is difficult for the average person to understand civil disobedience itself—though our country was founded on civil disobedience, and human history is full of such acts of conscience—from Socrates, to Jesus, to the early Christians, to the Boston Tea Party, to the Underground Railway, to Thoreau, to Gandhi, to the civil rights movement in the American South. Pacifists and other war resisters today point out that the Nuremberg Tribunals, set up after World War II primarily by the United States, found Germans guilty because they did *not* engage in civil disobedience, because they used as their defense that they were "only obeying orders" or "obeying the law" or "doing what we were told." Americans should be able to understand civil disobedience in the light of these historical traditions.

However, it is even more difficult to understand the acts of noncooperation; even many pacifists are puzzled, because they believe a civil disobedient should cheerfully accept the consequences of his act. A noncooperating demonstrator would reply that he is certainly willing to accept the consequences of his act, but that he does not believe in cooperating fully with what he considers an extension of the evil he is protesting. If he believes deeply that the law or government policy he is protesting against or refusing to obey is morally wrong, then he feels he cannot in good conscience cooperate with the police, courts, and prisons which enforce that law and that policy, and which are an arm of the government which he feels is doing wrong.

There are other reasons for noncooperation—probably the reasons are as many as there are individual noncooperators. Many believe that since the law—that is, police, courts, and prisons—have their ultimate authority in physical force and violence, it is wrong to voluntarily cooperate with these agents of violence. Many are convinced that prisons do not "rehabilitate" but only punish and degrade—they have seen this happen to many fellow prisoners. Others feel that prisons are primarily for the poor and those without influence and "respectability," and that this kind of discrimination ought not

Marjorie Swann, "Noncooperation," *Win*, June 16, 1967, pp. 3–4. Reprinted with permission.

to be condoned by voluntary cooperation. For the same reason, many pacifists refuse to post bail or pay fines; many poor people, they say, sit in jail for weeks or months for lack of $25 bail or fine, so why should those better off have special privileges?

There are many forms of noncooperation. One of the most common is refusal voluntarily to walk to any place the police or authorities wish one to go, and to refuse voluntarily to be finger-printed, photographed, and "processed." The risk of minor or serious injury is great, and many demonstrators have been hit, beaten, kicked, dragged and thrown. One of the Pentagon demonstrators, a young woman, was hit over the head with a nightstick by a guard at the Women's House of Detention in Washington on May 13. Most persons who act out of a commitment to nonviolence attempt to explain their actions to the police in such situations, and to assure them that no personal animosity is intended. Since the police are often frightened (of unknown circumstances) and frequently hostile, at least initially, any communication possible is to the advantage of both police and demonstrators.

Another frequent form of noncooperation is that of fasting—taking no food and no liquid except water, or perhaps fruit juice or coffee. While abstaining from food can be uncomfortable and eventually risky, abstaining from all food and liquid can be extremely dangerous almost immediately. Five or six days is probably the longest a human being can go without liquid before incurring brain damage and serious dehydration. Usually authorities watch persons who are "water fasting" closely and take steps to hospitalize them before serious consequences occur, because the authorities do not want either public disapproval or the distress of their own consciences which would follow upon neglect, but no demonstrator can ever count on such attention and should therefore be prepared to give up the fast or perhaps be allowed to die, as did several Irish freedom fighters during the Irish Rebellion.

Some demonstrators refuse to cooperate partially or wholly with court procedures: they may refuse to enter a plea, to retain or accept a lawyer, to stand up in court, to speak to the judge as a symbol of court authority (but rather speak to him as a fellow human being), to take the stand or question witnesses. They may make a speech to those assembled in the courtroom, or simply lie or sit on the floor if they are carried in, or attempt to leave if not forcibly restrained. The penalties for such noncooperation are often severe, because most judges take such action as a personal affront as well as an insult to the court, and contempt of court sentences are frequently handed down. Some judges, on the other hand, overlook such conduct, or attempt to communicate with the demonstrators, or [exercise] wide latitude, as do police and other authorities, and almost any disposition can be made of a case if there is urgent enough reason; there are always exceptions to the "rules" if a person in authority wishes to utilize those exceptions.

Probably the most commonly held reason for civil disobedience and nonco-operation is simply a deep moral conviction that individual human beings must throw their whole weight against the evil of a violent society and, at the present time, against the government of their country which is waging war and terror on helpless people in a far-away country. This war so agonizes many pacifists that they feel they must cry out with their whole being, "Stop!", and they must back up this cry with personal action commensurate to the wrong being done. They feel they must face their countrymen with the moral consequences of our national policy, and that the only way to change that policy is for individual citizens to take individual responsibility—take such responsibility in acts of love and determination.

DOCUMENT 34

The Pentagon, October 1967

The celebrated Pentagon demonstration on October 21, 1967, when several thousand demonstrators besieged a building in which the fathers of several of the demonstrators were employed, took place at a time of crisis and volatility in the antiwar movement. (See, generally, Gregory Nevala Calvert, Democracy from the Heart: Spiritual Values, Decentralism, and Democratic Idealism in the Movement of the 1960s *[Eugene, Oregon: Communitas Press, 1991], Chapter 8.)*

One emerging tendency took form at almost the same time in Stop The Draft Week in Oakland, California, October 16–20, 1967. Originally conceived as an action supporting the return of draft cards on October 16, the project drifted out of control of the pacifists who proposed it. On October 20, ten thousand demonstrators surrounded the Oakland induction center. Many wore helmets and shields. When the police advanced, the demonstrators used preplanned "mobile tactics" to melt away before them. Acting in small groups the demonstrators reassembled at street intersections outside the police lines, where they built barricades and for some time prevented buses from reaching the induction center. (See Michael Ferber and Staughton Lynd, The Resistance *[Boston: Beacon Press, 1971], pp. 140–145.)*

Likewise in planning for the Pentagon activity, advocates of tactics thought to be modeled on Black and Third World insurrectionary movements debated proponents of nonviolence like David Dellinger and Barbara Deming. The crux of the disagreement was how to regard the soldiers whom President

Lyndon Johnson had called out to deal with the emergency. Some wanted to call them "fascists" and "enemies." Others urged an effort to win over the troops. The second approach prevailed.

> *The agreement was to add a "teach-in for the troops" during all the activities. We would address them as brothers who were being victimized by the war. Our slogans would be: "You are our brothers, join us" and "You are victims too, join us." And we would encourage everyone to reflect this in their individual contacts with the GIs. (David Dellinger,* From Yale to Jail: The Life Story of a Moral Dissenter [*New York: Pantheon Books, 1993*], p. 303.)

As the following documents narrate, this agreement was carried out the next day by means ragged, improvised, and magnificent. The encounter between demonstrators and soldiers lasted thirty-three hours. At one point, someone "placed a flower in the bayonetted gunbarrel of one of the soldiers. Soon others followed his example, and before long the demonstrators were sharing not only flowers, but cigarettes, coffee, and friendly words with the soldiers." (Ibid., p. 306.) The new fraternity toward those in military service that was acted out at the Pentagon foreshadowed resistance by servicemen themselves later in the Vietnam War (see Document 36).

A. Maris Cakars and Others, "The Siege of the Pentagon"

"We will enter the Pentagon and sit down in offices, in meeting rooms, and across hallways. If this seems impossible, we will block doorways and entrances. If police and armed forces make this impossible, we will clog service roads, preventing deliveries and obstructing vehicles."

This was the plan of the National Mobilization Committee's Direct Action Committee. The response of the government was to call out a total of 8,500 soldiers—military police and members of the 82nd Airborne Division who had seen action in Vietnam, the Dominican Republic and Detroit—to protect the Pentagon. It was the first time since 1932, when Herbert Hoover called in 1,000 cavalry and infantrymen under Douglas MacArthur to put down the Bonus March, that federal troops were called to the nation's capitol. But the

Excerpts from "The Siege of the Pentagon" by Maris Cakars and others, *Win*, Oct. 30, 1967, reprinted in 10th Anniv. Issue, Apr. 29, 1976 and May 6, 1976, pp. 34–39. Reprinted with permission.

troops were only the most dramatic aspect of the hard position that the government had taken towards the peace demonstration. In negotiations for the permit necessary to hold the march and rally, the government at first announced that no permits would be granted unless the Mobilization Committee publicly renounced plans for civil disobedience. When it became clear that the Mobilization would not do that, the government, in the person of Henry Van Cleve, General Counsel for the General Services Administration and chief government negotiator, changed its position. Nevertheless, it categorically denied the Mobilization the use of more than one bridge to get from Washington to the Pentagon, permission to picket the building in any more than one area, access to the picketing of "activity" area except during very limited hours, a march route wide enough to enable the march to reach the Pentagon in a reasonably short amount of time, and the area for a rally that the Mobilization considered most suitable.

To a certain extent the precautions on the part of the government must have been the result of the rumors of violence that circulated widely prior to the demonstration. The New York based "Revolutionary Contingent" had circulated a leaflet calling on everyone to participate in a snake dance that it would hold at the Pentagon. There were reports of groups planning to bring lead pipes for "self defense." The hippies, it was said, were planning to come with water pistols. And then there was the memory of Newark and Detroit.

Against this backdrop, some 150,000 Americans arrived in Washington on October 21 to demonstrate their repugnance for the war in Vietnam. They came to hear speeches by Dr. Spock, Lincoln Lynch, Clive Jenkins of the British Labor Party, and many others. They came to exorcise the Pentagon and "do their thing." They came to shut down the Pentagon.

—Maris Cakars

The head of the march arrived in the Pentagon's North Parking Area about 3:30. The scheduled departure from Lincoln Memorial had been delayed in order to give the General Services Administration extra time to remove a fence separating the North Parking Area from the Mall. Only a small portion of the fence was removed so, half an hour late and equipped with ten wire cutters, the march stepped off. The marshals had their hands full. Trained by Cordell Reagan, one of the original Freedom Singers and the chief marshal of the Meredith March and other civil rights demonstrations, they struggled with the press, obstructionist Nazis, and Josef Mlot-Mroz, the eternal counterpicket.

By 4:00, when the second rally was starting, perhaps a thousand people had already gone over to the Mall, tearing down a good deal of the fence as they went. Donald Duncan, Carl Davidson and others spoke at the rally, but all attention was focused on the steps to the Mall entrance to the Pentagon. Even as the speakers spoke, people kept streaming over to what was called in the permit the "Post-North Parking Rally Activity Area." By 4:30 the leaders—Dellinger, Spock, Robert Lowell, Dwight MacDonald, Father

Rice—were ready to lead the civil disobedience. They walked in a group to the Mall and found the steps to the entrance packed with people. So, in order to encourage blocking doors on the other four sides of the building, they went up on Washington Boulevard, the highway running along the west side of the Mall and the Pentagon, and attempted to get to the heliport side. As they advanced, a line of soldiers stationed across the highway began to advance. The notables and the 50 or so people accompanying them, myself included, sat down. Only Dellinger remained standing and, bullhorn in hand he addressed the troops. Then Noam Chomsky of MIT took his turn, but as he was speaking the troops once more advanced. Robot-like they came forward, one slow step after another until they were almost on top of the seated pacifists. Then a remarkable thing happened. They advanced right over and around us. Stepping carefully to avoid hurting anyone they passed right through the crowd and went right on down the highway. Chomsky turned to follow and now the whole group was following the troops, going away from the Pentagon. After a minute or two we reversed ourselves and began marching back towards our original destination. Again we were confronted by a line of soldiers, again we sat down. The second line was not so gentle. After advancing to the point where it was stepping on people, it turned over the job of making arrests to the US marshals who, with a little more force than necessary, proceeded to do their job. (US marshals had been assigned the task of making arrests and made virtually all of them that weekend). They took people off in three ways, but left Spock, MacDonald, Lowell and Rice. Even the military is sensitive.

Had anyone else been arrested at this point, it would have been an irrelevant action. As it was, the demonstrators were deprived of some of their leadership. Not that these were the only leaders, or that leadership was so badly needed; but given the size of the crowd, if leaders were to lead there had to be many of them. As it turned out, the people hardly needed leaders, but they thought they did, and their absence contributed to a general feeling of insecurity and lack of definition in the situation.

—*Maris Cakars*

To the left, cheers are raised as a stream of protestors head to the corner entrance. Not a soldier from these in front of us runs over. There are cries as the troops pour in front of them; a Negro and a young girl climb underneath the flatbed truck separating our groups. Both are bloody. Another fellow with a camera comes out from under the truck but beyond the marshals' line; a marshal begins to club him while he is on his hands and knees; the marshal in front of me edges into this marshal, throwing him off balance and giving the kid a chance to get free; the marshal I had been facing winks and offers me a mint.

—*Allan Solomonow*

Suddenly there were cries from the top of the stairs. We grabbed hands and ran back, hearing rumors that an MP had defected. What excitement, we left just as the most important event occurred. Everyone was shouting: Join us, Join us. We could not make it up one stairway so tried the other side, and got right to the front by the press trucks. Later, there were other reports of another, then another defector.

—*Susan Kent*

Up among the demonstrators everyone seemed to be giving orders over bullhorns. EVERYONE WHO HAS A BULLHORN BECOMES A POLICY-MAKER. Those with better bullhorns were paid more attention. One seemed to be controlled mostly by SDS people. Theirs was much better than that of the pro-NLF committee, but these people had their flags up on the large flat truck that was parked to the left of the upper platform. Most of the night a lone anarchist stood holding a black flag directly over the line of troops beside the truck.

It was during a relatively quiescent period (as I remember it) that the MPs all put on gas masks. Only individuals had been rushing between the MPs from time to time, most of them being dragged back to the other side by the MPs, roughly but not with bloody violence. One soldier or MP was moving back & forth (after the gas masks had been put on) with a gun that looked like a contrabass bassoon. Then, without warning, one tear gas shell burst with a dull thud among the crowd in front of the MPs. Most of the crowd retreated a little way back from the line of MPs, but a scarf across my nose seemed sufficient to avoid anything except a slight burning sensation in the nasal passages—at least, this was my experience. Many around me were coughing, choking, their eyes were tearing copiously, however. I don't know whether this was because they'd been nearer to the original burst (it didn't seem much more than 10 feet away from me). Crowd surges took place several more times, but the tear gas shells seemed to be set off in the quiescent periods (at least twice more) and not when the movement of the crowd up to the MPs was strong. . . .

[Later.] A sort of speakers' stand is operating now (after 2:00 am) on the top of the parapet between the two levels. Greg Calvert of SDS speaks over the bullhorn: "We're boxed in again. This is all a failure? Perhaps but its still beautiful. We've desanctified this institution." Then, addressing the government leaders: "The troops you employ belong to us and not to you. They don't belong to the generals. They belong to a new hope for America that those generals never could participate in. The real enemy is not here (the troops) but there (the generals etc.)—not those who take orders but those who give orders"—then suddenly: "WHO IS THAT BEING BROUGHT IN ON A STRETCHER—IS HE ALIVE OR DEAD???"

Now on the right bullhorn, Sidney Peck saying that "we're the soldiers' brothers. Let's show the troops that if we have the option of accepting arrest, we'll accept it." Asks for some people in authority. I don't get the names.

A boy on the left parapet cries out that they just hit a girl. That it was horrible. Covers eyes. Someone else on another bullhorn addresses troops: "When you go home tonight, think about this. Why does a man with a gun hit someone who is doing nothing?" Orion and the moon are bright overhead. . . .

—*Jackson Mac Low*

By now the tension was very high. The police were inching forward crowding us back. On the speakers we were being told to link arms and crowd close together. And sit down. Behind us at the edge of the steps many were standing and throwing things at the MPs in spite of protests from all of us.

At this point some girl got on the bull horn and said it was dangerous and everyone should leave and gather around the fire. We all shouted, "No!" Bob Greenblatt, national coordinator of the Mobilization, got on and said those in the front wanted to leave and were all being prevented by the militants standing at the rear. We all shouted, "No!" and we stayed, but all felt our "leadership" had sold us out. Instead of supporting us, it helped cause mass desertions.

Using typical military strategy, the MPs were pushing hardest in the middle to divide the group in two. There would be a noise from the middle, the press would turn their lights on the area, while we all had a good view of the MPs kicking the seated and intertwined demonstrators. It was not always clear what the demonstrators were doing, because they were now on the ground, but they certainly were not given a chance to be violent if they wanted to, as feet kicked and billy clubs and rifle butts were smashed into people's heads.

It was terrifying to watch people who were only sitting there being beaten badly and carried out with concussions and broken bones. Many of the people sitting got up and ran. Those standing threw things. Those of us sitting bunched closer together, and sang softly, We shall overcome, We shall live in peace, We are not afraid, Soldiers are our friends, Kumbaya, my Lord, Kumbaya. . . . We talked with the soldiers in front of us, looking at them pleadingly: "You don't want to hurt us, will you do that, will you have to, please don't hurt us, arrest us, but don't hurt us, we mean no harm to you. . . ."

In the middle people were slowly being beaten and removed from the line to paddy wagons. The scene was terrifying; many ran. Everyone was shouting, "Get the girls out of there," but we stayed, afraid but wanting to stay, to stay with and support our men, to eliminate the violence, not to run and excuse ourselves from a dangerous position, to show the soldiers we were sure they would not hurt us, to make our position clear, about the war, to fight it here.

The police wedge broke through the middle. People ran. Those we thought most committed to staying ran in the face of brutality. We were surrounded. In keeping with the pacifistic approach of our small section, we realized there was no point in keeping our arms linked, we couldn't stop the advance of the troops and would only get hurt ourselves, and cause others to have to hurt us. We let go and covered our heads. A boy behind me put his hands on my head to protect me. The marshal lifted us out of the line carefully, one by one. The violence was gone. It was over for us.

—*Susan Kent*

The last few hours of the demonstration were the most agonizing, traumatic, and the most beautiful. By then the 150,000 had been reduced to a few hundred who had been through a lot together. They had faced the cold night, tear gas, beatings, indecision. And they came through it all with a new respect for themselves, a real (not just slogan-level) sympathy for the troops, and the beginnings of an understanding of what was needed in a confrontation with the American government. They found that linked arms, missiles and violent charges gained them no ground against the army, that they resulted only in bloodied heads. Many who had started out years ago as pacifists, then abandoned nonviolence for the rhetoric of Che and Giap, saw once again that a violent struggle gains nothing. Self-protection and—even more important—communicating with the troops we were facing—turned the whole group to a nonviolent stance. This was not something that the pacifists in the crowd imposed. Jerry Rubin and Stewart Albert, no pacifists in anyone's book, were the most eloquent in pleading for nonviolence. Stew even called for any of the soldiers who intended to use violence to raise their hands (one did).

The Mobilization's permit expired at midnight Sunday. In the last few minutes, as the demonstrators sang "We Shall Overcome" and "America the Beautiful," several hundred more soldiers emerged from inside the Pentagon and took up positions in front of the demonstrators. Then a voice from within the building announced over and over that the permit was about to expire, that those who remained would be arrested, that those who wished to leave could take buses supplied by the government. No more than two dozen left, most choosing to walk. About two hundred stayed and were gently arrested.

—*Maris Cakars*

The actions then turn into a blur of images in my mind, held in a matrix of terror and warmth and pity and confusion and something akin to a feeling of exultation. The clouds of tear gas and a choking sensation. Troops forming at the side of the Pentagon and marching down with bayonets pointed directly at us. A dialogue in fear between them and the demonstrators who instinctively sat down in their path. The twitching of the soldiers' jaws on their otherwise immobile faces when needless taunts came at them from the crowd. An impulse to turn and run away, mixed with the urge to bravely act the way the books on the theory of nonviolent power suggest. Trying to see, somewhere, that tiny nugget of humanity underneath in those guards who beat and dragged defenseless demonstrators. A girl walking from soldier to soldier at bayonet point, offering each one a flower—and then the image of that flower, lying in the dust at their feet. Of five men guarding one of the little embankments, two who had the decency not to put on their gas masks when the toxic fumes drifted over, standing with the same tears in their eyes that we had in our own. People wandering through the crowds, passing out water and apples and damp wash rags. The beautiful sight of hundreds sitting close together in front of the doors to the massive fortress. The sound of singing. The glow of bonfires in the dark. And the Sunday bright sun, shining on the tired, courageous people who had stayed throughout the night and were still sitting there, waiting their turn to be arrested—and who had won the battle of the Pentagon.

—Dorothy Lane

B. Gregory Nevala Calvert, *Democracy from the Heart*

Under the banner of "From Protest to Resistance," the Pentagon demonstration was scheduled for Saturday, October 21, 1967, the day after the end of the Oakland Stop-the-Draft-Week. I spent that week in non-stop meetings preparing for the largest, most militant demonstration against the war yet to take place. Plans for the demonstration included a rally at the Lincoln Memorial followed by a march across the Potomac to a second rally a short distance from the Pentagon and then a final march, by the most determined, right up to the Pentagon itself where civil disobedience was planned.

I was in a quandary about what to do. The new mood of militancy fed by the ghetto riots of the previous summer was creating the same dynamic on the East Coast that fueled the events in Oakland. I was approached by friends of several persuasions arguing that events in the black community demanded an equally militant response by white activists and specifically that the situation required that whites prove their ability and willingness to fight with the police in the street. The example of the Japanese Zengakuren's tactics of using bamboo poles in street confrontation with police was held up for Americans to emulate. In the Washington, D.C., office of the Mobe, Jerry Rubin, former Berkeley activist who had been brought onto the Mobe staff at the urging of Dave Dellinger to be a project coordinator for the Pentagon action, argued that after the initial rally marchers should sit down *en masse* on the Washington freeways and provoke the disruption of the entire Eastern Seaboard's transportation system. Several members of the "SDS house" in Washington, including Cathy Wilkerson and Tom Bell, wanted to organize a spray-painting spree targeting downtown buses. Students of former-Trotsky-

From Gregory Nevala Calvert, *Democracy from the Heart: Spiritual Values, Decentralism, and Democratic Idealism in the Movement of the 1960s,* pp. 224–251. Copyright 1991 by Gregory Nevala Calvert, Communitas Press, Publishers Services, P. O. Box 2510, Novata, CA 94948. Reprinted by permission.

ist-turned-anarchist Murray Bookchin who constituted the Up-Against-the-Wall-Motherfucker Lower Eastside of New York chapter of SDS wanted to trash downtown Washington in Zengakuren formations.

As I shuttled from New York to Washington, D.C., for Mobe meetings and negotiations with the GSA (the General Services Administration in charge of the capital's five police forces) I had long talks with Dave Dellinger about the necessity of adhering to the principles of nonviolence if the Movement was to maintain its balance and humanity and not self-destruct in adventuristic violence. Dave Dellinger had become a beloved friend and perhaps my closest ally. In addition, he was a true teacher whose vision of revolutionary nonviolence seemed increasingly to me to provide the only framework which could guide the Movement in a sane direction. Although I came to have serious differences with Dave Dellinger about strategic initiatives in the following year, he was one of the most important influences on my life and thinking and I credit him with having helped me maintain my political equilibrium at a crucial moment.

Another practitioner of nonviolence and Movement theorist, Barbara Deming of the CNVA (Committee for Non-Violent Action), also provided me with important guidance at this critical juncture. During a long conversation from New York to the GSA headquarters in Washington, Barbara Deming asked me more significant and provocative questions than I was accustomed to in a month. This brilliant and humane woman raised precisely the kinds of psychological and political issues that I was asking myself. I did not have a male friend in the Movement with whom I could freely share my convictions on psycho-sexual-political questions. As a result of her prodding, I began to conceive of the idea of a teach-in to the troops at the Pentagon. In retrospect, I have wondered if what I shared with Barbara Deming for that short period of time was a non-heterosexual perspective on the issues of masculinity and manhood-proving, which made us both question the wave of violence-prone machismo threatening to overwhelm the Movement. Barbara Deming later presented some of her insights in a brilliant article, "On Revolution and Equilibrium," which was the first major challenge in print to the politics of Black Power by a Movement radical. Her views were later elaborated in a book, *Revolution and Equilibrium.* Dismayed by the force of sexism and machismo in the Movement, Barbara Deming later became a radical separatist feminist.

Bolstered by my contacts with these advocates of radical nonviolence, I faced my comrades at the SDS House in Washington on the day before the demonstration and announced that if they were going to rampage through downtown D.C., I was going to join Dave Dellinger at the Pentagon and get arrested performing civil disobedience. They were appalled.

When I made it clear that I was absolutely serious, I became an instant outcast, but I remained firm and knew where I stood. I fully expected to be arrested the next day. If I was not able to prove to my friends that this was the only sane option, at least I wanted to make clear that in a choice between adventurism and moral protest, I had come down squarely on the side of nonviolence. At that point, I did not have a clear notion of how nonviolent action in such a situation could be infused with radical content and I was resigned to being liberal-baited out of the New Left. (The gay-baiting was already making my life quite painful in any case.)

That evening (Friday, October 20) while Berkeley radicals were celebrating the "victory" of mobile tactics and street fighting, I sat down for dinner with Dave Dellinger to discuss the morrow's action. Also present was a man I had not known before, Arthur Kinoy, one of the brightest and most dynamic lawyers I ever met, who worked as legal counsel for the Mobe. For two hours the three of us pondered the situation with agonized concern over the splits that were happening in the Movement and might get dramatically worse the following day. I explained the painful dilemma I was in and my decision to stand with Dave Dellinger on the question of nonviolence even if it meant the end of my career in SDS. Kinoy painted a picture that dispelled my gloom. He presented two interrelated and compelling arguments for the correctness of our decision to go to the Pentagon and demonstrate nonviolently. First, he justified the target by arguing that the U.S. government had itself drawn the line at the Pentagon by stationing troops inside and also by putting all U.S. military on alert from the East Coast to Colorado. Secondly, he argued that nonviolence was appropriate because it was the only way to maintain the "unity of the Movement." By the end of dinner, the three of us were elated. Arthur Kinoy and I went off to the SDS House where for two hours we argued the necessity of maintaining the unity of the Movement through nonviolence and the necessity of confronting the state at the Pentagon where it had chosen to demonstrate its military power.

We slowly won over the audience. Those who were not absolutely convinced by one or the other argument had been forced to think twice about the other alternatives. At no point did the argument degenerate into the false dichotomy between ineffective nonviolent moral protest and trashing (or other forms of violence or adventurism.) Militant, radical nonviolence seemed to have won out over the impulse toward tactical adventurism and fighting with the police. There were, however, rumblings of discontent. My female companion of the preceding six months, Karen Ashley (later of the Weather Underground), would not speak to me because, she said, I had betrayed the Movement. I sensed that what I had really betrayed was her dream of being the partner of a revolutionary hero.

THE PENTAGON PARADOX

On Saturday, October 21, perhaps 50,000 people gathered in front of the Lincoln Memorial to rally against the war. The crowd was restive. Just what did it mean to move "from protest to resistance"? For many it meant at least doing something more than easing their consciences by listening to speeches at rallies. The need "to put their bodies on the line," that act of determination in the New Left which had always expressed its sense of ultimate existential commitment, was a driving force for many as they filed out from the first rally and marched across the Potomac to a second site where yet more speeches were to be heard. The official plan of the Mobe was to make the second rally an opportunity for those who wanted to do civil disobedience at the Pentagon to participate one last time with the bulk of the demonstrators before separating and continuing on.

As soon as we had crossed the Potomac and long before reaching the second rally site, Tom Bell grabbed me by the arm and yelled: "Let's Go!" Almost before I knew it, I had become part of the new line of march which was half running towards the Pentagon. After about half a mile, we discovered that the GSA had carried out its threat to build a chain-link fence between the second rally site and the Pentagon in order to prevent demonstrators from reaching the building itself. The first canisters of tear gas were already being thrown by police. It was both exciting and somewhat frightening. When we reached the fence, Tom Bell, whose years as a full-back on the football team in high school and college had conditioned him well for physical confrontations, started to overwhelm the fence with sheer force. My many years as a farm boy had taught me much about both building and tearing down fences and I threw myself into the task.

With the fence now partially flattened, we ran straight for the Pentagon steps, avoiding the clouds of tear gas as best we could. Ahead of us was a group of adventuristic crazies, the "Revolutionary Contingent" from New York armed with long bamboo poles held upright and flying Viet Cong flags. We started up the Pentagon steps with hundreds of demonstrators now following behind us. The rank of marchers we now were part of included Marilyn Buck and Cathy Wilkerson.

When we emerged onto the great terrace between the top of the stairs and the actual doors of the Pentagon perhaps fifty yards away, we were facing a long line of federal marshals standing shoulder to shoulder with their billy clubs drawn. In front of us the Revolutionary Contingent was using its flag-topped bamboo poles to try to provoke a violent confrontation with the marshals. I was very afraid that the marshals would be provoked into firing tear gas into the crowd which, had it panicked and attempted to flee back down the steps, would almost certainly have trampled people in the surging mass that now poured up the stairs.

My instinctive reactions, formed by a childhood fraught with physical violence, were fear and the compelling need to get the situation under control in order to prevent bloodshed and violence. Tom Bell's reactions, conditioned by years on the football team, were to rally the team and urge them to head for the doors of the Pentagon. Some far-sighted SDSers had commandeered a set of bull-horns and Tom Bell grabbed one of them. Now standing on a balustrade, waving and yelling through the bullhorn for the crowd to charge ahead to the doors, he was suddenly faced with a federal marshal, baton in the air and ready to strike. With the grace and strength of a true athlete, he grasped the baton in mid-air and slowly twisted it out of the marshal's hand. The frightened cop slowly backed away and Tom Bell again began to urge the crowd to press ahead and break through the line. At the same time, the Revolutionary Contingent was still trying to provoke violence and a lone determined pacifist was trusting his throat against a cross-held billy club, taunting a marshal and trying to get arrested.

It was one of the tensest moments of my life. I was scared and I hated football, and Tom Bell appeared to me totally possessed by the heroic gridiron role he had played out for years. With fear in my guts and a certain sadness in my heart, I jumped up beside him, looked straight in his eyes, and told him with all the force I could summon to stop before someone got killed and to get down off the balustrade. "This is *not* a fucking football game," I yelled. He faltered, began to deflate, and slowly got down. I took the bullhorn and began urging the crowd to sit down. Paul Millman, another SDSer with a bullhorn, did the same from another balustrade a hundred feet away. Slowly what could have been a violent confrontation became a mass nonviolent sit-in and teach-in to the hundreds of troops who had suddenly appeared from the doors of the Pentagon and replaced the federal marshals with three ranks of young soldiers. The forces of the state had indeed been called to act by using the Army to defend the Citadel of American Imperialism. It was a serious error on their part.

Suddenly the anti-war movement was faced with the same young men it had been urging to resist the draft and not to fight in Vietnam. We were nose-to-nose with the very soldiers to whom we wanted to talk. Instead of provoking them to bloodshed we were able to exercise the most powerful tool a radical nonviolent movement has—the appeal to the human heart—and we communicated a very clear and compelling message: "You don't belong to the generals up there in their offices. You belong with us. This is their war, not yours or ours." And then with a tremendous shout that rang over and over through the afternoon and evening air we chanted the most beautiful mantra I have ever heard: "Join Us! Join Us! Join Us!."

A few did—throw down their arms and join us.

Later that night, after being forced to change its wavering contingents of youthful soldiers several times, the generals in the Pentagon ordered a squad of fresh troops to drive a wedge into the seated crowd and to beat and arrest all who resisted. Some speakers took the bullhorn and begged for mercy, asking that they be allowed to be arrested peacefully. That seemed to me a psychological disaster, which threatened to turn a radical victory into a liberal defeat. It seemed to me that a radical nonviolent movement needed to be able to claim its victory and then call for a retreat. It did not need to deliver itself into the hands of the state.

I climbed up on the balustrade once again and gave a speech claiming a victory in which I sincerely believed. I addressed myself to the troops with the same message of solidarity that had been embodied in the appeal to "Join Us!" Then I said we should retreat—until we returned one day as part of a larger movement of the majority of the American people who would come to dismantle the Pentagon together with the structures of power and empire for which it stood. Most of the crowd responded with relief and simply walked away. A small minority, largely pacifists, stayed and got arrested. Later that night Jerry Rubin denounced the "SDS sell-out" of the demonstration. Later still he met with a man named Abbie Hoffman and together they made plans to join forces in the Youth International Party (a media-oriented radical group.)

I left the Pentagon that night absolutely convinced radical nonviolence had worked and was the salvation of the Movement. Furthermore I was convinced that we had demonstrated that it was possible to confront the state nonviolently and effectively without falling into adventuristic tactics of street-fighting with police or trashing property. The event changed my life. It was another step in the completion of a new political gestalt that has guided me ever since. Others experienced the event in very different ways and drew very different conclusions than I did. There is no doubt in my mind that this moment in the history of the New Left, not just at the Pentagon but in the weeks preceding and following it across the country, marked the Great Divide in the Movement of the 1960s. I have recounted the story in personal, experiential terms because I believe no account of abstract ideas can explain the fate of the New Left. Only the lived experience of its participants holds the key to understanding its power and its self-destruction.

Part of what happened to me at the Pentagon was the deepening of an understanding that I found most clearly expressed years later when I read an interview with Jean-Paul Sartre, who said quite simply: "The real revolution will happen when we can all tell the truth about ourselves."

DOCUMENT 35

Ultra Resistance

On October 26, 1967, less than a week after the Pentagon demonstration, Father Philip Berrigan, Rev. James Mengel, Thomas Lewis, and David Eberhardt walked into the Selective Service offices in the Baltimore, Maryland Customs House and poured blood over the files. They did not try to escape;

they stood quietly until they were arrested. A few days later they were arraigned on charges of damaging government property, mutilating govern- ment records, and interfering with the functioning of the Selective Service System. Francine du Plessix Gray, writing in The New York Review of Books, *named the Baltimore Four and the groups that followed them the "ultra resistance." (See Michael Ferber and Staughton Lynd,* The Resistance *[Boston: Beacon Press, 1971], Chapter 14.)*

On May 17, 1968, Philip Berrigan and Thomas Lewis, with Philip's Jesuit brother Daniel Berrigan, and six other Catholic priests and laymen, destroyed 378 draft files at the Catonsville, Maryland draft board. Document 35A is the statement the Catonsville Nine released to the press.

Dozens of ultra resistance actions followed during the remaining years of the Vietnam War, and after. (See for example, Liane Ellision Norman, Hammer of Justice: Molly Rush and the Plowshares Eight *[Pittsburgh: PPI Books, 1989], an account of a 1980 action in which Molly Rush [see Introduction], Philip Berrigan, Daniel Berrigan, and others nonviolently invaded a General Electric plant that made nuclear warheads.)*

Document 35B is an account by a man who was inspired by the example of Daniel Berrigan to burn draft files in San Jose, California, on Christmas Eve, 1970. We do not know his name.

A. Daniel Berrigan, Philip Berrigan, and Others, Statement of the Catonsville Nine

(The following is a press statement released by the undersigned on the occasion described below.)

Today, May 17, 1968, we enter Local Board #33, Catonsville, Maryland, to seize the Selective Service records and to burn them outside with homemade napalm. (The recipe for napalm we took from the Special Forces Handbook, published by the Army's School of Special Warfare at Ft. Bragg, North Caro- lina.)

As American citizens, we have worked with the poor in the ghetto and abroad. In the course of our Christian ministry, we have watched our country produce more victims than an army of us could console or restore. Two of us face immediate sentencing for similar acts against Selective Service. All

---

Statement of the Catonsville Nine from *Daniel Berrigan: Poetry, Drama, Prose,* edited by Michael True, pp. 155–157. Copyright © 1988 by Daniel Berrigan. Reprinted by permission of Orbis Books.

of us identify with the victims of American oppression all over the world. We submit voluntarily to their involuntary fate.

We use napalm on these draft records because napalm has burned people to death in Vietnam, Guatemala, and Peru; and because it may be used in America's ghettos. We destroy these draft records not only because they exploit our young men, but because these records represent misplaced power, concentrated in the ruling class of America. Their power threatens the peace of the world; it isolates itself from public dissent and manipulates parliamentary process. And it reduces young men to a cost-efficiency item through the draft. In effect—if not in intent—the rulers of the United States want their global wars fought as cheaply as possible.

Above all, our protest attempts to illustrate why our country is torn at home and harassed abroad by enemies of its own creation. For a long time the United States has been an empire, and today it is history's richest nation. Representing 6 per cent of the world's people, our country controls half the world's productive capacity and two-thirds of its finance. It holds Northern and Southern America in an economic vise. In fifteen years time, economists think that its industry in Europe will be the third greatest industrial power in the world, after the United States and the Soviet Union. Our foreign profits run substantially higher than domestic profits. So industry flees abroad under Government patronage and protection from the CIA, counter-insurgency, and conflict management teams.

The military participates with economic and political sectors to form a triumvirate of power which sets and enforces policy. With an annual budget of more than 80 billion dollars, our military now controls over half of all Federal property (53 per cent, or 183 billion dollars) while U.S. nuclear and conventional weaponry exceeds that of the whole remaining world.

Peace negotiations with the North Vietnamese have begun in Paris. With other Americans, we hope a settlement will be reached, thus sparing the Vietnamese a useless prolongation of their suffering. However, this alone will not solve our nation's problems. The Vietnam War could end tomorrow and leave undisturbed the quality of our society, and its world role. Thailand, Laos, and the Dominican Republic have already been Vietnams. Guatemala, the Canal Zone, Bolivia, and Peru could be Vietnams overnight. Meanwhile, the colonies at home rise in rage and destructiveness. Our black people have concluded that after 350 years, their human acceptance is long overdue.

Injustice is the great catalyst of revolution. A nation that found life in revolution has now become the world's foremost counter-revolutionary force, not because the American people would have it that way, but because an expanding economy and continuing profits require an insistence on the *status quo*. Competitive capitalism as a system, and capitalists in general, must learn the hard lessons of justice, or a country may be swept away and humanity with it.

We believe that some property has no right to exist. Hitler's gas ovens, Stalin's concentration camps, atomic-bacteriological-chemical weaponry, files of conscription, and slum properties have no right to exist. When people starve for bread and lack decent housing, it is usually because the rich debase themselves with abuse of property, causing extravagance on their part and oppression and misery in others.

We are Catholic Christians who take the Christian gospel seriously. We hail the recent Papal encyclical, *The Development of Peoples*. Quotes like the following give us hope:

No one is justified in keeping for his exclusive use what he does not need, when others lack necessities.

A revolutionary uprising—save where there is open, manifest, and long-standing tyranny which does great damage to fundamental personal rights and dangerous harm to the common good of the country— produces new injustices, throws more elements out of balance, and brings on new disasters.

It is a question of building a world where every man, no matter what his race, religion, or nationality, can live a fully human life, freed from slavery imposed on him by other men or natural forces, a world where the poor man Lazarus can sit down at the same table with the rich man.

The hour for action has now sounded. At stake are the survival of so many children and so many families overcome by misery, with no access to conditions fit for human beings; at stake are the peace of the world and the future of civilization.

Despite such stirring words, we confront the Catholic church, other Christian bodies, and the synagogues of America with their silence and cowardice in the face of our country's crimes. We are convinced that the religious bureaucracy in this country is racist, guilty of complicity in war, and hostile to the poor. In utter fidelity to our faith, we indict religious leaders and their followers for their failure to serve our country and humankind.

Finally, we are appalled by the ruse of the American ruling class invoking pleas for "law and order" to mask and perpetuate injustice. Let our President and the pillars of society speak of "law and justice" and back up their words with deeds. Then there will be "order." We have pleaded, spoken, marched, and nursed the victims of their injustice. Now this injustice must be faced, and this we intend to do, with whatever strength of mind, body, and grace that God will give us. May He have mercy on our nation.

Rev. Daniel Berrigan	Majorie Bradford Melville
Rev. Philip Berrigan	Thomas Melville
Bro. David Darst	George Mische
John Hogan	Mary Moylan
Thomas Lewis	

B. "The Burning of Paper Instead of Lives"

Dan Berrigan once said, "Apologies, good friends, for the fracture of good order, the burning of paper instead of lives." I got the recipe for homemade napalm from a Special Forces handbook. I wanted to save lives by using a substance that was killing people in Vietnam. I wanted to show what draft files really were—death certificates, part of the paper process that sent people to kill and be killed.

I picked Christmas Eve as a symbol of hope. It is the Christians' festival of light, when light comes into the world with the birth of Jesus. My action would be my gift to Jesus and the community, like the Magis'.

A week before burning the draft files, I went to the San Jose Selective Service Office during regular office hours to case the joint. First, I walked into the front office and saw that the files were beyond a wall that was behind the counter. Several typists sat between me and the files. It would be difficult to reach the files, especially since I wanted to make sure I wouldn't start a fight getting to them.

I left the office and went around the corner to find a bathroom. I noticed another door. I put my hand on the doorknob and turned it. It opened, and there, to my surprise, was the file room. The file cabinets were only three feet away.

When I went in that back door on Christmas Eve, several file drawers were open, so it was simply a matter of pouring the napalm onto the files and lighting it. None of the people working in the office rushed to stop me. I went to a typewriter and tried to break off the "I" and "A" keys, I-A being the classification for people to be drafted, but I could only bend them. While the staff hid in the next room, I waited until the police and the FBI showed up to arrest me. I accepted the idea that I should be accountable for my actions.

I was taken to Santa Clara County jail, where I was taunted by the deputies with remarks like, "Hey, here's the big man for peace." Finally, after more than an hour of insults, I swore at the deputy who was fingerprinting me. Instantly, I felt ashamed because it was a negation of nonviolence. It was also just what they were waiting for. The deputy immediately laid into my face with sharp blows. I went down. He picked me up, pinned my hands behind my back, and then put a choke hold around my neck. Finally, I was thrown in the drunk tank for seven hours.

From *The Strength Not to Fight* by James W. Tollefson. Copyright © 1993 by James W. Tollefson, pp. 55–57, 180–182. Reprinted by permission of Little, Brown and Company.

I refused to let the jail nurses clean me up before I was taken to the U.S. commissioner for my arraignment. I showed up there with my mouth caked in blood. The commissioner was very disturbed by my condition. The newspapers reported that I had been roughed up. The sheriff's department responded by charging me with assault and battery. They said I had become unruly, wiped my inky hands on the deputy's shirt, lost my balance, and fell, striking my mouth. Later, a judge found me guilty of assault and battery.

After my arraignment, I was taken to a maximum security cell. As I was being led there, I passed a large cell block with a television on. Suddenly the guys started pointing to the TV and to me. Though I couldn't hear them through the security glass, it was clear they were saying they had seen me on TV. That was my first awareness that there was a hubbub about my action.

After a couple of days in the Santa Clara County jail, I was moved to San Francisco County jail. It was much rougher there, filled with poorer prisoners, and very overcrowded. The cells were filled with bunk beds, and mats filled the floor between the beds. There was a lot of tension and arguments, like, "Hey, don't put your hand on my towel. Don't put your hand on my blanket." The food was out of Dickens's *Bleak House,* watery, pasty gruel. Oatmeal gruel in the morning, hot water with a few things floating in it for lunch and dinner. In shame, one sheriff bought us oranges out of his own pocket.

We had an absolute lack of privacy, even for bodily functions. The lights were always on. The noise was incessant. I had no pattern of sleep. I couldn't ask, "Could I have some quiet, please?" So I just summoned up my inner resources and endured. After three months, about ten days before my trial, I was finally able to make bail—$50,000. My parish priest had raised it for me.

My trial began in late March 1971 and lasted four days. I came into it physically and emotionally exhausted from being in jail, deprived of sleep and food. I was incredibly nervous about speaking in front of the court but I felt I had a mission, a vision. I wanted to be accountable for my actions.

My defense was to admit that I had burned the files, but to argue that I had done it to stop a greater harm. I said that I broke into the draft office in order to stop the crimes of the war, the killing and the destruction. The judge said there was no evidence that the Selective Service System was committing a crime. He told the jury that it didn't matter why I burned the files. So the jury decided in only three hours that I was guilty of destruction of government property and interference with the Selective Service System—felonies. "We the jury find the defendant guilty as charged in the first indictment. We the jury find the defendant guilty as charged in the second indictment. We the jury find the defendant guilty as charged in the third indictment."

I asked that the jurors be polled individually. Several cried, one saying, "Sorrowfully, this is my verdict." I was sentenced to six years. The judge also ruled that I should be taken into custody immediately because I was a threat to society.

The image of my trial that has stuck most in my heart: as I was surrounded outside the courthouse by U.S. marshals taking me through the dark evening back to jail, one of the sobbing jurors stretched her hand out to me and said, "I'm sorry."

On the hundredth day of my imprisonment, I was transferred along with three other prisoners from Santa Clara County jail to Lompoc Federal Prison. We were quite a sight during the transfer. Our handcuffs were attached to a chain around our waists, with another chain running to leg irons that kept our feet from being more than a foot apart. It was difficult to move. I remember riding through the Valley of the Flowers, very conscious that it was the last time I'd see it for a long time. At the prison, I glanced up at gun towers as we drove through a fence with barbed wire on top. We stopped at an ugly, long, gray cement building. That was to be my home for the next two and a half years. . . .

I burned the files on December 24, 1970, and I was released on May 11, 1973. During that time, I spent twenty-eight and a half months in federal prison.

If you want to find out what it's like being in jail, get a board, go into your bathroom, put the board over the tub and some kind of mattress on top, leave the light and the radio on all the time, and have somebody stick your meals through the door. Try it for a weekend. You'll have a little better understanding of prison.

On the day of my release, I went into the dressing room to finally take off my prison khakis, the uniform I had worn for more than two years. I was given an old pair of blue jeans. Because of the sensory deprivation in prison, the jeans seemed like the brightest blue I had ever seen. Then I looked over the shirts and I picked out a bright red one.

My friends met me at the gate. I remember we went to a grocery store. It was incredible, seeing the stacks of food. I could get anything I wanted to eat. It was stunning. I was in a state of shock.

On my second day out of jail, Dan Berrigan coincidentally was not far away, giving a speech. We got together to visit. We did a radio interview and talked at his hotel. Later, Dan invited me to the University of Manitoba, where he was teaching classes in religion. I remember getting on the train in California and waking up the next morning in Klamath Falls, Oregon, with snow all around. Then we were in Vancouver, and then traveling across Canada. I had never before been out of the States. Or that far north. It was like a slap in the face, entering a world that seemed to me very different. The accents were different. The color of the money was different. From the train, I remember seeing herds of elk in the open fields.

Dan treated me like royalty. He's a gourmet cook, and stuffed me with food and wine. I spoke to his classes about my experiences. I relaxed. And I met a woman there and fell in love. It was wonderfully healing, everything my soul needed.

I finally felt, "I'm out of prison. I'm out. I'm really out."

I never forgot the tearful juror who held her hand out to me as I was being taken away to jail in handcuffs and waist and ankle chains. While I was in prison, she mailed a prayer card to me that said, "What do grace and glory mean except that we can endure in the midst of absolute fire, in the midst of incomprehensibility."

About three months after my release, I contacted her to see if she would be interested in talking about the trial. I wanted her to see that I had gone to prison and that I had survived. I wanted her to understand that I did not blame her. I wanted her to know I believed I had been imprisoned because of what I had done.

Eventually, I met at her house in the Bay Area with five of the jurors. We talked about things we hadn't been able to talk about during the trial, especially the war, which was still going on, and how we might respond to it. We talked about how juries were used to give legitimacy to a process where the defendant was essentially already guilty when the trial began. They talked about how the trial had made them more aware of the war, and of their own responsibilities. They told me how the trial had changed their lives.

Several years after my release from prison, I met a woman who told me that her son had gotten a letter from the draft board saying his files had been destroyed, and so he was not drafted. Because people like me burned draft files, perhaps he didn't have to die. Perhaps he didn't have to kill.

For many years now, I've been active with the Catholic Worker Movement. I cofounded the Family Kitchen, its feeding program. I helped start the Pacific Life Community, which undertook the campaign against the Trident submarine. Since Vietnam, I've been jailed about a dozen times for civil disobedience, the longest time for three months.

In the early 1980s, I was arrested for cutting some of the fences at the Trident submarine base and was sentenced to ninety days in jail for destruction of government property. Unlike my incarceration for burning draft files, this time I decided not to cooperate. I went limp and was dragged down the stairs from the federal courthouse to the county jail, and then through the halls to my cell. I decided not to eat or to leave my cell, and to do nothing except my bowel movements, which, with a little fasting, would not be an issue for long.

But there was one guard who took it as a personal affront that I wouldn't leave my cell. He made up his mind I was going to obey his orders. Every day, he came into my cell, threatening me. Finally, one day, he cranked the cell door open, grabbed me by the shoulders, and forced me up against the wall. He was probably expecting me to resist or to struggle with him, perhaps throw a punch, and then he could do whatever he wanted to me. But I did nothing. I just looked down at the floor. He became ashamed at what he did, let go of me, and left the cell very hurriedly. He came back later and apologized.

Arrest has never been important to me. Burning the draft files was important. Cutting the fence at the Trident base was important. Trespassing at the Trojan Nuclear Power Plant was important. When I took those actions, it was good to say "no" to death, and it was good to say "yes" to life.

DOCUMENT 36

Soldiers Against War

As the following selections demonstrate, a remarkable difference between resistance to World Wars I and II, and resistance to the Vietnam War, was that many of those resisting the Vietnam War were active-duty servicemen. Department of Defense figures show that between 17,000 and 18,000 members of the armed forces applied for noncombatant status or discharge as conscientious objectors between 1965 and 1973 (Charles C. Moskos and John Whiteclay Chambers II, The New Conscientious Objection: From Sacred to Secular Resistance *[New York: Oxford University Press, 1993], pp. 42–43, and sources cited on pp. 241–242). Countless others deserted, or resisted in other ways.*

Document 36A is the account of a young man who enlisted in February 1967. He trained as a combat medic at Fort Sam Houston, Texas, where about a third of the trainees were conscientious objectors. Then he was stationed at Fort Lewis, Washington, caring for paraplegics and quadriplegics just back from Vietnam. He filled out an application for conscientious objector status early in 1968. Later in the year he went AWOL. On October 12, 1968, he became one of the Presidio 27, prisoners at the Presidio, California stockade who sat down, sang "We Shall Overcome," and refused to fight in Vietnam.

Others, like Brian Willson (Document 36B), changed after they experienced the Vietnam War. Willson was a self-described "redneck." His father sympathized with the American Nazi Party, and looked down on Catholics, Jews, Italians, and Blacks. When Willson graduated from high school, he wanted to become an FBI agent. He enlisted in the Air Force in 1966, was sent to South Vietnam, and there was assigned to travel to villages after they had been bombed to assess the effectiveness of the raids. On one such occasion, he relates,

> *I looked at the face of a young mother on the ground whose eyes appeared to be open as she held two children in one arm, another child*

in the other. Upon closer examination I realized she and her children had been killed by bomb fragments. . . . I looked at that mother's face, what was left of it, and it flashed at that point in my mind that the whole idea of the threat of Communism was ridiculous. Somehow I couldn't see Communism on her face. I remember looking at that woman's face and thinking, "I wonder what a Communist looks like?" All I saw was the face of a mother no older than twenty holding her children.

After the end of the war, Willson's anguish led him to a moment when he sat down in front of a train that was transporting munitions to be shipped to Central America, was run over, and lost his legs (see Document 48).

Other veterans sought to exorcise their pain and guilt by symbolically separating themselves from all things military. At an occasion in January-February 1969, christened "Dewey Canyon III" for reasons explained in the narrative that follows (Document 36C), over 1,000 anti-war Vietnam veterans convened in Washington, D.C. Some in wheelchairs and on crutches, they sought to enter Arlington Cemetery, but were denied entrance. They proceeded to set up a campsite on the Washington, D.C. Mall. Notwithstanding an injunction approved by the Supreme Court of the United States, the veterans refused to move. After three days of lobbying, the veterans cast down their medals and ribbons on the steps of the Capitol.

A. The Presidio

I was born in Missouri and was a student at the University of Missouri in 1966. I believed everyone should do their duty. I had no feeling that there was anything wrong with being in the military. When I dropped out of school late that year, I knew I'd be drafted, so I went to the army recruiter to enlist. I told him I wanted to be an occupational therapist. He looked in his book and said that an occupational therapist was 91-A, so he gave me my written guarantee that I would be a 91-A. I enlisted in February 1967. I soon learned that 91-A was basic combat medic. That was my first lesson that something was wrong with the military.

The military concentrates on the worst macho aspects of eighteen-year-old boys. As time passed, most of us, including myself, got more and more stupid—more chauvinistic and more racist. After I did basic training, I went to medics' training at Fort Sam Houston in Texas, where a third of the guys were COs. They were in sharp contrast to the rest of us—thoughtful, introspective, and gentle. Over time, they became my friends. I learned to play the harmonica from one CO.

After leaving Fort Sam, I was stationed at Madigan General Hospital near Fort Lewis. I took care of paraplegics and quadriplegics, guys fresh back from the field who had caught a fragment in the spine or had other injuries. They were young guys, seventeen, eighteen, or nineteen years old, whose whole lives had been changed forever. They were very bitter. They'd lie there and tell me how they had been assigned to duties in Nam like guarding somebody's rubber plantation. None of them felt that they had sacrificed for a worthy cause. They hated the war.

For several months, I spent every day at work with those guys—who couldn't turn the pages of a book, who couldn't even shit by themselves, who begged me to kill them. All of us medics had discussions about whether we should kill our patients. I had been an Eagle Scout, a churchgoer, a good, clean American kid from generations of military people in small Missouri towns. But at Madigan, I became filled with a sense of betrayal, and outraged by the duplicity and ugliness underneath the grinning mask of Disneyland America.

About halfway through my year at Madigan, I decided to apply for CO status. I told my commander, who tried to argue me out of it by promising he'd never ask me to pick up a weapon. I believed him, but I persisted, and filled out the CO application in early 1968.

The army rejected my application and sent me orders to report to Vietnam. I probably would have gone to Nam, but then something happened that enraged me: I got orders to report to the rifle range. I reminded my commander that he had promised man-to-man that he would never make me pick up a gun. But he just grinned and said *he* wasn't giving me the order—the colonel was.

Out on the range, a major ordered me to pick up the rifle. I refused. He warned that I could get five years in prison, but I still refused. Instead of prison, they confined me to base, gave me an Article 15—a nonjudicial punishment—and took away my stripes. I felt betrayed.

I had a forty-five-day leave before going to Vietnam. I spent the time in Berkeley. It was the summer of 1968, and the country was on fire. I remember sitting around the kitchen table in our little apartment, listening to the radio reports from Chicago during the Democratic Convention. It was like a picture from behind the Iron Curtain, everybody huddled in the twilight as the announcer described kids being beaten and gassed by the police. Then suddenly the announcer began coughing, yelling, "Oh! Oh! You pig!" as the police attacked him.

At Bay Area antiwar demonstrations, where I served as a medic, I saw that the cops were very brutal. Once, I watched cops go for a pregnant woman and poke her in the belly. This was not the America I had grown up believing in. I felt I was getting cheated out of my America the Beautiful.

I thought about refusing to get on the plane to Vietnam, but the army's practice was to throw resisters on the plane, and then no lawyer in the world could help you. So on the advice of my lawyer, I went AWOL. It was a legal tactic to keep me in the United States long enough to appeal my CO application. I'd be dropped from my unit and my case would be delayed while new orders were cut. And I would be punished for the relatively light crime of being AWOL rather than the heavy charge of five years in jail if I refused an order to go to Vietnam.

After being AWOL for forty-five days, I turned myself in at a demonstration in San Francisco called GIs and Veterans March for Peace. I was one of four AWOL GIs who gave speeches and then stepped across the line at the Presidio military base. I remember it was my father's birthday, Saturday, October 12, 1968.

In the Presidio stockade, I linked up with a guy named Darrel, the leader of a group of nine AWOL GIs who had been in jail after they chained themselves to clergymen until MPs used bolt cutters to arrest them. We met with other guys and decided we'd have a sit-down strike on the following Monday.

On Monday morning, about a hundred prisoners were in the yard in formation. At the planned moment, at a certain point in the roll call, twenty-seven of us walked to a corner, sat down, and began singing "We Shall Overcome."

The guards shit bricks. They ordered us to return to formation, but we sang louder. Then the commander read us the articles of mutiny, a capital crime with no maximum sentence. One guy stood up and read our demands, which included an end to the war, opposition to racism, and better treatment in the stockade. A fire truck arrived, but the firemen refused to squirt us. Then a company of MPs in full riot gear and gas masks arrived. I thought, "Oh, boy, they're really going to fuck us up now." Using various amounts of impoliteness along the way, they carried us bodily back to the stockade and threw us in a common cell.

Two days later, we were charged with mutiny. Our case was called the Presidio 27. It got a lot of publicity. Nearly every issue of *Playboy* magazine in late '68 and all of '69, in the section on civil liberties, mentioned our case.

The first trial took place in early 1969. I was supposed to be in that group, but I got hepatitis and so the judge sent me to the hospital, delaying my trial. Darrel had escaped and in the hospital I considered doing it, too, with a friend. At night, we sawed the bars, then put soap and dirt in the marks. It was right out of *The Great Escape*. But then a Catholic priest visited me. He said that I was the only ringleader left, and it wasn't right that we who had organized the protest would leave everyone else behind to do time in prison. He was right, and so I chose to stay — though I helped finish the sawing and eventually waved goodbye to my friend.

One of the lowest points in my life was when the convictions in those first trials resulted in sentences of sixteen to eighteen years in prison. Because I was a ringleader, I expected to be treated even more harshly. When I heard about the sentences, suicide entered my mind for a nanosecond. I thought about setting myself on fire like the Buddhist monks in Vietnam, hoping to get attention so the other guys would get off. But I wasn't so sure it would help, and anyway, I didn't really want to commit suicide.

I finally went to trial along with thirteen other guys at Fort Ord near Monterey. By then, there had been a lot of publicity and so the military backed off harsh sentences. I got fifteen months in Leavenworth Federal Penitentiary.

Prisons are worse than most people think. When I tell people about my experience, they tend not to believe me, or they think I'm exaggerating. I went to a play once about a guy who was arrested and brutalized by the police. For me, the play was very real. Standing in the street afterward, still covered with sweat from the intense experience, I overheard people say the play was overdone and not believable. I realized then that people don't believe the real shit about prison. I personally witnessed guards break people's fingers. One night, all the prisoners in solitary confinement had their legs broken by the guards. People got raped by other prisoners. People committed suicide. I saw people do horrible self-mutilation. There are plenty of horror stories. It's a joke that prison is supposed to teach prisoners how to live in society by treating them in a subhuman way. It's a joke.

One thing I learned, though, is that it's not that hard to be a pacifist in prison. I found I could take a beating with the best of them. It's not any worse to be beaten up in prison than it is to be beaten up in high school. In fact, for pacifists, in some ways it's easier, because at least your head is clear.

Prisoners understand if you refuse to be complicit with society's bullshit. Prisoners know better than anybody how ugly America is. If you're in jail saying, "I ripped the mask off of America," everybody goes, "Right on!" You get more respect in prison than you do on the streets.

If you know what you're standing for and you're consistent, you can create a kind of moral authority in prison that people will respect. For example, one day, this naked gay prisoner about to get raped came screaming to me and climbed up on my bunk. All these ruffians surrounded us. I thought, "Oh, fuck, should I help him or just stay out of it?" I decided to get into my lotus position and I started chanting and chanting to beat the band. All the guys just stood there, caught off guard, looking at each other and shaking their heads. One guy finally said, "Man, we almost did a bad thing." Then most of them shuffled off. Two guys sat down and chanted along with me. It was a bizarre scene in the sixties, even in prison.

I learned that there are a hell of a lot of good people in jail, especially among nonwhite prisoners. In a country with few opportunities within the system for nonwhites, people who have anything on the ball sometimes find ways to advance themselves outside the system. Unfortunately, they may get caught and end up in jail. In a way, they're the cream of the crop, not the dregs.

I remember one amazing African-American guy who was there for having killed his commander in Vietnam. He had memorized Chairman Mao's Little Red Book. He would chant it in the style of African signifying. Another guy had been a student in junior college in Sacramento when he became fascinated with the cables sent by the U.S. embassy in Moscow during the Russian Revolution. He fell in love with the revolution and became an intellectual Communist. He didn't know any other Communists or any organizations. Eventually, he quit school and was drafted. When he got orders to go to Vietnam, he refused because he said he couldn't fight against his comrades. Of course, they threw the book at him.

One of the hardest times was in solitary. You want human interaction so badly. You want to be treated like a human being. Sometimes, a guard would slip you a cigarette. You'd think, "Wow, a human kindness!" But a short time later, that same guard, with a few others, would come in and beat you up. Then a few days later, he'd say he's sorry, he was only following orders, and he'd offer you another cigarette. If you take that cigarette, you're setting yourself up for a very painful experience. When an asshole treats you like a dog and doesn't pretend to like you, you can harden your heart to him, but when you feel connected to someone, there's a deep human pain when he hurts you. . . .

One day, I opened up *Life* magazine and saw a photograph of what was billed as these crazy people called hippies living in San Francisco in a strange place called Haight-Ashbury. The article condemned them, but when I saw that picture, I realized there were other people in the world who felt just like me. I had never thought about growing my hair long, I didn't know anything about dope, and I was in the army. But there was something about the people in that picture that made me feel for a moment as if I was not alone.

When I was in medics' training at Fort Sam Houston, one of the COs had a poster of Jesus carrying a rifle slung over his shoulder. The message was that it wasn't good enough just to refuse to be personally complicit in the war. If your country has gone crazy, then you must act—even if you sacrifice your own path to heaven by being violent. The crimes of the country were so great that it wasn't good enough just to be an individual pacifist.

I settled down in Leavenworth prison to do my time. I didn't know then that the Presidio 27 was held in such high esteem by other GIs. A lot of the soldiers knew about us. All the while, our support committee on the outside kept pushing and pushing and pushing, and never let go of the issue.

Finally, with all the publicity, the government decided it was better to release us. One day, an official came to me in prison and said I would be paroled. I was sure they wouldn't do it. "Forget it. I don't want it. Only suck-butts get parole."

They tried to make me go through the prerelease ritual of taking classes about readjusting to society, but I refused. I figured they were going to dangle parole on a string in front of me and make me jump for it and jump for it while they laughed. Fuck that. I had gotten tough enough in prison to protect my emotions.

But, sure enough, within a couple of weeks, they released all of us. My wife, who had moved to Kansas to be near me, was waiting for me. It was winter 1970, and they gave me a little car coat, a suit, a bus ticket to Kansas City, and twenty-five dollars. Of course, everybody in the town of Leavenworth knew I was just out of jail, because I had the same stupid car coat that everybody else had. I figured the first thing I needed to do was to get rid of that stupid coat.

I was officially on parole, but I never did any of the parole classes or met any of the other requirements. The military just cut me loose.

I was still a pretty gentle person, but after being in prison, I was definitely down for the revolution. I drove to San Francisco with my wife, where I immediately began working with the Pacific Counseling Service, which was made up of people who had organized support for the Presidio 27. At Pacific, I worked against the war and helped GIs who wanted to become COs. We differed from the traditional CO organizations because we were perfectly willing to help people who didn't really fit the CO rules. We figured if someone applied for CO status, that helped to clog up the system. We offended some of the other CO organizations, which were concerned that the CO law might be eliminated if it was abused.

I stayed in San Francisco for six months, and then I left to open a new counseling office near Fort Lewis and to work on an underground GI newspaper, the *Lewis-McChord Free Press*. I worked there for a couple of years, but by then I was in my mid-twenties, and I felt I was getting a little old for GI work. That sounds silly now that I'm in my forties. But the GI movement was made up mostly of young GIs. So I left and got a job in a factory.

Most of the Presidio 27 were working-class guys. Our actions didn't help us a bit personally. We couldn't use the GI Bill. We didn't get any veterans' benefits. But none of us, as far as I know, has ever expressed the slightest regret. We were the government's worst nightmare, individuals within the military who followed orders on the basis of conscience. That's what Nuremberg was about. Even though we did the confinement, Uncle Sam was the loser. We helped to end the war. I have no regrets whatsoever. Absolutely no regrets.

I remember during my medics' training feeling very inspired by a photograph of Dr. Howard Levy, an army officer who refused to train Green Berets. In the picture, he was being hauled off to jail, this little shrimp of a guy carted away in handcuffs by big, beefy MPs. The picture was obviously taken to denigrate him, but I found it inspirational and stuck it on my locker at Fort Sam. I also had a poster of a reservist from the Bay Area who refused to be activated. In the background of the picture were three guys called the Fort Hood 3, some of the earliest GI resisters to the war. The caption said, "I followed the Fort Hood 3. Who's going to follow me?" Well, I was the one who followed. And many more followed me.

Years later, I met a guy at a party. I had never seen the guy before, but when he heard my name, he suddenly started pumping my hand. It turned out that he was the army's company clerk who had read my CO application. He hadn't cared one whit about the war, but across his desk came my application, and when he read it, it turned him around. He became a GI resister.

In the sixties and seventies, my generation was going to make a new society. We thought we would hand the torch to the next generation, and together we would march toward a better future. Well, we looked back, and that next generation wasn't there. It went into yuppiedom.

Once you step in shit, you always recognize the smell. When *The Deer Hunter* came out, several of my buddies and I thought the movie smelled. We figured it was trying to rewrite the history of Vietnam and would help lay the basis for another war. So we passed out leaflets in front of movie theaters, saying the movie reversed the good guys and the bad guys in the war. Most people thought we were just being stupid veterans who couldn't lay Vietnam to rest. "Put it behind you, man. It's over. The United States isn't doing that shit anymore." Several of us went to the Academy Awards in Los Angeles, where we got our heads caved in by the LAPD. I was charged with two felony counts of assaulting their clubs with my head. The charges were later dropped.

During the 1980s, I worked against the use of white phosphorus in El Salvador. I know what white phosphorus does, because as a medic I took care of people who were burned by it. White phosphorus takes the moisture out of your skin by sucking the oxygen from the water molecules. So when that stuff spews out of an antipersonnel weapon, you can cover the burn, but you can't extinguish it. The phosphorus will use the moisture from your flesh to fuel the fire. It will burn down to the bone, and beyond, until it's exhausted. I knew it was being used in El Salvador, but we couldn't convince the American people that they needed to speak up. That was a very lonely time for me.

Like many guys, I have had to fight with one hand against the military, and the other hand against my family. My father was a career military officer, who couldn't handle the fact that I went the opposite way. So he cut me off completely. He literally wrote me out of his will. When my children were born, he refused to recognize them as his grandchildren.

I no longer have much contact with my parents. Twenty-five years after I refused to fight in Vietnam.

B. Brian Willson, Vietnam

After two years of studying law and penology, I was drafted in 1966 into the United States military. I chose the alternative of enlisting in the Air Force

From S. Brian Willson, *On Third World Legs* (Chicago: Charles H. Kerr, 1992), pp. 16–20. Reprinted by permission.

as an officer, a four-year commitment that I believed would be easier, more educational, provide more income, and likely be a lot safer than an Army tour in Vietnam.

My first two years in the Air Force were served in a relatively plush assignment as a member of the Inspector General's staff of a major command headquartered at Andrews Air Force Base near Washington, D.C. My enthusiasm began to wear off as I observed incompetence and, in the perception of this "country boy," licentious behavior among many of the officers and their wives and girl friends. I even wondered whether in fact decisions about going to war, and how to fight once engaged in war, could be made with careful thought by the kind of men with and around whom I was working. Occasionally I began to wonder whether the Vietnam War itself was legitimate. For the most part though I continued to believe in "America," its dreams of the good life, and the morality of the war against Communism being waged 12,000 miles west of my home town.

Then I received my orders to Vietnam. A clue that something new was brewing inside me emerged during the special three-month training our unit underwent in Kentucky before deployment to Vietnam. I found the bayonet training repulsive, a surprising response for a fairly macho, very athletic guy who supported United States wars and the military necessity to fight them. I continually refused actually to plunge the bayonet into the dummy and was reprimanded. More importantly I began seriously to question the war in Vietnam and expressed this concern to my superiors. I was reprimanded further.

When the time came to deploy I accompanied the six fire teams of six men each and a mortar crew under my command. Before I knew it we had flown across the Pacific Ocean and were landing for our mission assignment at Binh Thuy Air Base, nearly 100 miles south of Saigon (now Ho Chi Minh City) on the Bassac River in the Mekong Delta near the city of Can Tho. During 1969 I served as Section Leader of the combat security police unit protecting the base, with the rank of First Lieutenant. We were protecting the airplanes so they could launch their bombing missions at neighboring villages and return safely to a well-protected base.

Binh Thuy was a frequently attacked base. It was the sometimes headquarters for the South Vietnamese Air Force, and its fleet of small fighter/bombers needed the extra security we were supposed to provide. Vietnamese Vice President and former commander of the Vietnamese Air Force, Nguyen Cao Ky, used to fly his own plane in and out of Binh Thuy on a regular basis.

Shortly after we arrived, the Vietnamese base commander, Col. Anh, asked me, the officer in charge of the special combat security unit, to perform some additional security and "intelligence" functions. I was to travel fairly routinely to different designated hamlets and villages as well as to Can Tho City to meet with identified Vietnamese in order to gather information that might be helpful in determining when and from which direction Binh Thuy might be attacked on the ground or by mortars and recoilless rifles. Also, I was occasionally to travel to villages within hours after they had been bombed by South Vietnamese pilots in order to conduct a ground assessment of the "success" of the raids as measured by damages and deaths, and to double check the reliability of air reconnaissance. Normally I would be accompanied by a trusted South Vietnamese lieutenant. Apparently they didn't trust their own Vietnamese pilots so they wanted a U.S. officer to go with a Vietnamese officer into the villages to assess the success of the bombing missions.

Col. Anh explained that this was to be a "quiet" assignment, probably because of its quasi-official nature. I said, "Fine." I thought this extra assignment was a bit strange, but it sounded interesting, and I would meet English-speaking Vietnamese of whom there were a surprising number in the Delta.

Meantime Binh Thuy was attacked on the average of about once a week. The base regularly received bodies, usually already in body bags, of Vietnamese and United States dead on their way to the morgue in Saigon. The smell of death was everywhere. I came to feel an affinity with the Vietnamese as people, and soon was identified by other officers as a "gook lover." I was beginning to know why the bayonet drill had so repulsed me. Why were we half way around the world killing people we knew little and cared less about? What did we really know about the history of the Vietnamese people, their culture, their religion, politics, mores, etc.? What did we as people of the United States know about anything outside our borders? What did it matter to us? What did we really know about our own history? Killing and maiming thousands of human beings by weekly bombings began to seem bestial, barbaric to me. I started speaking out against the war to my superiors.

One day I encountered an old Vietnamese man fleeing his village as it was being bombed. I was driving near the village as the bombing started, not knowing in advance that I was about to be in harm's way myself. I was in a bit of shock because of it. The old man's eyes and my eyes met at about forty yards' distance before he fled in a different direction. I sped off in my jeep thinking that I was merely experiencing a nightmare. I had an impulse to tell the man, whom I have come to call Hue, that I was terribly sorry about the bombing, that I didn't know why we were causing this destruction. I just wanted to go home to scream and weep. Such insanity! I couldn't believe I was really experiencing it. It must be a nightmare. Please let it be a nightmare! I jabbed the palm of my hand with my Swiss army knife. I drew a drop of blood. I was not waking up from a bad dream.

Not long after, while assessing the "success" of a bombing mission in a small village south of Sa Dec, I looked at the face of a young mother on the ground whose eyes appeared to be open as she held two children in one arm, another child in the other. Upon closer examination I realized she and her children had been killed by bomb fragments. Napalm had apparently burned much of her face, including her eyelids. I stared into her eyes from a close distance, leaning over to do so. Tears streamed down my face. Many other bodies, including the bodies of farm animals, were strewn about. All the small houses (that we called "huts") had been leveled by direct hits or by fire. Subsequently I learned that over 90% of the victims of U.S. firepower were civilians, the majority women and children.

I looked at that mother's face, what was left of it, and it flashed at that point in my mind that the whole idea of the threat of Communism was ridiculous. Somehow I couldn't see Communism on her face. I remember looking at that woman's face and thinking, "I wonder what a Communist looks like?" All I saw was the face of a mother no older than twenty holding her children. All of them were dead. I said, "My God, this bombing, this war, is a lie. I've been living a lie. What does all this mean? These people are just persons, just human beings." I knew then that I didn't know anything.

The Vietnamese lieutenant accompanying me asked why I was crying. I stood straight up and turned to him and replied, "Because she is my sister, and these are my children, too." I have no idea from where that feeling and response came. It must have been a very deep and previously unknown place within me. The lieutenant angrily responded: "They are just Communists." I didn't say anything. I knew that I was in a different place. A different Brian Willson was emerging. I did not know how to talk. I did not know how I was going to survive emotionally or intellectually. We rode together in stone silence the hour or so back to Binh Thuy.

Back at Binh Thuy the eyes of the mother on the ground were etched in my consciousness. I have come to call her Mai Ly. I am sorry my dear Mai Ly, I said. I am sorry. You have penetrated my soul, forever.

I was never to be the same again. During these days and weeks in April and May of 1969 I was "born again" in the most meaningful of senses. Sometime in late May, I was enjoying dinner with a Vietnamese family in Can Tho City. The family was very political, and together we were expressing our outrage at the barbarism being unleashed on the Vietnamese by the United States. I came to have dinner with this family because one of its members worked in the Air Force Base library. She noticed the books I borrowed, and discerned that I was at odds with the other Americans at the Base.

After dinner the family sang some songs, one of which, accompanied by musical instruments, they translated into English specially for me. The song was dedicated to, and about, a North American hero to the Vietnamese people—Norman R. Morrison. Four of the lines went something like this:

> The flame which burned you will clear and lighten life
> And many new generations of people will find the horizon,
> Then a day will come when the American people
> Will rise, one after another, for life.

I was initially stunned. It was like being in shock. When Norman in protest of United States bombing of Vietnam burned himself to death in front of the River entrance to the Pentagon a little after 5 p.m. on Tuesday, November 2, 1965, it had had very little impact on me. At the time of his death I was in my Washington, D.C. apartment, studying my daily law school assignment.

It did not register for a while that this was the same Norman Morrison who had also graduated from Chautauqua High School, and had been the first Eagle Scout I ever knew. I thought in 1965 that what Norman did was a foolish act, and felt sorry that Norman had cracked, and shamed himself.

But now I was in a pleasant room with compassionate Vietnamese people sharing my own outrage at the war. "And many new generations of people will find the horizon." I broke into tears, trembling with emotions in the midst of some kind of metaphysical, spiritual experience, for the first time sensing a profound connection with Norman. This connection, and power, has remained with me ever since.

While still serving in Vietnam I began to write letters and memorandums against the war, citing the Hague Convention, the Geneva Convention, and the Nuremburg Principles. I was shipped back to the United States after 151 days in Vietnam. There was no explanation. I knew why; they didn't have to specify the reasons.

I served one final year in the military with the rank of Captain as the supply squadron executive officer at England Air Force Base in Alexandria, Louisiana. I played a lot of basketball while anticipating that formal charges might be brought to trial. Nothing did happen. I was honorably discharged.

I had started my journey as a recovering white male.

C. Operation Dewey Canyon III

Operation Dewey Canyon I took place during January and February 1969. During a five-day period in February, elements of the Third Marine Division invaded Laos. Operation Dewey Canyon II was the name given to the first seven days of the South Vietnamese invasion of Laos in February 1971. The name of the operation was subsequently changed. Operation Dewey Canyon III took place in Washington, D.C., April 19 through April 23, 1971. It was called "a limited incursion into the country of Congress."

Sunday/April 18, 1971

Anti-war Vietnam veterans from nearly every state begin filtering into West Potomac Park. By nightfall, only 900 have registered and the veteran leaders are worried that they will not have the requisite numbers for the desired impact.

"Chronology: Operation Dewey Canyon III" from *The New Soldier,* edited by David Thorne and George Butler, Collier Books, 1971.

Monday/April 19, 1971

About 1,100 veterans move across the Lincoln Memorial Bridge to Arlington Cemetery, some in wheelchairs, some on crutches. Mothers who lost their sons in Vietnam (Gold Star Mothers) head the procession.

A brief ceremony for the war dead on both sides is conducted by Reverend Jackson Day on the small plot of grass outside the Cemetery beneath the Tomb of the Unknown Soldier and the grave of John F. Kennedy. (Reverend Day had resigned his military chaplainship a few days before.)

After the ceremony, a small delegation of mothers and veterans is barred from entering the Cemetery and lays two memorial wreaths at the entrance. The march re-forms and makes its way to the Capitol.

The march reaches the Capitol steps. Congressman Paul McCloskey, who joined the march en route, and Representatives Bella Abzug, Donald Edwards, and Ogden Reid address the crowd. Jan Crumb, member of the executive committee of VVAW, formally presents sixteen demands to Congress.

The veterans march to the Mall and establish a campsite on a small grassy quadrangle between Third and Fourth streets. Some veterans go directly into the halls of Congress to lobby against the war.

Washington District Court of Appeals lifts an injunction barring veterans from camping on the Mall. The injunction had been requested by the Justice Department.

Tuesday/April 20, 1971

About 200 veterans attend hearings by the Senate Foreign Relations Committee on proposals to end the war.

Veterans lobby all day in Congress.

A contingent of 200 veterans, feeling that the affront of the day before cannot be overlooked, marches from the Mall back to Arlington Cemetery. They march single file across the Lincoln Memorial Bridge. The Superintendent tries to stop the veterans at the gates but then backs down.

In the afternoon, a guerilla theater performance is given on the steps of the Capitol.

Senators Claiborne Pell and Philip Hart hold a fund-raising party for the veterans. During the party, it is announced that Chief Justice Warren Burger has reversed the decision of the Court of Appeals—allegedly, the speediest process of an appeal to the Supreme Court on record. The injunction is once again in effect and the veterans are given until 4:30 the following afternoon to break camp.

Wednesday/April 21, 1971

A contingent of fifty veterans marches to the Pentagon to turn themselves in as war criminals. They are not arrested.

Lobbying on Capitol Hill continues all day. Guerilla theater is performed in front of the Justice Department.

At 4:30 PM, the appointed hour of eviction from the camp, an alarm clock rings over the microphone on the speaker's platform. No police are in sight. The area is packed with curious onlookers. The Supreme Court is meeting in special session.

At 5:30 PM, Ramsey Clark announces that the Supreme Court has offered the veterans an option: Stay on the Mall, don't sleep, and the government won't arrest you; or sleep on the Mall and the government will arrest you. The veterans retire into their various delegations and vote, in effect, on whether to sleep or not to sleep. By a close vote a majority choose to sleep. All agree to abide by that decision.

Washington Park Police state they have no intention of inspecting the campsite during the night. The cast of the musical *Hair* entertains the troops.

Senator Edward Kennedy makes a midnight visit to the Mall. He remains for one hour, talking and singing with the veterans.

The veterans sleep on the Mall without interruption.

Thursday/April 22, 1971

A large group of veterans march to the steps of the Supreme Court to ask the Court why it has not ruled on the constitutionality of the war. They sing *God Bless America.* One hundred and ten are arrested for disturbing the peace and are led off the steps with their hands clasped behind their heads.

John Kerry testifies before a special session of the Senate Foreign Relations Committee for two hours.

Lobbying on Capitol Hill continues all day.

A District Court judge angrily dissolves his injunction order, rebuking Justice Department lawyers for requesting the court order and then not enforcing it.

Veterans stage a candlelight march around the White House. A huge American flag is carried upside down as a signal of distress. The march ends back at the camp when the flag carriers mount the stage.

Friday/April 23, 1971

Veterans cast down their medals and ribbons on the steps of the Capitol.

Congressman Jonathan Bingham holds hearings with former intelligence and public information officers over distortion of news and information concerning the war.

Senators George McGovern and Philip Hart hold hearings on atrocities committed by U.S. soldiers in Vietnam.

Veterans begin breaking camp. A tree, donated by the veterans, is planted as a symbolic plea for the preservation of all life and the environment.

The quadrangle on the Mall is vacant. Not one act of violence has been committed. They came in peace.

The war in Indochina continues.

It was the absolute top of the mountain. This was the final act of contempt for the way the executive branch is forcing us to wage war. It was like two hours before I could stop crying. It was very, very, very heavy.

—Rusty Sachs
Vietnam Veteran

My parents told me that if I really did come down here and turned in my medals, that they never wanted anything more to do with me. That's not an easy thing to take. I still love my parents.

My wife doesn't understand what happened to me when I came home from Nam. She said she would divorce me if I came down here because she wanted my medals for our son to see when he grew up.

I'm not proud of these medals. I'm not proud of what I did to receive them. I was in Vietnam for a year and our company policy was to take no prisoners. A whole year we never took one prisoner alive. Just wasted them with the door gun, dropped down to check their bodies for maps or valuables, and split. If it was dead and Vietnamese, it was a VC.

—Ron Ferrizzi
Vietnam Veteran

PART XI

A NEW CATHOLICISM

DOCUMENT 37

Dorothy Day

Dorothy Day (1891–1980) helped to found the Catholic Worker movement in 1933. Her previous experience included working for the New York Socialist daily, The Call, *and hunger-striking for ten days along with other suffragettes in prison during World War I (see Document 12). She became a Catholic in 1928.*

The inspiration for the Catholic Worker movement came from Peter Maurin (1877–1949), a French working-class intellectual. In Document 37A, Dorothy Day describes how Peter Maurin came into her life. He advocated a variety of self-help strategies whereby the poor, even in the depths of depression, could begin to build a new society within the shell of the old. Maurin proposed a newspaper that the poor could read and afford; houses of hospitality to serve the unemployed with food and shelter; the creation of rural communities for those no longer needed by urban capitalism; and voluntary poverty. All these ideas became realities. The paper, The Catholic Worker, *soon had a circulation over 100,000; over thirty houses of hospitality were established, as were nine farming communes.*

At a time when Marxism, socialism, and communism enjoyed wide support, Dorothy Day told the unemployed that religion is not—or need not be—the opiate of the people (Document 37B).

Dorothy Day and The Catholic Worker *consistently challenged the tradi-tional advocacy of "just war" theory by the Catholic Church. They said that Catholics should be conscientious objectors to all wars. At the suggestion of Ammon Hennacy (see Document 15A), Dorothy Day and others refused to take shelter during New York City's air raid drills for so-called civil defense in the late 1950s. She went to jail as a result (Document 37C). In August 1963, the* Worker *called what may have been the first United States demon-stration against the war in Vietnam, a picket outside the residence of the South Vietnamese government's observer to the United Nations. At a demonstration against the war on October 15, 1965, Catholic Worker activist David Miller burned his draft card rather than give a speech. His was apparently the first draft card burning following enactment of a law by Congress making destruction of a draft card a felony.*

Here we can only give glimpses of a prophetic woman and movement that had enormous influence on nonviolence in the United States. (For more, see among other sources Voices from the Catholic Worker, *ed. Rosalie Riegle Troester [Philadelphia: Temple University Press, 1993], and the biographies and histories therein cited.)*

A. Peter Maurin

I was living with my younger brother, John, and Teresa, his Spanish wife. Our kitchen looked out on a back yard where there were no silanthuses—that tough weed of a tree—but fig trees, carefully cultivated and guarded by Italians, who corseted them in hay and burlap against the cold during the winter. In the summer the trees bore fruit. There were peach trees, privet hedges growing as high as trees, and rows of widow's-tears. Petunias and marigolds gave us a small riot of color—and delightful fragrance, too, when-ever the rain washed the air clear of the neighborhood cooking smells.

We were in the third year of the depression. Roosevelt had just been elected President. Every fifth adult American—twelve million in all—was unemployed. No smoke came from the factories. Mortgages on homes and farms were being foreclosed, driving more people to the city and loading them onto the already overburdened relief rolls. In New York long, bedraggled breadlines of listless men wound along city streets. On the fringes, by the rivers, almost every vacant lot was a Hooverville, a collection of jerry-built shanties where the homeless huddled in front of their fires.

An air of excitement, of impending social change, with the opportunity to implement our social ideas, buoyed up all who were young and had ideas. We met, we talked endlessly, feeling that this was the time to try new things. I had just come back from Washington, where I was covering the story of the Hunger March of the Unemployed Councils for *Commonweal* and the story of the Farmers' Conference for *America*. I had been a journalist most of my days, and I was earning my living by freelance writing of articles about the social order.

Sitting in the kitchen one afternoon, I was working on a book about the unemployed—it was to be a novel—when a knock came at the door. Tessa was just starting supper. John was getting ready to go to work—he was a copy boy on a Hearst paper at the time. They were both twenty years old and expecting their first baby. Tessa had a warm, radiant look, a glowing look. John was more reserved.

Tessa, who was always very hospitable, welcomed the man at the door. A short, broad man (he was fifty-seven, I found out later, but my first impression was that he was older) came in and started talking at once—casually, informally, almost as though he were taking up a conversation where it had been left off. There was a gray look about him: he had gray hair, cut short and scrubby; gray eyes; strong features; a pleasant mouth; and short-fingered, broad hands, evidently used to heavy work, such as with a pick and shovel. He wore the kind of old clothes that have so lost their shape and finish that it's impossible to tell whether they are clean or not. But Peter Maurin, agitator and soon to be founder of what came to be known as The Catholic Worker movement, was, as I later learned, always neat.

Tessa went on with her work and the newcomer stood before me, declaiming one of what John named his "Easy Essays":

> People go to Washington
> asking the government
> to solve their economic problems,
> while the Federal government
> was never intended
> to solve men's economic problems.
> Thomas Jefferson says that
> the less government there is
> the better it is.
> If the less government there is,
> the better it is,
> then the best kind of government
> is self-government.
> If the best kind of government
> is self-government,
> then the best kind of organization
> is self-organization.

When the organizers try
to organize the unorganized,
then the organizers
don't organize themselves.
And when the organizers
don't organize themselves,
nobody organizes himself,
and when nobody organizes himself
nothing is organized.

He actually spoke this way, using repetition to make his points. He phrased these points so simply that they sounded like free verse (and to this day people talk about "Peter's verses").

Tamar, my little daughter, had been calling me from the next room. She was down with measles, and she wanted orange juice and me. For his part, Peter wanted a listener and a disciple, so he went on talking to a doctor who had just come in. When the doctor left, he talked to the plumber, to the gasman reading the meter, to Tessa at the kitchen sink, and to John, while he was shaving before the kitchen mirror.

I learned from Tessa that he had actually come to see me. Tessa had a wonderful serenity, but I felt torn apart. The doctor, Tamar, and Peter all wanted my undivided attention at this moment, and I was dulled by my own fatigue as well. Peter had come a few times before to see if I was back from Washington, and Tessa had welcomed him; but John, solid American that he was, had not been so sure whether Peter was someone I would want to see or a crackpot from Union Square. Peter had told Tessa—his French accent made him hard to understand at first—that he had read articles I wrote in Catholic magazines and had come to suggest I start a newspaper to bring about "clarification of thought." Clarification was the first "point" in his program. Men must think before they act. They must study. "There could be no revolution without a theory of revolution," he had quoted Lenin as saying, and what he himself was interested in was the "green revolution," the back-to-the-land revolution, not the red one, which emphasized industry. It was because I had just come back from Washington that he had delivered to me his "People go to Washington" essay, but in my mixed roles as cook, dish-washer, nurse, and mother, as well as writer, it was hard for me to grasp what he said immediately.

It was a long time before I really knew what Peter was talking about that first day. But he did make three points I thought I understood: founding a newspaper for clarification of thought, starting houses of hospitality, and organizing farming communes. I did not really think then of the latter two as having anything to do with me, but I did know about newspapers. My father and three brothers worked on them all their adult lives. When I was eleven, we children had started to type out a little family newspaper. We all liked to write, and I had been taught early to write personally, subjectively, about what I saw around me and what was being done.

Tamar was not very sick. She was content for a few days to play with dolls and kittens and modeling clay, and Peter took advantage of my confinement at home to come back and continue my indoctrination.

"He who is not a Socialist at twenty has no heart, and he who is a Socialist at thirty has no head," he was fond of quoting from a French author. Since I had been a Socialist in college, a Communist in the early twenties, and now a Catholic since 1927, I had a very definite point of view about poverty, unemployment, and my own vocation to try to do something about it all. I had no doubts about the Church. It was founded upon Saint Peter, that rock, who yet thrice denied his Master on the eve of His crucifixion. And Jesus had compared the Church to a net cast into the sea and hauled in, filled with fishes, both good and bad. "Including," one of my non-Catholic friends used to say, "some blowfish and quite a few sharks."

Peter Maurin spoke to me often of his ideas about hospitality, a concept I understood well because I had lived so long on the Lower East Side of New York—and the poor are noted for their hospitality. "There is always enough for one more," my brother's Spanish mother-in-law used to say. "Everyone just take a little less." Poor families were always taking in other needy ones. So, when Peter began talking about what "we need," it sounded clear and logical:

> The Catholic unemployed
> should not be sent to the Muni
> [municipal lodging house].
> The Catholic unemployed
> should be given hospitality
> in Catholic Houses of Hospitality.
> Catholic Houses of Hospitality
> are known in Europe
> under the name of hospices.
> There have been hospices in Europe
> since the time of Constantine.
> Hospices are free guest houses;
> hotels are paying guest houses.
> And paying guest houses or hospices
> are as plentiful
> as free guest houses or hospices
> are scarce.
> So hospitality, like everything else
> has been commercialized.
> So hospitality, like everything else,
> must now be idealized.

Some of Peter's other ideas were less readily understandable, but his verses probably helped people grasp the sense and spirit of what he had to say. He fancied himself a troubadour of God, going about the public squares and street corners indoctrinating his listeners by a singsong repetition, which certainly caught their attention. Being a born teacher, he did not hesitate to repeat his ideas over and over again. He even suggested to the young students and unemployed who flocked around him and accompanied him to Columbus Circle that there should be a sort of antiphonal chant. Peter would sing out, "To give and not to take," and the chorus would respond, "That is what makes man human," and so on, through the entire essay.

He was good as bread. He was not gay or joyful, as others have described him, but he was a truly happy man, with the happiness a man feels when he has found his vocation in life and has set out on the way and is sure of himself: and sure, too, that others are searching for and willing to undertake their task in life, striving not only to love God and their brother but to *show* that love. Peter had faith in people as well as in ideas, and he was able to make them feel his faith in them, so that they gained confidence and overcame the sense of futility that so plagues the youth of today. In fact, he gave me so great a faith in the power of his ideas that if he had said, "Go to Madison Square Garden and speak these ideas," I would have overcome all sense of fear and would have attempted such a folly, convinced that, though it was the "folly of the Cross" and doomed to failure, God Himself could take this failure and turn it into victory.

Certainly there was nothing in Peter's physical appearance to impress his hearers. His dusty, unpressed, ill-fitting suit bulged with books and pamphlets; yet he gave no impression of carelessness, for he invariably wore a felt hat (not too wide-brimmed), a shirt (rough-dried), a tie, and sturdy shoes. He was not the bearded, sandaled, hatless fanatic—he had no appearance of an apostle. Neither was he establishing a personality cult; it was the primacy of the spiritual that Peter always emphasized. He was happy when people listened to him, yet he did not want people to follow him because of the influence he himself exerted but only because of the strength and beauty of the idea.

The idea of poverty, for instance. How glowing a thing it is in Franciscan literature, and how many illusions people have about it! But Peter *lived* it. He literally possessed nothing. He lived in an old hotel on the Bowery where he paid fifty cents a night for his lodging. He ate, when he had the money, in the "horse markets" of the Bowery, cheap cafés serving stew and hot weak coffee, very sweet. He was used to living on soup and bread.

Among his ideas it was the one of publishing a paper which most immediately appealed to me. "But how can it be done without money?" I wanted to know.

"In the Catholic Church one never needs any money to start a good work," Peter replied. "People are what are important. If you have the people and they are willing to give their work—that is the thing. God is not to be outdone in generosity. The funds will come in somehow or other."

Did he really say this? I cannot be sure now, and I suspect that he passed over my question about money—it was not needed in the Church. The important thing was work.

I had been reading the life of Rose Hawthorne Lathrop. She was a daughter of Nathaniel Hawthorne, the nineteenth-century American novelist. Rose, with her husband, had become a convert in 1891. She had started a cancer hospital for the poor and homeless—such institutions were a rarity in those days—in three dark, airless rooms down on the East Side. Her beginnings had been as humble as ours would be if I started the work Peter wanted. Indeed, when Rose herself fell ill with grippe, her very first patient had to take care of her. But from that simple start her work had grown until there are now a half dozen of those hospitals, run by the Dominicans, scattered around the country. A new order of nuns, wearing the Dominican habit, came into being as a result.

Reading about Rose Hawthorne Lathrop and listening now to Peter so inspired me that I was quite ready to believe that in the Church no money was necessary. I was all for plunging right in. After all, I had a typewriter and a kitchen table and plenty of paper and plenty to write about. The thing was to find a printer, run off the first issue and go out on the streets and sell it. Beginnings are always exciting.

B. "Letter to the Unemployed"

For two and a half months I have been traveling through the country, visiting Detroit, Cleveland, Chicago, Los Angeles, San Francisco, New Orleans, and stopping off at country places in between. And everywhere I have been meeting the unemployed—around the steel mills, the employment agencies, the waterfronts, around the "skid rows" and Boweries of this country, out in the rural districts where the sharecroppers and tenant farmers face lean months of hunger.

Now I am back on Mott Street, and as I get up at six-thirty there you are, a long line of hungry men extending all the way to Canal Street, waiting for the coffee and apple butter sandwiches we have to offer.

I remember how hard it was last Christmas to face you men. How could one say "Merry Christmas" to you who are gaunt and cold and ragged? Even

---

"Letter to the Unemployed" by Dorothy Day from *Dorothy Day: Selected Writings* edited by Robert Ellsberg. Copyright © 1983, 1992 by Robert Ellsberg and Tamar Hennessy. Reprinted by permission of Orbis Books.

the radio with its recipes and offerings of clothes on the installment plan, interspersed with music, did little to brighten things.

It is hard to preach the Gospel to men with empty stomachs, Abbé Lugan said. We are not a mission. We turn off the melancholy religious offerings on the radio in the morning. Religion is joy in the Holy Spirit. "Religion is a fire; it is like the coming of the Paraclete, 'a mighty wind rising'; it is a passion, the most powerful passion known to man. For religion is 'mighty to God unto the pulling down of fortifications.' Religion is a battle," writes Father Gillis.

Because it is a battle, and because you are not weaklings, we fight our own inclinations to feed only bodies to the small extent we can and let this editorial go. But it is a battle to hang on to religion when discouragement sets in. It is a battle to remember that we are made in the image and likeness of God when employers, treating you with less consideration than animals, turn you indifferently away. It is a fierce battle to maintain one's pride and dignity, to remember that we are brothers of Christ, who ennobled our human nature by sharing it.

But that very thought should give courage and should bring hope.

Christ, the Son of Man, lived among us for thirty-three years. For many of those years He lived in obscurity. When He was a baby His foster father had to flee with Him into Egypt. Joseph was a carpenter, a common laborer, and probably had no more savings than the majority of workers. When he tramped the long weary road, in the heat and dust of the deserts, he, too, and Mary and the Child were doubtless hungry. Do any of those hitchhikers, fleeing from the dust bowl into southern California across mountain and desert, remember, as they suffer, the flight into Egypt?

George Putnam, who has charge of our Los Angeles house, told me of picking up a man in the desert so starved that for the remaining days of the trip he could hold neither food nor water. Occasionally they had to stop the car and let him lie out on the ground to still the convulsive agony of his stomach. While I was in Los Angeles a young couple came to our place carrying a month-old baby and leading another eighteen months old. Some kindly worker had given them a lift on the last lap of their journey and turned his room over to them since he worked nights and could sleep days. That traveler, the father of the two little ones, was also a carpenter. Did anyone see Joseph in this unemployed man? Did they see the Holy Family, epitomized in this little group? Did they see Christ in the worker who helped them?

Christ was a worker and in the three years He roamed through Palestine He had no place to lay His head. But He said, "Take no thought for what ye shall eat and where ye shall sleep, or what ye shall put on. Seek ye first the Kingdom of God and His righteousness and all these things shall be added unto you. . . . For Your Heavenly Father knoweth that you have need of these things."

For one year now, our coffee line has been going on. Right now we are making seventy-five gallons of coffee every morning. There are too many of you for us, who wait on the line, to talk to you. We must think of the other fellow waiting out in the cold, as you remember, for you are very prompt in finishing your breakfast and making way for them. It is a grim and desperate struggle to keep the line going in more ways than one.

It is hard, I repeat, to talk to you of religion. But without faith in each other, we cannot go on. Without hope we cannot go on. Without hope we cannot live. To those who are without hope, I remind you of Christ, your brother. Religion, thought of in terms of our brotherhood through Christ is not the opiate of the people. It is a battle "mighty to God unto the pulling down of fortifications." Do not let either capitalist or Communist kill this noble instinct in you.

December 1937

C. Protesting Civil Defense

For years we at the Catholic Worker performed all the works of mercy except visiting the prisoner. We had tried to accomplish the equivalent of this through working for the release of political prisoners and speaking in their behalf. We had a chance to practice this act of love in another way in recent years, when we made our stand against the yearly war game of taking shelter during the air-raid drill by refusing to comply with the law. We visited prisoners by becoming prisoners ourselves for five years running, until the Civil Defense authorities dropped the compulsory drills.

It was Ammon Hennacy's idea to go out into the city parks to distribute literature calling attention to the penance we need to do as the first nation to use nuclear weapons at Hiroshima and Nagasaki. Pointing out on good authority that there could be no shelter against nuclear attacks, he always dwelt on the duty of civil disobedience in order to call attention to the hideous dangers hanging over the world today, and our personal responsibility to do something about them.

It was not a question of obedience to the law or to duly constituted authority. Law must be according to right reason, and the law that made it compulsory to take shelter was a mockery. In our disobedience we were trying to obey God rather than men, trying to follow a higher obedience. We did not wish to act in a spirit of defiance and rebellion. Ours was a small matter compared to the problem confronting the German, for instance, when he was called upon to obey Hitler. We were free to make our witness, and our jail sentences were light—five days on one occasion, thirty days on another, and fifteen days the last time. Fellow pacifists have spent months in jail since then—some for protesting the building of a missile base, some, the launching of nuclear submarines; others served many months in a prison in Hawaii for illegally sailing into the Pacific testing area.

We were setting our faces against things as they are, against the terrible injustice our basic capitalist industrial system perpetrates by making profits out of preparations for war. But especially we wanted to act against war and getting ready for war: nerve gas, germ warfare, guided missiles, testing and stockpiling of nuclear bombs, conscription, the collection of income tax—against the entire militarism of the state. We made our gesture; we disobeyed a law. The law we broke was the Civil Defense Act, one provision of which stipulated that everyone must take shelter for ten minutes during a sham air raid. We always gave the Civil Defense authorities, the police, and the press notice of what we intended to do. Among us in 1957, for instance, were Ammon Hennacy, Kerran Dugan and Deane Mowrer from The Catholic Worker. Judith and Julian Beck, heads of the Living Theatre group, called up the night before to say they were joining us. Judith had begun by distributing leaflets with us two years before and had been arrested with us then. We were held in jail overnight and later given suspended sentences. The second year we had served five-day sentences. This year the group included five Catholics, two Jews, two Protestants, and three who were of no faith. Richard and Joan Moses of the Fellowship of Reconciliation picketed independently in Times Square, thinking that ours was a Catholic demonstration; they received the same sentence. We truly represented a pluralist society. We regretted only that there were no Negroes among us.

At the Women's House of Detention, where we were held, five doctors are in attendance, also nurses and nurses' aides. First, preliminary tests and examinations, X-rays, cardiographs, blood tests, smears, and so on are taken. Every morning for the duration of one's stay, the shout "Clinic!" reverberates through the corridors. Girls leave their workshops or their cells to vary the monotony of their days by waiting in line for an aspirin, heat rash lotion, gargle, eyewash, or other innocuous remedies. In addition they have the refreshment of a visit with inmates from other floors.

Play is encouraged: bingo, basketball, interpretive dancing, and calisthenics—but sexual play is the most popular and is indulged in openly every evening on the roof, when the girls put on rock 'n' roll records. Living two to a cell does not help matters; yet the authorities have denied any overcrowding, ever since a new ruling was passed granting ten days off a month for good behavior for the long-term women. Just before we pacifists came in to serve our thirty-day sentence, a great many prisoners were released on this basis. All the same, most cells on our floor held two cots, which made our six-by-nine rooms more crowded than the tiniest hall bedroom.

One stout woman with a cell to herself was so cramped on the very narrow cot on which she was supposed to sleep that she hitched it up against the wall by its iron chain, spread a blanket out on the cement floor, and slept there.

We four political prisoners had cells next to each other. We were two in a cell, on the most airless corridor, with the darkest cubicles. We had a dim, twenty-five-watt bulb in ours, Judith Beck and I, until the last week of our thirty days, when a tall young colored woman brought us a fifty-watt bulb from a neighboring cell just vacated. Our windows faced north and look out over the old Jefferson Market court. We felt that we had been put there because the picketing meant to call attention to our imprisonment was going on along the south side of the jail. From the other corridors we might have seen the line. Our windows were small, and there was no cross-ventilation. Opposite us the showers steamed with heat. One of the captains said she thought that by putting us in this "good" corridor, next to each other, she was doing us a favor; but it was so obviously the least desirable, the most airless and dark, that I do not see how she could honestly have thought that. Perhaps she did. I do know that, from the time one is arrested until the time one leaves a prison, every event seems calculated to intimidate and to render uncomfortable and ugly the life of the prisoner.

I couldn't help thinking how entirely opposite is the work of the Good Shepherd nuns, who care for delinquent girls after they have been sentenced by the state. Their Mother Foundress said that her aim was to make the girls happy, comfortable, and industrious; she surrounded her charges with love and devotion, and with the expectation of good.

"Here we are treated like animals," one girl said to me, "so why shouldn't we act like animals?" Animals, however, are not capable of the unmentionable verbal filth that punctuates the conversation of prisoners. So these prisoners are, in a way, pushed below the animal level. I can only hint at the daily, hourly repetitive obscenity that pervades a prison. Shouts, jeers, defiance of guards and each other, expressed in these ways, reverberated through the cells and corridors even at night, while, gripping my rosary, I tried to pray. Noise—that is perhaps the greatest torture in jail. It stings the ear and stuns the mind. After I came out it took me at least a week to recover from it. The city itself seemed silent. Down the corridor from me was a strong, healthy Polish woman who should have used her great vitality rearing children instead of dissipating it in prostitution and drugs. She often held her head in her hands and cried. Even to her the noise was torture. Yet she herself, almost without knowing it, was one of the worst offenders. When she started screeching her ribald stories at night, her voice reverberated from cell to cell. "But this place was not made to live in," she said, pointing to the iron bars, the cement, and the walls. "The ceilings are low, the sounds bounce around."

Everything *was* exaggeratedly loud. Television blared from the "rec" room on each floor in the most distorted way. One heard not words or music, only clamor. The clanging of gates—seventy gates on a floor—the pulling of the master lever, which locked all the cells in each corridor at one stroke, the noise of the three elevators, the banging of pots and pans and dishes from the dining room, all these made the most unimaginable din, not to mention the shoutings of human voices.

The guard (there is one to a floor) has to have strong lungs to make herself heard; ours was one who could. She looked like a stern schoolteacher; she seldom smiled and never "fraternized." The women respected her. "She's an honest cop," one of them said of her. "She's just what she is and does not pretend to be anything else." That meant that she did not become friendly with the girls—neither honestly trying to help them nor becoming overly familiar.

I saw a few of the guards being treated with the greatest effrontery by the prisoners, who kidded them and even whacked them across the behind as they went in and out of the elevator. Much of this was greeted by the guards with smiling tolerance.

On the other hand, a "good" officer had to know just how far to go in severity, too: just how firm to be and just how much to put up with, to overlook. I saw one guard trying to hasten a prisoner's exit from the auditorium, where the inmates had just put on a show, with what we took to be a friendly push. The prisoner turned on her viciously, threateningly. On such occasions the officers do not press the point. They realize they are sitting on a volcano. They know when to back down. But a number of times, witnessing their humiliation, I was ashamed for them. The hostility of the Negro for the white often flares up then. Helpless as the prisoner may seem to be, she knows, too, that she has the superior numbers on her side, that she can start something if she wants to and maybe get away with it. She is also aware of the worst she can expect. In many cases the worst has already happened to her: she has undergone the "cold turkey" treatment.

While in prison I received a letter inviting me to speak on television. It had already been opened by the censor and commented on all over the House of Detention. The girls came to me and begged me to plead their case to the world: "You must tell how we are put here for long terms, and about the cold turkey cure, too; about how we are thrown in 'the tank' and left to lie there in our own vomit and filth, too sick to move, too sick even to get to the open toilet in the cell."

One girl added, "I had to clean out those cells." They are called tanks because they are kept bare of furnishings and can be hosed out, I suppose. The "cooler," on the other hand, is the punishment cell; there are several of them on various floors. Here a recalcitrant prisoner is kept in solitary for brief periods, until she "cools off."

I heard stories of padded cells; of cells with only ventilating systems but no window, no open bars, in which a girl sits in the dark; of cells where water can be turned on in some kind of sprinkler system to assist the process of cooling off. I heard of girls being thrown naked into these cells on the pretext that they might use some article of clothing to make a rope to hang themselves. I heard of girls breaking the crockery bowls and using the shards to try to cut their throats or their wrists. I heard of girls who had tried to hang themselves by their belts. But I know none of these things of my own knowledge. From the open elevator door, as we journeyed to and from clinic or workshop, I saw only the gruesome steel-plated doors, ominous indicators of the presence of these punishment cells.

Most cells for the five hundred or so prisoners, or girls held in "detention," are cemented and tiled halfway up the front, and then barred to the ceiling; about ten bars across the front of the cell, perhaps five bars to the gate, which is so heavy one can hardly move it. It is the crowning indignity for the officers to shout, "Close your gates!" and to have to shut oneself in. The open bars at the top enable one to call the guard, to call out to other prisoners, to carry on some friendly intercourse. The "cooler" is meant to be a place of more severe punishment than the cell, so it is completely closed in.

"Tell how we are treated!" they cried to me. I can only tell the things that I have seen with my eyes, heard with my ears. The reports of the other prisoners will not be considered credible. After all, they are prisoners; why should they be believed? People will say, "What! Do you believe self-confessed thieves, prostitutes, drug addicts, criminals who are in jail for assault, for putting out the eyes of others, for stabbing, and other acts of violence?"

Perhaps it is a little too much to believe that twenty girls have died in the House of Detention from the cold turkey cure these last two years, as one inmate charged. But there have been grim stories which appeared in the *New York Times,* and in other New York papers. I heard one young addict tell the story of a girl who died in the cell, after her "cellie," as the roommate is called, had cried out over and over again for the officer to come and administer to the sick girl. When the doctor finally came, hours later, after the cells were unlocked, she was dead. Two prisoners assaulted the doctor and kept her head poked down the open toilet while another prisoner kept flushing it in an attempt to drown her. "Her head shook from that time on, as though she had palsy," one of the other girls said, with grim satisfaction.

I repeat, these are tales I heard told and repeated. They may be legends, but legends have a kernel of truth.

Ill treatment? How intangible a thing it sometimes is to report! Whenever I was asked by the officers and captains and the warden himself how I was making out, how I was being treated, I could only say that everything was all right so far as I was concerned. After all, I was only in for twenty-five days, what with the five days off for good behavior. I had no complaint to make against individuals, and yet one must complain about everything—the atmosphere, the attitude, the ugliness of it all. "After all, we don't want to make this place glamorous," the guards protested. How many times when a prisoner was released I heard them say, "You'll be back!" as if to set a stamp of hopelessness on any effort the prisoner might make to reform.

Listening to the prisoners talk about the kick they got out of drugs, I saw how impossible it was for them to conceive of themselves as "squares" (people who go to work every day) and how hopelessly they regarded the world outside, which they nevertheless longed for hourly. They made me feel, too, that without a "community"—in the early Christian sense—to return to, their future was indeed bleak.

But, I wondered, must the attempt to keep the place "unglamorous" cause so many small indignities to be heaped on each prisoner? Why cannot they be treated as they are in the Good Shepherd Homes (where they are sentenced for two years or more), as children of God, and made happy and comfortable? The very deprivation of freedom is sufficient punishment. For the prisoners the breaking of vicious habits is difficult enough.

I have received letters from *Catholic Worker* readers who have been prison officers and officials which showed the same lack of understanding, and I could only think, What if *they* were treated as prisoners? What if they were crowded into a bullpen, a metal cage, awaiting trial, then transported in a sealed van with no springs where they are tossed from seat to ceiling in real danger of broken bones and bruised spines; or stripped naked, lined up, and prodded rudely, even roughly, in the search for drugs; or dressed in inadequate garments coming only to the knees, and then, with every belonging from rosary to prayer book to Testament taken away, led off to a permanent cell and there locked behind bars? Envisaging our critics, our chaplains, our catechists under such circumstances, seeing *them* shivering nakedly, obeying blindly, pushed hither and yon, I could not help but think that it is only by experiencing such things that one can understand and have compassion for one's brother.

Yet many priests and nuns around the world have had these experiences in Russia, Germany, and Japan in our generation. In the face of the suffering of our time one is glad to go to prison, if only to share these sufferings.

Our friends and readers will remind us of the beatings, the torture, the brainwashings in the prisons of Russia and Germany. As for beatings, third-degree methods are generally accepted in our own land. I have read of them, heard of them from parole officers as well as from prisoners. In the case of sex offenders and offenders against little children, brutality is repaid with brutality. One prisoner, a drug addict, told me that she had been so beaten by members of the narcotics squad trying to make her tell where she had gotten her drugs that they were unable to arrest her for fear they themselves would be held criminally liable for her condition—which goes to show that if beating is not accepted in theory it is nonetheless practiced.

Some time ago the magazine section of the *New York Times* carried a long article on the treatment of drug addicts in Great Britain. There they are regarded not as criminals but as patients and are so treated, through clinics and custodial care. Here they are made into criminals by our "control" methods, which make the drug so hard to get that the addict turns to crime to get it. Many criminologists believe that we should reform our thinking in this regard. At a recent meeting one prison official said that nowadays a prison term is a life sentence on the installment plan. And so it is with drug addicts. The girl who told of the beating and other ill treatment had started to use drugs when she was twelve and became a prostitute at that time. She had been in prison sixteen times since and was now twenty-two.

As for the problem of prostitution, most of the girls openly admitted it. "I'm a pross," they would tell us. "I was money hungry." Or "I wanted a car," or "I wanted drugs." They felt the injustice of the woman being arrested and not the man. They despised the tactics of the plain-clothesmen who solicited them to trap them. The grossest misconception held not only by prostitutes but also by some pious people is that were it not for the prostitute there would be far more sex crimes. I heard this statement made by Matilda, a girl down the corridor, one evening when she was in an unusually quiet and philosophical mood. Matilda pointed out that, in their demands on prostitutes, jaded men want to explore every perversion, to the disgust of what society considers the lowest of women, whores and dope fiends. These are not pretty words nor are they pretty thoughts. But everything comes out into the open in jail. "The more I see of men," one girl said, "the more I'd prefer relations with a woman." And another pretty girl added wistfully, "I've got to get used to the idea of men, so that I can have a baby."

Cardinal Newman once wrote that not even to save the world (or to save good women and little children) could a single venial sin be committed. When I lay in jail thinking of these things, thinking of war and peace and the problem of human freedom, of jails, drug addiction, prostitution, and the apathy of great masses of people who believe that nothing can be done—when I thought of these things I was all the more confirmed in my faith in the little way of St. Thérèse. We do the things that come to hand, we pray our prayers and beg also for an increase of faith—and God will do the rest.

One of the greatest evils of the day among those outside of prison is their sense of futility. Young people say, What good can one person do? What is the sense of our small effort? They cannot see that we must lay one brick at a time, take one step at a time; we can be responsible only for the one action of the present moment. But we can beg for an increase of love in our hearts that will vitalize and transform all our individual actions, and know that God will take them and multiply them, as Jesus multiplied the loaves and fishes.

Next year, perhaps, God willing, we will go again to jail; and conditions will perhaps be the same. To be charitable, we can only say that the prison officials do the best they can according to their understanding. In a public institution they are not paid to love the inmates; they are paid to guard them. They admit that the quarters are totally inadequate, that what was built as a house of detention for women awaiting trial is now being used as a workhouse and penitentiary.

When the girls asked me to speak for them, to tell the world outside about "conditions," they emphasized the crowded and confined surroundings. "We are here for years—to work out our sentences, not just for detention!" Shut in by walls, bars, concrete, and heavy iron screenings so that even from the roof one's vision of the sky is impeded, mind and body suffer from the strain. Nerves clamor for change, for open air, more freedom of movement.

The men imprisoned over on Hart Island and Riker's Island can get out and play ball, can work on the farm or in the tree nursery. They can see all around them—water and boats and seagulls—and breathe the sea air coming from the Atlantic. The women have long been promised North Brother Island as a companion institution. But that island is being used to confine teen-age addicts. And there are other seemingly insuperable obstacles in the way. Money figures largely. There is money for civil defense drills, for death rather than for life, money for all sorts of nonsensical expenditures, but none for these least of God's children suffering in the midst of millions of people who are scarcely aware of their existence. "Nothing short of a riot will change things," one warden told us. Was he perhaps suggesting that we pacifists start one?

If those who read this will pray for the prisoners—if New York readers, when they pass the Women's House of Detention, will look up, perhaps wave a greeting, say a prayer, there will be the beginning of a change. Two of the women, Tulsa and Thelma, said that they never looked out through those bars; they could not stand it. But most of the other prisoners do, and perhaps they will see this gesture; perhaps they will feel the caress of this prayer, and a sad heart will be lightened, and a resolution strengthened, and there will be a turning away from evil and toward the good. Christ is with us today, not only in the Blessed Sacrament, and where two or three are gathered together in His Name, but also in the poor. And who could be poorer or more destitute in body and soul than these companions of our twenty-five days in prison?

DOCUMENT 38

Letter from Father Thomas Merton to James Forest

Monk, writer, and poet Thomas Merton (1915–1968) became a Catholic in 1941, and soon after joined a Trappist monastery in Kentucky where he lived the rest of his life. His spiritual autobiography, The Seven Storey Mountain *(1948), is said to have sold 600,000 copies in the original hardcover edition.*

Peace and nonviolence were central preoccupations for Merton, especially in the 1960s. In 1962 he joined the peace organization PAX, and edited

"Letter from Father Thomas Merton to James Forest," reprinted with permission of James Forest and the Merton Legacy Trust.

an anthology titled Breakthrough to Peace. *In 1965 Merton edited* Gandhi on Nonviolence.

James Forest is an example of the younger persons on whom Merton had great influence. In 1964 Forest together with Philip Berrigan (see Document 35A) and another young Catholic Worker activist, Tom Cornell, founded the Catholic Peace Fellowship. That same year these three, together with A. J. Muste, Daniel Berrigan, and others, attended a retreat on "The Spiritual Roots of Protest" at the Trappist abbey where Merton lived. In September 1968, Forest became one of the Milwaukee Fourteen who burned some 10,000 draft files in Milwaukee.

Do not depend on the hope of results. When you are doing the sort of work you have taken on, essentially an apostolic work, you may have to face the fact that your work will be apparently worthless and even achieve no result at all, if not perhaps results opposite to what you expect. As you get used to this idea, you start more and more to concentrate not on the results but on the value, the rightness, the truth of the work itself. And there too a great deal has to be gone through, as gradually you struggle less and less for an idea and more and more for specific people. The range tends to narrow down, but it gets much more real. In the end, it is the reality of personal relationships that saves everything.

You are fed up with words, and I don't blame you. I am nauseated by them sometimes. I am also, to tell the truth, nauseated by ideals and with causes. This sounds like heresy, but I think you will understand what I mean. It is so easy to get engrossed with ideas and slogans and myths that in the end one is left holding the bag, empty, with no trace of meaning left in it. And then the temptation is to yell louder than ever in order to make the meaning be there again by magic. Going through this kind of reaction helps you to guard against this. Your system is complaining of too much verbalizing, and it is right.

. . . [T]he big results are not in your hands or mine, but they suddenly happen, and we can share in them; but there is no point in building our lives on this personal satisfaction which may be denied us and which after all is not that important.

The next step in the process is for you to see that your own thinking about what you are doing is crucially important. You are probably striving to build yourself an identity in your work, out of your work and your witness. You are using it, so to speak, to protect yourself against nothingness, annihilation. That is not the right use of your work. All the good that you will do will come not from you but from the fact that you have allowed yourself, in the obedience of faith, to be used by God's love. Think of this more and gradually you will be free from the need to prove yourself, and you can be more open to the power that will work through you without your knowing it.

The great thing after all is to live, not to pour out your life in the service of a myth: and we turn the best things into myths. If you can get free from the domination of causes and just serve Christ's truth, you will be able to do more and will be less crushed by the inevitable disappointments. . . .

The real hope, then, is not in something we think we can do, but in God who is making something good out of it in some way we cannot see. If we can do His will, we will be helping in this process. But we will not necessarily know all about it beforehand. . . .

Enough of this . . . it is at least a gesture . . . I will keep you in my prayers.

All the best in Christ,
Tom

DOCUMENT 39

James W. Douglass,
The White Train

Jim Douglass narrates in the following document how he helped to found a community in Bangor, Washington to protest the nuclear-armed Trident submarines at a nearby base (see also the closing paragraphs of Document 35B). He tells how the protest naturally grew to include a witness against the transport of nuclear warheads and missile propellants from distant factories to the base by railroad.

After the events described here, Douglass has written, the White Train stopped coming altogether. The missile propellant shipments were now going to a different Trident base on the coast of Georgia. To get to their Georgia destination the nuclear materials traveled on railroad tracks through Birmingham, Alabama. With the support of their Ground Zero community in Bangor, Jim and his wife Shelley Douglass decided to move to Birmingham.

We all share the responsibility today for choosing either the end dictated by our age, annihilation, or a nonviolent beginning (already begun) whose end is the world's transformation. The strange calling we have experienced at Ground Zero is that seeing the means of our annihilation has compelled us to seek transformation.

When did we first see the White Train? Some of us feel we saw it first in Franz Jagerstatter's dream.

Jagerstatter was an Austrian peasant who refused to fight in Hitler's wars because he believed that the Nazi movement was anti-Christian. He was beheaded by the Nazis in 1943. The story of his solitary witness[1] has been told and retold as a way of life in an age of death.

REFUSING THE TRAIN TO HELL

The train Jagerstatter saw in a dream five years before his martyrdom (and which he wrote about shortly before his death) corresponded to the White Train we saw passing our homes and exploding in our dreams:

> At first I lay awake in my bed until almost midnight, unable to sleep, although I was not sick; I must have fallen asleep anyway. All of a sudden I saw a beautiful shining railroad train that circled around a mountain. Streams of children—and adults as well—rushed toward the train and could not be held back. . . . Then I heard a voice say to me: "This train is going to hell."[2]

The train to hell in Jagerstatter's dream was a symbol of cooperation in the Nazi movement. Our White Train to hell was both symbol and reality. It contained the annihilation it symbolized.

For the sake of his soul Jagerstatter had to refuse to board his train to hell. For the sake of our souls and of life itself, we felt we had to stop the White Train.

We began tracking the White Train, although we did not know it existed then, when we moved into our house alongside the railroad tracks entering the Trident submarine base at Bangor, Washington.

We saw the house by the tracks for the first time in 1977, while seeking a piece of land that could become Ground Zero Center for Nonviolent Action. The house we discovered by the tracks was too remote to serve as such a center, but it brought another possibility to mind. It stood on a hill overlooking the gate where railroad shipments enter the Trident base. By living in such

---

1. This is the title of Gordon Zahn's biography of Jagerstatter: Gordon Zahn, *In Solitary Witness: The Life and Death of Franz Jagerstatter* (New York: Holt, Rinehart and Winston, 1964).

2. Ibid., pp. 111–12.

a house one could, simply by being there, begin to break through the invisibility and silence of one critical means toward nuclear holocaust: the missile shipments that travel the United States by rail, analogous to the boxcars that moved unchallenged through Europe in the '40s on the way to an earlier holocaust.

Through a series of miracles, Shelley, our son, Tom, and I moved into the house by the tracks four years later. The intervening time had been marked by my knocking on the door of the house every six months or so to ask if the couple living there ever planned to sell it; a friendly no was always the answer. Then one day I knocked on the door to no answer at all, and saw through its window a house empty of both people and furniture. From that moment on, the miracles took over. Through the grace of God and the gifts of many wonderful friends, we were able to buy the house by the tracks and move into it in July 1981. At the same time the Agape Community was born.

We held a workshop at Ground Zero that month entitled "Christian Roots of Nonviolence" and included a pilgrimage around the fence of the base. It ended at the railroad tracks with a meditation on the trains entering Bangor and on their parallel meaning to the trains entering Auschwitz and Buchenwald. As a part of the meditation we named some of the cities and towns along the tracks, as they wound their way up from Salt Lake City, near the Hercules Corporation, source of Trident's missile propellant shipments. (At the time we knew nothing of the White Train's journeys to Bangor from the Texas Panhandle.) When we finished our litany of the tracks, we realized that most of the workshop participants lived along those same tracks.

We all recognized that this was a workshop whose community could truly be deepened in meaning by our going home and becoming an extended nonviolent community in our various towns along the Trident tracks. We decided to become the Agape Community and adopted a community statement which said in part: "We believe the spiritual force capable of both changing us and stopping the arms race is that of *agape:* the love of God operating in the human heart." By this definition, we were basing our community especially on Martin Luther King's understanding of *agape.*

As we tracked and opposed Trident missile propellant shipments through Utah, Idaho, Oregon, and Washington in 1981–82, two truths found a special life in the Agape Community. The first is that systemic evil shuns the light. The government and the railroads did their best to keep us from seeing the missile shipments. The second truth we experienced is that once evil is brought into the light, it can be overcome by God's love operating in our lives.

Evil's power lies in darkness, our own darkness. Evil's power to destroy life comes from our denial of its presence and our refusal to accept responsibility for it. The essence of our life-destroying evil lies in our unseen, unacknowledged cooperation with it. As we began to claim personal responsibility for the missile propellant shipments and sought to express our love for the train employees, we experienced the faith to overcome the evil which was in us and on the trains: faith in the redeeming power of nonviolent love, faith in the cross. Our growing community of faith and nonviolent action made the tracks linking us a double symbol—of not only holocaust, but hope.

But we were about to experience a deeper sense of these realities along the tracks.

THE WHITE TRAIN

On December 8, 1982, I received a phone call from a reporter asking if we knew anything about a special train carrying nuclear warheads that was on its way to the Trident base. It had been spotted in Everett, Washington, two days before: an all-white, armored train, escorted by a security car traveling along highways.

I said we knew nothing of such a train. It bore no resemblance to the missile-propellant shipments that we witnessed going into the base every week. After the phone call I walked down our front steps to the tracks. I could see signs of unusual activity across the tracks at the base gate. More security cars than I had ever seen for an arriving train were parked by the gate, waiting for something. I went back in the house, loaded film in our camera, and came down the steps just in time to see the train approaching.

Perched outside the first Burlington Northern engine was a man, like a film director scanning his set. After the second engine came a string of all-white, heavily armored cars. Each of the two rail security cars had a high turret, like a tank's. Sandwiched between the security cars were eight middle cars, lower in height, white, and armored. When the final security car came opposite me, the armored flaps on the side of the turret clanked open, and an object was extended in my direction.

The White Train passed by, a train to holocaust, and I remembered the train of Jagerstatter's dream and the words: "This train is going to hell."

In response to the news of the White Train, the Agape Community grew rapidly. We surmised the source of the train must be the Department of Energy's Pantex plant in Amarillo, Texas, final assembly point for all United States nuclear warheads. A friend and railroad buff, Tom Rawson, drew up a likely rail route between Pantex and the Bangor base. We then sought old and new friends along this hypothetical White Train route, sharing with them the Agape Community's vision of love toward the people on the trains and nonviolent resistance to their cargo. As we contacted more train-watchers, we waited for the White Train to come out of its Bangor lair—and, we hoped, follow our route.

It did so on January 5, 1983, rolling past our house in the opposite direction. As friends along the tracks monitored the train, we confirmed that it was traveling the route Tom Rawson had drawn up. The train returned to Amarillo via Spokane, Denver, and Pueblo; it was seen entering the Pantex plant the night of January 12 by Les Breeding of Northwest Texas Clergy and Laity Concerned.

"It was a haunting sight," said Les, "this white train moving slowly into the distance where amber lights were glowing with a light fog all around. It brought to mind a phantom train bound for Hades."

The White Train may be the most concentrated symbol we have of the hell of nuclear war. It carries a world-destructive power within it, guarded by Department of Energy "couriers" who, according to a DOE spokesperson, are armed with machine guns, rifles, and hand grenades, and are trained to shoot anyone who threatens the train. Yet there is another side to all this, as indicated by an experience Les Breeding had with the "phantom train bound for Hades."

On the night of January 12 Les had a unique, forty-five-minute conversation in the middle of the Amarillo switchyards with the head security guard of the White Train, prior to the train's final movement to Pantex. The White Train watcher and White Train defender discussed issues of interest to them both: peace, the nuclear freeze movement, and the Soviet threat. After this conversation Les lost the White Train when it moved out of the switchyards into the darkness. He pursued it by car, discovering it again just outside Pantex. There was a tense moment when he drove up to the train and a searchlight suddenly glared at his car. He got out of the car and heard the security guard say, "Hey, Les, is that you?"

At the heart of perhaps the greatest outward symbol we have of nuclear war, this train bearing instruments of hell, there is a human voice asking if we are there. The question alters our sense of the train as absolute evil. There are people inside the train. We must stop this White Train to hell, but we can stop it only through a truthful, loving process which affirms the sacredness of that life within it. The security guard and his question to us are at the center of the tracks campaign.

For three years Ground Zero and the Agape Community tracked the White Train back and forth across the United States as it carried thousands of hydrogen bombs to their destinations. Half of these cargoes went to Bangor on the West Coast, the other half to the Charleston Naval Weapons Station in South Carolina, the East Coast base for Poseidon submarines. Hundreds of people were arrested for sitting in front of the White Train. Hundreds more vigiled by the tracks at all hours of the day and night, as Ground Zero notified people in each town along the various routes when the White Train would be coming.

Karol Schulkin of Ground Zero describes one such "coming of the train" and the deepening and widening of the community by the tracks:

On Wednesday, February 22, 1984 a call came from a reporter in Emporia, Kansas: a local man there had just reported seeing the White Train traveling north through town on the Santa Fe/Wichita rail line. It was a little after noon in Washington when the call came. By 10 p.m. on Friday, February 24, the White Train was locked behind the fences of the Trident submarine base at Bangor. It was not to pass there unnoticed. What followed that message from Emporia is a story of vigilance and waiting, of prayer and protest.

From Emporia, Kansas to Bangor, Washington throughout Nebraska, Wyoming, Idaho and Oregon this all white heavily guarded train was sighted and tracked by a network of peace-loving people. Shortly after the first call, a second sighting was made. Looking out the window of the Acapulco restaurant just south of Topeka, a customer saw a train pass by. Having seen the previous White Train, this man knew what was passing before his eyes. He notified his local peace group which notified Ground Zero. Phone trees throughout Kansas and Nebraska were immediately activated and people closest to the train headed to their stretch of tracks. Soon more eyewitness accounts gave the details: 17 white cars—10 weapons cargo cars, four buffer cars, and three turreted security cars—plus two engines and a caboose. The train was traveling fast. Throughout Nebraska, people driving alongside the train would clock it at speeds between 50–60 mph. A handful of residents in Frankfort, Kansas, because of their rapid response, managed to witness the train's passage before it headed on to Nebraska. The chain of vigils had begun.

By 7 p.m. as the train sped toward Hastings, Nebraska a group of 18 vigilers with signs, candles, and Bibles were waiting in the snow by the tracks. Singing hymns beneath a street light, these people in the heartland of America stood in witness to this train. A few days later Ken Gonsior, OSC, a brother at Crosier Monastery, wrote of how the train had moved within his life:

"At this point, I'm still coming to grips with the fact that the train actually passed through our town. Initially, when I first saw the articles in *Sojourners* and saw Hastings listed on the train map, I figured it would be rare for it to actually hit here. . . . I never dreamed that the interest that I expressed to your group in my first note to you would be called upon to act. I was plain afraid after you telephoned that one evening—what could I do? What did I want to do? What would the ramifications be for me personally, for us as a religious community in this conservative diocese in this conservative state? These questions and others haunted me for days. I discussed it with friends here; I prayed about it; I delayed acting upon it. Fortunately, I finally contacted the Marshes here in town and we shared similar apprehensions about involvement—we were all afraid, but yet we were all concerned about the reality of what the train was carrying and the arms race in general. I am thankful for finally having the courage to reach out to the Marshes. I am thankful to you for having prodded me along in describing the needs your organization had for common folk to work together in witnessing opposition to the train. I am thankful that our apprehensions and fears were re-created into a prayerful witness broadcast to the public.

People were touched, I know, and at least the public's consciousness was raised. . . ."

An hour later, when the train barreled through Kearney, Nebraska the number of vigilers had doubled to 35. At North Platte, Ogallala, Sidney and Kimball people kept watch.

It was morning now of the second day. In the pre-dawn darkness of Cheyenne, 100 people stood waiting for the train. Unknown to them, the train stood outside town for an hour; the crew was changed. At 2 a.m. the vigilers moved to a viaduct overlooking the railroad yard. From this windy vantage point they watched for another hour singing "This Land Is Your Land," "I've Been Workin' on the Railroad," and "America the Beautiful." It was 3:30 a.m. when the train finally passed and the vigilers tossed their flowers onto the top of the train. There were tears and prayers and the linking of arms as the train rolled on to Laramie where 50 more vigilers waited. In Rawlins, Rock Springs, and Granger the train was met again and again with protest and prayer. It was noon of the second day. The train was entering Idaho.

It was on the second day of the train's trip, February 23, 1984, that the *New York Times* released a story headlined, "Bishops Protest Train Carrying Atom Weapons." The story told of a statement signed by 12 Roman Catholic bishops in the West, ones through whose states the White Train is likely to pass. They urged direct action to impede the deployment of nuclear weapons and urged their parishioners to join in prayer vigils along the route of the train. In an interview given during these days, Bishop Lawrence Welsh of Spokane, Washington said:

"Protesting the train may be a small step, but it is an important one. It questions the good of nuclear weapons. To say nothing is to fall prey to moral apathy. To let these weapons pass through our towns without any response is to welcome them as friends. That is wrong. Our salvation comes not from weapons, but in God alone. I speak out against the preparation of nuclear weapons. I stand in union with those who vigil and pray."

In Spokane, a city through which the train did not travel this time, but might have, a vigil was held nonetheless. Near a railroad trestle on the edge of town, 18 people stood beneath an Air Force recruiting billboard and joined hands in a circle of prayer, songs, and readings. From Thursday evening through Friday evening they kept vigil, taking turns throughout the snowy night.

In other towns where the train did not go vigils were also held. In Pueblo, Colorado and Billings, Montana people of faith and good will stood together in opposition to the momentum of the arms race. There was a vigil of solidarity and concern in Sheridan, Wyoming with the group holding a large banner which asked, "Why 480 Hiroshimas?" [This was the vigilers' estimate of the nuclear firepower on the current White Train as compared to the Hiroshima bomb. They probably underestimated the train's cargo by as much as fifty percent. A more likely equivalent for the train's destructive power was 960 Hiroshima bombs.[3]] Throughout the South a chain of prayer was activated in support of those facing the train on the western route. The people in the South knew that when next the train leaves Pantex it is likely to head their way en route to the Charleston Naval Weapons Station in South Carolina.

On through Pocatello the train traveled, heading west to Shoshone, where 40 people waited with a candlelight vigil. At Gooding, a family stood together on the soil of their own farm holding up signs to the passing train. It was nearly 11 p.m. when the train went through Mountain Home, Idaho, a military town in which 40 people stood to publicly speak their "NO" to the weapons-carrying train.

It was in Orchard, Idaho that this train first encountered people on the tracks. In sub-freezing temperatures a vigil of 70 people had gathered here, a number driving in from nearby Boise. When four elderly women walked onto the tracks several minutes before the train's arrival the state police and sheriff's deputies moved in quickly to remove them. One deputy confided to one of the women as he led her away that if it weren't for their positions, many of the officers would be in the vigil line. No charges were brought against the women. Due to the openness of the demonstration planners in Orchard, the location and plans of the group were announced on the six o'clock news. Eight women in a bridge club heard this announcement, put down their cards, and went to the vigil. Two of the women had never been to a public protest before.

Although a police roadblock prevented the people at Orchard from driving on to Nampa to again meet the train, there were, nonetheless, about 80 people waiting in Nampa when the train reached there at midnight. Living out an action they had planned for over eight months, eight people crossed a police barricade in an attempt to reach the tracks. Seven were arrested and charged with trespass. As they were taken to a police van the others sang "We Shall Overcome." The train barreled through town at 50 mph. Cathy Posey, one of those arrested, explained the reasons for her action:

"I'm a simple homemaker, not a public figure. I choose to make my public statement by standing on the tracks. I have two children, seven and eight years old. I am convinced that if they are to have a chance

3. The February 1984 White Train to Bangor consisted of three security cars, four buffer cars, and ten cars designed to carry nuclear weapons. Each of the train's weapons cars is divided into three sections. A former nuclear weapons worker has estimated that each of these sections holds four warheads—thus twelve per car, and 120 warheads in this ten-car train. The Trident-1 nuclear warhead then being delivered to Bangor has an explosive equivalent of one hundred kilotons of TNT, or roughly eight times the power of the Hiroshima bomb, which was about 12.5 kilotons. A White Train carrying 120 Trident-1 warheads would therefore have the explosive equivalent of 960 Hiroshimas.

to grow up . . . our government will have to take the initiative in leading the world toward peace. Building nuclear weapons doesn't make the world more secure. It leads the world to war."

As the train crossed into Oregon about 1:00 a.m., 15 members of the Interfaith Peace Fellowship held a prayer vigil in the Ontario depot. In Baker, a dozen people waited for two hours until the train passed at 2:20 a.m. Two feet of snow covered the ground. Two hours later in LaGrande 28 people ranging in age from three to fifty met the train with large signs and banners reading "Give Peace a Chance—Stop the Arms Race" and "We Believe in Peace." In the Amtrak station in The Dalles 50 people held hands in prayer; the train passed at 10:22 a.m. Half an hour later 40 people vigiled in Hood River as the train passed headed toward Portland.

Then the unexpected happened. The train was stopped. It was two-and-a-half hours before it would move again. In northeast Portland 200 people stood together on the tracks. Some 80 police and security officers worked to remove the protesters, only to find that once removed, they would return again and again to the tracks. In the end, 35 people were arrested and charged with trespass. Despite rain and a chilling wind, spirits remained high. At 3:30 p.m. the train made its way out of Portland and into Washington.

At Kelso, Castle Rock, Chehalis, and Centralia the train was again met as the people of the state of Washington added their signs and prayers to the litany of protest which preceded the train. It was now 6:30 p.m. In Elma a group of 80 people lined both sides of the tracks. Carrying candles, they joined together in a liturgy of resistance and hope. As eight people attempted to make their way onto the tracks they were dragged off by officers. They were not charged.

The train was reaching the end of the line—Bangor. Just outside the fence of the Trident submarine base several hundred people had waited for hours into the night. They lined the final stretch of tracks, holding candles and lanterns, listening to readings, joining in songs and prayer. This vigil had actually begun the day before in Seattle, where members of the Seattle Agape Community maintained a vigil outside the corporate offices of Burlington Northern Railroad. Rebecca Johnson, an Agape member, explained, "We're asking people to just go see it. It will change their lives to see the White Train. It did mine."

Now everyone had gathered at Bangor. The train, expected at 3 p.m., was long overdue. About an hour before the train appeared a group of nine persons walked onto the tracks. Holding a large wooden cross in their midst, they stood facing the vigil line beside the tracks. Together, the vigilers on the tracks and those beside them sang songs of hope and prayed for a faith deep enough to end the violence which sends the trains. Then the nine knelt facing the on-coming train. The vigil line stood in silence. The nine were removed from the tracks and driven away by the sheriff's deputies as the train, with its spotlights now dimmed, passed into the darkened base. It was 10 p.m. on the third day. The crowd encircled the tracks, proclaiming together an affirmation of faith and breaking bread. There were songs. There were tears. There was a deep sense of connectedness along the tracks. Another train had passed through our lives. It had not passed unnoticed. One person standing with a candle was enough to pierce the darkness, one voice enough to break the silence. There had been many such gestures in the preceding three days.

It's hard to determine which is the greater danger, the moral or the physical one. These trains, with their deadly cargo of nuclear warheads, make visible the reality of an arms race propelling us toward destruction. These trains travel through our midst bringing the bombs close to us—right through our towns, right into our lives. They are no longer figures on a budget sheet or lines inching their way up a weapons production chart. They are here: in Topeka and Sheridan, Pocatello and Baker, in Jonesboro and Memphis, Birmingham and Jesup. The arms race has come home.

All across this country people are deciding they will not ignore this passage of destruction. These White Trains are not a matter for indifference or apathy. People of faith have roused themselves. They are bearing witness. There is a place for prayer and for resistance. One place they meet is by the tracks where the White Train travels.[4]

GOVERNMENT RESPONSES: REROUTE IT, REPAINT IT, STOP IT

The Department of Energy responded to the tracks campaign, first of all, by rerouting the White Train. The DOE command center for the White Train, located at Kirtland Air Force Base in Albuquerque, New Mexico, changed the train's route periodically onto whatever was perceived to be the track of least resistance. The result was an ever-widening and deepening nonviolent campaign, as hundreds of people on new routes became vigilers to the train. Because of people's willingness to stand in testimony to a power greater than this awesome train, lives were being transformed.

The DOE's next step was to repaint the train to make it less noticeable and less notorious. A secret July 30, 1984, DOE memorandum headed "Color Change of Safe-Secure Railcars" (obtained through the Freedom of Informa-

---

4. Karol Schulkin, "The Arms Race Has Come Home," *Ground Zero,* vol. 3, no. 2 (May/June 1984), pp. 5–7. For a subscription to the Ground Zero newspaper (four issues per year), write to Ground Zero Center for Nonviolent Action, 16159 Clear Creek Road, N.W., Poulsbo, WA 98370. A beautiful videotape, "The Arms Race Within," has been made of the February 1985 White Train arrival at Bangor. It is available from Idanha Films, PO Box 17911, Boulder, CO 80308.

tion Act) reads: "We recognize that the painting of these railcars will not stop dedicated protesters from identifying our special trains. However, it will make tracking our trains more difficult and this, we believe, enhances the safety and security of our special trains." The cars of the "White Train" were therefore painted red, green, gray, and blue. (They remained white on top for safety reasons, to reduce heat inside the cars.) As the DOE memorandum recognized, this was not a very effective camouflage. The train's armor and turrets remained conspicuous. Its Pantex source and nuclear cargo were too widely known by this time for the train to return to obscurity. Moreover, it was being watched vigilantly at Pantex by Hedy Sawadsky, a Mennonite woman of deep faith, who had moved to Amarillo at Ground Zero's invitation to be a light to unmask the darkness (Eph. 5).

Resistance to the multicolored Nuclear Train continued to grow. Reporters kept calling it the White Train, explaining that the government had painted it to try to evade protesters. In February 1985, 146 people were arrested in the course of the train's journey to Bangor. In June, a jury from our conservative Kitsap County returned a "not guilty" verdict for the twenty who had sat on the tracks at the Bangor gate in front of the February train. The county government then decided to stop charging people who were arrested for resisting the federal government's unpopular weapons trains. It was a waste of local taxpayers' money.

In the face of such developments, the Department of Energy stopped sending the White Train. Its nuclear weapons were put on trucks instead. The H-Bomb trucks have in turn been followed and vigiled in an effective campaign coordinated by Nukewatch of Madison, Wisconsin.

We learned from a Department of Energy statement that the White Train had been on the rails for more than twenty years before the nonviolent campaign arose that drew public attention to it. A question immediately presents itself: How did a heavily armored, all-white train carrying holocaust weapons across the United States remain virtually invisible for more than twenty years?

The question brings others to mind: How did boxcars carrying millions of Jewish people across Europe in the 1940s remain invisible until after the victims had gone to their deaths? How did radiation victims of our nuclear testing remain unnoticed by us until recent years? Have we always known instinctively that if we choose to see systemic evil, it will open an abyss that can only be bridged by faith?

A white light of annihilation is carried in the cars of the White Train. It is an evil so inconceivable in its effect that it calls forth an opposite kind of power.

We remember again Franz Jagerstatter's train to hell, and most important, his refusal to board that train. His resistance to it was a choice of the kingdom of God. It is said that Jagerstatter's eyes shone with such joy and confidence in the hour before his death that the chaplain who visited him in prison was never able to forget that look.

We remember the kingdom of God in Jagerstatter's eyes when he chose life. Out of the nightmare of a White Train to the end of the world can come an awakening to our Nonviolent God.

DOCUMENT 40

Shelley Douglass,
"A World Where Abortion Is Unthinkable"

Probably most participants in the movements of the 1960s supported a woman's "right to choose" whether or not to bear a child. In a major historical irony, the direct action tactics of the 1960s were widely used in the decades that followed by opponents of abortion, who supported a fetus' "right to life."

Shelley Douglass is associated with a thoughtful variety of the right to life movement exemplified by the following "Seamless Garment Statement": "We the undersigned are committed to the protection of life, which is threatened in today's world by war, abortion, poverty, the arms race, the death penalty and euthanasia. We believe that these issues are linked under a consistent ethic of life. We challenge those working on all or some of these issues to maintain a cooperative spirit of peace, reconciliation and respect in protecting the unprotected."

Unlike some in the right to life movement who seemed more concerned about unborn babies than about children after they are born, Shelley Douglass advocates changing the society we live in so that childbirth would not need to be feared.

My background is this: I have four kids. Two of them I bore myself and two of them are adopted. I realized, not too long ago, that the two that I actually bore myself would today be good candidates for abortion. Paul, who's the oldest, was conceived almost on my wedding night, when I was still an undergraduate. He did make it hard to finish my degree, I'll have to admit, but there was never any question of not having this child. Thomas, born

"A World Where Abortion is Unthinkable," from *Harmony: Voices for a Just Future,* vol. 2, no. 3 (May & June 1989), pp. 14–19. Reprinted by permission of Shelley Douglass and *Harmony.*

about four or five years later, came along right after the legalization of abortion. At the time I was pregnant with him I was in the middle of a marriage break-up, living at a Catholic Worker house, with an income of about $50 a month, and another of the children living with me. There was strong pressure from the people in the Catholic Worker house for me to have an abortion. That's not par for the course for Catholic Workers, but it's what happened to me. It really wasn't something that I seriously considered, because I wanted to have the child. But when I thought about it later I realized that both of those children would have been candidates for abortion today.

My other two children are adopted. They were both adopted before the liberalization of the abortion law, and they're so called "hard-to-place" kids—they're interracial—so of course they might have been kids who wouldn't have come to term either. I know those experiences color my response to the abortion debate. Those kids are now adults themselves; some of them have had happy lives, some of them have had troubles, but I can't say that any of them shouldn't have been born, or that the world would be a better place without them, or that I would be a better person. The whole question is a personal one for me, reflecting on the choices that I made; it's hard for me to look at it from a purely intellectual perspective, because it's so tied up with my own life.

I've had a fair amount of experience with discussion of abortion, as many of us have. I've been in several feminist support groups. Even back in the '60s there was a lot of discussion of pregnancy, people with very different perspectives on what it meant to bear a child to term. I can agonize on almost any side of the question if you give me a chance because I've thought through a lot of situations with a lot of people.

One of the most telling experiences I had happened in King County Jail, in Seattle. One of the valuable things about going to jail is that you meet people you'd never meet otherwise. In this particular instance, I was in jail for anti-nuclear actions with 8 other activists, all of us white. Everyone else in the jail was Black, Native American, or maybe Hispanic; maybe 70 of us all told.

You know how it is when you're in jail, you'd do anything to get out of your cell, it's boring in that cell! There was a women's health collective that came in every two weeks to do education on health care for the prisoners; you could go or not, whatever you wanted to do. We always went, because at least it was a change of scene and something different to talk about.

One day we walked in and the presentation was on abortion. It really made me think differently than I'd thought before. The two women who came in clearly believed what they were saying, felt that they were bringing something that would make life better. There's no question—they were not out to do these women in. They had no financial interest that I know of in any decision these women might make. They really did want to share that abortions were normal, an easy thing, a very simple thing to do, that you really ought to consider it, especially if you were financially embarrassed. Everyone in jail is, of course—that's why they're there. They explained about abortion and there was a silence, and one of the women from the streets said, "But why would I want to kill my baby?"

The answer was, "Well, it's not really a baby yet, it's not a big thing, you might as well do this because then you won't have little children to support." One of the visitors finally said, "Well, you know, it's simple; I got pregnant when I was writing my thesis and I just couldn't do both, so I had an abortion, and it was fine, and I got my thesis in."

What I remember about that is the total puzzlement of the women in jail, like a complete cultural divide, no meeting at all. And there is truth on both sides: there is an economic pressure that makes it very hard for people to bear children, especially people in the ghetto who have no options to get out. (Most of the women we were with were prostitutes.) There was definitely that truth of economic reality; on the other hand there was a very instantaneous human response: Why would I want to kill my baby?

For me those truths sum up two important things: the society is evil, or fallen, or sinful, and it creates a struggle between the mother and the unborn, so that the mother feels she must abort in order to survive. There is also a very basic truth in the assumption that the unborn is a developing child, and why would we want to kill it?

That leaves me with a lot of questions.

What is it that we're trying to do? What are we working for, where do we want to go with all this? We ask that question a lot in our community, which is part of the anti-nuclear movement. Where do we want to wind up when we're done?

I've had some answers that are really visions. One is that we're trying to create a new world—and there are a number of kind of worlds that can be created by people's energies. I'm aware that when I imagine a world where abortion is unthinkable, it isn't necessarily what other people think of! I need to be specific when I say, "a world where abortion is unthinkable." WHY is abortion unthinkable, what makes it that way? I've met people who were projecting a world where abortion is unthinkable because we were so regimented and women were so oppressed into being breeders that there was no freedom; all children would be carried to term, and there were no other ways to decide. That's not what I mean when I think of a world where abortion isn't considered.

What I think of is a world where all human people, all humankind, are valued, just because they're human; where they're welcome, just because they're human. A world of generosity. I think of Catholic Worker homes, where there is always room to pull up another chair to the table, always a little more to go around, a world where there is welcome for people.

It would be a world of responsibility, where we think about what we're doing and take the consequences of our acts. A world of peace, where it's assumed that everybody will be sustained at a basic level, not a world where some people will be floating in superfluous wealth and other people starving.

A peaceful world, where there are other ways of solving conflicts than killing each other, a world where rape was also unthinkable, and where economics did not force women into sexual activity.

I think, if we were able to create a world where those were the assumptions, it would go a long way toward a world where abortion wouldn't happen; it wouldn't be in the picture, it wouldn't be necessary. King talked about the Beloved Community. That's the kind of world we work for, where everybody is beloved. He talks about a world where Black children and white children, gentiles and Jews, Protestants and Catholics—and so on—everybody, all the children, could play together and work together and have enough to eat and be respected.

That's the world I hope some day to create. I find it really hard to imagine a world like that. It's very hard for me to imagine a world where being human is enough to guarantee being fed, clothed, educated, given medical care and a chance to fulfill your vocation. It's hard to imagine how that could happen, or what it would be like if it did.

When I discuss abortion in my head, there are two levels that are points of conflict, flash points. One conflict is the violence and injustice with which we live. Our system is a racist system, it's a sexist system; it's a system against those who are poor. Poverty is being feminized, and living, for poor women, is getting harder and harder. That's economic violence. There are other kinds of violence: rape, prostitution, the use of sex against women as a form of power, and the use of economics to force women into sex, in various ways. There is a violence in our lack of child care facilities and medical care, so that people with the least resources have the greatest demands made upon them to be superhuman parents. We are not hospitable to children as a society—we shunt them off. It doesn't make sense to think about a world where abortion is unthinkable unless we talk about a world where the system has changed so that children are made welcome. Women must not be made to feel that they will suffer if they nurture; men must be allowed to nurture without losing face. There has to be a systemic change in what happens to those children after they're born. What happens to the children of those women in jail who couldn't imagine abortion? Those women were turned back on the streets with no new skills, no help, nothing; some of them were back in a week, for turning tricks again. What happens to their children?

The other flash point is this: how do we think about people? When I try to imagine where violence begins, it seems to me that it begins in an individual's life at the point where a parent looks at a child and says, "This is a boy. He will be strong and powerful and a leader. He will never cry." Or, "This is a girl. She will be feminine and gentle and soft, and she will cry a lot and be very loving." When we do this kind of thing we warp the child's personality from the very beginning. We also teach that there are two kinds of people, and that one kind is more acceptable, more important, than the other kind. The same thing happens with race, where in the earliest days, or even before birth, the decision is made by society that this person is not valuable because of the color of her/his skin. How do we think about people? Once you begin dividing and discounting people you can go anywhere. It gets easier and easier to find new divisions, new groups to discount. It doesn't matter whether you start with women, or Native Americans, or Communists; it's a bad idea.

It may be the cradle of violence, right there.

The problem for people like us, middle class people, is that we have the most to lose. We are acceptable types, and we have a lot more than our share of the world's goods. As long as we believe that people like us are more important than others, it's going to be very hard to solve the world's problems. We have the most to lose.

The fact is, when I go out to talk about disarmament, I have to say that I don't think there can be disarmament without a commitment to total economic justice. A big part of the problem of violence is injustice. I've had some very honest people say to me, "Well, I agree with you about disarmament; I don't want to get blown up. But if you're saying that in order to disarm I have to give up my boat, my extra TV, my RV, my VCR—I'd rather take my chances!" And they really mean it. We all mean it on one level or another. It's very hard for anyone to imagine the kind of change that would have to be worked out in order to disarm the world; it's especially hard for us.

I think the same thing is true, in a different way, on the question of abortion. It's really hard to imagine the kind of justice, economic justice and justice for women, that would have to exist for there really to be a world where abortion was unthinkable. Not illegal: unthinkable! It's a spiritual question. It's as though our souls would have to be pulled out of our bodies and remade and put back in; we would need to change our heart of stone for a heart of flesh. When I'm talking such a world, I'm a little bit shaky, because I know that somewhere inside me, there's that one thing that I don't want to change, don't want to give up, and I'm not sure what it is. But I know it's there. It's that one thing that I have to fight with and learn to give up before the new world can come to be.

One of the guidelines for nonviolence is that, if you want to go someplace, you have to go by getting there. If you want the world to be one way, you have to live that way, and that helps the world become that way. Imagine a world where war and abortion are both unthinkable, and then start to live as if we lived in that world—that moves us along the path.

Question: there's a Biblical quote that goes like this—"If you can't love your brother, whom you have seen, how can you love God, whom you have not seen?" If we can't love our sisters, whom we have seen, how can we love their children, whom we have not seen? It seems to me that we start by learning to love those we can see.

In nuclear weapons issues, where I work, one of the hardest things for us to do is to love our brothers and sisters whom we can see, who are driving into the Trident base to put the missiles on the submarines. It's really hard because we think they're about to destroy the world. How can we have an attitude of love and respect and at the same time resist what they're doing?

There's no easy answer to that. It's a matter of prayer, a matter of self criticism, it's a matter of staying home sometimes if you're not in the right mood. It's also a matter of living there and getting to know people, being present to them in their lives apart from submarines.

I don't know if there's an analogy or not, if this translates into the abortion issue. What we discovered from being at the Trident base is that first of all people are very defensive. They have to do this for all kinds of reasons—because the Russians will come, or because they don't question the commander, whatever. When you're there a little longer and they realize you're not calling them murderers, but you're listening to what they have to say, then they start saying, "Well, you know, I really don't believe in what I'm doing, I'm not sure this is the right thing to do but I need to do it because of my job and family"—there's always a reason. Eventually the question comes up: Why not leave the job? There is a constant presence, being there, listening, giving our reasons, and listening to their reasons, working together in the PTA and the soup kitchen. Somehow that presence allows a respect that wasn't there when we just arrived a few times a year to demonstrate. There is some communication that wasn't possible before. What we're trying to do is to live in the world that we want to achieve, a world where instead of bombing each other we go out and talk to each other.

In small ways that approach has borne fruit; we have changed and we have seen changes in base workers. Some of them actually wind up coming out and being part of the peace movement. One former worker vigiling or being arrested, one person saying, "No, this is wrong, and I'm going to leave."—that's tremendously encouraging. But it's taken maybe 2 1/2 years for that decision to be reached.

That means that it's also excruciating because we know where those weapons are going and that people are starving NOW because of the money we spend on them. When you work so slowly, what about the violence that happens in the meantime, while we're building relationships? It's a constant tension that we can only handle by trying to be faithful, and saying, "Well, we're doing the best we can, if we could speed it up we would but we can't think how to do that and remain consistent with our aims." We just have to do what we can do, and pray that we're approaching the point where the spirit of the age is changing, and more and more people will be walking out of these bases.

I have some questions for all of us that I want to throw out, questions that have arisen for me as I've pondered these issues in relation to nonviolence. I'd like to share them with you because I don't have any answers to them, and I think we need to be discussing them.

First, is there an analogy between wars of liberation and the struggle over abortion? It seems to me that women today are involved in what could be called a war of liberation, a struggle against overwhelming odds to find out what it means to be fully human, and then to live that. The unborn are like the "collateral civilian damage" in a war: it's not that anyone has actual hostility to them, generally speaking. The problem is that they get in the way and have to be removed. I would say that's true of both sides, in the sense that women and men seeking liberation remove them as obstacles to the woman's (or even the man's) path, while on the other side the so-called "pro-life" position is often one that makes life for a single parent, or a poor parent, or a gay parent, untenable, and thus creates a climate where abortions continue, illegal or legal.

In a way I think arguing over the collateral civilian damage is beside the point: in our society as it is now abortions are going to happen. The real question, it seems to me, is the question of the struggle for liberation for people, all people, but especially women, to be able to make choices in their lives, to be supported by their society, to be respected and allowed to become full persons. (That does not mean to become what men have had to become; it means to become fully human, whether we're men or women.) So the question here is: how can we win that struggle for all of us, and how can we avoid collateral civilian damage to anyone as we do it?

Another question is the question of choice and control: are we meant always to be in control of our lives? Is there some place where our control ends and the life process, or the Holy Spirit, or whatever you call it yourself, takes over and may bring things you'd never choose or plan, but that ultimately are growing and learning, albeit painful, experiences? I do believe that we have the responsibility to think and plan, to use whatever methods of birth control are morally acceptable to each one of us, to make decisions based on our reason and understanding. But we have become such a controlling and technological society that I wonder if many of our plans block out the very life process we're trying to nurture. Maybe we each have to find the point at which we acknowledge that we have to give up control and accept a larger process in which we are only a small part. For me one place where that control ends is with a positive pregnancy test. It ends also when I reach the point where it's clear that a law must be broken and the consequences borne if I'm to be true to my conscience about war and weapons.

In my life the Spirit frequently speaks by pushing me into doing things I didn't want to do, and wasn't ready to do. I don't want to say that everybody should always do what they don't want to, but there definitely is a sense in which we don't know what we're going to do, or what we can do, until we're forced by circumstances to do it. If we are able to control our lives too thoroughly I think we might find that we aren't fully human any more, because we've closed off our flexibility, our openness to unexpected change.

These are spiritual problems. I don't believe they can be addressed legally, and a big question for me is whether or not the legal arguments around abortion are fruitless precisely because they so seldom get to the roots of the questions, which have no solutions in law. Maybe we should talk about things entirely differently. And the last question is: how can we hear the truth in what people on "the other side" are saying, and how can we make that truth part of our own?

DOCUMENT 41

Helen Prejean,
Dead Man Walking

Executions in the United States were temporarily blocked by the Supreme Court in 1967. In 1972, the Supreme Court declared in Furman v. Georgia *that the death penalty as applied by the State of Georgia was constitutionally-prohibited "cruel and unusual punishment" under the Eighth Amendment. The decision effectively invalidated all state death penalty statutes throughout the nation. In 1976 the Supreme Court reinstated the death penalty as constitutionally-permissible punishment and executions were resumed in some states in 1977.[1]*

Shortly before his retirement in 1994, Supreme Court Justice Harry A. Blackmun concluded that "the death penalty cannot be administered in accord with our Constitution." In the administration of the death penalty, he wrote, the goals of individual fairness, reasonable consistency, and absence of error cannot be achieved. Among the reasons he mentioned was that "race continues to play a major role in determining who shall live and who shall die." Justice Blackmun cited a "highly reliable statistical study" that demonstrated: "blacks who kill whites are sentenced to death 'at nearly 22 times the rate of blacks who kill blacks, and more than 7 times the rate of whites who kill blacks.' " "From this day forward, I no longer shall tinker with the machinery of death."[2]

A call to join a National Pilgrimage for Abolition of the death penalty, May 5 to May 19, 1990, sponsored by the Lighting the Torch of Conscience Campaign, stated:

Selected passages from pp. 3, 5, 6, 20, 22, 89, 94, 101, 131, 133, 136, 138, 144, 149, 179, 181, 223 and 226 from *Dead Man Walking* by Helen Prejean. Copyright © 1993 by Helen Prejean. Reprinted by permission of Random House, Inc.

1. The Friends Committee on National Legislation, "A History of the Death Penalty in the U.S." (August 1993).

2. *Callins v. Collins,*—U.S.—, 127 L. Ed.2d 435 (1994), Blackmun, J. dissenting.

In recent years, more than 100 people have been executed at the hands of state officials.

More than 2,300 others remain under sentence of death. Each year about 200 more are added to their number, selected almost randomly from the year's 20,000 homicide cases.

Almost *randomly. The fact is that nearly all of those selected to die are poor. Half of them are people of color. Some are insane, mentally retarded or juveniles. Mostly they are those whose victims are white. And some of them are innocent.*

But these are not the only ones who suffer because of capital punishment. We all do. Our preoccupation with the death penalty keeps us from dealing with the real causes of violent crime. It demeans us in the eyes of other Western democratic nations, all of which have now abolished capital punishment. And its astounding cost robs taxpayers while it undercuts funding for social needs.

This tragedy calls out for response from the community of faith. And that community is answering the call, through the effort called Lighting the Torch of Conscience.

Lighting the Torch of Conscience is a campaign sparked by the hope that in the hearts of religious believers, love is stronger than hate—compassion stronger than revenge.

Its purposes are to rekindle the religious community's long-held commitment to abolition of capital punishment. . . . [3]

"Dead man walking" is the expression called out by guards when a prisoner is taken from his or her cell for execution. In her book by that name, Sister Helen Prejean describes her experiences as she accompanied Patrick (Pat) Sonnier and Robert Willie to their executions. Pat and Eddie Sonnier, sons of Gladys Sonnier, were convicted for killing Loretta Bourque and David LeBlanc. Pat was sentenced to death, Eddie to life imprisonment. Robert Willie was sentenced to death for the killing of Faith Hathaway. Vernon Harvey is Faith Hathaway's stepfather, and Elizabeth Harvey her mother.

———————

When Chava Colon from the Prison Coalition asks me one January day in 1982 to become a pen pal to a death-row inmate, I say, Sure. The invitation seems to fit with my work in St. Thomas, a New Orleans housing project of poor black residents. Not death row exactly, but close. Death is rampant here—from guns, disease, addiction. Medical care scarcely exists.

I've come to St. Thomas to serve the poor, and I assume that someone occupying a cell on Louisiana's death row fits that category. . . .

———————

3. "Anti-death penalty campaign, Lighting the torch of conscience," *Peace & Justice Journal* (Dayton, Ohio: American Friends Service Committee, Feb./March 1990), p. 10.

I came to St. Thomas as part of a reform movement in the Catholic Church, seeking to harness religious faith to social justice. In 1971, the worldwide synod of bishops had declared justice a "constitutive" part of the Christian gospel. When you dig way back into Church teachings, you find that this focus on justice has been tucked in there all along in "social encyclicals." Not exactly coffee-table literature. The documents have been called the best-kept secret of the Catholic Church. And with good reason. The mandate to practice social justice is unsettling because taking on the struggles of the poor invariably means challenging the wealthy and those who serve their interests. "Comfort the afflicted and afflict the comfortable"—that's what Dorothy Day, a Catholic social activist said is the heart of the Christian gospel.

In 1980 my religious community, the Sisters of St. Joseph of Medaille, had made a commitment to "stand on the side of the poor," and I had assented, but reluctantly. I resisted this recasting of the faith of my childhood, where what counted was a personal relationship with God, inner peace, kindness to others, and heaven when this life was done. I didn't want to struggle with politics and economics. We were nuns, after all, not social workers, and some realities in life were, for better or worse, rather fixed—like the gap between rich and poor. Even Jesus Christ himself had said, "The poor you will always have with you." Besides, it was all so complex and confusing—the mess the world was in—with one social problem meshed with other problems. If you tried to get a handle, say, on improving housing for poor people, you found yourself in a morass of bureaucracy and waste in government programs, racist real estate and banking policies, unemployment—a mess.

Enlightenment had come in June 1980. I can remember the moment because it changed my life. My community had assembled at Terre Haute, Indiana, to grapple with directions of our ministries for the 1980s, and the chief speaker was Sister Marie Augusta Neal, S.N.D.deN. A sociologist, she described glaring inequities in the world: two thirds of the peoples of the world live at or below subsistence level while one third live in affluence. Did we know, she asked, that the United States, which comprises about 6 percent of the world's population, consumed 48 percent of the world's goods? What were we to do about such glaring injustices? She knew her facts and I found myself mentally pitting my arguments against her challenge—*we were nuns, not social workers, not political.* But it's as if she knew what I was thinking. She pointed out that to claim to be apolitical or neutral in the face of such injustices would be, in actuality, to uphold the status quo—a very political position to take, and on the side of the oppressors.

But it was the way she presented the message of Jesus that caused the most radical shift in my perspective.

"The Gospels record that Jesus preached good news to the poor," she said, "and an essential part of that good news was that they were to be poor no longer." Which meant they were not to meekly accept their poverty and suffering as God's will, but, instead, struggle to obtain the necessities of life which were rightfully theirs. And Jesus' challenge to the nonpoor, she emphasized, was to relinquish their affluence and to share their resources with the dispossessed.

Something in me must have been building toward this moment because there was a flash and I realized that my spiritual life had been too ethereal, too disconnected. I left the meeting and began seeking out the poor. This brought me one year later to the St. Thomas housing development.

Later, in the months ahead, Patrick Sonnier will confide his terror to me of the death that awaits him, telling me of a recurring nightmare, always the same: the guards coming for him, dragging him screaming toward the chair, strapping him in with the wide leather straps, covering his face with the hood, and he is screaming, "No, no, no . . ." For him there can never again be restful, unbroken sleep, because the dream can always come. Better, he says, to take short naps and not to sink into deep sleep.

I cannot accept that the state now plans to kill Patrick Sonnier in cold blood. But the thought of the young victims haunts me. Why do I feel guilty when I think of them? Why do I feel as if I have murdered someone myself?

In prayer I sort it out.

I know that if I had been at the scene when the young people were abducted, I would have done all in my power to save them.

I know I feel compassion for their suffering parents and family and would do anything to ease their pain if I knew how. I also know that nothing can ease some pain.

I know I am trying to help people who are desperately poor, and I hope I can prevent some of them from exploding into violence. Here my conscience is clean and light. No heaviness, no guilt.

Then it comes to me. The victims are dead and the killer is alive and I am befriending the killer.

Have I betrayed his victims? Do I have to take sides? I am acutely aware that my beliefs about the death penalty have never been tested by personal loss. Let Mama or my sister, Mary Ann, or my brother, Louie, be brutally murdered and then see how much compassion I have. My magnanimity is gratuitous. No one has shot my loved ones in the back of the head.

If someone I love should be killed, I know I would feel rage, loss, grief, helplessness, perhaps for the rest of my life. It would be arrogant to think I can predict how I would respond to such a disaster. But Jesus Christ, whose way of life I try to follow, refused to meet hate with hate and violence with violence. I pray for the strength to be like him. I cannot believe in a God who metes out hurt for hurt, pain for pain, torture for torture. Nor do I believe that God invests human representatives with such power to torture and kill. The paths of history are stained with the blood of those who have fallen victim to "God's Avengers." Kings and Popes and military generals and heads of state have killed, claiming God's authority and God's blessing. I do not believe in such a God.

In sorting out my feelings and beliefs, there is, however, one piece of moral ground of which I am absolutely certain: if I were to be murdered I would not want my murderer executed. I would not want my death avenged. *Especially by government*—which can't be trusted to control its own bureaucrats or collect taxes equitably or fill a pothole, much less decide which of its citizens to kill.

Albert Camus' "Reflections on the Guillotine" is for me a moral compass on the issue of capital punishment. He wrote this essay in 1957 when the stench of Auschwitz was still in the air, and one of his cardinal points is that no government is ever innocent enough or wise enough or just enough to lay claim to so absolute a power as death.

> Society proceeds sovereignly to eliminate the evil ones from her midst as if she were virtue itself. Like an honorable man killing his wayward son and remarking: "Really, I didn't know what to do with him" ... To assert, in any case, that a man must be absolutely cut off from society because he is absolutely evil amounts to saying that society is absolutely good, and no one in his right mind will believe this today.

Camus addresses the moral contradiction inherent in a policy which imitates the violence it claims to abhor, a violence, he says, made more grievous by premeditation:

> Many laws consider a premeditated crime more serious than a crime of pure violence ... For there to be equivalence, the death penalty would have to punish a criminal who had warned his victim of the date at which he would inflict a horrible death on him and who, from that moment onward, had confined him at his mercy for months. Such a monster is not encountered in private life. (p. 199)

A guard called Slick comes through the front door. He is a big, burly man with a shiny bald head and he is carrying a small canvas bag. Rabelais comes and asks me to step out into the foyer. Slick, accompanied by two other guards, goes into the cell with Pat. I quietly walk up and down the foyer. I look down at my black leather pumps. I walk back and forth, back and forth. "Please, God, help him, please help him."

A chaplain named Penton approaches me. He is dressed in a bright green suit. I have the feeling that he has worked here for a long time. He tells me that he is here "in case the inmate might need my services at this time." Then he tells me to prepare myself for the "visual shock" of Pat's shaved head. "They must remove the hair to reduce the possibility of its catching fire," he says. I keep walking slowly up and down the foyer and he walks alongside me. I am thinking of Gandhi. I am thinking of Camus. "Resist, do

not collaborate in any way with a deed which you believe is evil . . . resist
. . ." In his *Reflections* Camus tells of a Russian man about to be hanged by
the Tsar's executioners who repulsed the priest who came forward to offer
a blessing: "*Go away and commit no sacrilege.*" (p. 224)

Camus says about Christians:

> The unbeliever cannot keep from thinking that men who have set at
> the center of their faith the staggering victim of a judicial error ought
> at least to hesitate before committing legal murder. Believers might
> also be reminded that Emperor Julian, before his conversion, did not
> want to give official offices to Christians because they systematically
> refused to pronounce death sentences or to have anything to do with
> them. For five centuries Christians therefore believed that the strict
> moral teaching of their master forbade killing. (p. 224)

I talk to Penton about a phone call I received from one of the Catholic
prison chaplains several weeks ago. The priest had asked me which funeral
home would pick up Pat's body if the execution were to take place. Before
I got this call, Pat had told me that the old priest had approached him in his
cell and said brightly, attempting humor, "Well, Sonnier, what are we gonna
do with the body?" Pat had said angrily, "Don't you call my mama and ask
her that. Don't you dare upset her. Call Sister Helen." And so the phone call
had come to me, and I had said I had no idea who would pick up the body.

I see how easy it is for chaplains, on the payroll, to play their part in this
"uncomfortable but necessary business," and I ask whether it should be the
role of the chaplain to collaborate with the prison in planning the "disposal
of the remains" of the person the state has killed. Penton tells me he will
think about that. (He does. Later he sees to it that chaplains no longer make
burial arrangements for executed prisoners.)

Rabelais comes to tell me that I can go back now to Pat.

I move to my side of the visitor door and wait for Pat to come from the cell.

Slick and crew are just coming through the door from the tier. One of the
guards is carrying a towel and small broom, another a brown paper bag with
Pat's curly black hair in it. Slick is zipping up his canvas shaving kit. He
moves quickly. I look at Pat as he comes back to the metal chair. His head
looks whitish gray and shiny. His hair is gone now, eyebrows too. He looks
like a bird without feathers. I see that they have also cut his left pants leg
off at the knee. "They shaved the calf of my leg," he says, and he holds out
his leg for me to see. I see a tattooed number.

"What's that number?" I ask.

"That's from when I was at Angola before," he tells me. "In case anybody
killed me, I wanted them to be able to identify my body."

I notice that he is wearing a clean white T-shirt.

I look at my watch and Pat looks at his. It is 10:30. Everything is ready
now. All Pat needs to do now is die. He asks the guard for a pen and

writes in his Bible, up in the front, where there is a special place for family history—births, marriages, deaths.

"There," he says, "I wrote it in my own hand."

The guard unlocks the door and hands me the Bible. I look at the front page. He has written loving words to me, words of thanks. Then I see under "Deaths" his name and the date, April 4, 1984.

I remember Jesus' words that we do not know the day nor the hour. But Pat knows. And in knowing he dies and then dies again.

Two guards inside the tier stand on stepladders and hang black curtains over the windows along the top.

"They don't want other inmates to see the lights dim when the switch is pulled," Pat tells me. He is smoking and talking now, his talk a torrent, a flood, all coming together now, snatches from childhood and teasing Eddie and school and the sugar-cane fields gleaming in the sun and Star, what will happen to her, and his Mama, to please see about his Mama, and Eddie, will he be able to keep his cool in this place, and if only he knew when the current first hit that he would die right away . . .

He begins to shiver. "It's cold in here," he says, and the guard gets a blue denim shirt from the cell and puts it around his shoulders, then goes back to his position at the end of the tier.

. . . Mr. LeBlanc and Mr. Bourque must be here. What are they going through? Will this help heal their loss? I wonder. I hear the toilet flush in Pat's cell.

Rabelais summons us back to the door. Pat comes from his cell, his legs and hands cuffed. Anger flickers in his eyes. "A grown man, and I have to leave this world with a diaper on," he says.

"I'll be free of all this," he says, shaking his handcuffs. "No more cells, no more bars, no more life in a cage," he says.

He reaches in his pocket for a cigarette. He turns and shows the guard, "Look, the last one. It'll see me out."

Warden Maggio approaches us. He is flanked by six or seven very large guards. It must be midnight. "Time to go, Sonnier," Maggio says. One of the guards takes Bill out to the foyer, another tells Millard to follow him. I stand to the side of the door. I will walk with Pat. I am holding his Bible. I have selected the Isaiah passage to read as we walk, the words that were in the song, words that Pat has heard and the words will be there for him to hear again, if he can hear words at all, when he will be trying to put one foot in front of another, walking from here to there across these polished tiles.

"Warden," he asks, "can I ask one favor? Can Sister Helen touch my arm?"

The Warden nods his head.

I am standing behind him. Guards, a mountain of blue, surround us. I put my hand on his shoulder. He is tall. I can barely reach. It is the first time I have ever touched him.

We walk. Pat walks and the chains scrape across the floor. God has heard his prayer. His legs are holding up, he is walking.

I read Isaiah's words:

> Do not be afraid . . . I have called you by
> your name, you are mine.
> Should you pass through the sea,
> I will be with you . . .
> Should you walk through the fire,
> you will not be scorched,
> and the flames will not burn you.   (43:2)

As we pass through the lobby the old priest raises his hand in blessing.

We stop. There is the oak chair, dark and gleaming in the bright fluorescent lights. There are the witnesses all seated behind a Plexiglas window. There is a big clock on the wall behind the chair. There is an exhaust fan, already turned on to get rid of the smell of burning flesh. Two guards have firmly taken hold of my arms and are moving me toward the witness room. I lean toward Pat and kiss him on the back.

"Pat, pray for me."

He turns around toward me and says, his voice husky and eager like a young boy's, "I will, Sister Helen, I will."

I see Millard then and I sit in the chair beside him. He reaches over and takes my hand. Mr. Bourque and Mr. LeBlanc are seated on the first row over to the right of us. Their faces are expressionless.

There is a small podium with a microphone on it and Pat is standing behind it. I can see past him to a wall of green painted plywood with a slit of a window behind which the executioner waits.

The warden is standing over in the right-hand corner next to a red telephone.

"Have any last words, Sonnier?" he asks.

"Yes, sir, I do," Pat says, and he looks at the two fathers, but addresses his words to only one of them. "Mr. LeBlanc, I don't want to leave this world with any hatred in my heart. I want to ask your forgiveness for what me and Eddie done, but Eddie done it." Mr. LeBlanc nods his head. Mr. Bourque turns to Mr. LeBlanc and asks, "What about me?"

Pat is in the chair now and guards are moving quickly, removing the leg irons and handcuffs and replacing them with the leather straps. One guard has removed his left shoe. They are strapping his trunk, his legs, his arms. He finds my face. He says, "I love you." I stretch my hand toward him. "I love you, too."

He attempts a smile (he told me he would try to smile) but manages only to twitch.

A metal cap is placed on his head and an electrode is screwed in at the top and connected to a wire that comes from a box behind the chair. An electrode is fastened to his leg. A strap placed around his chin holds his head tightly against the back of the chair. He grimaces. He cannot speak anymore. A grayish green cloth is placed over his face.

Millard says, "Father forgive them, for they know not what they do."

Only the warden remains in the room now, only the warden and the man strapped into the chair. The red telephone is silent. I close my eyes and do not see as the warden nods his head, the signal to the executioner to do his work.

I hear three clanks as the switch is pulled with pauses in between. Nineteen hundred volts, then let the body cool, then five hundred volts, pause again, then nineteen hundred volts. "Christ, be with him, have mercy on him," I pray silently.

I look up. His left hand has gripped the arm of the chair evenly but the fingers of his right hand are curled upward.

The warden says over the microphone that we will wait a few minutes for the doctor to make the "final check." Then the prison doctor, who has been sitting with the witnesses, goes to the body in the chair and lifts the mask and raises the eyelids and shines the light of a small flashlight into the eyes and raises up the clean white shirt and puts his stethoscope against the heart and listens and then says to the warden that, yes, this man is dead. Warden Maggio looks up at the clock and announces the time of death: 12:15 A.M. His eyes happen to look into mine. He lowers his eyes.

The witnesses are led from the room. As we walk through the lobby, I go over to the old priest and ask him to give me communion for "both of us," as Pat had requested. I go to where the witnesses are gathered to sign the papers. Everyone is silent. All you can hear is the papers being shuffled across the white tablecloth and the scrawling of ballpoint pens as people put their signatures on three copies of the official state papers.

As we are filing out of the room, Lloyd LeBlanc is behind me and I turn and look at him and he looks shaken and the rims of his eyes are red. I touch his arm but I have no words. It is all so overwhelming. What can I say? I am not sure why Pat addressed his last words to Lloyd LeBlanc and not to Mr. Bourque, but I suspect it's because Pat was trying to make his last words loving and he didn't trust himself to say anything to Bourque, who had been outspoken to the press about wanting to see him die. Who knows? But Pat's dead now. As dead as Loretta Bourque and David LeBlanc are dead, and I think of Gladys Sonnier waiting out the night. . . .

Who killed this man?

Nobody.

Everybody can argue that he or she was just doing a job—the governor, the warden, the head of the Department of Corrections, the district attorney, the judge, the jury, the Pardon Board, the witnesses to the execution. Nobody feels personally responsible for the death of this man. . . .

A young man, one of the marchers, touches my arm and points to the bottom of the steps where the counterdemonstrators are and says that a man says to tell me "to watch out or someone is going to hurt you." The man down there wants to talk to me. He says his name is Vernon Harvey. My heart tightens. Oh, God, not here, not now. "Someone wants to hurt me?" What does that mean? . . .

I don't *have* to respond to the invitation, I reason with myself. With the crowd milling about, I could pretend the message never reached me. Besides, maybe another time less confrontational than this would be better for our first meeting. *Any time* would be better than this.

The young man delivering the message looks at me expectantly. I know it would be cowardly not to respond to the invitation. I thank him for the message, my heart racing, and walk down the long, white steps to Vernon Harvey.

I introduce myself. He's a short guy with close-cropped gray hair, black-rimmed glasses. I brace myself for attack. He says he's heard I visit with death-row inmates and that I'd better watch myself with those "scum." "They'll just as soon slit your throat as look at you," he says. He's not shouting and he looks at me when he talks.

Relief. I was prepared for apoplectic rage, and here he is expressing concern about my safety.

We must have executions, he tells me, because it's the only way we can be sure these "mad dogs" don't kill again. He ticks off his favorite pro-death-penalty arguments, just as I tick off mine for abolition. I have to respect that he's out here at the foot of these capitol steps because he believes in his cause as strongly as I believe in mine. Maybe even more. I haven't had anyone close to me murdered. I tell him that I'm terribly sorry about his stepdaughter and ask if I may come to visit him and his wife. "Sure, come on over," he says, and he writes his telephone number for me on a piece of paper. . . .

Tragedies have a date and time. Tragedy in the Harvey family happened on May 28, 1980. . . .

Vernon recounts the scene and the murder. Both Willie and Vaccaro, he says, gave basically the same account in their confessions, except that each blamed the other for the stabbing.

Sometime in the early-morning hours of May 28 the two men met Faith outside a bar and offered her a ride home. Instead, they drove her down gravel roads to a remote place, made her take off all her clothes, blindfolded her, and led her down a ravine where they forced her to lie down and raped her. Then one of them stabbed her to death while the other held her hands. Some fingers of her right hand were missing where the knife had cut as she raised her hand to protect herself.

"The SOB, Vaccaro, got a life sentence," Vernon says, and he is crying again, "and it's been four years and they haven't fried Willie's ass yet. We've been waiting and waiting for justice to be done. I can't rest until justice is done. All you hear about these days is the rights of the criminal. What about our rights? Don't we have a right to see this chapter closed?"

I wonder how Vernon and Elizabeth would have fared emotionally if Robert Willie, like Vaccaro, had been sentenced to life imprisonment. He would have slipped into anonymity behind Angola's walls, his fate sealed, his crime punished, and maybe these grieving parents could, over time, have laid down their grief and carried on with their lives. But now they are like two deer paralyzed by headlights in the road. All they can think, all they know, all they want is the death of their child's murderer that the state has promised them. So they follow the case in the courts. They hold their breath each time there's a new appeal. They wait and wait, reliving their daughter's murder again and again. And the hope is that when Willie's death does come, it will ease their pain and their loss. At last, they will have *justice.*

The pale October sun has been sliding steadily downward and through the window I can see the trees turning into dark purple silhouettes. Inside, darkness has been slowly seeping into the room. Elizabeth gets up and turns on a lamp. I know I have to drive back across the lake, but time is standing still. In the presence of such suffering, it doesn't matter how late I get home.

"Let's go to the kitchen and I'll make us some coffee," Elizabeth says. As we walk to the kitchen, Vernon keeps talking, "Willie and I met face to face in the hallway during his trial. He was cocky. He said he'd never go to the chair. I told him I'd see his ass fry."

Then he picked up on the point he had made to me when I met him on the capitol steps—that the only way to be sure we get rid of someone like Willie is to kill him. Elizabeth agrees. "That's the only way we can be sure that he'll never kill again," she says. "In prison he could kill a guard or another inmate. Someone like Willie can escape from prison."

I disagree with these arguments, but the intensity of all the sorrow silences me. I do not offer counterarguments. I just let all the torrents of rage and loss and sorrow tumble over me.

"He's a mad dog, that's what he is," Vernon says, and he tells how Willie and Vaccaro, after killing Faith, had continued their reign of terror, kidnapping a teenage couple, raping the girl, tying the boy to a tree, stabbing him, shooting him, and leaving him for dead. "Miraculously he lived," Vernon says, "but he's partially paralyzed from the waist down."

Vernon has stopped crying. It's his anger talking now, which I welcome. At least he's not dissolving in grief and loss. I want him to survive this terrible sorrow. I want him to make it.

"Before their rampage was over," Vernon says, "Willie and Vaccaro drove through five states, stole four cars, robbing, raping, and killing all the way. The law had a bulletin out on 'em for the kidnapping, and that's what they first arrested them for. They had turned the young Madisonville girl loose, and she had gone to the police and described them. When the law arrested the two of them in Arkansas for the kidnapping," he says, "they didn't yet know they had killed Faith. That only came out as they confessed to the kidnapping."

I think of the young man I have just visited with the neatly combed hair and the quiet voice. I think of how he exhaled his smoke downward so that it didn't blow into my face.

"I am going to be Robert Willie's spiritual adviser," I tell them quietly. I have to say it. I have to let them know. We have made our way to the kitchen and now sit at the small table there. Elizabeth is pouring the coffee into our cups.

"He needs all the spiritual advisers he can get," Vernon says. "He's an animal. No, I take that back. Animals don't rape and kill their own kind. Robert Willie is God's mistake. Frying in the electric chair is the least of the frying he's about to do when God sends him to hell where he belongs," and he jabs his finger downward.

This Robert Willie, who is he? I recoil at the thought of him. How dare he calmly read law books and concoct arguments in his defense? He should fall on his knees, weeping, begging forgiveness from these parents. He should spend every moment of his life repenting his heinous deed. But, judging from my first visit, he seems to be in a world of his own, oblivious to the pain he has caused others. Remorse presupposes enough self-forgetfulness to feel the pain of others. Can Robert Willie do that? I doubt it and wonder whether his death sentence makes his own repentance even more difficult. *Someone is trying to kill him,* and this must rivet his energies on his own survival, not the pain of others.

A few days after visiting the Harveys I visit Robert for the second time. I have a notebook on the front seat of the car. I'm not allowed to take it into the prison (only attorneys and news reporters can bring writing materials inside), but afterward I'll jot down notes from our conversation. . . .

"I went to visit the Harveys," I say. "They told me about Faith's death. Robert, you raped and stabbed that girl and left her to rot in the woods. Why?"

"All right," he says, and he lights a cigarette. "I'm telling you what, ma'am, I'm real, real sorry that girl got killed, but like I told the police when they was questioning me, I didn't stab and kill that girl. Joe went crazy and started stabbin' her. I told them that when I gave my statement, and I offered to take a lie detector test then and there on the spot, but they wouldn't let me. I told them I don't kill women. I don't. But when Joe started stabbin' her, her hands went up and he told me to hold her hands and I did. But it was more instinct than anything, and with him slashing with that knife, there was blood everywhere, I was scared. I just did what he said, and afterwards we was runnin' around in those woods lost, goin' through brambles and mud and couldn't find the truck and I was some scared."

I groan inside. The truth. What's the truth? Not another one of those situations where two perpetrators each accuse the other and it's so difficult to ferret out the facts. He admits that he held Faith's hands. He did not come to her defense. Even if he's telling the truth and did not stab her himself, he is responsible for her death. Does he know what he did? And if he does, how can he live with himself?

"Robert," I say, "Vernon Harvey tells me that you taunted him in the courtroom. You said you'd never fry, is that true?"

"He said he'd see me fry and I said, 'The hell you will,' " Robert says. "I'd never show my inner feelin's out there in the courtroom, in public like that. Ever since I was a little boy I ain't ever showed my real feelin's. See, my daddy went to Angola when I was a baby. People would point to me and say, 'That's John Willie's kid,' and wham, there I am in a fight. My mama had her hands full in her own life, much less trying to take care of me. I don't blame her none for what's happened. She separated from my daddy when I was real young and married again, and me and my stepfather never got on too good. I'd stay with my grandmother sometime, my aunt and uncle sometime, my mother and stepfather sometime. By the time I was in seventh grade I was sniffin' glue, paint, gasoline, you name it. Me and Joe were loaded on Valium, acid, and booze when this happened with Faith Hathaway. I had this light airy feelin' inside. I hadn't slept in two nights."

I say, "Robert, drugs don't explain violence like this. Thousands of people take drugs and don't slash and rape and kill people. The Harveys told me about that young boy, Mark Brewster, and his girlfriend whom you and Joe kidnapped after you killed Faith. They say you raped the girl and stabbed the boy and shot him and tied him to a tree and left him to die. The boy's paralyzed now for the rest of his life and God knows about the emotional scars on the girl. Did you do that?"

I am keeping my voice low, but it's an effort. I am quivering inside.

He pauses. He always speaks in a measured way and softly. "Yeah," he says, "I let Joe Vaccaro call all the shots and I went along. I wasn't thinkin' straight." . . .

"Have you ever told the Harveys that you're sorry?" I ask him.

"Well, ma'am that's hard to do because Vernon Harvey keeps holding these press conferences, mouthin' off about how he can't wait to see me fry. Personally, I think the guy is his own worst enemy. He just needs to let it go, man. The girl's dead now, and there's nothin' he can do to bring her back. Even watchin' me fry ain't gonna bring her back, but he won't let it go and he's just makin' himself miserable, in my opinion."

"Robert," I say, "you understand, don't you, that you are the *last* person in the world with the right to say that to Vernon Harvey?"

"I guess you're right," he says, but he doesn't seem terribly convinced.

"Hell," Robert says, "it's hard, ma'am, to be having much sympathy for *them* when, here, they're tryin' to kill *me*. When somebody's after your hide, it kind of tends to occupy your mind, if you know what I mean."

"But look what these parents are going through," I say. "Their daughter raped and stabbed and left to die in the woods. What if someone did that to your mother? What would you want to do to them?"

"Kill 'em," he says. "I sure as hell would want to kill 'em."

I'm quiet then for a while.

I'm hoping he can take in his own words so he can feel the Harveys' pain. The quiet does not last long. He says, "I'm gonna be honest with you, ma'am, I believe in the death penalty in some instances, like for people who rape and torture little children. Messin' over adults is one thing, but little innocent kids? I'd pull the switch on them myself."

I have heard that prisoners are hardest on child molesters. I guess everybody's got a code of evil, a line beyond which they consider redemption impossible. But the irony jolts me. Here's a man condemned to death by the state and here he is defending the death penalty—not for himself, of course, only for *truly heinous* killers.

"If you do die," I say, "as your friend, I want to help you to die with integrity, and you can't do that, the way I see it, if you don't squarely own up to the part you played in Faith's death."

I tell Robert I've been talking to his mother on the telephone and he says that now she's his biggest worry. He can do it, he's "ready to go," but he doesn't know what he'll do if she starts "crying and breaking down" in the death house.

That was what Pat Sonnier had feared most, his mother breaking down and causing him to lose emotional control.

"You don't always have to be this tough Marlboro Man," I say to him. "Real men cry, you know."

He gives a little laugh, a nervous laugh, and I know he's listening.

"There's another mother who's suffering, Robert," I say. "Elizabeth Harvey. She and Faith were very close. They used to talk to each other almost every night on the phone. They used to go shopping together. She had her brother come to dig her daughter's jaw out of a body bag to do a dental check before she could accept that this daughter, whom she loved so much, was really dead. And she will live every day of her life knowing that her daughter died a terrible death—and alone. And, Faith—have you ever really faced her pain, felt it, taken it inside yourself? I'm saying all this to you because I'm your friend and I care about you and I just can't see you going to your death and not owning up to the part you played in Faith's death."

"I am sorry, I really am sorry about Faith," he says, "I hope my death gives the Harveys some peace. I really do. Maybe my death will help them get some relief, some peace."

His head is down and his voice is soft, and when he says this I say to him, just as I said to Pat Sonnier, that his last words can be words either of hate or of love and maybe that's the best thing he can offer the Harveys, a wish for their peace.

The guard comes to tell us time's up. As I am about to leave, I get a message that Major Kendall Coody wants to see me.

The major. That's top brass. This is the man in charge of death row who supervises inmates and guards. I brace myself. He probably wants to assess Robert's seriousness about escaping. Maybe he wants to know if Robert has a "cyanide finale" or something like that planned.

He asks me to pull the door behind me as I step inside his office.

"How's Willie doing?" he asks.

"Okay," I say, "I think he's okay."

He's seated behind his desk and I can't tell how tall he is. I'd guess he's in his late forties. He has a broad, square face, fair skin, and a thick brown mustache. His dark brown hair is neatly combed except for a thick shock that falls in the middle of his forehead. He has light brown eyes and wears glasses. He is a troubled man.

"I'm not sure how long I'm going to be able to keep doing this," he says. "I've been through five of these executions and I can't eat, I can't sleep. I'm dreaming about executions. I don't condone these guys' crimes. I know they've done terrible things. I don't excuse what they've done, but I talk to them when I make my rounds. I talk to them and many of them are just little boys inside big men's bodies, little boys who never had much chance to grow up."

He tells me that he talks to each inmate on the Row almost every day. In his job, that could be a serious occupational hazard—getting to know inmates personally, finding the little boy inside the man—dangerous territory indeed, for a man whose duty is to oversee their execution. One of the personnel at the prison had once told me about the orientation of guards at Angola, and that's the first rule they are taught: never relate on a *personal* level with inmates.

Coody tells me that he also serves on the "Strap-down Team," the guards who accompany the prisoner to the electric chair. That means he's not insulated from the "final process." He's not like the other guards who work day in and day out on death row, feeding men, talking to them, supervising their showers, delivering their mail—but never seeing the green room with the brown wooden chair. But five times now this man has been in the execution chamber at night and then back here on the Row for business as usual the next morning. He's never had to strap them in the chair, he says, but he's walked them to the chair and sometimes been the one to gather up their personal belongings—clothes, toilet articles, books—from the holding cell after they're dead.

"I get home from an execution about two-something in the morning and I just sit up in a chair for the rest of the night. I can't shake it. I can't square it with my conscience, putting them to death like that."

What a spot to be in. Major Coody is not like the governor, the head of the Department of Corrections, the warden, and most of the other guards around here. He can't persuade himself that he's just *doing his job*. My heart goes out to him, and I tell him how I felt watching Pat Sonnier die, and I say that it seems to me that he is someone who is unable to shield himself by rationalization and it may mean that he will need to find another job.

It is not a very long conversation.

"I respect you, Major Coody. I'll pray that you follow where your heart and conscience lead," I say to him as I am leaving, and his eyes look into mine as he reaches out for my hand.

It is the last time I see him alive.

I do not run into him again over the next weeks prior to Robert's execution, nor do I notice if he is one of the guards surrounding Robert as he walks to the chair. A couple of months after Robert's execution I hear that he has been transferred to another part of the prison, and then I hear that he has asked for early retirement, and then I hear that he has died of a heart attack.

Two years after Robert's execution, in 1986, our abolition group is sponsoring a weekend seminar on the death penalty at Loyola University. Not a big event by any means, attended by a hundred or so of those most dedicated to the cause. Proponents of the death penalty *never* attend these seminars.

Except the Harveys.

As we are about to begin the first session I look across the room and see them. I avert my eyes. All day I avoid them. Why have a confrontation over irreconcilable differences, a confrontation that can only lead to further estrangement and pain?

I make it through the whole day without meeting them. The day is ending. People are beginning to leave. Elizabeth is standing near the exit and I don't see her ahead of time and suddenly here she is and here I am and she says, "You haven't even looked at us all day. We haven't heard from you in such a long time. When are you coming to see us?"

I'm stunned. I tell her I'll be glad to come see them if they want me to come. Vernon, standing near Elizabeth, nods. Yes, they want me to come.

I realize that in their sorrow they must be lonely, but even more, I know it's rough going organizing victims' families in Louisiana. *They want me to visit.* It is an invitation for which I haven't dared to hope. I remember Vernon saying he liked apple pie. I decide to bake an apple pie. When sorrow and loss and conflict are overwhelming, bake a pie.

A few weeks later I drive up to the Harvey home in Mandeville across
Lake Pontchartrain. Same tall trees near the house. Same swing on the porch.
Vernon is recuperating from hip surgery. He's glad to get the pie. Elizabeth
says, "For disagreeing with somebody so strongly, you sure are tearing into
her pie." Vernon just smiles and eats. I sit in their kitchen and we talk and
drink coffee. I am glad to be in their company again. They talk about helping
victims' families—going with them to court, telling them what to expect,
educating them on their rights. "Which we have had to learn on our own,"
Elizabeth says, "because we sure didn't have anyone to teach us," and then
she says how they experienced two victimizations—one with Faith's murder
and the other at the hands of the criminal justice system. "All the rights of
the criminal are protected—they have lawyers appointed to them if they can't
afford one and their rights are all spelled out and they are told what those
rights are, but nobody told us our rights. We didn't even know we had rights.
Like the right to see the autopsy report and Faith's body. They kept me from
seeing Faith's body and then once the chance had passed it was too late. I
know they were trying to protect me but that was my decision, not theirs,
to make."

"What people don't know," Vernon says, "is that if they get stonewalled
by local law-enforcement people, they can call up elected officials—
politicians—and get some action."

"In dealing with the D.A. and the police," Elizabeth says, "you could
probably get more information when you get your car stolen than if your
child is killed because then you're the victim, but when someone's killed,
they figure the one killed is the victim, not you, and you're pushed to the
sidelines. You and what your needs are don't even count and you can call
them until you're blue in the face and they won't call you back. Some do.
Some are understanding, but not most of them. They're too busy prosecuting
the criminal to be concerned about the victim's family."

Elizabeth says that she tells victims' families to be calm and unemotional
when they telephone the D.A. or the police for information. "They don't deal
well with emotionally upset people, they just hang up on you, and it's real
important to keep lines of communication open with them. There's one case
I'm thinking of where the woman's daughter could talk to the police calmer
and easier than her mother, and so the daughter was the one who always
made the phone calls for information. I tell them that after they hang up the
phone, then they can cry and scream all they want, but not when they're
talking to law enforcement people."

Vernon says prosecutors may not even want victims' families in the courtroom. "After all their hard work they're scared some relative of a victim
might lose control and blurt something out and the jury will hear it and
they'll lose the case."

"Some people don't know that they can give a victim impact statement,"
Elizabeth says, "and most don't know about the victim assistance programs
that are available. Again, it's the sheriffs and D.A.'s who are supposed to let

folks know about these programs, but plenty of them don't get the word out. There's no votes in it for them. They don't get elected or reelected for helping victims. We're making progress and now more people do know about the programs, but not nearly enough."

Dealing with the law enforcement officials is one thing, Vernon and Elizabeth say, and the way they were treated had surprised them, but what had surprised them even more was the way all their friends and even Faith's friends stayed away from them after the murder. Few, they say, came to visit them and very few came to the funeral.

"I think everyone was denying that this sort of violent death could hit so close to home," Elizabeth says. "They didn't want to admit it had happened to Faith because then they'd have to admit that it could happen to them, and people don't want to face that."

Vernon talks about the abolitionist seminar they had attended at Loyola University. He says he had told Elizabeth, " 'We better watch that nun, we better watch her. She's gonna abolish executions if we don't watch out.' "

He says it half joking, half serious. It's easy. The conversation is easy—even with Vernon shingling in his favorite death-penalty arguments and my countering with my own. I tell them about Robert's last hours and his struggle to formulate his last words. I tell them that I believe he was sincere when he said that he hoped his death would relieve their suffering.

Vernon begins to cry. He just can't get over Faith's death, he says. It happened six years ago but for him it's like yesterday, and I realize that now, with Robert Willie dead, he doesn't have an object for his rage. He's been deprived of that, too. I know that he could watch Robert killed a thousand times and it could never assuage his grief. He had walked away from the execution chamber with his rage satisfied but his heart empty. No, not even his rage satisfied, because he still wants to see Robert Willie suffer and he can't reach him anymore. He tries to make a fist and strike out but the air flows through his fingers.

I reach over and put my hand on his arm. My heart aches for him. I sympathize with his rage. Reason and logic are useless here. In time, I hope Robert's final wish comes true: that Vernon and Elizabeth find peace. But I know that it will not be Robert's death which brings this peace. Only reconciliation: accepting Faith's death—can finally release them to leave the past and join the present, to venture love, to rejoin the ranks of the living.

PART XII

NONVIOLENT TRADE UNIONISM

DOCUMENT 42

Cesar Chavez

Historically, farm workers have been too scattered, too difficult to reach, and too transient to organize. Cesar Chavez (1927–1993) led a successful struggle to organize farm workers into trade unions. Deeply committed to nonviolence, Chavez and his associates used unconventional methods such as the hunger fast and the consumer boycott. One of his last campaigns was against the use of pesticides in commercial agriculture.

A 1965 march from Delano to Sacramento first brought Chavez to national attention. He is said to have begun the march with 70 persons and to have ended it, 300 miles later, with 10,000. The boycott of table grapes publicized by the march ended when growers agreed to a contract with the union in 1970.

Chavez fasted for 25 days in 1968, for 24 days in 1972, and for 36 days in 1988.

Between 1975, when the California legislature adopted an Agricultural Labor Relations Act, and the early 1980s, the membership of the United Farm Workers grew to 90,000. At the time of Chavez' death, the number of farm workers under contract was an estimated 9,000 to 22,000.[1]

In the documents that follow we glimpse the roots of Chavez' ideology, as he perceived them, in his mother's nonviolence and his father's militancy

---

[1] Bureau of National Affairs, *Labor Relations Reporter,* Aug. 30, 1993.

(Document 42A); his appeal to the growers in the manner of Dr. King's letter from Birmingham jail (Document 42B); and his highly unorthodox belief that a people's movement should not take money from outside sources, but seek financial support from those who are least able to give (Document 42C). "When you sacrifice, you force others to sacrifice. It's an extremely powerful weapon."

A.　Cesar Chavez Recalls

My mom kept the family together. She was the sort of woman who had time for her children, who would talk with us. She used many dichos—proverbs— and they all had a real purpose. "What you do to others, others do to you" was one of them. "He who holds the cow, sins as much as he who kills her." "If you're in the honey, some of it will stick to you." Though she was illiterate, she had a tremendous memory. I think most illiterate persons do because they must rely on their memories.

She also gave us a lot of consejos—advice. She didn't wait until something went wrong, nor was she scolding when she was doing it. It was part of the training. At first I didn't understand, but she would make it easy for us. She would say, "He who never listens to consejos will never grow to be old."

I remember her story of the stone freezing in the boy's hand. It was a very disobedient son who came home drunk and got real mad at his mother. He picked up a rock and was about to throw it at her when it froze to his hand. Her stories were about obedience and honesty and some of the virtues. There were others that dealt with miracles. The range was very wide.

When I look back, I see her sermons had tremendous impact on me. I didn't know it was nonviolence then, but after reading Gandhi, St. Francis, and other exponents of nonviolence, I began to clarify that in my mind. Now that I'm older I see she is nonviolent, if anybody is, both by word and deed. She would always talk about not fighting. Despite a culture where you're not a man if you don't fight back, she would say, "No, it's best to turn the other cheek. God gave you senses like eyes and mind and tongue, and you can get out of anything." She would say, "It takes two to fight." That was her favorite. "It takes two to fight, and one can't do it alone." She had all kinds of proverbs for that. "It's better to say that he ran from here than to say he died here." When I was young I didn't realize the wisdom in her words, but it has been proved

From Jacques E. Levy, *Cesar Chavez: Autobiography of La Causa* (New York: W. W. Norton, 1975), pp. 18–19, 32–33, 225–227. Reprinted by permission.

to me so many times since. Today I appreciate the advice, and I use quite a few of the dichos, especially in Spanish.

———————

Although my mother opposed violence, I think the thing that she really cracked down on the most was being selfish. She made us share everything we had. If we had an apple or a tiny piece of candy, we had to cut it into five pieces.

As she was an excellent cook, she baked pies out of anything, even potatoes, sprinkling brown sugar on them. She would try to give us equal shares, but if one of us complained, "I got the smaller piece," she would take them away from everybody. Then the others would put the heat on the one who complained. Eventually we got to the point where we would say, "Well, I got the smallest piece, but it doesn't matter."

She also taught us never to lend money to our brothers or sisters. "If you were really brothers, you wouldn't let money come between you. You'd trust them." So instead of lending, we'd give them the money. Even today, none of us really cares much about money. We never make loans. If we have it, we give it.

Since our beds were outside during the summer, we sometimes huddled under their mosquito netting, even though we burned pans of manure to drive away the thousands of mosquitoes. From that safe haven, we listened to the lively conversations between my parents and their relatives.

It was then that we found out about our uncles, our grandfather, and some of our other relatives who had died. Because many of my relatives were miners, there were stories of miracles in the mines—accidents, mines caving in, and people not getting killed because of their strong beliefs. We had some good storytellers who kept us on the edge of our beds with adventure tales or spooky ghost stories. Others told stories from the Bible.

Then we heard about the Mexican revolution, the battles fought by farm workers, and how they won and lost. There were stories—a lot of them—about the haciendas, how the big landowners treated the people, about the injustices, the cruelties, the exploitation, the actual experiences our uncles had had.

Most of my uncles had left Mexico when they were a lot older than my dad and could remember what they had seen and gone through. They could recall, for example, the foreman who told the people not to eat salt because they would become dumb. They would examine that story and point out that the real reason this was done was not because salt would harm you, but because salt was expensive, and the foreman would pocket the money instead of buying salt for the people. Others then recalled they had been told the same thing about butter.

Stories were told over and over again of how Papa Chayo escaped from the hacienda, how no one could speak out for their rights, how they feared for their lives, how they were driven to flight. They never talked about revolution, but still it was there just under the surface. We learned that when you felt something was wrong, you stood up to it. Later, for example, when we were on a job, my father considered it dishonorable to be fired for being lazy; but if somebody was fired for standing up for a person's rights, it was quite honorable. I remember my dad would stand up for the rights of others, so we automatically did too.

DiGiorgio didn't spend much time fighting us on the picket lines. As they were more mature than other growers, they spent their time gathering information, getting police to do their dirty work, and filing suits against us. Finally, on May 20, they obtained a court order restricting the number of pickets.

We believe that each worker must have the right to protest, and if he can't be on the picket line to do his own protesting, his right for effective striking is taken away.

We saw this injunction as especially unfair because there had been no violence on the picket line. It also threw all of our strategy into a turmoil, because we couldn't use our source of strength, which was the people. We began to struggle desperately for other ways of putting the pressure on the scabs and on the company.

But after several days of particularly futile picketing, people were getting impatient and discouraged. As I just couldn't come up with any solution, I called a meeting at the American Legion Hall in Delano.

The meeting soon got around to the idea that we were losing because we weren't using violence, that the only solution was to use violence. We spent most of the day discussing that. Then, although we had taken a vote at the beginning of the strike to be nonviolent, we took another vote. Except for one older fellow, all voted to continue nonviolently.

Before ending the meeting, I told them that I had run out of ideas of things to do, but I knew that in them, the people, there were answers, and I needed their help to find those answers.

They said yes, but still they left without suggesting anything.

A couple of hours later, three ladies said they wanted to see me. In those days the question of money was extremely severe. We just didn't have it. So the first thing that came to my mind was that the ladies wanted money for some very special personal need. I asked them to come into my little office.

First they wanted to make sure that I wouldn't be offended by what they wanted to tell me. Then they wanted to assure me that they were not trying to tell me how to run the strike.

After we got over those hurdles, they said, "We don't understand this business of the court order. Does this mean that if we go picket and break the injunctions, we'll go to jail?"

"Well, it means that you go to jail, and that we will be fined," I said.

"What would happen if we met across the street from the DiGiorgio gates, not to picket, not to demonstrate, but to have a prayer, maybe a mass?" they asked. "Do you think the judge would have us arrested?"

By the time they got the last word out, my mind just flashed to all the possibilities.

"You just gave me an idea!" I said, then I was away and running. They didn't know what hit me.

I got Richard and had him take my old station wagon and build a little chapel on it. It was like a shrine with a picture of Our Lady of Guadalupe, some candles, and some flowers. We worked on it until about 2:00 in the morning. Then we parked it across from the DiGiorgio gate where we started a vigil that lasted at least two months. People were there day and night.

The next morning we distributed a leaflet all the way from Bakersfield to Visalia inviting people to a prayer meeting at the DiGiorgio Ranch and made the same announcement on the Spanish radio. People came by the hundreds. You could see cars two miles in either direction.

We brought the loud-speakers and tried to get the people in the camp to come to the mass, but I don't think more than ten came out. Most of them were out at the fence looking and seeing a tremendous number of people. They were very impressed.

There also was so much confusion, our guys found themselves talking to our members inside the camp for the first time in about three weeks.

The next day at noon something very dramatic happened. When the trucks brought the people from the fields to eat at the company mess hall, about eight women decided to come to where we had the vigil instead of going into the mess hall. The supervisors got the trucks in the way to keep them from coming, but the women went way out through the vines and wouldn't be stopped. They knelt down and prayed and then went back.

That was the beginning.

The same evening about fifty women came. The next evening half of the camp was out, and from then on, every single day, they were out there. Every day we had a mass, held a meeting, sang spirituals, and got them to sign authorization cards. Those meetings were responsible in large part for keeping the spirit up of our people inside the camp and helping our organizing for the coming battle.

It was a beautiful demonstration of the power of nonviolence.

B.   "Letter from Delano"

Good Friday 1969

E.L. Barr, Jr., President
California Grape and Tree Fruit League
717 Market St.
San Francisco, California

Dear Mr. Barr:

I am sad to hear about your accusations in the press that our union movement and table grape boycott have been successful because we have used violence and terror tactics. If what you say is true, I have been a failure and should withdraw from the struggle; but you are left with the awesome moral responsibility, before God and Man, to come forward with whatever information you have so that corrective action can begin at once. If for any reason you fail to come forth to substantiate your charges, then you must be held responsible for committing violence against us, albeit of the tongue. I am convinced that you as a human being did not mean what you said but rather acted hastily under pressure from the public relations firm that has been hired to try to counteract the tremendous moral force of our movement. How many times we ourselves have felt the need to lash out in anger and bitterness.

Today on Good Friday, 1969, we remember the life and the sacrifice of Martin Luther King, Jr., who gave himself totally to the nonviolent struggle for peace and justice. In his *Letter From a Birmingham Jail* Dr. King describes better than I could our hopes for the strike and boycott: "Injustice must be exposed, with all the tensions its exposure creates, to the light of human conscience and the air of national opinion before it can be cured." For our part I admit that we have seized upon every tactic and strategy consistent with the morality of our cause to expose that injustice and thus to heighten the sensitivity of the American conscience so that farmworkers will have, without bloodshed, their own union and the dignity of bargaining with their agribusiness employers. By lying about the nature of our movement, Mr. Barr, you are working against nonviolent social change. Unwittingly perhaps, you may unleash that other force which our union by discipline and deed, censure and education has sought to avoid, that panacean shortcut: that senseless violence which honors no color, class, or neighborhood.

"Letter from Delano," from *The Universe Bends Toward Justice,* edited by Angie O'Gorman (Philadelphia: New Society Publishers). Reprinted by permission.

You must understand—I must make you understand—that our membership and the hopes and aspirations of the hundreds of thousands of the poor and dispossessed that have been raised on our account are, above all, human beings, no better and no worse than any other cross-section of human society; we are not saints because we are poor, but by the same measure neither are we immoral. We are men and women who have suffered and endured much, and not only because of our abject poverty but because we have been kept poor. The colors of our skins, the languages of our cultural and native origins, the lack of formal education, the exclusion from the democratic process, the numbers of our men slain in recent wars—all these burdens generation after generation have sought to demoralize us, to break our human spirit. But God knows that we are not beasts of burden, agricultural implements or rented slaves; we are men. And mark this well Mr. Barr, we are men locked in a death struggle against man's inhumanity to man in the industry that you represent. And this struggle itself gives meaning to our life and ennobles our dying.

As your industry has experienced, our strikers here in Delano and those who represent us throughout the world are well trained for this struggle. They have been under the gun, they have been kicked and beaten and herded by dogs, they have been cursed and ridiculed, they have been stripped and chained and jailed, they have been sprayed with the poisons used in the vineyards; but they have been taught not to lie down and die nor to flee in shame, but to resist with every ounce of human endurance and spirit. To resist not with retaliation in kind but to overcome with love and compassion, with ingenuity and creativity, with hard work and longer hours, with stamina and patient tenacity, with truth and public appeal, with friends and allies, with mobility and discipline, with politics and law, and with prayer and fasting. They were not trained in a month or even a year; after all, this new harvest season will mark our fourth full year of strike and even now we continue to plan and prepare for the years to come. Time accomplishes for the poor what money does for the rich.

This is not to pretend that we have everywhere been successful enough or that we have not made mistakes. And while we do not belittle or underestimate our adversaries—for they are the rich and the powerful and they possess the land—we are not afraid nor do we cringe from the confrontation. We welcome it! We have planned for it. We know that our cause is just, that history is a story of social revolution, and that the poor shall inherit the land.

Once again, I appeal to you as the representative of your industry and as a man. I ask you to recognize and bargain with our union before the economic pressure of the boycott and strike takes an irrevocable toll; but if not, I ask you to at least sit down with us to discuss the safeguards necessary to keep our historical struggle free of violence. I make this appeal because as one of the leaders of our nonviolent movement, I know and accept my responsibility for preventing, if possible, the destruction of human life and property. For these reasons, and knowing of Gandhi's admonition that fasting is the last resort in place of the sword, during a most critical time in our movement last February 1968 I undertook a 25-day fast. I repeat to you the principle enunciated to the membership at the start of the fast: if to build our union required the deliberate taking of life, either the life of a grower or his child, or the life of a farmworker or his child, then I choose not to see the union built.

Mr. Barr, let me be painfully honest with you. You must understand these things. We advocate militant nonviolence as our means for social revolution and to achieve justice for our people, but we are not blind or deaf to the desperate and moody winds of human frustration, impatience and rage that blow among us. Gandhi himself admitted that if his only choice were cowardice or violence, he would choose violence. Men are not angels, and time and tide wait for no man. Precisely because of these powerful human emotions, we have tried to involve masses of people in their own struggle. Participation and self-determination remain the best experience of freedom, and free men instinctively prefer democratic change and even protect the rights guaranteed to seek it. Only the enslaved in despair have need of violent overthrow.

This letter does not express all that is in my heart, Mr. Barr. But if it says nothing else it says that we do not hate you or rejoice to see your industry destroyed; we hate the agribusiness system that seeks to keep us enslaved and we shall overcome and change it not by retaliation or bloodshed but by a determined nonviolent struggle carried on by those masses of farm workers who intend to be free and human.

Sincerely yours,

Cesar E. Chavez

United Farm Workers Organizing Committee
A.F.L.-C.I.O.
Delano, California

C.   Talk on Nonviolence

"When we are really honest with ourselves we must admit that our lives are all that really belong to us. So, it is how we use our lives that determines what kind of men we are. It is my deepest belief that only by giving our lives do we find life. I am convinced that the truest act of courage, the strongest act of manliness is to sacrifice ourselves for others

---

From a talk by Cesar Chavez to a group of church people on October 4, 1971 at La Paz, the farm workers retreat center in Keene, California.

in totally nonviolent struggle for justice. To be a man is to
suffer for others. *God help us to be men!"*

What I'm going to say may not make much sense to you. On the other hand,
it may make an awful lot of sense. This depends on where you are in terms
of organizing and what your ideas are about that elusive and difficult task
of getting people together—to act together and to produce something.

Labor unions today have a heck of a time organizing workers. The church
has a heck of a time organizing people. The government has a heck of a
time organizing people. The Republican Party has a very difficult problem.
So does the Democratic Party. So does almost any institution have a heck
of a time organizing people. Why is it difficult? First of all, if these institutions
hadn't been successful, they wouldn't exist. There were churches that were
successful. There were unions that were successful. There were government
departments that were successful. Someone had the right idea. But that's in
the past. Talking about those successes is like getting up and telling workers
about the great and joyous campaigns in the 30's to organize workers. And
they say, "So what? What about us today?"

Organizing is difficult because in our capitalist society we believe the only
way things get done is with money. Let's examine this assumption by using
the farm worker struggle as an example. Since about 1898, there have been
many efforts to organize farm workers in California and other states. Almost
invariably, at the end of each struggle someone would report, "The workers
weren't ready for it. They didn't want the union. They didn't do their share
to get organized." But every report of organizing attempts also included a
more honest statement: "We had to stop the organizing drive, or we had to
temporarily disband, because we ran out of money." It's a shame.

There isn't enough money to organize poor people. There never is enough
money to organize anyone. If you put it on the basis of money, you're not
going to succeed. So when we started organizing our union, we knew we
had to depend on something other than money. As soon as we announced
that we were leaving the Community Service Organization (CSO), the group
that I worked with so many years, to organize field workers, there were
people who wanted to give us money. In fact one lady offered us $50,000
to organize workers. When I said, "No," she was very hurt. I told her, "If I
take the money now that would be the worst thing I could do. I don't want
the money. Some other time I will, but not now." $50,000 wasn't enough.
The AFL-CIO had just spent a million and a half dollars and they failed. So
why did we think we could do it with $50,000.

We started with two principles: First, since there wasn't any money and
the job had to be done there would have to be a lot of sacrificing. Second,
no matter how poor the people, they had a responsibility to help the union.
If they had $2.00 for food, they had to give $1.00 to the union. Otherwise,
they would never get out of the trap of poverty. They would never have a
union because they couldn't afford to sacrifice a little bit more on top of

their misery. The statement: "They're so poor they can't afford to contribute to the group," is a great cop-out. You don't organize people by being afraid of them. You never have. You never will. You can be afraid of them in a variety of ways. But one of the main ways is to patronize them. You know the attitude; Blacks or browns or farm workers are so poor that they can't afford to have their own group. They hardly have enough money to eat. This makes it very easy for the organizer. He can always rationalize, "I haven't failed. They can't come up with the money so [we] were not able to organize them."

We decided that workers wanted to be organized and could be organized. So the responsibility had to be upon ourselves, the organizers. Organizing is one place where you can easily get away with a failure. If you send a man to dig a ditch 3 feet by 10 feet, you'll know if he did it or not. Or if you get someone to write a letter, you'll know if he wrote it. In most areas of endeavor, you can see the results. In organizing, its different. You can see results years later, but you can't see them right away. That's why we have so many failures. So many organizers that should never be organizers go in and muddy the waters. Then good organizers have to come in and it's twice as hard for them to organize.

We knew we didn't have the money. We knew farm workers could be organized and we were going to do it. We weren't going to accept failure. But we were going to make sure that workers contributed to the doing of this organizing job. That has never been done in the history of this country.

We started out by telling workers, "We are trying to organize a union. We don't have money but if you work together it can be done." 95% of the workers we talked to were very kind. They smiled at us. 5% asked us questions and maybe 1% had the spirit and really wanted to do something.

We didn't have any money for gas and food. Many days we left the house with no money at all. Sometimes we had enough gas to get there but not enough to come back. We were determined to go to the workers. In fact at the very beginning of the organizing drive, we looked for the worst homes in the barrios where there were a lot of dogs and kids outside. And we went in and asked for a handout. Inevitably, they gave us food. Then they made a collection and gave us money for gas. They opened their homes and gave us their hearts. And today, they are the nucleus of the union's leadership. We forced ourselves to do this. We kept telling ourselves, "If these workers don't get organized, if we fail, it's our fault not theirs."

Then the question came up, how would we survive? My wife was working in the fields. We used to take the whole family out on Sundays and earn a few dollars to be able to survive the following week. We knew we couldn't continue that way. And we knew that the money had to come not from the outside but from the workers. And the only way to get the money was to have people pay dues.

So we began the drive to get workers to pay dues so we could live, so we could just survive. We were very frank, very open. At a farm worker's convention, we told them we had nothing to give them except the dream that it might happen. But we couldn't continue unless they were willing to make a sacrifice. At that meeting everyone wanted to pay $5.00 or $8.00 a month. We balked and said "No, no. Just $3.50. That's all we need." There were about 280 people there, and 212 signed up and paid the $3.50 in the first month.

90 days from that day, there were 12 people paying $3.50. By that time we had a small community. There were 6 of us—four of us working full time. There were a lot of questions being asked. Some said, "They're very poor and can't afford it. That's why they're not paying." And a few of us said, "We're poor too. We're poorer than they are. And we can afford to sacrifice our families and our time. They have to pay."

I remember many incidents when I went to collect dues. Let me tell you just one. I'd been working 12 years with the mentality that people were very poor and shouldn't be forced to pay dues. Keep that in mind. Because that comes in handy in understanding what you go through when you're not really convinced that this is the way it should be.

I went to a workers home in McFarland, 7 miles south of Delano. It was in the evening. It was raining and it was winter. And there was no work. I knew it. And everyone knew it. As I knocked on the door, the guy in the little two room house was going to the store with a $5.00 bill to get groceries. And there I was. He owed $7.00 because he was one full month behind plus the current one. So I'd come for $7.00. But all he had was $5.00. I had to make a decision. Should I take $3.50 or shouldn't I? It was very difficult. Up to this time I had been saying, "They should be paying. And if they don't pay they'll never have a union." $3.50 worth of food wasn't really going to change his life one way or the other that much. So I told him, "You have to pay at least $3.50 right now or I'll have to put you out of the union." He gave me the $5.00. We went to the store and changed the $5.00 bill. I got the $3.50 and gave him the $1.50. I stayed with him. He bought $1.50 worth of groceries and went home.

That experience hurt me but it also strengthened my determination. If this man was willing to give me $3.50 on a dream, when we were really taking the money out of his own food, then why shouldn't we be able to have a union—however difficult. There had never been a successful union for farm workers. Every unionizing attempt had been defeated. People were killed. They ran into every obstacle you can think of. The whole agricultural industry along with government and business joined forces to break the unions and keep them from organizing. But with the kind of faith this farm worker had why couldn't we have a union?

So we set out to develop exactly that kind of faith. And by the time the strike came, we had that kind of resolution among members. Only a small percentage of the workers were paying dues. But it was ingrained in them that they were going to have a union come hell or high water. That's the kind of spirit that kept us going and infected other farm workers—this little core of people who were willing to stop talking and sacrifice to get it done.

That was seven or eight years ago. We had different problems in the Union then than we have today. But the kind of problems we had then were problems like not having enough money to pay rent. We told the workers, "If you're buying a house, leave it. Better get a smaller house where you pay little rent because we can't pay much rent." It was a lot of sacrifice and they did it. And we won the strike.

DOCUMENT 43

Jim Sessions and Fran Ansley, "Singing Across Dark Spaces: The Union/ Community Takeover of the Pittston Coal Company's Moss 3 Coal Preparation Plant"

Appalachia has been the scene of some of the most violent labor conflicts in United States history. "Bloody Harlan" County derives its name from the class wars endemic there. Viewers of the movie "Matewan" will recall the violence that afflicted one coal town in West Virginia in the early 1920s.

Reverend Jim Sessions and his wife, law school professor Fran Ansley, took part in an extraordinary episode of nonviolence during the United Mine Workers' strike against the Pittston coal company in 1989. Sessions was an invited participant in the nonviolent occupation of Pittston's Moss 3 coal preparation plant, serving as the occupiers' chaplain. Ansley swelled the crowd of supporters who gathered and camped outside the plant during the occupation.

Jim Sessions and Fran Ansley, "Singing Across Dark Spaces: The Union/Community Takeover of the Pittston Coal Company's Moss 3 Coal Preparation Plant," from *Fighting Back in Appalachia: Traditions of Resistance and Change,* edited by Stephen Fisher (Philadelphia: Temple University Press, 1993), pp. 195–222. Reprinted by permission.

THE TAKEOVER OF MOSS 3

The occupation of the Moss 3 coal preparation plant happened only after the courts and National Labor Relations Board had effectively closed off an entire range of peaceful, nonviolent tactics the union was attempting to pursue. With injunctions blanketing the coalfields, mass actions had ceased, and coal production was picking up again. Local citizens risked arrest merely by traveling their own roads. Astronomical fines and increasingly stiff sentences against the union and individuals were handed down by state and federal judges, who confusingly claimed simultaneous jurisdiction over the strikers' conduct. State troopers were everywhere. Frustration and indignation were setting in as the coalfields faced the winter under what amounted to martial law.

It was becoming clear that the miners could not win unless they could somehow retake the initiative, slow coal production, and challenge the legitimacy of the legal rules that were being used to cripple the strike. Against this background the union decided to take the dramatic move of physically seizing Moss 3. Only too aware that Pittston would attempt to cast the miners as violence-prone thugs, local leaders asked Jim if he would join them as a witness to the nature of the action. Jim's personal account begins the night before the takeover.

September 16

JIM: Sleep does not come easily. My anticipation and apprehension are both at a high pitch. Hours from the coalfields, safe and sound in my own bed in Knoxville, my images of what may be coming seem almost unreal. I know that tomorrow I will be joining a group of miners in the unprecedented step of attempting to take Pittston property and to stay for as long as we can manage a productive way to dig in. But I do not know where the action is to occur, whether we will be in a building or a coal mine, how many others will be with us, or how we will gain entry.

Security is tight, to say the least. For months southwest Virginia has looked as though it were under military occupation. The heavy-handed police presence is designed to ensure that coal production continues in spite of the creative disorder the mineworkers have managed to bring about through massive civil disobedience and community mobilization. The union's use of this strategy is one of the main things that makes the Pittston strike unique.

An early indication for me of the depth and seriousness of the UMWA's new resolve to mount a nonviolent and community-based strike came on June 7 when I was asked to go to Roanoke to visit three union leaders who had been jailed for contempt. They had refused to promise a federal judge that they would tell UMWA members to stop engaging in civil disobedience, and they were consequently sitting in jail. After being allowed to visit these local leaders, I realized that something extraordinary was going on.

The three men had begun a hunger strike to protest their treatment by the judge. During our time together I urged them to be mindful of their health and relayed a message from the union that community support was strong. As we talked, the three reflected on the union's strategy for this strike. They reported that they and other union staffers had committed the time to read *Parting the Waters,* Taylor Branch's book on the civil rights movement in the South, and that they were devoting special study to the thought and the political practice of Martin Luther King, Jr. They were drawing lessons from the mass mobilizations mounted during that era by black students and community members.

Though union leaders had been uncertain how the membership would receive the idea of civil disobedience, the members and their families had responded en masse. On April 18 women broke the ice. Some had been miners themselves. Others were wives, widows, daughters, other kin, and friends of miners. They staged a sit-in at Pittston's local headquarters in Lebanon, Virginia. A week later, two hundred union members sat down in the road at the Lambert Fork mine to block passage of coal trucks. They were arrested by state police. Another three hundred sat in at the McClure mine, and a thousand more outside the Moss 3 preparation plant. Rough handling of arrested demonstrators by state police shocked and angered many participants and community people, but did not dampen people's resolve.

Day after day, the miners took to the roads and streets to make their voices heard. As family members and friends of the miners began to join them in civil disobedience, the police became visibly nonplused. Soon over three thousand people had gone to jail. By the time the three staffers were jailed for contempt, the strategy of massive civil disobedience had won broad community support and appeared to be spreading.

At this point, in fact, on the eve of the takeover, the commitment has become strong enough that union orators sense they can speak forcefully at gatherings without fear of provoking undisciplined responses. The strike has begun to carry an air of simultaneous nonviolence and militance that is extraordinary.

The strikers' favorite speaker, UMW vice-president Cecil Roberts, a fourth-generation West Virginia coal miner, was originally sent by the union's president, Richard Trumka, to head the strike when the local leaders were thrown in the Roanoke jail, and has been here directing the strike ever since. He has developed a ritual opening for his frequent speeches at mass meetings: "Welcome to class warfare in southwest Virginia!" Cecil pronounces this greeting, and the crowds roar. He often continues in something like this vein: "All you need to know about this war is this: You work; they don't. You ought to be on our side, because working-class people have been taking it on the chin for the past ten to fifteen years. It's time to stop being quiet. Every major union in this country has taken a stand and recognized this battle for what it is. It's class warfare."

Cecil's other oratorical claim to fame is his unabashed use of the word "love" and his admiration for Dr. Martin Luther King. He has begun quoting entire passages of King's speeches from memory, and his Appalachian audiences have listened in rapt attention.

It is Pittston's own actions that have set the stage for the community to embrace both sides of this militance/nonviolence coin. The company took on new management, which entered the scene with guns blazing. The newcomers first engineered Pittston's withdrawal from the BCOA. Then they refused to enter into serious negotiations with the union over a new contract, leading many to conclude that they were in fact trying to provoke a strike and break the union. When the miners did go out, Pittston responded by throwing down the gauntlet eighties style: it announced that the mines would stay open, operated by replacement workers. With the strike focused on the survival of the union itself and continuation of health-care benefits for pensioners, entire communities—three and four generations deep—have now mobilized to support the striking miners.

If coalfield communities are committing themselves to broad-based nonviolent disruption, the state and federal authorities now appear equally committed to stopping them. As the strike has worn on, the miners and their families have been hauled repeatedly into court. Overlapping layers of injunctions from both state and federal courts are now imposed on the miners and their communities. If a picket line already has nine people on it, a person wandering too close on some related or unrelated errand may get arrested on the grounds that he constitutes the forbidden tenth picketer. Out-of-state strike supporters have been astounded to find themselves pulled over to the side of the road and searched for no apparent reason. Law enforcement personnel escort coal trucks loaded with coal mined by strikebreakers from the mines to their destinations. As a part of the evolving nonviolent strategy, "rolling roadblocks" have developed almost spontaneously, and now numerous people have been arrested for driving too slowly on the curvy mountain roads, because they are thereby impeding the movement of nonunion coal.

As time passes, and thousands of arrests and millions of dollars in fines have piled up, people's inventiveness has been increasingly taxed to find anything effective they can do that won't land them in jail. Despite the union's unprecedented and courageous willingness to keep on in the face of staggering legal penalties, morale has begun to wane. Many families have reached the end of savings and are beginning to lose houses and cars when payments cannot be met. Fall is approaching, and people know from experience how hard it is to be on strike during the winter. Some have begun to question the wisdom of nonviolent civil disobedience.

The union is receiving support from community groups, labor unions, and church organizations around the country. It has developed a creative "corporate campaign" that has tried to take the hardships and issues of the strike to the company's affluent home in Greenwich, Connecticut. Bake sales, soup kitchens, singing groups, quilting raffles—everything anybody can think of is being done.

But the company is still mining coal, and court injunctions continue to narrow the miners' alternatives. It is out of this sense of crisis that the action for tomorrow is being planned. But the crisis atmosphere itself makes me wonder as I lie here whether we will get very far with our plans.

In addition to the state and federal law enforcement presence, Pittston has hired its own private troops. Where local residents often take a moderately tolerant attitude toward the state troopers and even the federal marshals, their hatred for Pittston's private guards, the Vance Asset Protection Team, is clear and unqualified. The Vance guards are seen by union families as modern-day successors to the gun thugs hired to terrorize mountain communities when the union was first trying to organize. These "professionals," with their bright blue jumpsuits and their high-tech hardware, are another important element in the increasingly militarized atmosphere in the coalfields.

Given this highly charged, security-saturated context, it is hard to envision how we might actually be able to "take over" Pittston's property. I have told Fran in strictest confidence the general outlines of what I know, purposefully downplaying the significance of what we may achieve. "Realistically" I expect to get promptly arrested, and then to be out on bond and home again by evening tomorrow or the next day. Still, I have grown to respect the savvy and the seriousness of the strike leadership, and I secretly harbor romantic notions that we might actually be able to take a position, hold it long enough to affect coal production, and gain a wider audience for the miners' demands. Finally I drift off to sleep.

September 17

JIM: I get up early and set out for Virginia. It is the 170th day of the strike, a sunny, summerlike Sunday. My destination is Camp Solidarity, a tent community that has sprung up during the strike on land donated by a local union sympathizer. It has become a gathering place for local strikers and community members and for the constant stream of visitors who come to offer support and to witness for themselves what is happening in this amazing strike.

The preparation of communal meals at Camp Solidarity is an important contribution by local women. Role-stereotyped or not, this assignment puts them in the thick of strike activity and creates an opportunity to meet with neighbors, find out the latest strike news, and participate in group plans and discussions about evolving union and community strategy. Sitting around a table one evening over sausage, biscuits and pinto beans, you might find an auto worker from Michigan, an Eastern Airlines flight attendant from California, a British labor journalist, a Free Will Baptist preacher, and a Jesuit priest discussing the future of the U.S. labor movement and its relation to justice for unemployed workers in Latin America. It is a pretty amazing atmosphere.

Complementing the activity at Camp Solidarity are the efforts of women at the Binns-Counts Community Development Center on the McClure side of the mountain, where hundreds of miners are fed each day, and where many formal and informal gatherings take place. (The Center is funded in part by church groups and is named for Deaconess Margaret Binns, a longtime mountain minister, and for Mary Kathleen "Cat" Counts, who died in the McClure explosion of 1983, the first woman coal miner to be killed on the job in Virginia.) The Center is less isolated than Camp Solidarity and has therefore been more vulnerable to official and unofficial harassment: as the strike has worn on, the Center's doors have been shot out three times, workers have arrived to find the carcass of a dead dog at the doorstep, a bomb threat has been received, and the oppressively close police presence has kept everyone's nerves on edge. None of these stresses have succeeded in cowing those who labor to keep the Center open and vital.

As I approach Camp Solidarity, I think of all the people who have helped to keep it and the community center flourishing. I soon realize that I have joined a thin but almost constant stream of traffic moving toward the camp. We all pass through a system of checkpoints set up along the public road, before finally emerging into the open bottom land of Camp Solidarity. There I meet the camouflage-clad figures who will take part in the action planned for today.

The camouflage clothing has become a signature of the strike. The idea grew primarily from the experiences of UMWA strikers in the ill-fated A. T. Massey strike, where men were frequently arrested and convicted on the strength of descriptions of the clothing they had worn on a picket line or in a demonstration. Someone got the idea that the strikers should all try to look alike, and the notion caught fire. Practically everyone in the coalfields already owned some camouflage, since hunting is popular, so it was a natural choice for generic strike wear. Local stores (at least at the beginning) could easily supply more. And people soon discovered that the wearing of their colors helped their morale and provided a spirit-lifting way to show solidarity. Between camo regalia and the yellow "hostage" ribbons that soon appeared on car antennas, mailboxes, and the doors and windows of local small businesses, the towns of the area have come to wear a look that is somehow dead serious and festive all at the same time.

As I join the gathering crowd, I learn how others have come to be there. Very few know as much as I do about the plans for the day. Those invited to join this brigade were selected with care. The primary criterion was that each man (and all were men) must have demonstrated a personal willingness to accept the discipline of a nonviolent strike and an ability to keep cool under pressure. Planners took the particular situation of each man into account. Each had been asked if he would be willing to help do "something serious" on that day, and each had said yes. Over the weekend each man got a short phone call with the code words: "Kiss the wife and kids goodbye." They knew only that those words meant they were to be at Camp Solidarity at 2 p.m. on Sunday, packed to be gone "for a while."

There are 125 of us assembled. The leadership holds discussions about and with each miner, culling those with pending court cases because of strike activities or with critical family obligations. When this process is completed, a hundred men are left: ninety-five miners, four union staff members, and me. The strikers are divided into "Red," "White," and "Blue" teams, based primarily on each one's state of origin. They have been purposefully selected from West Virginia, Kentucky, and Virginia, so that each state with Pittston miners on strike is represented, even though the focus of the action will be here in southwest Virginia, the most active area of the strike. Eddie Burke (the union staff member with primary responsibility for the occupation) and I are not assigned a team, but are to stick together and help each other and the teams as needed.

A big U-Haul truck pulls up, and the back opens. As we look inside, we begin to realize the scale of what we are involved in, and the level of planning and preparation that has already taken place. The U-Haul is filled with 105 backpacks and bright orange vests. Each pack has ten days' worth of rations and supplies. The union has already bought a share of Pittston stock in each of our names, and when we arrive at our destination, we will announce that we are there "to inspect our property." Accordingly, we begin to call ourselves the Stockholders Brigade. The entire scheme is finally laid out in an old army tent. We learn that the plan is to take over the third-largest coal preparation plant in the world. Not one man backs out.

The giant Moss 3 facility is near the small town of Carbo in Russell County, Virginia. It is Pittston's largest coal preparation plant and ordinarily handles about 22,000 tons of coal a day. When it is shut down, every Pittston mine in the area ceases production. If the men can occupy this plant and stop coal from moving through it, they will be successfully pursuing a strike "the old-fashioned way"—by stopping production. Wall Street has at several important junctures cheered Pittston on in its effort to roll back longstanding agreements with the UMWA and has been quite sanguine about Pittston's power to have its way. Hurting Pittston's ability to process and deliver coal would surely send a message in a language these players could understand.

We pull out of Camp Solidarity packed into two U-Haul trucks and an old school bus with the seats removed, our pulses racing and hopes high. As we head toward Carbo, additional inconspicuous caravans of striking miners are also winding their way through the mountains from a number of assembly locations. They do not know where they are going or what they will find when they get there, but most people apparently suspect (and hope) that it is something big. The strike *needs* something big. The caravans stop periodically while leaders open their next set of sealed instructions to learn which fork in the road to take. At the same time a decoy group is sent ostentatiously to a mine in McClure, Virginia. Fake leads and deceptive rumors about an action in McClure are put out over car radios to be picked up by "the Vance" and the state troopers. Trees mysteriously fall across roads after the false leads are followed, significantly slowing the process of retreat.

Meanwhile the various caravans heading for Moss 3 are converging. They are to pass certain checkpoints at given moments along the way. Timing is critical, not only for the sake of surprise and successful entry, but also so that supporters will arrive immediately after our entrance, to secure the gates against attempts to evict us. Although there are some tense moments, we arrive on schedule at 4:10 p.m.

The road leading to the preparation plant is beginning to fill with hundreds of supporters and some media representatives, alerted at the last moment. We pile out of the vehicles, and everything begins to happen very quickly. We see the giant plant looming up before us. Amazingly, the gates are wide open. Eddie picks up his bullhorn and urges us on our way. We walk quickly through the open gates as planned, team by team, our hands high in the air to indicate we are unarmed. Two Vance Security men are the only guards anywhere in evidence. They take one look at our group and run to the shelter of their pickup truck, where they roll up their windows, hunch down in their seats, and stare out at us with hostile eyes. To see the swaggering Vance bullies cowed and surprised is a tremendous boost to everyone's spirits.

No reinforcements appear in time to hamper our entrance. The timing has been planned to catch the state troopers during a shift change. As things turn out, the troopers are caught six miles away from Moss 3 and are forced to tail after the train of supporters who are by now streaming toward the plant. The troopers are the last to arrive.

As we actually step through the plant gates, a huge crowd behind us is cheering us on. We are concerned about a panicked overreaction from the guards, and Burke keeps announcing over and over on the bullhorn, "This is a peaceful action. . . . We are an unarmed group. . . . I repeat, we are unarmed. No person or property will be harmed. We are simply here to inspect our property." We have been told that if shots are fired, we are to kneel and hold our ground until told to proceed.

The union has done everything its leaders could think of to prevent any of us or anyone else from being harmed. One man in each team is equipped with a gas mask and heavy gloves; these are "chuckers," who are to handle tear gas canisters if any are used. A helicopter hovers overhead, in radio contact with us and ready to help if anything unexpected happens. But it turns out that more contingencies were planned for than actually develop. We have caught them completely off-guard. There are a small number of supervisors inside the plant. We ask them to leave peacefully, assuring them that they will not be harmed in any way, and they quickly comply.

The gates we enter open directly onto County Road 600. From there a narrow bridge crosses a creek onto the Pittston property. From the bridge to the plant is a span of about two hundred yards with two giant silting ponds between. The plant is six stories of ramshackle steel plates and girders that enclose massive coal crunching machinery. Narrow steel stairs wind up through the machinery and connect the six floors of the plant. As we enter the plant, we climb single file up four flights of those stairs to the central control room.

The last man mounts the last step, and we look at each other and grin. Incredible: we are inside, and in control. The entire takeover has taken about twenty minutes, and has gone thus far without a hitch. Quickly everyone is deployed to secure the doors; watches are appointed to scan in every direction. Communications are set up, using two-way radios, with prearranged posts on the outside. In fact, throughout the occupation we are in constant communication with numerous checkpoints. (The union's expertise in communication is only one of several ways in which the Vietnam experience common to many of the miners will prove relevant during this nonviolent occupation.)

Soon after we enter, strike leaders speak to us about the great Flint sitdown strike that gave birth to the United Auto Workers and the CIO during the Depression. Auto workers took over and occupied the Fisher body plant in Flint, Michigan, in 1937, and the event marked a turning point in the development of the industrial union movement. Organizers give the Moss 3 takeover the code name "Flintstone" to honor that historic event and claim lineage from it. The men begin to challenge one another to break the Flint record of a forty-four-day occupation (later we learn that union press releases mentioned that record as well). In our hearts, though, we are hoping mainly to make it until nightfall.

We try to make ourselves at home, despite the fact that the environment is far from inviting. A coal preparation plant is a dirty place. Coal dust is literally everywhere. We become smeared with black coal dust, seemingly without touching a thing. There is also the—for me—unnerving combination of electricity and trickling water everywhere. We pick up trash and begin what will come to seem like an eternal sweeping at the ever-present coal dust.

Some men come back from scouting to report that they have discovered a way to the roof. This turns out to be important, because on the roof there is a balconylike area big enough for us to gather in such a way that we can see back down toward the bridge and the road where the crowd of our supporters is still growing, as it will continue to do throughout the occupation.

Someone checks his watch and lets out a whoop. *We have been in for an hour: victory!* But how soon will the troopers move to take us out? There is a good crowd out front, but are there enough to stop an evacuation? And will our supporters be willing to engage in civil disobedience to prevent or delay our removal? (Later we will realize that we were probably at our most vulnerable point at that moment, just barely settled in the plant, with many strikers and potential supporters not yet aware that anything was afoot. But the numbers were increasing, and it would soon become clear that the response of other rank-and-file miners and the surrounding community would play a crucial role in determining how long the occupation would last.) We have made a dramatic move and have important work yet to do, but the initiative now is shifting from us to the company and to other miners and the community.

If the men have doubts about whether their fellow unionists and neighbors will support them, our first visit to the roof removes them. We emerge into the light and squint across the distance to the bridge and the road beyond. One of the men spray-paints "UMWA FOREVER" in huge letters on the side of the building behind our walkway on the roof, and an enthusiastic cheer goes up from the crowd. Even at our distance we can tell the crowd is growing, and the surge of feeling in that cheer is powerful.

As dusk falls, we have our first visit from representatives of the company, escorted by UMWA vice president Cecil Roberts. From the beginning of the occupation, the men have assured the company that the coal plant is safe in their hands, and that the union will be happy to arrange inspections so that management can confirm the safety of its equipment.

Nevertheless, when Cecil enters the facility with two troopers and the Moss 3 superintendent, the latter is visibly tense and hostile. It is funny to watch his surprise when he is introduced to one of our number, Chuck Blevins. Chuck was specially recruited for this action because he had been the plant operator at Moss 3 for twenty-two years. Two years earlier Pittston had shifted him to a small one-man plant on top of a nearby mountain, but Chuck is still minutely familiar with the operation at Moss 3. Six or seven other members of the takeover team are employees from the plant as well. The union was serious when it assured Pittston that it could take proper care of the plant and its equipment.

The Pittston supervisor relaxes visibly once he realizes the expertise on hand. Throughout the plant occupation these orderly inspections continue, each time revealing that the facility is being kept in perfect working order.

As the light fades from the sky, we are summoned out to the roof again and have our first exposure to what will become a nightly ritual: our evening serenade. A mass of enthusiastic supporters have gathered just on our side of the bridge connecting the plant to the county road, getting as close to us as the union's own security team will allow. They are equipped with bullhorns, as well as just plain strong voices, and soon we are trading chants:

"We are!"

"Union!"

"We are!"

"Union!"

The crowd is singing to us, yelling to us, chanting to us, and roaring its approval. It seems to us that if we were state troopers, we would not want to try to wade through that particular crowd on that particular evening. Maybe we will be spending the night after all.

As true dark is coming on, we check our flashlights in readiness for the night. We soon learn that the water to the plant has been cut off. We, of course, have brought water with us in our packs. But the loss of the bathroom is a serious hardship. Back inside the plant we begin to explore our packs in greater detail. Each of the three teams has been provided with checkers, cards, a Bible, a small television. Everyone's individual pack has flashlights, extra batteries, hand lotion, dried food and fruit for ten days to two weeks, two bottled drinks, five canteens, toilet paper, soap, cleaning cloths, and notebooks and pens for keeping personal journals (the notes from one of which you are now reading). All of us take delight in the loving precision with which all these things have been planned. People start autographing the team Bibles.

I decide to try to sleep in the transformer room under constantly blinking red and green control panel lights. It is like bedding down under a giant 4,160-volt Christmas tree that I hope may hum me to sleep. But first Eddie is holding a crackling radio signal next to my head. The message is garbled, but I understand them to be saying that they are trying to get through to Fran, Elisha, and Lee to let them know that I am okay.

FRAN: All day long on Sunday, I feel on edge. For all we knew when Jim left this morning, he might end up with a handful of other hardy souls somewhere down in a coal mine in the wilds of southwest Virginia. Somehow a coal mine does not seem like the kind of place you'd like to be caught by a group of state troopers or Vance security guards. By five o'clock, though, a staff person at the District headquarters in Castlewood, Virginia, has called to say that the men are above ground inside the Moss 3 coal preparation plant, and everything is all right.

Next we start monitoring the news media and calling friends to alert them to what is happening. The children and I are proud and excited to be even indirectly involved in this important action. It is hard to put my full weight down all evening.

At about 9:30 the telephone rings, and I jump. When I pick up the receiver, a friendly voice says, "Hello, I am John Hawks with the United Mine Workers of America. I'm calling to tell you that your family member is safe tonight. Everything is going fine." It was almost like being tucked into bed. We would receive nightly calls for the duration of the occupation. They symbolize for me the care and attention to human-scale details we experienced throughout the takeover.

September 18

JIM: I try hard for sleep this first night, but without much success. I am just too energized. There is a ground cloth in my pack, but it and the sleeping bag are not much comfort on the steel-plated floor. About midnight I finally fall asleep, but awake about three and again at five, and finally get up. I wander out onto the roof. The company has big flood lights trained on the plant, and their glare blinds me so I can't tell much about the crowd. Scores and scores of state police headlights move endlessly back and forth to no apparent purpose. I expect we will be removed at dawn by the troopers and try to scan the scene for any sign that they may be about to make their move.

After all, it can't be in the state's or the company's interest for us to stay here long.

At dawn, as the mists begin to lift, I can discern people on the roads, now stretching as far as the eye can see. It is a beautiful sight. The men begin to rise and clean up. We pack all our gear so we can be mobile at any time, a pattern we are to repeat each morning.

As I pull my things together, I look around at the collection of men who have ended up in this odd position together. The oldest is sixty-one; the youngest, twenty-seven. There are members from all three states where Pittston miners are striking. Two black miners are in the group. There are 1,400 years of mining experience represented among the group.

One of the miners from West Virginia is a handsome black man named Doug Johnson. He is thirty-three years old and lives two miles from historic Blair Mountain in Logan County, scene of some of the most protracted and violent episodes in UMWA history. Doug tells me that when he was sixteen, he and his family lived just below the defective dam that collapsed in the 1972 Buffalo Creek disaster. One hundred and twenty-seven people died in that disaster, seven were never found, and 4,000 were left homeless. They were victims of gross negligence when the coal refuse dam, created by Pittston and owned by its subsidiary, Buffalo Mining Company, gave way and poured 130 million gallons of water through the narrow, crowded valley of Buffalo Creek in the worst flood in West Virginia history. Doug went to work for Pittston four years later when he was twenty. He now has a three-year-old son. He shakes his head, "That Pittston, it's got me coming and going."

Another member of the Moss 3 brigade is the Reverend Johnny Fred Williams of Dripping Springs Free Will Baptist Church. He lives in Haysi, Virginia. I ask him about his family and he tells me that his wife works. He also has three daughters: two are already married, and his "baby" is to be married this coming Friday. She wants him to perform the ceremony, but he assures me that if he is still in Moss 3 or in jail on Friday she will understand. He says his church is split between union and nonunion, but he feels certain that even the nonunion people will understand what he is doing and support him in standing "for what is right" by his own lights.

Rayford Campbell also talks about his family. He tells me that his father is Travis Campbell, a seventy-eight-year-old Free Will Baptist preacher with black lung disease. Rayford's grandfather also had black lung, and he died of it. Rayford says, "A man who won't take care of his family is worse than an infidel." He follows with a remark I will hear echoed many times: "It's a shame we have to go through this for a job."

T. Larry Ford, Jr., is the oldest of five boys. The other four all live nearby. Their father is a minister who died at the age of fifty-one on the first day of the strike, back in April. Larry thinks the company will fire him after the strike, no matter what. He is thinking of taking some other job when this is over. He has two kids: the one in the third grade is gifted and scores in the ninety-ninth percentile on tests she has taken. She loves music and science.

He was in the process of getting her a piano by trading a calf for it, but the deal fell through when the takeover began. He will sell the calf and get her the piano when he gets out of Moss 3, he says.

A brother and I concoct a game of horseshoes or quoits, tossing scrap gaskets and rubber belts over machinery parts that are lying all over the place. By radio a dozen roses are sent to the wife of one of the miners for her birthday, compliments of the union, since her husband won't be home tonight to celebrate it. Blood pressure medicine is ordered for another miner and arrives promptly.

Late in the afternoon the troopers and plant superintendent return. The troopers formally ask Eddie Burke if we will leave voluntarily. Eddie replies that he will not. The trooper asks then if that is true for everybody, and the answer comes back loud and clear: "Yes!" The troopers dutifully go on to inform us that we are trespassing. We figure the stage is set, and we had better be prepared. Some of the men begin to spray-paint the numbers of union locals on the outside wall of the plant, where our support crew can see them, along with "UMWA FOREVER," until every local represented in the takeover is honored. Even "Rev. Sessions" eventually makes it onto the wall, an unwitting reminder of the solitary individualism of professional clergy, maybe, but also a sign of the men's unfailing courtesy and inclusiveness toward me during the events of the week. The American flag and a camouflage flag are raised from the roof. If we have to go, we will go down with colors bravely flying. However, as evening falls once more, we are still here: we have made it through a second day and are facing another night and hopefully another dawn.

September 19

JIM: I am up by 5:30. Soreness from my steel mattress is setting in along with the routine of being in the plant, so sleep has become a goal that must be achieved, not a natural activity.

Anticipation about what might be coming next is also becoming routine. Maybe they will move today, but we said that yesterday. All the formalities have been completed and the orders have been given. What do they have to wait for? What is there to gain? The longer we stay, the greater the benefit for the strike, but also, everyone is realizing, the greater the potential personal consequences.

In the late afternoon, standing on the roof with a bunch of other men, I learn that Fran is here. I am surprised, because we had not talked about her coming up. She is somewhere over there among the perpetual knot of people near the bridge. We talk over the radio, but I cannot make out which little figure she is.

FRAN: By Tuesday, I just can't stand it any more. I know that the site of the building occupation is only three hours from home, and I have no classes to teach on Wednesday. When Rich Kirby volunteers to drive up to Carbo with me after my last class on Tuesday, that settles it. (Rich is a temporary neighbor, staying in Knoxville for a year. His home is in southwest Virginia, and since the strike began he has donated much energy and his considerable musical talents to innumerable strike gatherings of all kinds.) We take off about two-thirty in the afternoon and drive straight to Virginia, not knowing what in the world we will find when we get there. For all we knew, an evacuation might be launched at any time. We also have no idea how close we can get to the plant, and we fear we will be stopped at some point short of our goal by a roadblock of state troopers.

As we go deeper into the coalfields, Rich points out the signs of the growing mobilization that has seized the area since the start of the strike. There are signs in store windows (such as "We respectfully refuse to serve state troopers during the period of the UMWA strike"), slogans spray-painted on walls (such as "We won't go back"), bumper stickers everywhere (such as "Our Jobs, Our Kids, Our Union"), yellow hostage ribbons on antennas and mailboxes.

As we drive out of St. Paul and hit the last stretch before the coal preparation plant, things begin to change even more. We notice little clumps of men standing beside pickup trucks or parked cars at certain points on the road. They look relaxed but alert, as if they are planning to stay where they are indefinitely. Nobody is in any hurry. As soon as they see our yellow ribbon, these men wave and smile or give a thumbs-up sign. Still no troopers or Vance. As we continue, the clumps of people begin getting closer together, and pretty soon the isolated knots of vehicles became more like a broken line and then an unbroken one. Eventually it is as though both sides of the road have become a parking lot.

As we draw nearer to the plant, we get the feeling that we have stumbled into a giant cultural event, something like a cross between a bluegrass festival, a turkey shoot, and an oldtime revival. People are everywhere, standing and talking in quiet groups, strolling side by side down the road, or sitting on tailgates, drinking soft drinks and whittling.

We squeeze our car between two other bumper-stickered, yellow-ribboned cars beside the road, and begin to walk toward Moss 3. The excitement in the air is simply electric. As we cross the small bridge connecting the road with the Pittston property, we are finally stopped by two men in camouflage, each sporting a walkie-talkie and a big grin. "Sorry, we're not allowing anybody beyond this point. Can we help you?"

Suddenly it dawns on us. There *are* no troopers, no Vance, no police. The *union* is in control here. It is as though we have entered another country, another time, another dimension, right here on the ground that was forbidden to the miners by the company and the courts a few short days ago. Now it is UMWA territory.

One of the most extraordinary sensations is looking into other people's eyes, young and old, black and white, men and women. As gazes meet, even between total strangers, there is irrepressible pride and a kind of harnessed elation. I have the impression that *all* of us are thinking, "This is one of the most important experiences of my life. I will remember this until I die."

The boundary where we find ourselves, the line maintained by the union, turns out to be an amazing contact point, a permeable membrane connecting and separating the "inside" and the "outside." From this position, you can see across to a kind of balcony on the preparation plant, and many of the men occupying the plant are lined up gazing out at us. Someone has spray-painted a huge, bigger-than-life "UMWA FOREVER" on the side of the building. The two union sentries explain that they are in radio contact with the men on the "roof," and that if we want to wait our turn, we can talk to Jim.

I look around me and realize that I am not the only family member who has come to visit. At my left stands a woman in full strike regalia. She is covered in camouflage, all of it spanking clean and sporty. Her brand new camo T-shirt is topped off with a bead-fringed camo bandanna at her neck, and a pair of jack-rock earrings dangle from her ears. ("Jack-rocks" are the bent and joined nails that have shown up on the road since the company reopened the mines. They have been sprinkled in the path of union caravans as well as coal trucks, but they have come to symbolize union resistance to the company's provocative decision to run the mines with nonunion workers.)

The woman's young daughter is standing beside her with a camouflage bow in her neatly curled hair. The woman is squinting intently into a pair of binoculars at the roof across the way. Suddenly she begins to laugh. "He's got me in his glasses, and I've got him in mine!" she says. For a couple of long minutes she gazes through the binoculars, chuckling now and then in pure delight. Then the sentry makes radio contact for her. "Stockholder, stockholder, we've got a family member here. Can we talk to Lonnie Evans?"

In a minute Lonnie is on the other radio, and the woman next to me is talking to him at top decibel while the mob of us other miners and supporters appreciatively listen in. She tells Lonnie she is sending in a bag of fresh-baked brownies donated by a neighbor, that his brother has called from out of town to wish him well, that the dog's ailment is better, that she loves him. Next the daughter takes her turn, yelling into her end while her eyes are trained on the tiny figure of her father on the balcony. "Daddy, we're proud of you." Mother and daughter stand and wave for several minutes.

As they turn to go, replacements step up to the line. This is the Students' Auxiliary, a group of middle and high school students who have joined in strike activities to support fathers, brothers, uncles, grandfathers, friends, and neighbors on strike, and to make a statement for themselves about the kind of place they want to live in, the kinds of jobs they want to have when they get out of school.

The mobilization of this younger generation is one of the new developments in this strike, and one of the indications that the support of the community is more than superficial or passive. In the spring, students had staged a walk-out of classes at all three Dickenson County high schools to protest the troopers' rough treatment of the miners in the civil disobedience at the McClure mine. In the summer, kids had walked picket lines, written irreverent songs about particularly hated figures in Pittston management, and staged strike support rallies. On this evening they are there to sing to the Moss 3 brigade, and sing they do, at the tops of their voices. They sing the Appalachian labor hymn "Which Side Are You On?"—written by Florence Reece during the miners' strike in Harlan County, Kentucky, in the 1930s. They sing "We Shall Not Be Moved." They sing new songs about the strike against Pittston.

In a few more minutes, I get my chance on the radio, and with the help of intermediaries and lots of instructions about which button to push, I am soon talking to Jim and hearing his voice come crackling back into my ear. He waves his white hard hat in the air, and suddenly I can pick him easily out of the line-up of men on the roof. It is odd, being helped by strangers to establish this connection to my own husband, at once so intimate and so glaringly public. He seems utterly familiar and utterly transformed, like the liberated grass under our feet, like the occupied building across the way, like "Which Side Are You On?" in the throats of the teenagers of the Student Auxiliary.

Rich and I stand around a while more, watching the parade of visitors who come to pay their different kinds of respects. Then we decide to take a wider tour. We go back across the bridge and out onto the road, walking and mingling with the jubilant, almost dazed crowd. At one point I look around me and realize how many more men there are than women, how many more whites than blacks. Under most circumstances, a woman vastly outnumbered by a crowd of men on a rural road with night coming on would be seriously nervous about her own safety—for good reason. And under most circumstances, a black person vastly outnumbered by whites in that same situation would feel the same. But this is not "most circumstances." And I never felt safer in my life. These people are here to take care of each other and of the men inside, and one consequence of the bond they are feeling is that we all get a glimpse of what a less oppressive set of race and gender relations might one day look like.

This period just before dusk has a little of the feeling of visiting hours at a hospital. Clearly most people are there for the duration—like Jim's co-worker Tena Willemsma, who is out on the road, busy organizing food, helping to guard one of the gates, and holding down other tasks as well. They will be sleeping in the backs of cars and pickups, or maybe not at all. But others have come to pay their respects and will go home at nightfall: elderly women in Sunday clothes, tiny babies wrapped in blankets and passed from hand to hand or held up in the air and pointed toward the "UMWA FOREVER" sign on the side of the plant, older siblings pulling younger ones by the hand through moving streams of people.

In its own chaotic way, the instant city that has sprung up along this road is well ordered. Food is being provided to the crowd for free—purchased, organized, and kept moving by many of the same tough, overworked, and chronically underappreciated women who have provided the backbone of community support throughout the strike. One man tells Rich and me with obvious pride about his wife, who had gone home on Sunday evening and stayed up all night. She cooked five hams and took them to Camp Solidarity, where she met her comrades, and, "Those women had 1,700 ham biscuits here at Moss 3 by seven o'clock on Monday morning." (Later we will hear tales of women working round the clock at Camp Solidarity to feed the occupation support crowd, of women at the Binns-Counts Center cooking hot dogs and hamburgers for one thousand and bussing them over to Moss 3 when it looked as if food was running short.) Port-a-johns have been hauled in and set up. In all the sea of camouflage and pickup trucks, not a single beer is anywhere to be seen.

String musicians are scattered through the area making all kinds of music, along with various groups of supporters making films, shooting video, taping interviews. One of the bridges in the area is being held by members of the Amalgamated Clothing and Textile Workers Union from Pennsylvania. They arrived at Camp Solidarity for a visit just before the building occupation and have allowed themselves to be drafted into the effort. Now they say they wouldn't *think* of leaving while the men are inside. They have never been part of anything like this in all their lives. Neither have the rest of us.

Night is falling, and as we look across at the coal plant, we can see that the guys on the inside have come out on the roof again. This time they have their flashlights with them, and they look like a little swarm of radiant fireflies on the building opposite. A crowd has already gathered for the nightly ritual of chanting and singing back and forth across the no-man's land between the bridge and the plant itself. With bullhorns or enough raw voices, each side can make itself heard by the other.

A group of Kentucky miners arrive, and they have their own contribution. They get on the bullhorn, introduce themselves, and say they have planned a song they want to sing to the men in the plant. One of their members, a gifted singer, lines out "Amazing Grace" in the old style, for all those on both sides of the empty space to hear and join.

There is a resonant pause as we hear our own echoes fall away, and in a minute the musicians have launched us into "Solidarity Forever." As we on our side join raised hands and sway to the rhythm of the grand old song, we look over at the plant roof and see that the lights of the men across the way are also held high and are swaying in time to the music. Tears fall free and unashamed down many faces around me.

When the song is over, people on our side light matches and cigarette lighters and hold them up, so we can send light back across the space to the glowing beams on the roof across the way. Suddenly we realize that the flashlight beams are no longer swaying to the music or bobbing randomly. The men on the roof have trained their lights on the side of the coal plant, and the glowing ovals spell out in huge wavering letters "U-M-W-A." The crowd around me goes crazy. We are stomping and cheering and waving.

(After the occupation was over, the company would be quick to paint over the spray-painted slogans and local union numbers that the occupying miners had put on the side of the building. During an interview with Paper Tiger Television, however, James Hicks, president of Local Union 1259, would remember the night the men used their flashlights to spell out the name of their union. He said, "I can drive up there now after dark and the visualization of those flashlights shining on that tipple is still there. They can't paint over them. . . . And it's something to be proud of.")

Next a member of the Kentucky local asks everybody to kneel. All around me, men and women in camouflage kneel in the gravel road, and the miner-preacher from Kentucky calls down his God's blessing on this just fight.

The true night watch begins then, with a rally and brief speeches from the back of a pickup truck by the union leaders responsible for things on the "outside." Their themes are to welcome all newcomers (UMWA members and representatives of other unions are streaming into Virginia, and each person we talk to seems to have heard of some other caravan on its way from Michigan or Ohio or Texas), to restate again and again the union's stringent commitment to nonviolence (with cordial but clear instructions for any who cannot accept that discipline to leave the scene), to commend the men inside for the personal risks they are incurring by their action, and to urge upon the crowd that the fate of those inside depends largely on the staying power and solidarity of those outside.

Rich and I take one more lingering look at the astonishing scene and head out to where we are to spend the night. We will come back for one quick visit in the morning (assuming, of course, that the men are still here!), but we won't be able to stay long. I have to get back to my job and to the children, though all that seems a thousand miles away.

And of course things will be like that for everyone. "Life" will still go on. People's normal preoccupations and everyday concerns and warts and pettiness and racism and sexism and in-fighting and fearfulness and inertia and weariness are all perfectly real and powerful factors in their personal and political lives. That was true before Moss 3, has been true during Moss 3, and will without a doubt be true after Moss 3 is over, however this specific action turns out. Even a victorious strike will have its bitter side; even dazzlingly right choices will be followed by murky dilemmas with no clear solutions. The coal industry in particular and the American economy in general will still be in deep trouble. The press is likely to continue its shamefully sluggish and niggardly coverage of the strike. None of this can be denied.

But neither can it be denied that there are moments of transcendence that are capable of teaching us, of making us *feel* the possibilities that reside in us, in the people around us, and in the groups of which we are or can be a part. Walking the road and the bridge in front of Moss 3 tonight has been such a moment for me.

Many ingredients leading up to this night were just right: strong leaders who were subjected to the continuing tough and well-informed scrutiny of rank-and-file miners; a cumulative set of decisions by those leaders that convinced workers and communities step by step that the leaders were worthy of trust and respect; a membership knit closely together by kinship and cultural tradition; a union with a long history of militant struggles against management; a recently demonstrated ability to take repeated militant actions and to resist corporate and state authority over and over again; a similarly demonstrated ability to accept the discipline of nonviolence; brilliant tactical planning; adequate resources and a willingness to spend them; growing acknowledgment by union members that they could not win the fight by themselves, but needed the support of their spouses, children, elders, and other people beyond the coalfields; families and communities and outsiders who were willing to respond to the miners' call for support; and finally a decision to tap into two powerful American traditions of social struggle: the industrial union movement of the 1930s and the fight against racial injustice of the 1960s.

But on the road that night, I want to tell you that it didn't feel like correct ingredients. It felt like a mysterious and unexplainable gift of great love and power. I will never forget the look in people's eyes that afternoon or the sound of that singing across black space to and with the sparks on the other side.

The Night of September 19

JIM: New worries begin: the word is that misdemeanor charges are now felonies for us, and that (federal) Judge Williams in Abingdon may be vindictive. The amounts of fines and the length of jail terms are debated. Two or three men are smuggled out of the plant for personal reasons and are replaced with two or three new recruits. (Nothing is said about this silent transfer. It seems as though it is intentionally unnoted as part of our collective discipline. For all anyone knows, the new guys might have been there all along.)

In the mists of evening, people are winding down, going to their watches and dispersing, thinking about the rest of the evening. One very young miner is left on the edge of the roof with a now soft-sounding bullhorn. He is listening for a word from a barely visible lone figure on the bridge:

"Bobby, I love you."

"Connie, I love you."

"We're proud of you."

"I'm proud of you."

"Goodnight, honey."

"Goodnight."

Like two whippoorwills.

September 20

JIM: When the mists clear in the morning, the crowd can see that we have painted "Day 4" on the plant, and a roar goes up. Around eight o'clock in the morning, Fran and Rich make their way across the bridge. I spot them right away, and I interrupt Eddie, who is telling me how he became a Catholic because of the pastoral letter on labor. Fran is beautiful in a blue sweater over an amazingly white shirt. What a treat. We talk over the walkie-talkie. Lee and Elisha are fine and send their love. Friends and family have called. Sentiment and feelings are so much closer to the surface for all of us. Tears come easily.

At morning prayers, which have become a part of our routine, I ask Reverend Williams to pray. He is eloquent, but he pretty much breaks up before he can conclude. I take over the task then and ask for silent prayers for POW-MIA's, as a miner has requested, and for the casualties and sacrifices of all wars, including this one; I bid us to remember that all wars are in some ways class wars like this one. We end together with the Lord's Prayer, so our voices are together.

Water has been turned back on for the sake of the silting ponds. A brother tells me that he has fixed up a hose on the sixth floor, if I want to take a good cold shower in some privacy. I wash my shirt and socks while I am at it.

In the early afternoon a federal marshal and four troopers serve us with the federal judge's order to leave. Seven tonight is the deadline. There is no formal announcement; the court order is not read aloud, but everyone knows the deadline nevertheless. Word is that the state has a fleet of buses parked up the road at the power station, poised to take us to jail. We have a group meeting and Burke updates us. He thinks they will come tonight or in the morning. Be ready. They may try tricks. Watches are set for all night on all sides, and everybody is fully packed and ready. No resisting arrest. We feel strong, almost immune from police action. There is an incredible sense of security because of the giant crowd outside who have pledged that they will have to be taken first before the troopers or National Guard can get to us. All of us are aware of the moment when the seven p.m. deadline passes and still we have not moved.

There is the nightly serenade outside from our folks across the way. A beautiful female voice is singing original songs for this occasion. I murmur, "How beautiful," and Earl, standing next to me, says: "That's my wife, Jean." I know of Jean because she is one of the many women who have invented a new kind of leadership in this strike. She participated in the women's sit-down at the Pittston office. She and other women formed support squads for arrested demonstrators after mass actions. (They would scour the countryside to find out which jails demonstrators had been taken to, then set up a constant vigil outside those jails until people were released.) She has spoken at miners' rallies and traveled outside the coalfields to help build support. She has written songs about the strike and sung them with other women and alone on countless occasions.

As I listen to her that night, she stands in my mind for all the women who took up the new challenges posed by this strike, who cooked biscuits, wrote poems, traveled to strange cities, met totally unexpected new friends from far-away places, who threw themselves into the strike for the sake of those who had gone before, for those who would come after, for their men in the mines, and for the exhilaration of feeling and using their own new powers. Her voice is as clear and pure an Appalachian voice as you could hear anywhere, and carries like a bird across the space from the bridge.

But as we look in that direction, we realize that the flood lights on the road have been taken down. Is that to allow the night to cover their moves? Or ours?

After seventy-six hours our personal, family, real-life needs and loves have begun to focus again in our minds. Why do we have to do this? Why can't all this struggle and risk-taking be a dream? Why can't peace and justice, covenants and contracts, family and loved ones, home and work, be present realities, instead of being across "over there" and "not yet"? We and the crowd pray together over bullhorns and sing and chant, and we think our fourth night in Moss 3 has begun.

But the night is young. Cecil is especially worried about the supporters outside as the crowd has grown, night has fallen, and the troopers are preparing to move. Convoys of supporters and union members are headed into the state, with some people predicting fifty thousand supporters for the next day. The injunction deadline has passed. Law enforcement is going to have to move. But how can they?

Cecil and Eddie call a meeting of all of us. The announcement comes: leadership has decided that the time has come to end the takeover. At the present moment things are incredibly favorable for the union. Support from the community is at a peak. Discipline has been maintained. The plant is in perfect condition. No one has been hurt. The advantages of leaving on our own terms and during a high point are beginning to look significantly more attractive than the dangers of staying.

Nevertheless, the proposal is difficult for us to absorb. There are strong but quietly held feelings. Some want to stay: make *them* move; force *their* hand; why take them off the hook? We are doing fine—better and better, in fact. But there is also a corresponding sense of relief. The men know that the next move threatened by the court would strip them of their tie to the union and take away all their membership rights, including the right to union legal representation. Commitments, desires, ambivalence, and emotions are deep throughout the group. All of us would like to shed the tension of anticipating the personal consequences that will probably flow from continuing the occupation, but we also resist the idea of leaving before we are forced. We have dug into the place.

There are strong talks by Eddie and Cecil. The Moss 3 takeover has achieved its goals: it has reestablished the direction and momentum of the strike; it has dramatically reaffirmed nonviolent, militant civil disobedience as a commitment that works and strengthens the union. With the occupation of Moss 3, the union shut down Pittston's mines and halted production. By reviving a tactic that recalled the great sit-downs of the 1930s, the takeover has reinvigorated support, retaken the initiative, and accelerated the momentum of the strike; it has delivered a dramatic message to Pittston about the miners' seriousness and the depth, breadth, and militancy of their community support. Cecil stresses that this is not the final act of the union's strategy for the strike but only the beginning.

In the end, the same trust, solidarity, and discipline that brought these men here lead them to accept the decision proposed. Acting on the belief that the union leadership has earned their trust in matters of strategy, the men stand firm. The decision is made and reinforced by ninety-nine men moving together to leave, as well and as tightly and in as high spirits as when we entered.

Cecil asks me to close the occupation with prayer. It is hard. Despite all the prayers I have undertaken in this occupation, this one seems different. "I'm all prayed out," I joke, and it's really true. When I finally begin, though, I am blessed with the most heartfelt words that have ever come to me. They fly from my lips. None of us want to part.

But we do, and we are quick down the stairs once we begin. Eddie and I link arms, and we all move together, quickly across the open ground and bridge, with an American flag flying in the lead. We are immediately enfolded into the startled bosom of our favorite mob. Our hats and packs mysteriously vanish as we enter the crowd. Someone hugs me and says, "This isn't a union, it's a movement." Another grabs me and whispers, "This shows we can lead with our head as well as our heart."

There is a short rally of celebration that ends with one more pouring out of "Amazing Grace," and then we are gone. Eddie, Rick, and I pile into the back of a pickup truck that carries us along darkened roads lined for miles with people, cars, and trucks. We duck down like fugitives as we ease through a police roadblock, then happily encounter our own checkpoints, where we are greeted by friendly, fire-lit faces, and finally come safely to Camp Solidarity, where magically our packs, hats, and belongings are waiting for us. The occupation has ended.

AFTERWORD BY JIM

At a briefing for stock analysts the month after the takeover of Moss 3, Pittston president Paul Douglas admitted that the company had overestimated the ability of the courts to control the UMWA's strike activity. All Pittston coal production in Virginia had stopped for almost a week. That could happen again and again. But could Pittston ever know where or when?

Twenty-four days after the takeover, U.S. Secretary of Labor Elizabeth Dole stood in front of Moss 3 announcing that she had asked UMWA president Richard Trumka and Pittston president Paul Douglas to meet in her office the next day. There, after only ninety minutes, an agreement was reached to appoint a mediator, who eventually helped to negotiate an end to the strike.

The settlement was not perfect. Months after the settlement, as Fran and I write this memoir, some miners are still laid off. Some may never return to work. The company won more "flexibility" on work rules, thus eroding hard-fought union victories and shifting more control over the work process back to management. But the terms of the agreement were vastly more favorable to the union than anyone dreamed would be possible when Pittston first set out to break the union, to drop all health care obligations to retirees, and to bust up the BCOA. Although the coal industry in America and the UMWA are still in trouble and still in great conflict, the victories won in this strike, and the methods that won them, stand as a beacon and challenge to the entire U.S. labor movement and to all those in churches and in communities who care about the future of American working people, their families, and their communities.

That tense, emotional last meeting together inside Moss 3 is etched deeply in my memory, as I know it is in the hearts and minds of the other men. As I search for what the future may hold, and as I try to think about how we should move toward that future, I remember Cecil's closing words to us as we stood together in a circle for the last time: "We'll stay just one step ahead of the law. Effective actions don't get bogged down. The question can never be, 'How can we hang on?' but, 'What's next?' "

PART XIII

ANTI-IMPERIALISM

DOCUMENT 44

David Dellinger,
"The Future of Nonviolence"

Born in 1915, David Dellinger attended Yale College and Union Theological Seminary. In 1940 he refused to register for the draft (see Document 19) and served two terms in federal prison. After the war he helped to found the Glen Gardner community in New Jersey, where he made his living as a printer. Dellinger was one of the original editors of Liberation *magazine. During the Vietnam War, he became the principal leader of the national anti-war coalition known as "the Mobilization" after A. J. Muste's death. He was indicted for his role in organizing demonstrations at the 1968 Democratic National Convention in Chicago, and along with other members of the Chicago Eight, was tried, found guilty, and then acquitted on appeal. Thereafter he continued to inspire and take part in a variety of nonviolent actions (see Document 46).*

David Dellinger made several visits to Cuba after its 1959 revolution. Roy Finch, a fellow editor of Liberation *magazine, resigned in protest against what he considered Dellinger's support of the Cuban Revolution. In his*

From David Dellinger, "The Future of Nonviolence," *Studies on the Left* (Winter 1965), pp. 90–96.

autobiography, Dellinger describes the content of a speech about Cuba he made to a very hostile audience of Cuban refugees in Miami in 1964:

> *I say that during a recent visit to Cuba I observed things that I applauded and things that worried me. One thing that worried me was the one-party state, even though there seems to be more freedom within it than most people think. I say that every government needs to be challenged and freedom to do so is important. I found more freedom to criticize the Cuban government than I had expected but was told by some people who do so that they find it harder to get published or to get good jobs, even though they have not been arrested and thrown in jail for it. . . . I mention my concern with the persistence of sexist stereotypes in Cuba, as indicated by the continued absence of males as workers in child-care centers and the elementary schools. Things like that take time, I say. Then I praise the gains I had observed, mentioning the new housing, low rents, the free, consistently improving health care and thriving literacy campaign. And I quote Fidel Castro's recent condemnation of "blind subservience to the Soviet Union" . . .* (David Dellinger, From Yale to Jail: The Life Story of a Moral Dissenter [*New York: Pantheon Books, 1993*], pp. 183–184.)

The impact of Dellinger's encounter with revolutionary Cuba, and his desire to stand beside any group of persons seeking to throw off United States imperialism, are evident in the following essay. His central thesis is that a violent revolution against injustice may in time become nonviolent, but nonviolence can never be used to protect injustice and exploitation.

The theory and practice of active nonviolence are roughly at the stage of development today as those of electricity in the early days of Marconi and Edison. A new source of power has been discovered and crudely utilized in certain specialized situations, but our experience is so limited and our knowledge so primitive that there is legitimate dispute about its applicability to a wide range of complicated and critical tasks. One often hears it said that nonviolent resistance was powerful enough to drive the British out of India but would have been suicidal against the Nazis. Or that Negroes can desegregate a restaurant or bus by nonviolence but can hardly solve the problem of jobs or getting rid of the Northern ghettos, since both of these attempts require major assaults on the very structure of society and run head on into the opposition of entrenched interests in the fields of business, finance, and public information. Finally, most of those who urge nonviolent methods on the Negro hesitate to claim that the United States should do away with its entire military force and prepare to defend itself in the jungle of international politics by nonviolent methods.

I

There is no doubt in my mind that nonviolence is currently incapable of resolving some of the problems that must be solved if the human race is to survive—let alone create a society in which all persons have a realistic opportunity to achieve material fulfillment and personal dignity. Those who are convinced that nonviolence can be used in *all* conflict situations have a responsibility to devise concrete methods by which it can be made effective. For example, can we urge the Negroes of Harlem or the *obreros* and *campesinos* (workers and peasants) of Latin America to refrain from violence if we offer them no positive method of breaking out of the slums, poverty, and cultural privation that blight their lives and condemn their children to a similar fate? It is contrary to the best tradition of nonviolence to do so. Gandhi often made the point that it is better to resist injustice by violent methods than not to resist at all. He staked his own life on his theory that nonviolent resistance was the superior method, but he never counselled appeasement or passive non-resistance.

The major advances in nonviolence have not come from people who have approached nonviolence as an end in itself, but from persons who were passionately striving to free themselves from social injustice. Gandhi discovered the method almost by accident when he went to South Africa as a young, British-trained lawyer in search of a career, but was "sidetracked" by the shock of experiencing galling racial segregation. Back in India, the humiliations of foreign rule turned him again to nonviolence, not as an act of religious withdrawal and personal perfectionism, but in line with his South African experience, as the most practical method Indians could use in fighting for their independence. During World War I, not yet convinced that the method of nonviolence could be used successfully in such a large-scale international conflict, he actually helped recruit Indians for the British Army. By contrast, during World War II, after twenty more years of experimentation with nonviolence, he counselled nonviolent resistance to the Nazis and actually evolved a plan for nonviolent opposition to the Japanese should they invade and occupy India.

In 1956 the Negroes of Montgomery, Alabama catapulted nonviolence into the limelight in the United States, not out of conversion to pacifism or love for their oppressors, but because they had reached a point where they could no longer tolerate certain racial injustices. Martin Luther King, who later became a pacifist, employed an armed defense guard to protect his home and family during one stage of the Montgomery conflict. In 1963, one of the leaders of the mass demonstrations in Birmingham said to me: "You might as well say that we never heard of Gandhi or nonviolence, but we were determined to get our freedom, and in the course of struggling for it we came upon nonviolence like gold in the ground."

There is not much point in preaching the virtues of nonviolence to a Negro in Harlem or Mississippi except as a method for winning his freedom. For one thing, the built-in institutional violence imposed on him every day of his life looms too large. He can rightly say that he wants no part of a nonviolence that condemns his spasmodic rock-throwing or desperate and often knowingly unrealistic talk of armed self-defense, but mounts no alternative campaign. It is all too easy for those with jobs, adequate educational opportunities, and decent housing to insist that Negroes remain nonviolent—to rally to the defense of "law and order." "Law and order is the Negro's best friend," Mayor Robert Wagner announced in the midst of the 1964 riots in Harlem. But nonviolence and a repressive law and order have nothing in common. The most destructive violence in Harlem is not the bottle-throwing, looting, or muggings of frustrated and demoralized Negroes. Nor is it the frequent shootings of juvenile delinquents and suspected criminals by white policemen, who often reflect both the racial prejudices of society and the personal propensity to violence that led them to choose a job whose tools are the club and the revolver. The basic violence in Harlem is the vast, impersonal violation of bodies and souls by an unemployment rate four times that of white New Yorkers, a median family income between half and two thirds that of white families, an infant mortality rate of 45.3 per thousand compared to 26.3 for New York as a whole, and inhuman crowding into subhuman housing. (It has been estimated that if the entire population of the United States were forced to live in equally congested conditions, it would fit into three of New York City's five boroughs.) Many white Americans are thrilled by the emotional catharsis of a law-abiding March on Washington (or even a fling at civil disobedience), in which they work off their guilt feelings, conscious and unconscious, by "identifying" for a day with the black victims of society. But when the project is over the whites do not return home anxious to know whether any of their children have been bitten by a rat, shot by a cop, or victimized by a pimp or dope peddler.

Commitment to nonviolence must not be based on patient acquiescence in intolerable conditions. Rather, it stems from a deeper knowledge of the self-defeating, self-corrupting effect of lapses into violence. On the one hand, Gandhi did not ally himself with those who profit from injustice and conveniently condemn others who violently fight oppression. On the other hand, he temporarily suspended several of his own nonviolent campaigns because some of his followers had succumbed to the temptations of violent reprisal. In perfecting methods of nonviolence, he gradually crystallized certain attitudes toward the nature of man (even oppressive, exploitative, foreign-invader man), which he formulated in the terminology of his native religion and which he considered indispensable for true nonviolence. Just as his basic insights have been translated by religious Western pacifists (including Martin Luther King) from their original language to that of Christianity, so they can be clothed without loss in the secular humanist terminology which is more natural to large numbers of Northern Negroes and white civil rights activists.

The key attitudes stem from a feeling for the solidarity of all human beings, even those who find themselves in deep conflict. George Meredith once said that a truly cultivated man is one who realizes that the things which seem to separate him from his fellows are as nothing compared with those which unite him with all humanity. Nonviolence may start, as it did with the young Gandhi and has with many an American Negro, as a technique for wresting gains from an unloved and unlovely oppressor. But somewhere along the line, if a nonviolent movement is to cope with deep-seated fears and privileges, its strategy must flow from a sense of the underlying unity of all human beings. So must the crucial, semi-spontaneous, inventive actions that emerge (for good or ill) in the midst of crisis.

This does not mean that Negroes, for example, must "love" in a sentimental or emotional way those who are imprisoning, shooting, beating, or impoverishing them. Nor need they feel personal affection for complacent white liberals. But it is not enough to abandon the use of fists, clubs, Molotov cocktails, and guns. Real nonviolence requires an awareness that white oppressors and black victims are mutually entrapped in a set of relationships that violate the submerged better instincts of everyone. A way has to be found to release the trap and free both sets of victims. Appeals to reasons or decency have little effect (except in isolated instances) unless they are accompanied by tangible pressures—on the pocketbook, for example—or the inconveniences associated with sit-ins, move-ins, strikes, boycotts or nonviolent obstructionism. But for any lasting gain to take place the struggle must appeal to the whole man, including his encrusted sense of decency and solidarity, his yearnings to recapture the lost innocence when human beings were persons to be loved, not objects to rule, obey, or exploit.

This reaching out to the oppressor has nothing to do with tokenism, which tends to creep into any movement, including a nonviolent one. In fact, tokenism is a double violation of the attitude of solidarity, because it permits the oppressor to make, and the oppressed to accept, a gesture which leaves intact the institutional barriers that separate them. One can gain a token victory or make a political deal without needing to have any invigorating personal contact with the "enemy," certainly without bothering to imagine oneself in his place so as to understand his needs, fears and aspirations. But the more revolutionary a movement's demands, the more imperative it is to understand what is necessary for the legitimate fulfillment of the persons who make up the opposition.

"We're going to win our freedom," a Negro leader said at a mass meeting in Birmingham last year, "and as we do it we're going to set our white brothers free." A short while later, when the Negroes faced a barricade of police dogs, clubs and fire hoses, they "became spiritually intoxicated," as another leader described it. "This was sensed by the police and firemen and it began to have an effect on them. . . . I don't know what happened to me.

I got up from my knees and said to the cops: 'We're not turning back. We haven't done anything wrong. All we want is our freedom. How do you feel doing these things?' " The Negroes started advancing and Bull Connor shouted: "Turn on the water!" But the firemen did not respond. Again he gave the order and nothing happened. Some observers claim they saw firemen crying. Whatever happened, the Negroes went through the lines. The next day, Bull Connor was reported by the press to have said: "I didn't want to mess their Sunday clothes, all those people from church." Until now this mood of outgoing empathetic nonviolence has been rarely achieved in this country. It was only part of the story in Birmingham, where in the end a more cautious tokenism gripped the top leaders. But it is the clue to the potential power of nonviolence.

Vinoba Bhave indicates something of the same sort on the level of international conflict when he says: "Russia says America has dangerous ideas so she has to increase her armaments. America says exactly the same thing about Russia. . . . The image in the mirror is your own image; the sword in its hand is your own sword. And when we grasp our own sword in fear of what we see, the image in the mirror does the same. What we see in front of us is nothing but a reflection of ourselves. If India could find courage to reduce her army to the minimum, it would demonstrate to the world her moral strength. But we are cowards and cowards have no imagination."

II

The potential uses of nonviolent power are tremendous and as yet virtually unrealized. But it is important to understand that nonviolence can never be "developed" in such a way as to carry out some of the tasks assigned to it by its more naive converts—any more than God (or the greatest scientist) could draw a square circle. It would be impossible, for instance, to defend the United States of America, as we know it, nonviolently. This is not because of any inherent defect in the nonviolent method but because of a very important strength: nonviolence cannot be used successfully to protect special privileges that have been won by violence. The British could not have continued to rule India by taking a leaf out of Gandhi's book and becoming "nonviolent." Nor would the United States be able to maintain its dominant position in Latin America if it got rid of its armies, navies, "special forces," C.I.A.-guerrillas, etc. Does anyone think that a majority of the natives work for a few cents a day, live in rural or urban slums, and allow forty-four per cent of their children to die before the age of five because they love us? Or that they are content to have American business drain away five hundred million dollars a year in interest and dividends, on the theory that the shareholders of United Fruit Company or the Chase Manhattan Bank are more needy or deserving than themselves?

It follows that advocates of nonviolence are overly optimistic when they argue from the unthinkability of nuclear war and the partially proven power of nonviolence (in India and the civil rights struggle) to the position that simple common sense will lead the United States (the richest, most powerful nation in the world, on whose business investments and armed forces the sun never sets) to substitute nonviolent for violent national defense. In recent years a number of well-intentioned peace groups have tried to convince the government and members of the power elite that the Pentagon should sponsor studies with this end in view. But nonviolent defense requires not only willingness to risk one's life (as any good soldier, rich or poor, will do). It requires renunciation of all claims to special privileges and power at the expense of other people. In our society most people find it more difficult to face economic loss while alive than death itself. Surrender of special privilege is certainly foreign to the psychology of those who supply, command, and rely on the military. Nonviolence is supremely the weapon of the dispossessed, the underprivileged, and the egalitarian, not of those who are still addicted to private profit, commercial values, and great wealth.

Nonviolence simply cannot defend property rights over human rights. The primacy of human rights would have to be established within the United States and in all of its dealings with other peoples before nonviolence could defend this country successfully. Nonviolence could defend what is worth defending in the United States, but a badly needed social revolution would have to take place in the process. Guerrilla warfare cannot be carried on successfully without the active support and cooperation of the surrounding population, which must identify justice (or at least its own welfare) with the triumph of the guerrillas. Nonviolence must rely even more heavily than guerrilla warfare on the justice of its cause. It has no chance of succeeding unless it can win supporters from previously hostile or neutral sections of the populace. It must do this by the fairness of its goals. Its objectives and methods are intimately interrelated and must be equally nonviolent.

The followers of Gandhi were imprisoned, beaten and, on more than one occasion, shot by the British during the Indian independence campaign. Today, some Americans consider the death of a nonviolent campaigner as conclusive evidence that "nonviolence won't work" and call for substitution of a violent campaign—in which people will also be killed and the original aims tend to be lost in an orgy of violence. But instead of allowing the British in effect to arm them, thereby giving the British the choice of weapons, the Gandhians kept right on fighting nonviolently and in the end succeeded in "disarming" the British. A number of times the first row of advancing Indians was shot, but a second and a third row kept on moving forward until the British soldiers became psychologically incapable of killing any more, even risking death at the hands of their superiors by disobeying orders to keep on firing. Eventually it became politically impossible for the commanders and the Prime Ministers to issue such orders. Need I add that if the Indians had been shot while trying to invade England and carry off its wealth, it would not have mattered how courageously nonviolent they had been; they could not have aroused this response.

If a Medgar Evers or a Goodman, Schwerner, or Cheney is killed fighting for a cause that is considered unjust, he is quickly dismissed as a fanatic. Indeed, at this stage of the struggle that is exactly what many white Southerners have done. But if the nonviolent warriors freely risk death in devotion to a cause that people recognize, even against their wills, as legitimate, the act has a tremendous effect. Willingness to sacrifice by undergoing imprisonment, physical punishment or, if need be, death itself, without retaliation, will not always dislodge deeply engrained prejudice or fear, but its general effect is always to work in that direction. By contrast, infliction of such penalties at best intimidates the opposition and at worst strengthens resistance, but in any case does not encourage psychological openness to a creative resolution of the underlying conflict of views or values.

Perhaps we can paraphrase Von Clausewitz's well known observation that war is but the continuation of the politics of peace by other means, and say that the social attitudes of nonviolent defense must be a continuation of the social attitudes of the society it is defending. A little thought should convince us of the impossibility of keeping Negroes and colonial peoples in their present positions of inferiority once privileged white America is unable to rely on overt or covert violence. Secondly, it is ludicrous to expect such persons to join their oppressors in the uncoerced defense of the society that has treated them so poorly. (Even with the power of the draft at its disposal—backed by the threat of imprisonment and ultimately the firing squad—the United States found it necessary to make unprecedented concessions and promises to Negroes during World War II in order to keep up black morale.) Finally, there is the crucial question of how we can expect to treat our enemies nonviolently if we do not treat our friends and allies so.

On the crudest level, as long as we are willing to condemn two out of five children in Latin America to early death, in order to increase our material comforts and prosperity, by what newly found awareness of human brotherhood will we be able to resist the temptation to wipe out two out of five, three out of five, or even five out of five of the children of China in overt warfare if it is dinned into us that this is necessary to preserve our freedom, or the lives of ourselves and our own children? If we cannot respect our neighbors more than to keep large numbers of them penned up in rat-infested slum ghettos, how will we develop the sense of human solidarity with our opponents, without which nonviolence becomes an empty technicality and loses its power to undermine and sap enemy hostility and aggressiveness? How will we reach across the propaganda-induced barriers of hate, fear, and self-righteousness (belief in the superiority of one's country, race or system) to disarm ourselves and our enemies?

Barbara Deming,
"On Revolution and Equilibrium"

In this essay, Barbara Deming (1917–1984) established herself as a leading theorist of nonviolence in the United States. It appeared when certain late-1960s attitudes within the Left—uncritical enthusiasm for Third World revolutions, belief that social change "comes from the barrel of a gun," condemnation of policemen as "pigs"—were at the height of their influence and popularity.

Deming confronted these attitudes nonviolently but firmly. She gave special attention to books that advocated violent revolution such as The Wretched of the Earth, *by Algerian psychologist Frantz Fanon, and Carl Oglesby's* Containment and Change, *a reflection on the Vietnam War by the president of the Students for a Democratic Society (SDS). The heart of her argument is her doctrine of "the two hands":*

> *We can put* more *pressure on the antagonist for whom we show human concern. It is precisely solicitude for his person in combination with a stubborn interference with his actions that can give us a very special degree of control. . . .*

Those in nonviolent rebellion, Deming wrote,

> *are able at one and the same time to disrupt everything for [their adversary], making it impossible for him to operate within the system as usual, and to temper his response to this, making it impossible for him simply to strike back without thought and with all his strength. They have as it were two hands upon him—the one calming him, making him ask questions, as the other makes him move.*

Barbara Deming, "On Revolution and Equilibrium," *Liberation*, February 1968. Reprinted by permission.

> *"What we want to do is to go forward all the time ... in the company of all men."*
>
> *"But can we escape becoming dizzy?"*
>
> FRANTZ FANON
> *The Wretched of the Earth*

"Do you want to remain pure? Is that it?" a black man asked me, during an argument about nonviolence. It is not possible to act at all and to remain pure; and that is not what I want, when I commit myself to the nonviolent discipline. There are people who are struggling to change conditions that they find intolerable, trying to find new lives; in the words of Frantz Fanon in *The Wretched of the Earth,* they want "to set afoot a new man." That is what I want too; and I have no wish to be assigned, as it were, separate quarters from those who are struggling in a way different from mine—segregated from my companions rather as, several years ago in Birmingham at the end of a demonstration, I found myself segregated in the very much cleaner and airier white section of the jail. I stand with all who say of present conditions that they do not allow men to be fully human and so they must be changed—all who not only say this but are ready to act.

At a recent conference about the directions the American Left should take, a socialist challenged me: "Can you call degrading the violence used by the oppressed to throw off oppression?" When one is confronted with what Russell Johnson calls accurately "the violence of the status quo"—conditions which are damaging, even murderous, to very many who must live within them—it is degrading for all to allow such conditions to persist. And if the individuals who can find the courage to bring about change see no way in which it can be done without employing violence on their own part—a very much lesser violence, they feel, than the violence to which they will put an end—I do not feel that I can judge them. The judgments I make are not judgments upon men but upon the means open to us—upon the promise these means of action hold or withhold. The living question is: What are the best means for changing our lives—for really changing them?

The very men who speak of the necessity of violence, if change is to be accomplished, are the first, often, to acknowledge the toll it exacts among those who use it—as well as those it is used against. Frantz Fanon has a chapter in *The Wretched of the Earth* entitled "Colonial War and Mental Disorders" and in it he writes, "We are forever pursued by our actions." After describing, among other painful disorders, those suffered by an Algerian terrorist—who made friends among the French after the war and then wondered with anguish whether any of the men he had killed had been men like these—he comments, "It was what might be called an attack of vertigo." Then he asks a poignant question: "But can we escape becoming dizzy? And who can affirm that vertigo does not haunt the whole of existence?"

"Vertigo"—here is a word, I think, much more relevant to the subject of revolutionary action than the word "purity." No, it is not that I want to remain pure; it is that I want to escape becoming dizzy. And here is exactly the argument of my essay: we can escape it. Not absolutely, of course; but we can escape vertigo in the drastic sense. It is my stubborn faith that if, as revolutionaries, we will wage battle without violence, we can remain very much more in control—of our own selves, of the responses to us which our adversaries make, of the battle as it proceeds and of the future we hope will issue from it.

The future—by whom will it be built? By all those whom the struggle has touched and marked. And so the question of how it marks them is not irrelevant. The future will be built even, in part, by those who have fought on the losing side. If it is a colonial struggle, of course, a good many of the adversaries can be expected to leave at the end of a successful revolution; but if it is a civil struggle, those who have been defeated, too, will at least help to make the new society what it is. How will the struggle have touched them? How will it have touched the victors?

Carl Oglesby, in *Containment and Change,* quotes a Brazilian guerrilla: "We are in dead earnest. At stake is the humanity of man." Then he asks, "How can ordinary men be at once warm enough to want what revolutionaries say they want (humanity), cold enough to do without remorse what they are capable of doing (cutting throats), and poised enough in the turbulence of their lives to keep the aspiration and the act both integrated and distinct? How is it that one of these passions does not invade and devour the other?" Yes—the question is one of equilibrium. How does one manage to keep it?

Oglesby would seem to answer that, generally speaking, one cannot expect the rebel to have the poise he describes. "He is an irresponsible man whose irresponsibility has been decreed by others . . . He has no real views about the future . . . is not by *type* a Lenin, a Mao, a Castro . . . His motivating vision of change is at root a vision of something absent—not of something that *will* be there . . . a missing landlord, a missing mine owner, a missing sheriff . . ." Ultimately, says Oglesby, he must *become* responsible. But how? It is in the midst of the struggle that he must at least begin to be, isn't it? And so the very means by which we struggle, and their tendency either to give us poise or to leave us dizzy, is surely, again, relevant.

I think of the words with which Fanon opens the final chapter of *The Wretched of the Earth:* "Come then, comrades; it would be as well to decide at once to change our ways." I quote Fanon often—because he is eloquent, but also because he is quoted repeatedly these days by those who plead the need for violence. It is my conviction that he can be quoted as well to plead for nonviolence. It is true that he declares: "From birth it is clear . . . that this narrow world, strewn with prohibitions, can only be called in question by absolute violence." But I ask all those who are readers of Fanon to make an experiment: Every time you find the word "violence" in his pages, substitute for it the phrase "radical and uncompromising action." I contend that with the exception of a very few passages this substitution can be made, and that the action he calls for could just as well be nonviolent action.

He writes, for example: "Violence alone, violence committed by the people, violence organized and educated by its leaders, makes it possible for the masses to understand social truths and gives the key to them. Without that struggle, without that knowledge of the practice of action, there's nothing but a fancy-dress parade . . . a few reforms at the top . . . and down there at the bottom an undivided mass . . . endlessly marking time." "Knowledge of the practice of action"—*that* is what Fanon sees to be absolutely necessary, to develop in the masses of people an understanding of social truths, accomplish that "work of clarification," "demystification," "enlightening of consciousness" which is the recurring and the deepest theme of his book. This action could be nonviolent action; it could very much better be nonviolent action—if only that action is bold enough.

Here is Fanon as he argues the necessity for "mere rebellion"—which Oglesby has described—to become true revolution: "Racialism and hatred and resentment—'a legitimate desire for revenge'—cannot sustain a war of liberation. Those lightning flashes of consciousness which fling the body into stormy paths or which throw it into an almost pathological trance where the face of the other beckons me on to giddiness, where my blood calls for the blood of the other . . . that intense emotion of the first few hours falls to pieces if it is left to feed on its own substance . . . You'll never overthrow the terrible enemy machine, and you won't change human beings if you forget to raise the standard of consciousness of the rank-and-file."

THE SPIRIT OF INVENTION

The task involves the enlightening of consciousness. But violence "beckons me on to giddiness." I repeat Fanon's words: "It would be as well to decide at once to change our ways." Another man with whom I was arguing the other day declared to me, "You can't turn the clock back now to nonviolence!" Turn the clock back? The clock has been turned to violence all down through history. Resort to violence hardly marks a move forward. It is nonviolence which is in the process of invention, if only people would not stop short in that experiment. Fanon again: "If we want humanity to advance a step further, if we want to bring it up to a different level than that which Europe has shown it, then we must invent and we must make discoveries." It is for that spirit of invention that I plead. And again I would like to ask something of all readers of Fanon. Turn to that last chapter of *The Wretched of the Earth* and read it again. Is he not groping here visibly for a way that departs from violence?

He writes, "We today can do everything, so long as we do not imitate Europe." And earlier in the book he has reported, "The argument the native chooses has been furnished by the settler . . . The native now affirms that the colonialist understands nothing but force." He writes, "We must leave our dreams ..." And earlier he has written, "The native is an oppressed person whose permanent dream is to become the persecutor." He writes, "Leave this Europe where they are never done talking of Man, yet murder men everywhere they find them, at the corner of every one of their own streets, in all the corners of the globe. ... Europe has ... set her face against all solicitude and all tenderness. ... So, my brother, how is it that we do not understand that we have better things to do than to follow that same Europe ... When I search for Man in the technique and the style of Europe, I see only a succession of negations of man, and an avalanche of murders ... Let us combine our muscles and our brains in a new direction. Let us try to create the whole man, whom Europe has been incapable of bringing to triumphant birth. All the elements of a solution ... have, at different times, existed in European thought. But the action of European men has not carried out the mission which fell to them. We must try to set afoot a new man." And he writes, "It is simply a very concrete question of not dragging men toward mutilation ... The pretext of catching up must not be used to push man around, to tear him away from himself or from his privacy, to break and kill him. No, we do not want to catch up with anyone. What we want to do is to go forward all the time, night and day, in the company of Man, in the company of all men."

But how in the company of all men if we are willing to kill? In the passages I have quoted does Fanon not warn us again and again against murder, warn us that murder cannot possibly bring to birth the new man—that it was precisely Europe's propensity for murder that kept her from carrying out the mission we now inherit? What really but radical nonviolence is he here straining to be able to imagine? We must "vomit up" the values of Europe, he has written. Is it not above all the value that Europe and America have put upon violence that we must vomit up? He writes, "It is simply a very concrete question of not dragging men toward mutilation." Yes, very concrete, I urge, because it comes down to the means by which we struggle, comes down to a choice of *which* "practice of action" we are going to study.

At this point suddenly I can hear in my head many voices interrupting me. They all say: "Who among us likes violence? But nonviolence has been tried." It has *not* been tried. We have hardly begun to try it. The people who dismiss it now as irrelevant do not understand what it could be. And, again, they especially do not understand the very much greater control over events that they could find if they would put this "practice of action," rather than violence, to a real test.

What most people are saying just now of course is that nonviolence gives us no control at all over events. "After years of this," says Stokely Carmichael, "we are at almost the same point." Floyd McKissick expresses the same disillusion: all the nonviolent campaigns have accomplished essentially noth-ing for black people. They have served to integrate a token few into American society. Even those few cannot be said to have been absorbed into the mainstream; they still are not allowed to forget the color of their skins. And the great majority of black people are actually worse off than before. He declares, with reason, "We are concerned about the aspirations of the 90% down there"—those of whom Fanon spoke, the many "endlessly marking time."

PSYCHOLOGICAL FORCES

I won't try to pretend that progress has been made that has not been made. Though I would add to the picture these two men and others paint that there is one sense in which things hardly can be said to be at the same point still. If one speaks of psychological forces that will make a difference—the determination of black people not to accept their situation any longer, the determination of some white people not to accept it either, and a consciousness on the part of other white people that changes are bound to come now, doubts about their ability to prevent them—in these terms all has been in constant motion. And these terms—Fanon for one would stress—are hardly unimportant. Literally, yes, one can speak of gains that seem to mock those who have nearly exhausted themselves in the struggle for them. But I think one has to ask certain questions. Have gains been slight because nonviolent tactics were the wrong tactics to employ—or did many of those leading the battle underestimate the difficulties of the terrain before them? Did they lack at the start a sufficiently radical vision? Can those who have now turned from reliance upon nonviolence say surely that resort to violence over those same years would have brought greater gains?

There are those who are implying this now. One observer who implies it strongly is Andrew Kopkind, writing in *The New York Review of Books* in August about the uprisings in the ghettos. He writes, "Martin Luther King and the 'leaders' who appealed for nonviolence, CORE, the black politicians, the old SNCC *are all* beside the point. Where the point is is in the streets . . . The insurrections of July have done what everyone in America for thirty years has thought impossible; mass action has convulsed the society and brought smooth government to a halt." He itemizes with awe: they caused tanks to rumble through the heart of the nation's biggest cities, brought out soldiers by the thousands, destroyed billions of dollars worth of property. This violence (or as Dave Dellinger better names it, this counterviolence of the victimized) certainly called out the troops. One thing violence can be counted on to do is bring the antagonist forth in battle dress. The question that hasn't been answered yet is: did this gain the rebels an advantage? It gained them many casualties. The powers-that-be paid their price, too, as Kopkind points out. But it is one thing to be able to state the price the antagonist paid, another to be able to count your own real gains. Kopkind gives us the heady sense of an encounter really joined at last, of battle lines drawn. But in the days of Birmingham, too, people had the excited sense of an engagement entered. Kopkind himself grants, "It is at once obvious that the period of greatest danger is just beginning."

THE GHETTO CHALLENGE

I have slighted, however, one point that he is making, and a very central point: "Poor blacks," he writes, "have stolen the center stage from the liberal elites . . . their actions indict the very legitimacy of [the] government." Yes, this is a fact not to overlook: the people of the ghettos have thrown down a challenge to government that is radical. But Kopkind is writing about two things: the offering of radical challenge and resort to violence. And he writes clearly as though he assumes that such a challenge can only be offered violently. It is with this assumption that I argue.

It is an assumption many share. Carl Oglesby seems to share it. In *Containment and Change* he criticizes "the politics of the appeal to higher power . . . the same thing as prayer . . . a main assumption of which is that [the higher power] is not bad, only misinformed." He appears to see all nonviolent action as covered by this definition. "This way of thinking brought the peasants and priests to their massacre at Kremlin Square in 1905 . . . It rationalized the 1963 March on Washington for Jobs and Freedom. The Freedom Rides, the nonviolent sit-ins, and the various Deep South marches were rooted in the same belief: that there was indeed a higher power which was responsive and decent . . . The Vietnam war demonstrations are no different . . . The main idea has always been to persuade higher authority . . . to do something. Far from calling higher authority into question, these demonstrations actually dramatize and even exaggerate its power."

He goes on then to describe how the "whimsical" hopes that are entertained about the powerful evaporate: "Sometimes mass-based secular prayer has resulted in change. But more often it has only shown the victim-petitioner that the problem is graver and change harder to get than [he] had imagined . . . It turns out that the powerful know perfectly well who their victims are . . . and that they have no intention of changing anything. This recognition is momentous, no doubt the spiritual low point of the emergent revolutionary's education. He finds that the enemy is not a few men but a whole system whose agents saturate the society . . . He is diverted by a most realistic despair. But this despair contains within itself the omen of that final reconstitution of the spirit which will prepare [him] . . . for the shift to insurgency, rebellion, revolution . . . At the heart of his despair lies the new certainty that there will be no change which he does not produce by himself."

With this description I do not argue at all. It is a very accurate description of the education those protesting in this country have been receiving. May more and more read the lesson. I argue with the contention that nonviolent action can only be prayerful action—must by its nature remain naive. Too often in the past it has confined itself to petition, but there is no need for it to do so—especially now that so many have learned "change [is] harder to get than they had imagined." There have always been those in the nonviolent movement who called for radical moves. As Kopkind writes, "all that has come until now is prologue." But this does not mean that our alternatives have suddenly been reduced. The pressure that nonviolent moves could put upon those who are opposing change, the power that could be exerted this way, has yet to be tested.

POWER AND NONVIOLENCE

I have introduced the word "power" deliberately. When the slogan "Black Power" was first taken up, the statements immediately issued, both for and against it, all seemed to imply that "power" was a word inconsistent with a faith in nonviolence. This was of course the position taken by Stokely Carmichael: "We had to work for power because this country does not function by morality, love and nonviolence, but by power. For too many years, black Americans marched and had their heads broken and got shot. They were saying to the country, 'Look, you guys are supposed to be nice guys and we are only going to do what we are supposed to do. Why ... don't you give us what we ask?'. . . We demonstrated from a position of weakness. We cannot be expected any longer to march and have our heads broken in order to say to whites: come on, you're nice guys. For you are not nice guys. We have found you out."

Carmichael gives us: the humble appeal to conscience on the one hand, the resort to power on the other. If the choice were really this, anyone who wanted change would certainly have to abandon nonviolent action. For as Bradford Lyttle comments in a paper on Black Power, no, most people are not nice guys. "It isn't necessary to be hit over the head to learn this . . . Some Christians call the un-niceness of people 'original sin.' It's Freud's 'ego.' Naturalist Konrad Lorenz studies it as aggresiveness and argues convincingly that it's instinctive with men. Whatever the un-niceness may be, it is part of all of us, and our job is to minimize it."

The trouble is that advocates of nonviolence themselves often write in terms that seem to corroborate the picture Carmichael paints. When they actually engage in direct action, they pay great attention to other-than-moral pressures that can be and have to be placed on those with whom they are struggling. But on paper they tend again and again to stress only the appeal that can be made to conscience. Bradford, in his paper on Black Power, notes: "Carmichael's vision isn't limited to Negroes. Machiavelli had it: . . . 'A man who wishes to make a profession of goodness in everything must necessarily come to grief among so many who are not good. Therefore it is necessary ... to learn how not to be good.' " Then he pleads that to put one's faith in coercive power is tragic, and his argument is: "throughout history, those who have most deeply touched the hearts of hardened men have been the ones who chose not to defend themselves with violence." He, too, seems here to pose a narrow choice: resort to power (learning how not to be good) or appeal to conscience (learning, Carmichael would put it, to do only what we are supposed to do).

THE CHOICE IS WIDER

But the choice is very much wider than this (as Bradford of course knows); and the distinctions that seem to have been set up here are unreal. To resort to power one need not be violent,[1] and to speak to conscience one need not be meek. The most effective action *both* resorts to power *and* engages conscience. Nonviolent action does not have to beg others to "be nice." It can in effect force them to consult their consciences—or to pretend to have them. Nor does it have to petition those in power to do something about a situation. It can face the authorities with a new fact and say: accept this new situation which *we* have created.

If people doubt that there is power in nonviolence, I am afraid that it is due in part to the fact that those of us who believe in it have yet to find for ourselves an adequate vocabulary. The leaflets we pass out tend to speak too easily about love and truth—and suggest that we hope to move men solely by being loving and truthful. The words do describe our method in a kind of shorthand. But who can read the shorthand? It is easy enough to recommend "love." How many, even among those who like to use the word, can literally feel love for a harsh opponent—not merely pretending to while concealing from themselves their own deepest feelings? What *is* possible is to act toward another human being on the assumption that all men's lives are of value, that there is something about any man to be loved, whether one can *feel* love for him or not.[2] It happens that, if one does act on this assumption, it gives one much greater poise in the situation. It is easy enough to speak about truth; but we had better spell out how, in battle, we rely upon the truth. It is not simply that we pay our antagonist the human courtesy of not lying to him. We insist upon telling him truths he doesn't want to hear—telling what

1. Although those in the Movement who issued critical statements against use of the slogan "Black Power" seemed almost always to imply that "power" was an improper word, I couldn't help noticing that just that word had a way of slipping into their own publicity releases—an S.C.L.C. release, for example, repudiating the slogan but speaking the next moment of the "political power" they sought through pushing voter registration.

2. Sometimes, if one disciplines oneself to act upon this assumption, the feeling itself of love for one's enemy enters one, taking one by surprise—a kind of grace. Some readers may ask: why should one want to feel love for one's enemy? But I note that Fanon in *Black Skin, White Masks* writes, "I, the man of color, want only this: . . . That it be possible for me to discover and to love man, wherever he may be."

seems to us the truth about the injustice he commits. Words are not enough here. Gandhi's term for nonviolent action was "satyagraha"—which can be translated as "clinging to the truth." What is needed is this—to *cling* to the truth as one sees it. And one has to cling with one's entire weight. One doesn't simply say, "I have a right to sit here," but acts out that truth—and sits here. One doesn't just say, "If we are customers in this store, it's wrong that we're never hired here," but refuses to be a customer any longer. One doesn't just say, "I don't believe in this war," but refuses to put on a uniform. One doesn't just say, "The use of napalm is atrocious," but refuses to pay for it by refusing to pay one's taxes. And so on and so on. One brings what economic weight one has to bear, what political, social, psychological, what physical weight. There is a good deal more involved here than a moral appeal. It should be acknowledged both by those who argue against nonviolence and those who argue for it that we, too, rely upon force.

STOPPING SHORT

If greater gains have not been won by nonviolent action it is because most of those trying it have, quite as Oglesby charges, expected too much from "the powerful"; and so, I would add, they have stopped short of really exercising their peculiar powers—those powers one discovers when one refuses any longer simply to do another's will. They have stopped far too short not only of widespread nonviolent disruption but of that form of noncooperation which is assertive, constructive—that confronts those who are "running everything" with independent activity, particularly independent economic activity. There is leverage for change here that has scarcely begun to be applied.

To refuse one's cooperation is to exert force. One can, in fact, exert so very much force in this way that many people will always be quick to call noncooperators violent. How, then, does one distinguish nonviolent from violent action? It is not that it abstains from force, to rely simply upon moral pressure. It resorts even to what can only be called physical force—when, for example, we sit down and refuse to move, and we force others to cope somehow with all these bodies. The distinction to make is simply that those committed to a nonviolent discipline refuse to injure the antagonist. Of course if nonviolent action is as bold as it must be in any real battle for change, some at least of those resisting the change are bound to *feel* that injury has been done them. For they feel it as injury to be shaken out of the accustomed pattern of their lives. The distinction remains a real one. Perhaps there is another way it could be put. The man who acts violently forces another to do *his* will—in Fanon's words, he tears the other away from himself, pushes him around, often willing to break him, kill him. The man who acts nonviolently insists upon acting out his *own* will, refuses to act out another's—but in this way, only, exerts force upon the other, not tearing him away from himself but tearing from him only that which is not properly his own, the strength which has been loaned to him by all those who have been giving him obedience.

NONVIOLENT OBSTRUCTION

But the distinction I have just made is a little too neat. In almost any serious nonviolent struggle, one has to resort to obstructive action. When we block access to buildings, block traffic, block shipments, it can be charged that we go a little further than refusing obedience and impose upon the freedom of action of others. There is some justice to the charge. I nevertheless think it appropriate to speak of nonviolent obstruction, but I would revert to my original description as the definitive one: the person committed to nonviolent action refuses to injure the antagonist. It is quite possible to frustrate another's action without doing him injury.[3] And some freedoms are basic freedoms, some are not. To impose upon another man's freedom to kill, or his freedom to help to kill, to recruit to kill, is not to violate his person in a fundamental way.[4]

But I can imagine the impatience of some of my readers with these various scruples. What, they might say, has this to do with fighting battles—battles which are in dead earnest? How can we hope to put any real pressure upon an adversary for whom we show such concern?

A CREATIVE COMBINATION

This is the heart of my argument: We can put *more* pressure on the antagonist for whom we show human concern. It is precisely solicitude for his person

---

3. It is possible, but not always simple. When we stage an act of massive obstruction in a city, for example, there is always the risk that we will prevent some emergency call from being answered—prevent a doctor's car from getting through, perhaps. One has obviously to anticipate such situations and be ready to improvise answers to the human problems raised.

4. I am uneasy, however, at the way Carl Davidson of S.D.S. words his defense of obstruction. He writes in *New Left Notes* of November 13, 1967: "The institutions our resistance has desanctified and delegitimized, as a result of our action against their oppression of others, have lost all authority and hence all respect. As such, they have only raw coercive power. Since they are without legitimacy in our eyes, they are without rights. Insofar as individuals, such as recruiters, continue to remain in association with those institutions, they run the risk of being given the same treatment. . . . We can assert the Nuremberg decisions and other past criteria of war crimes as the criteria by which we, in conscience, decide whether or not an institution and individuals associated with that institution have lost their legitimacy and their rights." *Can* one give individuals the same treatment that one gives institutions—and deny them *all* respect? If he means that we need not grant individuals the right to oppress others, I am in agreement. But if he means that when we can identify an individual as an oppressor, then we need not treat him as though he had *any* human rights—he alarms me. This formulation would seem to me to lead into grim territory.

in combination with a stubborn interference with his actions that can give us a very special degree of control (precisely in our acting both with love, if you will—in the sense that we respect his human rights—and truthfulness, in the sense that we act out fully our objections to his violating *our* rights). We put upon him two pressures—the pressure of our defiance of him and the pressure of our respect for his life—and it happens that in combination these two pressures are uniquely effective.

One effect gained is to "raise the level of consciousness" for those engaged in the struggle—those on both sides. Because the human rights of the adversary are respected, though his actions, his official policies are not, the focus of attention becomes those actions, those policies, and their true nature. The issue cannot be avoided. The antagonist cannot take the interference with his actions personally, because his person is not threatened, and he is forced to begin to acknowledge the reality of the grievance against him. And those in rebellion—committed to the discipline of respect for all men's lives, and enabled by this discipline to avoid that "trance" Fanon describes, "where the face of the other beckons me on to giddiness," is enabled to see more and more clearly that (as Oglesby says) "the enemy is not a few men but a whole system," and to study that system.

THE TWO HANDS

The more the real issues are dramatized, and the struggle raised above the personal, the more control those in nonviolent rebellion begin to gain over their adversary. For they are able at one and the same time to disrupt everything for him, making it impossible for him to operate within the system as usual, and to temper his response to this, making it impossible for him simply to strike back without thought and with all his strength. They have as it were two hands upon him—the one calming him, making him ask questions, as the other makes him move.

In any violent struggle one can expect the violence to escalate. It does so automatically, neither side being really able to regulate the process at will. The classic acknowledgement of this fact was made by President Kennedy when he saluted Premier Krushchev for withdrawing nuclear missiles from Cuba. "I welcome this message," he said, because "developments were approaching a point where events could have become unmanageable." In nonviolent struggle, the violence used against one may amount for a while (indeed, if one is bold in one's rebellion, it is bound to do so), but the escalation is no longer automatic; with the refusal of one side to retaliate, the mainspring of the automaton has been snapped and one can count on reaching a point where de-escalation begins. One can count, that is, in the long run, on receiving far fewer casualties.

THE NUMBER OF CASUALTIES

Nothing is more certain than this and yet, curiously, nothing is less obvious. A very common view is that nonviolent struggle is suicidal. This is, for example, Andrew Kopkind's view: "Turn-the-other-cheek was always a personal standard, not a general rule: people can commit suicide but peoples cannot. Morality, like politics, starts at the barrel of a gun." (A surprising sentence, but by morality he means, no doubt, the assertion of one's rights.) The contention that nonviolent struggle is suicidal hardly stands up under examination. Which rebels suffered more casualities—those who, under Gandhi, managed to throw the British out of India or the so-called Mau Mau who struggled by violence to throw the British out of Kenya? The British were certainly not "nice guys" in their response to the Gandhians. They, the Indian troops who obeyed their orders, beat thousands of unarmed people, shot and killed hundreds. In the Amritsar Massacre, for example, they fired into an unarmed crowd that was trapped in a spot where no one could escape and killed 379 people, wounding many more. There was a limit, nevertheless, to the violence they could justify to themselves—or felt they could justify to the world. Watching any nonviolent struggle, it is always startling to learn how long it can take the antagonist to set such limits; but he finally does feel constrained to set them—especially if his actions are well publicized. In Kenya, where the British could cite as provocation the violence used against them, they hardly felt constrained to set any limits at all on their actions, and they adopted tactics very similar to those the Americans are using today against the Vietnamese. In that struggle for independence, many thousands of Africans fighting in the forest and many thousands of their supporters and sympathizers on the reserves were killed. Many were also tortured.[5]

One can, as I say, be certain if one adopts the discipline of nonviolence that in the long run one will receive fewer casualties. And yet very few people are able to see that this is so. It is worth examining the reasons why the obvious remains unacknowledged. Several things, I think, blind people to the plain truth.

First, something seems wrong to most people engaged in struggle when they see more people hurt on their own side than on the other side. They are used to reading this as an indication of defeat, and a complete mental readjustment is required of them. Within the new terms of struggle, victory has nothing to do with their being able to give more punishment than they take (quite the reverse); victory has nothing to do with their being able to punish the other at all; it has to do simply with being able, finally, to make the other move. Again, the real issue is kept in focus. Vengeance is not the point; change is. But the trouble is that in most men's minds the thought of victory and the thought of punishing the enemy coincide. If they are suffering

---

5. See *Mau Mau from Within* by Barnett and Njama.

casualties and the enemy is not, they fail to recognize that they are suffering *fewer* casualties than they would be if they turned to violence.

NONVIOLENT BATTLE

Actually, something seems wrong to many people, I think, when—in nonviolent struggle—they receive any casualties at all. They feel that if they are not hurting anybody, then they shouldn't get hurt themselves. (They shouldn't. But it is not only in nonviolent battle that the innocent suffer.) It is an intriguing psychological fact that when the ghetto uprisings provoked the government into bringing out troops and tanks—and killing many black people, most of them onlookers—observers like Kopkind decided that the action had been remarkably effective, citing as proof precisely the violence of the government's response. But when James Meredith was shot, just for example, any number of observers editorialized: "See, nonviolence doesn't work." Those who have this reaction overlook the fact that nonviolent battle is still battle, and in battle of whatever kind, people do get hurt. If personal safety had been Meredith's main concern, he could, as the saying goes, have stayed at home.

Battle of any kind provokes a violent response—because those who have power are not going to give it up voluntarily. But there is simply no question that—in any long run—violent battle provokes a more violent response and brings greater casualties. Men tend not to think in long-run terms, of course; they tend to think in terms of isolated moments. There will always be such moments that one can cite, in which a particular man might have been safer if he had been armed. If Meredith had been carrying a loaded pistol, he might well have shot his assailant before the man shot him. (He might also well have been ambushed by still more men.) Whatever one can say about overall statistics, some men will always *feel* safer when armed—each able to imagine himself the one among many who would always shoot first.

To recognize that men have greater, not less control in the situation when they have committed themselves to nonviolence requires a drastic readjustment of vision. And this means taking both a long-range view of the field and a very much cooler, more objective one. Nonviolence can inhibit the ability of the antagonist to hit back. (If the genius of guerrilla warfare is to make it impossible for the other side really to exploit its superior brute force, nonviolence can be said to carry this even further.)

And there is another sense in which it gives one greater leverage—enabling one both to put pressure upon the antagonist and to modulate his response to that pressure. In violent battle the effort is to demoralize the enemy, to so frighten him that he will surrender. The risk is that desperation and resentment will make him go on resisting when it is no longer even in his own interest. He has been driven beyond reason. In nonviolent struggle the effort is of quite a different nature. One doesn't try to frighten the other. One tries to undo him—tries, in the current idiom, to "blow his mind"—only in the sense that one tries to shake him out of former attitudes and force him to appraise the situation now in a way that takes into consideration your needs as well as his. One is able to do this—able in a real sense to change his mind (rather than to drive him out of it)—precisely because one reassures him about his personal safety all the time that one keeps disrupting the order of things that he has known to date. When—under your constant pressure—it becomes to his own interest to adapt himself to change, he is able to do so. Fear for himself does not prevent him. In this sense a liberation movement that is nonviolent sets the oppressor free as well as the oppressed.

THE GENIUS OF NONVIOLENCE

The most common charge leveled against nonviolence is that it counts upon touching the heart of an adversary—who is more than likely to be stony of heart. His heart, his conscience need not be touched. His mind has been. The point is that you prevent him from reacting out of fear—in mindless reflex action. You also prevent him from being able to justify to others certain kinds of actions that he would like to take against you—and may for a while attempt to take. Here one can speak of still another sense in which nonviolence gives one greater control. If the antagonist *is* unjustifiably harsh in his counter-measures, and continues to be, one will slowly win away from him allies and supporters—some of them having consciences more active than his perhaps; or perhaps all of them simply caring about presenting a certain image, caring for one reason or another about public relations. An adversary might seem to be immovable. One could nevertheless move him finally by taking away from him the props of his power—those men upon whose support he depends. The special genius of nonviolence is that it can draw to our side not only natural allies—who are enabled gradually to recognize that they are allies because in confrontation with us their minds are not blurred by fear but challenged (and they begin to refuse orders, as several soldiers did in October at the Pentagon). Even beyond this, it can move to act on our behalf elements in society who have no such natural inclination. When the Quebec to Guantanamo walkers were fasting in jail in Albany, Georgia, the men who finally put most pressure upon the authorities to release them and let them walk through town were clergymen not at all sympathetic either to the walkers as individuals or to the message on their signs and leaflets. Nonviolent tactics can move into action on our behalf men not naturally inclined to act for us; whereas violent tactics draw into actions that do us harm men for whom it is not at all natural to act against us. A painful example of this was Martin Luther King's act of declaring that the authorities were right in calling out troops to deal with the ghetto uprisings. John Gerassi provided another example in a talk I heard him give about revolutionary prospects in Latin America. He told how a plan on the part of a rebel group to gain support among the people by assassinating policemen backfired—because every slain policeman in that society of very large families had so many relatives, all unable to see the death as a political act that might help them, able to see it only as a personal loss. Violence makes men "dizzy"; it disturbs the vision, makes them see only their own immediate losses and fear of losses. Any widespread resort to violence in this country by those seeking change could produce such vertigo among the population at large that the authorities would be sure to be given more and more liberty to take repressive measures—in the name of "Order."

KNOWING THE ENEMY

Some readers might comment that such a development would be educational, for the underlying nature of the society would then stand revealed; and it is necessary to know the enemy. But it is necessary, too, to know that one had a certain power to affect those who stand against us. It would be easy enough to know the worst about them—by acting in a way that allowed them to behave toward us in the worst way that they could. It is more practical, even if it is more difficult, to act in a way that prevents this. If it is important not to be naive about their capacity for doing us harm, it is just as important not to be blind to our own capacity for moderating their action. In histories of the Chinese and Cuban revolutions, there are many accounts of generosity shown by the rebels toward enemy troops—resulting in widespread recruitment from among those troops. It proved very practical to act on the assumption that not all among them need be labeled permanently "enemy." Those engaged in nonviolent battle simply act on this assumption in the boldest degree. They declare, in the words of the Vietnamese Buddhist Thich Nhat Hanh—words that are startling and sound at first naive: "No men are our enemies." By this we do not mean that we think no men will try to destroy us; or that we overlook the fact that men from certain sections of the society are above all likely to try it. We mean, first, of course, that we are committed to try not to destroy them; but we mean furthermore that there is a working chance—if we do refuse to threaten them personally as we struggle with them—that in certain instances at least some of them may be willing to accommodate themselves to the pressure we put on them to change, and so both they and we may be liberated from the state of enmity. We mean that we refuse to cut ourselves off from them in any ultimate human sense—counting it as both decent and practical to do so.

KINDNESS AND REVOLUTION

I have been reading William Hinton's *Fanshen: A Documentary of Revolution in a Chinese Village,* and I have been struck by how many times in the course of his story he reports a decision taken by the revolutionary leaders that greater humanity shown this group or that group will advance the revolution. There is, for example, a decision at one point to be more lenient toward counterrevolutionary suspects among Catholic peasants. "They could never be won if they were isolated and discriminated against. They had to be drawn into full participation." In one dramatic instance it is decided that the attack on middle peasants has been overdone—that the land of many of these families has been wrongly expropriated, and that they must be reclassified as friends rather than enemies of the revolution. "We must make clear to them that they have their . . . rights." Because of this decision, too, things improved, the revolution gained momentum. The decisions which he reports are for the most part taken "to enlarge the united front of the people and to isolate as popular enemies only those diehard elements who could not possibly be mobilized to support a 'land-to-the-tiller' policy." One of the leaders explains, "In proposing any basic social change . . . revolutionaries had to decide who should be brought together and who isolated, who should be called a friend and who an enemy." Experience seemed always to be showing that the more people who were called friends, the better things went. I noted that as time went on leniency began to be advised even toward the gentry and the landlords; it was decided that here, too, the attacks had been at first overdone. "Families cannot be driven from house and home forever." As one leader put it: "We have to show everyone a way out."

This is of course just what nonviolence teaches—not to be naive about the fact that some men more than others will see it as in their interest to try to destroy us, and will often persist and persist in trying to; but to recognize that they never can see it in their interest finally to accommodate themselves to the changes we are forcing unless we give them the liberty to do so. And they will only believe that we offer this liberty, only be able to imagine new lives for themselves, if we have refused to threaten them with any personal injury.[6]

MAN VERSUS FUNCTION

I have had conversations with a Marxist who argues that it is absurd to claim we can avoid personal injury to others in any serious social struggle; for "men are reduced to functional elements": to threaten to deprive a man of his accustomed position in society is to threaten his very person. It will certainly be felt in many instances as just such a threat. But no man is ever

---

6. There is a cliché often applied to the enemy: "All he can understand is force." But men "understand" brute force in the most narrow sense only: They understand that they are being hurt, or may be hurt by it—and so that they had better either surrender or manage to hurt the other side even more. Brute force cannot make the other understand that in a new world he could find a new life for himself.

reduced quite in his entire being to a functional element in society. And precisely because the rebel who is nonviolent distinguishes, as he struggles with another, between the man himself to whom he offers a certain basic respect (simply *as* another man) and the role that man has been playing, which he refuses to respect, it becomes more possible for the other, too, to begin to make the distinction. It may indeed at first be literally impossible for him to see himself, if he tries to imagine himself functioning in any way but the way that he has been. But the fact that others seem to be able to, makes it easier—especially if so much pressure is put on him that it becomes impossible for him to see himself functioning comfortably any longer in the old way. It is necessary to remember—as Oglesby says—that "the enemy is not a few men but a whole system," to remember that when the men with whom we struggle confront us it is as functional elements in this system that they do so, behaving in a certain sense automatically. It is necessary to know this well. But it is precisely if we refuse to treat them as nothing more than this—if we insist on treating them not as parts of a machine but as men, capable of thought and of change—that we gain a very much greater control in the situation. It is practical, in short, always to be *talking* with the enemy.

Oglesby describes the rebel as one who is quite unwilling to talk. "The rebel is an incorrigible absolutist who has replaced . . . all 'solutions' with the single irreducible demand that . . . those who now have all power shall no longer have any, and that those who now have none—the people, the victimized—shall have all . . . 'What do you want?' asks the worried, perhaps intimidated master. 'What can I give you?'. . . But the rebel . . . answers, 'I cannot be purchased.' The answer is meant mainly to break off the conference." One reason the rebel wants to break it off, Oglesby explains, is that he has as yet no really clear vision of "the revolutionized, good society," and would be embarrassed to have to confess this. He is not yet a responsible man. Then Oglesby adds: Ultimately he must become so. I am not quite sure *how*—as Oglesby sees it—he is to become responsible. My own suggestion is, of course, that nonviolent battle in itself teaches one to be.

It is a more difficult way. It does, for example, complicate the process of defining for ourselves and others who can be expected to act as our allies and who can be expected to resist us as harshly as they dare when, of the latter, we have always to be making two points at the same time: (1) here are men toward whom we have to be on our guard and (2) here are men for whom we have to show human concern. It can be done, though, and in very few words. I remember James Bevel addressing a church audience in Birmingham: "We love our white brothers"—pause—"but we don't trust them."

THE FEEL OF AN ACTION

The trouble is that people tend to *feel* that they are taking bolder action when they disdain all conversations with the adversary. We had experience of this often on the Quebec to Guantanamo walk while we were in the South. There were any number of times when, at the edge of a town, we would find ourselves confronted by police who would inform us that we weren't going to be allowed to walk through. We had a constitutional right to walk through, and a few people in the group were always in favor of simply saying, "Try to stop us!" or saying nothing at all—and marching forward. What we actually did, always, was to stop the walk for an hour or two, drive into town and discuss the matter with the chief of police. We would talk very quietly and always show him courtesy, and respect for his *proper* authority (for example, where traffic control was concerned), but in the course of the talk we would let it become clear to him that he would save himself a lot of trouble by letting us walk through; we knew what our rights were and had been to jail before for them and weren't afraid of going again. Time and again, after a certain amount of bluster on the chief's part, we would be allowed to walk. A few people in the group were always dissatisfied with this way. For it *felt like* deferring to the authorities. If we had simply marched forward, of course, feeling very bold, we would not have made our way through the town—we would have made our way right into jail, the authorities doing with us what they liked. The action that felt less bold won us our way.

All this is relevant, I think, to discussions going on now in the Movement about how to pass from protest to resistance, from merely "symbolic" actions to "practical" ones. To define clearly which actions are symbolic—and which more than that—one has often to look twice. A bold foray that is absolutely certain to be stopped is, surely, symbolic action. For example, those who rushed up the steps into the Pentagon on October 21st—to be thrown back at once by the troops, and quite predictably—were surely engaging in symbolic action; whereas those who tried to communicate with the troops confronting them, and were able to cause at least two defections from those troops, were surely engaging in action that was more than symbolic. The whole subject is infinitely complex. I am hardly saying that bold forays are never in order; but I am saying that dialogue with the other side is deeply practical.

HOW MANY WILL ANSWER?

Again I can imagine certain readers interrupting—to remark that I am over-looking, in this essay, one fundamental point. It is all very well to talk of the advantages of nonviolence, they might say, but how many are going to answer the call to such battle? A certain form of struggle can hardly be called practical if one cannot recruit very many men to try it; and to get most men to fight, one has to offer certain things which nonviolent struggle does not offer. I have heard people state, for example, that men from the ghettos would never turn to nonviolence because it does not allow them to speak out the full measure of their hatred for the white man. I have heard others say that few people would turn to it because it does not offer them the chance to feel, for once, like men. How a certain action makes one *feel* is not irrelevant.

But if nonviolent action is boldly taken it does allow men to speak out their deepest feelings; and if it is boldly taken, it does allow them to feel that they are standing up to others like men. It may not permit them to act out their hatred for others by taking revenge; but it allows—it requires—them to act out all the truth they feel about what the other has done, is doing to them, and to act out their determination to change this state of things. In this very process, one's hatred of the other can be forgotten, because it is beside the point; the point is to change one's life. The point is not to give some vent to the emotions that have been destroying one; the point is so to act that one can master them now.

What is it to assert one's manhood—one's human rights? Let me quote Fanon again. He writes in *Black Skin, White Masks:* "I have only one solution: to rise above this absurd drama that others have staged round me," "I have one right alone: that of demanding human behavior from the other." This is, to me, a very accurate description of nonviolent struggle. He writes, "I will impose my whole weight as a man on [the other's] life and show him that I am not that ... [which] he persists in imagining," "What is needed is to hold oneself, like a sliver, to the heart of the world, to interrupt if necessary the rhythm of the world, to upset, if necessary, the chain of command, but ... to stand up to the world," "Man is human only to the extent to which he tries to impose his existence on another man in order to be recognized by him." He immediately adds, "If I close the circuit, if I prevent the accomplishment of movement in two directions, I keep the other within himself." He writes, "I do battle for the creation of a human world—that is, a world of reciprocal recognition." The battle for this world, I would plead, is one that *can* only be waged nonviolently.

It is true enough, however, that one of the chief difficulties those who believe in nonviolence must face is how to recruit others to trust themselves to this way. My own conviction is that one can recruit to this form of battle only by setting the very boldest kind of example. Those of us who believe in nonviolent action should listen closely to the words of those who mock it. For if the portrait the latter draw of it is a caricature, and reveals their own ignorance of what such action can be, it reveals, too, a great deal about our own failure to carry experiments with it far enough. We had better look hard at what it is men seek when they turn away from us.

The cry for Black Power, for example, was taken up with swiftness. Why? Because too many—though certainly not all—of the nonviolent actions taken to that date *had* been, as charged, essentially acts of petition; and the necessity of self-assertion was felt very deeply. The gestures of the slave had clearly once and for all to be put from them by black people. And the nonviolent actions in which they had taken part had too often seemed but to repeat those ancient gestures of submission—quite as Carmichael put it: Look, master, we are only going to do what we are supposed to do; we may be on the streets, but see, we're still your good niggers; won't you help us? In this context, the assertion of love for the other seemed too much an echo of the old defensive hypocrisy toward the master: Look, we are your loving servants—who love you, respect you, more than we love, respect our own lives. Only nonviolent actions daring enough to quite shatter that pattern could possibly release either side from the bondage of the old relation.

BOLD ACTION OR NONE

It is not only black people in our society who are suffering now from the sense that their lives are out of their control, and who are going to be satisfied only to take actions that give them some sense of beginning to assert such control. At this point in our history, nonviolent action had better be taken boldly or one need hardly bother to take it at all, for one will be taking it alone.

Those who believe in nonviolence face a sharp challenge. They must decide whether or not we really are engaged in a struggle that is "in dead earnest." If we are, certain consequences follow. One of them is that we must act boldly; another is that we can expect to be hurt. Those who commit themselves to violent struggle take this for granted—which gives them a certain advantage. In the very act of entering battle, they prepare themselves for this— knowing it, very simply, to be the nature of battle. We had better learn, too, to accept that it is. They can claim one other advantage: they are less apt to lose recruits. Fanon writes in *The Wretched of the Earth,* "You could be sure of a new recruit when he could no longer go back into the colonial system—because he had assumed 'the responsibility for violence' and committed some act that made him a hunted man."[7] It is easier to retreat from nonviolent battle. We face the challenge of persisting in spite of this.

THE NEED TO BE AGGRESSIVE

Yes, the challenge to those who believe in nonviolent struggle is to learn to be aggressive enough. Nonviolence has for too long been connected in men's minds with the notion of passivity. "Aggressive" is an ambiguous word, of course, and my statement needs qualifying. In this connection I recommend to all the book *On Aggression* by the Austrian naturalist, Konrad Lorenz. I have quoted Bradford Lyttle's reference to it: "Lorenz studies [the un-niceness of people] as aggressiveness and argues convincingly that it's instinctive with men." Actually, though Lorenz does argue that aggressiveness is instinctive—in men as in animals—he challenges the view that there is anything

7. I wrote earlier that one could substitute the phrase "radical uncompromising action" for the word "violence" in Fanon's text with the exception of a very few passages. This is one of those passages.

basically "un-nice" about that instinct. The correct translation of his original title, *Das Sogennante Bose,* would be *The So-Called Evil Instinct.* He argues that this instinct plays a very positive, life-*promoting* role among animals. Just to give one example: the instinct of each member of a species to fight for its own bit of territory "gives an ideal solution to the problem of the distribution of animals"—so that they don't all crowd into one place and eat up all the food available there and then starve. "The environment is divided between the members of the species in such a way that, within the potentialities offered, everyone can exist." "What a peaceful issue of the evil principle." Aggressiveness may "function in the wrong way" sometimes, by accident, he writes, and cause destruction, but "we have never found that the aim of aggression was the extermination of fellow members of the species." He writes of another, a very special instinct that has been developed in the process of evolution "to oppose aggression . . . and inhibit those of its actions that [*could* be] injurious to the survival of the species." He describes various ritualised "appeasing" gestures that are made by the weaker animal of the species at a certain point in any conflict, and describes how the stronger animal is then automatically restrained from taking advantage of the other and inflicting real injury upon him. He points out the "strangely moving paradox that the most blood-thirsty predators, particularly the Wolf . . . are among the animals with the most reliable killing inhibitions" (toward their own species, that is). For this "built-in safety device" was developed specifi-cally in those creatures who were born heavily armed. And he points out the special dilemma of Man. He is born "harmless," and so "no selection pressure arose in the prehistory of mankind to breed inhibitory mechanisms preventing the killing of his" fellows—and then he invented artificial weapons! Fortu-nately, Lorenz comments, "inventions and responsibility are both the achieve-ments of the same specifically human faculty of asking questions." Clearly the questions he has asked have, to date, resulted in a more rapid development of invention than of self-discipline, but Lorenz remains optimistic about Man, and sees him as still capable of evolving. "I assert," he writes, "that the long-sought missing link between animals and the really humane being is ourselves"—a hypothesis that I find persuasive.

A BALANCE OF INSTINCTS

What has very clearly worked, in the evolution of animals, to preserve and advance the life of each species, has been a particular *balance* of two instincts. The one, as it were, asserts the individual's right to exist. This is the so-called evil instinct. Lorenz names it "aggression." But just as I would substi-tute another word for Fanon's "violence," I would substitute another word here—and rename "aggression" "self-assertion." The second instinct restrains the first when it endangers *another's* right to exist. In human terms, the first amounts to respecting one's own person, the second to respecting the person of the other. Lorenz points out, by the way, that the only animals capable of love are those that are "aggressive." One can, it seems, *only* love another "as one loves oneself."

This life-serving balance—this equilibrium between self-assertion and respect for others—has evolved among animals on the physiological plane. In human beings it can be gained only on the plane of consciousness. And the plea this essay makes is precisely that we make the disciplined effort to gain it—all those of us who hope really to change men's lives, who, in Fanon's words, "want humanity to advance a step further," want to "set afoot a new man." My plea is that the key to a revolution that would "go forward all the time . . . in the company of Man, in the company of all men," lies in discovering within ourselves this poise. But it calls equally for the strengthening of *two* impulses—calls both for assertion (for speaking, for acting out "aggressively" the truth, as we see it, of what our rights are) and for restraint toward others (for the acting out of love for them, which is to say of respect for their human rights). May those who say that they believe in nonviolence learn to challenge more boldly those institutions of violence that constrict and cripple our humanity. And may those who have questioned nonviolence come to see that one's rights to life and happiness can only be claimed as inalienable if one grants, in action, that they belong to all men.

DOCUMENT 46

The Trial of the Winooski 44

On March 26th, 1984, the fourth anniversary of the assassination of Archbishop Oscar Romero of El Salvador, two hundred people walked into United States Senator Robert Stafford's office in Winooski, Vermont. They had come on the eve of a critical Senate vote on escalation of the contra war in Nicaragua, with two requests: that he stop voting for military aid to Central America, and that he hold a public meeting on the issue. He refused.

Three days later, still in his office, forty-four people were arrested and charged with illegal trespass. This is an unusual case inasmuch as the judge

From *Por Amor al Pueblo: Not Guilty! The Trial of the Winooski 44*, edited by Ben Bradley and others (White River Junction, Vermont: Front Porch Publishing, 1986), pp. 9–11, 22–29, 41–46, 48–50, 147–149, 151–152.

was willing to listen to a "necessity defense." As explained in the closing argument for the State of Vermont:

The common example of a necessity defense is where someone breaks a law in order to prohibit a greater harm. An example of it is where a passerby is walking along and he sees a building on fire and there is another person caught inside the building who is unable to leave, and the passerby has the ability [to] get that person out. Well, it's not his building. He can't simply go running into someone else's building. That may be a trespass. However, the law says that if the passerby goes in under certain circumstances that he may not be committing a criminal offense, or if he is committing a criminal offense he is absolved from it by virtue of the necessity defense.[1]

Through their own testimony and the testimony of Central American refugees and other expert witnesses, the defendants put United States war policy in Central America on trial. Their acquittal, by a jury of twelve Vermonters, attests to the power and eloquence of the defense testimony.

OPENING STATEMENT FOR THE STATE OF VERMONT

MS. SHINGLER: My name is Karen Shingler. I'm a deputy state's attorney.

We're here because the State of Vermont has charged the twenty-six Defendants individually with unlawful trespass; specifically, that on March 26th of this year they were in Senator Stafford's office in Winooski, an office that is located on the fourth floor of the Champlain Mill in Winooski, and that they were asked to leave after having stayed there for some period of time. They were asked to leave by Ray Pecor who is the owner of the Champlain Mill. They were asked to leave by Rey Post who is Senator Stafford's staff director. They were also asked to leave by two members of the Winooski police force, a Detective Michael Spaulding and Patrolman Barry Lawrence.

I'd like to give you some background. At about noon on March 23rd, that being a Friday, approximately a hundred and fifty demonstrators gathered outside of the Winooski Mall. This demonstration had been arranged and the demonstrators had notified both Mr. Pecor and Mr. Post of their intentions.

About an hour and a half later, at approximately one-thirty on Friday of March 23rd, many of those one hundred fifty entered the Champlain Mill, proceeded up to the fourth floor, and went to greet Rey Post at the Senator's office. Rey Post, knowing they were coming, had spoken to the Senator, had indicated what the demands of the protesters were, and he as well as the

---

1. *Ibid.,* pp. 132–133.

Senator had formulated a statement to be given to the protesters upon their arrival on Friday the 23rd.

This exchange occurred, and this group of individuals appeared unsatisfied with the statement that Senator Stafford had offered to them. They had two demands: that Senator Stafford was not to support military aid to Central America and that Senator Stafford was, as soon as possible, to convene a public meeting. Senator Stafford responded with a brief history of his votes on the Central America issue and stated that he was willing to gather with certain representatives of this group to discuss their problems and the issues at hand. The group was unsatisfied with Senator Stafford's responses, and they indicated to Rey Post that they were going to stay in the Senator's office. Rey Post said okay and proceeded to slowly remove his staff from the office. By this time it was approximately three, three-thirty in the afternoon and Senator Stafford's office was preparing to close down as in the normal course of business.

At approximately five, five-fifteen, Rey Post, as the last staff member present, left, indicating to the protesters, "I'm leaving. Senator Stafford's office is closed. Goodbye." He did not lock the doors. He did not turn off the lights. He left this group of individuals in the Senator's office. Throughout the weekend the sit-in continued.

I take you now to Monday morning, March [26], eight-thirty: the commencement of business hours at Senator Stafford's office. Rey Post arrives. They won't let him in his office, this group of individuals. Rey Post asks these individuals to please let him into his office and they say no. They demand a further statement from the Senator, and there is a little coming and going between Rey Post and the group of individuals as to how he is going about getting the statement if he can't get into his office. Rey Post comes back at approximately eleven-thirty in the morning and accompanying him is Ray Pecor and members of the Winooski Police Department. Rey Post conveys to the Defendants Senator Stafford's final response: that Senator Stafford is willing to meet with a specified group of individuals and once again states his record on certain rulings in the Senate with regard to Central America. The Defendants again express some anger or some dissatisfaction with Senator Stafford's response and once again they ask Rey Post, "Please, you have to talk to the Senator one more time."

Rey Post goes back, confers with the Senator who is in Washington. He comes back and says, "On behalf of the Senator and on behalf of myself, you have to leave. We cannot conduct business. You're violating the rights of citizens of the State of Vermont for access to their Senator." Accompanying him is Ray Pecor. Ray Pecor identifies himself as the owner of the Champlain Mill and indicates to the Defendants, "Please leave. Senator Stafford would like you to leave. You have been here all weekend. We have let you do what you want. You have to leave now." Some individuals leave. The Defendants remain in Senator Stafford's office.

A member of the Winooski police force, Michael Spaulding, says to the remaining group, "If you do not leave, you will be placed under arrest." They remained, and they were arrested by members of the Winooski Police Department as well as members of the Vermont State Police.

As this trial goes forward, you may be hearing something that lawyers call the necessity defense. It is my understanding that the focus of this necessity defense will be on Central America. Ladies and gentlemen, it really doesn't matter what you feel about Central America; and ladies and gentlemen, it does not matter what the Defendants feel about Central America. There may be things you will hear that may be upsetting about what is going on in Central America, things you may not like, things I may not like, things apparently the Defendants did not like when they heard them. Ladies and gentlemen, all I'm asking is that you please focus on our roles here throughout the rest of the week; that we're here because the Defendants broke the laws of the State of Vermont. We're not here for any other reason.

I'm confident, ladies and gentlemen, that you will find that the State has satisfied its burden that on March 26th of this year, twenty-six individuals who are sitting on the other side of this courtroom were in Senator Stafford's office, were asked to leave by Rey Post, by Ray Pecor, by Michael Spaulding and by Barry Lawrence. They chose not to, and I submit to you, ladies and gentlemen of the jury, to return a verdict of guilty. Thank you.

SONIA HERNANDEZ, having been duly sworn, testified as follows:

Direct Examination by MS. BAIRD

Q. Ms. Hernandez, could you state your name?
A. Sonia Hernandez.
Q. How old are you?
A. Twenty-seven.
Q. Where do you live?
A. In New York.
Q. What do you do there?
A. I am working.
Q. Could you tell the jury what kind of work you do?
A. Cleaning houses. I also work on the refugee committee.
Q. Can you describe the refugee committee's work for the jury?
A. We're developing programs to seek solutions to the problems which Salvadoran refugees are experiencing here in the United States.
Q. Ms. Hernandez, are there a number of Salvadoran refugees in New York City?

A. Yes, I do not know the exact number, but there's a large quantity of Salvadorans. We are working in Westbury and Hampton and there are twenty-two thousand Salvadorans in those two cities on Long Island.

Q. What kinds of work do you do for them?

A. For the most part, we are spending our time developing health programs, trying to establish a health clinic to meet the medical needs and health needs of the Salvadorans we are serving. We are also gathering various necessities such as clothing and medicine to send to refugees in Honduras and Guatemala.

Q. Are there refugees in Nicaragua as well?

A. Yes, there are.

Q. Where are you originally from, Ms. Hernandez?

A. Morazán province.

Q. In what country?

A. El Salvador.

Q. Perhaps Ms. Hernandez could point out to the jury where she is from in El Salvador. There is a map right there.

A. (Indicated.)

Q. How long did you live in that village?

A. Twelve years.

Q. And where did you go at the age of twelve?

A. I went to Morazán proper town. There was no special education for seventh, eighth and ninth grade [in the village].

Q. Your travels managed to take you to San Salvador [capital of El Salvador] as well?

A. I went to San Salvador afterwards to study, take my high school studies and to study nursing.

Q. Did your family stay in the village in Morazán?

A. Yes, they stayed there until 1981.

Q. Ms. Hernandez, could you describe what your village in Morazán was like? For instance, what is the major occupation in that area?

A. For the most part, Morazán is a farming community, with the exception of the town proper which is more or less urban.

Q. Is this area a prosperous region? A poor region? How would you describe it?

A. It has been prosperous; that is, people were able to survive and do more than survive in the area as farmers. They were renters. They do not own the land.

Q. By renters, do you mean sharecroppers?

A. No. No, a small number of proprietors owned the land and they paid the farmers for working for them.

Q. Is that area still prosperous?

A. The vast majority of the villages were destroyed and leveled by bombardment in military offensives. At this point in time, the small village which I am from originally no longer exists.

Q. And how did that happen?

A. In 1980 and 1981 a terrible repression began against the farming population.

Q. Repression by whom?

A. Repression by the government and its military forces.

Q. What forms did that oppression take?

A. The military offensives are composed of so-called cleanup operations
carried out on the presumed justification of the existence of guerrilla
soldiers in given areas. The outcome of a military cleanup offensive is
the destruction of towns and the death of civilians.

Q. Is this on the part of the government of El Salvador?

A. Yes.

Q. You say there are opposing guerrillas. Can you describe the guerrillas?

A. For many years a movement of increasingly organized resistance in opposition to the system of government in El Salvador has been growing,
as it has always been and continues to be an extremely unjust system
of government.

Q. And the opposition in your village had been growing, is that your testimony?

A. Yes. The farmers began to ask for increases in salaries, increases in pay,
and were met with firearms and repression of the kind I have been
describing.

Q. Is the church active in the formation of opposition?

A. Not really in the formation of opposition per se, though the church was
in agreement that the existing system required change.

Q. And as a result of this growing opposition in 1980 and 1981, there were,
you say, attacks on your village?

A. Yes.

Q. What happened to your family?

A. In one of these invasions, a great many civilians over the age of fifty
were taken out of their houses and rounded up—those who could not run
away, those over fifty-one, fifty-two years old—my father among them.

Q. What happened to your father?

A. They murdered him, burned him alive along with other elders like himself
and children who were not fast enough to get out of the village in time.

Q. Was your father a guerrilla?

A. No. He was an old fifty-two-year-old man who had no idea at all about
what that would be.

Q. At the time of this battle, Ms. Hernandez, where were you?

A. I was in San Salvador studying nursing. I didn't finish. They suspended
me at the school.

Q. Did you continue to work in San Salvador?

A. Yes, the kind of work I did was to attend to the refugees in the refugee
camps in San Salvador.

Q. What are these refugee camps in San Salvador? Can you describe them?

A. They were initiated by Archbishop Romero, who, in attention to the large numbers of countryside refugees coming to San Salvador, opened up the refugee camps.

Q. What is the purpose of refugee camps?

A. To give the thousands of farm workers displaced from their farms and their villages some shelter, a place to live, a place to survive.

Q. That's the church of El Salvador? They were helping in organizing these camps?

A. Yes. It is principally the church, with its various parishes, that has begun to create a program of refugee sanctuary, harboring of village refugees, in San Salvador.

Q. Is that what Archbishop Romero was active in?

A. Yes.

Q. Ms. Hernandez, were you in San Salvador when the Archbishop was assassinated?

A. Yes.

Q. Did you attend his funeral?

A. Yes.

Q. Can you describe the events of that funeral?

A. Six days after the death of Archbishop Monsignor Romero thousands of farm people, country people, gathered at the cathedral to bid their last farewell to the Archbishop. After all the people had gathered in the cathedral, a large shot, explosion, was heard and right after the loud shot or explosion, a great many people in the cathedral who were attending the funeral witnessed that directly across the street, from inside the national palace (which houses the Salvadoran army) soldiers were firing into the crowd.

Q. Were there deaths?

A. A great many. After everyone had left I went back and counted twenty-seven dead bodies. Just the same, I know a great many people, women, who left the cathedral running with dead children in their arms. It was a great and bloody ordeal with a lot of anguish for those present.

Q. How do you know that this was a government attack?

A. Because you could see the National Guard firing from up at the palace.

Q. Did you stay in San Salvador for a while after the death of the Archbishop?

A. Yes, I stayed there through the rest of 1980 and through 1981.

Q. And what was the atmosphere in San Salvador after the death of the Archbishop?

A. Great anger, but even greater anguish than anger, because Bishop Romero was a man who had offered a lot of hope, consolation and promise to the Salvadorans.

Q. Did the war in San Salvador continue?

A. Yes. There was a great deal of heavy fear and apprehension to the extreme at the funeral, within the processions and demonstrations of sympathy for Bishop Romero. It was discovered subsequently that a lot of people had been planted there to note civilians, take names, take photographs and a great many people disappeared as a result of that.

Q. When you say disappeared, what does that mean?

A. A great many homes are invaded and people removed from them. Subsequent to those kinds of operations the rest of the members of the family go into the streets of San Salvador the next day to look for the bodies of those who disappeared. Those bodies which are not found are counted as disappeared because no traces are found.

Q. Did there come a time when something happened to your fiancé? When was that?

A. In May of 1981. Despite all of the turmoil, I was determined to continue my relationship and get married. My fiancé was walking down the street one day and apparently at no provocation at all, several heavily armed men got out of a car. These men are known as the death squad and they savagely murdered my boyfriend at knifepoint, left him dismembered.

Q. How old was he?

A. Twenty years.

Q. What did he do for a living?

A. He was a student.

Q. Did you stay in San Salvador after that?

A. Yes, for the rest of 1981.

Q. Did you ever have access to your boyfriend's body? Was that ever found?

A. No, neither I, nor, I think, any of his family members ever had the courage to go and claim the body because that entailed danger since one is a marked person by going to claim a dead body.

Q. So, what was your life like after that in San Salvador?

A. Of course my life was shattered, but for a while I was able to join with friends who had suffered similar tragedies; that is, the loss of a brother, loss of a boyfriend, loss of some family members, and we managed to see each other through the next few months.

Q. Did events occur which caused you to decide to leave El Salvador, and what were they?

A. While I was still in San Salvador living with a lady who dearly loved me, I received a death-threatening phone call one night. They came to look for me one night. When they didn't find me, they took instead the seventeen-year-old son, one of two sons this lady had, and the only one who was home. The boy's intestines were—he was completely disemboweled. The lady more or less lost her mind. I understood, of course, that I was in imminent and crucial danger and that if I did nothing to try to save myself my chances were slim of carrying on.

Q. What did you do as a result of that evening?

A. Almost nothing. Nothing much one can do under those circumstances. No options, no alternatives for the simple reason that no one really wants to give shelter or harbor to someone over whose neck is hanging that kind of danger and stigma.

Q. Did you leave your country then?

A. I spent ten anguishing days going from one house to another, knowing that I was a curse to anyone's home. Those were ten terrifying days in which I lived very close to death. And it was amidst that situation, on the verge of madness myself, walking around alone in a war zone south of San Salvador, that I decided that the only thing for me to do was to leave my country.

Q. And at that time you left?

A. Sí. It is not as if I had any destination or particular direction in mind. The only thing that concerned me was to get out of El Salvador and so I did. The first place I went was Guatemala.

Q. You eventually went to Mexico as well?

A. In Guatemala, the situation was no different. The same kind of fear and repression permeated existence there, and so, seeing that, I decided to continue ahead to Mexico.

ANNIE GAILLARD, being duly sworn, testified as follows:

Direct Examination by MR. NELSON

Q. Annie, would you state your full name and your address please?

A. Priscilla Ann Gaillard and I live in Walden, Vermont.

Q. What is your occupation?

A. I am a farmer and a mother.

Q. And are you one of the Defendants in this case?

A. Yes, I am.

Q. And I take it that you admit that you were in Senator Stafford's office; is that correct?

A. Yes.

Q. Can you explain to the jury what brought you to Senator Stafford's office?

A. I had heard a lot of information about what was going on in Central America which disturbed me a lot. I had written a few letters to Stafford trying to explain my position and I called him a few times and had gotten run-of-the-mill form letters that just basically said he went along with Reagan's policy in Central America and he didn't seem willing to go into it in any more personal way as to why he felt that he had to follow Reagan's policy.

Q. Can you tell us some of the things that you heard that were disturbing to you?

A. At the time I was six months pregnant and the things that I heard about happening to the children, that seventy-five per cent of the refugees were children, that at least half, sometimes three-quarters of —

MS. SHINGLER: Objection, Your Honor. I was going to wait and see what this was going to be. Seems to be all hearsay. Question calls for a hearsay answer.

THE COURT: Mr. Nelson?

MR. NELSON: Your Honor, it's not being offered for the truth, but to show the witness' reasonable understanding.

THE COURT: Well, relying on Mr. Justice Peck's language in *State v. Shotton,* testing what is reasonably conceived by the Defendant to have been a necessity, I will allow the question and the answer but with a caution for the jury that it is to be considered by them only as to the witness' reasonable perception of a situation of necessity and not for the truth of any of the matters asserted.

Q. Go on. You were, I think, in the middle of an answer.

A. Let's see. In a family of five children, three of them would probably die before the age of five through either malnutrition or murders or things like that. That the military will torture children to torture the parents who are made to watch. One instance I heard, through a Guatemalan refugee, was that the children were held by their ankles and swung around until their heads hit a wall or tree or something which killed them and the parents were made to watch this.

Q. This last one you say you heard from a Guatemalan refugee?

A. Yes, I did.

Q. How about the statistics that you were giving us earlier? Where did you get those from?

A. I think some of them were in books and also information groups like CASA.

Q. You say you have made efforts before this to contact the Senator?

A. Yes.

Q. How many such efforts did you make?

A. I would say there were probably two phone calls and two or three letters.

Q. And you found satisfactory responses to that?

A. No. It was just usually the form letter. If it was a phone call they would just ask what I was calling about and I would say what I was feeling and they would just say what's your name and your address and then that was all and about a week or two weeks later I would get the same form letter back.

Q. I think you told us briefly what brought you to Senator Stafford's office. What was your purpose in being there? What was your intention?

A. I guess I was feeling frustrated by not getting anywhere with writing, the usual way that you contact your elected officials, and this was like a last resort.

Q. You're a citizen of Vermont?

A. Yes, I am.

Q. And a constituent of the Senator's; is that right?

A. Yes.

Q. Did you feel that you had legal authority to be in his office during work hours?

A. Yes, I did.

MR. NELSON: No further questions.

PHILIPPE BOURGOIS, being duly sworn, testified as follows:

Direct Examination by MS. BAIRD

Q. Would you state your name?

A. Philippe Bourgois.

Q. Where do you live?

A. New York City.

Q. What's your occupation?

A. I'm an anthropologist. I'm currently writing my doctoral dissertation at Stanford University.

Q. You're currently working on your Ph.D.?

A. Yes, I am writing my doctoral dissertation on Costa Rica.

Q. Could you explain what that means?

A. Sorry. I'm doing a history of the nationality and racial and cultural history of the population along the Atlantic coast of Costa Rica showing how it changed over the years.

Q. Have you done research in other areas of Central America?

A. Yes, I have been working in Central America ever since college. It's been about eight years now. My honors thesis at Harvard was on Belize. It's a small country in Central America on the coast next to Guatemala. And my Master's thesis was on the Mopan Maya Indians in Belize. I did field work also among the Miskito Indians in Nicaragua.

Q. And would you say that you're fluent in Spanish?

A. Yes.

Q. Did you take a trip to Central America in 1981?

A. Yes, I did. I was looking into the feasibility of doing my doctoral dissertation on Salvadoran refugees in Honduras.

Q. And where did you go at that time?

A. I had been interviewing refugees in the refugee camps in Honduras. These are Salvadorans who crossed over the border into Honduras and sought refuge. I had just begun doing the interviewing when the refugees kept telling me, Look. You keep asking us where we used to grow up. It's only ten miles away. Go ahead, it's right across the river.

Q. For what reason are you interested in these refugees?

A. Well, they are the bulk just in terms of numbers. The largest number of refugees that were accessible in this camp were from that region. As an anthropologist, I decided to focus on that particular area.

Q. You heard testimony before that there are refugee camps in El Salvador. Your testimony is that there are some refugee camps outside of El Salvador; is that true?

A. Yes, I thought it would be safer to do field work among the refugees outside the country, because of the situation in El Salvador today.

Q. What situation?

A. Well, it's very dangerous. There is a civil war going on and a lot of people are getting killed.

Q. What were your interviews, what did they consist of?

A. Well, I was just asking straightforward questions. I was asking the farmers what they grew, what they did when they harvested it, how much rent they paid for their land, how much wage work they did and those kinds of questions. Just the straightforward questions about the mechanics of their life.

Q. Your questions centered on their life in El Salvador?

A. Yes, I was getting history of their particular region to look at what had been happening to them, because I was trying to figure out why there was a civil war going on.

Q. There is a map down here, Mr. Bourgois. Where were you in Honduras?

A. The refugee camps are right here; and this is Honduras. This is El Salvador. This is the border right there. There it is. That's exactly where I was.

Q. Are Honduras and El Salvador friendly governments?

A. They aren't [historically]. They had a war in the '60s but recently that's been changing and as you will see from my testimony the Honduran government actually collaborated with the Salvadoran government.

Q. At this point they are not at war and they are friendly, would you say?

A. Yes.

Q. And they have welcomed refugees into their country?

A. No. Luckily the United Nations High Commission for Refugees has been overseeing the camps in Honduras and trying to ensure the safety of Salvadoran refugees, although there have been cases of kidnaps of Salvadoran refugees in Honduras. It's dangerous for them.

Q. Are there also refugee camps in Nicaragua?

A. Yes, I think every single country in Central America except Guatemala has Salvadoran refugees in it. Belize does. Honduras does. Costa Rica does.

Q. After you did your interviews, what were your findings on the refugee camps in Honduras?

A. Well, it was all very preliminary. I was hoping to do about nine months worth of field work, and I hadn't done even three weeks yet.

Q. And then what did you do after that?

A. Well, I made the mistake of crossing into El Salvador.

Q. Why did you do that?

A. As I was saying, I kept asking them these questions and they kept looking at me and saying, hey, go over there, it's just across the border, it's only ten miles away. And so I did. I crossed over there. I was planning on staying forty-eight hours, just a quick visit to get a feel for the land, to find out if they lived in homestead villages or clustered villages, and so forth.

Q. What was the nature of the border?

A. There is no border crossing there. There is no guard or anything, and there is just a path that the local peasants use and have always used. So I just went across there.

Q. How long did it take you to get over the border?

A. Oh, it took about six hours.

Q. Where did you go in El Salvador?

A. Well, I reached the region exactly below where I pointed on the map, that is known as the province of Cabañas. And I was just going around interviewing small farmers in that region. It's a region of small farmers.

Q. How would you describe that area?

A. Well, it's very typical of any small farming region.

Q. Like Vermont?

A. As a matter of fact, it is a lot like Vermont. It would be like further up north toward the Canadian border, for example. Well, of course, a lot poorer. The basic crops are corn and beans, and the land is owned essentially by a few large landlords, and the bulk of the population sharecrop their land. It's a strange relationship of sharecropping because they have to give a number of days worth of labor to the landlord in return for having access to growing corn and beans which is their subsistence crop.

Q. Could you describe that economic system as feudal?

A. Well, actually, to tell you the truth it's a big debate in anthropology. It's a technical debate about what to call it.

Q. What would you call it?

A. Well, it's certainly a bad deal for the farmer.

Q. Why don't you go on. What do you mean by that?

A. Well, what happens is that the small farmer has to stay in good with the landlord in order to even be given a plot of land to cultivate; and if the landlord just doesn't like him, the landlord won't give him access to any land and he will starve. They're living very close to starvation level. It's not like here. There is no electricity. There is no running water. There are no roads even, and so they're in a desperate situation.

Q. Also no money?

A. Well, money circulates, but they're very short of money.

Q. How about literacy?

A. Oh, about ninety percent illiteracy. Only about ten percent of the population can even read.

Q. Is that area religious?

A. Very religious.

Q. What kind?

A. It's Catholic.

Q. How long were you there?

A. Well, I was planning on staying forty-eight hours.

Q. What happened?

A. At dawn of the day I was supposed to be leaving, the Salvadoran government launched one of it's military operations against that region and I was trapped.

Q. Were you expecting that?

A. No, the region had been calm for eight months. There hadn't been a shot fired. As a matter of fact, that's one of the reasons why I thought, well, this area is safe, I will just make a quick trip in and out. And that was my mistake. It wasn't safe.

Q. What happened?

A. Well, it was at dawn and a little boy came running into the hut where I was sleeping. I was staying with a farming family.

Q. Describe the house that you were in.

A. It was shingled. It was a clay shingled house with mud walls and mud floor. It was actually a little better than the typical house there was. Some of them are thatched roofs.

Q. Was there electricity?

A. No, no electricity. No running water. As a matter of fact, there wasn't even an outhouse in this house. And you had to walk about a mile to get to the well.

Q. What happened on this morning that you were talking about?

A. A little boy came running in saying that Salvadoran government troops had surrounded the entire region and that Honduran troops had massed along the river which divides El Salvador from Honduras.

Q. Could you show it?

A. See, this is the river that runs along between the two countries, and Salvadoran government troops had circled this thirty-square-mile region like this, and the Honduran troops had lined up along here; so we were trapped and there was no place we could go.

Q. Why did the Honduran troops do that?

A. They were shooting into the river with the machine guns so that the civilians, the noncombatant regular farming population wouldn't be able to run out and become refugees.

Q. So this young boy told you this?

A. No, he came running in. He was in tears actually saying, "They're coming, they're coming. We're surrounded." I still hadn't quite figured out what was going on.

Q. How do you know who they were?

A. Well, I didn't. I was confused. I had been reading about the region so I knew that there was a civil war going on and I had been interviewing people, but I didn't think it was going to happen to me. And what happened was when the sun got high enough the first helicopter came. It was what they call a Huey helicopter. That's a U.S. helicopter. Everyone in my hut went running out.

Q. Going back to the Huey. It's something that the jurors might not be familiar with.

A. Well, it's actually not too different from the traffic helicopters they use in New York City. It's a big helicopter. They are what were used in Vietnam. It's a standard United States Army helicopter. And they went running out of the hut where I was and I was still standing there trying to let it sink in. They grabbed me and said, Get out of here, we've got to go into hiding. I did. We ran about a hundred yards away, and sure enough when the helicopter got above the hamlet where I was staying, they opened up fire with their machine gun. They were just strafing the entire area with machine-gun fire.

Q. Where were you at this time?

A. We were safe by a clump of trees and boulders and there was a cave that they had dug out of the side of the hill, and so we put ourselves in that cave. I have a picture of it.

Q. When you say "we"?

A. Oh, this was the family. I was with the family that I was staying with. There were several women, and their children.

Q. Were there any soldiers with you?

A. In the region there was armed opposition to the Salvadoran government. Basically these were the young men and young women farmers. They meanwhile had gone down to the periphery of that thirty-square-mile region and they were preventing the Salvadoran government troops from being able to come on foot and kill us.

Q. What did they have as weapons?

A. They had big weapons, formal weapons, and then hunting rifles. Some just had pistols. I'm not really an expert on weapons.

Q. They have any helicopters?

A. No, no.

Q. How old were these soldiers?

A. Basically they were kids. Teenagers. The way I understood it the people with the best eyesight, the fastest runners, healthiest people were the ones carrying the guns because they had very few, and the rest of us—just the normal grandmothers, grandfathers, mothers, children, men and so forth—we were just sort of helpless. The armed opposition had nothing to be able to fire at the helicopters or the airplanes. And the worst was that the Salvadoran government started sending in helicopter after helicopter and airplanes on us dropping bombs on us and then they started lobbing us with mortar fire. They kept this up and we couldn't stand the barrage. At night when the helicopters couldn't circulate and the airplanes weren't flying anymore they would increase the tempo of mortar fire. It seemed like they were doing it indiscriminately throughout the area.

Q. How long?

A. Well, what we would do is, we would be running back and forth from the cave where we were taking refuge when the helicopter and the planes would pass, to the hut where the cooking fire was, to try to eat something. And so we were basically in sort of a state of semi-panic running back and forth trying to find refuge. There were a couple of times when I found myself inside the cave and the cave was full because there were already people inside it. They told me whatever you do, don't panic and run. Stay still, because the helicopter shoots at anything that moves. Motion attracts the eye of the gunner and the gunner opens fire on what is moving.

Q. Did there come a time when you evacuated from that area?

A. Yes, after four days the armed fighters who were protecting us came back to us and said, look, we're running out of ammunition, we're getting desperate. More and more people were getting wounded. Several of us normal civilians had been hit by the mortar fire. They said, you have to get out of here, you have to evacuate.

Q. Going back to the wounded, was there any care for them?

A. No, that was the tragedy. They basically didn't have any real medical care.

Q. Any pain killers?

A. There were no pain killers. There was a little boy—I will never be able to forget—had a mortar scrap in his legs and they just held his feet and pulled out the mortar scrap. He later died. We buried him along —

Q. When it came time to evacuate, what happened?

A. We assembled together. There were about a thousand of us regular, normal small farmers.

Q. You have some pictures of people you were with?

A. Yes. It was grandmothers, grandfathers. There was a blind woman with us. There were several pregnant women. Many babies and two women actually gave birth during the flight. I have a picture of one of the women just after she gave birth. . . .

Q. These pictures portray people you were with? What kind of people were they?

A. Well, these are the people, these are the farmers that lived in this region. These are just the local inhabitants of this area.

Q. And there were women as well as men?

A. Yes, people of all ages and all farmers, as a matter of fact.

Q. What happened after you evacuated that region?

A. We had a hard time evacuating. There were about a thousand of us, and we were filing single file trying to sneak out of the area and go into hiding. And the hope was that the fighters, the people protecting us, the boys, were going to do a diversionary tactic and get the Salvadoran government troops to attack them. They were going to make a lot of noise, shoot their guns off to our left and we were going to run out as fast as we could on the right and hopefully go into hiding. What happened, though, is when we got right to that line of fire, the babies that the mothers were carrying started to shriek and cry because of the fright of the gunfire. And at that point the Salvadoran government troops changed the direction of their machine-gun fire and started shooting into the sound of crying babies. Now, at that point it was pandemonium, grenades were landing on us. Machine gun fire was coming on us. We were hitting the dirt, getting up and running as fast as we can, and the babies shrieking, and the fire getting stronger and stronger.

Q. And women carrying the babies?

A. Yes, you see the mother has to carry her own baby, because if a stranger picks up the baby, someone the baby isn't familiar with, the baby shrieks even louder. So the mother is the only person that can try to quiet her baby. That was our biggest risk.

Q. Why was that?

A. Because Salvadoran government troops—well, it appeared that they wanted to just do away with all forms of life in this region, and the sound of screaming babies was attracting their machine fire.

Q. Did you somehow escape?

A. Yes. I was running at one point and a grenade went off about from me to where the jury is and I hit the ground and the mud and the rocks are flying all over. I got on to my feet and was running forward and there was a little boy, the grenade had landed on him and taken off his legs—I'm sorry, it's a horrible story to tell—had taken off his legs and that was my first immediate contact with that, and I stood up and grabbed my head and I was saying what do I do, carry him? He was not dead yet, and I was sort of trying to figure out what was going on when someone came up behind me, pushed me hard so I fell down and then I heard, "Keep running, you're in the line of fire. You can't do anything for him," and I kept on running.

Q. Where did you run to?

A. Well, about three quarters of us, about six, seven hundred of us managed to run out into a ravine a few miles away. And when dawn was breaking, we found ourselves huddled into the ravine. They were patrolling up above us looking for us, and thank God they didn't find us.

Q. Did you stay in the region very long?

A. Basically for the next eight days we ran at night and we hid during the day. You see, we had to run at night, because at night the helicopters couldn't circulate and the helicopters were the big risk for finding us.

Q. Did you go to the Honduran border?

A. No, we wanted to become refugees. It's logical for civilians to become refugees in a state of war like that, but we couldn't because of Honduran troops lined along the rivers. So we actually had to flee away from the border during that first period. We were just zig-zagging and trying to make sure that the government troops' foot patrols wouldn't catch up, and each night we would have a different place or, as much as we could, a better place to hide and we had no food.

Q. Or water?

A. Well, we had a hard time with the water. There were streams we drank
out of, but since there were so many of us and many people were wounded
by this time we kept contaminating the water. As a matter of fact, that
was one of the reasons we had to move.

Q. Did there come a time when you went back into that region?

A. Yes, after eight days of this flight we thought it was over, and we started
to file back into the region we fled out of, and the first thing that hit us
as we were walking back was the stench of rotting meat, because what
the Salvadoran troops had done is they had killed every living creature
that they had been able to get their hands on. They were even killing the
cats and the dogs, the pets. They had tried to rip down the houses. They
had ripped apart the granaries. The granaries seem to be the first thing
that they went for, and they actually tried to stop the harvest. It was a
period of bean harvest which is a very important harvest for Salvadorans,
and they had zapped that, and that's what we walked into.

Now, what happened was a Salvadoran battalion which is trained by
the United States participated in this invasion, and they were using what
they called the new Green Beret-style, Vietnam-style tactics of leaving
behind small groups of armed men to do ambushes after you finish the
basic invasion. We didn't realize this, and the next thing we knew we
were ambushed and again they surrounded us. For another two days we
were submitted to the mortar fire, to the fire by the Huey helicopters and
to bombardment by the airplanes.

Q. Did you see many deaths during that time?

A. I didn't during those last days, I didn't see any more deaths. No other
people were blown up next to me, but by that time we had a serious
number of wounded people and trying to care for them was a big problem.
Our other big problem was the babies, because the mothers' milk by this
time was drying up because of the lack of food, and the dehydration from
terror. And the babies were crying a lot, and that was dangerous for us
because once again it gave away our exact position to the patrols.

Q. Eventually what happened?

A. Well, what happened was, an NBC film crew had gone just by luck to
the Salvadoran refugee camps and they were doing a regular public story
about refugees and the situation of refugees. While they were there, they
heard this bombing and strafing and so they said, well, let's see what is
going on; and they walked down to the border which was only about five
miles away. And that's what forced the Honduran troops to get out of
that border area and cleared it so we civilians could come out into safety;
and that's what we did. As soon as we found out the path was clear to
the refugee camps we just ran. It was an all night run for me. I made it
out just as dawn was breaking. Most of the people were mothers carrying
their children. They went much slower. And they were hit once again.
Daylight caught them when they were still in El Salvador, and they were

hit once again with the strafing by the helicopters. And they didn't get out until later that afternoon and some even until the next day.

Q. How many days did this go on?

A. It was fourteen days.

Q. You ended up in a refugee camp again in Honduras?

A. Yes.

Judge's Charge to the Jury

Citizens, therefore, have a right to petition their government for redress of grievances. They have a right to peaceful and orderly expression of their views in settings traditional for civic debate. They have a right to assemble together to instruct their elected representatives. They have a right to request that their elected representatives be accountable to them. If you find that the Defendants were engaged in the exercise of these rights, and they were arrested because of their activities, you may not find them guilty of unlawful trespass unless the State also proves beyond a reasonable doubt that the State's actions in restricting their exercise of these rights, served a significant State interest and, further, that their regulation of these important rights were reasonable as to time, place and manner.

The defense of necessity is well recognized in the law and was explicitly recognized as being the law in the State of Vermont by our own State Supreme Court within the past year. It is a defense with a long history. However, it is a doctrine which is one of specific application, as a defense to criminal behavior. This is so because, if the qualifications for the defense of necessity are not closely delineated, the definition of criminal activity may become uncertain and even whimsical. So it is important in applying the defense that has been presented, the defense of necessity, that you do it in terms of four well-established, analytical elements of that defense which have been laid down by our State Supreme Court. In other words, it is not a political referendum or an election. It is a legal principle and must be analyzed by you in terms of the legal criteria set forth by our Supreme Court for analyzing that defense. Essentially, the defense of necessity will apply if the four elements apply to the factual situation. And with regard to these elements, it is also the burden of the State to prove beyond a reasonable doubt, necessity did not exist or apply.

The four elements which must prevail are as follows: first, there must be a situation of emergency arising without fault on the part of the actor involved; in other words, without fault of the Defendants.

Secondly, this emergency must be so imminent and compelling as to raise a reasonable expectation of harm, either directly to the Defendant or upon those he was seeking to protect.

Thirdly, the emergency must present no reasonable opportunity to avoid the injury without committing the unlawful act; in this case, the alleged unlawful trespass.

Fourth, the injury impending from the emergency must be of sufficient seriousness to outweigh the criminal wrong that has been alleged, the criminal wrong of unlawful trespass.

The first element is a situation of emergency arising without fault on the part of the Defendant. I think that's pretty much self-explanatory.

Secondly, this emergency must be so imminent and compelling as to raise a reasonable expectation of harm upon those the Defendant was seeking to protect. In this regard I'd like to look at both the concept of imminent, and the concept of harm. The emergency must reasonably appear to the Defendant to be threatening to occur immediately, near at hand in terms of time, though not necessarily geographically. The harm need not be unique or one of a kind, or a one-shot type of harm. However, it must be a harm which is reasonably certain to occur. It's not a harm which is merely speculative or uncertain.

Third, this emergency must present no reasonable opportunity to avoid the injury without committing the unlawful trespass. And the question that you have to ask there is, was it reasonably conceived by the Defendant to have been a necessity? In other words, the test is one of reasonable subjectivity. Did the Defendant in fact conceive that his or her actions were a necessity, and was the Defendant reasonable in so conceiving the situation?

Fourth, the injury impending from the emergency must be of sufficient seriousness to outweigh the criminal wrong, or the unlawful trespass. And this element involves a weighing of values. Did the emergency which the Defendants claim they were responding to, was that of sufficient seriousness to outweigh the alleged criminal trespass? And here again, the test is one of reasonable subjectivity, and the relevant question is, did the Defendant reasonably believe that the need, as the Defendant conceived that need to be, outweighed the criminal wrong?

It is also necessary to ask, did the Defendant reasonably believe that his or her action would avoid the harm? And in this regard, it is not important whether the Defendant was ultimately successful or not in meeting the emergency situation.

In this situation of determining whether or not the impending injury from the emergency situation was of sufficient weight to outweigh the alleged unlawful trespass, you should understand that the threatened harm that was perceived by the Defendant need not have been a criminal act, or a crime. An emergency situation of that type could be, as one of the attorneys described, a fire in a house. On the other hand, you may, if you choose, consider whether or not the government of the United States was violating international law with regard to the alleged emergency situation which the Defendants indicated that they perceived. That is appropriate for you to consider in weighing the values involved under this fourth element.

You should understand that international law is law. It is law which is binding on the United States of America and on the State of Vermont, and so it is appropriate for your consideration. Some of the principles of international law which are relevant for your consideration in this regard include the Resolutions of the United Nations which were supported by the United States of America, as well as provisions of the Charter of the Organization of American States of which the United States of America is a signatory. Under those it is a principle of international law binding on the United States of America and the State of Vermont, and no state or group of states has the right to intervene directly, or indirectly, for any reason whatsoever, in the internal or external affairs of any other state or nation. This principle applies not only to armed forces, but to any other form of interference, or attempted interference. International law specifically prohibits the organization or the encouragement of the organization of armed bands for incursion into the territory of another state or another nation, the undertaking or encouragement of activities calculated to foment civil strife in another nation, or the undertaking or encouragement of terroristic activities in another nation.

Also under the Geneva Protocols, which are binding on the United States of America, it is a violation of international law for one country to associate in the crimes of another state. And under the Geneva Protocols, any indiscriminate act of terror aimed at civilians is a violation of international law, and such an act of terror includes violence to life and person, murder of all kinds, mutilation, cruel treatment, and torture.

The taking of hostages, outrages upon personal dignity, and humiliating or degrading treatment, are violations of international law. Acts of terrorism and collective punishments against civilian populations are likewise violations of international law. And it is appropriate for you to consider those legal principles in weighing the relative value of the injuries which the Defendants claim they saw impending from the perceived emergency in Central America against the seriousness of the criminal trespass allegedly committed by them.

THE DELIVERY OF THE VERDICT

Jury returns to the courtroom.

THE COURT: Mrs. Bedard, has the jury reached a verdict, ma'am?
MRS. BEDARD: Yes.
THE COURT: Very well. If the Defendants would please stand and face the jury? The jury would please stand and face the Defendants.
Mrs. Bedard, as to the Defendant Jeanne Keller, how does the jury find—guilty or not guilty?
MRS. BEDARD: Not guilty.
THE COURT: Please, please. As to the Defendant Joy Hammond, how does the jury find the Defendant—guilty or not guilty?

MRS. BEDARD: Not guilty.

THE COURT: As to the Defendant, Melrose Huff?

MRS. BEDARD: Not guilty.

THE COURT: As to the Defendant, Sylvia Lane?

MRS. BEDARD: Not guilty.

THE COURT: As to the Defendant, Joseph Moore?

MRS. BEDARD: Not guilty.

THE COURT: As to the Defendant, David Dellinger?

MRS. BEDARD: Not guilty.

THE COURT: As to the Defendant, Phil Fiermonte?

MRS. BEDARD: Not guilty.

THE COURT: As to the Defendant, Annie Gaillard?

MRS. BEDARD: Not guilty.

THE COURT: As to the Defendant, Robin Lloyd?

MRS. BEDARD: Not guilty.

THE COURT: As to the Defendant, Gil McCann?

MRS. BEDARD: Not guilty.

THE COURT: As to the Defendant, Paul Markowitz?

MRS. BEDARD: Not guilty.

THE COURT: As to the Defendant, Celia Oyler?

MRS. BEDARD: Not guilty.

THE COURT: As to the Defendant, Nancy Powell?

MRS. BEDARD: Not guilty.

THE COURT: As to the Defendant, John Rogers?

MRS. BEDARD: Not guilty.

THE COURT: As to the Defendant, Gary Sisco?

MRS. BEDARD: Not guilty.

THE COURT: As to the Defendant, Jennifer Strickler?

MRS. BEDARD: Not guilty.

THE COURT: As to the Defendant, Barr Swennerfelt?

MRS. BEDARD: Not guilty.

THE COURT: As to the Defendant, Leonara Terhune?

MRS. BEDARD: Not guilty.

THE COURT: As to the Defendant, John Van Raalte, Junior?

MRS. BEDARD: Not guilty.

THE COURT: As to the Defendant, Nicholas Velvet?

MRS. BEDARD: Not guilty.

THE COURT: As to the Defendant, Abby Yasgur?

MRS. BEDARD: Not guilty.

THE COURT: As to the Defendant, Joanna Rankin?

MRS. BEDARD: Not guilty.

THE COURT: As to the Defendant, Jean Pineo?

MRS. BEDARD: Not guilty.

THE COURT: As to the Defendant, Rose Reilly?

MRS. BEDARD: Not guilty.

THE COURT: As to the Defendant, Jeani Lowell?

MRS. BEDARD: Not guilty.
THE COURT: As to the Defendant, Eric Brocque?
MRS. BEDARD: Not guilty.
THE COURT: Very well. And so say you all, ladies and gentlemen?
THE JURY: Yes.

DOCUMENT 47

Sanctuary

During the summer of 1980, a group of Salvadorans was found in an Arizona desert where they had been abandoned by their "coyote" (a person who, for a fee, smuggles Central Americans across the United States border). Several church groups in Arizona set out to aid the survivors, only to find that the U.S. Immigration and Naturalization Service (INS) was preparing to deport them to El Salvador. INS obstruction to Guatemalans and Salvadorans achieving political asylum turned out to be widespread and systematic.

Concerned volunteers in Tucson, Arizona arrived at the idea of sanctuary. The most urgent need of the Central American refugees was not legal assistance after they were captured and deported; it was to avoid capture in the first place. "Confronted with Central Americans showing the marks of torture and telling horrific tales of persecution, religious workers along the U.S.-Mexico border concluded that these immigrants were clearly refugees entitled to safe haven in the United States, regardless of INS policy." In 1981 the All Saints Church in Tucson decided to house undocumented Central Americans. Other churches followed. (See Susan Bibler Coutin, The Culture of Protest: Religious Activism and the U.S. Sanctuary Movement *[Boulder: Westview Press, 1993], pp. 25–31.)*

Meanwhile, a group of clergy in Berkeley, California had independently come to a similar conclusion (Document 47A). Among the religious groups in Berkeley that eventually joined in were several East Bay synagogues (see Document 47B). The impetus for their affiliation was the decision of a Tucson, Arizona synagogue to join the movement in 1984. The rabbi of the Tucson synagogue recalls:

I decided that this was the most important issue that everything else depended on, and I prayed to God, I prayed to let it go through. And I decided that if it didn't pass, I would give up my rabbinate. So, when

Yom Kippur came around, which is one of the most important Jewish holidays, I didn't write a normal sermon, and I didn't speak from notes. I walked away from the pulpit and I preached a sermon facing the congregation eye-to-eye. And the president of the congregation walked out halfway through the sermon. But afterwards, a man came up to me with tears in his eyes, and he said, "Now I know why I belong to a synagogue."

Several months after the Tucson synagogue declared, Bay Area Jewish activists invited its rabbi to come and speak about his congregation's experience. One who heard him recalls:

There was a rabbi from Arizona who came out to speak at a Jewish Community Center near here to over 100 people—it was packed. And it was the most moving thing. And after that they said, "Whoever wants to help get Jews involved in sanctuary, please come up to the front." So I went. I mean, I was crying, that's how moving it was. He related it all to the Holocaust . . . (Coutin, The Culture of Protest, *pp. 32–33).*

As of 1992, thirty-one faith communities from the East Bay had covenanted together in this ministry.

A. "A History of East Bay Sanctuary Covenant"

East Bay Sanctuary Covenant began with the first declarations of sanctuary for Salvadoran and Guatemalan refugees on March 24, 1982. Five churches in the East Bay, along with one in Tucson, Arizona, and another in Washington D.C. publicly declared their commitment to provide sanctuary for refugees fleeing violence and persecution in El Salvador and Guatemala. All seven congregations coordinated their declaration of sanctuary and chose the second anniversary of the assassination of Salvadoran Archbishop Oscar Romero as an appropriate date to publicly announce their covenant.

REFLECTIONS

In the East Bay, sanctuary for Central American refugees was first discussed in a weekly gathering of pastors. Each week ministers of several churches

Irene Litherland, "A History of East Bay Sanctuary Covenant" (Berkeley, CA: 1991). Reprinted by permission.

near the U.C. Berkeley campus met (as they still do today) to discuss the lectionary readings for the week, share their thoughts on the significance of the passages for today's world, and discuss how best to present them to their congregations. In 1981, this group of pastors was studying the prophets of the Old Testament and trying to interpret the prophets' message for their churches in the East Bay. Specifically, the prophets identified three groups of people who needed special attention and assistance from the church: orphans, widows, and strangers. The pastors reflected on the question, "who are the current strangers in our midst".

At the same time, several events made them aware of the increasing violence in Central America. Church workers were returning from Central and South America describing the poverty, inequality, and injustice they had witnessed. Archbishop Romero in El Salvador wrote to President Carter in 1980 requesting him to stop the military aid being sent from the U.S. to El Salvador. Romero's assassination in March of 1980, and the killing of the four U.S. religious women in El Salvador in December of 1980, made many aware of the violence in El Salvador. In addition, several incidents of tragic deaths of refugees who had been abandoned in the Southwestern desert after being smuggled across the border also received much publicity. Along with others in the U.S., the clergy in Berkeley learned that violence and injustice were prevalent in Central America, that people trying to flee this violence were coming to the United States, that their journey was one of many dangers and sometimes death, and that, even if they made it here safely, life in the U.S. was extremely difficult for them without legal status.

The pastors discussed the Judeo-Christian concept of "sanctuary" in which a sanctuary is defined not just as a holy place of worship, but also a place of refuge and protection. Sanctuaries of many religions have served as places where people accused of crimes or fleeing violence could find safe haven. In the early 1970's, more than twenty churches in the Bay Area had offered sanctuary to members of the U.S. military who wanted to end their military service on the basis of conscientious objection. Thus the concept of sanctuary was not new to many of the Berkeley churches.

In November of 1981, the pastors from the discussion group held a workshop for other clergy on the concept of sanctuary and the situation in Central America. Then in January, 1982, another workshop was held with members of seven congregations. In February, five of these congregations decided to participate in a public declaration of sanctuary for Central Americans. On March 24, 1982, sanctuary was declared by Newman Hall-Holy Spirit Parish, St. John's Presbyterian Church, St. Mark's Episcopal Church, Trinity United Methodist Church, and University Lutheran Chapel.

PUBLIC DECLARATIONS

St. John's Presbyterian Church had already received a young Salvadoran couple into sanctuary before their public declaration. At the press conference on March 24 it was announced that three young Salvadoran men had moved into University Lutheran Chapel. The five churches stated that the refugees would remain in the building with support from the congregations until four goals were achieved: $5000 was raised, 500 letters were written to the U.S. President, 100 people had volunteered to attend deportation hearings in San Francisco, and 20 people were recruited to receive paralegal training to assist refugees in applying for asylum. Between Wednesday, March 24 and Sunday, March 28 all four goals were met. That Sunday processions were made from the five churches to St. John's Presbyterian Church where the five churches announced that the immediate goals had been reached and that the three men would be moving into housing provided by St. Mark's Episcopal Church.

From its inception in 1982, EBSC's decision-making body was a Steering Committee composed of one or two representatives from each sanctuary congregation. Some activities were organized by several congregations through the Steering Committee, while others were the projects of a particular congregation. Not every congregation directly assisted a particular Central American refugee or refugee family. Each congregation decided for itself how to carry out its sanctuary commitment.

Sanctuary was defined as providing "protection, support, and advocacy" on behalf of Salvadoran and Guatemalan refugees. Some congregations took an individual or family "into sanctuary" and worked to find them housing, services, and employment. Others raised money to secure the release of refugees who had been detained by the U.S. Immigration and Naturalization Service (I.N.S.), and helped them apply for political asylum. Others helped find housing, food, clothing, furniture, and jobs for Central Americans.

When sanctuary for Central American refugees was first declared in the East Bay, it was clear there was risk involved in assisting people who had not been legally admitted into the U.S. We believed U.S. immigration practices to be immoral and unbiblical, and declared our intention to assist Central American refugees as an act of faith. Immigration lawyers also pointed out that the U.S. had recently passed the Refugee Act of 1980 which adopted as law the standards of the United Nations 1951 Convention Relating to the Status of Refugees and the 1967 Protocol Relating to the Status of Refugees. All three define a "refugee" as anyone with a well-founded fear of being persecuted for reasons of race, religion, nationality, political opinion or membership in a particular social group, if that person is outside his or her own country. The U.S. law and the international agreements state that people who meet this definition of "refugee" should not be forced to return to their country of origin. Since Salvadorans and Guatemalans who fled violence and persecution in their countries clearly met this definition of "refugee", the sanctuary congregations stated that this stand was both moral and legal. We recognized that the U.S. government did not share this view, and each new congregation considering declaring sanctuary was encouraged to meet with a lawyer and become familiar with the possible legal ramifications of publicly declaring sanctuary. Elsewhere in the U.S., the legal questions of sanctuary have been viewed differently. Some areas have emphasized sanctuary as a form of resistance to U.S. laws and policies. Others focused on sanctuary work being a form of "civil initiative" in which citizens establish legal precedents by openly carrying out laws which the government is violating. Here in the East Bay, sanctuary congregations have viewed our work as lawful and the government's deportation of Salvadoran and Guatemalan refugees as being in violation of U.S. law.

REFUGEES GIVE DIRECTION

Soon after sanctuary first began in the East Bay, refugees in the Bay Area told us that as difficult as the situation was for them to live without legal status in the U.S., the situation for Salvadorans and Guatemalans still in Central America was much worse. They asked us to try to assist them. Thus our Visitor Program was established. In May of 1982, two months after the first declarations of sanctuary, we sent our first delegation to visit refugee camps in Honduras. For fourteen months, we had an ongoing presence in Honduras, serving as international visitors in the refugee camps. We later resumed this program several times in later years as well. Delegations of two to five people would go on two-week trips, spending their time in one or more of the refugee camps. Their role was to provide an international presence because when outsiders were present there was less chance that Honduran soldiers would enter the camps to harass, hurt, capture or kill refugees, or that they would allow Salvadoran or Guatemalan soldiers to enter the camps.

At the same time that our visitors were providing some form of safety for the refugees in the camps, they were becoming acquainted with the refugees and the effects of the war on their lives. Visitors were also observing the refugees' priorities in organizing their own communities in the refugee camps. Over 200 Bay Area visitors to the camps returned more deeply aware of the violence and poverty in Central America and impressed by the refugees' strong faith and determination to work together for peace. Our sanctuary work in the East Bay was strongly affected and strengthened by these early experiences in the refugee camps. This resulted in a dual focus in our sanctuary work. We sought to respond to refugees still living in Central America as well as Salvadoran and Guatemalan refugees in the United States.

In 1983, Central American refugees in the Bay Area decided to form their own organization to assist more effectively members of the refugee community and to educate the public about the situation in Central America. They formed the Central American Refugee Committee (CRECE), and began to organize the refugee community to meet its own needs. CRECE raised money to pay the bonds for Central Americans who had been detained by the I.N.S., provided housing for Central Americans, and distributed food and clothing to the refugee community. Since East Bay Sanctuary Covenant believed it preferable for Central Americans to be in charge of the delivery of services to their own community, we funneled resources such as donations of furniture, clothes, food, money, job referrals, and housing possibilities to CRECE.

CRECE also formed a speakers bureau with which we worked closely. When a new church or synagogue approached us about declaring sanctuary, a refugee speaker from CRECE accompanied a sanctuary representative to speak to the congregation. CRECE members gave public testimonies about their own experiences that caused them to flee Central America. These testimonies were often a congregation's first contact with Central Americans and the effect that violence had on an individual's life. We found our continued partnership with CRECE to be very instructional and we often looked to CRECE for guidance on how best to assist refugees.

A RANGE OF ACTIVITIES

In 1985, EBSC worked with officials in the city of Berkeley, leading the city to declare itself a city of refuge for Guatemalan and Salvadoran refugees. Then, in 1986, EBSC worked closely with other local organizations to convince Oakland's City Council to declare Oakland a city of refuge for Haitian, South African, Guatemalan, and Salvadoran refugees. Many other cities across the country were declaring themselves cities of refuge as well. All were instructing their city offices not to inform the I.N.S. of their clients' legal status.

EBSC often received news of people captured or threatened in El Salvador, Guatemala, or the refugee camps. In 1985, we began an "urgent action system" to respond to these human rights violations. Sanctuary workers made phone calls or sent telegrams to government officials in Central America, urging the release and humane treatment of refugees and church workers. Later, in 1988, we began a prepaid telex system which allows people to pay us in advance to send telexes in their names in response to alerts we received. We now respond to an average of three alerts every week.

In 1986, Salvadorans recently displaced from their homes but still inside El Salvador decided they did not want to accept the demoralizing life in resettlements they saw other displaced people enduring. Instead, they decided to insist on their right to return to their places of origin and live on their own land. They began what is now called the repopulation movement. They had been "depopulated" from their towns due to military activity. They were now "repopulating" those same areas. They asked for international supporters, especially from the religious community, to go with them as they moved back and rebuilt their destroyed villages.

Many people from the East Bay responded to their call and provided what became known as "accompaniment". The term was new but the concept was already familiar to people from EBSC as "accompaniment" was what our visitors were doing when they provided an international presence in the refugee camps in Honduras. In 1987, refugees in one of the refugee camps in Honduras also decided to return to El Salvador and their home villages. This was the first "repatriation"—similar to the repopulations except that these Salvadorans were returning from outside the country. EBSC worked to raise money and send delegates on several repatriations and repopulations, and to support the communities after they returned. Several EBSC congregations then formed "sister parish" relationships with particular repatriated communities.

In 1986, EBSC helped launch a new campaign to stop U.S. funding of the war in El Salvador. Many sanctuary activists participated in the campaign, and half of the congregations endorsed the campaign. However, EBSC as a whole decided not to endorse it at this time as there was uncertainty about whether all sanctuary congregations would view this lobbying effort as part of their sanctuary commitment. Later, in 1989, congregations were given informational materials and several months to discuss this issue. After requesting input from every congregation, EBSC's Steering Committee approved a "clarification of intent of the covenant of sanctuary" to include opposing war-related aid to both El Salvador and Guatemala.

GROWTH, CHALLENGES, TRANSITIONS AND CHANGE

East Bay congregations had been declaring sanctuary and joining EBSC since 1982. The indictments against sixteen sanctuary workers in other parts of the country in early 1985 only encouraged more congregations to consider offering public sanctuary to Central Americans. Several Jewish synagogues and organizations joined EBSC in 1985, bringing with them a deep understanding of what it means to be a people facing persecution. Today we have thirty sanctuary congregations of Protestant, Catholic, Jewish, Unitarian, Quaker, and Buddhist faiths.

Since 1982 EBSC has had an office and staff to help coordinate the activities the EBSC congregations decided to do together. Peggy Argueta was EBSC's only employee from 1982 until 1985. Much of her time was spent coordinating the biweekly delegations to Honduras. Graduate school students and seminary interns assisted the sanctuary congregations with overall coordination. Later, other staff were hired to coordinate assistance to refugees in detention, a health referral and advocacy program, and other direct services to refugees. In 1985, Marilyn Chilcote was hired as Director. Later, an office manager and a fundraiser were hired.

In 1988, EBSC found itself with shrinking income as funding of Central America issues was declining. This prompted us to go through a process of evaluation and reflection, looking at what our work had been and discussing whether to continue, and if so, in what form. It was a difficult time, but in retrospect it was very useful as our economic crisis forced us to think about the needs of Central American refugees and our commitment.

We decided to continue our dual focus on both responding to the needs of Central American refugees here in our midst, and supporting people still in Central America. We also agreed to continue to focus on combining services with advocacy for justice. Yet we had less income and so could not afford to maintain the staff of six we had then. We decided to drop our budget to a level of income that we could depend on from donations from individuals and our member congregations. This allowed us to have two staff positions: a coordinator of our refugee rights program, Sr. Maureen Duignan, to assist refugees in detention and those with asylum hearings pending, and a general coordinator, Irene Litherland, to facilitate our other programs.

NEW PROJECTS

Although staffing was decreased, several new projects were soon undertaken. In 1989, EBSC worked in coalition with local Afro-American and Asian American organizations and public leaders to stop a private company from building an I.N.S. detention center in Oakland. This was an exciting association and an important victory. We then assisted a coalition in Vallejo as they also defeated the location of the detention center there.

We had long been aware that we were placing more time and energy on activities regarding El Salvador than Guatemala. We had had more contact with Salvadoran refugees in Honduras than with Guatemalan refugees, more people had been to El Salvador, and there wasn't an organization of Guatemalans in the Bay Area educating us and proposing projects to us. In 1989, we started a Guatemala Committee to make a concerted effort to learn more and do more about the situation in Guatemala. At the same time, a Guatemalan organization had formed in San Francisco, the Guatemalan Unity Committee. Our committee began to coordinate our activities with the Guatemalans' organization. Our committee focused on educating sanctuary workers about the complexities of Guatemala and U.S. involvement there, supporting the development of the Guatemalans' organization, marketing crafts from Guatemala, and raising funds for a women's project in rural Guatemala.

In 1990, another refugee organization was founded: the East Bay Central American Refugee Committee (CRECE). We welcomed this new CRECE organization to the East Bay. The CRECE group that began in 1983 had moved to San Francisco and, although we still worked closely with them, we were glad to have a Central American organization providing services on our side of the bay. East Bay CRECE was soon distributing food boxes each week to fifty and later eighty families. They also try to help these families find services and employment. CRECE sponsors English classes and a mental health clinic. Their members have recently arrived from Central America and speak about the situation they were forced to flee.

In November 1989, the Salvadoran opposition launched a major offensive which resulted in government bombing and massive repression of the general population in El Salvador. On November 16, six Jesuits, their housekeeper and her daughter were brutally killed. Many church leaders and workers were captured by the Salvadoran military. It was a frightening time for sanctuary workers who had met people in El Salvador, not to mention for Salvadorans here who had family there. We held a round-the-clock vigil for three days and then held weekly vigils for several months. We also redoubled our efforts to end war-related funds sent by the U.S. government to El Salvador.

VICTORIES AND MORE WORK AHEAD

In 1990, we had several important legislative victories. U.S. aid to El Salvador was withheld for the first time ever. President Bush quietly approved the release of the aid early the following year on the same day the war in the Persian Gulf began. But the first step toward cutting U.S. funding of the war in El Salvador had been made. Current bills assume the language and conditions of the 1990 bill as a starting point.

Also in 1990, a landmark settlement was reached in a lawsuit filed in 1985 by 40 religious and refugee organizations, including many sanctuary congregations. The U.S. government recognized its past failure to grant asylum fairly and agreed to reconsider all cases of Guatemalans and Salvadorans denied asylum since 1980. Also in 1990, the U.S. Congress passed a bill that gave Salvadorans 18 months of "temporary protected status" from deportation. Both outcomes were tremendous victories for the sanctuary movement. However, Guatemalan refugees still do not have "temporary protected status". Neither do these gains benefit the numerous Salvadoran and Guatemalan refugees currently arriving in the United States. As war and human rights abuses continue in both Guatemala and El Salvador, our work to assist Central American refugees remains essential.

Most of the activities begun in EBSC's history continue today. We are still working to provide services to refugees in the Bay Area, through our own programs and referrals and by supporting East Bay CRECE as they develop programs. We also continue to educate ourselves about El Salvador and Guatemala, learning and working with the Guatemalan Unity Committee and both CRECE organizations. Our work to respond to the war and violence in Guatemala is increasing at the same time that we continue to watch and respond to the situation in El Salvador. This work includes advocating for a change in U.S. policy and responding to alerts from both Guatemala and El Salvador. Most of all, EBSC continues to search for the most appropriate and effective ways to carry out the covenant of sanctuary signed by our thirty member congregations.

Irene Litherland
September 5, 1991

B.   "Jewish Covenant of Sanctuary"

For the past several years the United States has become a place of uncertain refuge for men, women and children who are fleeing for their lives from the vicious and devastating wars in Central America. Many of these refugees have chosen to leave their country only after witnessing the murder of close friends and relatives.

The United Nations has declared these people legitimate refugees of war; by every moral and legal standard, they ought to be received as such by the government of the United States. The 1951 United Nations Convention and the 1967 Protocol Agreements on refugees—both signed by the U.S.—established the rights of refugees *not* to be sent back to their countries of origin. Thus far, however, our government has been unwilling to meet its obligations under these agreements. The refugees among us are consequently threatened with the prospect of deportation back to El Salvador and Guatemala, where they face the likelihood of severe reprisals, perhaps including death.

The plight of these refugees powerfully reminds us of our own history. Hundreds of thousands of Jews who could have been saved from Hitler's ovens did not meet the U.S. immigration requirements, nor those of virtually any other land. With all sanctuary denied them, our people were forced to wander as illegal aliens. Their return to Hitler's Europe almost always meant their death. Against this denial of safety there were a few courageous voices— the righteous gentiles—who followed their consciences and provided safe haven.

Our historical experience of the Diaspora has given us a profound appreciation for the exiled and the homeless among all people: black slaves who fled north to freedom, all the immigrants who fled desperate oppression. In their name we now seek to answer the call from our own tradition.

"When a stranger sojourns with you in your land, you shall do him no wrong. The stranger who sojourns with you shall be as the native among you, and you shall love him as yourself; for you were strangers in the land of Egypt." LEVITICUS 19:33–34

"Give council, grant justice; make your shade like night at the height of noon; hide the outcasts, betray not the fugitive. Let the outcasts of Moab sojourn among you; be a refuge to them from the destroyer." ISAIAH 16:3–4

The words of the Torah, the demands of the prophets, the ethics of the Talmud and the centuries of Jewish response are clear. Therefore we join in

---

East Bay Sanctuary Covenant, "Jewish Covenant of Sanctuary." Reprinted by permission.

covenant to provide sanctuary—support, protection, and advocacy—to Central American refugees who request safe haven out of fear of persecution upon return to their homeland. We do this out of concern for the welfare of these refugees, regardless of their official immigrant status. We understand that sanctuary is a serious responsibility for all persons involved. Although we recognize that legal consequences may result from our action, we do not acknowledge that the provision of sanctuary is an illegal act. We enter this covenant as an act of conscience and moral imperative.

DOCUMENT 48

Brian Willson,
"The Tracks"

After his transforming experience as a soldier in Vietnam (Document 36B), Brian Willson attempted to resume professional life as a lawyer and penologist. From 1974 to 1978 he coordinated a campaign for a National Moratorium on Prison Construction. He began to read Gandhi, King, Tolstoy, Thoreau, and A. J. Muste. From 1978 to 1980 he and his wife operated a dairy in New York State.

At this time Willson began to conceive what he later came to call the American Way of Life, or AWOL.

This country consumes more than 40% of the world's production of natural resources with about 6% of the population, a disparity that is both practically and morally indefensible. The result of massive production is massive filth far beyond the absorbing capacities of our environment. Water in the U.S. is being polluted on an unprecedented scale. Modern technology such as that present in western New York is already pressuring nature with thousands of synthetic substances, hundreds of new ones being added each year, many of which resist decay—thus poisoning people, animals, plants, and minute but necessary organisms.

"The Tracks" from S. Brian Willson, *On Third World Legs* (Chicago: Charles H. Kerr, 1992), pp. 67–82. Reprinted by permission.

What was needed, Willson concluded, was small, simple, labor-intensive, safe, "non-violent industries," which did not produce hazardous or toxic substances, either for sale or as by-products (S. Brian Willson, On Third World Legs [Chicago: Charles H. Kerr Publishing Co., 1992], p. 26).

In 1983, Willson helped to organize the Veterans Education Project in western Massachusetts. Distressed by the recruiting of Green Berets in local high schools, he and other veterans successfully sought access to high schools and colleges to tell their side of the story.

> *I estimate that in the course of this work I spoke to nearly 7,000 students in over sixty classes. I talked about war, about its insanity. I offered the principle that we always have choices. I told them about the ideas of cooperation in Kropotkin's* Mutual Aid. *I quoted Eugene Debs' words: "I would no more teach children military training than teach them arson, robbery or assassination" (Willson,* On Third World Legs, *p. 28).*

In January 1986, Willson resigned from his job with a Veterans Outreach Center in order to visit Nicaragua, where he attended a Spanish language school in Esteli.

> *After I had been in Esteli about ten days, the contras began to attack about four kilometers to the west of the city. For three nights in a row I could hear the machine gun fire and see the tracers.*

Willson felt he was experiencing another Vietnam.

> *At least eleven campesinos were murdered that week. Some of the bodies were brought into Esteli for burial on horse-drawn wagons. Standing alongside the street watching the procession to the cemetery I could see the open caskets containing mothers and children. Five women! I had been here before. Two children! I had been here before. I found myself moaning, quivering inside, with tears rolling down my cheeks (Willson,* On Third World Legs, *pp. 55–56).*

After returning to the United States, Willson and three other Vietnam veterans conducted a fast on the steps of Congress. The Veterans' Fast for Life began September 1, 1986, and ended October 17, 1986. Thereafter Willson returned to the war zones of Nicaragua as part of a group he helped to organize called Veterans Peace Action Teams. Early in 1987 a team of nine veterans and two non-veterans walked 73 miles from Jinotega to Wiwili on one of the most dangerous roads in Nicaragua. It was a road where a land mine explosion in October 1986 had killed eleven persons and left twelve legless.

Willson went to hospitals and homes all over the country and spoke to more than four hundred persons who had lost limbs to United States land mines. "As I left one hospital where I had seen over two hundred amputees

I cried out, 'Jesus Christ, their legs are worth just as much as my legs! My legs aren't worth any more than their legs!' " (Willson, On Third World Legs, p. 64).

Document 48 tells what happened to his legs several months later.

NUREMBURG ACTIONS

A relative of mine had been a young military officer who served with the United States prosecution team at Nuremburg. The chief United States prosecutor there, Justice Robert H. Jackson, grew up in the Jamestown, New York area, a few miles from Ashville. Upon signing the London Agreement of 1945 creating the International Military Tribunal, Jackson stated: "For the first time, four of the most powerful nations have agreed not only upon the principle of liability for war crimes of persecution, but also upon the principle of individual responsibility for the crime of attacking international peace."

When I returned from Nicaragua in the late spring of 1987, a number of friends and I decided to try to interdict the flow of arms from the United States to Central America. Charlie Liteky and I put out a leaflet in which we called for "thousands of people to participate in sustained strategic actions in the United States to block the flow of arms to Nicaragua." Later a group of us organized Nuremburg Actions at the Concord Naval Weapons Station in California.

The Concord Naval Weapons Station (CNWS), at Port Chicago about thirty five miles northeast of San Francisco, is the largest munitions depot on the West Coast. Its bunkers store a variety of bombs and munitions, including nuclear weapons. Many of these means of war are transported by train and truck from storage areas to the pier, for shipment by boat to their destinations. The train, consisting of a locomotive pulling box cars, has to pass through an area open to public use on its way from one piece of government property to the other.

During the Vietnam War, anti-war activists blocked both trains and trucks in the Bay Area. Members of the Berkeley Vietnam Day Committee sat down on the tracks in front of trains carrying soldiers bound for Vietnam. There were four such blockades in August 1965 alone. In May 1966, four women in San Jose blocked trucks loaded with napalm bombs for seven hours outside a trucking company. When they returned to the same location the next day, a truck driver told them that the company had decided to stop bringing napalm through that point. The women then moved on to an enormous bomb storage facility in nearby Alviso. There they had some success in delaying the loading of bombs onto barges for transit to Port Chicago. Marches, lengthy vigils, and frequent blocking of trains and trucks also occurred throughout the Vietnam War at CNWS itself.

We decided to revive the historic Bay Area focus on the Concord Naval Weapons Station. We had a copy of a contract with the government of El Salvador (procured through the Freedom of Information Act) disclosing that a number of bombs, white phosphorus rockets, and other munitions had been shipped to El Salvador from CNWS in June 1985. I had learned of substantial bombings of villages in El Salvador during my trips to Nicaragua and El Salvador. An item in the July 1987 *Harper's* indicated that 230 Salvadoran villages had been bombed or strafed by the Salvadoran Air Force in 1986. This behavior is a grotesque violation of international law. Furthermore, I had spent time with Eugene Hasenfus, both on a visit to the crash site and while he was imprisoned in Nicaragua in November 1986, and learned of the air drop routes used to transport United States military supplies from bases in El Salvador to the contras in Nicaragua. (Hasenfus, a Wisconsin native and ex-Marine in Vietnam, had previously participated in secret missions over Southeast Asia for the CIA-owned airline, Air America. He was caught red-handed in October 1986 dropping supplies from the United States to contra terrorists in the interior of Nicaragua when the secret plane he was on was shot down by the Nicaraguan Army. He parachuted to safety before being captured.) We had plenty of reason to ask that CNWS refrain from any further illegal shipment of munitions to kill civilians in Central America.

On June 2, 1987, Chris Ballin and I wrote to the CNWS. "We are planning a nonviolent action beginning June 10th. We are writing you because we wish to maintain open contact with all law enforcement agencies and military personnel. . . . We welcome the opportunity to discuss in person why we feel so strongly about this matter and the plans for the on-going resistance."

CNWS personnel cabled to their superiors in Washington as follows:

> Brian Willson, coordinator of a pacifist organization known as quote veterans fast for life and veterans peace action teams unquote informed public affairs officer this command that on 10 June his organization will begin a perpetual attempt to block weapons station concord explosive rail and truck movement between the station's inland and tidal areas by permanently stationing personnel on rail track and in roadway. He further stated that when one person is arrested, another will take his or her place for as long as they have people remaining, with those arrested returning to the scene after release from custody to repeat action. Willson is same person who fasted in Washington, DC, earlier this year protesting U.S. Central American policy with resulting high visibility national media attention. Members of group have been seeking to buy or rent residence in area to house marathon protesters. Willson says they hope to keep effort going for at least several months. Since track and roadway involved easily accessible to public and under juris-diction of civil authorities, this situation could require permanent police presence and has serious safety and security implications.

The sustained vigil began on June 10. I was not emotionally or spiritually prepared at first to bodily block vehicles, risking likely arrest. The very first day we watched a locomotive hauling two dozen or so box cars loaded with lethal weapons move slowly by our solemn vigil at the train speed limit of five miles per hour. All of a sudden I burst into tears. In my mind I saw each box car stacked ceiling-high with bodies of Nicaraguans and Salvadorans. It was as if I were a German standing alongside a Nazi train loaded with Jews on their way to the death camps.

Truck blocking went on throughout June with regular arrests and erratic jailings by the police. I was a support person from the sidelines. Train blocking was part of the plans of Nuremburg Actions but had not happened by early July. A local insurance salesman, who had been present on several occasions to support the vigil but who had not taken the prescribed nonviolence training, stepped out on the tracks on his own, without giving notice, when few vigilers were present as a munitions train slowly moved toward him. The locomotive came to within several feet of this man and stopped. The spotters standing on front of the locomotive grabbed the sign from his arms and removed his body from the tracks.

Our presence continued throughout the summer, always at the same location on the Port Chicago side of the public highway at the place where the munitions trains cross the highway. There were nearly always more than one, and sometimes a couple of dozen, persons present during daylight hours from June 10 to September 1.

Sometime in early or mid July I made plans to escalate my own participation in Nuremburg Actions beginning September 1, 1987. On that day, the first anniversary of the beginning of the Veterans' Fast For Life, I and others would start a forty day water-only fast and begin blocking munitions trains. We would attempt to block movement of the trains for every day during that period. We would fast on the tracks adjacent to the location where we had regularly vigiled since June 10.

Others were invited to join and several persons agreed to participate. Duncan Murphy, a participant in the 1986 fast, also agreed to be part of the forty day fast on the tracks.

We had examined the history of people blocking trains and had concluded that the train would certainly stop. The base would be notified in advance of our action. I still have some of the photographs we collected: for example, *Life* magazine pictures in the October 8, 1956 and May 19, 1972 issues showing locomotives stopping for protesters.

A doctor was planning to monitor my condition throughout the fast. I expected to spend some or most of the forty days in jail and had briefed the doctor on my need for potassium supplements during the fast to protect nutrition of the heart, and asked that he talk to jailers about the importance of my receiving these supplements.

On August 21, 1987, I sent a letter to CNWS Commander Lonnie Cagle explaining in detail the nature and philosophy of the September 1 plans. The letter asked for a personal meeting at least four times.

> This letter . . . requests a personal meeting with you. . . . I want you to know in advance of this plan. . . . Because of the seriousness of these matters I ask that we have a personal meeting to discuss them. This action is not intended to harass you or any military or civilian person-nel. . . . I would like to discuss with you your views and response to our concerns. . . . I hope that you will respond so that we can set up a mutually convenient time to meet.

Copies of the letter were sent to the Contra Costa County Sheriff, the Concord Police Department, the California Highway Patrol, and a number of elected officials, including U.S. Senators Cranston and Wilson of Califor-nia, U.S. Representatives Boxer, Miller, and Edwards of California, and U.S. Senators Kerry, Kennedy, Leahy, and Jeffords of Massachusetts and Vermont, where I had lived most of my life since 1980. I had received no replies as of September 1.

On August 23, Holley Rauen and I were married. We committed ourselves "to be prepared for the risks and prices required, individually and collectively, to live and promote a radical transformation in our North American society."

Another cable from CNWS to Washington was sent on August 31. It revealed no confusion about our intentions and showed that the Navy was quite clear about our expressed plans.

> Received letter from group identified as veterans fast for life and veter-ans peace action teams advising that protesters plan to fast for 40 days on railroad track used to transport material between station inland and tidal areas. Letter and news article quoting protest principal, Mr. S. Brian Willson, States fast to begin 1 Sept and that fasters will not move for approaching rail traffic. Local sheriff and police officers aware of threat. Should potential interruption of rail service occur, they will be requested to remove protestor(s). Commanding officer's assessment: interruption of normal station operations not anticipated. . . .

SEPTEMBER 1, 1987

The morning of September 1 arrived. We planned a worship service on the tracks after a press conference announcing the formal launching of the fast and the train blockade. Having never been arrested or jailed before, I was a bit anxious. I was most concerned about the prospect that as the fast progressed and I grew weaker, I might be hurt in the arresting process by officers repeatedly removing me from the tracks. Fasting on the Capitol steps appeared easy in comparison to fasting on train tracks at the same time I was attempting to block munitions trains, and subjecting myself to continual arrests.

Besides Duncan Murphy and myself, David Duncombe, a World War II and Korean veteran and a chaplain at the University of California Medical School in San Francisco, would be fasting for forty days on the tracks. Others might join us for different periods.

My wife Holley and stepson Gabriel accompanied me as I drove to CNWS, along with fellow faster Duncan Murphy and another friend. Two photographer friends and a friend with a video camera were present to record the press conference, worship service, blocking action, and anticipated arrests.

There were only a few media representatives present for the press conference. We conducted a worship and meditation service with the thirty or forty fasters and supporters. I said the following:

My hope is that today will begin a new era of sustained resistance like the salt march in India and like the civil rights movement in the 1950s and 1960s where people, every day, realize that we, the people, are the ones that are going to make peace. Peacemaking is full-time. Warmaking is full-time. And so my hope is that we will establish or create a kind of action here that revives the imagery of the sustained resistance of the past such as in the salt march and the civil rights movement where people are committed every day to say, "As long as the trains move munitions on these tracks we will be here to stop the trains." Because each train that goes by here with munitions, that gets by us, is going to kill people, people like you and me.

And the question that I have to ask on these tracks is: Am I any more valuable than those people? And if I say No then I have to say, You can't move these munitions without moving my body or destroying my body. So today, from the spirit of a year ago on the steps and then for five months in Central America and coming back, the Nuremburg Actions and today, I begin this fast for atonement for all the blood that we have on our hands and that I have on my hands.

And I begin this fast to envision a kind of resistance, an empowering kind of spirit, that we hope to participate in with many people, saying, These munitions will not be exploded in our names and they will not be moved any longer in our names and we must put our bodies in front of them to say, stronger than ever, that this will not continue in our name. The killing must stop and I have to do everything in my power to stop it.

And I hope that when people ask us what they can do to support us: what they can do is they can come to the tracks and stand with us on the tracks to stop the trains. That's all we want. We want more people to join hands and say, This will not continue. And only we the people can stop it. Thank you.

At about 11:40 a.m. the three of us took our positions on the tracks. Two others held a large banner across the tracks just behind us that stated in bold letters: "NUREMBURG ACTIONS: Complicity in the Commission of a Crime Against Peace, a War Crime, or a Crime Against Humanity, Is a Crime Under International Law."

I experience what the doctors call regional amnesia. Though I'm told that I was conscious the entire time prior to and after being struck by the train, except for the time in the hospital under anesthesia during surgery, I have no memory over a several-day period. So I will finish my account of what happened on September 1 with this transcript of a cassette recording made by a friend.

VOICE: Okay. Here comes the train.

MALE VOICE: We're not leaving the tracks, right?

MALE VOICE: We're not leaving.

MALE VOICE: It's planning, preparation, initiation, waging a war of aggression or a war in violation of international [INAUDIBLE DUE TO TRAIN WHISTLE].

[TRAIN WHISTLE IS HEARD FOR NINETEEN SECONDS BEFORE IMPACT]

[TRAIN WHISTLE CEASES]

MALE VOICE: No.

FEMALE VOICE: Oh, my God! Oh, my God! Oh, my God! Stop the train! Stop the—Oh, my God!

MALE VOICE: Help.

FEMALE VOICE: Come help me!

FEMALE VOICE: Ambulance is here.

MALE VOICE: Look what you did, you're the murderers.

GABRIEL: You murderers! You killed my father! You killed my father!

MALE VOICE: Where's the fucking ambulance?

MALE VOICE: Get an ambulance.

FEMALE VOICE: My God!

[SIRENS]

[MULTIPLE VOICES—INDISCERNIBLE]

GABRIEL: You killed my father! Killed my father! You did that, by God!

MALE VOICE: Stay right there.

MALE VOICE: We love you, Brian.

HOLLEY: I'm holding the bleeding.

MALE VOICE: You want me to hold that [INDISCERNIBLE].

HOLLEY: Yes. You have to press very hard so that no more blood comes out.

MALE VOICE: Relax. Real, real hard.

HOLLEY: Right here.

[MULTIPLE VOICES—INDISCERNIBLE]

MAN OPERATING TAPE RECORDER: The train—there's total confusion. There's a fire truck that came. There's still no ambulance. It's been five minutes since the train came barrelling down the tracks, blowing its horn. The three men who were on the tracks had panic in their eyes and two of them jumped aside. One of them who was kneeling fell back under the train, had his foot rolled over and cut off. Was dragged and bumped and dragged again. His head split open. His other foot cut off. And finally bumped into the inside of the track where the train then pulled on and stopped 400, 500 feet down the road.

The—I never saw the eyes of the guys in the caboose. There were two guys on the cowcatcher, sort of screaming and yahooing and "Here we come." The Marine guards who are around with their M-16s look panic-stricken. Now there are several veterans who are enraged and yelling and screaming at the soldiers who are starting to surround the crowd and keep people off the tracks. There is still no ambulance. There's been a County Sheriff and a fire truck and a military vehicle of some kind with an official person with a radio coming around calling for things.

Holley, Brian's wife, is holding his leg trying to keep it from bleeding. His skull is open, you can see his brain inside. It's probably a four or five inch gaping hole in his skull. He's stunned. Stunned—fuck! Grief, all around.

The man from the fire department is attempting to suture and bandage what he can but he—the military keeps telling people to step across the fucking yellow line. I can't believe it.

Why don't you guys do something constructive? Jesus Christ!

MALE VOICE: The train was going full bore.

FEMALE VOICE: We heard the screaming. I [INAUDIBLE].

MALE VOICE: Didn't touch the throttle. Didn't even touch the throttle.

MALE VOICE: Fucking unbelievable.

MAN OPERATING TAPE RECORDER: They've attached something to his nostril. I just picked up a huge chunk of bone. Duncan Murphy is leaning over Brian, trying to hold on to life. Brian's eyes are closed. I'm not sure at this point.

Gabriel, Brian's stepson, is still distraught and screaming. As you look around, some of the responses are changing from shock and grief to anger.

Here comes the ambulance. Five, six, seven minutes later.

This was not a surprise. This had been a well-publicized protest. Brian had sent letters to some fifteen or twenty people, the base commander amongst others, last week. Everyone knew full well that this was going to be a day where the train was going to be stopped and the train did not stop.

Looks like military nursing personnel have arrived. He's still blinking, still holding on. Brian is such a strong character.

FEMALE VOICE: Let's get a small no-pressure dressing—bandage, a Kurlex.

MALE VOICE: I've got [INAUDIBLE]. I've got everything under control.

MALE VOICE: Okay.

MALE VOICE: John, is that the only way you can stop it, is with that?

MALE VOICE:—have a tourniquet.

MALE VOICE: Hold on, man.

VOICE: Let's make a hole.

MALE VOICE: Need anything, buddy?

MALE VOICE: No. Looking good. Looking good.

FEMALE VOICE: How you doing, guy?

MALE VOICE: Pretty good.

FEMALE VOICE: I'm Petty Officer McGee. I'm a Navy Corpsman, okay? Let us help you.

MALE VOICE: I couldn't tell you, myself.

FEMALE VOICE: Don't hold pressure. Just hold it there.

FEMALE VOICE: 110 over 80 bp, Bob.

HOLLEY: You're doing good. Your blood pressure is good, honey. You're hanging in there.

FEMALE VOICE: You're doing great, guy. You're doing great.

FEMALE VOICE: How're you doing? You doing all right?

FEMALE VOICE: Yeah.

MALE VOICE: Okay. Keep your hands [INAUDIBLE].

HOLLEY: I love you, Brian.

MALE VOICE: We all love you, Brian.

FEMALE VOICE: Brian. Brian.

MALE VOICE: How many victims do you have?

MALE VOICE: What?

MALE VOICE: How many victims do you have?

FEMALE VOICE: Two that I—there's one minor victim down there.

MALE VOICE: Where's the other one?

FEMALE VOICE: Everybody's making a circle around you for healing, Brian.

HOLLEY: Honey, you've gotta be brave, okay?

GABRIEL: Why didn't you dodge it? I wanted you to dodge. Why didn't you dodge it? Dodge it. You should have dodge—My God, that's a piece of him! That's a piece of him!

HOLLEY: Tell him you love him, Gabe. Just tell him you love him.

GABRIEL: My God, that's a piece of Dad.

MALE VOICE: It's all right.

HOLLEY: Just tell him you love him.

GABRIEL: That's a piece of my Dad!

HOLLEY: Tell him you love him. Bring him up here.

MALE VOICE: It's all right.

FEMALE VOICE: Dan, tell him you love him.

HOLLEY: Hey, Gabe, listen, I'm going to go to the hospital with Brian and—

VOICE: I want to go with you.

FEMALE VOICE: I'll take you there.

HOLLEY: Okay, they'll take you and you meet us at the hospital, okay?

FEMALE VOICE: I'll take you there, Gabe. I promise you.

FEMALE VOICE: Okay? Okay? Okay?

VOICE: God.

HOLLEY: He's going to be okay, honey.

GABRIEL: No, it's not going to be all right, that's my Dad.

HOLLEY: Yeah, we know. You know? I know, honey, I saw the whole thing.

FEMALE VOICE: Right now we need to get out of the way so they can [INAUDIBLE].

GABRIEL: God, you have blood all over you!

HOLLEY: I was stopping the bleeding on his legs, honey.

MAN OPERATING TAPE RECORDER: They brought a stretcher now. They're placing Brian's torso, that's what it is. His legs are gone below the knees. His head is wide open. He's still hanging on. His blood pressure is pretty good. People have formed a semi-circle around him, holding hands, trying to help pump life.

It's still a pretty confusing situation. Duncan Murphy is still hanging on as is Holley. And the Corps is working to strap him to a piece of plywood now to lift him up into the ambulance.

Now there are police vehicles everywhere. Highway Patrol, Concord Police, County Sheriff; as well as all the military police. Lots of little radios calling someone somewhere.

The train is still stopped, ironically, down the track some 500 feet, meters, I don't know: some distance down the road with this little triangle of explosive or dangerous cargo highlighting the back of it.

The engineer is still standing on the cab looking back. The two guys on the cowcatcher, I don't know where they are. They are behind the fence and the sentries so we can't approach them. It's on military property and they're making it very clear that we don't cross the yellow line.

The young Marine guards whose responsibility that is, initially came out here trying to look serious but sort of with a chuckle. This was another day, another job. And all of a sudden it's a different day.

People are yelling. Some of the veterans are angry and yelling at the—I don't know—at the air, at the fates, at the gods.

This whole thing had been orchestrated and planned and the train didn't stop. [*End of transcript*]

WHY DID THE UNITED STATES GOVERNMENT CONSIDER ME A TERRORIST?

When I became conscious, I saw Holley Rauen sitting next to my bed. I saw many green plants throughout the room. I thought this was a very unusual jail cell. It seemed more like a greenhouse. Holley explained to me that I was in John Muir Hospital, Walnut Creek, California. The train (on September 1 a locomotive hauling two box cars) had crashed into me and continued moving over my body until the last of the two box cars was inside the fenced base area guarded by United States Marines.

I asked what happened to Duncan Murphy and David Duncombe who were part of the blockade. I learned that David, who was crouching (not sitting like me), jumped out of the way just before the train would have hit him. Duncan, also crouching, made a mighty leap straight up—quite a feat for a sixty-seven-year-old veteran—and grabbed the cowcatcher railing, cutting his knee but otherwise escaping injury.

It took several days for this reality to sink in. I began to watch television news reports on the wall-mounted hospital TV, which continued to carry stories about the assault, including selected cuts from the amateur video footage provided the media by my friend Bob Spitzer. For several days I saw the speeding train with two human spotters standing on the platform above the cowcatcher barrelling down on the three of us on the tracks.

I began to comprehend the life-altering nature of my injuries. The most serious of my injuries were a severely fractured skull, missing a golf-ball-size piece from the right forehead area; a seriously cut and damaged right frontal brain lobe; a severed but sewn-back-on left ear; and two legs missing below my knees. That I was alive at all seemed the more remarkable when I learned that a United States Navy ambulance arrived on the bloody scene within the first few minutes after I was hurt but refused to provide medical assistance or transportation to a hospital, apparently because my body was not lying on government property.

People who were present told me that I was conscious throughout and talked with those attending to my very vulnerable body. Holley directed a series of emergency medical procedures with the aid of several horrified supporters, stopping the bleeding from my right leg stump, from my mangled and twisted left leg, from my almost severed ear, and from the hole in the right forehead portion of my skull. These procedures, in addition to the nourishing love of those present, kept my fragile being alive until the county ambulance arrived some twenty minutes later.

Why hadn't the train stopped, I asked? They knew we were there. Visibility was excellent. The speed limit was a slow five miles per hour.

Holley was as shocked as I was, as every one was. She said that as she was standing off to the side, carrying a political sign as part of the support demonstration of thirty to forty people, she saw the two human spotters standing on the front of the locomotive distinctly shaking their heads from side to side as if to say, "We are not stopping, no way!"

From the beginning a lot of people came up to me and said, "You know this couldn't have happened without it being designed and intended to happen that way." I'm not a very conspiratorial-thinking person, nor a particularly paranoid person. I'm kind of naive.

I started thinking differently after the Congressional hearing held on November 18, 1987. Navy officials admitted that they knew a lot about me. Navy Captain S. J. Pryzby told the Congressional committee that the Navy knew about me, about the fasts, the trips to Nicaragua, and my being at the tracks since June 10, and he seemed to be describing me as a man of my word. I sat there thinking, "They knew that I wouldn't get off the tracks."

Then I found the notes of the unsanitized Navy report that had not been made public lying on the table in the room next to the hearing room. I started reading them and thought, "My God, this is in the original report that they didn't release to the public." I put the notes in my briefcase.

Later I got a copy of the sheriff's report, which was not included in the Navy report. It contained interviews with the train engineer, who said he was under orders not to stop the train.

Finally, I learned that at the time of the assault I was being investigated by the government as a terrorist. I was in the ABC-TV studio in Washington, D.C. in November 1987. They showed me the FBI documents and said, "We want your face on camera looking at these documents." I hadn't known anything about them until then.

Let's restate what happened on September 1 according to what we now know. The protesters, including myself, began the blockade after elaborate prior notice at about 11:40 a.m. A few minutes later the munitions train came into view. Upon seeing three men blockading the tracks, the train stopped near the main gate to await further instructions. CNWS personnel notified the county sheriff. The sheriff told them it would take his forces thirty minutes to reach the scene.

Up to this point every one's actions were consistent with the expectation, which I confidently shared, that the locomotive would not move until the sheriff's men arrived and arrested us.

Just after 11:55 a.m. the train began to move forward again. The FBI concluded after examining Bob Spitzer's videotape that the train was speeding at about 17 miles per hour, over three times its legal speed limit of five miles per hour. It was a bright sunny day. There was clear visibility for at least 650 feet according to the Navy's report. Yet the locomotive not only did not stop, but seems to have accelerated after striking me, as evidenced in a photograph revealing a fresh burst of smoke issuing from its smoke stack at the time of impact and after, as I lay mangled under the train.

The train did not stop because the train crew had been instructed not to stop. Ed Hubbard, railroad supervisor at CNWS, says "he told the crew, if the protesters started climbing on the train, to continue until the train was inside the gates and the marines could take over." David Humiston, the engineer, and Ralph Dawson, one of the two spotters, said they received orders not to stop if the protesters started "boarding the locomotive or the cars it was pulling." The statements of the crew members are quoted in "Weapons train that maimed pacifist was under Navy orders not to stop," *National Catholic Reporter,* Jan. 29, 1988.

Now, of course, we who were on the tracks had no intention of boarding the train or climbing on the locomotive and box cars, and we never did anything of the kind. But it seems that the Navy expected us to do so. And because of this expectation, the crew was instructed not to stop until it reached base property, or perhaps, not to stop if we did anything causing them to think we might be about to board the train.

From what source did the Navy derive its apparent belief that those who sat down on the tracks on September 1 would also try to board the train? We had written to the CNWS commander, distributed leaflets throughout the area, and talked extensively with the media. In none of these many statements did we state or suggest that we might seek to do anything but sit quietly on the tracks. I believe the source for the Navy's mistaken anticipation may have been the FBI. On October 10, 1986, while the Veterans' Fast For Life was in progress, U.S. Senator Warren Rudman of New Hampshire released a letter stating in part: "In my opinion, their actions are hardly different than those of the terrorists who are holding our hostages in Beirut." See "Rudman Likens Fasting Veterans To Terrorists," *Boston Globe,* Oct. 11, 1986. In that same month the FBI directed its agents to begin an inquiry into the alleged terrorism of those conducting the Veterans' Fast For Life. FBI agent John C. Ryan told his superiors in a memorandum of December 4, 1986 that he refused to take part in the investigation of a group that had a "totally non-violent posture." He was fired after nearly twenty-two years of service. See "The cost of a fired FBI agent's journey to Catholic nonviolence," *National Catholic Reporter,* Nov. 27, 1987; "FBI Probe of Willson Reported," *San Francisco Chronicle,* Dec. 12, 1987.

These facts support the conclusion that the United States government expected "terrorists" like Brian Willson to try to seize the locomotive and its box cars, just as terrorists hijack airplanes; and therefore, at some level higher than the CNWS train crew and its supervisor, decided not to stop the train.

I continue to believe that the decision to move and accelerate the train on September 1, 1987, cannot be fully understood outside the context of the government's demonstrated interest in my activities before September 1. The precise relationship of this prior interest to the decision intentionally and recklessly to move the train has yet to be unravelled. At a minimum it created a milieu of lack of concern, contempt, and wanton disregard. At a maximum, it was attempted murder.

I have a lot of empathy for the train crew. First of all, they're all living the way I used to live; I believe they're brainwashed just as I was. Second, they probably do have traumatic stress (which is what they sued me for) because I think they were caught in a conflict between following their orders and following their consciences. They were on the lower end of a chain of command that's involved in a diabolical, criminal national policy. They're the grunt men, just as we were in Vietnam.

The solution to their stress is to endure a transformational process within themselves, not to sue me. But if they were going to sue, they should have sued the Navy, which gave the order and possesses money.

I condemn their action. I just plead with them to be open to transformation, which is the only way to heal their stress, and to tell the truth about who gave the order and as to their state of mind.

POSTSCRIPT. As of the date of this writing (June 1, 1992), Nuremburg Actions has steadfastly resisted movement of munitions trucks and trains at CNWS for 1,817 consecutive days, temporarily blocking well over a thousand such trucks and trains, weathering cold, rain, 1,700 arrests, a number of jail terms, and hostile and violent responses from local residents. Rev. David Duncombe, himself having narrowly escaped injury or death on September 1, 1987, has continued his participation in Nuremburg Actions, being present *every* Thursday since that date when not in jail. He has been arrested numerous times for blocking the movement of munitions trucks and trains, while continuing to maintain his position as Chaplain and Professor at the University of California at San Francisco Medical School. He has been convicted twice in jury trials, serving a number of weeks in jail on each sentence. In both trials the judge excluded from jury consideration the violations of international (and therefore United States Constitutional) law by the United States government, and its agent, the United States Navy, in committing war crimes, crimes against peace, and crimes against humanity in the murdering and maiming of innocent civilians in Latin America.

DOCUMENT 49

Sharon Hostetler, Witness for Peace

In April 1983, thirty members of the Carolina Interfaith Task Force on Central America stood 200 yards from Honduras in El Porvenir, a tobacco farm in northern Nicaragua that was under attack by the contras. "They have stopped shooting because they can see you," a young militia man told the group.

In October 1983, on a stairway landing of a dilapidated office building in Durham, North Carolina, Betsy Crites set up a make-shift office out of which she expected to organize a few groups to go to Nicaragua. Ten years

Sharon Hostetler, "Old Commitments, New Directions," *Witness for Peace Newsletter,* vol. 10, no. 2 (Summer 1993), pp. 4–5. Reprinted by permission.

later, Witness for Peace (WFP) had organized 253 delegations that took more than 4,500 delegates to see the war in Nicaragua for themselves.

Witness for Peace maintained the longest nonviolent presence in an active war zone in United States history. In April 1986 a picture of WFP witnesses holding crosses and markers of sorrow and hope with names of Nicaraguans killed by the contras appeared on the front page of every major newspaper in the United States.[1]

In the following document, the coordinator of WFP work in Nicaragua reflects on what it meant and where it is going.

"Witness for Peace has a future here ... Your action has been very much related to the poor of the world, to the oppressed people, to the small, the smallest of the Third World nations. You have to remain. Trust the inspiration which gave form to Witness for Peace to find the new directions."

Father Cesar Jeréz,
former rector of the Central American University

Our commitments are deep; they are rooted in our hearts where we ponder the pain and injustices we see reflected in the eyes of a people who have suffered for centuries the results of U.S. policies which have waged war on the poor. Thousands of us have come to Nicaragua since the beginning of Witness for Peace in 1983. We came to bear witness and to respond by going into a war zone to say "no" to an immoral policy.

We heard a grandmother from Teotecacinte tell how her four year old granddaughter, Suyapa, was killed by a mortar when she ran from the bomb shelter to rescue her pet chicken. We stood in silence at the cross which marks the place where Suyapa took her last step. In Jinotega we saw the remains of a civilian transport truck blasted into a ravine after it passed over a land mine. Thirty-five people were killed—14 women, nine men and 12 children, including three infants. Petrona Torres wept as she told us that her 22-year-old daughter, Maria, was running for shelter with her young niece when they were both gunned down. The WFP Long Term Team and Short-Term Delegates documented almost 500 civilians killed by contras supported by our government.

We accompanied mourners at all-night wakes, and we still can remember the smells—the stench of death mixed with the odor of wilted flowers that covered the coffins and the smell of fresh dirt at the cemeteries. The cries of "Presente!" ring in our ears as we remember the sound of dirt hitting the

---

1. For the facts in the first three paragraphs of this headnote, see *Witness for Peace Newsletter,* vol. 10, no. 2 (Summer 1993), pp. 3, 10–11.

crude wooden boxes of all sizes holding the victims of the U.S. government-sponsored aggression. Our arms still feel the weight of the crosses and markers we carried along the road to San Juan de Limay. We planted them at the sites where innocent road workers and others were murdered with weapons bought with our tax dollars. Our mouths still open and close as we try to utter words of comfort.

Our commitments found expression in non-violent actions directed at stopping the war and changing our government's foreign policy toward Nicaragua. We accompanied people in cooperatives and communities when they predicted imminent attacks. We travelled roads that often held the threat of ambushes and land mines. We accompanied priests and nuns who knew that to continue their mission could mean death. We drove an ambulance in an area where it was not safe for a Nicaraguan to drive. We chartered a small fishing boat and headed out to the Pacific Ocean to confront a U.S. warship, protesting that Nicaragua was not a threat to the security of the United States. We set out on a mission of peace on the beautiful San Juan River knowing that contra soldiers had orders to fire on any boat that passed beyond a certain point. We vowed that we were willing to risk our lives for peace as many had risked their lives for war.

Our deep commitments were not a guarantee of success. We were not able to stop the suffering, death and destruction that the U.S. policy of low-intensity warfare imposed on the Nicaraguan people. The U.S. Congress continued funding the contras until the Arias Central American Peace Plan was signed by the five Central American presidents. We were not successful in stopping the economic embargo or the blocking of loans from international lending agencies. Those policies changed only after the U.S. massively intervened in the 1990 elections and ensured the election of "our" candidate.

After the elections, one of our partners declared, "Witness for Peace needs to reflect on the true meaning of peace. The military war is over, but there is still violence—unemployment, poverty, and instability. Is this peace? Witness for Peace needs to reflect on the actual U.S. policy toward this poor country and educate the people in the U.S. about its effects on the people of Nicaragua."

Our commitments call us to engage in a process of deep reflection and analysis. The military manifestations of the U.S. policy and its consequences on the civilian population which motivated our initial response are gone. However, U.S. Latin American economic policy in the 1990s—neo-liberal economics, the North American Free Trade Agreement, GATT, etc.—taken together kill the poor just as surely as did the military policy of the 1980s. We no longer go to all-night wakes; or document ambushes, kidnappings, and murders; or plant crosses and markers in the cemeteries. Yet everyday we see the pain of a different kind of violence. We know that 60 percent of the work force, many of whom are single mothers, are unemployed; we see the disastrous effects of U.S. AID policies that provide no credit for small and medium-sized producers; we see the suffering that results when 69 percent of the population, of which more than half are children, suffer severe nutritional deficiency. We see the disintegration of a society where children no longer can afford to go to school or to the neighborhood health clinic. We realize that our struggle has only begun.

We look into the future and know that we must find new ways to join hands with poor and marginalized people in Central America and in the U.S. where our government and our economic forces deny the right to justice. Gilberto Aguirre, Executive Director of CEPAD and long time friend and advisor to Witness for Peace, recently said, "We need your solidarity now more than ever. Before solidarity was perhaps too easy. You could see the bombs, the ambushes, and count the number of people killed in the war. Now the consequences of U.S. policy—the slow torture of starvation—are more hidden and dangerous. The alarming economic situation is due in large part to the pressures of the U.S. government through the World Bank and the International Monetary Fund. Seventy percent of the aid appropriated by the U.S. Congress to Nicaragua actually goes back to your country to pay for the balance of payments deficit, leaving no money for production. Together as people of faith we must find new ways to respond."

PART XIV

THE GULF WAR

DOCUMENT 50

Statements Refusing Military Service

During the buildup and war in the Persian Gulf in 1990–1991, between 1,500 and 2,500 active-duty members of the armed forces and mobilized reservists applied for conscientious objector status. More than sixty of these applicants were court-martialed for refusal to deploy overseas. Amnesty International adopted thirty-two persons as "Prisoners of Conscience" after they refused to fight in the Persian Gulf War. Three cities—San Francisco, Berkeley, and Oakland, California—declared themselves sanctuaries for Gulf War objectors in 1991. In addition, a number of churches in Atlanta, Boston, New York City, the San Francisco Bay area, and Seattle, offered sanctuary. (See Charles C. Moskos and John Whiteclay Chambers II, ed., The New Conscientious Objection: From Sacred to Secular Resistance *[New York: Oxford University Press, 1993], pp. 4–5, 227 notes 5, 6, 243–244 notes 93–95; CCCO News Notes, v. 44, no. 2 [Spring 1992] and v. 44, no. 3 [Summer 1992].)*

A. Lynda Reiser,
An Inexcusable Reason to Sacrifice a Life

I object to participation in war in any form. I believe in the preservation of life at all costs, and I have a strong commitment to human life. Human life is a precious gift that should be strongly coveted and treated with the highest regard. This belief is central to my being, and as a result I have devoted myself, as a physician, to the preservation and care of others' lives.

I have a strong respect for each individual's right to life and feel that each individual has an equal right to life. Therefore I am against anything which impinges on another's right to life. Because of this, I am strongly opposed to violence. Violence is cruel and unnecessary use of physical force that jeopardizes human life. It disregards human life and opposes my values of human kindness and compassion.

War is violence on an even greater scale. It is violent in that it typically involves the destruction of masses of innocent people for no good reason. Its violence is also evident in the employment of technologically advanced weapons created solely for the purpose of large-scale destruction.

For these reasons, I cannot participate in war, either as a combatant or as a non-combatant, because my doing so would represent my agreement with war.

My beliefs developed progressively over the past seven years, beginning from my initial training during ROTC in college. I applied for the Army Scholarship in March, 1983, due to the strong encouragement of my parents. I felt forced to apply because the financial burden of my college education was overwhelming. I was very distraught and confused. I felt my personality would not be compatible with military life. I had always viewed myself as a compassionate person who felt a strong sense of responsibility toward others.

When I applied for the scholarship I feared that the military principles of war and fighting would somehow dominate my personality and cause me to lose human compassion. I was uncomfortable with the prospect of military training because I had always been opposed to weapons as a child and adolescent. However, I was somewhat naive and did not have a realistic concept of my role as a military officer. I had no desire to disappoint my parents, and I did not want them to bear the burden of my education, especially with seven siblings at home. Thus I submitted my application and was awarded the scholarship.

Lynda D. Reiser, M.D., ". . . an inexcusable reason to sacrifice a life," edited version of her claim for discharge as a conscientious objector published in *CCCO News Notes*.

My military training was particularly influential toward the development of my beliefs. My most vivid experiences, and those which had the most impact on me, occurred when I attended ROTC Advanced Camp during the summer of 1985. Here I went through extensive training which included weaponry training, military drills and simulated war exercises. I loathed every bit of the training, especially that which involved the use of weapons.

Most of the other cadets became very excited by the training and actually enjoyed it. I was in disbelief. I couldn't comprehend how people could have fun playing "war games" and pretending to kill others.

I also became very disturbed by the chanting that occurred during my camp training—the marching rhymes we were taught and expected to routinely sing. Many of these were based on the "kill, kill" motto. I couldn't believe that people actually sang about killing. It seemed very barbaric to me. It also bothered me that these mottoes were widely accepted by the other cadets and sung incessantly by them.

Many of my commanding officers expressed to me that I should show more enthusiasm. However, no matter what they said, I could not pretend to enjoy this training. These experiences were in opposition to my basic character and beliefs. Even more frustrating, I believed there was nothing I could do to reverse the situation. I felt trapped in the military and believed that my only hope was that I could attend medical school and serve the military in a more humanistic capacity, as a physician.

Medical school, however, led to further development and strengthening of the feelings I held against war during ROTC. I began medical school in September, 1986, and during that period I had little contact with the military. However, my experiences during medical school heightened my moral beliefs and my commitment to helping others.

I attended medical school at Temple University in North Philadelphia, a poverty-stricken area of the city where crime and violence run rampant. As a result, I was often exposed to the consequences of violence through the patients I took care of, and each experience caused me to become more disgusted by it.

One particular situation during my third year had a grave impact on my feelings against violence. I was doing a surgery rotation and had been called to the emergency room for a trauma code. The patient was a sixteen-year-old male who had been shot in the chest during a drug-related "war." The team worked diligently to save him, but was unfortunately unsuccessful.

As I observed this scene, I became completely filled with remorse for this youth who had died unnecessarily. He died as a result of a conflict, an inexcusable reason to sacrifice a life.

I became very frightened and repulsed by this experience. I was frightened by the fact that human beings could actually do these horrible things to each other, and repulsed by the blatant savagery involved. Following this and many similar experiences, I found myself dwelling more and more on violence, to the point where I often had nightmares involving many of these scenes. I became more and more opposed to violence and the use of weapons.

At this point I began to review my obligation to the military even more closely. I realized that my growing beliefs were in obvious conflict with the military principles of war.

As I began the application process for residency, during my fourth year of medical school, I decided to participate in a rotation at Trippler Army Medical Center in order to review my future obligation as a military physician. While at Trippler I came to realize that my roles as a physician and military officer were contradictory. I realized that while I was in the military uniform, I was expected to disregard my own beliefs and replace them with the principles of war and destruction which the military is based on. Even though I might never be directly involved in any type of violent activity, I felt that my simple employment in the military represented my agreement to all its principles. This was impossible for me to accept based on my strong moral beliefs, and thus led me to my conviction as a conscientious objector.

Over the next several months, during my senior year, I began to read books and seek out movies which dealt with war and violence, in order to help me make a decision about my future obligation. Particularly influential to my decision to seek separation was the book *Slaughterhouse Five,* by Kurt Vonnegut, and the movie *Born on the Fourth of July.*

These works helped me to put into perspective what war actually encompasses. I was appalled by the outright and uncontrollable violence and the amount of destruction that occurred. It was evident to me that those who participated in war had a complete disregard for human life. As I watched and read, I knew that I could never be a part of this activity, whether on the front line or caring for those injured.

Since realizing that I am a conscientious objector, I have become more confident in myself as my beliefs have strengthened. Ever since I accepted the ROTC scholarship, I have been very distressed about my future service with the military. Now, since my beliefs as a conscientious objector have been clarified, I feel immensely relieved of guilty feelings and stronger because I am taking a stand for my beliefs.

My beliefs have also allowed me to view the world, in general, differently. I feel that now I am more aware of the "wrongs" in the world and I have a sense of responsibility to make an attempt to change them. Since I became a conscientious objector, I have become even more socially aware, and now have a strong desire to become involved in community service and the anti-violence movements with groups like Physicians for Social Responsibility. Particularly, I would like to be involved in movements aimed at banning and increased regulation of personal weapons.

I feel that my role as a physician best exemplifies my beliefs as a conscientious objector. Through familial experience and the teachings of my parents,

I learned at an early age the value of helping others. I always knew that I wanted to pursue an occupation that would allow me to be of some service to humankind. This desire became focused, at the age of thirteen, when I decided to pursue a career in medicine.

My commitment further developed when I worked in a convalescent home during college, and ultimately through my medical school experiences. I have come to hold the deepest respect for life and feel honored that as a physician I will be directly responsible for the care of others' lives. I object to forces which oppose my responsibilities, as a physician, to the preservation of life, and therefore I object to violence and war.

B. Jeff Paterson, Public Statement

Good Afternoon

My name is Jeff Paterson.

I'm a CPL in the USMC.

I have served 3 yr., 10 mo. in the military with a relatively clean record, have received various awards, and have consistently received above average job proficiency and conduct ratings from my superiors. I have seven months left to serve before my End of Active Service Date. My MOS is that of a Field Artillery Fire Direction Controller, however, for the past two years I have been able to keep myself posted as a supply clerk to reduce the internal conflicts within myself. The recent moves by our government in the Persian Gulf has made my attempt to fulfill the remainder of my contract in a benign way impossible.

As we speak tens of thousands of servicemen are being mobilized to defend for the first time in American memory a blatantly imperialistic economic interest stripped of the State Department's beloved specter of international communism. Although the U.S. is facing off against a truly despicable man in Saddam Hussein, the reality is that U.S. foreign policy created this monster.

It was the U.S. who tacitly endorsed the Iraqi invasion of Iran ten years ago.

It was the U.S. and West Germany who sold Hussein chemical weapons throughout the war.

It was the U.S. who remained silent when Hussein used these weapons on his own populations.

And after all of this, it was the U.S. who gave Hussein safe passage through the Persian Gulf and the Strait of Hormuz by shipping Iraqi oil under the flag of Kuwait thus protecting it from Iranian attack by U.S. escorts.

Fax by Corporal Jeff Paterson of the U.S. Marine Corps, released at a press conference on August 16, 1990.

As usual the world banks were delighted to assist Iraq in its invasion of Iran by handing out blank checks to be payable for by the blood of the people after Iran would be crushed into submission. It was these banks that actually financed the carnage of the half million dead resulting from that war. It was this enormous war debt owed by Iraq that forced Hussein in my opinion to make the following choice:

Impose harsh austerity measures on his people and face the downfall of his regime, or, with a little military maneuvering take Kuwait and in one fell swoop double the amount of oil produced by Iraq.

Although there are great differences in this interventionist policy and that of U.S. support for the death squad regimes in El Salvador and Guatemala, there is the underlining motive of corporate profit throughout. Unfortunately the American people have fell for a big lie—that corporate interests are always in the best interests of the people, this is rarely true. What is the equation that balances human lives and corporate profits?

In my opinion no such equation exists, except in the minds of those that are preparing to fight this war.

The United States has no moral ground to stand on in the Persian Gulf.

We created this monster and pointed him in this direction.

We pour millions into the coffers of the Israel's military to wage a war against stone-throwing youth seeking a country to call their own once again.

I can not and will not be a pawn in America's power plays for profits and oil in the middle east. I will resist my scheduled departure, tentatively Sunday, by immediately filing for conscientious objector status, and physically refusing to board the plane. And of course if I am drug out into the Saudi desert, I will refuse to fight.

C.   Erik Glen Larsen,
Statement of Refusal to Participate in Interventionist Wars

Hello and good morning:

My name is Erik Larsen. I am a Lance Corporal in the United States Marine Corps Reserve and a radar mechanic for the HAWK missile system. I am stationed in Hayward, California with the Fourth Light Anti-Aircraft Missile Battalion, Fourth Marine Aircraft Wing.

On April 21, 1986, I joined the Marine Corps to defend the American dream, which first attracted my parents to this country in 1958. I emerged from boot camp three months later, a fully indoctrinated fighting machine

---

From "Statement of Refusal to Participate in Interventionist Wars" by Marine Corps Corporal Erik Glen Larsen, August 28, 1990.

willing to go anywhere in the world to defend the ideals and freedoms stated in the Constitution of the United States of America.

I first became aware of the realities of U.S. policies through student activists at Chabot Community College. They introduced me to alternative newspapers and books, and exposed me to the writings and speeches of Archbishop Oscar Romero of El Salvador.

I learned about a Central American history of U.S.-sponsored exploitive policies motivated by corporate and personal greed. 70,000 Salvadorans have been killed over the last ten years as a result of U.S. policies. I realized that I could no longer blindly follow orders from my Commander-in-Chief but that my actions were ultimately accountable to a higher authority—namely God.

My deeply rooted moral convictions have led me to declare my objection to the escalation of tensions and seemingly inevitable war in the Middle East.

It sickens me to hear Mr. Bush announce that 40,000 of my fellow reservists and 80,000 of my active duty brothers and sisters are going to wage war in the Middle East to protect "our American lifestyle." Oil imports could be cut in half if a sound energy policy focusing on renewable resources and conservation was in effect.

Our oil consuming western lifestyle is destroying the earth and it is our wasteful society that has brought the world to the brink of a preventable war.

Our presence in the Middle East has destroyed any hope of any of us ever receiving a peace dividend. We are wasting more than 24 million dollars a day in Saudi Arabia while the Oakland school system is still in shambles, while homeless people still walk the streets, and while the S&L criminals are still on the loose.

I've been listening to a lot of experts on public radio and they share my concern that the use of chemical and tactical nuclear weapons is a possibility in the event war does occur.

I have experienced first hand the frightening power of chemical weapons and I never want to go through that again. I had two buddies who were involved in a chemical incident when I was on an exercise this summer at Dugway Proving Grounds in Utah. They were rushed to an aid station while a decontamination team swept the area.

While standing upwind from the contaminated area which had been the site of chemical testing for the last fifty years I made a vow to my buddies. Never again will I allow myself or others to be put into a chemical environment.

The suggestion that nuclear weapons could be used in addition to chemical weapons scares the hell out of me. The use of chemical-biological agents and nuclear arms is completely unjustified.

Eight years ago the Reagan-Bush administration encouraged the sale of chemical weapons to Sadam Hussein. Bush said nothing at the time about human rights when Hussein used the weapons on his own people. Bush wants us to forget that he turned his eyes when innocent men, women, and children were being gassed.

Now he wants the American public to turn our eyes and forget about humanity, as he prepares to use me and others in the service as fodder for his cannon. I spent three long months in boot camp to learn to view human beings as targets. It has taken me almost three years to begin to see people as individuals once again. And I'll be damned if I'm going to be a part of this militaristic feeding frenzy.

I will refuse orders to activate me into the regular Marines.

I will refuse orders to ship me to Saudi Arabia to defend our polluting, exploitive lifestyle.

I will refuse to face another human being with a gas mask covering my face and my M-16 drawn.

I declare myself as a conscientious objector.

Here is my sea bag full of personal gear. Here is my gas mask. I will return them to the government. I no longer need them; I am no longer a Marine.

DOCUMENT 51

Ramsey Clark, "Letter to Secretary-General Javier Perez de Cuellar"

Son of a Justice of the United States Supreme Court, Ramsey Clark served as Attorney General under President Lyndon Johnson in the late 1960s. When the Nixon Administration took office in 1969, Clark became a private citizen, and began a long career as attorney for unpopular defendants and expert witness for the defense in cases against anti-war protestors.

In 1991, Clark made four trips to Iraq during and after the Persian Gulf War. One of these trips from February 2 to 8, 1991, is reported in Document 51. As in the case of Witness for Peace in Nicaragua (Document 49), going into a war zone while hostilities were still in progress so as to report the human dimensions, was itself a form of nonviolent resistance to war.

Ramsey Clark, "Letter to Secretary-General Javier Perez de Cuellar," *War Crimes: A Report on United States War Crimes Against Iraq* (New York: The Commission of Inquiry for the International War Crimes Tribunal, 1992), pp. 227–233. Reprinted by permission.

On his return to the United States, Clark issued an urgent call on forces in the United States and around the world opposed to the war in the Persian Gulf to "intensify their efforts to demand (1) an end to the bombing, (2) the immediate withdrawal of all U.S. and 'allied' troops, and (3) that the U.S. get out of the Middle East."[1]

February 12, 1991

Secretary-General Javier Perez de Cuellar
The Secretariat
United Nations Plaza
New York, NY 10017

Dear Mr. Secretary General:

During the period February 2 to February 8, 1991 I traveled in Iraq to assess the damage to civilian life there resulting from the bombing and the embargo, including civilian deaths, injuries, illness and destruction and damage to civilian property. I was accompanied by an experienced camera team that has filmed war and its destructiveness in many countries including Afghanistan, Angola, Cambodia, El Salvador, Nicaragua, the Philippines and Vietnam. Their film documents most of the damage I mention in this letter and some I do not. In our party was an Iraqi-American guide and translator who has family in Baghdad and Basra and is personally familiar with those cities and many other areas of Iraq. He had last visited Baghdad, Basra and Kuwait City in December 1990.

We traveled over 2,000 miles in seven days to view damage, learn of casualties, discuss the effects of the bombing with government officials, public health and safety agency staffs and private families and individuals. We had cooperation from the government of Iraq including Ministers, Governors, health and medical officials and civil defense personnel. The bombing in all parts of Iraq made travel difficult, requiring caution for bomb craters and damage to highways and roads and making night driving especially hazardous.

The damage to residential areas and civilian structures, facilities and utilities was extensive everywhere we went. Every city and town we visited or that was reported to us had no municipal water, electricity or telephone service. Parts of Baghdad had limited delivery of impure water for an hour a day.

The effect of damage to municipal water systems on health and safety is tremendous. The Minister of Health considered potable water for human consumption the single greatest health need in the country. Tens of thousands

---

1. From Warren A. J. Hamerman, "Ramsey Clark: 'Stop the Slaughter' ", *The New Federalist,* Vol. V, No. 9 (March 4, 1991), p. 1.

are known to suffer diarrhea and stomach disorders. There are believed to be hundreds of thousands of unreported cases. Several thousands are believed to have died.

There is no electric lighting in the cities, towns and countryside in daytime or the long winter nights, except for a few interior spaces like hospital emergency rooms where gasoline generators are available. The meaning of this is brought home most painfully in the hospitals at night.

In the hospitals, there is no heat, no clean water except limited quantities for drinking supplied in bottles, no electric light in wards and hospital rooms, and inadequate medicine, even for pain alleviation, in the face of a great increase in critically and severely injured persons. Doctors we talked with in four hospitals are deeply concerned over the absence or shortage of needed medicine and sanitary supplies. Surgeons and medics treating wounds cannot keep their hands clean or gloved, and work in the cold, in poor light with greatly increased numbers of patients in unrelieved pain. Seven hospitals are reported closed by bomb damage. Many if not most have had windows shattered.

Schools are closed. Homes are cold. Candles are the principal lighting. Telephone communication does not exist. Transportation is extremely limited. Gasoline is scarce. Roads and bridges are bombing targets. There is no television. Radio reception is limited to battery powered radios which can receive short-wave signals, a few transmissions from Iraq stations or nearby foreign stations. According to the Ministry of Health, hospital officials and the Red Crescent, there is a substantial increase in falls, home accidents, stress, nervous disorders, shock, heart attack, miscarriage and premature births and infant mortality. Nightly air raids, the sounds of sirens, anti-aircraft fire and the explosion of bombs have placed a great strain on the society as a whole, but particularly on children and individuals with nervous system or heart disorders.

Dr. Ibrahem Al Noore has been head of the Red Crescent and Red Cross of Iraq for ten years. He is a pediatrician by training who interned at Children's Hospital in London, later headed Children Hospital in Baghdad and served in the Ministry of Health for some years, rising to Deputy Minister. Dr. Noore estimates that there have been 3,000 infant deaths since November 1, 1990 in excess of the normal rate, attributable solely to the shortage of infant milk formula and medicines. Only 14 tons of baby formula have been received during that period. Prior monthly national consumption was approximately 2,500 tons.

One of the early targets of U.S. bombing was the infant and baby milk processing facility in Baghdad. No Iraqi with whom we talked assumed this was a coincidence. The U.S. claim that the plant manufactured chemical warfare material is false. A French company built it. The twenty or more people whom we interviewed, who operated it, who visited it before its destruction and who have examined it since without ill effect all say it was a plant processing infant and baby milk formula. In a lengthy and unrestricted examination of the plant, we saw no evidence to the contrary.

In all areas we visited and all other areas reported to us, municipal water processing plants, pumping stations and even reservoirs have been bombed. Electric generators have been destroyed. Refineries and oil and gasoline storage facilities and filling stations have been attacked. Telephone exchange buildings, TV and radio stations, and some radio telephone relay stations and towers, have been damaged or destroyed. Many highways, roads, bridges, bus stations, schools, mosques and churches, cultural sites, and hospitals have been damaged. Government buildings including Executive Offices of the President, the Foreign Ministry, Defense Ministry, Ministry for Industry and Justice Ministry have been destroyed or damaged.

Ambassadors of member states should ask themselves if their capitals, major cities and towns were similarly destroyed and damaged by such bombing, would they consider the targets to be permissible under the International Laws of Armed Conflict. Imagine the reaction if water, electricity, telephones, gasoline, heating and air conditioning, TV and radio were denied to Lima and Arequipa, Lagos and Ibadan, Washington and Chicago, Paris and Marseilles, New Delhi and Calcutta, to Canberra and Sydney, while civilians were bombed in their homes, business, shops, markets, schools, churches, hospitals, public places, and roadways.

How can destruction of municipal electricity for Mosul, the telephone system for the people of Baghdad, the municipal water supplies for Basra, or shooting defenseless public buses and private cars on the road to Jordan and elsewhere possibly be justified as necessary to drive Iraq from Kuwait? If it can be so justified, then the United Nations has authorized the destruction of all civilian life of a whole nation.

The effect of the bombing, if continued, will be the destruction of much of the physical and economic basis for life in Iraq. The purpose of the bombing can only be explained rationally as the destruction of Iraq as a viable state for a generation or more. Will the United Nations be a party to this lawless violence?

I will briefly describe destruction to residential areas in some of the cities and towns we visited. In Basra Governor Abdullah Adjram described the bombing as of February 6 as worse than during the Iran-Iraq war. We carefully probed five residential areas that had been bombed.

1. A middle class residential area was heavily damaged at 9:30 p.m. on January 31. Twenty-eight persons were reported killed, 56 were injured, 20 homes and six shops were destroyed.

2. On January 22, an upper middle class residential neighborhood was shattered by three bombs destroying or extensively damaging more than 15 homes and reportedly injuring 40 persons, but without any deaths.

3. On January 24, an upper middle class neighborhood was bombed, killing eight, injuring 26 and destroying three homes and damaging many others.

4. On February 4, described by officials as the heaviest bombing of Basra to February 6, at 2:35 a.m., 14 persons were killed, 46 injured and 128 apartments and homes destroyed or damaged together with an adjacent Pepsi Cola bottling plant and offices across a wide avenue. The area devastated was three blocks deep on both sides of streets. At least fifteen cars were visible, crushed in garages. Small anti-personnel bombs were alleged to have fallen here and we saw what appeared to be one that did not explode embedded in rubble. We were shown the shell of a "mother" bomb which carries the small fragmentation bombs.

5. On January 28, about eighteen units in a very large low cost public housing project were destroyed or severely damaged, killing 46 and injuring 70. The nearby high school was damaged by a direct hit on a corner. The elementary school across the street was damaged.

On the evening of February 5 at 8:30 p.m. while our small group was dining alone by candlelight in the Sheraton Basra, three large bomb blasts broke glass in the room. We went upstairs to the roof. From there I saw one bomb fall into the Shaat-Al-Arab beyond the Teaching Hospital to the South throwing a column of water high into the air; another bomb hit near the Shaat. As agreed upon earlier, civil defense officials came to take us to the blast sites. They were 1.2 km down the street near the Shaat-Al-Arab. I had walked by the area about 6:30 p.m.

We found two buildings destroyed. It is an apartment and residential home area. One was a family club, the other a night club. If either had been open scores of people would have been killed. Palm trees were sheared off and shrapnel, rocks, dirt and glass covered the street for several hundred feet. We were unable to enter the buildings that night.

We returned the next morning and were told both buildings were empty at the time by the owners who were looking at the damage. The teaching hospital, about 150 yards distant, which had been closed for a week following earlier bombing, was without windows. It apparently received no new damage. As with all the other civilian damage we saw we could find no evidence of any military presence in the area. Here, there was no utility or facility that are frequent, if illegal, targets either. There were only homes, apartments and a few shops, grocery stores and other businesses found in residential areas, plus two small bridges connecting the hospital to the mainland.

We were informed by a variety of sources including visual observation during extensive driving in Basra, that many other residential properties had been hit and that the five areas we filmed were a minor fraction of the civilian damage that had occurred.

At the central market where more than 1,000 shops and vendors sell fruits, vegetables, fish, meat, foodstuffs and other items, a bomb leaving a huge crater had demolished a building with a grocery store and other shops and damaged an entry area to the market at about 4:00 p.m. It reportedly killed eight persons and injured 40.

We examined the rubble of a Sunni Moslem Mosque, Al Makal, where a family of 12 had taken sanctuary. The minaret remained standing. Ten bodies were found under the rubble and identified by a family member who had returned from his military post when informed of the tragedy. The dead included his wife and four young children.

In Diwaniya, a smaller town, we examined the same types of civilian damage we witnessed elsewhere and that was reported everywhere. In the town center, apparently seeking to destroy the radio telephone relay equipment in the post office, bombing had damaged the tower and the office. We saw many similar, or identical relay towers in the region that had not been attacked. Adjacent to the Post Office on the central circle of the city, three small hotels of 30 to 50 rooms were destroyed together with a host of shops, cafes, and offices including those of doctors and lawyers. We were told 12 people were killed and 35 injured. More damage could be seen across the circle among business and apartment buildings from one or more bombs that fell there.

Near the outskirts of town, four more-or-less contiguous residential areas had been bombed. Twenty-three persons were reported killed and 75 injured. Two schools were badly damaged. There was no water, electricity or telephone service. A water irrigation station was destroyed. Other damage was witnessed while driving around the town. On the outskirts an oil tank was on fire, one of more than a dozen we saw burning during our travels.

Baghdad has been more accessible to foreign observation than Basra and other places in Iraq. It will only be highlighted. We examined extensive damage on a main street in the blocks next to and across the street from the Ministry of Justice which had all its windows on one side blasted out. I know that area as a busy poor commercial residential area from walking through it on the way to the National Museum and visiting the Justice Ministry. A large supermarket, eight other stores and six or eight houses were destroyed or badly damaged. Across the street, one bomb hit on the sidewalk and another was a direct hit on housing behind the street front properties. Six shops, a restaurant and several other stores plus 9 or 10 homes were destroyed, or badly damaged. We could not get an agreed account of casualties from the 40 or 50 people standing around the damage. Some said as many as 30 died and many more were injured.

We visited a residential area where several homes were destroyed on February 7. Six persons in one family were killed in an expensive home and several others in adjacent properties. One 500 lb. bomb had failed to explode and the tail was seen above the thick concrete roof when a member of our team first drove by. When we returned, the bomb had been removed. Our camera team visited the hospital where the injured were taken later that afternoon. The critically injured father from the home where the bomb failed to explode was there. This was one of four hospitals treating persons injured in bombings that we visited.

A bus station was hit by a bomb and the stained glass in a nearby mosque shattered. We were unable to learn if any one was killed though 40–50 people were at the station near midnight when we drove by on our arrival.

We saw five different damaged telephone exchanges while driving around Baghdad and many destroyed and damaged government and private buildings.

Bridges in Baghdad were a frequent target though damage to them was minimal when we left. The bridges are not a legitimate military target. Even Defense Ministry buildings are occupied by non-combatants. The telephone exchanges run by civilians are overwhelmingly processing non-military calls. The military has the most extensive independent communications capacity in the country. These are not legitimate targets and the effort to bomb them necessarily takes civilian lives.

Damage in Basra appeared to be considerably more extensive than in Baghdad and the actual bombing there was much more intensive than at any time we were in Baghdad. There were civilian deaths every night we were in Baghdad.

Visits to the towns of Hilla, Najaf and Nasseriya by press corps representatives and our crew found civilian casualties in residential areas of each, damages to a medical clinic, 12 deaths in one family, and 46 deaths in one night of bombing in one town. A small town was bombed a few minutes before we passed through on our drive back from Basra. We saw no military presence there. Smoke could be seen from three fires.

Over the 2,000 miles of highways, roads and streets we traveled, we saw scores, probably several hundred, destroyed vehicles. There were oil tank trucks, tractor trailers, lorries, pickup trucks, a public bus, a mini-bus, a taxicab and many private cars destroyed by aerial bombardment and strafing. Some were damaged when they ran into bomb craters in the highways or road damage caused by bombs and strafing. We found no evidence of military equipment or supplies in the vehicles. Along the roads we saw several oil refinery fires and numerous gasoline stations destroyed. One road repair camp had been bombed on the road to Amman.

As with the city streets in residential, industrial and commercial areas where we witnessed damage, we did not see a single damaged or destroyed military vehicle, tank, armored car, personnel carrier or other military equipment, or evidence of any having been removed. We saw scores of oil tank cars driving between Iraq and Jordan and parked in Jordan, as well as five or six that were destroyed by planes on the highway. We saw no evidence of any arms or military material on or around the destroyed and burned out tank trucks, or those not hit.

No one in the press corps or among the civilians we encountered reported to us that they had seen any evidence of the presence of military vehicles having been hit on the highways or having been in the vicinity of civilian property, or private vehicles hit before, during or after an aerial strike. We saw no evidence of any military presence in the areas of damage described in this letter.

It is preposterous to claim military equipment is being placed in residential areas to escape attack. Residential areas are regularly attacked. The claim reveals a policy of striking residential areas, because it purports to establish a justification for doing so. If there had been military vehicles in the civilian areas we examined, or on the roads and highways we traveled when bombing occurred, it is inconceivable that among all that debris we would not find some fragments of military vehicles, material, equipment or clothing. Not only did pinpoint precision fail to hit military targets in civilian areas, they were not collaterally damaged in the attacks on civilian life. Had they been present they would have been hit.

The government of Iraq has vastly understated civilian casualties in Iraq. This is not an uncommon phenomenon for governments in wartime.

The inescapable and tragic fact is thousands of civilians have been killed in the bombings. The bombings are conducted with this knowledge.

Dr. Noore, with more than four decades in medical service and ten years as head of Red Crescent, estimates 6,000 to 7,000 civilian deaths, and many thousands of injuries from bombings. Red Crescent vehicles transport medicine and medical supplies into Iraq from Jordan and Iran. They make deliveries as often as two to three times a week to some cities and hospitals but regularly to hospitals throughout the country. These contacts and hospital requests for medicines and supplies along with the relationships established over the years provide a solid base for his opinion.

He adds to the toll thousands of deaths from failure to obtain adequate supplies of infant formula and medicine, from contaminated water and from increased death rates from stress, heart attacks and similar causes.

While I applaud your recent initiative in designating a U.N. mission to Baghdad to carry medical supplies and ascertain the health needs of the Iraqi people, I urge you to seek major funding now or release of Iraqi funds for supplying 2,500 tons of infant and baby milk formula, greatly needed medicines and sanitation supplies, municipal water system restoration and water purification.

The bombing constitutes the most grievous violation of international law. It is intended to destroy the civilian life and economy of Iraq. It is not necessary, meaningful or permissible as a means of driving Iraq from Kuwait.

No UN resolution authorizes any military assault on Iraq, except as is necessary to drive Iraqi forces from Kuwait. The bombing that has occurred throughout Iraq is the clearest violation of international law and norms for armed conflict, including the Hague and Geneva Conventions and the Nuremberg Charter. It is uncivilized, brutal and racist by any moral standard. With few if any exceptions we witnessed, the destruction is not conceivably within the language or contemplation of Security Council Resolution 678/44.

I urge you to immediately notify the Member States of the General Assembly and the Security Council of the information herein provided. I urge you to ask for the creation of an investigative body to examine the effect of U.S. bombing of Iraq on the civilian life of the country. Most urgent, I ask you to do everything within your power to stop the bombing of cities, civilian population, public utilities, public highways, bridges and all other civilian areas and facilities in Iraq, and elsewhere. If there is no cease fire, bombing must be limited to military targets in Kuwait, concentrations of military forces in Iraq near the border of Kuwait, operational military air fields or identified

Scud launching sites or mobile missile launchers in Iraq. If a cease fire is not achieved, the immediate cessation of this lawless bombing of civilian and noncombatants is essential.

The use of highly sophisticated military technology with mass destructive capacity by rich nations against an essentially defenseless civilian population of a poor nation is one of the great tragedies of our time. United States annual military expenditures alone are four times the gross national product of Iraq. The scourge of war will never end if the United Nations tolerates this assault on life. The United Nations must not be an accessory to war crimes.

We have 6–7 hours of video tape of much of the damage to civilian life and property described above. It includes painful hospital interviews with children, women and men injured in these assaults. The tape was not reviewed or in any way examined by anyone in Iraq before we left, and the actual filming was largely unobserved by any Iraqi official. This footage is being edited. I will send you a copy as soon as it is ready within the next few days. If you wish to have the entire tapes reviewed, let me know and I will arrange a screening.

Copies of this letter are being sent to President Bush and President Hussein and the United Nations Ambassadors for the United States and Iraq.

Sincerely,
RAMSEY CLARK

DOCUMENT 52

Howard Zinn,
"Just and Unjust Wars"

Howard Zinn, activist historian, has been a lifelong participant in movements for civil rights and peace. During the early 1960s he was one of two adult advisers to the Student Nonviolent Coordinating Committee, and wrote SNCC: The New Abolitionists. *He spoke and wrote against the war in Vietnam, and*

Howard Zinn, "Just and Unjust Wars," *Failure to Quit: Reflections of an Optimistic Historian* (Monroe, MA: Common Courage Press, 1993), pp. 99–115. Reprinted by permission.

after the war ended, testified as an expert on civil disobedience in several
trials of ultra resisters opposed to the nuclear arms race. His very influential
People's History of the United States *helped to prepare the ground for*
widespread opposition in 1992 to celebration of the quincentennial of Christo-
pher Columbus' landing in the Western Hemisphere.

In this talk, Zinn protests the Persian Gulf War and declares his opposition
to any foreseeable war that might be fought by the United States. Reflecting
on his own participation in World War II as a bombardier, he writes: "I
suppose I've come to the conclusion that war, by its nature, being the indis-
criminate and mass killing of large numbers of people, cannot be justified
for any political cause, any ideological cause, any territorial boundary, any
tyranny, any aggression."

––––––––––––––––

... The generous reader will recognize and perhaps forgive the loose and
easy style of an extemporaneous talk, in this case given at the University of
Wisconsin in Madison, at the close of the U.S. military action in the Persian
Gulf. It was a hard time for anti-war people, with most of the nation, whipped
up by the government and the media in their customary collaboration, exultant
at our "easy victory" (few American casualties; who cared about Iraqi casualties?). The anti-war minority was not silent; there were mass demonstrations
in Washington, D.C., and other cities, thousands of small actions all around
the country, some heroic refusals of participation by men and women in the
military, who faced court-martial and prison. I tried to put the short war into
a longer historical perspective.

1991

I think that the great danger of what has just happened in the Gulf is what
the Administration wanted to happen, that is, to fight a war that would make
war acceptable once more. The Vietnam War gave war a bad name. The
people who lead this country have been trying ever since to find a war that
would give war a *good* name. They think they've found it. I think it's
important for us to sit back and think about not just the Gulf War, not just
the Vietnam War, not just this or that war, but to think about the problem of
war, of just and unjust war.

We've had all these conferences. All of you who were around at the
beginning of the twentieth century remember the Hague Conferences and the
Geneva Conferences of the 1930s limiting the techniques of war. The idea
was: you can't do away with war, all you can do is make war more humane.
Einstein went to one of these conferences. I don't know how many of you
know that. (We like to bring up things that people don't know. What is
scholarship, anyway?) Einstein was horrified at World War I, as so many

were, that great war for democracy, for freedom, to end all wars, etc. Ten million men die on the battlefield in World War I and nobody, at the end of it, understands why, what for. World War I gave war a bad name. Until World War II came along.

But Einstein was horrified by World War I. He devoted a lot of time to thinking and worrying about it. He went to this conference in Geneva. He thought they were discussing disarmament, to do away with the weapons of war and therefore to prevent war. Instead, he found these representatives of various countries discussing what kinds of weapons would be suitable and what kind of weapons needed to be prohibited. What were good weapons and bad weapons, just weapons and unjust weapons? Einstein did something which nobody ever expected. He was a very private man. He did something really uncharacteristic: he called a press conference. The whole international press came, because Einstein was, well, he was Einstein. They came, and he told this press conference how horrified he was by what he had heard at the international conference. He said, "One does not make wars less likely by formulating rules of warfare. War cannot be humanized. It can only be abolished."

We still have that problem of just and unjust wars, of unjust wars taking place and then another war takes place which looks better, has a better rationale, is easier to defend, and so now we're confronted with a "just" war and war is made palatable again. Right now the attempt is to put Vietnam behind us, that unjust war, and now we have a just war. Or at least a quick one, a real smashing victory.

I had a student a few years ago who was writing something about war. I don't know why a student of mine should write about war. But she said, "I guess wars are like wines. There are good years and bad years. But war is not like wine. War is like cyanide. One drop and you're dead." I thought that was good.

What often is behind this business of "we can't do anything about war" and "war, be realistic, accept it, just try to fool around with the edges of it" is a very prevalent notion that you sometimes hear a lot when people begin discussing war. Fourteen minutes into any discussion of war someone says, "It's human nature." Don't you hear that a lot? You just get a group of people together to discuss war and at some point somebody will say, "It's human nature." There's no evidence of that. No genetic evidence. No biological evidence. All we have is historical evidence. And that's not evidence about our nature—that's evidence about circumstance.

There's no biological evidence, no genetic evidence, no anthropological evidence. What is the anthropological evidence? You look at these "primitive" tribes, as anthropologists call them, look at what they do, and say, "Ah, these tribes are fierce." "Ah, these tribes are gentle." It's just not clear at all.

And what about history? There's a history of wars and also a history of kindness. But it's like the newspapers and the historians. They dwell on wars and cruelty and the bestial things that people do to one another. They don't dwell a lot on the magnificent things that people do for one another in everyday life again and again. It seems to me it only takes a little bit of thought to realize that if wars came out of human nature, out of some spontaneous urge to kill, then why is it that governments have to go to such tremendous lengths to mobilize populations to go to war. It seems so obvious, doesn't it? They really have to work at it. They have to dredge up enormous numbers of reasons. They have to inundate the airwaves with these reasons. They have to bombard people with slogans and statements and then, in case people aren't really persuaded, they have to threaten them. If they haven't persuaded enough people to go into the armed forces, then they have to draft them.

Of course the persuasion into the armed forces also includes a certain amount of economic persuasion. You make sure you have a very poor underclass in society so that you give people a choice between starving or going into the military. But if persuasion doesn't work and enticements don't work, then anybody who doesn't want to sign up for the draft or who goes into the army and decides to leave is going to be court-martialed and go to prison. They have to go to great lengths to get people to go to war. They work very hard at it.

What's interesting also is that they have to make moral appeals. That should say something about human nature, if there is something to be said about human nature. It suggests that there must be some moral element in human nature. Granted that human beings are capable of all sorts of terrible things and human beings are capable of all sorts of wonderful things. But there must be something in human beings which makes them respond to moral appeals. Most humans don't respond to appeals to go to war on the basis of "Let's go and kill." No, "Let's go and free somebody. Let's go and establish democracy. Let's go and topple this tyrant. Let's do this so that wars will finally come to an end." Most people are not like Theodore Roosevelt. Just before the Spanish-American War, Theodore Roosevelt said to a friend, "In strict confidence" (you might ask then, how did I get hold of it; you read all these public letters that now appear and they all start "in strict confidence")—"I should welcome almost any war, for I think this country needs one." Well. No moral appeal there. Just we *need* a war.

You may know that George Bush, when he entered the White House, took down the portrait that Reagan had put up there to inspire him. It was a portrait of Calvin Coolidge, because Reagan knew that Calvin Coolidge was one of the most inspiring people in the history of this country. Coolidge had said: "The business of America is business." Bush took down the portrait of Calvin Coolidge and put up the portrait of Theodore Roosevelt. I don't want to make too much of this. But I will. What Theodore Roosevelt said, Bush might just as well have said. Bush wanted war.

Every step in the development of this Persian Gulf War indicated, from the moment that the invasion of Kuwait was announced, everything that Bush did fits in perfectly with, the fact that Bush wanted war. He was determined to have war. He was determined not to prevent this war from taking place. You can just tell this from the very beginning: no negotiations, no compromise, no—what was that ugly word?—linkage. Bush made linkage the kind of word that made you tremble. I always thought that things were linked naturally. Everybody was linked, issues were linked. I thought that even the countries in the Middle East were somehow linked, and that the issues in the Middle East were somehow linked. No negotiations, no linkage, no compromise. He sends Baker to Geneva, and people got excited. Baker's going to meet the Foreign Minister of Iraq, Tariq Aziz, in Geneva. What are they going to do? Bush says, no negotiations. Why are you going? Are you a frequent flyer? Amazing. No negotiations, right up to the end.

Who knows if Saddam Hussein in any of those little overtures that were made, I don't know how serious he was or what would have happened, but the fact is there were overtures that came, yes, even from Saddam Hussein, and they were absolutely and totally neglected. One came from a member of the Foreign Service of the United States who brought it personally from the Middle East and gave it to Scowcroft. No response, no response at all. Bush wanted this war.

But, as I said, there aren't a lot of people, fortunately, like Theodore Roosevelt and Bush. Most people do not want war. Most people, if they are going to support a war, have to be given reasons that have to do with morality, with right and wrong, with justice and lack of justice, with tyranny and opposing tyranny. I think it's important to take a look at the process by which populations are, as this one was in a very short time, brought to support a war. On the eve of war, you remember, before January 15, the surveys all showed that the American public was divided half and half, 46 percent to 47 percent on the issue of "should we use force to solve this problem in the Middle East." Half and half.

Of course, after the bombs started falling in Iraq, it suddenly became 75 percent and then 80 percent in favor of war. What is this process of persuasion? It seems to me we should take a look at the elements of that, because it's important to know that, to be able to deal with it and talk to people about it, especially since that 80 or 85 percent or now they report 89.3 percent, whatever, must be a very shallow percentage. It must be very thin, I think. It must be very temporary and can be made more temporary than it is. It must be shallow because half of those people before the bombs fell did not believe in the use of force. Public opinion, as we know, is very volatile. So to look at the elements by which people are persuaded is to begin to think about how to talk to at least that 50 percent and maybe more, who are willing to reconsider whether this war was really just and necessary and right, and whether any war in our time could be just and necessary and right.

I think one of the elements that goes into this process of persuasion is the starting point that the U.S. is a good society. Since we're a good society, our wars are good. If we're a good society, we're going to do good things. We do good things at home. We have a Bill of Rights and color television. There are lots of good things you can say if you leave out enough.

It's like ancient Athens. Athens goes to war against Sparta. Athens must be on the right side because Athens is a better society than Sparta. Athens is more cultured. Sure, you have to overlook a few things about ancient Athens, like slavery. But still, it really is a better society. So the notion is that Athens fighting Sparta is probably a good war. But you have to overlook things, do a very selective job of analyzing your own society, before you come to the conclusion that yours is so good a society that your unadorned goodness must spill over into everything you do, including everything you do to other people abroad.

What is required, it seems to me, is, in the case of the U.S. as the good society doing good things in the world, simply to look at a bit of history. It's only if you were born yesterday and also if today you don't look around very sharply that you can come to the conclusion that we are so good a society that you can take the word of the government that any war we get into will be a right and a just war. But it doesn't take too much looking into American history to see that we have a long history of aggression.

Talk about naked aggression. A long history of naked aggression. How did we get so big? We started out as a thin band of colonies along the East Coast and soon we were at the Pacific and expanding. It's not a biological thing, that you just expand. No. We expanded by force, conquest, aggression. Sure it says, "Florida Purchase" on those little maps that we used to have in elementary school, a map with colors on them. Blue for Florida Purchase, orange for Mexican Cession. A purchase. Just a business deal. Nothing about Andrew Jackson going into Florida and killing a number of people in order to persuade the Spaniards to sell Florida to us. No money actually passed hands, but we'll ignore that.

The Mexican Cession. Mexico "ceded" California and Colorado and New Mexico and Arizona. They ceded all of that to us. Why? Good neighbors. Latin American hospitality. Ceded to us. There was a war, a war which we provoked, which President Polk planned for in advance, as so many wars are planned for in advance. Then an incident takes place and they say, Oh, wow, an incident took place. We've got to go to war. That was also a fairly short war and a decisive victory and soon we had 40 percent of Mexico. And it's all ours. California and all of that.

Why? Expansion. I remember how proud I was way back when I first looked at that map and saw "Louisiana Purchase." It doubled the size of my country, and it was just by purchase. It was an empty space. We just bought it. I really didn't learn anything, they didn't tell me when they gave me that stuff in history class, that there were Indians living in that territory. Indians had to be fought in battle after battle, war after war. They had to be killed, exterminated. The buffalo herds, their means of subsistence, had to be destroyed, they had to be driven out of that territory so that the Louisiana Purchase could be ours.

Then we began to go overseas. There was that brief period in American history, that honest moment in a textbook where it has a chapter called "The Age of Imperialism." 1898 to 1903. There, too, we went into Cuba to save the Cubans. We are always helping people. Saving people from somebody. So we went in and saved the Cubans from Spain and immediately planted *our* military bases and *our* corporations in Cuba. Then there was Puerto Rico. A few shells fired and Puerto Rico is ours.

In the meantime Teddy Roosevelt is swimming out into the Pacific after the Philippines. Not contiguous to the U.S. People didn't know that. McKinley didn't know where the Philippines were. And Senator Beveridge of Indiana said, "The Philippines not contiguous to the U.S.? Our Navy will make it contiguous." Ours is a history of expansion, aggression, and it continues.

We become a world power. Around 1905–1907, the first books began to appear about American history which used that phrase, "America as a world power." That in fact was what we intended to do, to become a world power. It took World War I and then World War II. We kept moving up and the old imperial powers were being shoved out of the way, one by one.

Now the Middle East comes in. In World War II Saudi Arabia becomes one of our friendly places. The English are being pushed out more and more, out of this oil territory. The Americans are going to come in. Of the "Seven Sisters," the seven great oil corporations, five of them will be American, maybe one will be British. In the years after World War II, of course, the Soviet Union is the other great power, but we are expanding and our influence is growing and our military bases are spreading all over the world and we are intervening wherever we can to make sure that things go our way.

In 1940–41, at the beginning of World War II, Henry Luce, a very powerful man in America, the publisher of *Life* and *Time* and *Fortune* and the maker of presidents, wrote an article called "The American Century," anticipating that this coming century is going to be ours. He said, "This is the time to accept wholeheartedly our duty and our opportunity as the most vital and powerful nation in the world and in consequence to exert upon the world the full impact of our influence. For such purposes as we see fit and by such means as we see fit." He was not a shy man. So we proceeded.

While it was thought that anti-communism, rivalry with the Soviet Union, the other great superpower, was the central motive for the American foreign policy in the postwar period, I think it's more accurate to say that the problem was not communism, the problem was independence from American power. It didn't matter whether a country was turning communist or not, it mattered that a country was showing independence and not falling in line with what the United States conceived of as its responsibility as a world power. So in 1953 the government in Iran was overthrown and Mossadeq came into power. He was not a communist but a nationalist. He was a nationalist also because he nationalized the oil. That is intolerable. Those things are intolerable, just like Arbenz in Guatemala the following year. He's not a communist. Well, he's a little left of center, maybe a few socialist ideas, maybe he talks to communists. But he's not a communist. He's nationalized United Fruit lands. That's intolerable.

Arbenz offers to pay United Fruit. That proves that he's certainly not a real revolutionary. A real revolutionary wouldn't give a cent to United Fruit ... I wouldn't. I've always considered myself a real revolutionary because I wouldn't pay a cent to anybody like United Fruit. He offered to pay them the price of their land, the price that they had declared for tax purposes. Sorry. That won't do. So the CIA goes to work and overthrows the Arbenz government.

And the Allende government in Chile also. Not a communist government, a little marxist, a little socialist, quite a lot of civil liberties and freedom of the press, but more independent of the United States than the other governments of Chile. A government that's not going to be friendly to Anaconda Copper and ITT and other corporations of the U.S. that have always had their way in Latin America. That's the real problem.

That history of expansion, of intervention, is not even to talk about Vietnam, Laos, Cambodia. Not to talk about all the tyrants that we kept in power, of all the aggressions not just that we committed but that we watched other countries commit as we stood silently by because we approved of those aggressions.

Until Noam Chomsky brought up the name of East Timor into public discussion nobody had even heard of it. The CIA had heard of East Timor. Anyway, Indonesia went into East Timor and killed huge numbers of people. The invasion, occupation, and brutalization that Saddam Hussein committed in Kuwait was small in comparison to the enormous bloodshed in East Timor, done by Indonesia, our friend, and with military hardware supplied by the U.S.

The record of the U.S. in dealing with naked aggression in the world, looking at a little bit of history, is so shocking, so abysmal, that nobody with any sense of history could possibly accept the argument that we were now sending troops into the Middle East because the U.S. government is morally outraged at the invasion of another country. That Bush's heart goes out to the people of Kuwait, who are suffering under oppression. Bush's heart never went out to the people of El Salvador, suffering under the oppression of a government which we were supplying with arms again and again. Tens and tens and tens of thousands of people were being killed. His heart never went out to those people. Or the people in Guatemala, again, whose government we were supplying with arms. It's a long list.

The moral appeal of war is based on people's forgetting of history and on the ability of the mass media and the Administration to obliterate history, certainly not to bring it up. You talk about the responsibility of the press. Does the press have no responsibility to teach any history to the people who read its newspaper columns? To remind people of what has happened five, ten, twenty, forty years ago? Was the press also born yesterday and has forgotten everything that happened before last week? The press complained about military censorship. The big problem was not military censorship. The problem was self-censorship.

Another element in this process of persuasion is to create a Manichean situation, good versus evil. I've just talked about the good, us. But you also have to present the other as total evil. As the only evil. Granted, Saddam Hussein is an evil guy. I say that softly. But he is. No question about it. Most heads of government are. But if you want to bring a nation to war against an evil person, it's not enough to say that this person is evil. You have to cordon him off from all the other tyrants of the world, all the other evil leaders of government in order to establish that this is the one tyrant in the world whom we have to get. He is responsible for the trouble in the world. If we could only get him, we could solve our problems, just as a few years ago if we could only get Noriega, we could solve the drug trade problem. We got Noriega—and obviously we've solved the drug trade problem. But the demonization is necessary, the creation of this one evil shutting out everything, Syria, Turkey, Egypt, Saudi Arabia, not letting people be aware of them.

I didn't see the media paying any attention to this, to the latest reports of Amnesty International, in which, if you read the 1990 report of Amnesty International, they have a few pages on each country. There are a lot of countries. A few pages on Iraq, Iran, Turkey, Syria, Saudi Arabia, Kuwait, Israel. You look through those pages and all those countries that I have just named show differences in degree, but the same pattern of treatment of people who are dissenters, dissidents, troublemakers in their own country. In Israel, of course, it's the Palestinians. Israel has a more free atmosphere in the non-occupied, but in the occupied territories, Israel behaves the way Saudi Arabia behaves towards its own people and the way Syria and Turkey do. You see the same pattern in the Amnesty International reports, the same words appearing again and again. Imprisonment without trial. Detention without communication with the outside. Torture. Killing. For all of these countries. But if you want to make war on them, you single one out, blot out the others, even use them as allies and forget about their record. Then you go in. You persuade people that we're against tyranny, aren't we? We're against brutality, aren't we? *This* is the repository of all the evil that there is in the world. There are times when people talked that way. Why are we at war? We've got to get him. We've got to get Saddam Hussein. What about the whole world? Saddam Hussein. Got to get him.

I would like to get him. I would like to get all of them. But I'm not willing to kill 100,000 or 500,000 or a million people to get rid of them. I think we have to find ways to get rid of tyrants that don't involve mass slaughter. That's our problem. It's very easy to talk about the brutality. Governments are brutal, and some governments are more brutal than others. Saddam Hussein is particularly brutal. But in addition, Saddam Hussein uses chemical weapons and gas. That kept coming up. I remember Congressman Stephen Solarz, the great war hawk of this period: Saddam Hussein used gas, used chemical warfare. True, ugly and brutal. But what about us? We used napalm in Vietnam. We used Agent Orange, which is chemical warfare. I don't know how you characterize napalm. We used cluster bombs in Iraq. Cluster bombs are not designed to knock down military hardware. They are anti-personnel weapons which shoot out thousands of little pellets which embed themselves in people's bodies. When I was in North Vietnam during the Vietnam War I saw x-rays of kids lying in hospital beds showing the pellets in the various organs of their bodies. That's what cluster bombs are. But gas? No. Chemical weapons? No. Napalm, yes. Cluster bombs, yes. White phosphorus, yes. Agent Orange, yes. They're going to kill people by gas. We're going to kill people by blowing them up. You can tell who is the cruel wager of war and who is the gentlemanly wager of war.

You can persuade people of that if you simply don't mention things or don't remind people. Once you remind people of these things they remember. If you remind people about napalm they remember. If you say, the newspapers haven't told you about the cluster bombs, they say, oh yes, that's true. People aren't beastly and vicious. But then information is withheld from them and the American population was bombarded the way the Iraqi population was bombarded. It was a war against us, a war of lies and disinformation and omission of history. That kind of war, overwhelming and devastating, waged here in the U.S. while that war was waged over there.

Another element in this process of persuasion is simply to take what seems like a just cause and turn it into a just war. Erwin Knoll used that terminology. I have used that terminology, and both of us, because we're so wise, seem to come to the same conclusions. That is, that there's this interesting jump that takes place between just cause and just war. A cause may be just: yes, it's wrong for Saddam Hussein to go into Kuwait, it's wrong for this and that to happen. The question is, does it then immediately follow that if the cause is just, if an injustice has been committed, that the proper response to that is war? It's that leap of logic that needs to be absolutely avoided.

North Korea invades South Korea in 1950. It's unjust, it's wrong. It's a just cause. What do you do? You go to war. You wage war for three years. You kill a million Koreans. And at the end of the three years, where are you? Where you were before. North Korea is still a dictatorship. South Korea is still a dictatorship. Only a million people are dead. You can see this again and again, jumping from a just cause to an overwhelming use of violence to presumably rectify this just cause, which it never does.

What war does, even if it starts with an injustice, is multiply the injustice. If it starts on the basis of violence, it multiplies the violence. If it starts on the basis of defending yourself against brutality, then you end up becoming a brute.

You see this in World War II, the best of wars. The war that gave wars such a good name that they've used it ever since as a metaphor to justify every war that's taken place since then. All you have to do in order to justify war is to mention World War II, mention Churchill, mention Munich. Use the word "appeasement." That's all you need to take the glow of that good war and spread it over any ugly act that you are now committing in order to justify it.

Yes, World War II had a good cause. A just cause against fascism. I volunteered. I don't like to admit that I was in World War II, for various reasons. I like to say, "I was in a war." I suppose I admit that I was in World War II so that people won't think I mean the Spanish-American War. I volunteered for World War II. I went into the Air Force and became a bombardier and dropped bombs on Germany, France, Czechoslovakia, Hungary. I thought it was a just cause. Therefore you drop bombs.

It wasn't until after the war that I thought about this and studied and went back to visit a little town in France that I and a lot of the Air Force had bombed, had in fact dropped napalm on. The first use of napalm that I know of was this mission that we flew a few weeks before the end of World War II. We had no idea what it was. They said it was a new type of thing we were carrying, the bomb. We went over and just bombed the hell out of a few thousand German soldiers who were hanging around a town in France waiting for the war to end. They weren't doing anything. So we obliterated them and the French town near Bordeaux on the Atlantic coast of France.

I thought about that, about Dresden, the deliberate bombing of civilian populations in Germany, in Tokyo. Eighty, ninety, a hundred thousand people died in that night of bombing. This was after our outrage, our absolute outrage at the beginning of World War II when Hitler bombed Coventry and Rotterdam and a thousand people were killed. How inhuman to bomb civilian populations. By the end of World War II we had become brutalized. Hiroshima, Nagasaki, and even after that.

I have a friend in Japan who was a teenager when the war ended. He lived in Osaka. He remembers very distinctly that on August 14, five days after the bomb dropped on Nagasaki, the Japanese agreed to surrender on August 15. After Nagasaki it was very clear that they were about to surrender in a matter of days, but on August 14 a thousand planes flew over Japan and dropped bombs on Japanese cities. He remembers on August 14, when everybody thought the war was over, the bombers coming over his city of Osaka and dropping bombs. He remembers going through the streets and the corpses and finding leaflets also dropped along with the bombs saying: the war is over.

Just causes can lead you to think that everything you then do is just. I suppose I've come to the conclusion that war, by its nature, being the indiscriminate and mass killing of large numbers of people, cannot be justified for any political cause, any ideological cause, any territorial boundary, any tyranny, any aggression. Tyrannies, aggressions, injustices, of course they have to be dealt with. No appeasement. They give us this multiple choice: appeasement or war. Come on! You mean to say between appeasement and war there aren't a thousand other possibilities? Is human ingenuity so defunct, is our intelligence so lacking that we cannot devise ways of dealing with tyranny and injustice without killing huge numbers of people? It's like the police. The only way you can deal with a speeding motorist is to take him out of his car and beat the hell out of him, fracture his skull in ten different places? It's a sickness of our time. Somehow at the beginning of it is some notion of justice and rightness. But that process has to be examined, reconsidered. If people do think about it they have second thoughts about it.

One of the elements of this process of persuasion is simply to play on people's need for community, for national unity. What better way to get national unity than around a war? It's much easier, simpler, quicker. And of course it's better for the people who run the country to get national unity around a war than to get national unity around giving free medical care to everybody in the country. Surely we could build national unity. We could create a sense of national purpose. We could have people hanging out yellow ribbons for doing away with unemployment and homelessness. We could do what is done when any group of people decides and the word goes out and the air waves are used to unite people to help one another instead of to kill one another. It can be done. People do want to be part of a larger community. Warmakers take advantage of that very moral and decent need for community and unity and being part of a whole and use it for the most terrible of purposes. But it can be used the other way, too.

The reason I've gone into what I see as this process of persuasion and the elements of persuasion is that I think that all of them are reversible. History can be learned. Facts can be brought in. People can be reminded of things that they already know. People do have common sense when they are taken away briefly from this hysteria which is created in the time of war. I can only describe what's happened in these last few months as a kind of national hysteria created by the government and collaborated with by the media. When you have an opportunity to lift the veil of that hysteria and take people away from under it and talk to people, then you see the possibilities. When you appeal to people's sense of proportion: What is more important? What is it that we have to do? People know that there are things that have to be done to make life better. People know that the planet is in danger, and that is far more serious than getting Saddam Hussein out of Kuwait ever was. Far more serious.

I think people also may be aware in some dim way—every once in a while I think of it, and I imagine other people must think of it, too—that here it is, 1991, and we're coming to the end of the century. We should be able, by the end of this century, to eliminate war as a way of solving international disputes. We should have decided, people all over the world, that we're going to use our energy and our resources to create a new world order, but not *his* new world order, not the new world order of war, but a new world order in which people help one another, in which we divide the enormous wealth of the world in humane and rational ways. It's possible to do that. So I'm just suggesting that we think about that. I feel that there's something that needs to be done and something that *can* be done and that we can all participate in it.

PART XV

HEALING GLOBAL WOUNDS

DOCUMENT 53

Seabrook

The Clamshell Alliance was founded in 1976 in New Hampshire after the Public Service Corporation announced its intention to go ahead with plans to build a nuclear power plant on the New Hampshire coast in the town of Seabrook. The Alliance adopted the principle of nonviolence, agreed to make all decisions in small groups by consensus, and held a series of occupations of the Seabrook nuclear site.

After two small occupations in the summer of 1976, efforts were directed toward a mass occupation which was held in April 1977 and is described in the following documents. More than 2,000 people occupied the site, and more than 1,400, after being told to leave by Governor Thompson, remained to be arrested. Protesters were taken to seven armories throughout New Hampshire, where most remained for two weeks.

The Clams, as they called themselves, inspired dozens of other alliances against nuclear power elsewhere in the United States. The largest of these was the Abalone Alliance, also organized in 1976, in Northern California, which organized successive occupations of a proposed nuclear power plant in Diablo Canyon. An offshoot of the movement against nuclear power confronted nuclear weapons research at the Lawrence Livermore Laboratory of the University of California through the Livermore Action Group. (See, as to all the above, Barbara Epstein, Political Protest and Cultural Revolution: Nonviolent Direct Action in the 1970s and 1980s *[Berkeley: University of California Press, 1991], pp. 10–12, and for Seabrook, Chapter 2.)*

*As Barbara Epstein comments (*ibid. *at pp. 12–13, Chapter 5), the Clamshell Alliance and its successors saw themselves as "developing a feminist way of doing politics." Consensus decision making, characteristic of the early 1960s, had faded with the advent of Leninist models of organization at the end of the decade; the Clams revived it. Affinity groups were an extension of the consensus idea. The concept had been introduced to the New Left (according to* ibid., *p. 66) by the philosopher Murray Bookchin, who found it in his studies of Spanish Anarchism. Quakers introduced the idea of affinity groups to the Clamshell. When masses of people were to engage in civil disobedience, they divided voluntarily into small groups each of which pledged to stay together throughout the demonstration, supporting and gently disciplining its members. A final organizational innovation was "the discouragement of any institutionalized leadership through the rotation of representatives, or spokes, who would convey the decisions of the local group to a spokescouncil" (*ibid., *p. 98).*

A.   "Declaration of Nuclear Resistance"

WE THE PEOPLE demand an immediate and permanent halt to the construction and export of nuclear power plants.

Nuclear Power is dangerous to all living creatures and their natural environment. It is designed to concentrate energy, resources and profits in the hands of a powerful few. It threatens to undermine the principles of human liberty on which this nation was founded.

A nuclear power plant at Seabrook, New Hampshire—or elsewhere in New England—would lock our region on this suicidal path. As an affiliation of a wide range of groups and individuals, the CLAMSHELL ALLIANCE is unalterably opposed to the construction of this and all other nuclear plants. We recognize that:

1. The present direction in energy research and development is based on corporate efforts to recoup past investments, rather than on meeting the real energy needs of the people of America.

2. There is a malignant relationship between nuclear power plants and nuclear weapons. The arms industry has used the power plants as a shield

---

"Declaration of Nuclear Resistance," *Win*, June 16 and 23, 1977, p. 3. Reprinted by permission.

to legitimize their technology, and the reactor industry has spawned nuclear bombs to nations all over the world, as well, potentially, to "terrorist" groups and even organized crime.

3. Nuclear plants have proven to be an economic catastrophe. They are wasteful and unreliable, and by their centralized nature, tend to take control of power away from local communities.

4. The much-advertised "need" for nuclear energy is based on faulty and inflated projections of consumption derived from a profit system that is hostile to conservation. The United States is 6% of the world's population consuming 30% of its energy resources. With minimal advances in conservation, architecture and recycling procedures, the alleged "need" for nuclear energy disappears.

5. The material and potential destructiveness of nuclear power plants is utterly horrifying. It ranges from cancer-causing low-level radiation to the possibility of major meltdown catastrophes to the creation of deadly plutonium which must be stored for 250,000 years, to the destruction of our lakes, streams and oceans with hot water. The murderous contingencies have already filled many volumes, and they cannot be countenanced by a sane society. No material gain—real or imagined—is worth the assault on life that atomic energy represents.

WE THEREFORE DEMAND:

1. That not one more cent be spent on nuclear power reactors except to dispose of those wastes already created and to decommission those plants now operating.

2. That American energy resources be focused entirely on developing solar, wind, tidal, geothermal, wood, and other forms of clean energy in concert with the perfection of an efficient system of recycling and conservation.

3. That any jobs lost through cancellation of nuclear construction be immediately compensated for in the natural energy field. Natural energy technology is labor intensive (as opposed to nuclear, which is capital-intensive) and will create more jobs—permanent and safe—than the atomic industry could ever promise. Any dislocation caused by the shift from nuclear to natural energy must be absorbed by capital, not labor.

4. That a supply of energy is a natural right and should in all cases be controlled by the people. Private monopoly must give way to public control.

5. That in concert with public ownership, power supply should be decentralized, so that environmental damage is further minimized and so that control can revert to the local community and the individual.

We have full confidence that when the true dangers and expense of nuclear power are made known to the American people, this nation will reject out of hand this tragic experiment in nuclear suicide, which has already cost us so much in health, environmental quality, and material resources.

The CLAMSHELL ALLIANCE will continue in its uncompromising opposition to any and all nuclear construction in New England.

Our stand is in defense of the health, safety and general well-being of our selves and of future generations of all living things on this planet.

We therefore announce that should nuclear construction still be in progress at Seabrook, New Hampshire on MAYDAY WEEKEND, 1977, we will mobilize the citizenry and march onto that site and occupy it until construction has ceased and the project is totally and irrevocably cancelled.

B.   Murray Rosenblith,
"Surrounded by Acres of Clams"

More than a month after the occupation of the Seabrook nuclear power plant construction site, it sometimes is difficult to keep the event in proper perspective. There is a sense that it was a mystical event; something greater than a well planned and executed direct action project. Some have hailed Seabrook as the opening of a new era for social change activism in the US. That it may be, but there is no magic about it. The Seabrook occupation was the result of many hours of hard work by hundreds of people.

Organizing for the mass occupation at Seabrook began last year with the arrests of 180 people after they occupied the site on August 22, 1976. The people of New Hampshire had been fighting the Seabrook nuke to no avail by legal means for many years through the courts, town referenda and lobbying the Public Service Company. The first direct action against the nuke occurred in January 1976, when a Weare, NH resident, Ron Rick, climbed a weather tower on the Seabrook site and spent 32 hours there in sub-zero degree weather. For most people outside of New Hampshire, publicity of this action brought the Seabrook nuke to their attention for the first time.

Continuing this history of opposition, the Clamshell Alliance began to plan for the mass occupation. The affinity group structure, which had functioned successfully at the earlier occupation, was central to the organization. The affinity group had been the basic organizational unit of the anarchists during the Spanish Civil War. Operating on the principle that people function best in a situation in which they are familiar with and trust the people immediately around them, the group provides everyone with ongoing feedback into any decision. All participants in the April 30 occupation were members of an affinity group and all groups received nonviolence training before occupying.

Friday night before the occupation was clear and cold. That night and Saturday morning were a blur of last minute meetings, training sessions, repacking gear. People were, generally, well supplied. National guard officers

---

Murray Rosenblith, "Surrounded by Acres of Clams," *Win*, June 16 and 23, 1977, pp. 4–8. Reprinted by permission.

would later comment we were better equipped then they were, looking out over a field of people hoisting 40 and 50 pound packs I could believe it.

A count finished around 2 am Saturday morning showed that just over 1200 people were camped out at the five staging areas. Another 500 were expected from Boston early in the morning, and people continued to arrive all through the night.

We did not move out until after 1 pm, Saturday. We woke hours before, ready to roll then, but there were meetings and last minute details to clear up. And, the Clam people reported, there were still people pouring into the Marigold Ballroom, the last minute staging area south of the site.

Clam organizers had been worried about provocateurs all week, particularly after the Labor Committee, a vehement supporter of nuclear power, became the main source of the violence reports that Meldrim Thomson quoted in the days right before the occupation. However, there was no trouble from provocateurs, and poison ivy, sunburn and blisters became our greatest threats. Most people marched between two and six miles, with heavy packs, to reach the site. Even with good hiking shoes, there were a sizable number of people gingerly limping around the encampment on Saturday night.

Midday Saturday the marches moved out from Hampton, Newton, the Marigold Ballroom and the North and South Friendly areas bordering the nuke site. A small group boated in through the estuary and landed on the eastern edge of the site.

Miraculously enough, they all converged on the site within minutes of each other. The western march, composed of the Hampton, Marigold and Newton groups numbering over 1000, had to go through the front gate. The only obstructions were a few sawhorses and a private security guard making a rather tentative request that people not trespass on the site. The main group paused at the gate to allow stragglers to catch up and then swept in.

Just ahead of the march several dozen newspaper and TV photographers struggled to catch a clear picture of the group while walking backwards. The reporters were actually the first trespassers. Some of them would be arrested with everyone else the next day. Only the AP and UPI correspondents, who had some kind of sweetheart deal with the state, were immune. They wandered around the site in funny helmets with flashing lights on top, looking like refugees from a Flash Gordon fan club.

The site itself is not very attractive. It is the former Seabrook town dump (they still haven't found another place to put their garbage), covered over with a sandy landfill. There are some temporary construction buildings and a five story cement mixer. In all, it looks like a disaster already occurred there.

Clam organizers had not found out until late Friday night that we might be allowed to actually enter the site. The original injunction had covered the entire site, but under the altered injunction only a small, central construction area was fenced off. The change in the injunction indicated that the state might be realigning their tactics. Unfortunately, the organizers had not really worked out a scenario for this possibility.

Once on the site, there was a quick meeting to decide where to camp out. After that we trooped onto the enormous parking lot and pitched camp. The choice of the lot for the campsite would later turn into one of several "mistakes that didn't have time to become mistakes."

As the Clam organizers had not worked out an on-site scenario, the inertia of the situation was to do nothing. Many people, particularly those who were veterans of other direct actions, chafed at the inactivity. The occupation was an aggressive action but somewhere along the way, without a general consultation, some of the more active proposals for confrontation were shelved. Once we got on the site, the energy to do anything seemed to dissipate. Not only did the Clam not have plans for being on the site, but the nonviolence training had emphasized passivity as the proper reaction to any new situation.

Many of the trainers had given the impression during the sessions that nonviolent direct action was more inaction than anything else. Among their examples had been how to nonviolently stop people from breaching the interior fence. Many of us who have been active in the nonviolent movement for a while were surprised at the reappearance of this concept. We didn't get to hold the site long enough to work out these problems, though we did seem to be moving in the right direction. Fortunately, the next two weeks gave many people ample opportunities to explore the possibilities and illustrate the theories of active nonviolence.

After we were on the site there were immediate and constant spokes and DMB (the Decision Making Body, a smaller group supposedly constituted to make quick, emergency decisions on the march) meetings. The meetings went on into the evening.

For a while the affinity process appeared to have been inverted. Decisions were supposed to come from the affinity groups with the spokes meeting for coordination and feedback. But late Saturday afternoon it seemed that spokes were coming back to their affinity groups with "orders" from above. The discontent among many occupiers was immediate and grew rapidly. People also pointed out that the DMB was supposed to cease functioning once we occupied the site; so why were there DMB meetings?

By Saturday night, however, the tide was turning. Spokes carried peoples' anger to their meetings, and there was a growing awareness that the occupation should not continue in a passive vein.

However, there were a significant number of people who felt the occupation's purposes were best served by just sitting tight. The debate began Saturday night. Most of the proposals for action were aimed at Monday morning when workers were to resume construction at the site. The conclusions never came; the State of New Hampshire took the next step.

Police and security activity had followed the site occupation. The fenced-off, injuncted construction area was heavily patrolled by the over 300 state police (Vermont, Maine, Connecticut and Rhode Island had also supplied members of their state forces to patrol the site, and ultimately, assist in the arrests) and private guards leading Doberman Pinschers. Police and national guard vehicles were constantly coming and going. And helicopters taking off from a cleared area behind the fence continually buzzed the camp site.

Despite the authorities' good aerial surveillance of the entire area, they still couldn't judge the size of the occupation. On Sunday afternoon, when at least 1500 people were encamped, the commander of the state National Guard, Adjutant General John Blatsos, flew over the site and estimated there were between 200 and 300 occupiers. The general's statement was a good indicator of how poorly the state was prepared to deal with the large number of occupiers.

Their lack of preparation was ironic, as the Clamshell had never made a secret of anything it was doing or planning. Earlier in the week, Clamshell organizers had informed Colonel Paul Doyon, commander of the New Hampshire State Police, that they expected approximately 1800 people to occupy the Seabrook site. The media widely reported that this figure was based on a "mystical formula"—that the Clam was returning with ten times the number of people arrested in the last occupation. In reality, the figure was based on the number of people who had participated in the nonviolence training sessions prior to coming to Seabrook.

It would come out later in testimony in federal court that New Hampshire officials refused to believe the scope of the Seabrook protest until the latest possible moment. They chose to believe unreliable sources and even seemed set on denying what was happening right before their eyes. Colonel Doyon testified that he had expected 400 to 800 people in this occupation. When Clamshell media organizer Cathy Wolff asked him outside the courtroom why he had not believed the figures she had told him before the occupation, he turned away without answering.

As the state was totally unprepared to deal with the over 2000 people who occupied on Saturday, they decided to play a waiting game, choosing to see if the numbers would evaporate during the night.

Some groups did leave during the night, but by police estimates there were still well over 1000 people on the site by sunrise, Sunday, May 1, and as the day passed, people continued to arrive.

Governor Thomson, who had been at the site briefly on Saturday, was growing tired of trying to wait the occupiers out. Meldrim Thomson's reputation was a law 'n' order man and a strategy of appeasement went against his grain. Flown in again by his helicopter, the Governor arrived on the site to consult with Doyon, Attorney General David Souter and other officials on a course of action.

When they were informed of his visit, the Clams decided to send a delegation to seek a meeting. They didn't believe they would change the Governor's mind about nuclear power or anything else, but making the human contact was in keeping with the general spirit of the occupation.

They chose six people, one representing each march route. The meeting was short, terse, but cordial. Thomson immediately informed the Clam representatives, "You have a right to your opinion, but we cannot permit a violation of the law. We have been patient and tolerant. I doubt that I can persuade you and I doubt you can persuade me; but we all have a place we can go to decide this—to the polls."

The Clams pointed out that a Seabrook town meeting had voted against the power plant. Thomson retorted that the townspeople had originally approved the plant. This is only half true, as no one in the Public Service Company had told Seabrook residents that the original plans were for a proposed *nuclear* power plant.

Thomson finished with a flourish, "We cannot, as public officials, allow this breaking of the law; it is, after all, Law Day."

"It's also May Day, Governor," one of the Clam reps replied.

After once more asking the Clams to leave, Thomson flew off, and Colonel Doyon stepped in. He offered the use of buses, which the police had been stockpiling all morning behind the site, to carry people out to a local destination of their choice. One way or another we would be riding those buses out of the site.

It was about 2:15 pm. Doyon waited until 3 when the Clam representatives returned after a hasty, but spirited spokes meeting. Elizabeth Boardman, a long time Quaker activist from Acton, Massachusetts, spoke for the Clams, "We have good news for some of us, we're staying."

At 3:09, Doyon announced that anyone remaining on the site after 30 minutes would be arrested. The weekend's tactical debates all became moot. The buses rolled onto the site 40 minutes later; police emerged and began the arrests. They would continue taking people from the site until 7:30 am, Monday, arresting 1414 people in all.

Arrest was followed by a bus ride to the Portsmouth National Guard armory, where a mass booking facility had been established. We were processed and fingerprinted then herded into a roped off holding area.

Louisa Woodman, a bail commissioner for Hampton District court, was there to tell us we could all bail out immediately on personal recognizance [pr]. She assured us that this arrangement had been worked out with Clamshell legal representatives. People were tired, anxious, confused and the deal didn't sound right. We had discussed bail solidarity in affinity groups before and there was general agreement that people should not pay any bail and go free unless everyone got out on pr. But this, which sounded like what we wanted, also sounded too easy.

Ms. Woodman and the other Hampton court officials didn't understand why people were balking at the deal. They assured people that everyone would be released in this fashion.

New buses, each carrying about 20 people, arrived every five minutes and the holding area quickly became crowded, adding to everyone's confusion and frustration. While some affinity groups, particularly the first ones arrested, were reunited in the holding area, most people were still separated from their groups.

Manny Krasner, a Clam lawyer, finally arrived and tried to explain the pr procedure. He thought it was a good deal and argued earnestly for people to accept. As a show of good faith, Ms. Woodman offered to process Medora Hamilton, a third time occupier from central New Hampshire, so that people could see it was a square deal.

It looked like Krasner was making progress. Some people were still suspicious, but many seemed anxious to get out and regroup. After arrest and release people planned to return to the Hampton camping area to consider the next move. Since a few people held out against consensus, however, most people were reluctant to begin processing.

While the bail debate raged on, Ms. Woodman returned to the holding area; she was obviously agitated. She announced that the pr arrangement was scuttled. District court judges had arrived, people would be arraigned and some bail would be required.

What she didn't announce was that Governor Thomson was at the armory. Several people, including me, saw him walk through and heard the arrival and departure of his helicopter. He had obviously been displeased by what he saw, both at the site and here at the armory. People started to realize that the stakes for this game might be higher than we anticipated. Thomson wanted to "teach us a lesson" and this was one of the first instructions.

With two, and later three, judges sitting, people were arraigned ten at a time. Despite this revolving door justice, the arrestees backed up faster than the court could handle. Some people ended up spending the night in open trucks and unheated buses outside the armory, waiting for their turn before the law.

In the first arraignment, Manny Krasner asked that people be released on pr, but assistant attorney general James Cruse demanded cash bail, claiming the state had evidence showing that people who were released would immediately reoccupy the site. He never proved this, but the judge was satisfied and set $100 bail. Everyone pleaded not guilty, if they pleaded at all, and no one paid bail.

The state would later contend that bail solidarity was part of a Clamshell plot to further hurt the state and damage the criminal justice system. They also tried to prove people were coerced to refuse bail. State officials never understood the discipline of individuals acting in group solidarity. It seemed to them that such a large group of people acting together obviously had to be getting orders from some central authority. When they later attempted to prove this theory and came up against a wall of denials, they wrote that off to further conspiracy. The men from the attorney general's office admired the Clams' discipline but failed to ever comprehend its actual source.

While Judge Gray assigned $100 bails, Judge Flynn in the next room handed out $200 price tags for peoples' freedom. It was an excellent lesson in even-handed justice for people participating in their first bust. Bail for second and third time occupiers was set at $500. Later, however, when the strain on the state's capacities mounted, New Hampshire residents were urged to take pr. When they refused, some were literally thrown out of the court. They had pr whether they wanted it or not.

General Blatsos says he had not had any plans for holding arrested occupiers in the state's national guard armories until 6 pm Sunday, May 1. The first armory he opened was in Somersworth. The buses rolled out of Portsmouth for there just after 9 pm. Buses left Portsmouth all night until the armories at Somersworth, Manchester, Concord and Dover were brimming with arrested Clams. Later in the week, the state would move people out of Somersworth and Dover back to the Portsmouth armory to relieve overcrowding in those places.

People arriving at the armories reformed affinity groups or created new ones. The structures differed from place to place, but each group established a process for group decisions. In some armories people stuck with the affinity group, and spokes structure; in others they went from affinity groups to mass "town" meetings. It didn't seem to matter much, it could still take anywhere from 15 minutes to 2 days to reach a decision.

The first confrontation and resistance came the first night at Somersworth. Buses of occupiers were arriving every 15 minutes; by 11 pm there was no room left within the barricades the guard had erected by turning tables on their sides. The guard commander, Captain Dupee, told us that at least four more buses were due. When we protested the lack of space we were told that we would have to accommodate the newcomers somehow.

We'd just spent two or three nights in the spring chill, and the entire day awaiting arrest, being booked and arraigned, arguing about bail and tactics. We were edgy and pissed off, but we were also still disorganized.

However, when the next bus arrived, people sat down at the door and blocked the new arrivals' entry. They were just as tired and confused as we were, but after a quick explanation they sat down with us. The guardsmen, especially Dupee did not know how to respond to resistance; they had their orders, but to follow them they would have to use force. As the days passed we would realize how important it was for Dupee not to look bad to his superior officers; he would occasionally become absolutely frantic because he could never be sure if a new order would be obeyed. For now, he was just someone who seemed committed to an unreasonable course of action.

We weren't moving, though, and in 15 minutes another bus would arrive and add 20 more resisters to the confrontation. After a phone call to his superior, Dupee relented and moved the tables out to make more room.

We told him that we would accept two more busloads, not four, and then sit in again. He said he couldn't allow that, but never said how he would stop us. After two more buses arrived, there were approximately 200 people in the armory. We waited for another load and the confrontation. No further buses came to Somersworth, however, so we spread our sleeping bags on the concrete and rested on our apparent victory. That night had revealed the direction the imprisonment would take—resistance, some victories and some defeats.

Each Clam occupier was at the center of decisions; each guardsman was at the mercy of decisions from the top brass. Our "chains of command" clashed constantly. . . .

C. Cathy Wolff,
Reflection on the Seabrook Occupation

The National Guardsman stood with his feet slightly apart, his hands behind his back; separated from me by a table barricade in the Somersworth Armory.

"Have you been ordered not to talk with us?" I asked.

Silence.

"I hope you also haven't been ordered not to listen," I said and began to speak quietly about the danger of nuclear power and why more than 1400 people were willing to be arrested because of it.

While I spoke with the young guardsman, other nuclear opponents in the armory sang a song about love. We sang for three hours, protesting a decision to physically break up our affinity groups, the basic unit of strength of the Seabrook nuke site occupation.

"There's something I really need to know," I told the guard. "Would you please blink once if the answer is yes and twice if it's no? Are any of the guards here against nuclear power?"

The guard looked me in the eye and slowly blinked his eyes once.

It was the fourth day we had been held in the cement-floor armory; more than 200 of us crowded onto a space the size of a basketball court.

"Do you know that you are violating my civil rights?" one occupier asked a guard who had just told him his one telephone call would be severely censored.

"That may well be," the guard replied. "But I'm only following orders."

At the end of World War II, Norman Corwin wrote a radio play called "On A Note of Triumph." In it a low-level Nazi answers all questions about his war actions with the excuse, "I was only following orders."

On that fourth day of incarceration, a middle-aged occupier from Philadelphia also talked with a guard: "If the people of Germany had banded together and physically tried to halt construction of Hitler's crematories, perhaps they would never have been built. We consider the threat of nuclear power to be as great, if not greater, than Nazi Germany. That's why we occupied the Seabrook site."

Other people spoke with the silent guardsmen about the difference of their organization and ours. The Guard and much of our society is based on a

From "No Nuke of the North: Reflections on the Seabrook Occupation," *Win,* June 16 and 23, 1977, pp. 36–37.

hierarchy of order-giving and taking. But the people in the armories and the Clamshell Alliance believe that everyone must be involved in making the decisions that affect their lives, including decisions about nuclear power.

We have no officers; we follow no orders. We discuss, for hours sometimes, what to do until we reach a consensus everyone can live with. It's a little like town meetings.

Throughout the two-week ordeal in the five New Hampshire armories, we tried to let guardsmen know we considered them as fellow human beings, not enemies. The radiation and cost of suicidal nuclear power will hit them and their families as hard as us. We gave them literature on atomic power and suggested books they could read.

At the Dover Armory, a guard decided to name his new puppy No Nuke Luke. At the Concord Armory, at least one guard sat in on a workshop on nuclear power organized by the detainees. At Somersworth, I overhead a guard shout "No Nukes!" when a homerun was hit in a televised baseball game. Guards participated in some of our nightly talent shows; at Manchester they judged a mock fashion show. The night before we were released we took up a collection and gave the guards several cases of beer.

Hopefully, the guards realized we were not a band of terrorists or rich kids looking for a thrill. I'm sure they realized that being locked up for two weeks was not a picnic and none of us wanted to be there any more than they did. But most important, I hope some of the guards now will begin to think about nuclear power, if they haven't already, and realize that utilities and the federal government have not been upfront about the danger, cost and alternatives of nukes.

DOCUMENT 54

Judi Bari,
"The Feminization of Earth First!"

On May 24, 1990, a bomb exploded under Judi Bari's car as she and Darryl Cherney drove through Oakland on their way to an environmental meeting. Bari was nearly killed and suffered permanent injury. Cherney recovered

---

Judi Bari, "The Feminization of Earth First!," *Timber Wars and Other Writings* (106 W. Standley, Ukiah, CA: 1992), pp. 72–74. Reprinted by permission.

from his critical injuries. Both were active in organizing Redwood Summer,
a program of nonviolent protests against the logging of old growth redwood
trees, modeled after the civil rights Freedom Summer of 1964.

It is impossible to live in the redwood region of Northern California without being profoundly affected by the destruction of this once magnificent ecosystem. Miles and miles of clearcuts cover our bleeding hillsides. Ancient forests are being strip-logged to pay off corporate junk bonds. And bee-lines of log trucks fill our roads, heading to the sawmills with loads ranging from 1,000-year old redwoods, one tree trunk filling an entire logging truck, to six-inch diameter baby trees that are chipped for pulp. Less than 5% of the old growth redwood is left, and the ecosystem is disappearing even faster than the more widely known tropical rainforest.

So it is not surprising that I, a life-time activist, would become an environmentalist. What is surprising is that I, a feminist, single mother and blue-collar worker would end up in Earth First!, a "no compromise" direct action group with the reputation of being macho, beer drinking eco-dudes. Little did I know that by combining the more feminine elements of collectivism and non-violence with the spunk and outrageousness of Earth First!, we would spark a mass movement. And little did I know that I would pay for our success by being bombed and nearly killed, and subjected to a campaign of hatred and misogyny.

I was attracted to Earth First! because they were the only ones willing to put their bodies in front of the bulldozers and chainsaws to save the trees. They were also funny, irreverent, and they played music. But it was the philosophy of Earth First! that ultimately won me over. This philosophy, known as biocentrism or deep ecology, states that the earth is not just here for human consumption. All species have a right to exist for their own sake, and humans must learn to live in balance with the needs of nature, instead of trying to mold nature to fit the wants of humans.

I see no contradiction between deep ecology and eco-feminism. But Earth First! was founded by five men, and its principle spokespeople have all been male. As in all such groups, there have always been competent women doing the real work behind the scenes. But they have been virtually invisible behind the public Earth First! persona of "big man goes into big wilderness to save big trees." I certainly objected to this. Yet despite the image, the structure of Earth First! was decentralized and non-hierarchical, so we had the leeway to develop any way we wanted in our local Northern California group.

Earth First! came on the scene in redwood country around 1986, when corporate raider Charles Hurwitz of Maxxam took over a local lumber company, then nearly tripled the cut of old growth redwood to pay off his junk bonds. Earth First! had been protesting around public land issues in other parts of the West since 1981, but this was such an outrage that it brought the group to its first "private" lands campaign.

For years the strategy of Earth First!, under male leadership, had been based on individual acts of daring. "Nomadic Action Teams" of maybe 10 people would travel to remote areas and bury themselves in logging roads, chain themselves to heavy equipment, or sit in trees. There were certainly brave and principled women who engaged in these actions. And a few of the actions, notably the Sapphire six blockade in Oregon, even had a majority of women participants. But by and large, most of the people who had the freedom for that kind of travel and risk-taking were men.

I never consciously tried to change Earth First!, I just applied my own values and experiences to my work. I have nothing against individual acts of daring. But the flaw in this strategy is the failure to engage in long-term community-based organizing. There is no way that a few isolated individuals, no matter how brave, can bring about the massive social change necessary to save the planet. So we began to organize with local people, planning our logging blockades around issues that had local community support. We also began to build alliances with progressive timber workers based on our common interests against the big corporations. As our successes grew, more women and more people with families and roots in the community began calling themselves Earth First!ers in our area.

But as our exposure and influence grew, so did the use of violence to repress us. And in this far-flung, rural, timber-dependent area, it was easy to get away with. At one demonstration an angry logger punched a 50-year old non-violent woman so hard that she was knocked cold and her nose was broken. In another incident, my car was rammed from behind Karen-Silkwood-style by the same logging truck that we had blockaded less than 24 hours earlier. My car was totaled and my children and I and the other Earth First!ers who were riding with us ended up in the hospital. In both these cases, as in other incidents of violence against us, local police refused to arrest, prosecute, or even investigate our assaulters.

Earth First! had never initiated any violence throughout all of this. But neither did we publicly associate our movement with an overt non-violence code. After all, that would contradict the he-man image that Earth First! was founded upon. Yet I did not see how we could face the increasingly volatile situation on the front lines without declaring and enforcing our non-violence. And, considering the rate at which the trees were falling and the overwhelming power of the timber corporations, I did not see how we could save the forest with just our small rural population and the small group of Earth First!

So, drawing on the lessons of the Civil Rights Movement, we put out a nationwide call for Freedom Riders for the Forest to come to Northern California and engage in non-violent mass actions to stop the slaughter of the redwoods. We called the campaign Redwood Summer, and, as it became clear that we were successfully drawing national interest and building the infrastructure to handle the influx, the level of repression escalated again.

As Redwood Summer approached, I began to receive a series of increasingly frightening written death threats, obviously written in the interest of Big Timber. The most frightening of these was a photo of me playing music at a demonstration, with a rifle scope and cross-hairs superimposed on my face and a yellow ribbon (the timber industry's symbol) attached. When I asked the local police for help they said, "We don't have the manpower to investigate. If you turn up dead, then we'll investigate." When I complained to the County Board of Supervisors they replied, "You brought it on yourself, Judi." Finally, on May 24, 1990, as I was driving through Oakland on a concert tour to promote Redwood Summer, a bomb exploded under my car seat. I remember my thoughts as it ripped through me. I thought "this is what men do to each other in wars."

The bomb was meant to kill me, and it nearly did. It shattered my pelvis and left me crippled for life. My organizing companion, Darryl Cherney, who was riding with me in the car, was also injured, although, not as seriously. Then, adding to the outrage, police and FBI moved in within minutes and arrested me and Darryl, saying that it was our bomb and we were knowingly carrying it. For eight weeks they slandered us in the press, attempting to portray us as violent and discredit Redwood Summer, until they were finally forced to drop the charges for lack of evidence. But to this day, no serious investigation of the bombing has been conducted, and the bomber remains at large.

There were indications in advance that the attack on me was misogynist as well as political. For example, one of the death threats described us as "whores, lesbians, and members of N.O.W." But soon after the bombing, a letter was received that left no doubt. It was signed by someone calling himself the Lord's Avenger, and it took credit for the bombing. It described the bomb in exact detail and explained in chilling prose why the Lord's Avenger wanted me dead.

It was not just my "paganism" and defense of the forest that outraged him. The Lord's Avenger also recalled an abortion clinic defense that I had led years ago. "I saw Satan's flames shoot forth from her mouth her eyes and ears, proving forever that this was no Godly Woman, no Ruth full of obedience to procreate and multiply the children of Adam throughout the world as is God's will. 'Let the woman learn in silence with all subjection. But I suffer not a woman to teach, nor to usurp authority over the man, but to be in silence (Timothy 2:11).' "

Other misogynist hate literature about me was also distributed while I lay devastated in the hospital. The worst was from the Sahara Club, an anti-environmental group who wrote in their newsletter, "BOMB THAT CROTCH! Judi Bari, the Earth First bat slug who blew herself halfway to hell and back while transporting a bomb in her Subaru, held a press conference in San Francisco. . . . Bari, who had her crotch blown off, will never be able to reproduce again. We're just trying to figure out what would volunteer to inseminate her if she had all her parts. The last we heard, Judi and her friends were pouting and licking their wounds."

But meanwhile out in the forest, Redwood Summer went on without me. Before the bombing I was one of a very few women who had taken a prominent leadership role in Earth First! But after the bombing, it was the women who rose to take my place. Redwood Summer was the feminization of Earth First!, with 3/4 of the leadership made up of women. Our past actions in the Redwood Region had drawn no more than 150 participants. But 3,000 people came to Redwood Summer, blocking logging operations and marching through timber towns in demonstrations reminiscent of those against racism in the South. And despite incredible tension and provocation, and despite the grave violence done to me, Earth First! maintained both our presence and our non-violence throughout the summer.

Being the first woman-led action, Redwood Summer has never gotten the respect it deserves from the old guard of Earth First! But it has profoundly affected the movement in the Redwood Region. It brought national and international attention to the slaughter of the redwoods. The 2000-year old trees of Headwaters Forest, identified, named and made an issue of by Earth First!, are now being preserved largely due to our actions. The legacy of our principled and non-violent stand in Redwood Summer has gained us respect in our communities, and allowed us to continue to build our local movement. And our Earth First! group here, recently renamed Ecotopia Earth First!, is probably the only truly gender-balanced group I have ever worked in, now equally led by strong women and feminist men.

I believe that the reason I was subject to such excessive violence was not just what I was saying, but the fact that a woman was saying it. I recently attended a workshop in Tennessee on violence and harassment in the Environmental movement. There were 32 people in the circle, drawn from all over the country. As we each told our tale, I was struck by the fact that the most serious acts of violence had all been done to women. And of course this is no surprise. Because it is the hatred of the feminine, which is the hatred of life, that has helped bring about the destruction of the planet. And it is the strength of the women that can restore the balance we need to survive.

DOCUMENT 55

Western Shoshone Nation and
the Global Anti-Nuclear Alliance

*It became increasingly clear to Native Americans in the 1970s and 1980s
that chemical fertilizers and toxic pesticides are being used indiscriminately
against indigenous peoples throughout the "Fourth World."*[1] *Seventy percent
of all uranium reserves in the United States lie beneath Indian lands, where
they are mined without regard to the health of those who live on the land or
work in the mines.*[2] *All nuclear testing is done on indigenous people's lands:
for example, the Marshall Islands in the Pacific; and the land in Nevada
where over 700 bombs have been exploded, and Shoshone, Paiutes, and other
downwind communities suffer from cancer, leukemia, thyroid problems, and
birth defects.*[3] *In the United States, "having already plundered and poisoned
native lands to acquire the raw materials needed by a wasteful and throw-
away culture (oil, coal, uranium, etc.) federal officials and corporate sharks
now seek out tribal leadership willing to take on toxic waste incinerators,
toxic dumps, and high- and low-level nuclear waste dumps."*[4]

*Nonviolent direct action against these conditions has developed from small
beginnings. In 1977, as thousands were walking onto the Seabrook nuclear
power construction site in New Hampshire (Document 53), the National
Indian Youth Council and the Citizens Against Nuclear Threats held a joint
press conference to protest nuclear contamination of drinking water by uranium mining on Navaho and other Indian lands.*[5] *Healing Global Wounds
was an international nonviolent direct action that took place January 31 to*

---

1. Carlos Rainclouds, "Chemical Warfare Against Native Peoples," *Win*, Mar.
31, 1977.

2. Raymond D. Yowell, Chief, Western Shoshone National Council, to Dear friends,
*The Western Shoshone Nation and the Global Anti-Nuclear Alliance call to Healing
Global Wounds*, Oct. 2–12, 1992, p. 3.

3. Raymond D. Yowell to Dear friends, *ibid.*

4. Jennifer Viereck, "Next Year is the 501st," *ibid.*, pp. 6–7.

5. "Native People Oppose Uranium Mining in New Mexico," *Win*, July 20, 1978,
p. 8.

October 12, 1992. The project was initiated in the autumn of 1991 by leaders of the Western Shoshone Indians. It consisted of two walks, one from New York City, the other from Georgia, to Las Vegas, Nevada, and a civil disobedience demonstration at the Mercury nuclear bomb testing range at which approximately 600 people were arrested for trespassing.[6]

The following documents set forth the purpose and participation guidelines of the Healing Global Wounds project.

A.   Purpose Statement

We mourn what began on this continent on October 12, 1492. We invite people, corporations, and governments to apologize to all indigenous peoples for centuries of injustice.

We seek to understand American history from the perspectives of American Indians, African-Americans, Asian-Americans, political prisoners, and all other oppressed people.

Standing in solidarity with indigenous peoples everywhere, we honor Mother Earth. We support all indigenous peoples' rights to use of and title to their own lands.

We support the demands of Native Nations to receive a voice in the United Nations, as no indigenous nation on earth has a seat in this global political institution.

We demand immediate political decisions to protect the religious freedom of indigenous people worldwide.

We demand the immediate repeal of Public Law 93-531, which has advocated the forced relocation of the Dine (Navajo) people from their homeland to make room for corporate mining of coal and uranium.

We demand the immediate release of Leonard Peltier of the Lakota (Sioux) Nation (and all political prisoners), whose only crime is defending the rights of his people and the survival of Mother Earth.

We call for an end to nuclear testing, all of which occurs on lands of indigenous peoples, as a severe violation of human rights and a threat to life.

As we seek sustainable lifeways, we look towards indigenous cultures to offer us practical knowledge which could help secure the future of all life.

---

6. "Healing Global Wounds," *Midwest Pacifist Commentator,* vol. 8, no. 3 (May 29, 1993).

From "Healing Global Wounds," *Midwest Pacifist Commentator,* vol. 8, no. 3 (May 29, 1993), p. 2.

We walk across the land we call America to generate a spirit of compassion for Mother Earth.

B. Participation Guidelines

For the purpose of building trust, creating a foundation of safety, and so that we will know what to expect from each other, the Western Shoshone National Council has asked us to observe the following guidelines during Healing Global Wounds:

1) I will act nonviolently, with respect for all people and other living beings I encounter. I will seek to express my feelings without verbally or physically abusing anyone. If a conflict does arise, I will seek a designated Peacekeeper to arbitrate.

2) I will conduct myself with respect for other people's beliefs, religious affiliation, race, nationality, and sexual preference.

3) Out of a desire to make all participants comfortable at these events, I will be thoughtful and sensitive in my conduct and dress, and refrain from nudity.

4) I will not bring or use non-prescription drugs including alcohol at these events. Alcohol or drugs can endanger myself and others legally and physically. It can also hamper my ability to communicate and work with clarity.

5) I will not bring firearms or other weapons to these events.

6) I will take responsibility for my presence in the fragile desert environment, and avoid harming plants, animals, rock formations, etc. I will pick up trash, cigarette butts, etc. when the occasion arises, and refrain from having fires, smoking, or driving except in designated areas.

DIRECT ACTION GUIDELINES

7) If I choose to risk arrest at the Test Site, I will participate in site specific nonviolence training beforehand, to prepare and orient myself and to receive necessary action specific information.

8) If I risk arrest, I recognize that I may face legal consequences as a result of my actions, and I am prepared to accept these consequences.

"Healing Global Wounds Participation Guidelines," *The Western Shoshone Nation and the Global Anti-Nuclear Alliance call to Healing Global Wounds,* Oct. 2–12, 1992, p. 17.

9) I agree that I will not destroy property at the Test Site. However, many activists in the nonviolence resistance movement recognize the validity of direct disarmament actions.

10) The action planning meeting (spokescouncil) is the coordinating and decisions-making body for direct action tactics. I agree to follow its decisions.

DOCUMENT 56

Simon J. Ortiz,
"This America Has Been a Burden"

Simon Ortiz is a Native American poet and writer from Acoma Pueblo, New Mexico. In his book Woven Stone *(Tucson: University of Arizona Press, 1992, pp. 353–363), he describes how he grew up in the Southwest just as uranium was beginning to be mined for the nearby Los Alamos Laboratories. "Right out of high school I worked in the mining and millage region of Ambrosia lake," he relates. "Mostly, I worked at the Kerr-McGee millsite. ... There was always a haze of yellow dust flying around and even though filtered masks were used, the workers breathed in the fine dust." He concludes that the poor and workers of this nation "will have to be willing to identify capitalism for what it is, that it is destructive and uncompassionate and deceptive."*

We must have passionate concern for what is at stake. We must understand the experience of the oppressed, especially the racial and ethnic minorities, of this nation, by this nation and its economic interests. Only when we truly understand and accept the responsibilities of that understanding will be able to make the necessary decisions for change.

Only then will we truly understand what it is to love the land and people and to have compassion. . . .

This America
has been a burden
of steel and mad
death,
but, look now,
there are flowers
and new grass
and a spring wind
rising
from Sand Creek

The future will not be mad with loss and waste
    though the memory will be there;
eyes will become kind and deep,
and the bones of this nation
will mend after the revolution.

That dream
shall have a name
after all,
and it will not be vengeful
but wealthy with love
and compassion
and knowledge.
And it will rise
in this heart
which is our America.

INDEX